T5-BPZ-273

BLAST-POWER & BALLISTICS

Concepts of Force and Energy in the Ancient World

Jack Lindsay

BLAST-POWER & BALLISTICS

Concepts of Force and Energy in the Ancient World

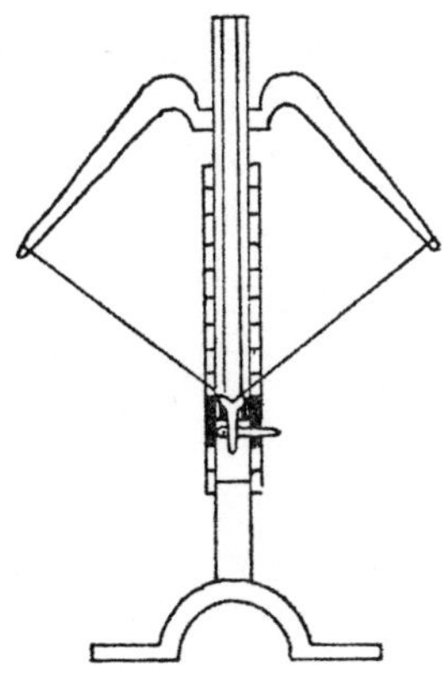

First published in the United States 1974 by
Harper & Row Publishers, Inc.
Barnes & Noble Import Division

ISBN: 06 494292 9

Printed and bound in Great Britain

To my son Philip

How take the world to pieces, then
put it alive together again?

The problem's crashed upon us all
since Humpty Dumpty had his fall
crackt from the bumptious abstract wall—
since consciousness of human fate
made us feel direly separate
yet merged with something far more great:
our lives a fragmentary part,
yet pulses of a single heart.

Only in momentary vision
the trick's been done: the bits defined
in analytic lockt precision
inside the seamless unity
both ultimate and immediate
with ceaseless changes, fiery, free,
which form the stable stormy whole.

But now the breaking-point is near
and we must use our better wits,
not merely count more bits and bits
in treacherous ghost-infinities,
a world where nothing human fits.
Yes, we must choose the harder goal
and grasp the method that will bind
both vision and analysis
in steady focus, till we see
the quarrelling aspects one:
the leap
into new wholes, the structures struck
from the extending symmetries
where number breeds and plays its role
ever more complex in division,
but under unity's clear control.
No need for atomising fear:
Courage will give us back our luck.

There is no forward way but this.

Contents

Illustrations

Foreword

I started this work with the aim of carrying on the analysis and exposition of ancient science which I began with my books on the Origins of Alchemy and of Astrology. I found however that it required many comparisons between ancient and modern concepts of Force and Energy; and that in order to make these comparisons properly effective, I needed a larger focus still—an inquiry into the fundamental ideas or motives of science from the earliest days. The book remains essentially what I had intended, a discussion of concepts of Energy and Force in the ancient world, but it has gained a much enlarged perspective and thus emerges in the last resort as a general critique of science. It was with something of a shock that I arrived at my over-all thesis: that the developments culminating in the atomic bomb, jet-propulsion, and the rockets may be said to have been programmed many millennia back by the shamans who added their fantasies of blast-power to the actually existing projectiles. And I would ask the reader to consider the evidence here set out before he reacts with incredulity at what might appear to be a wild generalisation.

Jack Lindsay

Energy Ancient and Modern

I

Nothing could more clearly bring out the differences between ancient and modern attitudes to nature than the uses made of the concept of energy. On the one hand we have the complex philosophical concept of *energeia* in Aristotle; on the other, the concept of a body's power of doing work by virtue of its motion, which Carnot and Joule elaborated in the first half of the nineteenth century. A comparison of the two concepts clarifies both the strengths and the weaknesses in each of the approaches.

The word *energeia* is made up of *en*, in, and *ergon*, work. Herodotos has the adjective *energos* with the meaning *active*. The noun came into full play with Aristotle, but it is unlikely that he invented the word or its philosophic use. In his *Metaphysics* he attacks the Megarean school for arguing that there is potentiality only where there is energy and that where there is no energy there is no potentiality: "For example, that the man who isn't actually building lacks the capacity to build, but he has the capacity as he actually builds, and it's similar with other matters." The founder of this school was a disciple of Sokrates, Eukleides, who, with other followers, took refuge at Megara when the master was put to death in 399 at Athens. Aristotle lived from 384 to 322 B.C.; and though it is possible that the Megareans had taken to arguing about *energeia* after he had developed his use of the term, it is perhaps more likely that the term had come up in the early fourth century B.C. and that Aristotle took it over and gave it an important place in his system. We do not know of its use by Demokritos or Plato.[1]

Aristotle himself uses it in several senses: in his *Ethics*, for activity as opposed to mere disposition, *hexis*, and in his *Rhetoric*, for vigour of style. He uses the verb *energein* as meaning: "to be in action or activity, to operate." But his main use of the noun is in a strict philosophic sense: to express actuality as distinct from potentiality, *dynamis*. He speaks of substance, *ousia*, as *energeia*: that is, substance in the sense of actuality. And he opposes it to mere matter, *hyle*, as also to the full working-out of an action or movement, *entelecheia*.[2]

In thus identifying actuality with *energeia*, he is expressing his belief that actuality by its very nature is in ceaseless motion of some sort, is always involved in working something out. The term *ergon* is not present in the word by chance; the stress is always on the notion of work, of activity, of production. Without this motion and work there is no actuality. The movement inherent in *energeia* is a ceaseless transition from the potential into the actual, with *entelecheia* as the state to which the process of *dynamis-energeia* directs itself. Because, then, of the deep difference between the Aristotelian and the modern concepts of energy I shall continue to use *energeia* for the most part when speaking of the former, with *dynamis* for potentiality.

Dynamis was not a new coinage. Homer knew it, especially in the sense of bodily strength. From this limited application it expanded to express power in all spheres, above all in war and in politics. Thus Herodotos speaks of "the *dynamis* of Kyros", the political and personal power of the Persian king. The original meaning is not "a substance that has power", but "a substance which *is* a power, which can assert itself, and by this simple act of asserting itself, by being too strong, stronger than the others, can cause trouble" (Peck). In medical theory this meant that a *dynamis* required not suppression by a stronger power, but counterpoise by an equal. Plato used the term with an interiorised meaning: to express the inner power or faculty possessed by a man. He knew it also as a mathematical term: a power, generally a second power or squared number. Here he was doubtless drawing on Pythagorean terminology, Aristotle uses the word philosophically in two senses: the power of one thing over another, its power to produce some sort of change in the other thing—and the power in a thing of passing from one state into another. Without this latter *dynamis* in objects we cannot explain change at all. Not that he sees *dynamis* as existing by itself as a sort of abstract power in the object. *Energeia*, he says, is prior to *dynamis*, both logically and in the sense that A is not potentially B unless it can come to be actually B. And so the very *dynamis* of A, its potentiality of being B, presupposes an actualisation which is the transition into

B. *Dynamis* everywhere and always presupposes, and is rooted in, *energeia*. A man is capable of knowing something new because he already knows something else; in this sense all knowledge comes from, and through, already-existing knowledge.[3]

Dynamis and *energeia* do not thus link together in an abstract way, or anything might result. Their union can only be understood if we know the end they serve and to which they move. Potentiality points to actualisation, not the other way round. A man has the faculty of sight in order to see; he doesn't see so that he may have the faculty of sight. To grasp Aristotle's concept of *energeia* we must then look at his theory of form and of final cause. In the account of any event, human or natural, of any object made by man or by nature, he insists that we must take four factors into consideration. If we are dealing, say, with a chair, we must keep in mind (*a*) its material, here wood (*b*) its form, the particular shape that distinguishes it (*c*) its moving or efficient cause, here the carpenter (*d*) its final cause, the purpose expressed in its completed form, the function of the chair as a seat. Or to take a human being as an example of living creatures: (*a*) the matter is supplied (he thought) by the mother (*b*) the form is that which makes up the matter into a human organism (*c*) the moving cause is the father (*d*) the final cause is the perfected state of growth which the individual in question will attain. Each of the four factors is seen as a cause; all four are necessary for the actualisation of any object or creature.

It follows that Aristotelian Physics must include much more than mere mechanical causation. A distinction is made between the final cause in man and the final cause in natural objects. Purpose is conscious in man (who is said to have a superadded form, the active reason—though the ultimate ideal is pure contemplation); but there are no conscious aims in nature. The ends of nature are immanent, are directly inherent, in plant and animal; the fullgrown tree is the purpose of the seed. In nature process takes place "always or for the most part"; that is, nature sometimes fails in its ends, but in general succeeds. It thus reveals order and regularity, and these aspects may be considered to show a final cause at work.

Aristotle does not see a demiurge or a divine mind at work controlling natural or human changes from without, or involved with processes as some sort of immanent force. (He has a God, an Unmoved Mover, but because this God lacks all *dynamis*, he is not the precipitator of *energeia*. He cannot have *dynamis*, Aristotle thinks, since to have the potentiality of being is also to have that of non-being. He is thus an abstraction of the final cause, the perfected existence to which all things aspire; but does not in effect intrude on the system.) Aristotle, with all his stress on the final cause, is deeply interested in the way that that cause is arrived at or works out—in the first three causes, the actual processes of nature and man as they can be grasped in their *dynamis* and *energeia*. Hence his readiness to include mechanical causation among his interests, while in biology his concern for final causes leads on to the study of function—his formal and final causes then corresponding to the structure and the function of the part or organ. His efficient cause, which he defines as "primary source of change", suggests the use of the causal law as an instrument for discovering causal connections in nature. Further, some aspects of the formal cause hold hints of the mathematical formulation of natural laws: thus "the ratio 2:1 and number in general are causes of the octave".[4] But it was the final cause, in which the purpose of change was located, that was taken as overwhelmingly important; and the teleological approach it stimulated dominated the physical sciences, especially dynamics, till the seventeenth century.

Here we touch on the abstract and obstructive side of Aristotle's ideas, of which we shall have more to say later. For the moment, it is enough to note that the stress on form and final purpose pervades all his thinking. Form turns the matter into particular things and thus constitutes their essence; but it is inseparable from final purpose. The chair is a chair because of its form, but the form is determined by the function. Form is eternal, but only in virtue of the ceaseless succession of its embodiments. Form indeed has many meanings for Aristotle. At times it refers to sensible shape, as when a sculptor is said to impose a form on his material; but philosophically it refers to the inner nature of a thing, which is expressed by its definition, the plan of its structure. And even sensible objects could be thus expressed: e.g. the statue by a mathematical formula, though a complex one. *Eidos*, form, is then intelligible structure, and synomyms for it are *logos* (word, formula, definition) and *to ti ēn einai* (the what-it-was-to-be-so-and-so.)[5]

Besides the four essential causes which bring about a creature or thing and develop it into its *entelecheia*, there are four kinds of changes which substance or the substratum undergoes in the transition from *dynamis* to *energeia*. These changes are local (involving locomotion), qualitative alteration, quantitative change of size, and substantial change (involving generation or passing away).

There is yet another fourfold aspect of reality. All things are made up in varying combinations out of four simple elements: fire, air, water, earth. Each of these is seen in turn as a combination of two of the four primary qualities or opposites: cold, hot, wet, dry. Thus earth is cold and dry, water cold and wet, air hot and wet, fire hot and dry. (*Hygron* and *xeron* have a wider range of meanings than wet and dry in English; *hygron* refers to both liquids and gases, *xeron* mainly but not solely to solids.)[6]

Aristotle wants to account for the sensible qualities of physical objects. So his theory is qualitative, derived from observable changes in those objects, which are all in varying degrees hot or cold, wet or dry. Changes such as that of boiling water to steam seemed to show the point of decisive change or transformation from cold and wet to hot and wet, from water into air; and condensation seemed to show air turning into water. The fourth book of the *Meteorologika* discusses the properties of many physical bodies which are combustible, which are not combustible, which can be melted, which can be solidified, and so on. Aristotle tries to classify natural substances according to which of the simple bodies predominates in them; but he makes no attempt to define or control by experiment the precise combinations, the proportions of the simple bodies in each compound. The system of transformations is very schematic. All the four primary or simple bodies keep passing into one another in a cycle. The quickest and easiest change is for one simple body into that next above it in the series (earth, water, air, fire); the most difficult is that in which a step is missed out, so that a change in both qualities is required. A third way of change is when two simple bodies, taken together, pass into a third by each dropping a quality, e.g. fire and water can produce earth or air according to which quality each drops—only, the elements combined must not be consecutive or one would be left with two identical or two opposite qualities.[7]

We may say then that Aristotle sees nature as holding an innate impulse to movement, to a ceaseless transformation of *dynamis* into *energeia*. (The Stoics developed this notion of the innate impulse. Cicero, describing Zenon's ideas, states that "Universal nature has all her motions voluntary, has affections and desires, called *hormai* by the Greeks, which are productive of actions agreeable to them, as to us who have sense and understanding to direct us".)[8] In a rough way it might be claimed that *dynamis* and *energeia* correspond to the potential and the kinetic energy of nineteenth-century science. But the Greek terms have so much wider a sphere of reference that the analogy breaks down. The modern concepts are purely quantitative and mechanical, while Aristotle's concepts cover the totality of a situation—not only the quantities and the mechanics, but also the qualities of the substances involved, the structure of the developments in which they play their part, the direction of the developments, and the new integrations or forms of organisation that appear at certain nodal points of change. The modern concept of energy, sharply delimiting its sphere of reference, arrives at precise mathematical formulations, while the ancient concept of *energeia* remains at philosophical generalisations, simplified logical classifications, and momentary intuitions of the fullness of process.

There is one slight nuance in the word *ergon,* and so in *energeia,* which we have not noted. Strictly, there is no Greek word for work in our sense of the term (defined by the Concise Oxford Dictionary as "expenditure of energy, striving, application of effort to some purpose"—with particular reference to the productive sphere). *Ergon* signifies for each thing or being the product of its specific virtue, its *aretē*. There is also the term *ponos*, which lays stress on effort, labour, with a suggestion of something painful, difficult, toilsome; it came indeed to mean simply pain. In the parable of choice, Herakles had to turn to a life of pleasure or one devoted to *ponos*. The verb connected with *ergon, ergazesthai,* is mainly linked with two aspects of economic life: work in the fields (as in the title of Hesiod's poem, *Works and Days*) and financial activity. In some ways the word that comes nearest to our concept of work is *technē*, craft or art. Words with the root *tek-* are linked with craft-activity, the making of things. The word for the maker is *poiein* (from which comes *poietes*, poet, a word with a wide connotation of "makings"), while the verb that suggests *ergon* is *prattein*, to do or act in general. Natural activity leads to *ergon*, the expression of one's natural being, one's *aretē*; the craftsman's work is thus, in contrast with *ergon*, a *praxis*. In Plato's *Charmides*, Kritias (probably following the sophist Prodikos) deals with the difference between activity and production, *prattein* and *poiein*. The kind of action expressed by *ergazesthai* belongs to the domain of *prattein* as opposed to that of *poiein*, just as *ergon* is opposed to *poiēma*. The fact that craftsmen are called *demiourgoi* does not run counter to these definitions; it means in Homer "public workers, workers for the people"; that is, men who do not work inside the *oikos* or estate of the landholder; and includes prophets, heralds, poets (perhaps even beggars), as well as smiths and carpenters.

The contrast between craftsman and peasant or farmworker, implied by the term *demiourgos*, gets a new emphasis with the growth of the city-state, its industries and mercantile activities. The number of craftsmen increase, but, despite some cult-connections with Athena and Hephaistos, they lack a proper place in the traditional systems, which are largely based in agriculture or orchardry. Because in the latter spheres things are grown, not made, there is a feeling that men cooperate with the gods in bringing the products about. Many aspects, such as the weather, are outside human control; and so without the aid of the gods men feel helpless. The same situation appears in warfare, with its many uncertainties and incalculable results. The farmer-soldier thus appears as a quite different character from the craftsman, who, given his material, produces an object wholly by his own initiative, aim, and skill. Xenophon stresses the special aspects of farmer and warrior. Agriculture is above all a form of activity that allows a certain type of *aretē* to express itself. Here it is not enough to own powers and gifts; one must put them into action, *ergazesthai*. This life of energy is contrasted with the life of idleness and softness. But it is also contrasted with the artisan's life—in a workshop, shut in, and bent over a bench or forge. It hardens men for war and so has nothing disgraceful about it. "I never go to dine," says Kyros, "without having made myself sweat by labouring at some soldierly or rural work." In wartime, put the farmers and the craftsmen in two groups and ask what they will do. The farmers will decide to fight; "the craftsmen, not to fight, but as their education has accustomed them, to stay quiet without hardship or danger." Agriculture has nothing secret about it; it needs no special apprenticeship. But "those who practise the other *technai* hide more or less all the essential secrets of their *technē*". In war and farming men feel their dependence on the gods; no one would carry on a campaign or set about agriculture without seeking to conciliate the divine powers. "The Earth, being a divinity, teaches justice to those capable of learning it. It's to those who cultivate [or pay her a cult] best that she accords in return the best fortune."

We shall have more to say later of this distinction of farmer and craftsman, country-worker and city-worker. For the moment it is enough to point out how Aristotle's concept of *dynamis* issuing in its proper *energeia* and leading on to full actualisation of its aim is linked with the meaning we have noted in *ergon* as the expression of the *aretē* of a thing or person, the essential nature. Hence the way in which the emergence of *energeia* in men represents also their harmony with nature, their cooperative activity with natural process. It reflects the union of man and nature in growing things for human use rather than the craft-activity which appears as a separation from nature.[9]

We need now to look at the modern concept, not only because a more detailed consideration will help to bring out more thoroughly the differences we have noted, but because it also helps us to understand the crucial importance of the social situation in determining the direction of thought in these matters. The modern concept, derived from the work of men like Carnot, Benjamin Thompson (Count Rumford), and Joule, arrived rather late on the scientific scene set by Galileo and Newton; it depended on the growth of methods for measuring mechanical energy and heat-energy in systems such as heat-engines.

Rumford made the first rough effort to work out a universally applicable doctrine of energy. He had worked in the military arsenal at Munich, superintending the boring of cannons, and was struck by the amount of heat that was generated by the action of the boring bar on the brass castings. Experiments led him to conclude that heat came solely from friction and that the supply of it was inexhaustible; hence it was not a substance. About the same time Davy showed that two bits of ice could be melted by being rubbed together in a vacuum. But to what precise dynamical quality heat corresponded was a problem not yet raised.

Sidi Carnot was born in 1796, two years before Rumford published his paper in the *Philosophical Transactions*. He began his career as an army-engineer in 1814, only to find his hopes of rapid advancement ended by Waterloo.

His father Lazare had prepared the way for the direction his thought was to take. A military engineer before the Revolution, he had written on those aspects of mathematics and mechanics which concerned the army of that time; he entered a wider sphere with an essay on the mathematical theory of the infinite which failed in 1786 to win a competition of the Berlin Academy; but, when printed, soon went into a second edition and in a few years was translated into five languages. He welcomed the Revolution and became one of the three most powerful members of the Committee of Public Safety during the Terror; and later he was a leading member of the Directory of the Republic. Deposed in 1797, he returned in 1800 from exile to become Napoleon's Minister of War. An ardent Republican, he soon resigned. As a revolutionary general he had played a key rôle in organising the popular armies and forming them into large masses able to strike heavy crushing blows; he had thus abandoned the idea of attempting to build defences at all points and rejected the Prussian tradition then dominant in Europe. As a military man, Lazare Carnot thus pioneered the way leading to Napoleon's strategies. As Minister of War he did much to reduce military expenditure and reform administration; he refused all the customary gifts from contractors. Napoleon did not want to let him go, but Carnot was opposed to his monarchical ambitions. Freed from official work, he gave himself up to scientific inquiry and survived the refusal to nominate Napoleon as First Consul for life. Still, he preferred him to the restored royal line, rallied to his cause during the Hundred Days, and was exiled after Waterloo. In his writings he specialised in matters of fortification, but he also published *On the Correlation of the Figures of Geometry*, 1801, *Geometry of Position*, 1803, and *Fundamental Principles of Equilibrium and Movement*, 1803. He thus moved from problems directly concerned with logistics, with defensive and offensive systems of strategy, into those which dealt with the abstract conceptions behind such matters. He developed a theory of machines and assisted in the gradual development towards concepts of work and energy. His approach to geometry and calculus was influenced by his engineering experience. Above all, his analysis of hydraulic machines was translated by his son Sidi into an analysis of heat-engines.

With such a father Sidi had the impulsion both to grapple with military matters and to seek for principles of action and movement in a wider field. Thwarted in his plans, he was kept for long to the mere drudgeries of his service; but in 1819 he obtained a lieutenancy and studied mathematics, chemistry, natural history, technology, and political economy, as well as maintaining a keen interest in music and the fine arts. In 1827 he became captain in the Engineers, but left the army next year and in 1832 died of cholera. The only work he published was *Reflections on the Driving Power of Fire and on the Machines suited for Developing this Power* (puissance motrice), 1824. Here he founded the science of Thermodynamics, though what interested him was the practical possibilities of the power-engine rather than the theory. Further extracts of his manscript were added by his brother in the 1878 edition of the essay; these showed that he had not only grasped the significance of heat but had noted down for trial many systems for finding its mechanical equivalent, such as were later devised—e.g. the perforated piston used by Joule, the friction of water and mercury, and the forcing of gas through a porous plug, used by Kelvin. Steam engines were coming into common use and had to be fed with fuel, in return for which they did work. Carnot wanted to find out precisely how much work was got for a given expenditure of fuel; his aim was to gain a maximum of work from the expenditure. He thought of work as the raising of a weight through a height, and he saw the concept of heat as interchangeable with that of work.

It had been noted that in steam engines only part of the absorbed heat was transformed into work or the energy of movement of the machine; the rest of the heat reappeared in the condensor steam, which was waste. Naturally men at first thought the loss was due to the inefficiency of the machine; but Carnot realised that there was an absolute limit to the portion of heat convertible into work, however excellent the machine. So he introduced the scheme of an Ideal Machine, which depended solely on the amount of heat flowing from a source at a given temperature to a receiver at a lower temperature, and on the difference in temperature. In such an ideal system the flow of heat into work could be exactly reversed to give a flow of work into heat—that is, when a slightly more powerful engine drove the first one backwards. Carnot concluded that "no heat-engine constructed by man can produce more available work from heat than the ideal [reversible] engine working under the same conditions". He thus propounded his concept of a reversible process entirely in engineering terms, so that it took some time for the working-out of the quantitative mathematical aspects of the thermodynamical principle he had invoked. Applied universally in the 2nd Law of Thermodynamics, this principle assumes that entropy is everywhere to be found, that in every system, animate or inanimate, there is a loss of thermal energy for conversion into work, and that the universe is steadily and irreversibly running down to the point where no more energy at all will be available. The universe is thus imaged as a vast steam-engine in which heat is all the while disappearing; in the end no more work will be possible and there will result a total deadlock or equilibrium. We see the philosophical consequences of a world-model based on the power-systems employed by industrialism.[10]

In 1842 R. Mayer tried to determine the mechanical equivalent of heat produced when air was compressed; but he omitted the possibility of heat being consumed in the process within the air itself or of its being generated by the transformation going on in internal potential energy. Joule of Manchester, pupil of Dalton, carried on more successfully. Already in 1840 he had shown that when electric current was produced by means of a dynamo-magneto-electric machine the heat generated in the conductor (when no external work was done by the current) was the same as if the energy used in producing the current had been converted into heat by friction. He also determined an approximate value for the mechanical equivalent of heat out of these experiments; and he extended his investigation to currents produced by batteries. He defined his unit of work (the footpound) as the work done in raising a pound weight through a foot; his unit of heat (the calorie), as the heat that raised a pound of water through a degree of the Fahrenheit scale. He showed that there was a fixed relation between the two units so that one unit of heat always yielded the same definite number of units of work: of what was later called the mechanical equivalent of heat. He thus proved that heat and work were interchangeable at a fixed rate, and determined what the rate was.

In 1843 he published *On the Calorific Effects of Magneto-Electricity and on the Mechanical Value of Heat.* Work could be done by other agencies than heat, by electrical and radiant energy. There was a kinetic energy of motion, called by Joule *vis viva*, a living force, and a potential energy such as the energy of a raised clockweight. Joule found that these two energies were interchangeable at fixed rates. In 1844–5 he published a series of researches into the compression and expansion of air, showing that Mayer's assumption was correct in practice—though later researches by Joule and by Kelvin showed the incorrectness of the claim that no internal work was done when a gas expanded or contracted, even if the amount was very small with gases (oxygen, hydrogen, nitrogen) which can be liquefied only by intense cold and high pressure. In 1847 he announced: "Experiment has shown that when living force is apparently destroyed, whether by percussion, friction, or any similar means, an exact equivalent of heat is restored. The converse is also true. Heat, living force, and attraction through space (to which I might add light, where it is consistent with the scope of the present lecture) are mutually convertible. In these conversions, nothing is ever lost." Also, nothing is ever gained.

In the same year von Helmholtz in a pamphlet set out the same conclusion; but by an abstract argument against the possibility of perpetual motion. About the same time William Thompson (later Lord Kelvin) began to study these matters mathematically and to build up out of them a consistent theory. Every material, it had now been shown, contained a pool of heat, living force, and so on, which represented its capacity for doing work, and each aspect could change into another at fixed rates of exchange. The total stayed the same throughout all transformations, except in so far as it was increased or diminished from outside. Kelvin described the pool as Energy, a term brought into physics by Young in his *Lectures on Natural Philosophy*, 1807.

Joule's principle could now be expressed in the thesis that energy was conserved. He had been concerned in the main with mechanical forces and heat, but had shown that the same principle applied to electrical power. In 1853 Julius Thomsen found that energy was conserved in chemical transformations. Thus a general principle of the conservation of energy was established in physical science, where it formed a fitting companion to the principle of the conservation of mass. Energy like mass was seen to be of a constant total amount; all the changes in the universe were the result of redistribution of the pools of energy and mass which never changed their total amounts.

Kelvin proposed a precise scale of measuring energy or heat. Accepting the theory that heat was a random motion of the particles of a body, he proposed that temperatures be measured from a zero point at which there was no such motion: the absolute zero of temperature. Considerations set out by Carnot showed that this would be the same for all substances; and experiments set it at −273° C. But it was not possible to ask how the molecules and atoms of a substance must function so as to endow the substance with its observed physical properties. After attempts by others, James Clark Maxwell in 1859 took the problem up and tried to find what the average speed of molecules would be if the disturbing effect of collisions was allowed for, and also how the average speed of individual molecules would be distributed about the general average. His conclusion, known as Maxwell's Law, was gained by fine mathematical intuition rather than by rigorous analysis.

General ideas about heat, motion, and conservation of energy had indeed been coming up ever since the start of the new science in the sixteenth and seventeenth centuries. Bacon declared his belief that heat consisted of a kind of motion or "brisk agitation" of the particles of matter. "The very essence of heat, or the substantial self of heat," he said in his *Novum Organum*, "is motion and nothing else." Newton divined the principle of conservation of energy in so far as it applied to mechanics. But what became of work done against friction and such non-conserving forces remained obscure, while the chemical doctrine that heat was an indestructible substance led to the idea that it was lost. Early writers did not distinguish heat and temperature. Joseph Black, the Scottish chemist (1728–99), showed that the distinction existed and that heat could be measured, thus opening the way to the linking of heat with the mechanical scheme. But it was not till industrialism had made much progress with the use of steam-power that the Carnot–Joule synthesis arrived. Black, however, had been the first to make an accurate measurement of heat, in terms of the rise of temperature when heat was absorbed by a given mass of water; he thus devised a product-unit of measurement, which worked out as defining heat-energy as the mass of water multiplied by the rise in temperature. Joule used this work by Black; but Black's method did not yield any direct relation between the energy supplied by an engine as heat and the energy got from it as mechanical work. Joule was the man who made the connection between the two units. Industrialisation had made considerable progress in the use of steam-power between the days of Black or Carnot and those of Joule.[11]

It seemed from the work of Rumford, Carnot, Joule, Maxwell and Kelvin that conservation of energy was mechanically established and that everything in the universe moved and changed by a set of relationshipships which could be thus quantatively set out. In fact the conservation described and proved in these terms was valid only for small motions such as are encountered in engineering problems and their applications.

We need not discuss here the strains on the system from the days of Planck and Einstein, and the problems raised by the behaviour of particles; but we may note how, with quantum mechanics, energy, hitherto conceived in terms of mass and velocity, or of the ability to produce velocity in a mass, has become directly related to frequency of oscillation. One result is a ghosting of nature. "The limiting of energy interchanges as between one system and another to complete 'packets' or *quanta* imports into physics an operation which seems inconceivable except as the bare outcome of a piece of mathematical formalism" (Whiteman). The elementary particles can be taken to exist in a certain position only at the instant when the experimental effect appears; and the wave function characterising any atomic system represents only a set of possibilities, one of which will be actualised, in an unpredictable way, under particular experimental circumstances. The actual controlling or organising system cannot be expressed as anything definite in physical space.[12]

These problems we can for the moment ignore. But, returning to the Laws of Thermodynamics, we may note an odd contradiction between the 1st and the 2nd. The 1st insists on the conservation of energy, which is never created or destroyed, only transformed from potential to kinetic. The original states of say coal or gunpowder store potential energy, which is released as kinetic energy when the coal is burned or the powder exploded. The 2nd Law denies that a simple process of transformation occurs when heat is involved. Heat is seen as energy which is scrambled or randomised over all the molecules in matter; the degree of disorder thus produced is represented by the temperature produced by the heat, and the disorder will never of its own accord move towards order. So on the one hand energy is merely being transferred from one form to another without any loss; on the other hand energy is producing a steady decrease in order and organisation. That there is any counter-process, organising or formative, at work is expressly denied because the mechanical systems from which the concept of energy is derived have no place for it; they can express disintegration, but not integration.

A few more points about the Joule–Kelvin system need to be noted. Energy is defined as accumulated mechanical work. A charge of gunpowder has energy as it can do work in exploding; a bent spring has energy as it can do work in returning to its natural form; a Leyden jar charged with electricity has energy as it can do work in being discharged; a magnet in attracting other bodies does work during their movement towards it. The motions of bodies or of the ultimate parts of bodies also involve energy, since the stopping of them becomes a source of work. But energy is not just the capacity to do work, since we cannot always bring about the change which actually does work. So we may call it that which diminishes when work is being done, by an amount equal to the work in question. Kelvin differentiated available energy from diffuse energy: that is, useful work can be got from a system by simply connecting visible portions of it by a train of mechanism.

The notion of potential energy, we may add, had been developed by applied mathematics in the eighteenth century; such energy was determined by simple multiplication of weight-lifted by height-raised. Following Savory, Watt found out by trial how many footpounds of mechanical work his engine could provide every second. The footpounds of such work supplied by a good horse, in the same length of time, had already been determined; it was thus possible to make an exact comparison of horse-power and engine-power. In mechanical systems the working stresses in operation between the parts may be defined when the relative positions of all the parts are known; and the energy that a system possesses by reason of such relative position, or by its configuration, is its latent or potential energy. Kinetic energy, the energy of motion, is owned by a system of two or more bodies by reason of the relative position of the parts. The concept of velocity is essentially relative, so that any property a body owns by reason of its motion may be effectively defined only in relation to those bodies in respect to which it is moving. Our choice of the base of measurement then intimately affects the estimate of kinetic energy.[13]

Carnot was much indebted to Watt for the insights represented by his work on the expansive power of steam and his separate condensor. Watt led physicists to think along the lines which he had found profitable, e.g. the fact that heat flowed from a hot object to a cold one. Carnot also drew on the concepts of efficiency and reversibility evolved in hydraulic engineering. Indeed we cannot overstress the close relation between the theory of energy and the industrial processes developing from the sixteenth century onwards. Here we touch on the essential difference between ancient and modern thought in such matters. Mining had played a considerable rôle in the new technology. In Agricola's *De Re Metallica*, 1561, apart from a slight use of water-power, animals supply the primary motive force. By the later seventeenth century scientists were seeking an alternative source of power, especially for driving pumps. Capitalist relations in industry were growing and the Cromwellian Revolution had broken through the feudal system in England. Samuel Morland, Master Mechanic to Charles II, had served in Parliament under Cromwell and written a history of the Piedmont Protestant Churches (whose persecution evoked a sonnet from Milton); he also constructed hand fire-engines of various kinds and devised calculating machines, a capstan, and the speaking trumpet. He was aware of the great power available in steam, though it could not yet be harnessed. In 1685 he wrote:

> Water being evaporated by fire, the vapours require a greater space, about 2,000 times that occupied by the water. And rather than submit to imprisonment it will burst a piece of ordnance. But being controlled according to the laws of statics, and by science reduced to the measure of weight and balance, it bears its burden peaceably, like good horses, and thus may be of great use to mankind, especially for the raising of water.

1. Animate power (goats in treadmill, men on capstan wheel) with windmill in distance: Agricola's *De Re Metallica*, 1561

Note the stress on steam's explosive power and the idea of it as a surrogate for horses. Morland understood that the full mechanics of the problem had yet to be worked out. "The measure of weight and balance" is felt to hold the capacity to transform the explosive violence, the war-aspect. into something that will serve men "peaceably". The existing patents show how many men were struggling to overcome the problem. T. Savory's first condensing engine, a pistonless steam-vacuum pump, was patented in 1698; he was a military engineer like Carnot. In his engine, heat-energy from the boiler was partly converted into potential energy of the water raised from a low level by a pump; but there was still no effective alternative to animal power.[14]

The first steam piston-engine of which we know was built near Wolverhampton in 1712; it did work equivalent to seven normal horses. The question of horse-power was very much in men's minds. Early steam-engines, though more dependable than windmills and easier to handle than large teams of draught animals, were cumbrous, unwieldy, lacking in flexibility. The machines had to be popularised and proof given that they were superior to other methods; their progress depended on the working-out of more compact and flexible power-units. Hence the concern for precise relations to horse-power. Mechanical energy is measured by the product Force Exerted x Distance Moved by Point of Application of the Force. Watt established that a typical horse could do mechanical work at the rate of 33,000 feet x pounds per minute. Whether or not the equation would apply today to horses, it gave a definite quantitative unit for measuring the rate at which a prime mover, animal or mechanical, was able to do work. Using Rankine's *Useful Rules and Tables* we may estimate that while ox, mule, ass, man (pumping or turning winch) worked at a rate well under that of a horse, the overshot 18-foot waterwheel worked at a rate of 2 to 5 horse-power, a post-windmill at a rate of 2 to 8, and the early stationary steam-engines at a rate of 7 to 1,000. We see how the computations about horse-power, linked with the need for more efficient working of steam-power, led on to the ideas of Carnot.

The war-aspect was never absent. In 1770 Cugnot designed a Steam Artillery Carriage. Far back in 1690 Papin had considered whether the expansion of gases that occurred at the igniting of gunpowder might not be used to drive a piston in a cylinder. The same image lies behind the later more successful attempts that led on to the internal combustion heat-engine. Patents for gas ignition-engines date from 1794 on, but it was not until 1860 that Lenoir constructed the first engine that made effective use of the expansive thrust of hot gases when an explosive mixture is sparked off. Petrol motor-vehicles appeared round 1876–8 through the work of Otto and Benz. Carnot in 1824 had described an internal combustion-engine devised by French engineers, Messrs Niepce, which involved the formation of a mixture of air and lycopodium powder in a cylinder. The mixture inflamed when ignited and provided an expansive thrust on the piston. At this time the costly powder (fern spores) was needed to supply a very finely divided inflammable solid, which left little or no ash on combustion. Carnot himself refers to the possibility of igniting mixtures of air with hydrocarbon vapours in piston-engines.[15]

A related use of the expansive powers of hot gases appeared in developing force by letting the gas react in the blades of a turbine. Successful steam-turbines were introduced by de Laval and by Parsons in 1882–4. If hot gases are let out through a jet, a backward thrust is exerted on the vessel from which they emerge. Here we meet also the basis for gaining a driving force from heat-energy to propel jet aeroplanes and rockets.

The idea of using gunpowder to provide a jet motive-power for propelling rockets goes far back. Rockets were known in Europe from about 1380 when they were used in a battle between Genoese and Venetians. Giovanni di Fontana in his *Metrologum de Pisce Cane et Volucre*, about 1420, deals with clocks capable of measuring very short periods of time, which were to be operated by moving models (of fish, bird, hare) powered by rockets. He states: "I have seen and experimented with the tube filled with gunpowder which flies through the air. When it is ignited, indeed, it is sent upwards by the force of the fire that is emitted behind, until the powder is consumed." He speaks of a flying dragon constructed with a thick long tube in the inside of its belly along its length, the fire surging out through the anus. (Here we see blast-power directly connected with bodily flatus.) Such experiments in fact go back to ancient ideas and models, which were never developed because the social and economic situation provided no basis for their application.[16]

More on Aristotelean *Energeia*

II

We now have a general idea of the difference between Aristotle's *Energeia* and Joule's Energy, and of the way in which the post-1600 economic situation stimulated the efforts to find a link between the power-engine and mechanical theory. But Aristotle's positions were more complex than we have yet shown, and their strengths and weaknesses were greater. On the weak side we may point to his belief that the world of the celestial sphere was one of natural circular motion and so quite different from that of the earth; and to his failure, shared with other ancient thinkers, to link his concepts with any evolutionary perspective. The final cause or function is considered to have been implanted in, say, a seed as if by some predetermining system. The seed is simply there, and with it the whole process of *dynamis-energeia* which will turn it into a tree. To explain the seed Aristotle would have to fall back on his theory of the way in which simple bodies come together; a certain composition of two or more of them happened to form the seed, but no method for grasping in precise detail just how the composition came about was available or even attempted.

There were thus all sorts of metaphysical divisions cutting his concepts off from the concrete processes he sought to grasp and define. Matter was seen as inseparable from form; but the lack of any evolutionary perspective prevented Aristotle from developing a concept of matter which gave it a formative force in its own right and which allowed effectively for the interaction of forces. Form was imposed on passive matter, just as the father was considered to put into the passive womb the active form that produced the child's organism. Still, when we have pointed out these limitations, we can wonder at the richness of the system and at the way in which only a step more is needed to break down the metaphysical divisions and arrive at a truly unitary and dialectical concept of change, movement, growth, development.

A closer view of the concepts will show how the system is in one sense continually trying to overcome its own limitations. Aristotle begins the third book of his *Physics* by raising the question of what *kinēsis*, movement, is. "Since nature [*physis*] is the principle [*archē*] of *kinēsis* and change [*metabolē*] and our inquiry is about nature, we must understand what *kinēsis* is; for if we don't know that, we shall not know what nature is." Commentators agree that he is here using movement and change as synonyms, and that is true, though *metabolē*, like our change, has a wider sphere of reference than has movement. Neither movement nor change is itself an existent. "There is no such thing as *kinēsis* over and above the things."[1] Change is always with reference to something. "That which changes, changes always with reference to an *ousia*", a self-subsisting individual, "or to quantity or to quality or to place". And *physis* has as its primary meaning "the genesis of growing things". The subject, *ousia*, is a natural being—one to whom *kinēsis* belongs by its very essence. And this *kinēsis*, as we saw, always entails on the one hand a potentiality and an end-state. It is not movement in an isolatable way, reducible to mechanics.

Because of the way in which we tend to make that reduction, the term movement is not an adequate translation of *kinēsis*. *Kinēsis* is a process of transition aimed at the achieving of a particular end, and we do not possess any single word able to compass the full reach of this meaning. *Kinēsis* is a process of achievement. And yet here again we have to be careful. *Kinēsis* is not a first motion, a process that carries on—and then, emerging out of it, the existence of the natural object. Such a view treats *kinēsis* as something existing by itself apart from the object as a sort of abstract mover, an external force; it leads either to mechanics or to the notion of some transcendental power operating from outside nature. It contradicts the fundamental idea of a being in nature as one that involves *kinēsis* in its very *ousia*. Potentiality and actuality cannot be separated; they must be seen as making up an integral whole, in a polar relationship.

Dynamis and *energeia*, we see, cannot be simply opposed to one another. *Dynamis* implies a potency to move or change, but it also implies that which is capable of being actualised by the motion. Motion is always the motion of something, of an *ousia*; and so this *ousia* as the subject of the motion is always involved in the *dynamis*. The *ousia* must itself be in some respects actual. Pure potentiality by itself would be merely the capacity to move without the process of moving in fact taking place. So *kinēsis* is the process of attaining, in contrast to the end-state or that which is attained; it actualises the *dynamis* and is a full being "in-act", *energeia*. Aristotle says: "*Kinēsis* takes place when the full achievement itself exists, and neither earlier nor later. The achievement of the potentially existent, when it is a fully achieved being in act, not *qua* itself, but *qua* moveable, is *kinēsis*."[2]

Physis or Nature, we saw, is that which has the principle of motion in itself, and *kinēsis* is thus in its essence an aspect of Nature. Nature itself then appears as not a sphere of mere flux or random change—change which just happens. To understand the change manifest in the kosmos we must see it as based in the very being or *ousia* of natural or physical process. The fundamental change is the *kinēsis*, which is the process involved in the actualisation of existents. So every physical existent is in constant process of actualisation, and that process is not something added or driving it on from outside; it resides in its very being. A physical being does not exist as simply actual; it exists as in-actualisation, *energeia*. Existence and process are one and the same thing, and process consists of three forms of change: qualitative, quantitative, and positional. The transition constituting actualisation can be analysed into one or other of these, but most likely consists of all three in union. (The heavenly bodies alone were thought merely to change positions.) Locomotion, *phora*, is only one form of *kinēsis* and cannot in the Aristotelian system be separated from the full range of quantitative and qualitative changes going on in any object or group of objects.[3]

In his system Aristotle is working out with particular fullness a view of nature which was generally held by the Greeks: the view that nature has in itself the *archē* or principle of movement and that this principle lies at the heart of the process bringing about the universe with its manifold forms and compositions. Nature is the sensible bodily-extended, with movement essentially related to all being, *ousia*. We may call this outlook both unitary and organic; we may also call it materialist as long as we understand that matter for the Greek thinkers is not the ghostly quantitative abstraction that it has become since the seventeenth century, but is seen as implying physical and sensory existence in its fullness. When Aristotle said that the *physiologoi*, the philosophers of *physis*, identified nature with matter, *hylē*, he was thinking in a much larger and richer sphere of reference than the term "matter" now suggests or implies.

Let us look closer at the word *physis*. *Phyein*, the verb, is used in both *Iliad* and *Odyssey* for bringing forth, producing, especially of the vegetable world; in the passive, for growing, springing up. The *Odyssey*, once, has the noun: Odysseus says of the herb moly, a pharmakon or magico-medicinal substance, "Hermes showed me its nature." *Physis* gained its wider sense through the *physiologoi*; the word appeared in titles of books by Xenophanes, Herakleitos, Philolaos in his publication of the Pythagorean treatises, Gorgias, Epikouros. It was used for the regular order of nature Demokritos, Herakleitos) and for nature as an organising power (Herakleitos, Aristotle); Plato generalised it as elementary substance, followed by Aristotle; Archelaos used it for nature in opposition to human conventions, and Plato used it for natural law as opposed to chance. The Hippokratic writers used it to mean growth, but also for the natural place or position of bone or joint. Empedokles used it to mean origin as opposed to end, as well as for a person's nature or character. In general then we may say that the word had a strong sense of growth, of springing up or out, and also of a regular or orderly system determining the ways or forms of growth. Aristotle defines *physis* as "that immanent part of a growing thing from which its growth first proceeds". It is the *archē*, source or principle, of all living things.[4]

For the early Milesian thinkers what is, is extended bodily. So *physis* must be something extended—water, for example—and we arrive at the concept of the *ousia*, the being or essence of thngs. That is natural which has its *physis* in itself, by virtue of what it is. So for Aristotle *physis* is the *ousia* of natural things; but he also uses the term collectively to denote all things that are natural, that thus have a nature by virtue of what they are. Soul and spirit, *psyche* and *pneuma*, were taken to be extended existences like everything else, even though they might be of finer stuff. The physical universe was the bodily-extended universe, not an aspect of the universe isolated as definable in terms of mechanics.

The weakness of this line of thinking, as set out in the pre-Sokratic *physiologoi*, was that all existence was seen, so to speak, at the same level; differences in structure were merely the result of simpler or more complex compositions made up out of the unitary stuff. The crisis emerging out of the unrealised contradictions here came to a head with Plato, who, in the name of hierarchy and function, broke up the unitary concept and put in its place a dualism of extended things, known to the senses, and non-extended things, known to the mind. Life is split in half, and the formative and organising elements of process are handed over to an otherworld, that of the spirit and of the stars, while the earthly sphere is controlled, moulded, given form and meaning, only by the otherworld. In that latter world reside the Forms or *Eidē* which provide significant structure and purpose to what is otherwise a passive, meaningless flux. Socially we see reflected in these ideas and attitudes the breakdown of Athenian democracy, the lapse of faith in human (social) process unless it is controlled autocratically from above; but at the same time we see a genuine inner crisis in the concept of nature and movement, change and actualisation. If we examined Plato's work in detail we should find, not only the despairing turn to transcendental factors for an explanation of the organisation of life, but also a quest for the dialectical principles through which the split between spirit and matter can be overcome.

And so we find the next two great schools of thought, the Aristotelean and the Stoic, each in its own way, attempting to resolve the Platonic contradictions and to regain a unitary and organic outlook without losing what was valuable in the Platonic critique.

Plato in the *Timaios* had made a distinction between actual physical existence and its *archai*, its sources and principles; for him the *archai* were the transcendental Forms and the recipient of form, the imperfect earthly reflection of archetypal structure and function. Aristotle took over this distinction, omitting the transcendental aspect and identifying the recipient with *hylē*, matter. Form he saw as inherent in substance, not as something imposed on a formless flux by forces from outside our world. But the ghost of the Platonic split persisted, revealing itself in the metaphysical form into which Aristotle had to cast his new version of the unitary stream of being. In the later applications of Aristotelian doctrine the tendency to treat form and matter as distinct or separable realities increased, as we see clearly expressed in medieval scholasticism attempting to carry on his systems; and this tendency, together with the reasserted influences of Plato in the Renaissance, led to the two *archai* being taken in the seventeenth century as themselves actual existents: material substance and spiritual substance. The new science of Galileo and his fellows stressed dualism with a vastly enhanced force. So the question of the *archai* was removed into ever greater abstraction; in this split world of thought God had to be seen as the sole *archē*. Leibniz protested at the fallacy of the *deus-ex-machina* brought in to solve oppositions and contradictions, but himself couldn't in the end resist it. Then from the eighteenth century God dropped out except as a pious appendage; and with him went all question of an *archē* at all. Matter as a mechanical system filled the picture, with physical existence as a sensory reality omitted or relegated to a secondary place as something merely subjective. The inevitable result of such a development is a science which ends by relying on mathematical constructions for which no models can be found in the physical, sensory world and which cannot be described in physically comprehensible terms. The illusion that this is the natural form of a highly advanced science accompanies the progressive movement into abstraction.[5]

We can bring out the way in which Aristotle struggled to achieve a system at once unitary and dialectical if we look at his treatment of time. As the process of becoming or actualisation is continuous, it is eternal and cannot be said to have ever come into existence or to imply that it will ever reach an end. "It is impossible that *kinēsis* should either have come into being or cease to be (for it must have always existed), or that time should. For there could not be a before or an after if time did not exist. *Kinēsis* also is continuous, then, in the sense in which time is; for time is either the same thing as *kinēsis* or an attribute of it."[6]

Time then for Aristotle is not some kind of separate existent as it has been taken in post-Newtonian doctrine, or in the recent variation of that doctrine in which, as in Einsteinian Relativity, time is linked with space, though the abstraction remains, in a more refined and complex form. For Aristotle, time is an aspect of *kinēsis*, of the fundamental process by which physical existents are actualised; it is an aspect of the ceaseless enaction of physical existence. It is thus continuous, but its continuity is not an abstract mathematical one. The actualisation is concrete and may be said to occupy a durational stretch as well as an extensive volume.

But "that which has potency need not actualise it", since *dynamis* entails a capacity for either being or non-being. So the ultimate acting and form (the two *archai*) need a third factor to provide the necessity of actualisation. *Dynamis* implies a *telos* or end, but a specific *telos* is not contained in *dynamis* as such. The third factor cannot be transcendental, as in religion, for what is needed is a further coordinate with the two *archai*. In Aristotelian terms it is pure actuality or enaction, a specific and individual enaction. It is both *ousia* and *energeia*. What Aristotle is saying can easily be misunderstood, because of the way in which his terms are entangled with the astronomical ideas of his day; but if we get at the essence of what he means, we can make out two key points. First, all physical existents must derive their purpose or end from the actuality which is the source of all such purpose or end. Secondly, the purpose or end is not simply and individually received directly by each physical existent, but is received in mediation through the entire structure of all physical existents in relation to one another.

That is, what is entailed is not just a simple two-term relation between each individual physical existent and the source of its end. Such a relation could not explain the specific content and direction in movement of each physical existent. The relation is a highly complex one, which in the last resort includes all other existents in its scope—each according to its perspective from the existent in question. We see then, on the one hand, that there is a conjoint operation of all three *archai* in the process; and, on the other hand, that the total interrelation of all physical existents involves a general order of extensive relatedness which in its working-out becomes increasingly and progressively more specific —ending in the specific set of causes, compositions, that appear in the particular object with its own nexus of time and place, and with its own definite relations to other existents. Each specific end is therefore entailed in the general relatedness as a limit.[7]

We see, then, Aristotle struggled hard to hammer out a philosophy of process in which a concept of unitary *physis* was maintained, which also grappled with the problem of development and structure, and which, while working out a general pattern of movement and change, tried to show how specific objects or events appeared within it.

One more point: the way in which Aristotle defined infinity. Since enaction is eternal, pure actuality is infinite, yet the concept of the infinite cannot pertain to the actual as an attribute. The actual as such is complete, while the concept of infinity implies the absence of wholeness; it implies that which it is always possible to go beyond in some respect. Infinity therefore pertains only to process, "that which is gone through". Eternal *energeia* is such a process, and so infinity may be said to pertain to the process of enaction, which is never complete.

The becoming or *kinēsis* of physical existence is also a process; its *archē* is pure potency, the ultimate substratum acting. This acting, because it is necessarily conjoined with the other two *archai*, is eternal; and so the process of *kinēsis* is infinite. But physical existence itself is infinite only in relation to *kinēsis*.

It follows that we cannot look on the physical universe as infinitely extended; for extension is a relation, not an attribute. A relation cannot be infinite since it entails terms.

> In the light of these issues, the modern conception of the physical as matter has been shown to entail a separation of continuity from the discrete, of the finite from the infinite, of the mathematical from the physical, separations which are bridgeable only by an appeal to a transcendent *archē*. To the extent to which this conception of the physical is retained, explicitly or implicitly, these implications will continue to have their effect on thought. The consequences in contemporary science are considerable.
>
> What is needed is a conception of nature as essentially in becoming (and not as a changeless actuality), that is involving a process of *kinēsis* (and not merely moving from place to place), and as having the *archē*, source, of its *kinēsis* in itself (and not transcendent)—an *archē* which must be understood in a threefold aspect (Leclerc).[8]

For Aristotle, then, the physical is matter in movement, but this movement is not in its full nature mechanical—however much it may at one level involve the mechanical analysis. It is a movement from a potential state into *energeia* and through *energeia* into a full actualisation of the potentiality. But the latter is not simply inherent in the moment entailing enaction; it is itself a resultant of an endless threefold process and at each moment its enaction is related to the world outside in a threefold fashion, in an endless chain which in the last resort involves the whole universe, but in which certain factors will have a stronger influence or effect than others, according to a hierarchy determined by the nature and time-place of the *ousia*, the individual physical existent in question. There is nothing fated in the movement, nothing predetermined by the fusion of form and matter at the outset of the process; for potentiality is not compelled by a simple necessity into *energeia*. It can be held back or prevented from issuing into *energeia*, and the full enacting can itself be thwarted or frustrated in varying degrees.

Aristotle's system is thus a very subtle mixture of the concrete and the abstract, the dialectical and the metaphysical. We can find in it an embryonic form of the dialectical concept, worked out by Hegel and Marx, of the unity and the conflict of fundamental opposites, which bring out the movement into a new synthesis, a new unity with its specific qualities. Or we can trace aspects of the concept, worked out by L. L. Whyte, of the presence of an element of unbalance or asymmetry in all physical existence, so that an *ousia* in its complex set of inner and outer balances and unbalances is driven continually to reassert symmetry on a new level, with extended self-organisation. But such systems are not here consistently developed; the concept of relatedness remains primitive and insecure (except in terms of purely logical exposition); the full body of unified theory and practice never appears. Yet, when the worst is said, we must admit that here is an attempt on a grand scale to work out a theory of process which deals always with wholes in a concrete way. In this theory *energeia* is a universal aspect of process, which simultaneously involves both the qualities and quantities of objects; in modern theory energy is entirely quantitative, a matter of mechanics, a measure of a body's power of doing work by virtue of its motion.

The idea of conservation is present throughout a great deal of Greek thought. We find a belief in the *homologia* or agreement of the elements, which comes about through *isomoiria*, equal proportion, and *isodynamia*, equal power. Heavy and light, hot and cold, are equally balanced in their totalities, so that there is an underlying *isonomia*, equal distribution, balance, equilibrium. (The word is used by Herodotos and Thoukydides for equality of political rights, and the latter opposes it to *dynasteia* or power exercised by an oligarchy. *Homologia* also has the meaning of pact, truce, terms of peace, and the Stoics used it to express conformity with nature.) These concepts were doubtless first worked out in part by the Pythagoreans with their interest in proportions; but in extant texts the key passage is to be found in Plato's *Timaios* where he tells how the demiurge, called the *xynistas*, the combiner or arranger, set water and air between fire and earth, and "bestowed on them so far as possible a like ratio, *logos*, towards one another—air being to water as fire to air, and water being to earth as air to water. Thus he fitted together and constructed a heaven visible and tangible. For these reasons and out of these materials, such in kind and four in number, the body of the kosmos was harmonised by proportion and brought into existence. These conditions secured for it amity, *philia*, so that, being united in identity with itself, it became indissoluble by any agent except him who had bound it together."[9]

The author of *On the Kosmos* later sums up the conservation-view:

> Even the unexpected changes are accomplished in due order: the winds of all kinds that clash together, thunderbolts falling out of the heavens, storms that burst violently out. Through these the moisture is squeezed out and the fire dispersed by air-currents; in this way the whole is brought into harmony [*homonoia*] and so established. The earth too that is crowned with plants of every kind and bubbles with springs and teems with living creatures everywhere, that brings forth everything in season and nurtures it and receives it back again, that produces a myriad shapes and conditions—this earth still keeps its never-ageing nature unchanged, though it is racked by earthquakes, swamped by floods, and burnt in part by fires.
>
> All these things, it seems, happen for the good of the earth and give it preservation from age to age: for when it's shaken by a quake, there's an upsurge of the winds transferred within it, which find ventholes through the chasms; when it's washt by rain it's cleansed of all noxious things; and when the breezes blow round about it, the things above and below are purified. More, the fires soften things that are frozen, and frost abates the force of the fires. And of the particular things on earth some come into being when they're in their prime and others are perishing, and generation is set in the balance against destruction and destruction

lightens the weight of generation. There's one single principle of preservation sustained uninterruptedly among all these things that interchange with one another, dominating and then being dominated; and this keeps the whole system safe, eternally indestructible.

The only important dissentients were the Stoics, who believed in a periodic destruction of the universe. The thinkers who upheld the eternity of the universe, from Aristotle to Timaios of Lokroi, all based themselves one way or another on the conservation-principle. The elements mingled with an orderly system of give-and-take in the transformations, a system dictated by proportion and equality. Philon of Alexandreia was a strong exponent of this outlook; the pseudo-Aristotle of *On the Kosmos*, we saw, insists on the equal balances within the system of change. The link with political concepts is brought out by such remarks as that of Timaios of Lokroi: "Those things composed according to the best proportions are in a power-equality, none defeats, or is defeated by, others through its share."

However, the idea of the conservation of the elements or forces in the universe remained general and no attempts were made to demonstrate quantitatively how the conservation worked.

If we turn to the question of heat, we find that the Greeks were well aware of its importance, especially in biological matters and in the transformations brought about by craft-activity. Plato remarked that "heat and fire, which generate and sustain other things, are themselves begotten by impact and friction". Men had long known that by rubbing sticks together they could produce fire, and that they could produce heat by rubbing hands, churning water, having sexual intercourse, or getting in the way of blows.

But it was a more difficult matter to work out methods of converting heat into mechanical energy—a conversion which, as we saw, is never complete. That organic life, with its genesis, growth, and development, was intimately connected with heat-processes, was well known in the pre-Sokratic period. Anaximandros is said to have thought that living creatures originated from the wet acted upon by the sun. Aristotle observes of Thales' theory that water was the primary substance: "He probably derived his opinion from noting that the nutriment of all things is moist, that even actual heat is generated from it, and that animal life is sustained by it—though the first principle of all things is that from which a thing is produced; and doubtless for this reason also he held such a theory: both from the fact that the seeds of all things own a moist nature and that water is first principle to the nature of humid things." Parmenides, holding that there were two elements, declared that "according as the hot or the cold predominates does the understanding vary, there being a better and purer understanding derived from the hot; yet even such knowledge requires a certain proportion" or *symmetria.* The Pythagorean Philolaos held the body to be made up of the hot, with no share of the cold; at birth it began to cool through the intake of the surrounding cold. With this cold the body's heat had to find a balance or harmony. The Hippokratic *On Regimen* discussed the thesis that generation occurs through the interaction of the hot and the wet; *On Fleshes* pointed out the connection of humidity and vital heat. Aristotle's biological works are full of allusions to the action of 'innate heat" in maintaining the processes of life; digestion is consistently seen as a kind of cooking. Innate heat (a Hippokratic term) was thought by Galen to be the cause of metabolism.[10]

No attempts were made, however, to measure heat, though doctors attempted relatively precise accounts of heat-states in patients. Doctrines based on hot and cold, dry and wet, were much used in diagnosis and treatment; but the author of *On Ancient Medicine* noted the difficulties that arose, and suggested that hot and cold were the least important of the body's *dynameis.*[11] There was much argument as to which bodily homours were hot and which cold, and also as to whether women as a sex were hotter or colder than men. Empedokles held that the factor differentiating sex in the womb was heat; males apparently formed in the hotter parts, females in the colder. Other thinkers, probably led by Parmenides, argued that women, not men, were the hotter sex. As heat was considered superior to cold, Aristotle tried to assert the greater heat of males by an argument which assumed that what in females is the menses is semen in males; he declared that blood may be more or less pure, more or less concocted, and that semen, though smaller in quantity, was purer and more concocted than the menses, which is an impure residue. Behind the argument lay his belief that women were deformed males. Thick and hot blood conduced to strength, thinner and colder blood to sensation and intelligence. Best of all was to have blood that was both hot, thin, and clear: a combination creating courage and intelligence. Hippokratic writers argued that males, because of their regimen and because females purged their bodies monthly of heat, were hotter and drier; logically they should have argued that females grew drier monthly. But the author of *On Regimen*, for example, wanted to equate males with fire and females with water. There were arguments also as to whether land-animals or sea-animals were hotter or colder.[12]

The Stoics attempted to work out a more thorough and consistent theory of the function of fire and heat. For them the life-force or *pneuma* was composed of air and fire; the identification seems to have been helped by the analogy of *pneuma* with a warm puff of breath. They allotted only one quality to each of the four elements, and fire and air were the active pair.[13] We now enter the sphere of force rather than that of energy, and soon will have much to say about it. Cicero provides a convenient summary of Stoic ideas about fire and heat. "Zeno," he says, "gives us this definition of nature: Nature is a Craftsmanlike Fire proceeding methodically to the work of generation. For he thinks that to create and beget are special properties of art, and that whatever may be wrought by the hands of our craftsmen is much more skilfully performed by nature: that is by craftsmanlike fire, which is the master of all other arts. According to this manner of reasoning, every particular nature is craftsmanlike, as it operates agreeably to a certain method peculiar to itself; but that universal nature, which embraces all things, is said by Zenon to be not only crafts-

2. Creation of Life: Deukalion and Pyrrha forged by smithgod Hephaistos (same sarcophagus as figure 11, page 153: once at Villa Panfili)

manlike but absolutely the craftsman, ever thinking and providing all things useful and proper." The Greek term here translated to express the generative and shaping powers of heat would be *technikos*. (Greek has no word for art; there is only *technē*, craft, to express all things made by men's hands, whether they are tables or statues.)[14]

The Stoics, in using the term *technē* for the operations of natural process, were merely putting in concentrated form what Aristotle had said in setting out his four causes. The craftsman needs material, sets to work on it, and produces an object which has its specific form and function. Only, by seeing the process as the work of fire rather than as the result of matter and form united in producing actuality, they are laying more stress on the creative or formative aspects of change and development; they are seeking to get rid of the metaphysical ghost lurking in the distinction of matter and form.

Cicero goes on, now probably drawing on his teacher Poseidonios:

> It's a fact that all beings which take nourishment and grow, contain in themselves a power of natural heat without which they could not be nourished or grow. For everything of a hot and fiery nature supplies its own source of motion and activity. But that which is nourished and grows possesses a certain regular and uniform motion. And so long as this motion remains in us, so long do sense and life remain; but the moment it abates and is extinguished, we ourselves decay and perish.

He says that Kleanthes, another Stoic, showed how great was the power of heat in all bodies.

> He observes that there's no food so gross as not to be digested in a night and a day, and that even in the excremential parts, which nature rejects, there remains a heat. The veins and arteries, by their continual quivering, seem to resemble the agitation of fire; and it has often been noted that when an animal's heart has just been plucked from the body, it palpitates with such visible motion as to resemble the rapidity of fire. Everything therefore that has life, animal or vegetable, owes that life to the heat inherent in it. It is the nature of heat that contains in itself the vital power extending throughout the whole world.

He continues in this vein. Every division of the world is sustained by heat. He notes that fire is got from stones by striking or rubbing them together, that "the warm earth smokes" (an old Latin verse), and that water is drawn warm from well-springs—especially in winter, when, he thinks, the heat in earth's caverns is made denser. All seeds originate and grow through "the temperature and regulation of heat". Every liquid "has a mixture of heat in it", as is shown by its congealing when the heat goes, and by its liquefaction when heat is reapplied. Earth likewise may be frozen hard and dissolved. The sea grows warm when agitated by winds, showing that "there is heat included in that vast body of water; for we cannot imagine it to be an external and adventitious heat, but it is such as is stirred up by agitation from the deep recesses of the sea. And the same thing takes place with respect to our bodies, which grow warm with motion and exercise." Even air is not lacking in water, and "the fourth part of the universe is wholly fire". So "the hot and fiery principle is so diffused over universal nature that there is contained in it a power and cause of generation and procreation". He adds:

> The world's heat is purer, clearer, livelier, and thus better adapted to move the senses than the heat allotted to us, and it vivifies and preserves all things within the compass of our knowledge. So it's absurd to assert that the world, endowed as it is with a perfect, free, pure, spiritual [pneumatic] and active heat, is not sensitive, since by this heat men and beasts are preserved and move and think. More especially, this heat of the world is in itself the sole principle of agitation and has no external impulse, but is moved spontaneously. For what can be more powerful than the world, which moves and raises the heat by which it subsists?

We see that there is no effort made to distinguish solar heat or fire from the heat or fire obtained by friction or the heat which accompanies all living process. True, all these heats in the last resort own the same nature; but in ancient thought—indeed in all thought up till the breakdown of the Phlogiston Theory in the eighteenth century—fire is conceived as a "thing", a physical existent or substance. Hence the way in which men can speak of innate heat in bodies as if the heat were an ingredient in the same way as earth, water and air. Still, there is a clear idea that heat is doing work as well as being produced by work (friction and so on); and a conviction that the movement involved is measurable—of a "regular and uniform motion"—while itself exercising some sort of regulative function. But there is no suggestion that any attempt should be made to define these regularities.[15]

Though inevitably the rôle of heat in living processes claimed most attention, its relation to inanimate things was not ignored. Aristotle in the fourth book of his *Meteorologika* examined the part played by heat and cold in their construction. Innate (*symphyton*) heat was linked with *pneuma*, the life-force, in all its aspects. And one of Aristotle's problems was to explain how the heavenly bodies emit light and the sun emits heat, when, according to his theory of the *aithēr*, they could not themselves be hot. He tentatively suggested that light and heat were produced by the friction of their movements without the bodies becoming themselves hot.

The Greeks had a profound sense that the same formative process could be seen at work in the structural systems developed by nature and the constructive or creative works of men. They did not mean that the growth of a tree from a seed could be equated with the construction of a table or a statue out of the wood of the tree; but they believed that the same principles of movement, of growth and change, operated in the different spheres. Herein indeed lay their greatest strength, their insistence on dealing with the full concrete situation and on seeking for the unity of the various elements brought together in any given moment of change or development. But this line of approach also determined their limitations, their inability or refusal to isolate aspects of the moment and submit them to quantitative measurement in any consistent way.

We note how the Stoic phrase *technikon pyr*, going on its way to *genesis*, in effect put in a concentrated form the ideas behind the Aristotelian scheme of fourfold causes inherent in all substance. Both the Stoics and Aristotle reflect the attitudes of a craftsman who makes whole things with his hands—a state of things in which fragmentation of the labour-process is minimal. Take the carpenter making a chair. He considers the material at his disposal and the form he is going to impart to it. The material and the mental form are brought together as soon as he starts to work, and all the while he works he is guided by his idea or plan of the structure he has in his mind; and the use to which the finished object is to be put when the job is completed and he has made the material express or embody his idea to the best of his ability. In the job *dynamis* passes into *energeia*, which ends in *entelecheia*; all the while he works, there is movement, not merely the movement of his hands and tools, but also the *kinēsis* or becoming of the object, the wood changing into table.

The four causes thus correspond to stages in the work of a craftsman, which they generalise. Production in the Greek world is individual and concerned with thoroughly understood wholes. In larger works of construction, such as the building of a temple, many men collaborate, but the craft-approach is still much the same. For each man his part is a comprehensible unit, even if he and the others are working under the general plan of an architect.

Aristotle has an interesting passage in the introduction to his treatise on the Parts of Animals, in which he uses the analogy of artistic and natural process in order to defend a scientific concern with even the lowliest forms of life or the most obscure corners of nature:

> It remains to treat of the nature of living creatures, omitting nothing, whether of higher or lower dignity. For even in the case of creatures, the contemplation of which is disagreeable to the sense, Nature, who fashioned them, affords all the same an extraordinary pleasure to anyone with a philosophic disposition and capable of understanding causes. We take delight in looking at representations of these things, because we observe at the same time the art of the painter or sculptor who created them; and it would be strange that contemplation of the works of Nature should not yield a still greater satisfaction when we can make out their causes. Hence the consideration of the lowlier forms of life should not excite a childish repugnance.
>
> There is a story that some strangers wanted to meet Herakleitos but halted on finding him warming himself at the kitchen stove. He told them to come boldly in, for "there also there were gods". In the same spirit we should approach the study of every form of life without disgust, knowing that in each of them is something of Nature and of Beauty. For it's in the works of Nature above all that design, in contrast to random chance, is manifest; and the perfect form, which anything born or made is designed to realise, holds the rank of beauty.[16]

We see there the linkage of craft and natural process together with the basic assumption that the aim of science is to study the total organisation and function of an object or creature. There are gods in the kitchen oven because it is a source of heat and because the heat is used to bring about transformations through cooking. Other ovens are used by potters or smiths to bring about other kinds of transformation. Aristotle himself used the facts of cooking to illuminate the processes of digestion; but he did not go on to measure the heat-points at which the various transformations occurred. His failure in interest here was helped by the lack of any instruments for potters or metallurgists to measure temperature; they used signs or computations inherited in the lore of their crafts, but had no precise methods for marking critical moments of change in the materials they handled.

From Aristotle's viewpoint the mechanical aspects existed and had importance in their own place as helping to explain certain aspects of the way things work, move, affect one another, and change. But the abstracting method could not advance far; by excluding the full reality in order to deal with certain aspects of configuration and motion in isolation it ran counter to the whole trend of ancient thought. Since Galileo there has been a dominant tendency to see all kinds of change as caused by—indeed as—epiphenomena of movements in space: what Aristotle calls locomotions. Thus the moving parts of a thing, which we cannot see, are considered more real than the perceptible and tangible characteristics. Robert Boyle, as an apostle of the new science, in his work *On the Excellence of the Mechanical Principle*, praised "those two most grand and most catholic principles of bodies, matter and motion". But motion here means mechanical movement in space, not qualitative change, and matter has shrunk to the mere medium of such motion, with space as a sort of container. not an integral element of substance in its changes. For Aristotle, as for Greek thinkers in general, change was an observable process involving all the qualities of the object as a whole, not the definition of the changing locations of its miniscule parts. The ancient world did indeed know one branch of science that attempted to look away from the object as a whole and to reduce reality to the miniscule parts: the atomism of Leukippos and Demokritos. But the inquiry remained on a purely theoretical level, with some guesswork about the movement of atoms and their geometrical shapes. (This atomism was in fact a molecular theory—if we could imagine molecules as the indivisible small objects making up reality.)[17]

We have said that it was because of the Greeks' attempts to concentrate on the totality of process that they could not achieve the abstractions needed for the development of mechanics. Yet that is not the whole truth. As we shall see, the Greeks went much further than is usually thought in the applications of mechanical principles in machines or models. What happened was not so much an inability to develop mechanics as a refusal to do so. Not of course a conscious refusal, but a decision expressed none the less in the whole bias of their culture and social attitudes. As a result they did not free their minds (or severely limit them) so as to achieve the sort of generalisations and precisions of mechanical law that began with the sixteenth century and found an important extension in the work of Carnot and Joule. We shall keep on examining this point.

Aristotle tried to distinguish physics from mathematics, to find their points of contract, and to define their respective aims. Both

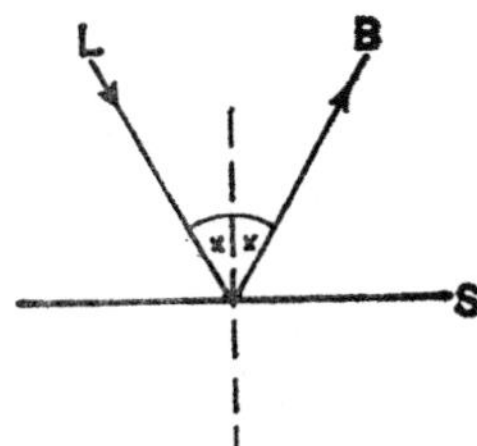

3. Heron's Optical Principle: The ray of light, to go from L to B via the mirror, takes the shortest path

disciplines study "planes and solids and lines and points", but mathematics is not concerned with them as "limits of a physical body". The objects of mathematics are studied in abstraction from movement; the mathematician indeed makes abstraction of everything sensible—weight and lightness, hardness and softness, heat and cold. He leaves only what is quantitative and continuous, and its attributes as such. Arithmetic deals with discrete or unextended quantity; geometry with quantity extended or continuous. Geometrical objects have a certain matter, but pure extension, intelligible pattern, not sensuous, physical, or moveable matter. Aristotle has glimpses of a dynamic continuum, such as the Stoics developed: "They say a moving line generates a surface, and a moving point a line."[18]

A difficulty arises with the application of mathematics to

astronomy, optics, harmonics: "the more physical parts of mathematics". Here thinkers seem to treat of physical bodies, but do so with a mathematical method; and Aristotle finds that these fields are generally ranked as branches of mathematics, though he himself puts them on the whole among physical sciences. However, with regard to such matters as the shape of sun or moon, he thinks that they come under the headings of both physics and mathematics—the latter discipline treating them "not as the limit of a physical body". That is, mathematical astronomy and the like are concerned only with certain attributes abstracted from the concrete object or situation. Aristotle envisages a hierarchy of disciplines in which the higher ones study the reasons for the facts studied by the lower. He thus wavers towards an attempt to work out a method which will combine both the physical and mathematical aspects; but the idea of contemplation as the supreme form of mental activity intrudes, to divide the study of facts from the understanding of causes, as if the causes could be deduced by a general system of logic and the facts collected as things in themselves.

So we return to the logical systems which are expected to extract the secrets of composition, structure, and development from the facts of observation and the like. The physicist, says Aristotle, studies nature for both matter and form, and it is shallow to think that he is concerned solely with matter. Art or craft requires knowledge of form and to some extent of matter; a doctor needs to know both the nature of health and that of the "gall and phlegm" in which health is embodied. The same science studies both ends and means. But there is no idea as to how to make the analysis of means precise. Mathematical analysis, in so for as it exists, carries on in a sort of parallelism with the physical analysis, not in fruitful interaction. Though a valuable rôle is played by mathematics in explaining the phenomena in astronomy, optics, harmonics, and though the doctor and the artist do actively unite theory and practice, no general lessons are drawn to provide a stable basis for scientific work or to link that work consistently with technology.[19]

For Aristotle *energeia* is a release of energy, since it stands for the actualisation of the potentiality of an organism or situation; but nothing could be further from his mind than to define it specifically as a body's power of doing work by virtue of its motion, or to go on to arrive at the equation that this power may be expressed as half the product of the mass with the square of the velocity. The author of *On the Universe*, probably written by a Peripatetic drawing on many neo-Pythagorean ideas as well as some Stoic ones, in the later last century B.C., states that God, residing in the highest place, by his *dynamis* "penetrates the whole of the kosmos, moves the sun and moon, turns the entire heavens, and is the cause of the preservation of all things on earth. He has no need of the contrivance or support of others as do rulers among men who need a host of workers [literally a hand-host] on account of their weakness. The most divine thing is to produce all kinds of results easily by means of a single motion, as do the machine-operators who produce many varied *energeiai* by means of the machine's single release-mechanism."

There are many points to be noted here. We meet *energeia* used in the sense of force producing work. The various *energeia* no doubt refer to the interaction of different parts of a single machine, not to multi-purpose machines; but the use of the term is none the less interesting. Operator, *mechanopoios*, is a term most often used for military engineers—recall Savory and Carnot; *schasteria* is used for the release-mechanisms of catapults and ballistae, but also for that of automatic machines such as Heron's device for producing holy water. The term for machine here is *organon*, and this, taken with *mechanopoios*, suggests a reference to something like a catapult, a war-mechanism. The author goes on, however, to speak of puppets. "In the same way the men who work puppet-shows, by pulling a single string, make the creature's neck move, and his hand and shoulder and eye, and sometimes every part of the body, according to a rhythmical pattern. So also the divine nature, with a single movement of the nearest element, distributes its *dynamis* to the next part and then to the more remote parts until it permeates the whole. One thing is moved by another, and then itself moves another in regular order, all things acting in the manner appropriate to their own constitution; for the way is not the same for all things, but different and various, in some cases quite opposite, though the key of the whole movement, as it were, is set by a single note."[20]

Philon also uses the puppet-simile: "If we leave the understanding out of sight, the remainder of our soul is divided into seven parts, namely five senses, the faculty of speech, and that of generation. All these, as in puppet-shows, are drawn with strings by the understanding, now resting, now moving, each in the attitudes and with the movements appropriate to it." Here however the puppet-master represents the *hegemonikon* or directing faculty which dominates in the soul, so that there is no simple analogy with the passage from *On the Kosmos*, except in so far as the *hegemonikon* in the individual reflects the governing principle of the universe. The passage in Philon, with its numerological discussion of Seven, suggests a neo-Pythagorean source, as does the musical metaphor (*endosis*, the striking of a key-note) in *On the Kosmos*, though the ideas of the *hegemonikon* and of the dynamic unity of the kosmos give a Stoic touch.[21]

In one sense we might claim that the author of *On the Kosmos* is anticipating the concept of the Celestial Mechanism of the eighteenth century; but the *energeiai* set off by the central or unifying *dynamis* are conceived as bringing about process in its fullness, not merely releasing motions that are mechanically measurable. Still, the very use of the machine-metaphor does show a tendency to stress the latter aspect—a tendency which in the ancient world could not develop very far. In Carnot and Joule, as in Galileo and Newton, we see an immensely advanced power of abstraction, which seeks for mechanical laws that can be tested and applied in experiment. This power comes in the last resort from the replacement of craft-activity by machine-production, the steady replacement of the individual craftsman by the mass-proletariat or hands, the enormous extension of the rôle of money (that abstract medium with a common denominator to which all the processes of production and distribution can and must be reduced by the nature of the capitalist system), the increasing division and fragmentation of labour. This development had a long history, going back into later medieval times and gaining momentum in the sixteenth century. The systems of capitalist production and distribution in Galileo's world were still relatively simple, but they were already sapping the old bases. In Holland the national war against the Catholic power of Spain had deep effects, begetting the first society with the burgesses in power; and soon England was to make the decisive break with feudal forms and controls in the 1650s. Even to glance at this situation is to realise how different was the whole social and economic environment of

Galileo and Newton from that of Demokritos and Aristotle. We can grasp how it was that the concepts of force and energy were worked out on quite different lines from those of *dynamis* and *energeia*.

Opposites III

Ideas of the unity or conflict of opposites played an important part in the Greek concept of movement, change and development, and we need some understanding of the way they arose and worked out. The roots of such ideas went far back in the tribal society that lay close behind the Greeks of history; the strength with which the ideas were inherited was revealed by the persistence, in continually changed forms, of certain tribal systems and outlooks in Greek society—until the climax came with the recreation of the tribal assembly of all free men in Athenian democracy. Characteristic of tribal societies all over the world is some form of what may be called the dual organisation, which may appear in simple or highly complex systems, but which owns as its constant and essential principle the division of the tribal group into symmetrically arranged sections. There may be only two of these sections or there may be many multiples of two, but the fundamental idea remains the same. The dual organisation is often linked with myths of twin heroes, with a totemic system of relationships to the animal or plant worlds, and with systems of taboos which are applied in particular to the totemic object and to marriages within the same section of the group. Whatever the origin and full explanation of the taboos, their effect is to maintain the symmetrical subdivisions.

The origin of the dual organisation itself is lost far back in prehistoric time; but we may divine behind it the first stages of man's consciousness of having separated himself out from nature (generally identified with the ancestral spirits). The deep sense of an overriding duality in life—of man set over against nature—expresses both a conflict and a harmony between the two parts: a conflict and a harmony that exists within the higher unity of the life-process. And this sense of duality is in turn expressed in the linked and opposing sections that compose the unity of the tribe;

the human world, it is felt, should reflect within itself the conflict-and-harmony that exists outside it. The individual thus has a dual pattern inherent in his life: he is on one side a member of the divided yet united group, and he is on another side, as a human being, both inside nature and yet separated from it, opposed to it. Behind this kind of system there also perhaps lies an embryonic yet true intuition of the polarities deep inside reality, polarities expressed most obviously in the opposing sexes of the group, which need one another for the perpetuating of the species. Hence in what we may call the fundamental tribal ideas there is a primitive but powerful form of the dialectic of united opposites that determine growth and development. In any event, the complex of ideas growing up around and out of the dual organisation begets a deep sense of polarities and provides the basis for a more systematic working-out of the dialectic. An important point is that while all ancient societies carried on and developed the ideas in question in varying ways, it was the Greeks who first proceeded to use them for the creation of philosophy and science on a grand scale.[1]

In tribal societies the concept of linked opposites is at times extended to take in everything in the universe. Thus in Australia, in the Ngeumba tribe, not only the people but everything whatever belongs to one or other of the two phatries; the subtotems amount to a division of the whole universe between White and Black Cockatoo. In some tribes all things are either male or female. A Kimberley group, seeking to control the intrusions from the modern world, allotted aeroplanes to one world-half and lorries to the other.

The groups of opposites are thus often linked with the opposing groups in the tribe or society. Among the folk of Amboyna, Indonesia, the following basic opposites are set out: Left, Female, Coast or Seaside, Below, Earth, Spiritual, Downwards, Exterior, Behind, West, New—as against Right, Male, Land or Mountain-side, Above, Heaven or Sky, Worldly, Upwards, Interior, In-Front, East, Old.[2] Such sets of opposites are often linked with orientations. In Amboyna the Male is East, the source of light, the place of the rising sun, while the Female is West, the place of the setting sun, of death. Among the Nuer we find weakness, west, femaleness and evil on one side, with strength, east, maleness, goodness on the other. The young men of this African people put their left hand out of action for a long time by binding it with metal rings, because the left is the evil side. Among the Chinese left was Yang, superior; the right was Yin, inferior; and there are other examples of these positions. Fourfold systems are common among the Amerindians, connected with orientations, the seasons, colours, and the quarters of the tribal camp (which is seen as a microcosm, embodying in its fourfold system the essential forces at work in the universe).[3]

Among the Greeks we find the early oppositions of sky and earth, light and darkness, up and down, white and black. There seems to be in Homer and Hesiod the idea of four world-areas: sky, sea, earth, and underworld (night). We may well see here the embryonic form of such later doctrines as that of Empedokles about the four elements. Homer uses the term *dieros brotos*, wet mortal, which seems to mean the same as *zoos brotos*, living mortal. On the other hand the dead are dry, dead men as well as dead trees. Athena, turning Odysseus into an old man, says that she'll dry up his fine skin. Cold also was associated with death and with emotions like fear; warmth with life, and so with joy and relief. These ideas are connected with the observation of dead wood drying and corpses growing cold; no doubt also with experience of strong heat and dryness in the Greek summer, chill and wetness in the winter. The correlation of wetness and life (and sexual desire) perhaps appears already in the rôle assigned in mythology to Okeanos, the primeval surrounding waters: Aristotle states that some thinkers saw Thales, with his concept of water as the primal substance, as rationalising the myth:

> There are some who suppose that the men who lived in the most ancient times, far earlier than the present generation, and who first formed schemes of theology, also entertained opinions after this manner about Nature. For these philosophers constituted both Okeanos and Tethys as the parents of generation and Water as the object of adjuration among the gods—called Styx by the poets themselves; for what is most entitled to respect is what is most ancient. Now an object of adjuration is a thing most entitled to respect. Whether there is this certain early and ancient opinion about Nature, in all likelihood would be an obscure point to decide. Thales indeed is said to have declared his sentiments in this way as to the first cause.[4]

Opposites of various kinds occur in Hesiod's *Theogony*: Night (and Erebos) against Day (and Aithēr), with the implication that Night was prior. We may also note the rôle of Heaven and Earth in the Sacred Marriage, and the pairing, in sexual terms, of male and female personifications. Myths indeed were concerned with origins rather than the existing situation, though we cannot truly speak of their events as located in the past, since they express an eternal present, which is renewed both in the patterns of natural process and in the forms of recurrent rituals. Still, the development from the mythical presentation to a rational analytic method was none the less significant. For example Anaximandros, dealing with definite origins in the past, held that living creatures arose from the wet acted on by the sun. He also gave the concept of opposites a new force, while linking them with social process, when he saw all movement and change as the result of a ceaseless struggle of justice and injustice—a struggle further conceived as involving a self-regulating and self-perpetuating system.[5]

If we look back at tribal societies we find that the dual principle, which in earlier phases is mainly concerned with equilibrium and polarity, comes more and more to express conflict as divisions deepen inside the group. In Polynesia and parts of New Guinea we find a dual chieftainship; one chief is often of war and one of peace. We may compare the consuls of Rome and the kings of Sparta for the duality, and the Two Cities on the Homeric Shield of Achilles (one of peace, one of war) for the social division. Ball games with two sides and dramatic dances of groups opposing one another develop with increased force and scope in symbolism and interpretation. In Persian religion the good and evil principles, Ormuzd and Ahriman, played a ball game; in pre-Columban Mexico *tlachatli* was played with a rubber ball in an enclosed court, associated with Xolotl: twin, double, shadow, especially the night-shadow dogging the sun. We see him playing ball with the moon; and the conflict of light and darkness was symbolised by bright and dark colours for the balls and the courts. The Omaha were divided into sky-people and earth-people, each with five subdivisions; the former were concerned with the creative and organising forces of social and personal life, the latter with the rites and duties of warfare. The two groups played a ball game: the sky-people camping to the north, the earth-people to the south. The Winnebago were divided into two exogamous halves, Those Above and Those Below. The clan-totems of the first group were birds, those of the second, land and sea animals; the leading clan of the first group was the Thunderbird of Peace, of the second the Bear of War. Conflicts and competition can thus invade productive life, as on Tiktopia in the Solomon Islands, where the two main geographical groups were rivals in flyingfish-netting, dancing, dart-hurling, and so on. We also find the two twin culture-heroes quarrelling and fighting, e.g. Romulus and Remus. These heroes often play the ball game, and are opposed as light and darkness (Iroquois), good and bad (Huron), right and left (Zuni); or they are given different colours, as are the camp-orientations. We may compare the pair of identical assessors who represent the morning and evening stars in Mithraic cult-representations, or the Dioskouric brothers of Helen in Sparta, one of whom is immortal, one mortal, or who alternate in death and life.

Aristotle gives us a list of the Pythagorean opposites. They held that the first principles were in ten pairs: The Bounded (or Limited), Odd Numbers, Unity, Right, Male, Rest, Straight, Light, Good, Square—as against the Unbounded (Infinite), Even Numbers, Plurality, Left, Female, Motion, Crooked, Darkness, Evil, Oblong. Aristotle adds that Alkmaion held similar opinions and he himself is not sure who originated the lists, since "Alkmaion had reached the age of manhood when Pythagoras was an old man". Alkmaion declared that "the greater portion of things human may be reduced to two classes, calling them opposites, not distinguished as these [the Pythagoreans] had distinguished them, but such as were any casual sort whatever, as for instance: White, Black; Sweet, Bitter; Good, Bad; Small, Great." He apparently held that everything had its opposite, and is said to have remarked that "most human affairs go in pairs." As he does not include Odd and Even, his list is not Pythagorean.[6]

We cannot date the Pythagorean table, but clearly it ties up with the sort of primitive systems summarised above. Similar attitudes assert themselves at highly sophisticated levels. Thus, Plato in the *Republic* in an eschatological myth describes the judges dividing the souls of men into two groups: the just going to the right, upwards through the sky, with the tokens of their judgments on their fronts, while the unjust go to the left, downwards (into the earth), with their tokens on their backs. Here are four of the pairs listed by the Amboynans. Attempts were made to apply the basic opposites in the interpretation of phenomena, e.g. the differentiation of sex in the womb. Parmenides thought that if a child lay on the right side, it became male; if on the left, female. Anaxagoras thought sex was determined by which side of the father's body produced the semen. In one theory (attributed to Leophanes) the determining factor was the side of the father's testicles sending out the semen. These fantasies entered into the Hippokratic treatises; and in all the variations it is assumed that the male is somehow linked with the right.[7]

Aristotle, appealing to observations made during anatomical dissection, denied these correlations and accused the testicle-theorists of basing their conjecture on a preconception. "They lie, stating what is likely, they guess what will happen, and pre-suppose that it is so, before they see what in fact *is*": an important vindication of direct observation and inquiry as against theoretical assumptions based on an untested generalisation. He is however himself much affected by such opposites as right and left, above and below, front and back. Right, above, and below, he argues, are the *archai*, not only of the three dimensions (breadth, length, depth), but also of the three main types of change (locomotion, growth, sensation) in living beings. He tries to prove that all locomotion proceeds from the right, using such dubious evidence as that men step off with the left foot and bear burdens on their left shoulder—the right side initiating movement—and that they defend themselves with their right limbs. He adds that it's easier to hop on the left leg and that men raise their right eyebrows more than their left.[8]

He declares that the heavenly sphere (which is alive) moves "from the right"; and since for him "upwards" is defined for organisms in relation to the part from which nutriment is distributed, he has to describe plants as existing upside down, the roots being their upper portion. He considers right, above and front to be more "honourable" than their opposites, and uses this principle in his anatomical analysis; e.g. in connection with the windpipe, oseophagus, the "great blood-vessel" (superior and inferior *venae cavae*, perhaps plus the right auricle of the heart), and the aorta. He thus faces a problem of explaining why the heart is on the left when he calls it the life-principle, the source of all movement and sensation in an animal. He stresses that it is rather to the front and in the upper part of the body, and tries to palliate its position by saying that it is put where it is to "counterbalance the chilliness of the left side". His idea of differences of temperature on the two sides of the body is mere fancy, though he uses it to explain other anatomical matters as well, e.g. the "watery" quality of the spleen. Indeed, after all his objections to the linking of sex with the left or right of mother or father, he comes down on a theory that hotter seed is likely to beget males and that it would come from the right side—though he belatedly adds that to make such a statement is "to seek the cause from too great a distance"—that is, without close observation of the actual way the organs behave. He considers that in general limbs on the right are stronger than those on the left; and where he has to admit exceptions, e.g. lobsters and the testaces, he looks on the species as deformed. He holds that in man alone the natural parts are in the natural positions, and the upper parts are turned to what is uppermost in the universe. Finding that the lower animals failed to comply with this ideal, he was confirmed in his belief of the superiority of the human structure.[9]

Plato takes a more rational view of such matters. In the *Laws* he recommends that children should be taught to use both hands equally and rejects the belief that right and left are naturally different, pointing out that the principle does not apply to the feet or lower limbs. He notes that athletes can become ambidextrous. Aristotle indeed admits this point, but thinks the equality is brought about in defiance of the natural strengths of the arms.[10]

Hot and cold, dry and wet, do not figure in the primitive sets of basic opposites, except that we find the seasons there with their changes in heat and cold, dryness and wetness. The first known reference to such pairs of opposites in philosophic writings occurs in fragments of Anaximandros, where they appear together with brightness and darkness, "much earth" and "innumerable seeds", in the primal mixture when "all things were together". They again appear with the rare and the dense, as separating off from one another in the rotation started off by *Nous*, Mind. Here we see the opposites making up an original unity broken up by a rotatory movement—imaged perhaps in terms of boiling, of whirlpool effects gained by stirring water, or circling movements of wind. (Aristotle points out that the similars as well as the dissimilars separate out.) Incidentally, we must not interpret *nous* here as the Mind of some transcendental or supreme God; it means no more than that a coherent and intelligible system operates in the whirl of substances: what Aristotle later called form and final cause.[11]

For the use of opposites in early cosmological theories we have to rely largely on the comments of Aristotle and Theophrastos, who probably simplified things through a wish to show how such theories led up to the Aristotelian thesis of the equilibrium of the opposites and the genesis of the four simple bodies through the interaction of the opposites on undifferentiated matter. The facts were doubtless more complex, though we may accept that in certain key-matters there was a genuine continuity in the tradition.[12]

In Anaximandros we again meet the separation-out of opposites. These opposites, however, were later described by Simplikios as "hot, cold, dry, wet, and the rest", while Aetios refers to hot and cold, and the author of the *Stromateis* says that what separates out is that which is "capable of generating hot and cold". The commentators may be to some extent recasting Anaximandros' formulations in terms of the familiar fire and mist, as we know that he saw the heavenly bodies as circles of fire enclosed in *aēr* (opaque mist), with holes or openings for sun, moon, stars.[13] From the fragments that survive of the early thinkers (Xenophanes, Herakleitos, Parmenides) the primary elements seem to be rather substances like water and earth, fire, light, and night—not the relatively abstract entities, hot, cold, wet, dry. Still, there is little doubt that Anaximandros spoke of opposites forming the universe by separating out from the boundless, from that which has no limits. We have already noted the fragment which describes the opposites as acting on one another with alternate aggression and reconciliation. Simplikios tells us of his thought: "Neither water nor anything else among the suggested elements was first principle of anything, but there is some other non-limited substance from which all the heavens and the worlds contained in them came into being. The source from which existing things derive their existence is also that to which they return at their destruction, according to necessity; for they give justice and make reparation to one another for their injustice, according to the assessment (*taxis*) of Time."[14]

The terms suggest that the "they" are equal, different, and correlative, and we may assume that they are the opposed substances composing the differentiated world. The imagery is social, drawn from class-conflict and presupposing an ideal of equilibrium between contending forces. The word *taxis* suggests the ordering of penalties by a judge or the assessment of tribute, as in the Athenian tribute-lists; in such cases what is assessed is the amount of penalty or payment. But Time as judge suggests further that a time-limit is set for restitution, plus perhaps a proportionate fine. It has been suggested that "the injustice of summer has to be made good within the roughly equal period of winter, that of night during the period of day, and so on. No uniform period can be meant: Time makes the assessment to meet the particular case" (Kirk-Raven). But the significance of Time is wider and deeper than any question of time-limits for reparation, though certainly there is a rhythmic element in the whole conception. Time here has an active character of the kind we shall discuss in the next chapter. We may compare the lines by Solon: "Why did I cease before I gained the objects for the sake of which I brought the People together? The Great Mother of the Olympian daimones would be my best supporting witness for this in the Court of Time: black Earth, whose boundary-stones, fixed in many places, I once removed. Once she was enslaved, now she is free." Earth will plead for him since he freed her from oppressive property-controls or limits by the nobles; Time will vindicate him, but not only in the sense in which later men might "appeal to posterity". Time is the active human process in which he, Solon, has participated; this Time is past, present, and future.

Other lines of Solon conjure up the social situation, and show how Anaximandros is speaking as a moderate democrat of the same type as the early Pythagoreans; his "equality" presupposes the putting-down of the nobles who are overweening, as well as the keeping of the commoners in their place. "Men are tempted to gain riches by unjust acts; they snatch from one another and they steal, nor sparing sacred property or public, not guarding themselves against the dread foundations of Justice who silently notes what's done, what was before, and comes in time to exact unfailing vengeance." Here Justice has the same function as Time in the other quotations; it embodies the whole of human time, past, present and future.

What gives force in such passages to the concept of balance or equal reparation is the dynamic nature of the situation from which they come and which they reflect: the tension between Time-Justice (embodying the ideas and aspirations of the thinker and his class) and the transgressors at each end of the balancing-beam, who keep on trying to upset the equilibrium. If in fact the equilibrium were ever statically fixed, there would be an end of all movement. The universe would fall into a total deadlock, or the process of composition would break down, with a return to the Unbounded. Socially that would mean a return to tribal fraternity, a reversal of the process of differentiation and inequality, an elimination of the "injustices" inherent in the cash-nexus which was driving the city-states forwards. Such a formulation as this by Anaximandros brings out clearly how the systems of polar opposites inherited from tribal society were being given a deepened philosophic content, and were being seen to embrace ever-larger spheres of reality, through the forms of social development in the Greek world. Parmenides also in his *Way of Seeming* calls the pairs of cosmological factors both opposites and equals; and he links with them hot and cold and other sets of opposites. Aetios attributes to him a system of interwoven rings made up of fire (or light) and darkness (or night) which further suggests the world-picture of Anaximandros.[15]

The theory of opposites found its justification also in the field of arts and crafts where the opposites were seen both in pairs and in fours. *On the Kosmos* tells us:

> Perhaps Nature actually has a liking for opposites; perhaps it is from them that she creates harmony, and not from similar things, in the same way as she has joined the male to the female, and not each of them to another of the same sex, thus making the first harmonious community not of similar but of opposite things.
>
> It seems too that *technē* does this in imitation of nature. For painting mixes its whites and blacks, its yellows and reds, to create images concordant with their originals; music mixes high and low notes, and longs and shorts, and makes a single tune of different sounds; by making a mixture of vowels and consonants grammar composes out of them the whole of its *technē*. This is just what

> Herakleitos the Dark [Obscure] meant when he said: Junctions are wholes and not wholes, concord and discord, consonance and dissonance. One out of All, All out of One."[16]

The four colours here mentioned are those of the restricted palette used by the four-colour painters, of whom the earliest recorded may be Polygnotos and the latest Aetiōn (at the time of Alexander the Great). It has been suggested that Empedokles, with his thesis of four elements, was inspired in his comparison of painting and creation by the four-colour school:

> Just as when painters are elaborating temple-offerings, men whom Metis [wisdom, craft, skill] has well taught their art—they, when they've taken pigments of many colours with their hands, mixing them with harmony, more of some, less of others, from them produce shapes that are like all things, making trees and men and women, beasts and birds and fires that live in the waters, yes, and gods that live long lives and are exalted in honour—so don't let the error prevail over your mind, that there's any other source of all the perishable creatures that appear in countless numbers. Know this for sure, for it's from a goddess you have heard the tale.[17]

Cicero mistakenly thought the four-colour system was a primitive limitation found in early Greek painting; but all its exponents we know were of the fourth century. So it is hardly likely that there was a school of them in the days of Empedokles. But the idea of four basic colours certainly has some connection with the philosophic theses we are discussing. The four primary colours of Demokritos were those used by the artists—other colours being interpreted as compounds of the four.[18]

The Aristotelean *Colour* opens by saying that "those colours are simple which belong to the elements, fire, air, water, and earth. Air and water are naturally white in themselves, while fire and sun are golden. The earth is also naturally white, but seems coloured because it is dyed." That leaves us with only two colours; but then we are told: "The colour black belongs to the elements of things that are being transformed into something else. The other colours are evidently due to mixture, when they're blended with one another." So we get two opposites with a third that represents the moment of transformation: when the two are dynamically fused but have not yet issued into the changed state. Plinius uses the term *tonos* of colours: "Those qualities that exist between these [light and *splendor*, probably highlight] and the shades are called *tonos*, while the joining-together and transition of colours is called *harmogē*"—a term used for fitting things together and also for tuning an instrument. No doubt Plinius is drawing on Euphranor and other Greek painters who wrote on their art. *Tonos* was a term much used by the Stoics. We may take it here to define the light and shadow in a painting, not as a mere technical relationship, but as a vital tension between two forces. As *tonos* among other meanings came to signify the pitch of voice or instrument, and the diatonic scale, while *harmogē* could refer to tuning, we see a strong sense of the unity of pictorial and musical composition, with stress on the dynamical aspect. Music, by joining high and low notes, long and short, also presents a fourfold system.[19]

The early medical writers described the hot and the cold, the dry and the wet, as the four primary qualities or components of things; but usually these were linked with the elements, not seen as things in themselves. Empedokles connected hot and cold, bright and dark, with some of his roots, but we do not know how thoroughly he worked out a scheme. In the Hippokratic *On Fleshes*, however, heat—"what the ancients called *aithēr*"—is taken as the principal element; earth is described as cold and dry, *aēr* as hot and wet, and "that which is nearest the earth" (water or sea) is wettest and thickest. *On Regimen* makes fire and water the basic component of all creatures, with the hot and the dry belonging to fire and the cold and the wet to water—though there is some moisture in fire and some dryness in water. The author tries to work out a fourfold scheme: Man has four ages, the first is hot and wet, the second hot and dry, the third cold and dry, the last (old age) cold and wet. But his wish to link the young man with fire and the old man with water makes him drop the normal link of death with dryness, though in an earlier chapter he referred to it.

The medical writers often attributed disease to the opposites or to their effects on other substances or parts of the body. *On Ancient Medicine* (later than Empedokles) attacked the extreme form of such theories; and earlier indeed Alkmaion had held that a balance or *isonomia* of the *dynameis* in a body gave health, while *monarchia* or single rule by one of them provoked disease. Here the image is political. The kingship (or tyranny) is identified with unbalance, while *isonomia*, which can mean equal rights, produces the balance of health.[20]

Aristotle defined heat as that which "combines things of the same kind", cold as that which "brings together and combines homogeneous and heterogeneous things alike", wet as that which, "being readily delimited" by something else, "is not determined by its own boundary", and dry as that which, "not being readily delimited, is determined by its own boundary". But elsewhere he divides the pairs into a negative and a positive pole, especially with regard to hot and cold. Hot is the positive term, cold the privative. Things are not so clear with dry and wet. Aristotle notes the link of humidity with life, dryness with death; yet at other times he suggests that wet is the inferior privative term, because of its correlation with female, left, and cold.[21]

We can construct a table of Aristotle's opposites: right, male, upwards, front, hot, dry—against left, female, downwards, back, cold, wet. To these indeed could be added light and rare, as against heavy and dense. Despite the contradictions and difficulties his prolonged analyses came up against, he held fast to the belief that such a system of opposites underlay the life-process. But though he introduced the notion of positives and negatives, he did not rise to the idea of a dialectical unity of opposites. The notion of a necessary equilibrium prevented him from striving to work out how the new emerged—a new unity or a new qualitative level. For him the factors involved in change were (*a*) that which produces movement (*b*) that which is moved (*c*) the time taken by the motion and (*d*) that from which and into which a thing is moved. In the last two factors are included not only the two places involved in locomotion, but also the two substantial changes involved in generation and perishing, the two sizes involved in growth and diminution, and the two qualities involved in alteration.[22]

Change is always between two opposites or between one opposite and an intermediate (which then stands for the other opposite), or between contradictories. Movement proper must be (*a*) from a positive to a positive (opposite) (*b*) from a positive to its contradiction (*c*) from a negative to its contradiction (*d*) from a negative to a negative. But (*d*) does not involve opposites and so is not truly change; (*c*) is generation; (*b*) is destruction or perishing. Then (*c*) is change but not movement, since only that which is and that which is in place, can be moved. And (*b*) is also change but not movement, since the opposite of movement is movement or rest, while the opposite of destruction is generation. So it seems that only (*a*) is in fact movement. Aristotle is here trying to restrict the sense of movement so that it excludes "change in respect to substance".[23]

Further, he recognises a fourfold system in dealing with qualities: state and disposition; natural powers and impotencies; affective qualities and affections (the qualities perceived by the particular senses); figure and shape. At times he argues that alteration is always change in respect to the third of this group; but in *Generation and Perishing* he adds the first and fourth as well.[24]

This sort of analysis is extended with much refinement; but it goes on at the level of logical constructions out of given principles rather than as an instrument of inquiry that is continually tested by application. And the given principles ensure that no true concept of development can arise. Alteration involves a new quality, but it takes place when there is a perceptible persistent substratum or where the new quality is a quality of the persistent substratum. In coming-into-being there is again a persistent substratum but one which is imperceptible—that is, prime matter; while if a perceptible quality persists, such as transparence in the generation of water from air, the new quality (coldness) is not a quality of this but a fellow-quality with it.[25]

> The processes by which things come into existence in this total sense may be divided into (1) change of shape, as with statues made of bronze (2) additions, as in things that grow (3) subtractions, as when a block of marble is chipped into a Hermes (4) combination, as in building a house (5) such modifications, *alloiōseis*, as affect the properties of the material itself.

But what Aristotle is not doing is to consider coming-into-existence in a total sense, since he begins with an "underlying subject and the form which the defining properties give to it", not with a process of evolution in which complex bodies have developed from simpler ones, with consequent changes in the whole qualitative and structural level of organisation. This limitation of outlook, however, he shared with all other ancient thinkers in one degree or another. "The term *alloiōsis*, in the Aristotelian sense, implies a hard and fast definition of identity and difference, with the identity residing in an unchanging essence, while the differentiae relate to the non-essential or accidental" (Heidel).

Thus the emergence of the new is not the result of fusion of opposites producing a new qualitative unity. It comes about through the variation in the mixtures of the simple bodies and their qualities. However the factors are juggled about inside the given schemata, the fundamental concept is that of a cyclic movement in which all sorts of complicated combinations occur, all sorts of changes of primal matter, but in which the new aspect arises only through some previously buried factor coming to the fore and some new relationship of the factors being established. Thus the expansion and contraction in bodies is explained in the same way as qualitative changes—as due to a matter capable of various states: that is, "of filling space with all possible degree of intensity". (Correctly enough, this doctrine has been compared to Kant's concept of the Real in "Anticipations of Perception.") Small cycles of generation-and-perishing occur, inside larger cycles, but the rule of equilibrium and conservation is such that nothing truly new can emerge. Behind Aristotle's physics there lies his ethical conviction that virtue "in respect of its definition and its essence is a mean". The virtue in the individual is thus linked with the concept of social equilibrium or *symmetria*, and with that of balance in physical process.

Aristotle's concept of unity is consequently weak; he finds it hard to get away from the idea of a thing as being more than the sum of its parts, a matter of geometrical contacts or additions of contiguous bits, though he admits a binding element, e.g. string tying faggots or glue holding pieces of wood together. (He comes closer to a dynamic note when he says that a thing is continuous "when its motion is essentially one and cannot be otherwise".) He describes composition, as in a mixture of barley and wheat, as resulting in a sort of minute mosaic arrangement of particles of each component. Mixture, he declares, "should be uniform throughout and, just as any part of water is water, so should it be with a mixture". There is no real fusion, only a dominance of the larger or stronger body. He tries to find a philosophic explanation by making a distinction between actual and potential existence: the components "capable of action and capable of being acted upon" combine to form a compound which is "actually" something different, while each component is still "potentially" what it was before the mixture. If one component predominates in bulk, the result is a change of the weak component into the stronger one. "A drop of wine does not mix with ten thousand measures of water, for its form, *eidos*, is dissolved and changes so as to become part of the total volume of water." Aristotle makes no attempt to define at what point the ratio of the components brings about a balance where mixture still has qualities depending on both the components, and at what point the weaker one is changed into the stronger. Any notion of chemical fusion and change is far from his mind.[26]

The definition of *alloiōsis* which we noted above required as its preconditions the arguments of the Eleatic school which defined unity in terms of identity, and the systems of logic developed by Plato and Aristotle. We cannot apply any sharp definitions to the positions among the pre-Sokratic thinkers, who tended to look on qualities as physical constituents or ingredients of things. To some extent their attitudes to change may be called a more primitive version of what was narrowed down into the Aristotelian *alloiōsis*; but at times it seems to hold deeper implications. This is particularly so with Herakleitos, who considered that conflict was the key-principle: "Cold things warm themselves, warm cools, moist dries, parched is made wet." And again, "Fire lives in the death of air, air in the death of fire, water in the death of air, and earth in the death of water." Here however the form is that of the hieratic aphorism, and we have little idea how Herakleitos would have worked out his positions if he had attempted a full-length exposition as did Aristotle. On the one hand he affirms the unitary outlook. "To God all things are beautiful, good, and right; men on the other hand think some things right and others wrong." But the unity exists as a living conflict. "God is day and night, winter and summer, war and peace, satiety and want. But he undergoes transformations, just as . . . , when it is mixed with fragrance is named according to the particular savour" which has been added. The missing word has been taken as fire, on account of the prominence of fire in Herakleitan thought; but we know of no case where fire is named according to the incense or spices thrown into it. More likely Herakleitos has in mind the oily base, or beeswax, used in making perfumes. In any event, despite the cyclic scheme of elements passing into one another, we feel a dynamic and dialectical note at the heart of the thinker's cryptic paradoxes. For this reason Aristotle several times accuses him of breaking the law of contradictions. But that meant merely that he did not grasp the way in which Herakleitos often fused opposites in a dynamic unity, using a dialectical logic even if in an intuitive way.[27]

Cycles of Time

IV

For the Greek the perfect movement was circular. Such a movement had no beginning, no end; and its cosmic significance seemed to be written large on the skies in the cycles of the heavenly bodies, which were considered to belong to a higher world because of their distance and luminosity, but above all because of what seemed their regular circular motions. Aristotle was driven to invent a fifth element, free from coming-into-being and passing-away, where everything moved in circles and where the straight line of earthly bodies was unknown. The universe consisted of a series of concentric spheres, with the earth stationary at the centre and the first heaven carrying round the fixed stars in a unified rotation once every twenty-four hours. Eudoxos had decomposed the apparent motion of sun and moon into three rotatory movements; Kallipos found it necessary to suppose five spheres to cover the motions of sun, moon, Mercury, Venus, Mars; and Aristotle took over these systems.

Plato in the *Timaios* saw a celestial demiurge at work, with a circular movement of the heavens and so of time—space being a given factor. Hermippos the comic poet summed up the prevailing ideas in his lines on the Returning Year, Eniautos:

> *He's round to look at and he revolves in a ring*
> *containing all things in himself. Round the whole earth*
> *he brings us men to birth, Eniautos his name,*
> *Being round, he has neither end nor beginning, and never*
> *will cease from wheeling round all of the day*
> *and every day.*[1]

Ultimately behind such ideas was the primitive notion of all life as cyclic. The tribesman dies and his spirit rejoins the ancestors, then is reborn in a child of the tribe; and the cycle of the year is the ceaseless expression of the recurrent system of life and its changes, its deaths and renewals. This endlessly repeated cycle is expressed in myth and initiation-ritual.

Thus, among the Arunta of Central Australia, the tribesmen recognised four more or less distinct periods in the Alcheringa, the Dream-time: a period located in the mythical past which is also the eternal present. In the first period, men were created; in the second, the rite of circumcision by a stone knife was introduced; in the third, the rite of subincision was introduced; in the fourth, the existing marriage-system was instituted. Here is expressed the sequence of crucial events in the life of an individual Arunta: birth, circumcision, subincision, marriage. That life repeats the mythic cycle.[2]

Or take the Djanggawul, a cult of north-west Arnhem Land:

> It is primarily a re-enactment of the principal features of the Brothers' and Sisters' original journey through north-eastern and north-central Arnhem Land, and an important form of expressing these is the totemic dancing in conjunction with the sacred *rangga*. All these are correlated with the basic theme. The main structure of the ritual refers symbolically to the sexual sequence which culminates in the act of childbirth; and this, in a variety of forms, is the focal point. It is completely orthodox, for in it is contained the core, the basic thesis of the Djanggawul myth. By re-enacting the primal birth of the ancestors, the Arnhem Landers convey the sense of "tribal" (clan or linguistic group) continuity; a continuity, moreover, which cannot be broken unless the actual performance of the *nara* ritual is interrupted or halted.

In re-enacting the primal birth the performer is also representing his own birth into the group and his rebirth through initiation into a fullness of union with nature and the ancestors. The rite also has its fertility-aspects; the Two Sisters are the original mothers of the various *dua* moiety clansfolk:

> Re-enactment of the initial birth of the people expressed their inherent fertility, which by grace of the Djanggawul can be diffused to embrace a concept of universal fertility. Moreover, it expresses the seasonal rhythm. The coming of the wet season, with its rains, germinates the soil; foliage and vegetable matter and all the natural species "are reborn". Because of the Djanggawul, the natural resources of the land are assured.[3]

Time has a rhythmic aspect; it is a circling rhythm with an organic pattern, embracing past, present, and future.

As an example of the same sort of thing as the Djanggawul in a sophisticated form we may take the Babylonian festival of the New Year, the Akitu, with its myth set out and recited in the *Enuma elish.* The festival repeated the timeless moment of creation with its terrible conflict between Tiamat (the salt waters of the seas) and the demiurge Marduk; and it was felt to establish the universe securely and prosperously for the coming year. But because the festival occurred as part of the rituals stabilising a well-developed state with its various social and political problems, the creation it envisaged was also a specific event during which Marduk and the other gods, assembling it seems in a Chamber of Destiny in Marduk's temple, the Esagila, decreed the destinies of the state for the coming year. At Akitu festivals elsewhere in Mesopotamia the same procedures apparently went on. The Hebrew account of creation was no doubt originally a text recited ritually in the seven days of the New Year Festival.

Incidentally we may note how inside the cosmogonies, whether primitive or sophisticated, "creation meant not only bringing a thing into existence, but also the ability to conceive its purpose and the power to decree that it should fulfil that purpose. Quite clearly the idea of the magical potency of knowing and pronouncing a name was operative here, although it also possibly involved some primitive analysis of conception and planning, together with the authority to achieve what was composed" (Brandon). The act of creation, which involves both purpose and the power to see that the purpose is actualised, has close affinities with Aristotelian process, with its *dynamis*, *energeia*, and *entelecheia*, as also with his fourfold set of causes. The notion of the creative name or word does not exist at the Djanggawul level, but appears only when forms of overriding authority have developed in a divided society; with the rationalising Greeks, however, the creative word has ceased to be a magical or theological concept. It is the logos of human reason and understanding.[4]

But to return to the primitive concept of time. The stress is on the concrete moment, time has the quality of what it brings. *Chronos*, time, is for Homer an experience, not a measurement. It is a point or moment in a series of similar points or moments; it expresses an indefinite duration, generally a long one. The noun is always in the accusative, with or without *epi* (for). A short duration is called "not much time". That is, to think of time involves an act of detachment from the stream of immediate experience, and so the "time" which is summoned up is necessarily endowed with a fairly long duration or perspective. Yet time never stands outside human life; it is always merged with some activity or condition. There is no sign of an abstraction existing outside experience as a system of objective measurement set over and against man: a system capable of division into definite units. Generally men become aware of time only when frustrated or rendered useless: weeping or caught up in some delay, separated and far from home. We might then say that it was through waiting that men discovered time—through something that divorced them from normal and satisfying action.[5]

A day for Homer is not a measurable length of time; it is a human event, usually differentiated only to mark some disaster: Hektor's fateful day is that day as experienced by Hektor, not a date in a calendar. We meet the terms: day of fate, day of perishing, day of necessity, day of slavery. It is "the cruel day". Only once do we find it used in conjunction with something happy and positive, but even there it appears in contrast with the unhappy actuality: Patroklos is going to deprive the Trojan women of their day of freedom.[6]

With Hesiod the day is still an experience, not a unit of measurement; but there is a rudimentary sense of time-divisions in that each day does belong to a numerical series. The poet is a farmer; he is involved with problems of work in terms of the changing seasons of the year. He has to see the days as a succession of varying tasks, though they exist for him primarily as propitious or ill-omened durations; their outstanding characteristic lies in the qualities they embody. Still, Herakleitos felt the linear element to be sufficiently present for him to declare in indignation: "Hesiod distinguishes between good days and evil days, not knowing that every day is like every other." Indeed he must have felt strongly that Hesiod innovated and degraded the sense of time; for he returned to the charge with the accusation: "Hesiod, whom so many accept as their wise teacher, did not even understand the nature of day and night; for they are the same." Here again is the reduction of all time-moments to the cycle; each moment is seen as complete in itself, not as linked with one another in a linear or measurable progression. There is no contradiction on the part of Herakleitos, we may note, when he also says that a new sun is born and dies each day; for while each time-cycle is in one sense the same as all the others, in another sense it is unique. Galenos explains the aphorism by saying that the sun is moulded afresh each morning from the waters surrounding earth and becomes one with the waters again when it drops into them at sunset—a direct leap from fire to water and back again, without the intermediate stage of air being involved. If this in fact is the Herakleitan image, the concept of a new creation is even more stressed; and what is claimed here for the sun is considered to be true for each moment of duration, for every experience with its unique element of concrete immediacy.[7]

We have some lines on time by Skythinos of Teos, a poet of uncertain date who versified the Herakleitan doctrines:

> *End and Beginning of all is Time, in it is All,*
> *it is and is not One, eternally it leaves*
> *and regains being by a contrary route, while in itself*
> *remaining the same. So for us tomorrow*
> *is in reality yesterday, and yesterday tomorrow.*[8]

The lack of a linear conception—time seen as moving in a single direction along a measurable line—is strongly brought out by the Homeric use of *opiso* or *opisthen* (behind) in relation of future events. Helen says of Paris: "He has not a sound heart nor will he have it behind" (that is, he won't have it at any time in the future). Time seems to be imaged as coming up, so that in the future the time which is now coming up will have gone past him. "Time is always coming and arriving, it is always on the move and active. There is no time that has stiffened up and died, which, as the past, could standing still for ever contain history. What is past is removed out of the reach of time. 'Of deeds rightly done or unrightly, not even Time the Father of all things can make undone the accomplishment' (*Odyssey* ii, 17). Time is only the future which wishes to become present and becomes present. It creates, destroys, preserves. *Chronos* is the creative power which produces all that is novel and different out of the inert matter of mere states, matter-of-fact and things: *Chronos*, the father of all things" (Fraenkel). Nothing could be further from the post-Galilean notion of time, like space, as a sort of abstract container or framework inside which events, mechanically measurable, occur.

If we move on from Homer and Hesiod to Pindar, we find much of the old qualitative element, and time is still coming up to us, bringing the things to be or impersonating what is to be. But there is now the idea that time is also a point capable of arrest, of fixation outside the flow that carries us along. Gradually an analytic linear attitude grows up, and round 400 B.C. it has prevailed so far that events are seen as a continuous series appearing in a regular succession inside time. But the old positions never quite yield.[9]

The time-attitudes reveal themselves further in the way that sentences are built. Homer's method is essentially appositional: that is, one word or phrase links with another, extending meaning but not moving forward in a linear way. The construction, which has been called ring-composition, is circular. Each circle or cluster represents a moment of qualitative experience. One circle supplants another and thus there is a forward movement; but the units are moments of self-sufficient apprehension. We might say that what happens is the obliteration of one circle by the next; the old one completes itself and closes up; the new one appears and expands on the same ground, a complete moment of sensory perception and meaning. Life indeed moves, but not so much by a linear time-succession as by spiralling through a series of qualitative moments which emerge, one on to another or inside another, as well as one after the other.

Just as the analytic attitude to time asserts itself and carries on a complex struggle with the systems of cyclic immediacy, so the appositional method of sentence-construction meets and is partly subdued by the paratactic constructions which suit the sense of time as made up of successive units. Thus Pindar keeps on using the appositional method when he wants to build suspense. We may note that originally the perfect tense of the Greek verb did not take an object, but expressed the present state of the subject; as it became transitive and took on an object, what it expressed was the state into which the object had been brought and in which it now was. Thus we see a change from concentration on the subject to that on the object. We may further note that among early Latin-speakers the time of night when nothing happened (as far as men were concerned) was *nox intempesta*, night with no time. Like many primitive folk the Romans left out of consideration that period of the year when (farming) activities ceased; the period, now equivalent to the months of January and February, was ignored.[10]

During the sixth century a deepened sense of Time as an active force had emerged, expressed in the passages from Anaximandros and Solon that have been cited. It appeared also in the cosmogony of Pherekydes (written in prose) which began according to Diogenes Laertes: "Zas and Chronos always existed and Chthonie. . . ." The life-principle is directly linked with Time as the basis of all things. Time makes fire, wind, and water out of his own seed. In the later stages of the cosmogony the primeval trio seem to have taken the more familiar form of Zeus, Kronos, and Hera. (The link of Chronos and Kronos, purely verbal, became common.) It has been argued that the idea of Time as a force creating worlds is too sophisticated for the mid-sixth century; but our discussion will have shown that this attitude fails to get inside the deep significance of Time from Homer onwards. We need not look, except perhaps in a very general way, for any eastern influences. The Iranian abstraction *Zvrab Akarana*, Unending Time, seems to find its earliest Greek reference in Eudemos, in the late fourth century. Time played an important rôle in Orphic theology; here the eastern derivation is brought out by its shape as a multi-headed winged snake. Such monsters began to appear in Greek art round 700 B.C., and went on being popular till the first quarter of the sixth century; but we know nothing of what ideas were attached to the imagery at this period. It is, however, possible that some general time-ideas were associated with the winged-snake in the archaic period, though the Orphic elaboration is certainly much later. In Pherekydes, Kronos and Ophioneus wage a cosmic struggle; and Ophioneus (*ophis*, snake) is a snake-monster of the type of Typhoeus. In general we may say that during the sixth century men became much more aware of what was implied by the prevailing notion of Time as a life-force. The unity of the concept began to break up. We meet a more abstract approach; but elements of the old concept survived in phrases like Pindar's "Time the Father of all things", and Time had something of an active rôle for the tragedians. With Plato it appeared in the *Timaios* as an abstract cosmogonic force.

In Empedokles Time is still an active force. He speaks of "alternate Time", *amoibaios*. Time is here the equalitarian or democratic justice of rotating office: with the four roots or elements taking their turn. Again Empedokles has the phrase "in the fullness of Time" (literally, "Time being fulfilled") where Time is the measure allotted to each root, not an abstract measurement but the active process bringing about the just change. Time is thus identified with Justice as the principle of dynamic cosmic order.

We have seen how the idea of cyclic time goes far back in human history; we can add that the idea of the circle itself has roots as ancient. Ultimately circular movement no doubt has an organic basis; we find it linked with ideas and images of birth and rebirth. The Latin for womb, *vulva*, has a root-meaning of revolving movement; and the Roman slave, in being freed, was turned round three times. We see from the Omaha Indians how the whirl of birth-rebirth (here in an initiation-rite) can be merged with a fourfold cosmic system. The priest carrying the child, who was to assume his tribal name, put him in turn on four oriented stones, turned him round and sang:

Turned by the wind goes the one I send yonder,
yonder he goes who is whirled by the wind,
goes where the four hills of life and the four winds are standing,
there in the midst of the winds do I send him,
into the midst of the winds, standing there.[11]

Here the birth-turn, whirl, vortex, is seen as one with the sky-circle with its four points, and is given its vulvic power by the four winds. We can see how the early Greek cosmogonic systems are generalisations and rationalisations on such a basis as this.

It was in the neolithic age that the circle started appearing in human constructions, on the rims of pots as well as in the roofs and foundations of huts; but it is with the Bronze Age that we see it coming fully into its own. The tree-trunk no doubt provided the idea of the cylinder, used both as a roof-support and as a roller; its circular section helped towards the formulation of the concept of the circle, as, no doubt, so also did the halves of gourds or coconuts and the like. "The basis of all mechanical invention and all solid geometry upon which applied science rests, consists of the circle, the sphere, the cylinder, and the ellipse. Rectangular shapes came much later, and are by no means so vital to the growth of mechanical ideas and inventions" (Casson). A neolithic city found some 115 miles south of Kiev, near the village of Maidanetskoye, in the bend of a small river, held some 20,000 people. It covered 700 acres, and its pottery showed the black spiral characteristic of the Tripolye culture. The city was built in a concentric pattern broken by radially oriented streets. Here we see in grand form the circular camp with four oriented sections of the Amerindians. Out of this obsession with the circle was born the cart-wheel, the potter's wheel, and spinning techniques.

Excavations at Myrtos in Crete have shown an Early Bronze Age settlement where the potters used turntables, clay disks flat on one side and slightly convex on the other. The centre of the convex side had generally been rubbed away; at times a slight groove round the disk-edge suggests the use of a cord to help the turning. No examples, however, had a hole in either face to indicate the use of a spindle and a freely rotating (fast wheel) disk. Most disks had a painted cross on one or both sides, and at times a band round the outer edge. The cross might have been used to ensure a vessel was correctly centred; in turning it would give the broken swastika effect we at times find on developed Bronze-Age pottery, e.g. from Samarra on the Tigris, showing how decorations sought to express dynamically the circular movement.[12]

The circle is a dynamic concept, and was born and developed in the dance; and as tribal dances have ritual bases and rich mythic content, the circle thus realised was not an abstract geometrical figure, but a movement imbued with meaning, with imagery of fertility and transformation. It united man with the cyclic movements of the universe, with the sky-movements and the seasonal rhythm. Throughout antiquity the motions of the stars were seen as a cyclic dance; and Pythagorean ideas of music and of harmony were linked with them. (Primitive music itself, like primitive story-telling, is based on a circling or spiralling system analagous to the appositional system of Homeric narrative. "Primitive melody, which is scarcely more than a continually repeated and varied motive, is regulated essentially by the tension between the beginning of the motive and its final note" (Schneider).) Plato in the *Timaios* describes "the choric dances of the stars and their crossings one of another and the relative reversals and progressions of their orbits. . . ." The *Epinomis* speaks of "the nature of the stars, the most beautiful sight of all; passing along, dancing the most beautiful and magnificent of all dances in the world, they perform their service to all living creatures." *On the Kosmos* says that heaven "is full of divine bodies that we call stars; it moves eternally and revolves in solemn choral dance with all the stars in the same circular orbit unceasingly for all time." And it adds the Pythagorean notion of the music of the spheres.

> The single harmony that is produced by all these as they sing and dance in concert round the heavens has one and the same beginning and one and the same end, in the true sense giving the whole the name of *kosmos* [order] and not *akosmia*. Just as in a chorus at the direction of the leader all the chorus of men, sometimes of women too, join in singing together, creating a single pleasant harmony with their varied mixture of high and low notes, so also in the case of the god controlling the universe: the note is sounded from on high by him who might well be called the Chorus-master; then the stars and the whole heavens move continually and the all-shining sun makes his double journey, dividing night from day by his rise and setting, and bringing the four seasons of the year as he moves forwards to the north and back to the south.

The author goes on about rains, winds, dewfalls, rivers, sea-swellings, tree-growths, fruit-ripenings, birth of animals, their nurture, prime and decay; the whole rhythm of life is seen as dependent on the ring-dance of the heavens.

4. Moon in the Chariot of the Sun rising from Sea, out of a Boat: Pan with fourfold torch leads, while Korybant or Koures dances, clashing shield. Red-figured krater in Louvre (*Annali* 1852 pl. F3)

The great astronomer Ptolemaios, to bring out his concept of uniform and circular motion as the basic element of heavenly kinetics, falls back on the dance-image:

> The parts of the planetary orbits are free to undergo translations and rotations in their natural positions in various ways, except that their movement is uniform revolution, like the chain of hands joined in a circle in a dance, or like the circle of men in a tournament who assist each other and join forces without colliding so as not to be a mutual hindrance. Our theory may be illustrated and made plausible by the construction of an apparatus which explains the eccentric and epicyclic motions; but should anyone use poles when explaining these motions, and insist on their being fixed, he will not arrive at an understanding of the principle of the whole thing nor of its arrangement and the way it works.[13]

The dance here seems the *geranos* or maze-dance (linked in myth with the Knossian Labyrinth) which has close affinities with the tournament or manœuvre-patterns of the Game of Troy at Rome. Such a dance is a part of initiation or funerary ritual; the successful passage through the winding or spiralling pattern, which involves the killing of the obstructive Minotaur, is the entry into a new life, a new level of life. So, to grasp the cyclic order of the heavens is felt by the observer to entail as it were the repetition of the original act of creation in which the demiurge defeats chaos or disorder—like Marduk killing the monster Tiamat. The recognition of the heavenly dance thus means the discovery of the principle of organisation in the universe, not in detached abstraction but in ecstatic participation. Men have created the dance as symbol and expression of the organising principle which they share with nature; they then find the movement-pattern in the sky and in their awe they transfer to the upper world the principle which originated in themselves.

As part of this system of thought and activity the circular hearth appears as the womb-shaped life-centre: *focus* in Latin. Circular or oval ovens, which are wombs of craft-transformation, belong to the same series. Here we meet the basis of constructional ideas of the utmost importance, which find their architectural culmination in domed buildings like St Sophia of Byzantion or the Gothic cathedral: structures seen as having a cosmic significance. They are images of the kosmos, and their roots lie in the primitive notion of the world as a hill or mound emerging out of the circle of waters. We already find among the Australian natives the totem-centre constructed as a stone or a mound in the middle of a circular hollow.[14] What gives such ideas and images their dynamic and stimulating force is the experience of the ring of dancers looking in on the sacred centre.

In Homer the image of the world is of a sky like a solid bowl (bronze or iron), no doubt polished shining, and a round flat earth, with equal distance between sky and earth's surface, and the surface and the foundations. Round the earth is the Ocean (shown on Achilles' Shield, a cosmic image, round the circular rim). There are ideas and images from the Near East and Egypt there, as well as native ones. In Egypt the primeval hill or mound rising at the middle of the waters was symbolised by the pyramid and various cult-centres—the temple was set on the holy mound of the beginning. We have a Babylonian map of the world, made to illustrate the exploits of Sargon of Akkad; we see a circular shape with the ocean (Bitter River) around it and seven triangles probably representing mountains. The early Greek maps (the first of which was said to be the work of Anaximandros) were similar, as we learn from Herodotos. "I smile when I see that many have drawn circuits of the earth, up to now, and none of them has explained the matter sensibly. They draw Okeanos running round the earth, which is drawn as with a compass, and they make Asia equal to Europe." That is, the maps had a circular plan, with known regions shown as roughly symmetrical segments. Anaximandros himself describes the earth as cylindrical in shape: "and its depth is a third of its width". Its shape "is curved, round, similar to the drum of a column; of its flat surfaces we walk on one, and the other is on the opposite side." The name *Okeanos* has been related to a non-existent Sumerian or Hittite *uginna* (ring); but it may in fact be connected with Aramaic *'ogānâ* (basin) or *ôgen* (rim). Pherekydes uses the form *Ogēnos*. Certainly the word seems non-Greek; Krates says the name Okeanos was used by many barbarians.

In thus attributing to the dance the origin of the concept of the circle we are speaking of something immemorially old, but also of something that still had its immediate effect and stimulus on the Greeks. They were the first people to develop precise and complex metrical forms in song and narrative verse because of the close connection of music, dance, and song in their culture while it was building up its mathematics, its geometry, its astronomy. It has

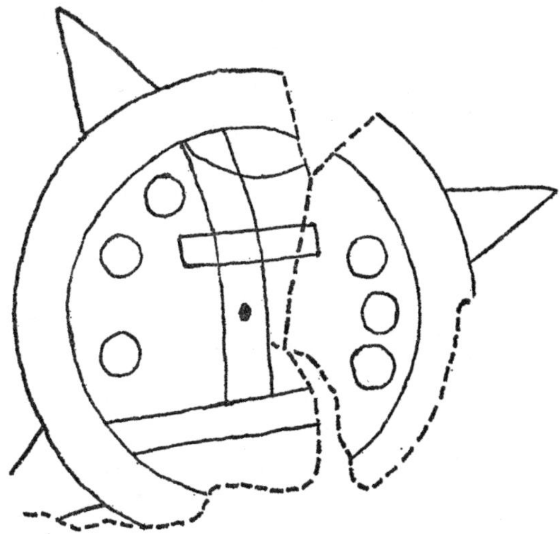

5. Babylonian Map of the Circular World (made to illustrate the campaigns of Sargon of Akkad): B.M. E 153: 92, 687. The inscription has been omitted

been pointed out that the dance, "among the arts the most complete, arithmetical and geometric, occupying simultaneously both time and space, manifesting itself simultaneously in rhythms and in figures", while finding its model in the circuit of the stars, was intimately related to the attitude and method of Greek mathematics. "The Greeks succeeded in overcoming difficulties, by a laborious but sure movement, holding to their over-concrete point of view" (Tannery). "Eukleid progresses slowly but in the open, while the operatory facilities of algebra bring us straight to the end, but by obscure abridgements" (Michel). The Greek stress on the concrete has many causes, but here in relation to the rhythms and figures, the steps by which movement of numbers and forms are defined, we find direct links with dance-evolutions, in-movements and out-movements, balancings and marshallings.

Time was seen as an endless series of cycle within cycle, as were the heavenly bodies in their circular movements. There were small cycles such as that of the day, larger ones such as that of the year; and as astronomy developed there were cycles that proved important for calculation, such as Meton's Nineteen Years. But there were also imaginary cycles, based on the idea of the periodic breakdown and renewal of the whole frame of things. Hesiod with his scheme of five ages, which traces a progressive decline in human life, was giving a semi-historical form to myth; Empedokles with his vision of a universe controlled by Strife and Love (Philia) gave a philosophical interpretation to the cyclic scheme—Strife and Love triumph alternately, then yield to the other. Love ends in the compacting of all things in a total mixture: "a god equal to himself and altogether eternal, a rounded Sphairos, complete, rejoicing in its aloneness." But then, "according to the oracle of Necessity", Strife stirs again and at last dissolves and disperses all things into a total vortex. Love awakes and starts linking things again, and so on. In the *Laws* Plato speaks of stages in a world-cycle, apparently occurring between one cosmic upheaval, e.g. the flood, and the next. Herakleitos, according to Aristotle, believed that in the cyclic movements a phase could be reached when "all things became fire"; but whether this phase entailed a total destruction is not at all sure.[15]

Cyclic concepts of cosmic destruction and renewal are common in complex tribal cultures, such as those of Mexico, where astronomy has been developed. The Aztecs believed in great cycles, each ending with cataclysm; their astronomy fixed dates in terms of a 52-yearly cycle. There had been Four Suns; the fourth ended in a flood and mankind lived in the fifth. The Chaldaians, with their advanced astronomy, believed in a Great Year, which covered the period taken by the seven known planets (in which were included sun and moon) in coming again into conjunction. The figure given was 36,000 ordinary years, though we cannot see any astronomical computation behind it. Traces of a similar doctrine can be found in ancient Iran and India. The Chaldaian formulation shows signs of a scheme of interacting elements; for when the conjunction of the planets occurred in Cancer all things were reduced to water, while when it occurred in Capricorn the reduction was to fire. The Greeks usually estimated the Great Year as lasting 18,000 or 10,800 years. The latter number was specially popular since it represented 30 (the average span between one generation and the next) multiplied by 360 (the formalised version of the number of days in a year); the Great Year thus symbolised a year of human generations, with the span between one generation and the next being reckoned as a day. The Stoics held strongly to a belief in *ekpyrōsis*, the cyclic destruction by fire.[16]

Even an upholder of the creed of the universe's eternity and its essential balance such as Aristotle believed in a cataclysmic flood and thought that philosophy and the arts had many times flourished and then disappeared. A fragment from a lost work of his declares that proverbs are the detritus from lost philosophies, surviving through brevity and wit. He repeats his general view on these matters in the *Metaphysics* and the *Meteorologika*: "We must say that the same opinions have arisen among men in cycles, not once, twice, not a few times, but infinitely often." He held that "just as there is a yearly winter, so after a certain long period of time there is a great winter with an excess of rain". His pupil Eudemos told his class of the Pythagoreans: "If we are to believe them, you will sit in front of me again and I shall be talking to you and holding this stick, just as we are now." Plato at the start of the *Timaios* recounts how an Egyptian priest tells Solon of earth's periodic catastrophes; a speaker in his *Laws* mentions the old traditions describing "many destructions of mankind by flood, disease and other causes, from which only a remnant survive". He goes on to depict a flood. An historian like Polybios assumes the same sort of thing, with continual destruction of civilisations. Porphyhrios says that Pythagoras held "that events recur in certain cycles and nothing is ever absolutely new."

The two main theories of the universe were then that it had always existed with perpetually changing but ultimately balanced elements or that it periodically reached a stage of unbalance or undue concentration of one element, which led to cataclysm and a new start. (We may compare the contemporary theories of the "steady state", at present out of favour, and the "big bang".) Diodoros in the first century B.C. tells us:

> Two views about the origin of mankind have been current among the most notable scientists and historians. One school, premising that the kosmos is ungenerated and indestructible, declares that the human race has always existed and there was no time when it began to reproduce itself. The other holds that the kosmos has been generated and may be destroyed, and that men similarly first came into existence at a definite time.

The second theory thus made possible the growth of ideas of evolution—though many thinkers imagined men as arriving as a matured species. Aristotle, with his concept of the fixity of species, speaks of "the first men, whether they were earthborn or survivors from some fatal calamity". Polybios tells of new populations, after a disaster, bringing about a revival of social life "as a crop come up from the ground". But a few thinkers fumbled at an evolutionary concept. Anaximandros pictured the earliest forms of life crawling painfully, shell-encrusted, out of the sea; and Empedokles imagined strange creatures, not to be found on his earth, who fought for life against adverse conditions and were beaten, destroyed, in the struggle.

For Aristotle the movement of which time is the measure may be that of generation or passing-away, growth, qualitative change, or locomotion. But movement is naturally measured by locomotion, the only kind of movement that need not change its pace. The primary kind of locomotion is that of a circle. Dealing with the formation of rain and its fall, he says: "We observe in nature a certain kind of circular process of genesis." And in his *Physics* he adds, "Even time itself is regarded as circular." This last idea was perhaps helped by the measuring systems; the clocks were all cyclic mechanisms, whether they consisted of the earth revolving on its axis, the skies revolving or water-clocks. Aristotle, like the other thinkers, could not move definitely into mathematics and treat time as merely a linear coordinate. That is, he could not close his eyes to the essential difference between linear distance and time—expressed by the fact that we measure distances by measuring-rods and times by clocks—and thus could not apprehend them both in the abstract as coordinates, as mere numerical quantities. He defined time as "the number of the movement in relation to earlier and later", and remarks that human affairs too constitute a kind of circular succession of events and that all things which in the order of nature pass from generation to decay move in a circle.[17]

Aristotle in his definition reached a high degree of abstraction, expressing both the link of time with change and the possibility of mathematically defining the change. He understood that a clock was the first condition of measuring time. The best measure was the movement of the heavens, regular and circular, "because the number of it is the best known". As usual he proliferated with logical distinctions. Time is not number in the sense of that by which we number: that is, the sense of pure number; it is number in the sense of that which is number—that is, it is the numerable aspect of movement. The analysis is often difficult, as when he seeks to show that as movement is recognised by observing a single moving body successively at different points, the passage of time is recognised by noting that the single character of "nowness" has been attached to more than one experienced event. Time depends on the Now both for its continuity and its differentiation into parts. But if it is by reason of its Nows that time is numbered, we must not suppose the Nows to be parts of time any more than points are parts of a line; there is no least time as there is no least line.

Aristotle makes three distinctions as to what can be meant by a thing being "in time". The thing may be when time is; it may be a part or attribute of time; it may be measurable by time. But he says that to be in time is not to be when time is, any more than to be in movement or in place is to be when movement or place is. Present, past, and future are in time as being parts of it. Events are in time as being measurable by it; they are contained in it just as things in place are contained by place. Since they are in time in this sense, there must be a time greater than anything that is in time. So things that are always, are not in time. As time is the measure of movement, it is also the measure of rest; only things in movement or at rest (that is, potentially moveable) are in time. Necessary truths are not in time. Time will never fail, as movement will never fail and as each Now is the beginning of a future as well as the end of a past. Though he does not identify time and change, he notes that time implies change. When our state of mind does not change or we are unaware of change, we do not think time has passed. When we notice change, we think that time has passed and vice versa. (Here there is a touch of the Homeric notion of time as a factor of derangement, of interruption in obsessed activity.) Spatial magnitude is continuous and so is the primary continuum. Movement is continuous since it is movement through continuous space; time is continuous since it is taken up by continuous movement. Before and After refer primarily to space, secondly to movement, thirdly to time.[18]

In the concept that events are in time as things in place are contained in place we come close to the post-Galilean concept of space as a mere container; but with Aristotle this aspect of being in time is not considered as the whole or the essential aspect, and so there is no tendency to abstract it and base on it a system of mechanics.

His pupil, Straton of Lampsakos, who showed signs of a leaning towards a dynamic-continuum theory, opposed Demokritos' idea of empty continuous space, though, on the grounds of experience, he admitted that small holes existed, discontinuously distributed, in the inside of bodies. He therefore objected to his master's use of the term "number" in his definition, as number was a discrete quantity while time was continuous. His own definition, according to Sextus Empiricus, was "the measure of motion and rest", but we also find it given as "a quantity that exists in all actions". He seems to have wanted to drop the term movement so as to escape a confusion of "actions", that is, of all kinematical aspects of physical phenomena (including rest), with the flux of time as constant and uniform—the uniform flux being that by which those aspects are supposed to be measured. An action is slow if not much happens over a long period of time, and vice versa. Aristotle had already made this point in his *Physics*; but it was Straton's formulation that led the Stoics to bring into their definition the function of time as the measure of slowness or swiftness. Zenon called time the "interval of movement in the sense in which it is sometimes called measure of swiftness and slowness", and Chrysippos expanded the point, adding to Zenon's definition the words: "or the interval proper to the movement of the kosmos; and it is in time that everything moves and exists".[19] Sextus was then referring to the Stoics when he stated, "Some define time as the interval of the motion of the Whole: meaning by Whole the Universe." (He adds that others define it as "the actual motion of the Universe". Aristotle also mentions this definition, which is Platonic. The *Timaios* speaks of "the vision of day and night and of months and circling years" which "has created the art of number and given us not only the notion of time but also the means of research into the nature of the universe". It declares as well that time came into existence with the heavens and that the demiurge made "an eternal image of that eternity which abides in unity, moving according to number; that which we have named time.")[20]

Chrysippos was no doubt defining what Newton called relative time, and had no notion of Newton's "absolute, true, and mathematical time". (Straton perhaps came closest of all these ancient thinkers to conceiving that absolute time.) The Stoics, like practically all the ancients, saw time as bound up with events; it was concrete whether considered as motion or interval. The question of the continuum and infinite division had long been raised; a crucial point had appeared with the paradoxes of Zenon of Elea (first half of the fifth century), which, denying the possibility of motion, had raised some of the basic issues linked with the idea of space as a continuum of points. Zenon argued that the ends and body of an arrow in flight must at each instant coincide with the points making up the trajectory; but if this happened for however brief a moment, there was immobility. Thus he opened up the question: how to reconcile a theory of space as made up of points with one of space as a continuum. Because of an approach largely based on a static geometrical outlook, the problem of the infinitesimal calculus could at first only be tackled deviously. Antiphon, a contemporary of Sokrates, seems the first to try to calculate a circle's area by the method of exhaustion, regarding the circle as the limit of a polygon with a vast number of sides. He spoke however only of the sides becoming so small that they coincided with the circle's circumference; so he seems to have been thinking of a finite process. Simplikios, nearly a thousand years after Antiphon, remarked that his position "would annul the geometric principle of the infinite divisibility of magnitudes". Bryson, about the same time as Antiphon, used both inscribed and circumscribed polygons; he also thought he could avoid the issue of infinite sequences.[21]

How much interest was aroused by such problems at the time is shown by some lines in Aristophanes' *Birds*: "These, said the astronomer Meton, are instruments for measuring the air. But you must know that Air has an Oven's shape. That's why, applying the top of this curved rule, then placing the compass, I'll use a straight rule and I'll take my dimensions so well I'll produce a Squared Circle."

Eudoxos generalised the method of Antiphon and Bryson, but still sheered off from infinitesimals; he also used exhaustion for computing volumes, though he didn't know how to evaluate the successive terms of the progression. He extricated geometry from its impasse, but the full problem of infinitesimals could not be tackled. Greek geometers thought it was by logical argument, not by mathematical method, that Zenon's paradoxes had to be refuted. They avoided in every way the direct use of infinity. Thus they did not take the step—later taken by Cavaliero, Fermat, and especially Pascal—of examining the nature of the progression which represented the decomposition of geometrical figures; they were so intent on ensuring the rigour of the method of exhaustion in each particular case that they had no room to develop, beyond the needs of the moment and the methods they used to prove the results; no room to create new systems. So they failed to take the road leading to the results of Leibniz and Newton.[22]

Aristotle tried to juggle with terms to evade the issue, e.g. to distinguish between number and magnitude in the problem of infinity. He considered all magnitude as finite, thus rejecting spatial atomism, but admitted its infinite divisibility. He admitted the extensible infinity of number, but *not* its infinite divisibility. He defined continuity as that which is divisible into parts that are always divisible. But the infinite exists only potentially, and not in actuality; and it doesn't exist even potentially except in the sense of infinite subdivision. It cannot exist even potentially in the sense of exceeding every finite magnitude as the result of successive additions. In effect he supports the Eudoxan method of exhaustion.[23]

Xenokrates, pupil of Plato and teacher of the Stoic Zenon, took a different line; he used the idea of atomic lengths to resist the arguments of Zenon of Elea by introducing the idea of a minimal length. As the atoms of Demokritos were impassive and without quality, he assumed that they had a length resisting further division. Demokritos himself seems to have thought of a solid as made of an infinite number of very thin layers. He was thus led to a paradox concerning a cone cut by a plane parallel to its base. What of the surface area of the sections? "If they were unequal, it would make the cone irregular as having many indentations, like steps, and unevennesses; but if they're equal, the sections will be equal and the cone will seem to have the qualities of a cylinder and to be composed of equal, not unequal, circles—which is quite absurd." There was no answer if atomic lengths were constituted in a static way, as consisting of constant magnitudes. Simplikios tells us that Demokritos considered his atoms to be mathematically divisible to infinity.[24]

The Stoics, with their concept of a dynamic continuum, could not but look far beyond the Eudoxan method of exhaustion. In his reply to Demokritos' paradox on the sectioned cone, Chrysippos declared, "The bodies will be unequal, since their surfaces are neither equal nor unequal." The term body here refers to the solid contained between two parallel sections of the cone.

> Let $A_1 < A_2 < A_3$ be the surfaces of three adjacent sections. Chrysippos' assertion is that volume defined by A_1 and A_2 is not equal to that defined by the surfaces A_2 and A_3, in spite of the relations $\lim (A_3 - A_2) = 0$ and $\lim (A_2 - A_1) = 0$. There is no indication that this proposition has been proved by Chrysippos, and it is most unlikely that a rigorous proof was given at that time. However, the proposition is necessary in order to assure that by the limiting process with regard to adjacent sections of the volumes bounded by these sections do not become equal, which would lead to a cylinder instead of a cone and thus restore the dilemma of Demokritos. (Sambursky)

Chrysippos was thus on the road to a deeper comprehension of the infinite sequences of inscribed and circumscribed figures than the Eudoxan method could yield. More, the Stoic conception swept away the static Aristotelean notion of place as the innermost motionless boundary of the containing body at which it is in contact with the contained body—a sort of surface of the container of the thing. The process of inscription and circumscription (used by Archimedes as an approximate method for calculating π) was turned by the Stoics into a rigorous definition of a given body set in a continuum. No static surfaces, definitely defined, could exist in that continuum, which was a medium for the transmission of physical actions and the exchange of forces. Bodies were seen as interdependent and there was a continuous transfer of *pneuma*-tensions throughout space.

> The Stoics therefore discarded the conception of the distinct surface of a body, or generally a distinct boundary of $(n-1)$ dimensions forming the surface of a figure of n dimensions ($n = 1, 2, 3$) and replaced it by an infinite sequence of boundaries defining the surfaces of inscribed and circumscribed figures which converge from both sides to the figure in question and thus define it as a dynamic entity. (Sambursky)

As a result of this approach the Stoics were aware of the main characteristics of the infinite set: the fact that it contains subsets which are equivalent to the whole.

> Man does not consist of more parts than his finger, nor the kosmos of more parts than man. For the division of bodies goes on infinitely, and among the infinities there is no greater or smaller nor generally any quantity that exceeds the other, nor do the parts of the remainder cease to split up and supply quantity out of themselves. (Ploutarch setting out Stoic doctrine.)

Later, this property of the infinite set was rediscovered by Galileo. Chrysippos, we may add, stated the essential difference between a denumerable aggregate made up of a definite number of "macrocosmic" and separable elements, and a continuous one, which cannot be described as composed of parts and which by its nature is incomplete and fluid. The continuum is a dynamic whole which is always in a state of becoming.[25]

We see then that Greek scientific thought, as it developed, was perfectly capable of grappling with the infinitesimal calculus if there had been an impetus or wish to build on the Archimedean basis, let alone on the concepts of the Stoics. "The mathematicians of the third century had an entirely modern attitude before the problems of the infinite. . . . The historians who have accused them of timidity and inadequacy, Montuela at their head, did not know the treatise of Archimedes on Method. The great mathematician of antiquity shows himself there as bold and as expert as his seventeenth-century pupils. Besides, these same historians did not know the modern axiomatic. They could not understand that the theory of proportions, on one side, and the method of exhaustion on the other, are the prototypes of our modern theories of the continuum and of the integral of Riemann. The technique of the Greek geometers is clearly inferior to ours, to that of even the seventeenth and eighteenth centuries: that is certain. Their axiomatic, or, as one liked to say once, their metaphysic, was caught up with and surpassed only at the end of the last century" (Itard). But we can indeed go further than that claim. The *concepts* of the Stoics, if not their mathematics, went far beyond the positions of Archimedes; and if they had been able to define them in systematic physics, they would have gone far beyond anything yet attained in the twentieth century. We must remember that they, more than any other ancient thinkers, saw process in its full concrete bearings. Faced with the Newtonian calculus and its claims, they would certainly have at once agreed with Berkeley, who, in *The Analysts* (1734), asked if the *dx* are zero or not zero, and called them "ghosts of departed quantities". They would have been fascinated by the method, but would have sought different applications, different concepts of just what truths were yielded, and consequently different points of departure.

We can add that their approach would have had close affinities with that of Marx's mathematical manuscripts (only published in part as yet). In commenting on an attempt to attack his method, he wrote in a letter to Engels (22 November 1882):

> Sam, as you have seen immediately, criticises the analytical method I have used by simply pushing it aside, and instead keeps himself busy with the geometrical application, to which I did not devote one word.
>
> I could in the same way get rid of the development of the proper so-called differential method—beginning with the mystical method of Newton and Leibnitz, then continuing with the rationalist method of D'Alambert and Euler, and finishing with the strictly algebraic method of Lagrange (which, however, always starts from the original principle of Newton-Leibnitz)—I could get rid of the whole historical development by saying that *practically* nothing had changed in the geometrical application of the differential calculus, that is, in the geometrical representation.

His approach thus shows affinity with that of Dedekind, who also tried to build up the calculus independently of the geometrical representation of the derivative. But Marx's critique went deeper than this point. He showed that the classical writers had the derivative ready prepared before the process of differentiation really began; he wanted a method that actually followed the process of variation of the variable and in this process itself defined the derivative as $0/0$, in which case it can be endowed with the new symbol dy/dx. The derivation, he insisted, should be performed by a process of differentiation, not be produced from the beginning by the binomial theorem; and he suggested a method avoiding the lack of internal development.

> Another important feature was his insistence on the operational character of the differential and on the search for the exact moment where the calculus springs from the underlying algebra as a new doctrine. "Infinitesimals" do not appear in Marx's work at all. In his insistence on the origin of the derivative in a real change of the variable he takes a decisive step in overcoming the ancient paradox of Zeno—by stressing the task of the scientist in not denying the

contradictions in the real world but to establish the best mode in which they can exist side by side. (Struick)

I do not cite these ideas of Marx on the calculus as saying the last word or as bringing out all the problems which it raises; they are useful however in showing an attempt to move in a more concrete direction and find ways of transforming the abstract approach of the mathematicians or mathematical physicists from Newton on. His analysis has the Stoic note and gives us at least a hint of what the calculus would be in a science that had truly moved beyond the abstractions ruling from Newton to Einstein. Since Marx's day the formal apparatus has been very much refined; but the difficulties he sought to overcome are still as central in the system.[26]

We may conclude this section by glancing at a few more ancient passages on time. Sextus says that, according to Demetrios the Lakonian, Epikouros defined time as a "concurrence of concurrences, concomitant with days and nights and seasons and affections and non-affections and motions and rests": an omnibus definition that plants human *pathos* and *apatheia* full in the midst of converging time-factors and motions. Proklos in the fourth century A.D. denied that the progress of time was straight and like a line that's infinite in both directions: "It is limited and circumscribed." Seneca sets out the cyclic view:

Our span of life is divided into parts; it consists of large circles enclosing smaller. One circle embraces and bounds the rest; it reaches from birth to the last day of existence. The next circle limits the period of our young manhood. The third confines the whole of our childhood in its circumference. Again, there is, in a class by itself, the Year. It contains within itself all the divisions of time by the multiplication of which we get the total of life. The month is bounded by a narrower ring. The smallest circle of all is the day; but even a day has its beginning and its end, its sunrise and its sunset. Hence Herakleitos, whose obscure style gained him his surname [the Obscure] remarked: "One day is equal to every day." Different persons have interpreted the saying in different ways. Some hold that days are equal in the number of hours; and this is true. If we mean by day the time of 24 hours, all days must be equal, inasmuch as the night gains what the day loses. But others maintain that one day is equal to all days through resemblance,

> because the very longest span of time possesses no element which cannot be found in a single day: namely light and dark—and even to eternity day makes these alternations more numerous, not different when it's shorter and different again when it's longer. So every day should be regulated as if it closed the series, as if it consummated and completed our existence.[27]

When we consider for instance the many biological time-cycles in our existence, we begin to realise the element of truth in the ancient emphasis on cyclic time. The strength of the cyclic concept lay in the element of immediacy, of full concrete apprehension, that it expressed and encouraged. It therefore impeded the movement towards mechanical abstraction, of the concept of time as a linear coordinate with space. A truly balanced science would need to recapture its element of truth without losing what benefits can be gained from the post-Galilean mechanical systems. Such a science would have many aspects in common with the Stoic theoretical approach.

Numbers and Atoms

V

Before we turn to the question of force or *pneuma* we need to glance at Pythagorean ideas of proportion and at the atomic theory, since without some understanding of them we cannot get inside the Greek universe. The teachings of Pythagoras or his early disciples are hard to make out. Born on Samos, he emigrated to southern Italy in the second half of the sixth century; he there gathered a fraternity living a communal life under a seal of secrecy. Not for more than a century later did any of the disciples begin revealing the creed of the sect. Certainly Pythagoras must have been concerned greatly with integral numbers; but his approach was essentially geometrical. Sets were arranged in geometrical forms; thus integers could be set down symmetrically in series of rows of points, one under the other. The numbers were shown and felt as points. Take thus an arrangement in which the first line had 1 point, the second 2 points, the third 3, the fourth 4, the fifth 5. We get a triangular shape, and by adding the numbers we find a series 1, 3, 6, 10, 15, and so on. Every triangular number is equal to the sum of all the integers from 1 down to the serial position of the number in question. Thus, 6, the third triangular number, is made up of 1, 2, 3, while 10, fourth in the series, is the sum of the integers from 1 to 4, and so on. By using pebbles or some such objects to represent the points, the Pythagoreans were stimulated to feel that numbers and their sequences were inherent in physical bodies; that in some sense they were themselves physical existents. The alternation of rows brought out the alternation of odd and even.

A number was thus seen as a concrete thing, occupying a determinate place in space, with its own qualities and affinities, both moral and physical. In their quest for groups of numbers that corresponded to spatial forms, the inquirers thought that the most satisfying system was provided by the gnomon or set-square. The

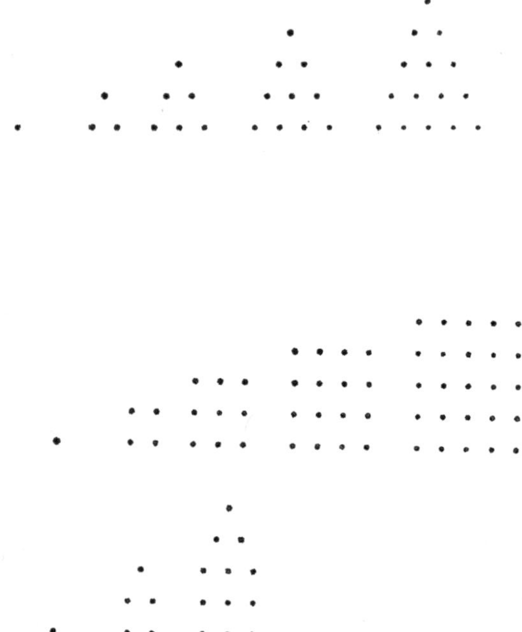

6. Pythagorean Pebble-systems for triangular, square and pentagonal numbers

gnomon, remarked Heron later, is that which, being added to a number or figure, gives a whole similar to that which has been added. Suppose a set of gnomons that fit into another set. If the first encloses one point, the second three points, and so on, it will be found that the sum of the odd numbers forms squares. If the gnomons enclose even numbers, the result will be rectangular, while the sum $1+2+3+ \ldots n$ of n consecutive numbers is a triangle.[1] That brings us back to the pyramidal form with which we started. Not only plane-figures thus correspond to numbers arranged in series; spatial figures do the same. Thus, by superimposing the triangular numbers, we get the pyramidal numbers 1, then $1+(1+2) = 1+3 = 4$, then again $1+(1+2)+(1+2+3) = 1+3+6 = 10$. These arithmetical-spatial concepts probably led to the classification into squared numbers (got by multiplying a number by itself), plane numbers (formed by two factors), and solid numbers such as the cube. Some numbers were considered perfect: that is, equal to the sum of their divisors (e.g. 6 = 1+2+3), while others were friendly: that is, such that each was equal to the sum of the divisors of the other.[2]

There was probably an eastern basis for the systems. The gnomon seems linked with the proportions of the Babylonian ziqqarats, ritual structures which were cosmic emblems of the sort we discussed in connection with the circle and the central mound. The gnomon number-series thus has a cosmic significance, which leads on to the cosmogonic schemes of the Pythagorean Philolaos and of Plato.[3] Indeed the philosophic theories worked out by the Pythagoreans have a close link with their arithmetic. We have already noted the table of their opposites. Those opposites can

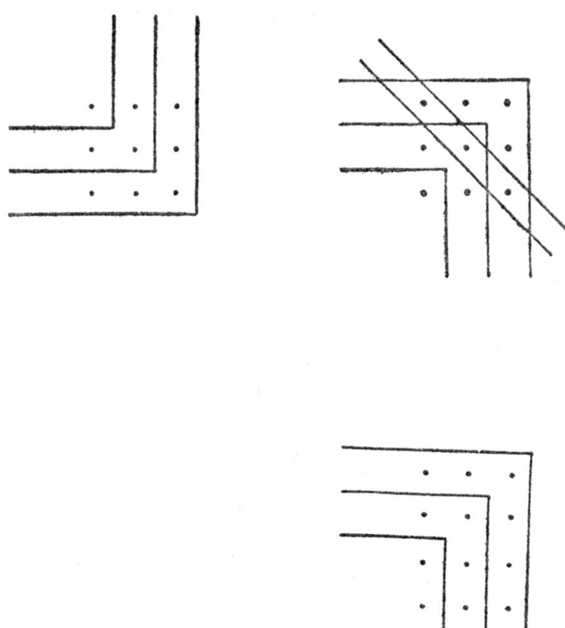

7. Pythagorean Gnomons, enclosing odd and even numbers: also figure showing how the sum of consecutive numbers $(1+2+3+ \ldots +n)$ beginning with 1 is a triangle; and another showing how to gain the pyramidal numbers $(1,\ 1+(1+2) = 4,\ 1+(1+2)+1+2+3) = 10$, etc.

be better understood if we look again at the gnomon. If we build up the odd numbers with it, we get a square: that is, a finite and complete figure, the sides of which have a ratio $\frac{n}{n}$ always identical and equal to unity. On the contrary, the construction of the even numbers gives a rectangle, a figure indefinite in the sense that its sides n and $n+1$ have a ratio changing with the value of n. The Pythagoreans also went on to consider that moral realities as well as physical existents were formed of numbers. Ten was the Tetraktys of the decade (the sum of the first four integers), and so was venerated; the most solemn oaths were taken by it; it was considered the fount of nature. The number 4, the square representing perfect equilibrium, was identified with Justice. The quest for other forms of equilibrium led to the three means: the arithmetic, such that $a+b = 2m$; the geometric, such that $m^2 = ab$; the harmonic, such that 2 over m = 1 over a+1 over b.

$$(1)\ \frac{a-m}{m-b} = 1 \qquad (2)\ \frac{a-m}{m-b} = \frac{a}{m} \qquad (3)\ \frac{a-m}{m-b} = \frac{a}{b}$$

But their system depended on all numbers being whole numbers; and they had to face a crisis with the discovery of the irrational $\sqrt{2}$ and with the paradoxes of Zenon. Eukleid in Books VII–IX of the *Elements* systematised the results obtained. He represented numbers as lengths and deduced their properties from those of the geometrical figures; he studied the rules for rational or whole numbers and indicated the rules for finding the greatest common factor and the least common multiple; he also studied fractions and geometrical progressions, and demonstrated that the number of prime numbers is unlimited. With Diophantos arithmetic becomes abstract, becomes algebra, unconnected with objects, and the problems are treated methodically. But the old way of looking at numbers died hard; Nikomachos insisted on considering that those of Diophantos were concrete. (The Greeks looked to the Egyptians for the origins of both arithmetic and algebra. A scholiast on Plato's *Charmides* speaks of parts of *logistikē* [science of calculation] as being "the so-called Greek and Egyptian methods in multiplications and divisions, and the additions and subtractions of fractions. . . . The aim of it all is the service of common life and utility for contracts, though it seems to deal with things of sense as if they were perfect or abstract.")[4]

The Pythagorean mystique of numbers strongly affected Plato and continued to haunt Greek thought. Thus Ploutarch tries to "Pythagoreanise" some aspects of Egyptian myth:

> The better and more divine nature consists of three elements: what is spiritually intelligible, the material, and the element derived from these, which the Greeks call the kosmos. Plato is given to calling what is spiritually intelligible the form and the pattern and the father; and the material he calls the mother, the nurse, and the seat and place of creation, while fruit of both he calls the offspring and creation. One might suppose that the Egyptians liken the nature of the universe especially to this supremely beautiful of the triangles which Plato also in the *Republic* seems to have used in devising his Marriage Figure. That triangle has a vertical of 3 units of length, a base of 4, and a hypotenuse of 5, which is equal, when squared, to the squares on the other two sides. The vertical should thus be likened to the male, the base to the female, and the hypotenuse to their offspring; and one should similarly view Osiris as the origin, Isis as the receptive element, and Horus as the perfected achievement.
>
> The number 3 is the first and perfect odd number; 4 is the square of the even number 2; 5 is analogous partly to the father and partly to the mother, being made up of a triad and a dyad. *Panta* [All] is cognate with *Pente* [5] and they say "to reckon by fives" for "to count". The number 5 forms a square of itself, which is the same number as the Egyptians have of letters and as the Apis [Bull] had of years to live.[5]

The Pythagoreans did much to develop a doctrine of proportions, in which they made the first attempts to apply mathematics to a basic physical phenomenon. In doing so, they carried out a number of experiments—for example, using strings in musical instruments of varying length and thickness, and changing the tensions by turning the screws to which the strings were attached. They also experimented with wind-instruments of different lengths and with vessels of identical shape filled with different amounts of water—thus creating vibrations of air-columns of different lengths. They felt the universe to be an ordered system which could be expressed in numerical ratios and which had yielded up its secret in the link between vibrating strings and their notes. They related these points to the planetary circles with their different distances from the centre and their different speeds. They used a craft-analogy to explain why we don't hear the notes uttered by the heavenly bodies in their harmonious motions: "Voice and silence are perceived by contrast, and so all humanity is undergoing an experience like that of a bronzesmith who by long habit becomes insensible to the din around him."[6]

Their glorification of the sphere and the circle played an important part in developing Greek astronomy and differentiating it, with its model-making, from Babylonian computations. Fragments attributed to Philolaos show how they felt that their theory of numbers provided a coherent basis for understanding the real relationships of things and the way in which opposing elements could work together without tearing the system to pieces. "Actually, everything that can be known has a number; for it's impossible to grasp anything with the mind or to recognise it without this." That is, the nature of a thing can only be known through its system of relationships; and the number gives the key both to the individual nature and to its living place in the kosmos. It gives the universe a consistent and intelligible structure. Again, "The things which were like and related needed no harmony; but the things which were unlike and unrelated and unequally arranged are necessarily fastened together by such a harmony, through which they are destined to endure in the universe." That is, the structure is not a static one; it has dynamic and tensional aspects.[7]

Eurytos, a disciple of Philolaos, worked out an odd way of relating numbers to forms. Some of the details are obscure; but we can make out that he smeared a wall with a substance capable of being impressed with the sketch of a human figure. Then he fixed into the outlines of face, hands, and so on, small pebbles of various colours, till they were used up. The amount of pebbles thus stuck into the form he called the causative number of the man. He used the same system for plants, and doubtless for other creatures besides man. Aristotle is not helpful as to the exact method adopted.

> In no sense has it been determined in which way numbers are the causes of substance and being—whether as limits (as points are of spatial magnitudes): that is how Eurytos decided what was the number of what (e.g. of man or of horse): by imitating the figures of living things with pebbles, as some people bring numbers into the forms of triangle and square—or is it because harmony is a ratio of numbers?

Theophrastos says that he used to claim "that such and such was the number of man, such and such that of horse, and such and such that of anything else". Alexandros gives further details:

> For the sake of argument let the definition of man be the number 250 and that of plant 360. Having settled that, he used to take 250 pebbles, some green, some black, others red, and, in short, of a variety of colours. Then he would smear the wall with unslaked lime and make a shaded drawing of a man or a plant. Some pebbles he set in the drawing of the face, others in the hands, and others elsewhere, until he had completed the drawing of a man in the number of pebbles equal to the number of units which he claimed to define man.

Eurytos, the leading Pythagorean of his generation, could hardly have thought the pebbles represented the unit-atoms of such objects as man or horse; Zenon had already made his strong criticism of earlier Pythagorean positions. Alexandros says that he decided on the definitive number before starting. It has been suggested that he set out to use the pebbles to define the form of man or horse so that the arrived-at figure could represent nothing but a man or a horse. He marked off the surfaces that were peculiarly those of a man or a horse, and the points that bounded those surfaces. Then he counted up the number of pebbles used and corroborated the equation of a man with a particular number. *Skiagraphia* suggests a shaded drawing, though at times he used merely an outline. He was thus thinking in three-dimensional terms, and by means of the shading was able to represent three dimensions on a flat surface. The different colours could be used to bring out the effect of a purposeful and intelligible representation, an archetechtonic form.

There seems some connection between the Pythagorean pebble-systems, taking on relations to organic forms, and the newly developed art of pebble-mosaic. Far back, in the late fourth millennium B.C., at Ur we find conical clay pegs driven into frontages, producing geometrical motifs of decoration; and about 2600 B.C. ornamental tesserae appear. But mosaic proper began when the Greeks started making designs out of floor-pebbles. Some remains of such a floor occur in the sixth-century temple of Athena Pronoia at Delphoi. In the late fifth century the first figure scenes come in, mostly of animals fighting; the earliest known complete depiction of a myth-scene is one of

Bellerophon on his winged horse at Olynthos, dated to the late fifth century. But in view of the difficulty in giving precise dates to such art developments or to early Pythagorean thought we can merely note the relationship.

Aristotle seems to be referring to later Pythagoreans such as Philolaos and Eurytos when he says that "some persons are in doubt even in the case of the circle and the triangle, considering that it isn't right to define these by lines and by continuous space, but that all these are to the circle or the triangle as flesh and bones are to men, and bronze and stone are to the statue; and they reduce all things to numbers and say that the formula of 'line' is that of 'two'." Note that in the citation above he spoke of points defining magnitudes. The early Pythagorean idea seems to have been that a line equals 2 because two extended points set side by side constitute a line; but after the Zenonian critique the idea was probably made less vulnerable by being reformulated as saying that a line was a stretch of continuous magnitude bounded by two points. In the light of these suggestions we can make sense of what Eurytos did. A tetrahedron could be defined by the number 4 since that was the number of points needed to bound its surface. Eurytos on this basis may have sought for the least number of pebble-points that could define a much more complex figure, that of a living three-dimensional object. The *ousia* of the object would then be this number, which defined its surfaces. Thus the Pythagoreans attempted to reformulate their doctrine of the imposition of limit upon the unlimited. (We might compare the modern designs or models, also using colours, to represent atomic structures or the lattices of crystal.)[8]

The scheme further illustrates the Pythagorean interest in canons of proportion. Their ideas in this matter had a wide influence. Galen tells us that Chrysippos linked the idea that beauty lay in the proportion of the body's parts, with the doctrine that health lay in a balance or correct proportion of the body's constituents, and adds that "all doctors and philosophers" (of his own day?) accepted at least the former view. The idea of health here stated was close to that of Alkmaion and of Philolaos. Galen finds the question of beauty as proportion best exemplified in the writings of the sculptor Polykleitos of Argos:

> Beauty he believes arises not in the commensurability [*symmetria*] of the constituent elements, but in the *symmetria* of the parts, such

> as that of finger to finger, and of all the fingers to the palm and the wrist, of these to the forearm, and of the forearm to the upper arm, and in fact of everything to everything else, just as it is written in the Canon of Polykleitos. For having taught us in that work all the proportions of the body, Polykleitos supported his treatise with a work. He made a statue according to the tenets of his treatise, and called his statue, like the work, the Canon.[9]

Philon Mechanikos uses the term "numbers" and cites Polykleitos as using it:

> Thus the statement made by the sculptor Polykleitos may be suitably repeated for the future. "Perfection," he says, "arises *para mikron* through many numbers." Indeed it happens in the same way in that art that, in finishing works off through many numbers, they make a slight deviation in each part and in the end these add up to a large error.[10]

The meaning of *para mikron* is not sure. It seems to mean here "from a minute calculation": that is, a very slight difference in measurements can make the difference between a perfect work and an imperfect one; but the phrase can mean "almost", "except for a little": implying that when all the correct measurements are made, still something more is needed to achieve true beauty.

We get a good idea of the sort of thing that Polykleitos worked out in the account of human proportions with which Vitruvius begins his section on the Planning of Temples. "Proportion consists in taking a fixed module, both for the parts of a building and for the whole, by which the method of symmetry is put into practice." Nature, he says, "has so planned the human body that the face from the chin to the top of the forehead and the roots of the hair is a tenth part . . ." and so on. He then says that the navel lies in the exact centre of the body. "If a man lies on his back with his hands and feet outspread, and the centre of a circle is placed on his navel, his fingers and toes will be touched by the circumference. Also a square will be found described within the figure, in the same way as a round figure is produced. For if we measure from the sole of the foot to the top of the head, and apply the measure to the outstretched hands, the breadth will be found equal to the height, just like sites that are square by rule."[11]

Though we do not know the details of transmission, the aesthetic canons were clearly derived from the Pythagorean system.

The Pythagoreans thus introduced two ideas of the greatest importance: that of a rhythm and of varying proportions in all movement, all phenomena, and that of a mathematical basis which can be found for all physical attributes. The full implications of these ideas are only beginning to be realised.

> No better proof of the Pythagorean idea that number underlies physical attributes could be found than the physical quantities which are expressed by dimensions. For a body is differentiated simply and solely by the sum total of these quantities which define its physical attributes: specific weight, specific heat, the constants of elasticity, viscosity, etc. . . . Certain quantities of this kind have a significance which goes far beyond the particular phenomenon in which they were discovered. Such quantities are called "universal constants. . . ." (Sambursky)

Such constants are the velocity of light which appears in mechanics, optics, electricity, and atomic theory; and Planck's quantum of action. There are also non-dimensional quantities, which have been called pure numbers, since they appear as ratios of quantities of the same dimension, e.g. the product of the velocity of light and Planck's constant has the same dimension as the square of the charge of the electron.

But this discovery of universal constants will need to be much extended, and the links between them will need to be realised, before we reach a science of full Pythagorean scope. And there is a further point. The Pythagorean linkage of numbers and their combinations with fundamental philosophic concepts (unity, multiplicity, and so on) and with moral ideas (the qualities of human life in all its concreteness) may have been naively set out; but the concept of a unitary dialectical process which lies deep in it is not naive in the least. It expresses the great truth we continually find in Greek scientific thinking—the unity of quantitative and qualitative elements in all natural and human process. A truth which they could for the most part set out only in general terms and in logical or theoretical expositions, but which is none the less valuable.[12]

The Pythagorean notion of number and substance meant that there were interstices in space, which might be an absolute void, but which these thinkers, like Epikouros later, preferred to consider as filled by air, *aithēr*, or some such rarefied medium. Still, their notion of number-substance as made up of discrete particles led straight on to atomism, though we do not know how much they themselves contributed to this development. No doubt the theories of men like Philolaos helped to some extent in this direction; but the enunciation of a definite atomic theory was associated with Leukippos and Demokritos. The atom was the indivisible (*a-tomon*) object or particle which was absolutely simple. No atom owned any internal properties that could distinguish it qualitatively from another; but atoms differed in form and magnitude, and had a weight proportional to their magnitude. Hence the variations in the natural bodies they formed. Their lightness or heaviness resulted from their collective whirling movement. Everything in the universe, including our emotions, thoughts, perceptions, occurs in a purely mechanical way in the sense that it results from the varying combinations and actions of atoms—direct contiguous actions at that. For example, we do not merely see something far off; the thing emits forces that impact physically upon us. These forces or effluences are of a very fine atomic composition, which preserves the shape of the emitting object and impacts directly on our visual organ. But there was a distinction between primary or objective qualities (weight, density, hardness), which lie in the object, and secondary qualities (colour, taste), which depend on the manner of our perception. The psyche was composed of fine tenuous atoms of an igneous nature; through their tenuity they tended to slip out of the body and be lost, but breathing renewed their number, sucking them back again. When breathing weakens, there is sleep or lethargy; when it stops, there is death. Thought is connected with the temperature and mobility of the atoms; an excess of heat or cold begets an inaccurate representation of reality.

The only further point in the development of the theory that we need to note is the effort of Epikouros to prove the freedom of the individual by including in his concept of the atom an element of spontaneity. He saw atoms as always in motion at a uniform speed, but held them to be capable of swerving slightly at any point of space or time. He argued that without the swerve they would "fall down through the bottomless void in straight lines like drops of rain; they would never meet or clash, and nature could never have brought anything to birth". He went on to argue that "living beings all over the earth are free" to make choices; but this freedom would be imperilled "if one movement necessarily always follows on another and the atoms never make a swerve to break the bonds of fate, to break the never-ending chain of causes and effects".[13] But in his eagerness to deny a fatalistic and mechanistic interpretation of cause and effect, Epikouros was not quite fair to Demokritos, who did not see the atoms, before they unite to form a kosmos, as falling in straight lines through space. They are engaged in a dance, which Cicero describes as a violent jostling, *turbulenta concursio*. At this point they are without weight; only when a multitude of them seize on a free space and begin the vortical movement, which creates the kosmos, do they gain weight.[14]

However that may be, the Demokritean system, if pushed further along the lines of reduction, could end in the world-vision of Galileo and Newton, where the mechanical relation is seen as alone solid and real, and all concrete human qualities are relegated to the level of the secondary and subjective. Epikouros is protesting against such a reduction; he insists on bringing back the principle of contradiction into a mechanistic world.

We have seen how in one sense pebble-numbers and atoms merge as abstract constituents of reality. Another equation appears between atoms, simple bodies, and the letters of the alphabet. A verbal equivalent of *atomon* is *stoicheion*, a collective noun for letters. Letters are like atoms in that they can be jumbled together, but when they are put together in a significant pattern they attain a new kind of unity. *Stoicheion* was also used for element or simple body, the ultimate ingredient of the universe. Plato uses the word in a double sense in the *Theaitetos*, pointing to letters as primary elements and to the syllables made out of them, which achieve meaning. In the *Sophist* he again uses the comparison, but now employing *gramma* for letter. Some things are able to combine with others, some are unable: as we see with letters.

Demokritos regarded the atomic character of the letters of the alphabet as expressive of the structure of the physical universe. In this connection we may note some words of Aristotle: "These philosophers say the differences in the elements are the causes of all other qualities. Those differences, they declare, are three:

shape and order and position. For they say the real is differentiated only by Rhythm and Intercontact and Turning; and of these, rhythm is shape, intercontact is order, and turning is position. For A differs from N in shape, AN from NA in order, and I from H in position." Here he too, dealing with physical theory, uses the Demokritean analogy of letters to demonstrate the construction of more complex units out of units that cannot be divided or cut up further. Lucretius uses the same analogy to show how simple bodies can be combined in larger units with their own special quality or meaning.

> *So it comes about that all things change their shapes,*
> *alter their colours, receive sensations, yield them,*
> *all in an instant. You may then realise*
> *how it matters with what others, in what position,*
> *the same* primordia *of things are held*
> *in union, what motions they mutually impart*
> *or get. So don't assume that what we see*
> *afloat on the surface of things, now born, now gone*
> *at once, can be a property inherent*
> *in eternal primal bodies. More, in our verses*
> *it matters greatly, with what other elements,*
> *in what kind of order, the various elements*
> *are set. The largest number, if not all,*
> *are similar; but the totals, composed of them,*
> *are made to differ much by the position*
> *of the elements. Thus in actual things as well*
> *when the clashings, motions, arrangement, position, shapes,*
> *of matter change about, the things too change.*[15]

The Pythagoreans gained the impetus to glorify the mean from their social rôle. Aristoxenos says that Pythagoras was the first man to advance the study of mathematics beyond the needs of trade. Kroton, where he operated, was a rich commercial city with a famous medical school, which produced Alkmaion, his younger contemporary. His order or fraternity for some time held political power in Kroton and several other cities of the region. But in about 450 B.C. the order was broken up and the members violently expelled. Their position seems to have been that of moderate democrats, not unlike that of Solon at Athens. Their rule coincided with the introduction of the coinage at Kroton; and we may claim that they represented the mercantile class, which also had industrial interests, and which established a sort of federal union for a number of city-states. They would have seized power one way or another from the landed aristocracy; and thus, standing between the nobles and the plebeians, they devised the doctrine of the mean for their political, ethical, and physical philosophies alike. They held that the upper and the lower parts of the kosmos "stood in the same relation to the centre, only reversed", and it is of interest that on Krotonian coins covering the period of Pythagoras there was a raised design on one side and on the other side the same design sunk in intaglio. On these coins they seem certainly to have been symbolising their concept of opposites. Their ideal was to preserve the balance of justice—as justice appeared to them in their rôle of separating upper and lower classes, and yet reconciling them. "Don't step over the beam of a pair of scales." Later they inevitably moved to the right against the growing pressures from below and were finally suppressed by the popular forces. We might take the discovery of irrational numbers as representing the turning-point in their development, which also led in general to a turning from arithmo-geometry to geometric solutions. By breaking down their mystique of integral numbers it also broke down the thesis of the golden mean in the terms in which they related it. It thus expressed a social as well as an intellectual crisis: the ending of the temporary hegemony of the merchant class with some sections of the landlords over the nobles and the commoners.

The Pythagorean idea of balance, then, involved a concept of proportional relations, which worked out as producing *harmonia*. Their discovery of concordant relations in music seemed above all to justify such a position: with ratios like $\frac{2}{1}$, $\frac{3}{2}$, $\frac{4}{3}$, in which pairs of unequal numbers appear. This kind of harmonic ratio differed from the idea of equality among the pre-Sokratic philosophers; and the Pythagoreans no doubt saw in life a conflict of good and evil which could only be kept under control through themselves as *sophoi* who held an understanding of the Odd Number, the Good Principle, which conferred on them the authority to govern the state.

Because of his use of opposites, Alkmaion, the medical theorist, has often been considered a Pythagorean. But Aristotle, we noted, declared that, while he shared their notion of life as composed of opposites, his system lacked their dogmatic systematisations.

Further, Alkmaion stated: "The bond of health is the *isonomia* of the *dynameis*, moist and dry, cold and hot, bitter and sweet, and the rest, while the *monarchia* of one of them is the cause of disease. . . . Health is the proportionate mixture of the qualities."

We cannot take "*isonomia*" as a Pythagorean term. On the one hand, philosophically it goes back to Ionian thinkers like Anaximandros (who does not however, it seems, use the word); on the other hand, politically it was bound up with the struggle for democracy. Its link is with *nomos*, law (originally customary right), rather than with *nemein*, to share. Indeed, if we go far enough back, we find the notion of rights and shares (fates) inextricably mixed; but in the early fifth century *isonomia* had strong connections with democracy and was the term used for that political form before *demokratia* was evolved. Herodotos shows it as meaning the rule of the masses in contrast with tyranny and oligarchy; and it is characterised by election-by-lot, the auditing of public officials, and the power of all free citizens to take part in the assembly to discuss and decide all matters of public policy. Its primary meaning is equality before the law rather than equality maintained by law. If we look back to Solon's constitution we find an unequal distribution of rights and privileges; magistracies were restricted to the upper-income classes, though every citizen was admitted to the courts before which suits could be tried and the magistrates themselves called to account. Solon called his ideal *Eunomia* (excellence or goodness of law). The Spartans also used that term, declaring Law was the Lord over their aristocratic system.

Isomoiria was the term for equal distribution of wealth (land). Such an equality was the aim of the insurgent peasants in Attika against their oppressors, the Eupatrid nobles. Under Solon the peasants got a partial share in political power, but in the economic sphere they had to be content with debt-cancellation and the release of those men who had been enslaved for debt. After that, the democratic call was simply for equal political rights, not for economic equality. (Only under the tyrant Peisistratos were the landless given Attic land by the state.) So *isonomia* had as one of its aspects the defeat of the poorer classes, of the landless peasant. It expressed the balance between the old class of hereditary nobles and the new plutocrats, with the commoners getting political rights plus economic subjection. Hence the idea that the law guarantees equality, but also equality guarantees the law; and that democracy represents the government by law as opposed to monarchy or oligarchy. In the Herodotean debate on constitutions, Otanes argues that *isonomia* will be the rule of law-abiding states free from the lawlessness of tyranny; and he bases his case, not on the old notion that the breakdown of justice is a matter of personal failure on the part of noble or king, but on the new concept that any concentration of power in individual hands corrupts. "Even the best of men" in the tyrant's place "would be changed from his wonted mind." The unequal powers in the non-isonomic state make the rulers, willynilly, act by force.

As we have noted, the fundamental concepts here go back to the Ionian philosophers, but their working-out belongs to the world in which the struggle against the nobles and the movement into democracy had begun and was being carried on. Alkmaion took over the Anaximandrian vision of universal process as one of struggle, of wrong-doing (over-stepping the limits of correct balance), justice, and reparation, and applied it to the human organism. For him, as for the Hippokratic medical theorists of Ionia or the Sicilian physicians of the Empediklean school, the normal functioning of an organism came about through the mixture of equal powers. How he himself saw the social relations of *isonomia* we do not know. He may have been one of the élite, the Thousand, of Kroton who yet had liberal views. But we can be sure he was not generalising from the political situation in Kroton where only the Thousand could attend the assembly; and it would certainly be wrong to see him as expressing an aristocratic position by condemning only *monarchia*. Whatever his personal political views, his ideas were rooted in the tradition leading from Ionian concepts of balancing factors in the kosmos to the attempt to realise such ideas politically in the developing mercantile city-state.

But though we must not identify Pythagorean proportion or *harmonia* with *isonomia*, that school had its own notion of the mean. They described a concord in music as "a coordination of opposites, a unification of the many, a reconciliation of dissentients". The terms for dissent and reconciliation are *dicha phronein* and *symphronasis*: both Doric, corresponding to the Attic *stasis* and *homonoia*, words derived from social relations and expressing party strife and civil war, and civil peace and concord. Philolaos, who fled to Greece after the forcible dissolution of the order, saw the soul as an attunement of the bodily opposites. Aristotle took over the idea of the mean, though from a much wider tradition than that of the Pythagoreans, and made it central in his philosophy. In one aspect or another it profoundly affected the whole of Greek thought. Aischylos, whom Cicero says was a Pythagorean, makes Athena cry in the *Eumenides*: "I bid my people uphold and honour the mean between the despot and the slave." But even if he was a Pythagorean, his views have been tinctured by the democratic struggles of his day; and he uses the slave as the antithesis of the despot. The social situation has grown more complicated.[16]

One important effect of this concentration on the mean, on a balance or equipoise between two extremes or opposites, was that Greek thought found itself, except fitfully and unstably, unable to lay hold of the idea of the dialectical unity of conflicting opposites, out of which a new stage of development occurs. In Herakleitos, Plato, some of the Stoics, we find that idea present, at times powerfully asserting itself, implied in concepts of triadic movement, yet never fully able to overcome the spell of the idea of balance and reconciliation. We shall find the key to this situation if we turn to Demokritos. In his work we see how the Greeks were advancing to the concept of universal natural law, of *anankē* or necessity, and in turn we find how the concept of necessity was bound up with the existence of slavery. The moderate democrat, the Pythagorean and his fellows, in fact advocated the class-war in so far as it broke the power of the landed aristocracy; that power was taken as an example of immoderate or extreme self-assertion. But having ensured the political power of the middle-class of merchants and industrialists, they wanted to halt the process there, and justified this arrest of the class-struggle as the expression of the golden mean. (At this stage we must not see merchants or industrialists as men exercising large-scale economic power or as composing a definite ruling-class. As always in the ancient world, the man with money sought to buy land, the primary source of wealth; and in that fact lay the aspect of compromise. The merchant did not want to dispossess the noble, only to curb his "immoderate" power; he himself wanted to join that class in its curbed condition.) No one therefore, except some of the early Stoics and Cynics, wanted to recognise the existence of slavery for what it was. If the class-war spread to the proletariat of craftsmen and sailors, in so far as such a class existed in the big mercantile city-states, it could not help drawing in the slaves—as happened at Pergamon round 130 B.C. and in Sparta under Nabis. And the democrat as much as the aristocrat saw such a development as the total collapse of civil society.

The concept of *anankē* thus had a dual aspect: men existed in a world of natural law which they could not alter; they also existed in a world where slavery assumed the character of a natural law and had to be accepted. The slave was slave by reason of *anankē*. The two aspects penetrated one another, and we may say that it was because of the recognition of the bond of social *anankē* that men were able to arrive at the generalisation of the inexorable rule of natural law.

The two key-concepts of that law, *anankē* and *aition* (cause), arrived in the latter fifth century. Leukippos, founder of atomism, declared: "Nothing happens at random, everything happens out of *logos* and by *anankē*." That is, there are universal natural laws, but they do not operate at random or sporadically; therefore they can be investigated and known. There is a coherent system in them, a *logos*, which can be grasped by human *logos* or reason. The concept was particularly developed by the medical writers: for example in the analysis of the causes of disease in the organism itself and in its environment, in *On Ancient Medicine*. The physicians were the men in whom scientific theory and practice could never be wholly divorced.[17]

Anankē was in many ways an Orphic figure; and Orphism, though a complex phenomenon, may be said primarily to express the deep divisions inside a society with extending slavery plus a continual strengthening of money-forces. The situation is reflected in the idea of a cleavage between soul and body, and in the hope of an afterworld in which the injustices of the present will be compensated for: a form of liberated life for the initiated without the iron rule of necessity. We meet Anankē as a figure in the works of Herakleitos and Parmenides, both influenced by Orphism, and of Empedokles, himself a sort of Orphic prophet. Herakleitos couples Anankē with Moira, Share or Fate; and Parmenides gives the same attributes to Moira, Dike (Justice), Anankē. A century later, in Plato's Republic, Anankē has taken over Moira's rôle and even holds her spindle. A man's Share or Fate, once strongly tribal and communal, has become the Necessity of slave-society.[18]

From Homer on, the idea of necessity and slavery had been closely connected. In Orphic paintings of the underworld, Sisyphos rolls his stone uphill while over him stands Anankē with lash in hand. The wheel of grief and misery from which the soul in the Orphic formula is released in death suggests the birth-death cycle seen in terms of the wheel to which slaves were tied in punishment, a wheel which was spun round. The turning of the wheel was an emblem also of unending toil. "I have flown out of the sorrowful weary wheel," was the first article in the Orphic confession of faith. The Pythagoreans saw in the cycles of transmigration, in which they believed, a wheel-compulsion. Diogenes Laertes says that Pythagoras was the first to declare that "the soul went round in a changing Wheel of Necessity, being bound down now in this, now in that animal". There was probably a wheel actually used in the Orphic rites, as we shall find later in the Egyptian temples when we come to Heron's *Pneumatics*. Clemens speaks of "the Wheel that is turned round in the precinct of the gods and that was derived from the Egyptians". Proklos says that the one salvation is that the spirit should free itself from the Wheel of Birth: "This is what those who are initiated by Orpheus to Dionysos and Korē pray that they may attain: to cease from the Wheel and breathe again from Evil." The torments of Prometheus in Aischylos' play are throughout described with reference to the idea of *anankē*."[19]

Thus in the divided self there is born the idea of a complete cleavage between mind or spirit and the body. The latter represents the servile principle, at the will of fate, chance, and all the ills of the flesh; the mind, setting itself against the body, can claim to be of a higher realm. The split appears strongly in Plato, in whose *Timaios* Mind, *Nous*, is confined by *Anankē* as an "errant cause", concomitant and corporeal, and is thus prevented from wholly effecting its purpose. Society cannot achieve true unity because of the deep alienations affecting everyone, master or slave; but men are unable to face the facts. There seems a blind and malicious principle of evil at work distorting their best aims and intentions. The dialectic of the problem of freedom in such a world is succinctly set out by Sophokles when his Chrysthemis tells her sister that she has decided "to obey her masters in all things in order to be free", while Electra, who asserts her independence and freedom, is treated like a slave. Later Tychē or Chance was linked with Necessity. This development may be paired off with the attempt of Epikouros to introduce the swerve of spontaneity into the rigorous world of Demokritean atom.

Demokritos himself was a complex character. His atom, from one angle, represents socially the increasing separateness and egoistic movement of the individual in the world of the cash-nexus; the *anankē* of the atom represents the inescapable need to accept slavery if Greek society is to go on functioning. But the act of recognising the essential nature of the situation has also its element of release, of detachment; and we find in the aphorisms attributed to Demokritos the declaration: "Poverty under democracy is as much to be preferred to so-called prosperity under an autocracy as freedom is to slavery." The aphorism is possibly his in substance, and in any event we feel in his personality a breadth of humanist sympathy that stands out among the positions of other early thinkers and gives him certain affinities with the Stoics, on whom also the problem of slavery weighed heavily. For him freedom is opposed to slavery, which is yet accepted as an institution, but the acceptance is linked with the readiness to struggle for "democracy" as the best way of life. His position is that of the Pythagoreans, but in a social situation which has grown more complex, where slavery is much more firmly rooted, and in which the class-struggle has a much more extended scope.[20]

In making these correlations, we must not be misunderstood as simply reducing *anankē* to slavery or the Pythagorean mean to middle-class politics. We are claiming that the social relations in question are a highly important factor in stirring men's minds and making them raise the general problems, and in determining the form in which those problems are formulated and answered. In short, that they play a vital part in the dialectics of the whole situation. But there is an objective aspect in the concepts of Pythagorean proportion and Demokritean necessity as well as a socially conditioned aspect; and this is what constitutes the element of release, or truth. Further, even the social aspect, of which the thinkers are only partially aware, is not subjective in the narrow way that personal rationalisations and fantasies are; it proceeds from a group which is doing its best to organise itself in the productive sphere, its best to understand its place in nature. It thus has close links with the ways in which humanity is being concretely realised and in which the group in its totality is actively developing its place in nature, through work and technology, through philosophy and the arts. (In this relation the group includes all who play a function inside it, slaves as well as freemen, peasants as well as traders, craftsmen as well as thinkers. We must think of a unitary development in which a complex set of factors all have a part to play, interacting on one another, though some are more important than others and there is a fundamental contradiction, between slaves and freemen, which operates all the while.)

To bring out our meaning here we may take a modern example which shows one of the direct social and economic forces at work on a thinker mentioned in our first chapter: Clerk Maxwell. It can be shown that he got the idea for the kinetic theory of gases from sociology: from Quêtelet's social physics through the intermediary of John Herschel. Quêtelet held that it was possible to found a science of society on the statistical regularity of the behaviour of large numbers of people. Behind such thinking in turn lay the need to find a secure basis of calculation for the insurance societies without which a matured capitalism could not function. So Maxwell, applying Quêtelet's ideas to gases and arriving at his kinetic theory, was following out a propulsion that originated in the last resort from the cash-nexus of maturing capitalism. A further example is the way in which Darwin was stimulated into constructing his evolutionary theory by the work of Malthus on the pressure of population, which had behind it the advent of the industrial proletariat and the question of its wages. Marx commented at the time: "It is remarkable how Darwin recognises among beasts and plants his English society with its division of labour, competition, opening up of new markets, inventions, and the Malthusian struggle for existence."[21]

But all that does not deny in the least an element of objective truth in the kinetic theory of gases and in the Darwinian thesis of evolution. It does mean however that if we recognise the social links we are in a better position to notice errors or limitations and to understand why they have crept in through the unconscious intrusion of prejudices and preconceptions. Further, we can get the whole work of a scientist in a fuller perspective, see why certain problems or methods were chosen instead of others, and thus understand the full implications of his thought. However, the recognition of the social links does not mean that the scientist's thought arrives by any simple process of derivation from the social forces that do much to direct the lines of his interest. The thought also belongs to its own sphere, its own discipline, which, even if not autonomous, has its own traditions and methods determining what questions will come up and how they will be tackled—though the tradition in turn has evolved in an endlessly complex way from a fusion of social pressures and intellectual systems.[22]

Air and Fire as Force

VI

It is clear by now that we cannot get far if we look for energy-concepts in the ancient world that correspond to the formulations of Carnot, Joule, or Kelvin. We have found that the ancients held a far more comprehensive idea of energy and force than is compassed by the mechanical approach. Though, as we shall see, they did not lack considerable skill in applied mechanics and knew of steam-power, these matters never became central in their thought or technology. We shall turn now to their ideas of force, many of which collected round the term *pneuma*—*pnoiē* is the Homeric form. *Pneuma* means blast or wind, any agitated movement of air; it is of the same root as *pnein, pneuein*, which refers to the blowing of winds. The word is first known in Anaximenes (about 546), who described the primal matter as air. "It differs in different things according to its rarity or density. In its rare form it gives rise to fire, and in its dense form it gives rise to wind, from which comes clouds and water, from which in turn comes earth, and from this come stones, and from them everything else." Heat has here its rôle; for fire, born from the most rarefied air, is at the top of the scale, at the bottom of which we meet the final chilling, the condensing or hardening of air to stone.

Pneuma appears as breath in Aischylos; as respiration it is common in the Hippokratic writers; in Aristotle and the comic poet Euboulos it has further the meaning of flatulence, or breaking wind. In the Hellenistic period it takes on the meaning of spirit; and in the Septuagint and New Testament it is used for the Spirit of God. We may compare the Latin *spiritus*, breeze, air, breath, spirit; also *anima*, wind, breath, soul, cognate with the Greek *anemos*, wind. Indeed the Greek complex of ideas and images is to be found practically everywhere among primtive folk.

> The West Australians used one word *wang* for "breath, spirit, soul"; in the Netels language of California, *piuts* means "life, breath, soul";

> certain Greenlanders reckoned two souls to man, namely his shadow and his breath; the Malays say the soul of the dying man escapes through his nostrils, and in Java use the same word *nawa* for "breath, life, soul". . . . The conception of the soul as breath may be followed up through Semetic and Aryan etymology, and thus into the mainstreams of the philosophy of the world. Hebrew shows *nephesh*, "breath", passing into the meanings of "life, soul, mind, animal", while *ruach* and *neshamah* make the like transition from "breath" to "spirit"; and to these the Arabic *nefs* and *ruh* correspond. The same is the history of the Sanskrit *atman* and *prana*, of Greek *psyche* and *pneuma*, of Latin *animus*, *anima*, *spiritus*. So Slavonic *duch* has developed the meaning of "breath" into that of soul or spirit. . . . (Tylor).[1]

The universal range of these ideas comes obviously enough from the correlation of breath with life, and then with all other movements of air. But what, as usual, is remarkable about the Greeks is the use they make of primitive concepts. Other tribal folk saw breath as life and wind, but only the Greeks built up such a vast structure of philosophic and scientific hypotheses on the analogies.

The term *psychē* also deserves a glance.

In Homer it has the meaning of life. The verb *apopsychein* means to exhale or breathe out; and there is the phrase *psychēn kapyssi*, to breathe out one's soul. The word has already reached an advanced stage of abstraction, and in some passages its meaning is obscure. Still, the link with breath and air appears in phrases like "his psyche flew out of his mouth" or "out of his body". There can be no doubt that psyche belongs to the same group as *pneuma*, *spiritus*, *anima*. Anaximenes certainly saw it as a form of air: "Just as our psyche, which is air, holds us together and rules us, so do *pneuma* and air encompass the whole universe." That is, he assumes that his audience will agree in linking *psyche* with breath, and then, after defining it as the cohesive life-force of the individual organism, he goes on to use *pneuma* to express the whole encompassing and binding force of the kosmos. The psyche in Homer we may add, is merely the animating force; the centre of consciousness, of thought, emotion, and understanding, is the breath-spirit in the lungs, the *thymos* in the *phrenes*. The *noos*, which effects reasoned thought, is also in the lungs. By the time of Herakleitos, the meaning of *noos* is not much changed; the word may be translated as sense or intelligence. But the *thymos* has become the seat of strong emotions (above all, anger and desire) that are not concerned with rationality; the psyche is the seat of feeling, and it gathers together a man's moral and intellectual qualities. But in all these changing ideas about *psyche*, *thymos*, *phrenes*, the importance of breath as a life-force is unaffected.[2]

Xenophanes is said to have argued against the thesis that the world breathes; he must have been thinking of some Ionian nature-philosophers. Possibly Anaximenes originated the idea. Aristotle says that among older Pythagoreans was a similar belief; its advocates connected it with the theory that the world contained empty space. Sextus says that the Pythagoreans and Empedokles based on it their creed that the fellowship of men is not merely with one another and with the gods, but includes animals: "For there is one *pneuma* which pervades, like a soul, the entire universe and which also makes us one with them." By adding the opposites dry and moist, hot and cold, to *pneuma*, thinkers were able to differentiate the *pneuma* of *psyche*, dry and warm, from the *pneuma* of *physis* (world of plants), moist and cold. Orphic theology represented the *psyche* as entering the newborn child on wings of wind.[3] We are not sure how far air was active or passive in early formulations. There seems a confusion in Aristotle and later writers, perhaps through a linking of air and water-vapour. Poseidonios makes moisture produce the chill of air over marshy ground; but his pupil Cicero stressed the caloric content of air. Ploutarch pointed to the active rôle of air in freezing water, and assigned air a mid-position between fire and water. The Stoics made air and fire active.[4]

Demokritos, perhaps in his lost main work, *Mikros Diakosmos*, wrote a passage cited by Clemens of Alexandreia: "Some of the wise men lifted their hands towards that place which we Hellenes call the Abode of Air, and said that Zeus holds converse with himself about all things, and that it is he who knows all things and gives and takes away, and he is king of all." It is clear that the wise men are not Greeks; probably they were Babylonians or *magousaioi* of Anatolia; but the Greeks are the ones who identify *aēr* with the sphere aloft.

With Herakleitos *psyche* includes the idea of consciousness, though we do not know if it had this meaning for Anaximandros, who was mainly concerned with its physical aspects—though his statement, "psyche rules us", suggests intellectual powers as well as vital essence. Diogenes of Apollonia, who followed Anaximandros' doctrines closely, certainly considered the air-principle to be animated and "knowing much". The variations in the soul derived from differences in the proportion of hot and cold, dry and wet, in the air. He stressed the differing degrees of warmth of psyche in human beings and animals, and argued that the vast number of possible variations in the mixture explained the observed diversity in form, way of life, and intelligence. These ideas of his influenced the Stoics. He related physical changes to modifications in the motions of the air: its becoming drier or moister, steadier or faster in movement. (Questions of speed came up not long after with Archytas, who explained the high or low pitch of notes in speed-terms.) Alkmaion held the soul to be immortal because of its ceaseless motion; for "all the divine things, moon, sun, planets, and the whole heavens, are in eternal movement".[5]

Pneuma appears as a cosmic force in the cosmogony of Pherekydes in the sixth century, which was halfway between myth and philosophic speculation. In his treatise *On the Genesis of the Gods* we saw that he sets out a triadic group: Zas, Chthonie, Chronos—the active principle of life (perhaps connected with what Demokritos called the Abode of Air), the earth-principle, and Time. Time created from his seed Fire, Pneuma, Water; another triad, from which came the gods.[6] Here *pneuma* seems to assume the rôle of air; but later with the Stoics, who made great use of the term, it signified a mixture of fire and air, which took over the active aspects of these two elements in more pronounced form.

The Stoics did not follow Aristotle in linking a pair of qualities with each element or simple body. For them fire was hot, air was cold, earth was dry, water was moist; but they agreed with him in stressing the active aspect of air and fire. They seem to have had two main reasons for this attitude of theirs, one physical, one biological. Men had known for some time that air had elastic properties; they had pressed on air-filled skins and proved its compressibility. (Later was to come an interest in the expansive powers of steam and other phenomena connected with vapour-tension. Aristotle several times cited air's elasticity, linked with pressure, as one of its active characteristics. And as we saw, the processes of life had long been connected with heat and its effects. By their concept of *pneuma* the Stoics took the big step of extending the dynamic function of fire and air to cover all natural phenomena, including those of physics. *Pneuma* now embraced all the active processes of the kosmos, whether they involved qualitative changes or mechanical motion. Here was an attitude implicit in certain aspects of Aristotle's thought, but never brought by him so boldly into the open, so dramatically generalised. However, before we examine the Stoic concept we had better look in more detail at the thought of Herakleitos, who in some ways was their forerunner and who at times brings out more clearly the basis from which the concepts developed.[7]

Some of his imagery is linked with the picture of the cosmogony given by Anaximandros. That picture may be made out on something like the following lines: Four elements in a sort of stratified form—earth covered with water, mist above, and fire encompassing all. Fire heats the water till it evaporates and dry land appears, but the heat also increases the volume of mist. Pressure grows to breaking-point. The fiery integument of the universe breaks and takes the form of wheels of fire enclosed in tubes of mist which encircle the earth and sea. The heavenly bodies whirling overhead are in fact holes, or gaps through which the enclosed fire glows; an eclipse is a total or partial closing-up of a hole. There are three distinct regions: in the nearest are the rings of the fixed stars, then comes the ring of the moon, furthest out is that of the sun. We have three accounts of the imagery:

> The heavenly bodies come into being as a Circle of Fire separated from the Fire in the Kosmos and enclosed by *Aēr*. There are breathing-holes [*ekpnoiai*], certain tube-like passages [*poroi aulōdeis*], at which the heavenly bodies show themselves. So eclipses occur when the *ekpnoiai* are blocked up. The moon is seen now waxing, now waning, according to the blocking or opening of the *poroi*. The sun's circle is 27 times the size of [the earth, that of] the moon [18 times]; the sun is highest, and the circles of the fixed stars is lowest. (Hippolytos).

> Anaximandros says the sun is a circle 28 times the size of the earth, like a Chariot-Wheel, with its felloe hollow and full of fire, and showing the fire at a certain point through an aperture [*stomion*] as through the tube [*aulos*] of a *prēstēr*.
>
> Anaximandros says that the sun is equal to the earth, but that the circle from which it has its *ekpnoia* and by which it is carried round is 27 times the size of the earth. (Aetios).

To get the full picture we must add the statement that he declared:

> That which is productive for the eternal of hot and cold was separated off at the genesis of the kosmos, and a kind of Sphere of Fire from this was formed round the air surrounding the earth like a bark round a tree. When this was broken off and shut off in certain circles, the sun and the moon and the stars were formed. (Pseudo-Ploutarch).

The sphere of fire was thus broken up, and each star, including the planets, gained its own wheel. The wheels were equal in diameter and inclined on countless different planes.[8]

What concerns us here however is mainly what is meant by saying that the vent or blow-hole was like the tube or pipe of a *prēstēr*.

Prēstēr generally means a special kind of storm, a tornado, but it has been taken here to mean the nozzle of a bellows, partly because of the reference to a tube (*aulos*) and partly because of a passage in the *Argonautika* of Apollonios Rhodios. In that passage Hera tells Iris to go to "the seabeaches where Hephaistos' bronze anvils are struck by sturdy hammers, and tell him to still the blasts of fire, till Argo has passed them by. Then go as well to Aiolos who rules the winds, children of the clear sky," and bid him still all winds but the western, which will blow the ship on its course to the Phaiakian Isle. She goes to Hephaistos and "quickly made him halt the clangs of his iron hammers. And the smoky *prēstēres* were stayed from their blast." Then on she went to stop the winds. Clearly the god's smithy is here seen as a place of elemental forces and changes. His bellows are the whirlwinds, the wild forces that he controls and uses for creative (craftsman) purposes. The most destructive forces are tamed and transformed to constructive ends. In the *Iliad* the bellows are *automata*, selfmoving; a detail which perhaps suggested to Apollonios his bold image. Note also that the task of Iris is to still both the *prēstēres*, the tornadoes, and the winds. The text here also uses the phrase *physai* (of fire), which is found in the Homeric account. *Physa* means breath, wind, blast, fart, stream of fire (*Hymn to Hermes*), and volcanic crater (Strabon).[9]

There can be no doubt that the word *prēstēres* was never used

8. Romano-Gallic Altar with Sky-Wheel and Thunderbolt (Maison Carrée at Nîmes)

for bellows except in this metaphor; it refers always to tornadoes. Anaximandros sees the heavenly fire as belching and raging out of a hole and down a tube (or in tube-form). He uses the contrast of stormy light and dark cloud-mist again in his account of thunder. Aetios says that he held thunder and lightning to be wind-caused: "When it's imprisoned in a dense cloud and escapes with violence, the disruption of the cloud produces the noise and the rent appears luminous in contrast with the darkness of the cloud." There is thus a strong analogy between lightning and the heavenly fire; both are produced by a body (wind) which is enclosed in cloud or mist (*aēr*) and then emerges from it.

Now let us turn to the Herakleitan aphorisms. In considering the fire and air of these early thinkers we must realise that it was the capacity of these elements for violence, agitation, furious and destructive effects, as well as for nurturing aids, which stirred their minds and impressed them as with a spectacle of primal power. Not tranquil air, but the air of wind and storm; not the mild heat that hatches the egg, but fire the great ravaging force. For Herakleitos fire is not a primary element, but is the most active and transforming force in the kosmos, aspiring to the height. It drives the universe irresistibly along and provides the impact that both destroys and creates; it is birth and death, and the curve of life rushing headlong in between. No doubt many particular aspects of fire played their part in the full concept: its power through combustion to effect changes in the constitution of things submitted to it; the way it frees from the consumed mass the particles thought to blend with it and thus to change their character; the stream of particles given off in the form of sparks and smoke; the differing times taken for the consumption (or conversion into fire) of various substances under given conditions. (Heat would not be seen as the chief characteristic; it was thought to vanish when fire was most condensed in the form of earth—the limits of the process of rarefaction and condensation being spoken of as kindling and extinguishing.) It was fire as a great transforming force that dominated the Herakleitan conception: "This universe, which is the same for all, has not been made by any god or man, but it always has been, is, and will be an ever-living fire, kindling itself by regular measures and going out by regular measures." Fire is not primal matter for Herakleitos, as Aristotle says; rather it is a rhythmic force, swinging between "craving and satiety".[10]

That description of its phases is only another way of expressing its driving and directive power, which works by regular measures and which in turn sets men on courses of alternating desire and repletion, too little and too much. The fire-rhythm is linked with the polarities inside natural process. "It throws apart and then brings together again; it advances and retires." Again, Herakleitos tells us: "The transformations of fire are: first sea, of sea half becomes earth, and half the *prēstēr*." *Prēstēr* is then an important moment in the transformations of fire. The saying is a difficult one. It seems certainly however to be describing the change of fire into water and earth and back again. There is a tornado, a violent attack or shock in which the sea breaks open, is transformed. The whirl of fire is no longer in the sky, creating what seem bodies of fire that send us light—and in the case of the sun, heat as well. The whirling tube has reached down and struck the earth.[11]

In view of the importance of the *prēstēr* as revealing the fire-force at its most complete and powerful, we had better look at the passages of ancient authors that describe it. Aristotle in his *Meteorologika* speaks of it as a variant of the *typhōn*, which is a whirlwind. Forming in a cloud, it is unable to break loose from it and so drags it down to earth as it descends. Aristotle calls it a *helix* (whirl, spiral, convolution) bringing a cloud down to earth. There can be no doubt that what he describes is a tornado or waterspout. A tornado is a whirl of small diameter. From the furiously agitated main cloudmass aloft there usually hangs at such a moment a writhing funnel-shaped cloud. When the latter swings over the sea the water rises in a cone to meet it; the result is a waterspout. The Mediterranean is one of the seas where waterspouts are most common. Lightning usually accompanies a tornado; at times it is seen with a spout. Aristotle says that the *prēstēr* is the same as a *typhōn* except that with it the wind catches alight.[12] He presumably means that the wind ignites it as it emerges, at least when it strikes or sets some object on fire.

In Hesiod's *Theogony* the monster Typhōeus, who fights with Zeus, is linked with violent forces, blasting or erupting. "And through the two of them heat grasped the dark blue sea, through the thunder and lightning, through the fire from the monster and the scorching winds and the blazing thunderbolt." Pindar tells of Typhos buried under volcanic Aitna. To see the monster or the related figure Typhon as merely a personification of tornado or volcanic eruption would be too simple; but those phenomena have certainly contributed essential imagery to the picture of a creature representing wild elemental forces at their most dangerous and threatening. We see why Hephaistos in his volcanic smithy, in the *Argonautika*, used *physai* and *prēstēres* tamed to his creative craft-will; and why for Herakleitos the *prēstēr*-moment was that of fire at its most critical turning-point, capable of shattering destruction but also bringing about a necessary transformation. (Fire in a smithy was actually carrying out metallurgical changes.)[13]

The word used for the critical moments is *tropai*, turns, which before the fourth century can be shown to have been used always in contexts of sudden and complete changes, not of gradual or small ones; e.g. it was used of the reversal of the sun's course on the ecliptic, but not of the normal revolutions of the heavenly bodies. Herakleitos says that half of the sea can be regarded as turning to earth (and replenished by earth), the other half as turning to *prēstēr* (and replenished by fire), the total remaining unchanged as sea. We may note that men of the time thought they could observe aspects of this sort of process. The sea was turning to earth when rivers and harbours were silted up—as was happening to the harbour of Ephesos in Herakleitos' own time. Xenophanes used his knowledge of marine fossils in Malta, Paros, Syracuse, to support his theory (perhaps held in slightly different form by Anaximandros) that the earth had once been all sea. Ploutarch spoke of

> the tradition that Typhon once ruled the domain of Osiris, since Egypt was then a sea. For this reason many shells can be found up to this day in the quarries and the mountains; and all the springs and wells, of which there are many, contain salty and bitter water as though a stale vestige of the former sea had collected there.

Then rain and the Nile drove out the sea; and the river still keeps on bringing up new alluvium and pushing the land further on. (In fact it is only the lakes and wells near the Nile Valley that are brackish.) The recurrent Ionian idea that earth had solidified out of a primeval island of mud no doubt arose from observations of this kind. Earth turned back into water when new streams broke out, when coastline was eroded, or when whole landmasses sank. Compare the mythical upheaval of islands like Delos and Rhodes for the change from sea to earth. The change from sea to fire was through evaporation. Aristotle and Theophrastos, wanting to refute Ionian ideas of the world coming to be or passing away, argued that if indeed "many places were now dry, which were once under water, the opposite also was true", and so a balance was kept.

9. Zeus attacking Typhon with Thunderbolt (Rumpf, *Chalkid. Vasen* no. 10)

Arrian in his account of a *typhōn* agrees with Aristotle and mentions the funnel. One difficulty of identifying the sky-vent of Anaximandros with the tornado is that the latter is more likely to suck things up than send them down. But this is a minor point, as also the fact that the tornado reaches right down to earth, whereas Anaximandros clearly visualises some sort of durable tube or tunnel of whirling *aēr*, which hangs down below sun and moon but does not come anywhere near the earth. It is no answer to say that now and then a tornado's funnel fails to reach earth or to draw up its water-cone. Anaximandros was merely using a general analogy; the image of the tube of whirling *aēr*, with fire inside it, is what matters. The tornado is cylindrical in form and has a spinning motion; also it does not provide a mere momentary effect as does lightning. It often lasts for minutes and occasionally for hours. And it has a rectilinear motion. The play of lightning round it however does not seem to give it a strong enough relation to fire; but eyewitness accounts show that the interior is an inferno of light.

A farmer in Kansas who found himself under the funnel of a tornado described his experience. "All wind had ceased and a pungent odour prevailed. A screaming, screeching sound poured from the end of the funnel," and he saw right up inside. "The circular opening, which he judged to be between fifty and one hundred feet across and to extend upward at least one-half mile, was brilliantly lighted by lightning zigzagging from side to side. Small twisters formed and writhed around inside the rim of the tornado." Another witness in Texas also saw up into the funnel, "the flashing lightning giving a shimmering fluorescent glow, the terrific whirling, and the horrendous road". He also noted that the whole column inside was "composed of rings or layers mounted one on top of the other much in the manner of a stack of automobile tyres at a service station. If a higher ring moved laterally, the ring immediately below slipped over to a position underneath again, and this rippling motion continued down the funnel."[14]

The other ancient references to a *prēstēr* do not help much to clarify the picture, but they show it an important phenomenon. Epikouros in his *Letter to Pythokles* seems to describe it as a whirlwind, and there is apparently a reference to a funnel; cloud is mentioned, but not that the *prēstēr* is emitted from it; fire is not noted. The Stoics, however, take the significant step of linking both lightning and *prēstēr* with the universal pervasive force *pneuma*. Diogenes Laertios says that Zenon in his treatise *On the Whole* declared:

> Lightning is a kindling of clouds from being rubbed together or being rent by *pneuma*. Thunder is the noise the clouds make when they rub against each other or burst. Thunderbolt is the term used when the fire is violently kindled and hurled to the ground with great force as the clouds grind against each other or are torn by *pneuma*.

Diogenes goes on to say that others declare the bolt to be "a compression of fiery air descending with great force. A *typhōn* is a great and violent *keraunos* [thunderbolt: here apparently a bad storm of thunder and lightning] that's like *pneuma* [*pneumatōdēs*] or a smoke-like *pneuma* from a burst cloud. A *prēstēr* is a cloud rent all round by fire with *pneuma*."

On the Kosmos deals with what the author calls exhalations:

> There are two exhalations from it [the *oikoumenē* or inhabited world] which pass continually into the air above us, composed of small particles and completely invisible, except that in early mornings some can be observed rising along rivers and streams. One of them is dry and like smoke; the other is damp and vaporous as it's exhaled from the wet nature [*physis*]. From the latter come mists, dews, the various kinds of frost, clouds, rain, snow and hail; from the dry exhalations come the winds and various blasts, thunder and lightning, *prēstēres*, and thunderbolts, and all the other things of the same class.

He goes on to discuss these phenomena and their causes. Of the dry exhalation, he says that "when it is forced to flow by the cold, wind is produced, for this is nothing but *aēr* flowing in quantity and in mass. It's also called *pneuma*. In another sense *pneuma* means the substance found in plants and animals, pervading everything, which brings life and generation." Though the author bases much on Aristotelian tradition, he draws on other schools, especially neo-Pythagorean; here he is thinking of the Stoics. He goes on to deal with rainbows and light-streaks in the sky. Shooting lights are generated by friction in the air that begets fire: "The fire moves rapidly, giving the impression of length because of its speed." Wind and fire burst from vents in the earth. The winds cause ecstatic inspiration, wasting disease, prophecy, even complete destruction; they cause earthquakes, which are divided into the horizontal, the heaving, the sinking, the splitting, the thrusting, the oscillating, and the roaring. But a wind can produce roaring without an earthquake, when it merely "lashes about, enveloped in the earth, with tumultuous force. Entering the earth, a wind also can be merely condensed. Similar effects occur in the sea."[15]

The *prēstēr*, we see, is classed with thunder and lightning, and with wind in its more violent effects; the wind born of dry exhalations is identified with *pneuma*. Lucretius gives us an extended picture of *prēstēres*:

They come down from above into the sea. For at times
it's as if a pillar were let down from heaven descending
into the sea and round it the surges seethe,
stirred by heavy blasts; and all ships caught in the turmoil
are dashed about and swung into uttermost danger.
It happens at times when the force of the wind aroused
can't break through the cloud that it attempts to burst,
but weighs it down; so it's like a pillar from heaven
let down in the sea, but gradually, as though
a thing were thrust down from above and outstretched by the fist
and push of the arm to the level of the waters;
and when the force of the wind has torn this cloud, it bursts
out into the sea and provokes a marvellous boiling
wild in the waves; for the whirling eddy descends
and brings down yonder cloud with its pliant body,
and as soon as it's forced it down, full-charged, to levels
of sea, the eddy itself plunges whole in the water
and stirs up all of the sea with prodigious noise
and compels it to boil. At times, also, the eddy
of wind wraps itself up in clouds and gathers
cloudseeds from air, and imitates, it seems,
the prester *let down from the heavens. And when this* prester
has let itself down to the land, it bursts and belches
a whirlwind and a storm of enormous fury.
But as it seldom happens, and on the land
the mountains can't help but obstruct it, it's seen more often
at sea with its wide prospect and open horizon.

Plinius speaks of a *turbo* or whirlwind bursting from the cavern of a cloud, and adds that "when it rages more fiery and fire-kindling, it's called a *prēstēr*"; just before that, dealing with sudden blasts (*flatus*), he may refer to a funnel. He also mentions related phenomena called the column and the *aulon*. So here at last we have definite evidence that the whirling vapour of cyclonic disturbances could be called a tube or pipe. Seneca takes the *prēstēr* to be a fiery whirl, an incendiary *turbo*, and says that it bursts into flame; the funnel is not mentioned. Ateius also implies some igniting effect, stating that a *prēstēr* is caused by "kindling and extinction of clouds", while Plutarch evidently thinks the *prēstēr* and the *keraunos*, thunderbolt, to be of much the same type.[16]

The word *prēstēr* has the same root as *prēthein*, to blow out, spout, swell out by blowing. It occurs in Homer; and in the passage from the *Theogony* cited above, which tells of the cosmic struggle of Zeus and Typhōeus, it describes the scorching or blasting winds which seem weapons of the monster as against the blazing thunderbolt of Zeus.[17] The reason for examining its usages here at some length lies in its importance for the early physical theories of Anaximandros and Herakleitos. We see the great significance attached to the more violent phenomena of fire and air, with thunderclap, thunderbolt, lightning and tornado taken as the supreme expressions of cosmic power. The tornado had a specially impressive aspect, for it could last quite a long time and it combined terrific noise and lightning-bursts with a circling motion. Therein no doubt lay the reason for Anaximandros' image of the heavenly bodies. The fact that the tornado came down from the clouds of storm to land or sea, connecting sky and earth (as it would seem), made it a portentous thing. We see why Herakleitos used it to express the most violent moment of transformation, of the active power of fire, and we begin to grasp something of the full force of his aphorisms. "Fire lives in the death of earth." Consider too: "The thunderbolt pilots all things." Seneca tells us of *fulmen*, the thunderbolt: "Some philosophers hold that it goes back after its fall." It thus linked heaven and earth in the same way as the tornado did.[18]

We must then understand that thunderbolt as cosmic pilot and *prēstēr* as a crucial moment of fire's transformations are essentially the same thing. Herakleitos is repeating his point when he says, "When earth has melted into sea, the resultant amount is the same as there had been before the sea hardened into the earth." But there he is putting the stress on the "regular measure" rather than on the dialectical moment of deep change. Several comments on Herakleitos by later writers show that evaporation was what he had in mind when he spoke of the change from earth to water, but the word they use, *anathymiasis*, may not have been that used by the early thinkers. (A passage in Aetios suggests that Thales already stressed evaporative process. Ploutarch, discussing the matter, scrupulously numbers his points, and the third doctrine he attributes to Thales is that "even the very fire of the sun and stars and indeed the kosmos itself is nourished by evaporation of the waters". Perhaps the early term was *ekpoia*, efflux, the use of which is attributed to Anaximenes: "We come into existence by an *ekpoia* from air."[19])

Inability to enter into the unitary nature of the thinking of the early philosophers has led to much barren dispute among commentators as to whether fire in Herakleitos is or is not simply a physical phenomenon. Certainly we may identify thunderbolt and *prēstēr* with wisdom: "Wisdom is one: to know the intelligence by which all things are steered through all things", wisdom which "is willing and yet unwilling to be called by the name of Zeus". In fact the Greek word *kybernatai* can be taken as either middle or passive in voice, so that we could translate "by which all things steer themselves through all things".

Later scholars, in a more divided society where terms had be-

10. Okeanos and Wind (Endymion sarcophagus: Robert iii 1, 20, 77)

come far more abstract, could not grasp the kind of unity of fire, wisdom, Zeus in the Herakleitan system. Hippolytos introduced the aphorism on the phases of fire by saying that Herakleitan fire "is characterised by intelligence and is responsible for the movement of the universe". Stobaios remarked: "Herakleitos held that the kosmos is generated, not by time, but by mind." Modern scholars have suggested that he did not consider all fire to be rational, but only fire of the purest and most ethereal kind. It has been argued that the kosmos *is* fire and so is not steered by it; therefore the directing fire must be the heavenly sort. Thus Kleanthes took lightning to derive from pure creative fire, which the Stoics distinguished from everyday fire.[20] Again, to get rid of what may seem the difficult statement that the thunderbolt pilots the universe, scholars have suggested that *keraunos* is used as an epithet of Zeus. We do indeed find Zeus Keraunos in a fifth-century inscription from Mantinea; in an Hellenistic inscription from Homs (Emesa); and in an Orphic hymn: a cult of Keraunos was instituted at Seleukeia in Pieria by Seleukos Nikator (*c.* 358–280 B.C.). Or *keraunos* has been taken to mean the weapon of Zeus—something hurled by Zeus, who is thus the motivator of all things. Less likely is the suggestion that there might be a reference to the Orphic belief that the thunderbolt was the instrument of fate driving souls into the cycle of births as a punishment for defilement. That the bolt was thought of as a kind of fire is shown by the common epithet for it in the fifth century: *pyrphoros*, fire-bearing.[21]

In Homer a man's mind "darts" from place to place when he is thinking of himself as somewhere else; and in Empedokles deity is not anthropomorphic, but "darts through the whole kosmos with swift thoughts". Herakleitans of the late fifth century held that the moving body of the world was traversed by something far quicker and subtler which "administered" all things and brought them to pass. Sokrates states that he has been told that this *dia-ion* (through-thing or force) is *to dikaion* (justice) and also Zeus, since all things happen DIA it—*dia* meaning both "through" and "Zeus" in the accusative. Beyond that point, he adds, there is no agreement; one person says the traversing force is the sun, but another mocks at him, asking if there can be no *dikaion* after sunset, and claiming that the force is fire. Herakleitos had declared: "How can one hide anything from that which never sets?" Plato clearly took "that which never sets" to be fire. It had to be something owning or able to invoke the power of punishment, like Dikē who "will overtake fabricators of lies and false witnesses". But when Kleanthes hymned Zeus as governing all things with Dikē and as guiding the world with his ever-living thunderbolt, he was breaking up the unity of the Herakleitan concept. In that concept Dikē, Fire, Thunderbolt, Prēstēr, and Wisdom are all one, but they are not attributes of an anthropomorphic god.

For Herakleitos *sophia* (*to sophon*) or wisdom still has a craft-note about it; it expresses the know-how of the man making things; it expresses also the dialectical structure of natural process, which knows how to get on with its job, making all sorts of changes in the universe and growing trees from seeds and so on. Nature has a *logos*, an intelligible structure and system, as much as the world that man has made, even if the two cannot simply be identified. The transformations go on by their own inner motive force, and yet man is entangled deeply in their systems, part of them and yet separate. The unity and differences of Zeus, Wisdom, Fire, express the strange way in which one system of the world of nature can become conscious of itself and its relations, can become humanised, and yet be only an aspect of the universal formative process. That is why Wisdom, the insight into the nature of the critical moment of change as into the difficult points of craft-activity or of a poem's composition, is both willing and unwilling to be called Zeus.

And so ancient commentators could argue that Herakleitan fire was rational or that it was merely material fire. Asklepios keeps referring to Herakleitos' fire in a way that shows he considered it to play a rôle corresponding to that of Thales' water or Anaximenes' air; he declares that Herakleitos and each of the Milesians took one of the physical elements as their fundamental principle. Alexandros of Aphrodisias shows a similar attitude, though he also calls Herakleitan fire both *archē* and *ousia*, principle and substance. Simplikios says that Herakleitos regarded fire as the primary bodily principle. But such views as these are as one-sided as those that try to abstract the fire as Wisdom or personify it as Zeus.[22]

Soul, *psyche*, for Herakleitos is substance, activity, and quality; all in one, because of his unitary concept. (He always speaks of *psyche* with the definite article.) Souls have their origin in what is moist; they are vapourised from the moisture. The terms used are those suitable for a vapourisation that is hot and even fiery; the burst of flame is merely the completion of the process. Vapour looks like smoke, which suggests fire. But vapour is also moist, so it reveals a counter-tendency to go down, to be transformed into water—and if the movement persists, into mud and earth. Soul then lives somewhere in the region between water and fire, capable of self-transformation in either direction. Alexandros says: "Wishing to make clear that souls, as they rise up in vapour, become intellectually aware, he represents them in the likeness of rivers. . . ." He also speaks of Herakleitos seeing the soul as "a perceptive exhalation". But Herakleitos said that "soul has its own principle of growth" (literally: Soul is a *logos* increasing itself). He stresses the struggle of dry and moist in the soul. "It is death to souls to become water, and it is death to water to become earth. Conversely, water comes into existence out of earth, and souls out of water."[23]

To maintain one's identity, one's humanity, is a ceaseless struggle, a ceaselessly involved motion. There is no escape by means of rest, withdrawal, isolation, abstraction. Herakleitos uses the analogy of the *kykeon*, the sacred drink used in the Eleusinian Mysteries and made of barley, grated cheese and Pramnian wine: "Even the sacred barley-drink separates when it isn't stirred." Only continual stirring maintains its character; only activity preserves the unity of the soul—not activity of *any* kind, but activity reaffirming the human essence and maintaining its vital relation with the universe. To let that activity stop amounts to breaking down the fusion of opposites which lies at the heart of all process. It is not by chance that Herakleitos uses the mystery-drink as his symbol for the active unity of the self, which in turn implies an integration with universal process. Theophrastos, explaining the aphorism, says that certain things hold together only when in motion; if the motion stops, they lose their essential nature. The composition of the soul is dynamic and involves a continual tension inside and outside.[24]

Sextus Empiricus tries to explain: "So it is by inbreathing the divine *logos* that we become intelligent according to Herakleitos. During sleep we are forgetful, but we become mindful again on waking up. For in sleep the pores of the senses are closed, so that the mind in us is shut off from what is akin to it in the surrounding world, and its connection with outer things is kept up only at vegetative level through the pores of the skin. Being cut off it loses its formative power of memory." Perhaps that last phrase is too strong a translation of *mnēmonikē dynamis*; but the Greek certainly stresses memory as an active power or organising force. "But when we wake up again, it [the mind] peers out through the pores of the senses, which serve us as little windows, and by thus entering into relations with what surrounds us, it regains the power of reason"—*logikē dynamis*. This last phrase means much more than the reasoning faculty in a limited sense; it means that the *logos* in man is liberated to find its unity with the *logos*, the coherent and significant structure, of all process, human or natural.

Not indeed that we take the statement by Sextus as echoing the terms used by Herakleitos, who would have made the points in a more concise and paradoxical way. But Sextus seems to be faithfully setting out a Herakleitan doctrine. He goes on with an illustration, which is far too detailed in its elaboration to be close to anything Herakleitos said; but again the idea seems genuinely Herakleitan and we may take the statement to be an expansion of an aphorism about fire and its surroundings. "Just as coals when brought close to the fire undergo a change that makes them incandescent, while if moved away they become extinguished: so likewise that portion of the enveloping substance that stays as a stranger in our bodies becomes well-nigh irrational owing to the separation, but through its union by means of the numerous pores it is made like in kind to the whole." Note the dynamic sense of reality. A man's body is partly merged with the environment (social and natural); it is being acted on all the while. But only when consciousness is awake and actively linked with human activity is the unity of the self realised.[25]

Soul is then here not soul in the later sense of some indwelling entity, which can be separated as such from the body. It is physical existence at certain stages of dynamic and dialectical development; and it functions only as long as it maintains the particular tension of fire and air, water and earth, out of which it has originated. So Aristotle was right when he took Thales' statement that all things are full of gods, to mean that "soul is diffused throughout the entire universe". Soul is the active principle, which in the human *logos* reaches consciousness of itself. That *logos* can then be called the divine *logos* since it penetrates to the core of the formative process. Simplikios, commenting on Aristotle's explanation, shows how hard it was for a man of the later centuries to enter into such a concept. He takes Thales to mean that "the gods are blended with all things", and adds, "This is strange." To Thales or to Herakleitos it was the simplest of matters; for gods, *psyche*, formative energy, intelligible structure or relationship (*logos*), were felt to be all aspects of the same reality. Something of the old meaning carries on in such passages as the following from *On the Kosmos*: "The *psyche*, by which we live and build houses and cities, though invisible, is perceived through its works; for all the conduct of life is discovered, arranged, and maintained by the soul: the ploughing and sowing of land, the inventions of *techne*, the use of laws, the order of a city's government, the activities of people in their own country, in war and peace with foreign nations." But it was only in the early period that thinkers could say with simple and entire conviction, as Herakleitos did: "Immortals become mortals, mortals become immortals, they live in each other's death and die in each other's life." Clemens of Alexandreia gave us his version of this: "Men become gods, gods become men." But to get the full taste of the words we must know that in the Greek the verbs are all left out. So the full aphorism begins: "Immortals mortals, mortals immortals. . . ." The meaning then is not that in the violent convolutions of change, in the *tropai* that beget *prēstēres*, a god dies and his soul-stuff turns into something else, while a man, dying, may be somehow compounded as a god. Rather it is that in the shattering *tropai* of human life a man may achieve such deep consciousness of cosmic unity, of the nature of process and his place in it, that he is a god for a while—since he shares the divine *logos*. And in the same way it can be said that the divine descends into the mortal at such a moment when the fire in the soul is at its strongest and purest.[26]

The thoroughness with which Herakleitos held fast to his idea that every organism is dynamically a part of its environment is brought out further by his aphorism: "In the circle the beginning and the end are common." Here is not only an affirmation of the cyclic nature of processes, of the dialectical unity of life and death, order and disorder; there is also a deeply revealing pun. *Xynos* for Herakleitos always means both "in common" and "with understanding": *xyn nōi* and *xynōi* ("with rational awareness" and "to that which is common"). What he is implying is that all deep awareness of the nature of things comes out of shared or social activity—not out of lonely contemplation.

A play on words of this type was felt by these men to have a subtle suggestiveness, a sort of cryptic proof of the argument in which it occurred. Thus Alkmaion a little later said: "Men perish because they cannot join the beginning with the end," the *archē* with the *telos*—which can also be read "first principle" and "governing or completing aim". Herakleitos' phrase does not have this particular double-meaning, for his terms are *archē* and *peras*. Here *archē* has the same double meaning as with Alkmaion, but *peras* signifies "end in the sense of limit". That is, the "end" which is "in common" with the *archē* involves a sense of the limit of the movement in question.

So the apparently simple aphorism sets out a belief that each movement, each launching of a new cyclic process, carries deep within itself a definite rhythm or pattern—its measure of energy (biological as well as mechanical) and so its own limit or death. And *archē* and *peras* are for humanity not only a rhythm and a measure which make up the living unity of a given process; they also necessarily involve a struggle of consciousness, an effort to understand what is happening in its fullness. And this struggle, as well as the understanding in which it culminates, is not something that happens to the individual as a separate and isolated being. It comes about because the individual is also a being acted on by endless forces, social and natural, and in turn acting on the world around him.

The strength of Herakleitos' conviction on these points is brought out by two more of his sayings. "Thinking is common to all." And then, in more elaborated form: "Men should speak with understanding [*xyn nōi*] and thus hold on strongly to that which is shared in common [*xynōi*]—as a city holds on to its law, and even more strongly. For all human laws are nourished by the one divine law, which prevails as far as it wishes, suffices for all things, and yet is something more than they."[27]

Herakleitos was opposed to the reduction of a complex living process to one of its aspects: which is a different matter from being ready to analyse any of the aspects while still insisting on the need to grasp the living totality. The opposition to reduction seems to lie behind the remark by Simplikios that he saw fire as irreducible fire and not as "composed of pyramids". It is not clear if Herakleitos himself attacked some primitive atomic theory that fire consisted of pyramid-like particles, or if Simplikios or someone else made the contrast. Aristotle knew the theory of pyramid-particles and considered it implausible. We gather that the shape in question was a tetrahedron (triangular-based), as this was the simplest of solid figures and so by ancient logic was taken as the basic element of all other solid figures as well as being the most piercing.[28] In another aphorism Herakleitos makes something of an anticipation of the doctrine of *energeia*: "The name of the bow is life, but its work is death." There is here another of his complex puns—on *bíos*, bow, and *biós*, life. Life and death are dialectically one. The tension represented by the drawn bow is life, but its work is death, in the sense both that the arrow kills and that the act of shooting ends the tension and achieves the aim of the act. *Dynamis* is released into *ergon*, which by completing itself ends both *dynamis* and *ergon*; only the result remains.[29]

Though Herakleitos resisted the reducing and abstracting pressures, his capacity to see into the nature of relationships and the conflicts inside process was in part due to the increasingly pervasive effects of the cash-nexus in his world. An aphorism which reveals a great deal about him and Greek philosophy is that which declares: "There is exchange of all things for fire and of fire for all things, as there is of wares for gold and of gold for wares." The reductive power of money is bringing the value of all things to a common denominator, facilitating the expansion of mathematics and of formal logic; and here for the first time a thinker realises what this reductive power implies. His imagery, and indeed his idea itself, are helped to emerge into consciousness by the way in which gold could be equated with the sun and its universal power. Pindar, opening the 5th *Isthmian* (about 476), cries: "O Mother of the Sun [Helios], Theia of many names, for your sake men even set a stamp upon gold as mighty beyond all else beside." Theia (Divine) is mother of the sun, moon, and dawn, in the *Theogony*; she is thus the principle of light, which gives gold its brightness and prompts men to stamp it as coins. Pindar goes on to say that through her influence wars are carried on by land and sea, for the gaining of treasure, of bright gold. To gain gold is to gain solar power, the life-principle—or rather, the alienating object which has usurped the rôle of that principle. Pythermos of Teos, Ionian poet, announced, "Nothing but gold is of account."[30] It was not by chance that philosophy originated in the Greek cities of western Asia Minor where mercantile activity was at is highest, and where there were many connnections with the more eastern regions; that it made fresh developments in the mercantile cities of south Italy and reached its height in Athens. Not that every mercantile centre seems to have had its philosophers; but the link of the cash-nexus with the new freedoms and detachments of thought was everywhere present.

Among the most obvious social effects was the breaking down of old limits or settled divisions of status. In terms of the new equalising or levelling trend all men are defined and judged in terms of their monetary wealth or power; a single criterion is brought into operation. And at the same time a new trend to inequality. Men are better or worse, stronger or weaker, according to the money-power they wield. (True, land is still the great source of power and status, and money tends to sink back into it. But the new unsettling force is at work on the land too, so that there is no way of land-power setting back fixedly into its old aristocratic systems.) Theognis of Megara bitterly attacked money as a levelling force in the later half of the sixth century; he saw it as breaking up aristocratic controls and ways-of-life, fusing what should be kept apart as eternal opposites:

In our rams, asses, horses we try to preserve
a noble breed; to mate them with good stock
we seek. Yet a noble has no scruple in wedding
a lowborn wife as long as she brings money.
And a woman won't refuse a lowborn suitor,
preferring riches to nobility.
What's valued is money. Into base families
the nobles marry, the baseborn into noble.
Wealth's mixed up birth. Don't wonder the citizen's breed
dies out; for noble now is mixed with base.

The impact of money was thus linked with a sense of limits breaking down in all spheres. Solon declared, "Riches know no limits," and he went on to the generalisation, "How hard to see the hidden measure of intelligence, which alone holds the limits of things." Thinkers felt that if they could only penetrate below the confused surface of things, they might find "the hidden measure" which would after all provide stability, clarifying the processes of nature and of man's place amid them. (Marx noted that the simple circulation of commodities is a means of satisfying wants, but "the circulation of money as capital, on the other hand, is an end in itself, for the expansion of value can only occur within this perpetually renewed movement. Consequently, the circulation of capital has no limits.")

Aristotle makes a comparison of money-making and craft-activity:

> Thus also there are no limits to the *technē* of medicine with respect to the health it attempts to procure; the same also is true of the other *technai*; no line can be drawn to terminate their bounds, the various professors of them desiring to extend them as far as possible. (But still the means to be employed for that purpose are limited; and these are the limits beyond which the *technē* cannot proceed.) So in the *technē* of acquiring riches there are no limits, for the object of that is money and possessions. . . .

But the drive to develop medical knowledge and the use of it, or to develop a craft as skilfully and fully as possible, can have no real comparison with the drive for money. He himself admits it by pointing out that under certain circumstances a man may have lots of money yet be unable to turn it into food. "With all his possessions he may perish of hunger, like Midas in the fable, who from his insatiable wish had everything he touched turned into gold." There is thus an unbridgeable gulf between money on the one hand and products with some sort of use-value on the other.[31] Money then is a power which though devised by men has its own uncontrollable laws and ways of impacting on people and affecting them. Alkaios, a member of one of the first states to coin money, declared, "Man is money"—whereas no one could or would say, "Man is medicine, man is shoes, man is a song." In other words, money usurps the human essence.

Sophokles, with his fine sense of the contradictory forces at work in Greek society, anticipated the Shakespearean sense, set out in *Timon*, of money as a transformative force turning all values upside down and steadily dehumanising:

> *Money wins friendship, honour, place and power,*
> *and sets man next to the proud tyrant's throne.*
> *All trodden paths and those as yet untrodden*

are scaled by nimble riches, where the poor
can never hope to reach their heart's despire.
A man illformed by nature and illspoken
is made by money fair to eye and ear;
money buys man his health and happiness
and only money cloaks iniquity.

And again:

Of all the evils thriving in the world
money's the worst. Money drives men from home,
plunders great cities, perverts the honest mind
to shameful practice, godlessness, and crime.

Isokrates said that the men who have gained great riches cannot rest content but are driven to risk what they have by reaching after more. Such judgments as those cited above must be linked with the endless complaints about *hybris* (overstepping of due limits) and the comments on the thin edge between prosperity and disaster. The Hippokratic school noted that extreme conditions of physical wellbeing were dangerous, as unable to remain stable; and Plato connected the unbalance with social revolution. "In the seasons, in plants, in the body, and above all in civil society, excessive action results in a violent transformation into its opposite."[32]

Herakleitos summed up his attitude to money-making with the aphorism: "May you have lots of wealth, men of Ephesos, so that you may be punished for your evil ways." He is not primarily speaking of punishment inflicted from outside, though money-getting may lead to crimes and penalties, and so on; he means that men of money will be punished by losing the human essence, by living stunted and distorted lives. It is Fire that will overtake them. "The sun will not overstep his measures; if he were to do so, the Erinyes, handmaidens of justice, would seek him out." The sun too must not distort its nature.

It was Herakleitos' own sure sense of the human essence, of man's place among his fellows and in nature, which made him the one ancient thinker secure in his recognition of the decisive aspect of conflict, of the unity of opposites, in all process. In setting out his image of life-death (decisive change or development) in terms of the bow with its tension in cord and wood, and the release of that tension by the flight of the arrow to its target, he was directly standing out against the Pythagoreans who admitted tension but wanted it relieved by attunement and harmony. He took the cord of the bow, they took the cord of the lyre. "They do not understand how that which is at variance with itself agrees with itself. There is a harmony in the bending back, as in the case of the bow and the lyre." Here he has appropriated their lyre and assimilated its with the bow. (There is a variant reading for "bending back"—"inverse harmony", *palintonos*, which would represent a use of musical symbolism against the Pythagoreans who relied so much on music in their theory of proportions.)[33]

Like Theognis, Herakleitos is against reconciliation; but not because he wants a rigid establishment of limits that must not and cannot be transgressed—a barrier against the mingling of noble and commoner. Rather, he wants an acceptance of tension and conflict as the law of life. "War is the father of all, and lord of all, and has made gods and men, freemen and slaves." Philodemos cites him as saying, "War and Zeus are the same thing". [By *polemos* he meant much more than warfare; he meant all forms of struggle, of *eris*, strife.] Simplikios tells us that Herakleitans considered that "if either of the opposites should fail, there would be complete and utter destruction of everything". Aristotle supports Herakleitos in a mild way by arguing that "there could be no harmony without both high and low notes, nor could life exist without both male and female".[34]

One last point: Theognis saw the social opposites as noble and commoner; Herakleitos saw them as freeman and slave. The class-struggle had deepened, and a different set of basic contraries had arrived. With it was being born the concept of *anankē* or necessity, complicating the issues. No thinker was again to face the issue of conflict and transformation with such frank and open confidence as Herakleitos had done.[34]

Pneuma as Force

VII

Though the later efforts to make out Herakleitos' Fire as the primary substance of the universe were certainly wrong, he endowed it with a dynamical and tensional quality that made it in many ways the driving-force of all movement and development. It is then not amiss to see in it the precursor of Stoic *pneuma*—especially when we realise how the thunderbolt and the tornado play a key-part as expressing and revealing the great critical moments of change. As a generative force it has the more genial qualities of the light and the heat of the sun; but as the violent driving-force that compels nature to the nodal-points or *tropai* of decisive development it is a sort of blast-power which only the thunderbolt and the tornado linking clouded sky and earth in a tunnel-whirl of dangerous lightnings can effectively symbolise. The Stoic descriptions of thunder and lightning, thunderbolt, typhoon, tornado, cited in the last chapter, showed that the force erupting and blasting in such phenomena was considered to be *pneuma*. But what Herakleitos set out in aphoristic paradoxes, obscure and hieratic in style, even liturgical, the Stoics explained at length in a thoroughly worked-out scientific philosophy. Though there was a deep and pondered system behind the Herakleitan pronouncements, there was clearly also a strong intuitive element. Herakleitos was connected with the temple of the Ephesian Artemis and dedicated his book there; he left a fraternity of disciples, the Herakleitidai. Ploutarch tells us of a poetess who, winning the prize at the Isthmia for her poems, deposited a scroll of them in the Delphic temple; and someone, whether or not the poet, dedicated Hesiod's poems at Mt. Helikon, where Pausanias saw them engraved on old tables of lead. Such acts were not uncommon, but in the case of Herakleitos we may be sure there was a serious purpose in his dedication.[1]

The Stoic kosmos had no void within it; but it existed itself within a surrounding void. What gave fullness and continuity to it was *pneuma*. Aristotle used the term *synecheia*, holding-together, to express continuity in a geometrical and topographical sense; the Stoics used *pneuma* to express a pervasive physical and dynamic force. They distinguished *pneuma*-like matter, cohesive and producing cohesion, with *hylē*-like matter, which lacked such powers. *Synetikē dynamis*, cohesive force, was their term for the quality of *pneuma*.[2]

The Greeks in general wanted to explain all movement, all impacts, including those on the senses, by the action of direct forces. So one of the roads leading to the pneumatic continuum came from the theories about sight. Theophrastos in his work on sensory perception says that the various opinions fell into two groups. Some inquirers ascribed perception to similarity, others to opposition. The first group held that it occurred through an effluence, *apporhoia*, by means of which like was borne to like; the second group held that it occurred through an alteration, in which opposites affected one another. Theophrastos then sums up Plato's opinion, basing his statement on the *Timaios*:

> He makes the organ of vision consist of fire; and that is why he regards colour also as a flame given off from bodies, having particles commensurate with the organ of vision. Assuming that there is this effluence and that [effluence and organ] must unite, he holds that the [visual stream] issues forth for some distance and coalesces with the effluence, and thus it is that we see it. His view may thus be said to lie halfway between the theories of those who say that vision falls on the object, and the theories of those who hold that something is borne from visible objects to the organs of sight.

Both Empedokles and Alkmaion held that the eye had fire within. "For when one is struck, it flashes out. Vision is due to the gleaming [transparent] character that is in the eye which reflects the object" (Alkmaion). Demokritos held that everything sent out ceaseless effluences, stressing the aspect of similarity in sense-perception. The Stoics, who carried on the principle of like to like, thought that an optical *pneuma* was emitted from the *hegemonikon* (ruling or directive principle) to the eye and excited the air by the pupil; the process of seeing was carried on by the air between the eye and the object. The air, linking eye and object, has a faculty of perception given to it by the light. This point explains why we cannot see in the dark.[3]

11. Prometheus creating Man as a Clay Image, while Athena animates him with a butterfly, *psyche*; also Hephaistos and Kyklopes, Eros and Psyche, Okean, Helios, Wind, Earth, Klotho and Lachesis, Night, Moon, Thanatos or Death, a Deadman, Fate, Hermes Psychopomp; one clay figure stands animated (*Annali* 1847 pl. QR)

In these various theories we see attempts to construct systems dynamically linking our senses and the world around us. With Demokritos we meet a world of endless effluences of all sorts. But we are still far from the coherent Stoic scheme in which *pneuma* pervades all things, acting in and on them. A key-word in that system was *tonos*, tension. *Tonos* was possessed by *pneuma*-like matter. "*Tonos* is the heat of fire," said Kleanthes, "which, originating in the soul in sufficient measure to accomplish the task, is called strength and force." Galen uses the term "vital tension"; and Stoics saw a release of sensory tension in sleep. But inorganic matter also possessed *tonos*. As *pneuma* pervaded the kosmos, it was *tonos* that made of the latter a single cohesive unit—a concept that has been compared with the use made of the aether from the seventeenth century on.[4]

How then was it that *tonos* operated to keep the various parts of the universe where we see them? There was an idea that heavy things were drawn in by a gravitational pull to the centre, but non-heavy things spread from the centre out. The in-movement created stability; the out-movement was the work of air and fire, which lacked gravity. All the physical qualities of matter were generated by *pneuma*. Thus the Stoics "generalised their continuum theory into a field theory; the *pneuma* is the physical field which is the carrier of all specific properties of material bodies, and cohesion as such thus gets a more specific meaning by becoming *hexis*, the physical state of the body" (Sambursky). *Hexis* (from *echein*, to possess) denoted the structure of inorganic matter, *physis* that of organic matter, and *psyche* that of the living being.[5]

Galen, strongly influenced by the Stoics, came near the concept of the bodily cell. Eratosthenes had spoken of a "small elementary nerve" or neuron, and Galen asks if that meant a "unit mass of living matter" or merely an agglomeration of atoms subject to mechanical law. He brings up some formal objections to either interpretation; but himself later used for the idea of Eratosthenes the term "body continuous throughout", where *soma* might be taken as corpuscle; and he goes on to refer to "homogenous fibres". He was advancing to the idea of the cell or corpuscle as a unit in the living and continuous whole.

There was a hierarchical series of inorganic structures: discrete, contiguous, and unified. From disorder came a discrete state allow-ing numerical determination (e.g. an army or chorus); then came elements joined together (e.g. links of a chain or stones of a house); finally an object with unified structure (e.g. a stone, a piece of wood, a metal). In *hexis* the elements or parts were not separable units, but interpenetrated to make up a whole which existed only because of the way they merged. Alteration of one aspect (mechanical, thermic, electrical and so on) affected all the others. The fusion was by means of *sympatheia*. Varying mixtures of fire and air produced variations in *pneuma* and so in physical properties.

It is perhaps revealing to pause a moment and take the summary by Diogenes Laertes of the views we have discussed above and note how difficult it is to translate effectively, because of the deep way in which metaphysical dualisms have become imbedded in our language.

> The kosmos, in their view, is ordered by *nous* and *pronoia* [reason or mind; and providence, forethought]. So says Chrysippos in the 5th Book of his treatise *On Pronoia* and Poseidonios in his book *On the Gods*, 3rd Book—inasmuch as *nous* pervades every part of it, just as *psyche* does in us. Only, there is a difference of degree; in some parts there is more of it, in others less. For through some parts it passes as a *hexis*, as is the case with our bones and sinews; while through others it passes as *nous*, as in the *hegemonikon* of the soul. Thus, then, the whole kosmos is a living thing, endowed with soul and reason [*logos*], and having *aithēr* for its *hegemonikon*. So says Antipatros of Tyre in the 8th Book of his treatise *On the kosmos*. Chrysippos in the 1st Book of his work *On Pronoia* and Poseidonios in his book *On the Gods* say that the Heaven, but Kleanthes that the Sun, is the *hegemonikon* of the kosmos. Chrysippos, however, in the course of the work cited gives a somewhat different account: that it is the purer part of the *aithēr*—the same which they declare to be pre-eminently god and always to have, as it were in sensible fashion, pervaded all that is in the air, all animals and plants, and also the earth itself, as *hexis*.

The Stoics could not be expected altogether to throw off the dualistic way of thinking brought to a head by Plato; but they were doing their best to regain the unitary outlook of the early thinkers without losing what was valuable in the Platonic and Aristotelian systems. When then they speak of *nous* or *logos* at work in the universe, they mean that there is a system of law, of intelligible process, which our minds can recognise; and they saw the act of recognition as also an act of union. What was recognised in the last resort was the unity of process inside ourselves and outside, in nature. The laws of development, of the unity of opposites, of conflict and its resolution, were the same in essence in humanity and in nature. *Nous* in the universe in general was the same as *psyche* in ourselves, and psyche was a corporeal principle. There was no simple gap between organic and inorganic, and in the last resort the two aspects came together in the life-principle. I have used the usual translation of "endowed with soul and reason" for *empsychos* and *logikos*, but the words convey something very different from the meaning of the Greek. The soul or life is not something with which the kosmos is endowed, as if there had been a gift in question; the life is something inherent. Indeed it *is* the kosmos; for life implies movement, conflict, unity, structure, development, change. And for us the word "reason" remains hopelessly dry, suggesting the application of an abstract instrument of thought to a given problem, whereas *logos* refers to the structure and meaning inherent in the life process and merely raised to a new level of consciousness by men. When we give a capital to god as the translation of *theos*, we lose sight of the fact that the Greek word is more or less the same as *theios*, divine, and does not intend to suggest a person or a transcendental principle; it refers to the dynamic essence of process; and its nature as an aspect of the physical universe is brought out by the discussion as to whether the cosmic *hegemonikon* is to be found in fire or *aithēr*. (A little earlier Diogenes remarked: "Fire has the uppermost place; it is also called *aithēr*, and in it the sphere of the fixed stars was first created.")

Diogenes goes on:

> The kosmos, they say, is one and finite, having a spherical shape, such a shape being the most suitable for motion, as Poseidonios says in the 5th Book of his *Physical Discourse* and the disciples of Antiptaros in their works on the Kosmos. Outside of the world is diffused the infinite Void, which is incorporeal. By incorporeal is meant that which, though capable of being occupied by body, is not so occupied. The world has no empty space within it, but forms one united whole. This is a necessary result of the *sympatheia* and *syntonia* [tension in an intense and harmonious form] which bind all things together in heaven and earth.

The Stoic Providence must not be interpreted as referring to some power standing outside process and guiding it or foreseeing its results. On the contrary it refers to a power inherent in the process, which guides it by its own dialectical laws. Chrysippos in *On Ends* wrote: "The dearest thing to every animal is its own constitution and its consciousness of it." The word usually translated as "consciousness" is *syneidēsis* which means knowledge which is shared; the stress is on communication but at the same time it expresses self-awareness. Chrysippos is then speaking of the way in which all living creatures grow aware of their constitution, their make-up, by living together with others and sharing their awareness. Foreknowledge is this sort of understanding of oneself and one's world, in which the laws governing the future are realised as one with the laws governing the past and the present. The aim of foreknowledge is to achieve harmony with all things by a perspective which embraces present, past and future.

> The term *kathēkon* [usually translated as duty] is applied to that for which, when done, a reasonable defence can be adduced, e.g. harmony in the tenor of life's process, which indeed pervades the growth of plants and animals. For even in plants and animals, they hold, you may discern fitness of behaviour. Zenon was the first to use this *kathēkon* of conduct. Etymologically it is derived from *kata tinas ēkein*, i.e. reaching as far as, being up to, or into, bent upon so and so. And it is an action in itself adapted to nature's arrangements.

Kathēkon, dealing originally with physical distance or scope, was thus used by Zenon to signify figuratively that which extends to us—that outside ourselves which reaches in to embrace us. He thus attempted to express the vital principle of harmonious balance and reciprocity. Man, we see, shares it with animals and plants.

To return now to the question of mixture, which much interested the Stoics. They wanted to show how *pneuma* permeated all things with its quality-giving cohesion. They distinguished three types of mixture: mingling or mechanical mixture, similar to Aristotle's composition; fusion, when individual properties or components were lost in the total effect, as in drugs; and between mingling and fusion, mixture proper—*krasis* for liquids, *mixis* for non-liquids—in which each component preserved its own properties, whether it was a large or small portion of the whole. The original proportion was then maintained and the components could be separated out again.[6]

The idea of total mixture (of a homogeneous distribution of components throughout the mixture) met much opposition. Despite Archimedes, the concept of specific density had not been truly grasped; critics refused to credit that substances could exist in differing densities according to differing physical conditions. The old notion of the opposites—heavy-light, wet-dry, and so on—was too strong; and thinkers were baffled or antagonised by the idea of rare and tenuous *pneuma* merging with bulkier bodies in a total mixture where every element of volume, however minute, would be homogeneous with regard to the mixing of the components. Their notion of mixture, however complete, continued to be one where bits of the components persisted side by side in a sort of mosaic-like system.[6] For the Stoics *pneuma* was forever at work on shapeless and inert matter—or rather, on matter that would have been shapeless and inert without the pervading *pneuma*. *Pneuma* imbued matter with its qualities; and in each quality there were fire and air in certain proportions. The sum total of the pervading *pneuma* defined the physical state.

That state could be defined in terms of itself and of something else outside it (the relative state), and also by means of a comparison of two states in the body as it underwent changes —the changes being the result of a continuous transition brought about by changes in the fire-and-air proportions. The theoretical system thus revealed is one that had the capacity of development into that of Newtonian mechanics.

> Here we have a system of bodies forming the substratum; the quality is given by the various traits exhibited by these bodies, such as spatial distribution, mass, velocity, etc. If the specific data of these traits are known for a given moment, the state of the system is hereby defined. This state can undergo changes with time and the new state is described in terms of the former which defines the relative. The relation, finally, between the states of two different systems at any moment determines the second subdivision of the fourth category, the relative state. (Sambursky)

But, as usual, we have to point out that the step into Newtonian mechanics was avoided, not through incapacity, but because of the different concept of quality involved. Newtonian mechanics is interested only in certain forms of movement abstracted from the total qualitative substance and its total relation to time-space, which include all and any aspects of inner and outer changes, all and any aspects of impact and influence involved in those changes. In the last resort the attention of seventeenth-century thinkers had been turned to the problems behind Galilean and Newtonian mechanics because they were problems inherent in the foundation and expansion of the technology of capitalist industrialism; the attention of the Stoics was concentrated elsewhere, on the whole man, on his total relationship to process.[7]

The questions of sense-perception, raised earlier in this chapter, had much importance for the Stoic position; for it was in this field that they developed the concept of the ruling or directing part of the psyche, the *hegemonikon*, which they identified with the heart. The *hegemonikon* was thought to control the power of speech, the five senses, the generative part of the body, as a centralising and co-ordinating organ, the seat of consciousness. (It thus had some likeness to the central nervous system, but with very much greater range and powers.) *Pneuma* moved between it and the rest of the body in an endless to-and-fro—not as the movement of countless particles, but rather as the expansion of an agitation in an elastic medium. For a *tonikē kinēsis*, a tensional motion, the Stoics used the image of ripples spreading out in rings from the point where a stone was thrown in water. In general that image served to express their idea of how movement went on in a continuum.

> The Stoics assert that air is not composed of particles, but that it is a continuum which holds no empty space. If struck by a puff of breath, it sets up circular waves that advance in a straight line to infinity, till all the surrounding air is affected, just as a pool is affected by a stone striking it. But whereas in this case the movement is circular, the air moves spherically. (Aetios)[8]

Stoics thus consistently thought in terms of fields of force. Tensional motion was propagation in a continuous medium, not a mere change of place by the movement of a body, not a mere flow of a current. Such motion could be defined as a "simultaneous movement in opposite directions", a movement in and out (connected in turn with rarefaction and condensation)—though we also hear of the alternation of two motions. Out of such positions Galen developed his idea of equilibrium, not as a state of rest, but as a rapid oscillation round a balancing point. The concept of the universal permeation of *pneuma* led on to the concept of the same laws operating everywhere and the first sketchy notion of universal gravitation. One of the speakers in Ploutarch's *On the Face in the Moon* remarks:

> If all heavy bodies converge to one and the same point, while each presses on its own centre with all its parts, it will not be so much *qua* centre of the universe as *qua* whole that the earth will appropriate weights, because they are parts of itself; and the tendency of bodies will be a testimony, not to the earth of its being the centre of the universe, but, to things which have been thrown away from the earth and then come back to it, of their having a certain and natural kinship [*symphyia*] with the earth. Thus the sun attracts all the parts of which it is composed, and in the same way the earth draws the stone to itself and makes it part of itself. . . .
>
> But if any body has not been allotted to earth from the beginning and has not been rent from it, but somehow has a constitution (*systasis*) and nature of its own, as they would maintain to be the case with the moon, what is there to prevent its existing separately and remaining self-contained, compacted and fettered by its own parts? For not only is the earth not proved to be the centre, but the way in which things here press and come together suggests the manner in which it is probable that things have fallen on the moon, where she is, and remain there.[9]

The idea of gravity here is certainly derived from the concept of tensional *pneuma*, as we can tell from the terms used. The Stoics could use that concept in order to answer arguments that a finite universe would fly apart. Their liking for words beginning with *sym-* (with), such as *sympathia*, *syntasis*, *symphyia*, *syneidēsis*, came from their feeling that they best expressed the dynamics of the cohesive *pneuma*, tensional and permeating.

In dealing with causes they broke through the simple scheme still found in Aristotle: X is caused by Y. They insisted instead that Y causes an effect Z to come about in X. They first stated the link of causal law and induction, and raised the question of the possible and its relation to the necessary inside the framework of actuality. They came close to the question of probability. They made the first movement from causal to functional thought. They saw everything capable of acting or being acted on as a body; continuity was made an essential aspect of causality. An uncaused event was an impossibility. The universe was an endless chain of causes extending everywhere in time and space. All things were ultimately interdependent.

But the chain is not one-dimensional. It is a many-dimensional concatenation of potential events, all of them equally possible inside the framework of fate—out of which only one course will actually come about. Clemens of Alexandreia notes their distinction between the asymmetrical cause-effect relation and the symmetrical relation of mutual cause and interaction. Here we meet the contrast of the interpenetration of pneumatic tensions and the equilibrium of forces acting between contiguous bodies—the way that virtues cause one another and are fused in their interdependence is an example given of the first kind of situation; "the stones of a vault which are each other's cause for remaining in place", as an example of the second.[10]

The realisation that the relation of cause and effect can be asymmetrical as well as symmetrical shows what a gulf divides the Stoic world of concepts from that of Newtonian mechanics where cause and effect are simply equal and opposite. It is not by chance however that the Stoic example of symmetrical cause-effect concerns a static situation. Archimedes limited the domain of theoretical mechanics to the study of problems of equilibrium, and thus established the foundation of statics and hydrostatics; but he made no attempt to enter the field of kinematics. Yet he was well equipped to do so if he had wanted, and his ballistical work had provided him with experimental material to be studied and theoretically analysed.

A physical state can run through a whole range of continuous changes: "*hexis* can be tightened or loosened." We return to the symbol of the lyre to explain the changes: "The same string, corresponding to its tension or relaxation, produces a high or a low pitch." But the Stoics also had in mind the way a rod can be bent or curved. They turned geometrical shapes into physical ones held together by pneumatic tensions, and completed the physicalisation of geometry begun by Archimedes.[11] At moments they showed intuitions of the calculus of variations, and such tendencies provoked Simplikios to cry out, "This would destroy the essence of mathematics which is static and free from every change and so also from tension". The Aristotelian system was turned upside down, and now it was motion that explained form.

The idea of the limit, so important for Greek social, political, moral and psychological thought, was developed by the Stoics, especially Chrysippos: we saw how he replied to the Demokritean paradox of the cone cut by a plane. He referred to the process of convergence towards the limit. But, as was typical in Greek thought, he argued his position in terms of logic, not of mathematics, putting it as a negation of the law of the excluded middle—a law that cannot but be violated if the static concepts of equal and unequal are applied to the problem of a dynamic approach to zero. He and other Stoics thus developed the idea of the infinitesimal as far as could be done in general terms of dialectical logic. They dropped the notion of the distinct surface of a body, or of a distinct boundary in general, and put in its place an infinite series of boundaries defining the surfaces of inscribed and circumscribed figures which are converging from both sides of the figure in question—and are thus defining it as a dynamic entity, not as a static isolated figure. As we noted, they discovered the idea of infinite sets. The continuum was seen, not as the sum of separate units or sequences, but as a dynamic whole in a ceaseless state of becoming. But, as we discussed, they could not set against concrete time an abstraction of absolute time (naively called "true" by Newton); and it was precisely this sense of a dynamic and concretely involved whole which lay behind their concept of the infinite and prevented them from separating out the abstractions of Newton and Leibniz.[12]

One last point about the Stoics. Their deepened and extended notion of the rule of universal law in nature and in human life alike raised acutely for them the moral problem of free will or necessity, and each of the leading Stoics had his own varying points of emphasis in the way he answered the problem. We see in them the last great attempt by ancient thinkers to grapple with the question of what necessity implied in nature and in human society. Coming after the breakdown of the free city-state, they had to face new questions about conformity to the world of political power (now increasingly autocratic), about the nature of necessity and slavery. Part of the Stoic answer was to glorify the life of "nature" against all convention and prejudice, against the accepted values of the "unnatural" world in which they lived. Take for example the comment by Zenon on the incest of Oidipous: "If she had been ailing in some part of her body and he'd done her good by rubbing it with his hands, it wouldn't have been shameful—was it then shameful for him to stop her grief and give her joy by rubbing her other parts?" (I choose this passage because it shows "rubbing" as a sexual term. We may compare the rubbing of a fire-stick in a hole in a piece of wood to produce heat and fire, and the Stoic passages cited earlier about the rubbing of clouds together to beget thunder and lightning, the thunderbolt—a sort of cosmic blast-orgasm.)[13]

But among early Stoics there was also a tendency to encourage social revolt in the name of equality, as we see in Blossius, who was with the Gracchi at Rome and later joined in the uprising that proclaimed the City of the Sun at Pergamon. Stoic attitudes appeared in utopias such as that of Iamboulos which set out the kind of brotherhood and equality that would rule in a "natural" society. Behind such positions there lay movements of popular discontent, such as we see importantly at work in Sparta under Agis IV, Kleomenes III, and Nabis—each phase leading to greater intransigence, till under Nabis debts were cancelled, private property in land and merchandise ended, communal meals and ways of living restored, and the class-distinctions of Spartiates, Neighbours, and Helots swept away. The triumph of Rome in the east crushed all popular movements, but in the period when Stoicism was adventurously creating its universe of thought it truly reflected the crisis, the new potentialities, of Greek society after Alexander the Great—a sense of universal humanity, which was soon cut across by increasing contradictions; a sense of deepening conflict between freedom and necessity; a vastly widened horizon. They expressed the full potentialities of the situation, but also were caught up in its limitations. The problem of slavery was insoluble in their society, so that the concept of unity, despite all the passionate efforts to grasp it in the fullness of its concrete relations, remained for the most part theoretical, only imperfectly related to practise, moral, political, or scientific.

The writings on Kingship by Zenon, Kleanthes, Sphairos, and Perseus are lost. The Stoics did not defend the absolute monarchy; they glorified the Wise Man as the one true leader, because, having achieved order inside himself, he owned alone the right to command, the royal *aretē*. They condemned the existing royalty, in principle, as not fulfilling the fundamental condition; but in order not to attract persecution or find themselves well out in the political cold, they declared that rulers could fill the gap by taking a Wise Man as counsellor. Panaitios and Posidonios, in the second period of Stoicism, were less concerned with an idealised character of kingship or sought to construct more eclectic and elastic political schemes; but brotherhood remained something that the Wise Man achieved internally by his sense of human unity, not something that needed to be politically actualised.[14]

The Sources and Bases of Greek Scientific Thinking

VIII

From the writings that have come down to us we can often make out how scientific ideas have arisen in the minds of the Greeks. Sometimes the source of an idea is directly stated; sometimes we have to infer it from the language used, from similes or metaphors. Inevitably the sources vary a great deal. Some ideas are closely linked with social experiences, others spring from direct observation of nature. However, there is one natural process which must be first considered, since it clearly played a major part in early cosmogonies. This is the process of evaporation, of rarefaction and condensation. The sight of the sun drawing vapour from water was one that could hardly fail to be noted; it deeply impressed thinkers brooding on unitary substance and the changes going on in things. Theophrastos referred to evaporation to explain Thales' assumption that all is water; and from Anaximandros on, every philosopher of significance made a large and increasing use of the phenomenon for his explanation of the kosmos. It provided an outstanding example of the diminution of one body and the enlargement of another by increments which in detail were beyond human grasp. It thus became the type of all effluences, exhalations, emanations. Next, the upward course of the vapours and the downward course of the precipitates exemplified the two-way movement of the elements. Thirdly, heat or fire emerged as an explanation of movement or change; for evaporation and condensation were identified with heating and cooling. By evaporation air and fire encroached on water and earth; and by precipitation water and fire encroached on air and fire. So here lay a scheme for explaining changes of one element into another. Later came the notion of differences consisting in the relative degree of density, though among the Greeks it never stood alone as the explanation of the varieties of concrete things (except perhaps for Diogenes of Apollonia). Empedokles, Anaxagoras and Leukippos attributed differentiation to composition and gave rarefaction and condensation a less important rôle; and this ultimately led to the assumption that the essential properties of things are the properties of mass.

But even in the earliest stages of broodings over nature, imagery and schemes from craft-activity provided organising concepts. To explain composition men had recourse to the idea of winnowing and sifting. Aristotle connected the *ekkrisis* (*apokrisis*) of Anaximandros with the winnowing of like to like—a process that derived from the everlasting motion, the whirl at the heart of things. Anaximenes called the process rarefaction and condensation. Evaporation lay behind the Herakleitan notion of change, and we may assume a central whirl, as is strongly suggested by the image of the potter's wheel attached to the process in a Hippokratic text. The notion of the whirl comes in part from observation of nature and circular movements of wind and water; but it also derives from the whirl in winnowing or sieving, and in craftwork where implements such as wheel or lathe turned and produced a current of air—just as ideas about evaporation were stimulated by the observation of boiling water.

Apart from the main phenomena of air, water, and fire, perhaps the most important sources of ideas lay in craft-processes and activities, which provided men with analogies for natural processes and sharpened their minds with an awareness of what to look for. Many times already the craft-relation has come up, in small or large matters. An example of the latter is the whole scheme of causes in Aristotle, which we noted was a generalisation based on the stages of a craftsman at work. It is of interest that while Greek philosophers in general expressed contempt for the manual worker and as a result saw the thinker's world to be one of contemplation, they were continually driven to the sphere of the crafts in order to explain the workings of the kosmos and of natural process. Not that contempt had always been there. The term for craftsmen is a laudatory one, going far back—*dēmiourgos*, worker for the people. And a hero like Odysseus is proud of his craft-skill; he describes how he built his "room of close-set stonework" round an olive bed, and put much care into the bed: "A great *sēma* is wrought into that complicated bed, and it was my work and mine alone." *Sēma* for Homer means a sign, such as the cairn that marks a hero's

12. Hephaistos in worker's cap making Achilles' armour; note gorgon-head on shield: redfigured amphora (Boston Museum of Fine Arts)

grave; but it has a special force as a sign from the gods. Odysseus also builds his raft in four days on Kalypso's isle; at Troy, with the aid of the best workers, Paris builds his own house; Laertes hoes and attends to his garden; Nausikaa washes the family linen; and so on. The slaves and the *thētes* (bondsmen, later hired workers) are in a very lowly position; but it is their lack of independence that is their real stigma. The *dēmiourgos* is called "divine" since his skills are inspired, even though he has a status far below that of the warrior. The Prometheus of Aischylos, who represents all the crafts without differentiation, seems to carry on the archaic spirit, when, despite the specialisations of the *dēmiourgoi*, Odysseus stands for an ideal all-round character capable of meeting any challenge.

So it comes about that Plato, for all his aristocratic disdain of manual work, has to use the word *dēmiourgos* for his god who constructs the universe, and we still use the term demiurge. He also calls this creator-god an architect or builder, *tektainomenos*, who makes use of models or patterns just like an earthly craftsman. *Tekton*, carpenter, is thus a synonym for the demiurge; and it seems that here lies the reason for making Jesus the (adoptive) son of a carpenter. Aristotle, speaking of the attempts to reduce the elements of the universe to a pair of opposites, rare-dense or hot-cold, comments: "These are the creative forces, *ta demiourgounta*, and the One underlies them as matter." Creative forces are "those things working like craftsmen".[1]

Aristotle sees *technē* as imitating nature and nature as following the same course as *technē*; and indeed these views became more or less a commonplace of Greek thought. A medical work attached to the Hippokratic tradition, written perhaps around 400 but more likely a couple of generations later, makes a considered attempt to use illustrations from the *technai* for the human condition. Some of its images may go back to Herakleitos —e.g. two men are sawing wood: "the one pulls, the other pushes, they are doing the same thing, but by doing less they are doing more." A passage from the Aristotelian *On Plants* shows how the heat-processes in craftwork were used to explain biological process:

> The growth of the plant is due to the earth, its solidity comes from water, and the union of its solidity from fire. We can see a good deal of this in earthenware pottery. For there are three elements there: clay from which the pot is made, the water that combines the clay, and the fire that causes the parts to set until by its means the creation [*genesis*] is completed. The demonstration of the unification by fire is found in the fact that the pottery consists of finely divided particles. When the fire has mixed these together, the wet matter is perfected, and the parts of the clay cohere, and the result is dryness instead of moisture. Owing to the mastery of fire a ripening takes place in every animal and plant and in metals. For ripening occurs wherever moisture and heat each reach their own proper limit.

Indeed this passage has a reference beyond heat-process in biology, for it shows one of the lines of thinking that led to the concept of transformation in general through the effects of fire, air, water and earth on one another, with the consequent emergence of new qualities.

Philon of Alexandreia shows the idea of God as a craftsman reasserted in the the world of dynamic tensions that the Stoics had expounded.

> Mind and sense-perception [*aisthēsis*] and sense-object [*aisthēton*], are three, with *aisthēsis* in the middle and mind and object at each extreme. But mind lacks the power to get to work; that is, to put forth its energies by way of *aisthēsis*; unless God wets and sends down the sense-object as rain upon it, nor is any benefit got from the rained-down object unless like a waterspring the mind extends itself to reach the *aisthēsis*, sets it in motion as it reposes, and leads it to grasp in turn the presented object. Thus the mind and the sense-object are always practising a reciprocity of giving: the one lying ready for sense-perception as its material [*hyle*], the other like a craftsman [*technites*], moving sense-perception in the direction of the external object, to produce an impulse towards it.[2]

We are reminded of the analogies drawn from the work of a machine-operator or a puppet-master to explain *hormē* (which in Stoic thought is inherent in the object or situation).

Dubarle has well remarked, in dealing with Aristotelean hylemorphism:

> The cosmology sketched-out by Plato in the *Timaios* and firmly established by Aristotle is based on the craft-universe of manufactured objects, utensils and tools; almost all the mechanical energies that appear at work in it are derived from living creatures, men or animals used for the motive force. This universe is further not limited to that first technological ensemble. The efficacy of fire gives rise as well to a complementary group of techniques: metallurgy, pottery, and so on. In addition, preparations already in some sort chemical—dyes, drugs, perfumes—give rise to diverse trades. In this second group of techniques, opening on physico-chemical perspectives rather than physical-mechanical ones, we meet relations of men with matter somewhat different from those that the techniques of manufacture and construction bring forward. The traditional philosophy of causality has based itself above all on the first aspect of the ancient universe of techniques, on the cycle of activities of the physico-mechanical type.

> In all ways the ancient universe of techniques is a universe *without machinery.* The main system of relations is that which appears between the craftsman bringing his production to a successful conclusion and the object he produces: a system, the analysis of which lays stress on the matter [material] of the object, the model and its utilitarian destination, the tools and intermediary operations of manufacture.

Thus the whole concept of creativeness, of the systems that have brought about the combinations or structures of the kosmos, is derived from craft-process. We see this link in both the general ideas and the particular working-out of problems. Aristotle gets his concept of *hyle,* undifferentiated matter, "that out of which", from the material used by artist or craftsman. *Hylē* itself cannot be isolated; it is known only by parallel. "The knowledge of this underlying nature [*physis*] is by analogy; for as the bronze is to the statue, the wood to the bed, or the *hylē* (the shapeless before receiving shape) is to the thing which has shape, so is this [*physis*] itself to substance [*ousia*]—that is, to "this" or to "that which is"—to particular being. The very word used for the underlying *physis* shows the basis of the idea in craft-activity; for *hylē* means forest, woodland, timber. Out of timber-in-general, timber which has no shape relevant to the finished product, is made the bed, which has a functional shape. Elsewhere Aristotle writes, "For at least in certain cases the substratum itself does not make itself change: that is, neither the wood nor the bronze causes the change of either of them, nor does the wood manufacture a bed

13. Masons at work: Rome, Latin Way, Tomb of Trebius Justus

and the bronze a statue; but something else is the cause of the change".

Dealing with stages of growth he declares: "Foundations must have come to be if a house is to exist, and there must be clay, if there are to be foundations. Does it follow that if the foundations have come to be, the house must necessarily do so?" In the same work, discussing how simple bodies are combined to form compounds, he mentions thinkers who do not make the composing elements "come to be out of each other, nor one from another taken singly, except in the sense that bricks come to be out of a wall". Shortly after that, dealing with views like those of Empedokles, he says: "They must maintain that the process is composition, just as the wall comes to be from bricks and stones. More, this mixture will consist of elements preserved intact but set side by side with one another in minute particles."[3]

The author of *On the Kosmos* uses the metaphor of the keystone in dealing with ideas of God. "He is truly like the so-called keystones of vaults, which lie in the middle and by their junction with each side ensure the proper fitting of the whole structure of the vaults and maintain its system and stability." He goes on with the anecdote about the statue of Athena on the Akropolis. Pheidias was said to have carved his own face in the middle of the shield, "and by some hidden trick of craftsmanship [*dēmiourgia*] attached it to the statue in such a way that if one tried to remove it, he inevitably destroyed and demolished the whole statue". The word for keystone, *omphalos*, means navel. In early Greek religion *omphaloi* could mean world-centres and be represented by a stone like that at Delphi. The *omphalos* stone or mound was thus a form of the primeval isle or hill rising out of the waters at the centre of things.[4]

The image of the universe as a sort of building, which finds its microcosmic representation in the temple, seems to go far back. Gudea, ruler of Lagash, was shown in a dream the plan of the temple he was to build (apparently on a heavenly pattern); and Babylonian *usurtu* meant "outline, plan, configuration, plan of building, immutable destiny." Plato described his demiurge at work as if he were a builder. Empedokles (not Anaximenes, it seems) spoke of the stars being fixed like nails in the crystalline; *petala* in the next entry would then be metal-plates, not leaves. He uses several metaphors from metallurgy. He compares Love's binding-force to fig-juice coagulating milk; the juice "rivets" and binds milk. (He is probably thinking of the mixing of male and female seminal fluid.) The mixing of the four elements is compared to the mixing of four metals. The sterility of mules comes through the seminal mixture being too hard "like copper mixed with tin". He also compares Love's action (probably in producing animal parts) to that of a baker making a mixture of barley-meal and water. For Aristotle nature both creates and decorates; it devises, *mechanasthai*. Plato uses the metaphor of irrigation channels to describe the vascular system, and thinks that the crisscrossing blood-vessels round the head play a part in binding head to trunk; Aristotle follows him in both images, adding the idea of wickerwork to the blood-vessels.[5]

The work *On Colours*, attributed to Aristotle but probably by some member of the school he founded, shows how the approach to questions of colour was determined by considerations drawn from dyeing processes. Here we meet an attempt to deal with colour in thorough detail instead of using general notions of fiery effluences and the like. The author has made many subtle observations of nature and is very interested in colour-mixtures: "We must inquire into all the variations of colour, finding similarity of colour in objects undergoing movement according to their actual appearance, finding similar explanations of the mixture in each case." But though he says that the inquiry must be made "not by mixing these colours as painters do", his whole method is based on ideas drawn from dyeing fabrics. What is mixed in colour is "the

14. House-painter, Pompeii (*Annali* 1881 pl. H)

light of the sun, and that which comes from fire, air, and water; for these, mixed in greater and less proportions, produce in a sense all the colours". He adds, "All colours are a mixture of three things: the light; the medium through which the light is seen, such as water or air; and thirdly the colours forming the ground, from which the light happens to be reflected." When he tries to apply these principles, what he has to say is that "all dyed things take their colours from what dyes them". Discussing what it is in nature that dyes objects thus, he remarks:

> The moisture, penetrating through them and washing all colours through with it, produces all the possible colours. And as this is warmed up in the ripening of the fruit by the sun and the warmth of the air, each of the colours becomes fixed by itself, some more quickly and some more slowly, as occurs in dyeing the murex. For when they have cut this open and drained all moisture from it, and have poured it out and boiled it in vessels, at first none of the colours is quite obvious in the dye, because as the liquid boils more and the colours still there get more mixed, each of them shows many and varied differences. For there is black and white and dull and misty, and finally all becomes purple when the boiling is complete, so that in the mixture none of the other colours is visible by itself. The same thing occurs with fruits.

Later he again makes the pervading metaphor explicit:

> The fruits, through their quantity of moisture, change at the time of their ripening into all their natural colours. This is clear, as said before, especially in the case of dyeing with colour. For sometimes to start off, when they're dyeing purple and put in the blood-red dye it becomes greybrown, black and skyblue; but when the dye is boiled enough, it becomes quite purple, gay and bright. In the same way many of the flowers must differ from the colours of the fruits, some getting an excess and some a deficiency of their natural colours, through the fact that in some the ripening is incomplete and in some complete.

Aristotle, we noted, linked cooking processes with what goes on in digestion. *On Plants* uses cooking to explain the growth of trees and plants through the action of solar heat:

> For instance, when the sun's heat begins to scatter the water-particles, the sun draws upwards the particles of moisture, and the ripening is a slow process, because the ripening of the fruit occurs only by congealing, and the leaves come out before the fruit by the

> addition of much moisture. In this case there is often much oiliness, when the mixture that's in the plant gets cooked, and a thick steam rises from it, and the air together with the sun attracts it. For from that moisture oiliness and fruit and leaves all emerge in one output.

The author approaches the idea of photosynthesis. He links colour in plants with the sun's effects on their moisture; light and heat mix with the moisture to produce the varying hues. Though there is no direct chemical concept apart from the dyeing metaphor, the author knows that green results from the sun's action on the leaf. He mentions also, with disagreement, that Anaxagoras believed in the breathing of plants.[6]

Medical writers used ideas drawn from cooking and from natural processes like condensation to explain digestion and metabolism. Those of the school of Kos, whose works have come down under the name of Hippokrates, knew the nature-philosophers' theories well; and the idea of mixture is dominant in their treatises, from which it invaded all areas of Greek thought, from the theory of education to that of the soul. Galen remarked that Eratosthenes had failed to grasp "in what sense the ancients spoke of digestion being similar to the process of *boiling*. . . . It is, he says, inconceivable that digestion, involving as it does such trifling warmth, should be related to the boiling process. It's as if we supposed the fires of Aitna had to be put under the stomach before it could manage to alter the food, or else that, while it was capable of altering the food, it didn't do this by virtue of its innate heat, which of course was moist, so that the word *boil* was used instead of *bake*. . . . He [Eratosthenes] should not have made himself ridiculous by a futile quarrel with a mere term, as though Aristotle hadn't clearly stated in the 4th Book of his *Meteorology*, as well as in many other passages, in what sense digestion can be said to be allied to boiling, and also that the latter expression is not used in its primitive or strict meaning."

The changes and fusions in metallurgical process inevitably attracted much attention. Aristotle tells us:

> When only one of the ingredients is susceptible to action, or is excessively susceptible, while the other ingredient is only slightly so, the result of the mixture of the two is no greater in volume or

> very little greater, as happens when tin and copper are mixed. For some things adopt a hesitant and wavering attitude towards one another. They appear to be only slightly mixable—one as it were, acting in a receptive manner, the other as form. This is what happens with these metals. The tin almost disappears as though it were a property of the copper without any material of its own, and, after being mixed, almost vanishes, having merely given its colour to the copper. And the same thing happens in other instances too.

Again dealing with growth as change in respect to size, he says:

> That which is moving changes its place as a whole, but that which is growing changes its position like a metal that's being beaten. For while it retains its place, its parts undergo local change, but not in the same way as the parts of a revolving globe. For the latter change their places while the whole remains in an equal space, whereas the parts of that which is growing change so as to occupy an ever larger space; and the parts of that which is diminishing contract into ever smaller space.

Ploutarch declares that inspiration and divination result from the fullness of fire in the soul; for, according to Herakleitos, the soul is dry: "Moisture not only dulls the sight and hearing; but when it touches mirrors, takes reflection away from them." Still, the prophetic powers may be made keener by a certain sudden cooling and condensation of the spirit, "as is the case with the tempering of iron". Further, "just as tin, being melted with it, constringes and solidifies copper, naturally soft and porous, and makes it brighter and cleaner, so the prophetic vapour, not improbably, owning a certain sympathy and affinity to the soul, fills up the soft parts of it, and cements and keeps them together. For different substances are congenial, with affinity to others, just as beanflower is thought to aid the murex dye, and natron to aid kermes, when mixed with it. 'Some of the blue crocus is mingled with flax,' as Empedokles has said." We see that in the quest for illuminating analogies men's thoughts flitted from natural process to craft-process and back again, and were always ready to bring in what they considered to be the nature of the soul and its composition as further examples to clarify what happened in nature.

Thus Alexandros of Aphrodisias, dealing with Chrysippos on mixture, cites drugs as bodies, the component parts of which undergo simultaneous destruction and union in a new substance. Mixture, which is no more than juxtaposition, is represented by beans and grains heaped together. "Many bodies preserve their qualities whether they are present in smaller or larger quantities, as can be seen with frankincense. When burnt, it becomes more rarefied, but still retains its quality." Some things expand when aided by others from outside; e.g. "gold when mixed with certain drugs can be spread and rarefied to an extent not possible when beaten out by itself". Men can be effective in union where they would fail by themselves; they can cross rivers by holding hands, lift greater weights. "The tendrils of the grape-vine which could not stand up by themselves can do so if entangled with each other." Certain substances "aid each other by forming a complete union such as to preserve their own qualities while totally interpenetrating each other, even if the mass of one is so slight that by itself it could not preserve its quality if spread out to such an extent"; e.g. a ladle of wine mixed with a large amount of water. (Other thinkers denied this point which the Stoics stressed.) Stobaios cites a mixture of wine, honey, water and vinegar as proof that the qualities of various mixed substances could persist. An experiment, he claims, can demonstrate this persistence. "If we put an oiled sponge into the wine mixed water, the water separates from the wine by returning into the sponge." Aristotle cites the wine-water mixture and the way in which fire seizes on inflammable material to help in explaining how food turns into flesh. Such examples as that of crossing rivers show how social life as well as craft-experience was drawn on for clarifying ideas of mixture and growth.[7]

The names of many geometrical figures suggest strongly that it was craftsmen who first noticed them and passed them on to geometers proper. The old name for ellipse was *thyreos*, connected with *thyra*, door, and used in the *Odyssey* for the stone propped against a door to keep it shut. It came to be used for an oval type of shield. Eukleid speaks of "a section of an acute-angled cone, which is like a shield". There was another figure called *arbēlos*, Shoemaker's Knife; a wedge-shaped solid is called *bōmiskos*, Little Altar, by Heron, and there is another figure called *salinon*, perhaps Saltcellar. *Tomeus*, a cutter, used for the sector of a circle, was also said to be suggested by the shape of a shoemaker's knife. A square is represented as a Racecourse formed by a series of natural numbers with 1 as the *start*, going up to *n* as *turning-point*, and

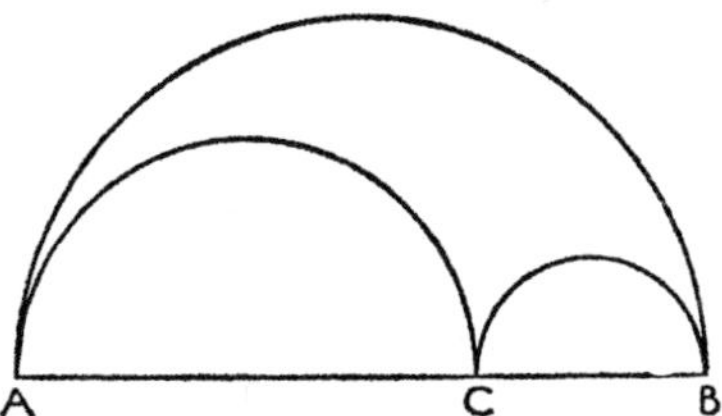

15. Geometrical pattern called *Arbelos* or Shoemaker's Knife; formed by dividing a straight line AB in two unequal parts at C, then describing semicircles with AB, AC, CB as diameters. The figure included between the three circumferences is the *arbelos*

returning through $n-1$, $n-2$ . . . to 1, the *goal.* The sum is made up of two triangular numbers with sides $n, n-1$, respectively, and so is equal to $\frac{1}{2}n(n-1)+\frac{1}{2}n(n+1) = n^2$. (This analysis occurs in Iamblichos' commentary on Nicomachos.) Among the names for solid numbers are Beam and Column: these have a square base, while the height is greater than the side of the square. In Tile the base is a square, while the other edge is less than the side of the square. Eratosthenes called his device for finding prime numbers the Sieve. Perseus, inventor of spiric sections, called one of his *speirai* the Anchor-Ring; and a section is called Horse-Fetter. It seems then that the custom of using such names for figures or numbers had become so strong that later mathematicians were pleased to find some craft-object or the like to which they could compare their discoveries.[8]

We may add that the father of Pythagoras of Samos is said to have been an engraver of seals. These owned a magical value and the glyptography of Samos was famous. It has been suggested that it was the stone-cutters who devised the regular polyhedra which the geometers took over and reasoned about. Further it seems that much of the *Elements* of Eukleid was derived from the craft of building. The definition of parallels as straight lines produced to infinity and never meeting may be an interpolation, as it jars against the need of Greek geometry to avoid the direct intervention of infinity. Certainly Eukleides should have defined parallelism as a function of the two lines' equidistance. He was generalising in geometrical terms the practice of architects, who for the construction of a wall used rectangular blocks cut so that they could be interchanged in their superimposition. The definition of a straight line is perhaps to be read in the light of the mason's practise of applying a stone rule coated with red oil to verify the facing of a chiselled surface; if the facing was perfect, the imprint of the rule appeared without any break. Hence a straight line was one "lying equally between its points". The Greeks glorified the straight line and the circle; and though they could give theoretical reasons for looking on these as the essential forms in the construction of reality, they were certainly also holding fast to the forms which could be produced by means of rule and compass—forms taken over from the crafts. For long they refused to consider any other forms, and such curves as the quadratrix of Hippias, the conchoid of Nikomedes, or the cissoid of Diokles remained on the margin of what was considered pure or true science. They were considered too mechanical because instruments other than rule and compass were needed to construct them—the link of rule and compass with mechanical crafts having been long glossed over. We may note that Plato attacked geometrical demonstrations in which mechanics entered as a degradation of the science by making it pass, like a fugitive slave, from the study of things incorporeal and intelligible to that of objects perceptible by the senses, and by using, besides pure reasoning, objects laboriously and slavishly fashioned by manual labour. Note his revealing phrase "like a fugitive slave", and the way he forgets the craft-basis of rule and compass.[9]

In matters of physiology or sense-perception we find thinkers attempting to grasp what went on in the body by looking for some tool or instrument that seemed to produce comparable effects. Empedokles declared, says Theophrastos, that "hearing results from sounds within [the head] whenever the air, set in motion by a voice, resounds inside. For the organ of hearing which he calls Fleshy Spring [*ozos*, the knot or eye from which a leaf or bunch grows] acts as the Bell of a Trumpet, ringing with sounds [like those it receives]. When set in motion, [this organ] drives the air against the solid parts and produces there a sound." It is unclear just what the picture is: whether the *ozos* is the concha of the ear or some trumpet-like portion less external, such as the ampullae with their conjoined canals, which might suggest a twisted trumpet. But we can see that he uses an image from nature, the eye-knot in the tree, and another from man-made instruments. Again, of the eye Empedokles says that it is of fire, with earth and air around. Through the latter, "the fire, by reason of its subtlety, passes like the light in lanterns".

Luckily we have Empedokles' own words:

> And as a man who decides to sally out into the stormy night, gets a lantern ready, a flame of flashing fire, fastening hornplates to it to keep out all manner of winds, and they scatter the blast of the winds that blow, but the light leaps out through them and shines across the threshold with its unyielding rays inasmuch as it is finer—just so did Love surround the elemental fire in the rounded pupil and confine it with membranes and fine tissues, pierced through and through with innumerable passages. They keep out the deep water that surrounds the pupil, but they let through the fire, inasmuch as it is finer.

The purpose of the simile seems to have been to give an account of the structure and composition of the eye, not to explain the purpose or function of the fire leaving the eye. The membrane round the fire has the function of separating the water in the eye from the fire there. Fire and water are the percipient elements; earth and air are present only as constituents of the protective membrane. (The round pupil of fire with the surrounding membrane and water is something of a miniature image of the Anaximandrian heavenly bodies.)[10]

Dealing with Demokritos' ideas of sight-impression, Theophrastos says, "It is as if one were to take a mould in wax." He criticises the use of both air-prints and effluences in the theory, though the air-print might be meant to explain how we see form, the effluence how we see colour. The Stoics took over the idea of the imprint. Kleanthes, apparently following Zenon, said that *phantasia* or presentation "is an impression on the soul or on the *hegemonikon*". *Typōsis* was taken in the literal sense "as involving depression and protrusion, just as does the impression made in wax by signet-rings". Chrysippos rejected this idea, saying that one impression would destroy or obliterate the proceeding one, just as a second seal obscured the impression of the first; he defined presentation as a modification of the soul, argued that this was what Zenon had meant, and used the analogy of acoustic effects.

> It is by no means absurd that the same body be submitted at one and the same time to a very large number of modifications. In the

> same way as air, when many sounds are uttered, is submitted to innumerable and different strokes, and holds at once many modifications, so the *hegemonikon* undergoes an equivalent experience when presentations are formed by it in various ways.

We may note the idea of continual modification going on inside a complex but unified process. The *heteroiōsis* of the soul involves changing dynamic states of the *pneuma*. "The superimposition

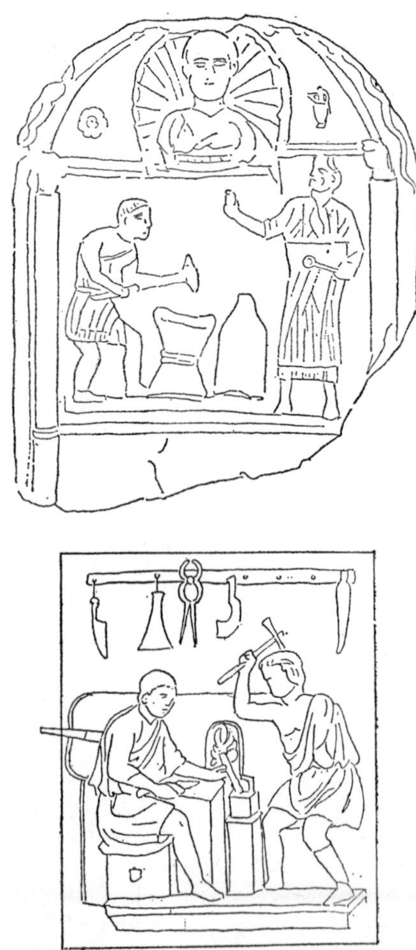

16. Striking coins and forging knives (*R.M.* 1907 pl. 4; *DS Dict.* fig. 2112–3)

of the modifications of the *pneuma* is of a specifically dynamic character since each modification is given by a definite movement of the *pneuma*. If we bear in mind that the Stoics had a clear conception of the wave character of sound, the analogy quoted might easily indicate that they already had an inkling of the principle of the superimposition of waves" (Sambursky).[11]

Typos, a blow or its effect, a mark or impression, was a term with a long and complicated history; and Zenon or Kleanthes may well have used it to bring out the idea of a strong impact on the soul from the outer world, which had the effect of forming it—without being concerned with the difficulty raised by Chrysippos as to how one impact merged with or displaced another. *Typos* was linked in meaning with *sphragis*, seal, and with *charaktēr*, something cut-in, stamped, impressed and came to signify a characteristic mark or likeness, an image. We find the Christian idea of Baptism as a *sphragis* impressing the new life on the convert and obliterating the old; and *typos* and *antitypos* are used in a complex dialectic by the late poet Nonnos. Recall the early Pythagorean coins with design raised on one side and impressed on the other.[12]

Behind the idea of an orderly revolution of heavenly bodies there was the image of the dance, but that of the wheel also played its part. We may repeat what Aetios says of Anaximandros' image of the sun: "a circle twenty-eight times the size of the earth: like a chariot-wheel with a hollow felloe [rim] full of fire; at a certain point the fire shines out, through an opening like a *prēstēr*-tube. . . . An eclipse of the sun results from the closure of the opening through which the fire appears." And of the stars: "they are compressions of air in the form of fire-filled wheels and they throw out flames through openings at a certain place." Parmenides seems to be following this sort of image when he sets out a system of heavenly bodies with a series of rings compounded of mist and fire—though he speaks of three different kinds of rings: one kind made of the rare (light) alone, a second of the dense (darkness) alone, and a third of the two elements combined. The image of the fiery wheel may have been suggested by someone swinging a torch round or by the use of a wheel-on-fire spinning in a fire-festival. Ixion, punished in Hades, was said to have been tied hands and feet to a wheel (like a condemned slave); the wheel is called fiery or winged and keeps on rolling forever in the air or in the lower world. Probably we have here an Orphic image, which may have been borrowed from the cosmogonies, though both Orphics and philosophers may have drawn on the sight of a fire-wheel spinning down a hill at a festival.

We have seen Anaximandros' fire-sphere like the bark of a tree. A different kind of circular image appears in Aristotle's account of the views of Anaximenes, Anaxagoras, and Demokritos on the flatness of the earth as the cause of its "staying still". The earth "doesn't cut the air beneath but covers it like a lid, which flat bodies evidently do; for they are hard to move even for the winds, on account of their resistance." (Another homely image is used for air as the earth-support, by Plato, who says that some physicists see it holding up the earth "like a broad kneading-trough".[13])

The act of swinging things round at the end of a cord also helped in building the idea of circular movement. Aristotle tells us: "Others agree with Empedokles that it is the excessive swiftness of the motion of the heaven as it swings round in a circle which prevents motion on the earth's part. They compare it to water in a cup, which, when the cup is swung round in a circle, is in fact stopped from falling by the same cause, though it often finds itself underneath the bronze and it is its nature to move downwards." No doubt the same sort of image lies behind Anaxagoras' idea of the centrifugal force in his cosmogony. With the earth as centre, "the sun and moon and all the stars are flaming stones which are carried round by the revolution of the *aithēr*". The swinging of a sling must also have contributed to these ideas. Cicero cites Chrysippos as noting that the cylinder and spinning top cannot start moving till given an impulse, then the cylinder goes on rolling and the top spinning according to its nature. Aulus Gellius makes the same point about a cylinder set off rolling down a steep bit of ground.[14]

We come back to tools proper with the lathe, *tornos*.

On the Kosmos, discussing the universe as a single continuously moving sphere, remarks, "But there are necessarily two points which are unmoved, opposite one another, just as in the case of a ball being turned in a lathe. They stay fixed, holding the sphere in position, and the whole mass revolves in a circle round them. These points are called poles," *poloi*. The straight line joining the poles is the *axon*, axle. How old the lathe was cannot be determined, but by Aristophanes' day it was sufficiently familiar for its action to be used figuratively: he speaks of "neatly turned verses". Aischylos knew the lathe; and the *Iliad* uses the verb which means to mark something (a barrow) off with a *tornos*. The whole stress of the root is on roundness and turning. *Torneuma* means a whirling motion such as that of a lathe; *toreus* is a boring tool. *Polos* is cognate with *pelein, polein,* to come into existence, to become, to be; *polein* is used for going about, revolving (Plato), while Hesiod uses it in the sense of turning up earth with a plough. Herodotos uses *polos* for a concave sundial (shaped like a vault of heaven) with a shadow-casting gnomon; Aischylos uses it for the sky-vault; Xenophon for the centre of a round threshing-floor; later it is used for capstan or windlass. Plato uses it for the axis of the heavenly sphere, and Aristotle for the pole of this axis. The root-meanings of *pelein* seem to belong to the same complex of ideas as we see in the Latin *volvere* and *vulva*: birth or coming-to-be as a rhythmic revolving motion. *Vortex* (*vertex*) in Latin, we may note, means a whirl or whirlpool, eddy; Lucretius, Livius, Virgil use it as whirlwind or coil of flame; it also means the highest point or peak, and Cicero and Virgil use it for the pole of the heavens. We are finding ourselves back with the *prēstēr*-image—the tornado-whirl now becoming the central whirl of the universe.[15]

The central whirl or eddy was as we saw, an important Greek

17. Cook at work (Rayet, *Mons de l'art ant.* pl. 84)

18. Sawyer at work (Boiotian terracotta, late sixth century)

concept. Aristotle says, "If the earth's rest is due to constraint, it must have been under the action of the vortex that it travelled to the middle." No doubt many other observed phenomena, as well as the shattering tornado, contributed to the idea. Men must have noted spirals of dust, the gyration of fallen leaves (from which they could estimate the direction of the velocity and its size at the various points of the whirl). Light dust was raised and carried along in a general rotary movement, while heavier bodies, hard for the wind to shift, stayed at the centre of the vortex, where they were joined by other bodies drawn in, in constantly decreasing circles, by a frictional movement. Anaximenes saw his earth, the result of condensation from *aēr* downwards, as a flat body riding on the air; exhalations from it produced the heavenly bodies, which were like flat leaves floating on air. They revolved round the earth "as a felt cap turns round our head".[16]

Observations from nature, we have seen, continually keep coming up and merging with observations from the world of men, especially of matters connected with craft-activities. In the quest for origins, for primordial elements, men felt that there were important clues in the seeds and roots of plants. Seeds helped to form the ideas both of seminal bodies and of atomic structures. Empedokles called his primordial elements *roots*. Aristotle tells us: "He says that the nature of Fire is to be borne upwards, and *aithēr* 'sank with its long roots into the earth'." As Anaximandros saw the tornado linking sky and earth, Empedokles saw the upper elements reaching down long roots.

Anaxagoras saw the cosmic constituents as *seeds* infinite in number and contained in the smallest quantity of matter. He asked how foods such as bread and wine could be turned into sinews, flesh, bones, hair, in the living body unless they themselves held something of these products; and the same argument must apply to the seeds. "One must believe that there are many things, which contain all kinds of shapes and colours and pleasant savours." Again: "For in everything there is a portion of everything . . . but each individual thing is most obviously that of which it contains the most." Aristotle says that for him fire, earth, water, air were composite, since each was, as they say, "a *panspermia* for things which have like parts". *Panspermia* is a mixture of all seeds.[17]

Empedokles made an attempt to correlate various forms of growth "Hair and leaves, and the thick feathers of birds, and the scales that grow on mighty limbs, are the same thing." Aristotle with more sophistication tried to link growth-processes with condensation and evaporation, observed, it appears, not in nature but in baths: "Just as in the bathroom the heat attracts the moisture and transforms it into steam, and this, being light, when in excess condenses into drops of water, so also in animals and plants the waste product rises from the lower to the upper parts and descends again from the upper to the lower." He further draws in as analogies the way that rivers appear underground from mountains, and refers to blood rising to the brain:

> For as some of it, owing to food, rises with the evaporation, so it is with all waters. A part of the salt water rises with it, which the heat dries, into the form of air, which is completely above all water both fresh and salt. We have found an example of this principle in many baths. When the heat affects the salt water, it lightens its parts and a vapour arises, which was formed at the bottom of the bath, and the solid particles of salt rise at the same time as the natural moisture (for this is not of the form of air), so that they follow the evaporation, which goes in the form of one cloud after another. When many have hurried upwards, the ceiling is thick with them, and then they collect and condense, and fresh water falls down; and so in all salt baths there is fresh water.

Seneca shows how ideas drawn from heating systems were applied to nature:

> Empedokles considers that water is warmed by fires which in many places the earth covers over, if they are set under the ground through

> which the course of the waters runs. We are wont to make *dracones*, cylinders and various other vase-forms, inside which are constructed tubes of thin copper arranged around in a sloping way, by aid of which the water, winding several times round the fire, has a long enough journey to get warmed up. It enters cold, it goes out heated. Empedokles declares that the same thing goes on under the earth, and his theory will be willingly accepted by those who know how to heat baths without fire. They introduce into the warming place heated air [*spiritus fervens*] which, circulating through channels just like the hidden fire, heats the walls and the vessels of the bath.[18]

At times an examination of language reveals a complex tension between mechanical and organic or social ideas. Thus in Empedokles's account of the fire in the eye, the term used for the rounded pupil, *kyklops kourē*, can be taken to mean also a round-eyed baby-girl, and the verb used defines the pupil's formation as either an ambush or an act of childbirth—the latter meaning is the more likely one. We are shown the formation of the eye (which is also described as a lantern) as the act of giving birth to a baby-girl. In the passage on respiration the terms used to describe the blocking of the water-vessel's neck and the pressure of air on the surfaces of the strainer can also be taken to mean: "the straits are blocked and the air commands the heights"—a metaphor from military operations. Some copyists have tried to extend the image by writing *isthmoio* for *ēthmoio*, so that "around the openings of the gurgling strainer" becomes "above the pass of the isthmus of ill-repute". Again in the lines "Kypris [Aphrodite], plying her pleasant task, moistened the Earth in water and then gave it to leaping fire to harden", the latter phrase has the connotation: "allowed fierce fire to conquer"; another military metaphor. *Kratynein* can mean both to harden and to conquer, and the epithet for fire, *thoos*, is often used by Homer in military contexts. We see then how an analysis of the diction often reveals how complex is the movement of thought in arriving at a generalisation.

We see that the ancients, while in general averse from carrying out and repeating experiments systematically under controlled conditions, were often ready to take advantage of some system or construction which did at least a certain amount of controlling for them. Hence the use of baths for observing evaporation and condensation. They watched such phenomena working on a large scale in nature, and drew general conclusions from them there, but they recognised that they could, or should, make more precise deductions from the same sort of processes in the bathroom.

It is then perhaps not an accident that Archimedes is said to have got the first clue to his definition of specific gravity—as the ratio of the weight of a body and its volume—by stepping into a bath and noting the displacement of water by his foot. Traditionally, he was brooding on the problem of how to detect the mixture of silver in a crown which Hieron of Syracuse had ordered to be made of gold; and he was so struck by having grasped the solution that he forgot to put on his clothes and ran off naked through the streets, shouting: "*Eurēka—I've found it!*" One main reason why such advances were made in linking observations with mathematical analysis in astronomy was because nature herself provided the laboratory with the moving phenomena inside it—the night sky.

Aristotle too watched things sinking or floating in water, not in a pool or stream, but in vessels. Discussing earthquakes he remarks that "no such cataclysm occurs in the parts of plants and animals, and especially in earthenware vessels, in glass and metals. For in a body that contains finely divided particles, it's usual for the evaporation to rise, since the air makes it light. We quite often see this when we throw gold or some heavy substance into water, and it at once sinks to the bottom; on the other hand, when we throw in thin or small wood, it floats and doesn't sink." He thinks the results are not due to differences in weigh, but come from variations in compactness and fine division in a body —that is to say, he touches on a view of specific gravity as resulting from molecular separation.

Speculations connected with water and floating or sinking bodies went far back. The primeval mount or isle set in the circle of waters, Okeanos, became for Thales a sort of ship. His world-picture "supposes that the earth is at rest because it can float like a log and similar substances, the nature of which is to rest upon water, though none could rest upon air". The image of the *skaphe*, bowl or rounded ship, was also called upon. "Thales said that the earth is carried by the water and moves like a *skaphe*. It's because of the water's movement that the earth moves in what is called an earthquake." Herakleitos seems to have seen the heavenly bodies as *skaphai*.

> Fire is fed by the bright exhalations, the moist element by the others. He doesn't make clear the nature of the surrounding element. But he does state that in it are bowls [*skaphai*] with their concavities turned towards us, in which the bright exhalations collect and produce flames. These are the stars. The sun's flame is brightest and hottest; the other stars are further from the earth and thus give less light and heat. The moon, nearer, traverses a region that isn't pure; but the sun moves in clear untroubled regions and keeps a proportionate distance from us. Eclipses of the sun and moon occur when the bowls are turned upwards; the monthly phases of the moon are due to the bowl turning round in its place little by little. Day and night, months, seasons and years, rains and winds and other similar phenomena are accounted for by the various exhalations. Thus the bright exhalation, set aflame in the circle of the sun, produces day; the opposite exhalation, getting the mastery, causes night. . . . He gives no account of the nature of the earth or of the bowls (Diogenes Laertes).

The more mythologised image in Mimnermos describes the never-resting Sun at night going across the waters in a winged "hollow bed", beaten by Hephaistos out of gold. Here the sun, Helios, is *in* the bowl-boat, whereas in Herakleitos the sun *is* the bowl. Later Herakles sailed on his westward journey in the bowl. He shot arrows at the Sun, who so admired his courage that he gave him a golden cup in which to cross the Ocean. Here the culture-hero undertaking the journey to the spirit-world in search of booty there (the golden apples) uses the sun-bowl to get over the sundering waters. The original meaning of *skaphe* was probably "something dug or scooped out". Aristarchos devised a sun-dial with the pointer set vertically in the middle of a concave hemispherical surface; the dial was called a *skaphe*.

Behind the idea of the sun-bowl there may lie the image of the Zoroastrian fire-altar, shown on reliefs of the sixth and fifth centuries B.C. The fire burned in a circular basin about a foot, or at most two feet, across; it certainly represented the sun—indeed in a way it *was* the sun (or the power that kept the sun going): hence the taboo against letting the sun's rays fall on it. Herakleitos declared that the sun's bowl was equal to the length of a man's foot. His whole conception here may have been derived

19. Ixion on Wheel (with Sisyphos and Rock, Tantalos and Water): sarcophagus (Reinach, *Rels*. iii 391); Herakles sailing in the Bowl of the Sun (Greek vase, J. H. *Themis* 371)

from a fire-altar which he had seen and which stirred his imagination. But he, or others, may also have assimilated the idea of the floating sun-bowl to that of a round boat, aware of Egyptian sun-images.[19]

We saw above how Empedokles linked underground water-streams with channels or tubes, or rather how Seneca thus interpreted his account. Certainly the image of such passages or pores became important for a large number of explanations concerning the operation and effects of effluences, and Empedokles led the way in this field. He believed all bodies to be full of invisible holes, through which effluences easily penetrated if the fit was right; his system of pores was used to explain physiological process, and he thought trees lost their leaves because the absorbing pores of the roots were smaller than the emitting pores of the leaves. Perception was caused by effluences coming in through pores that let in particles of a specific mixture without letting the blood out. We have his account, which shows how a game with a vessel called water-catcher helped him to arrive at his system:

> Thus all things draw in breath and breathe it out again. All have bloodless tubes of flesh stretched over the surface of their bodies, and at the mouths of these the uttermost surface of the skin is perforated all over with close-packed pores, to keep the blood in while a free passage is cut for the air to pass through. Thus, when the yield blood recedes from these, the bubbling with an impetuous surge rushes in, and when the blood runs back it's breathed out again.
>
> Just as when a girl, playing with a water-catcher of shining brass, puts the orifice of the pipe on her comely hand and dips the waterclock into the yielding mass of silvery water—the stream doesn't flow into the vessel, but the bulk of air inside, pressing upon the close-packed perforations, keeps it out till she uncovers the compressed stream. Then air escapes and an equal volume of water rushed on.
>
> Just in the same way, when water occupies the inside of the brazen vessel and the opening and passage is stopped up by the human hand, the air outside, striving to get in, keeps back the water at the gates of the sounding strainer, pressing upon its surface till she lets go with her hand. Then, on the contrary, just in the opposite way to what happened before, the wind rushes in and an equal volume of water rushes out to make room.
>
> Even so, when the thin blood that surges through the limbs rushes backwards to the interior, straightway the stream of air comes in with a rushing swell. But when the blood returns, the air breathes out again in equal quantity.

The exact interpretation is difficult; but Empedokles is certainly applying his idea that there are pores or funnels of the right size for one element, but too small for another. Here the pores somewhere at the base of the nostrils are of the right size for air to pass through, but too small for blood. The situation is not the same with the *klepsydra*, where the elements are air and water and both can pass through the perforations. Air in fact only enters through the neck at the top; water, however, does periodically pass through the perforations. When it doesn't do so, it is not because the perforations are too small, but because air beats back the water from within or presses on the perforations from outside. Empedokles is explaining what happens, not how it happens. He says that the *klepsydra* is filled alternately with air and water, just as the lungs or chest are filled alternately with air and blood. Air passes up and down the vessel's neck, just as air is breathed in and out through mouth or nostrils. Water passes in and out through the vessel's base just as blood wells up and then drops back through veins in the lung or chest. But we are here concerned, not with the detail of the Empedoklean theory of respiration, but with the use of the vessel in an experiment with air and water.

Anaxagoras repeated the same sort of experiment. He compressed air in wineskins, says Aristotle, and showed that it offered resistance when the skins were stretched; but he rejected the theory of pores and held to a belief in continuity. Aristotle himself sees present in matter "a kind of *dynamis*, as if it were a channel". He is discussing the growth of bone or flesh (form as well as matter): "So if matter is added, which is potentially a channel, these channels will also grow bigger." His term for channel is *aulos*, tube, pipe, which we saw with *prēstēr*. "If the form is no longer able to function, then (as water mixed with wine in ever-larger quantities finally makes the wine waterish and converts it to water) it will cause a diminution of the quantity, though the form persists." The tube-image, which had been expanded to cosmic dimensions in the tornado, here contracts to a minute invisible form running in a network through the body. In the latter form it was used by Aristotle for rectum, urinal duct, arteries and veins, and passages leading from the organs of sensation to the brain; and by Herophilos (third century B.C.) for the optic nerve. It thus helped inquirers to form ideas of systems pervading the body, such as veins and nerves.

Plato makes use of an experiment in capillarity to express the flow of thought. "How fine it would be . . . if wisdom were a sort of thing that flowed from the fuller man into the emptier, by our mere contact with one another, as water will flow through wool from the fuller cup into the emptier."[20]

The idea of a complicated tube-system in the body may be taken as a crude attempt to express the net work of nerves, veins, sinews and so on. A subtler image is that of the spiderweb, which is said to go back to Herakleitos: "In the same way as a spider in the middle of his web senses when a fly destroys one of the threads, and quickly hurries to the spot as if afflicted by the laceration of the thread, so does a man's psyche, if some part of his body is injured, move quickly there as if indignant over the injury done to the body with which it has a firm and proper connection." The Stoics saw that the simile would serve well to express their notion of the *hegemonikon* in the body: "In the same way as a spider in the centre of the web holds in its feet all the beginnings of the threads, so as to feel by close contact if an insect strikes the web, and where—so does the *hegemonikon* of the psyche, situated in the middle of the heart, check on the beginnings of the senses, so as to perceive their messages from close proximity." The image here is not of an actual movement or leap from centre to the outer boundaries of the body, not of contact in any crude way, but of the propagation of an impulse through a medium in a state of tension. Later we shall see how the engraved lines on the astrolabe were taken to represent a spiderweb snaring the whole heavens and expressing their movements.

We saw what an important part was played by letters and numbers in bringing about the concept of combinable atoms or simple bodies. But we must also allow for the observation that clods of earth could be crumbled, or rocks could be pounded, into small apparently-identical bits. Aristotle, arguing against the atomists, says, "It's odd there should be small indivisibles, but not large ones. It's natural to suppose the bigger bodies are more liable to be shattered than the small, since the former, like big things in general, are easily disintegrated as they come into collision with many other bodies. Yet why should indivisibility in general attach to small things rather than large? "He also discusses how, "when the body is being divided, a minute portion like a bit of sawdust is formed". He goes on to argue that it is impossible for magnitudes to consist of contacts and points, while indivisible bodies and magnitudes also raise unanswerable questions. "After dividing a piece of wood or some other object, I put it together again, it is again both equal to what it was, and a unity. The wood has therefore been divided, potentially, throughout. What then is in the wood besides the division? For even if there is some quality, how is it dissolved into these constituents [points of division and quality] and how does it come to be out of them?" We see how the breaking or cutting up of objects, by chance or in craft-activity, raised many questions as to relation of parts to the whole. Beaches made up of small bits of sand, and waves shattering into small droplets of spray would have raised similar questions.

Lucretius has an important passage that shows many of the lines of reasoning which led into the concept of atoms or were used to support it. He asserts that the *primordia* cannot be seen, then deals with bodies which, though invisible, are proved to exist by their activity.

> *The force of wind, aroused, beats on the harbours,*
> *overwhelms great ships, and scatters clouds. At times*
> *in a rapid whirling eddy it scours the plains*
> *and strews them with big trees, scourges mountaintops*
> *with forest-shattering blasts. So fiercely the wind*
> *raves with shrill howls, rages with threatening roar.*
> *Winds then are unseen bodies that sweep the seas,*
> *the lands, yes, and the clouds of heaven, tormenting*
> *and catching them up in sudden whirls. And streaming*
> *they spread destruction abroad as does the soft*
> *nature of water when all at once it's borne*
> *along in an overflowing gush, and a vast*
> *downfall of water from high comes swelling it*
> *with rains in abundance. . . .*

He draws a picture of the wild roaring elemental and destructive force of masses of water—and a similar one for the winds. He stresses the circling movements, the curling eddies and whirls, which carry things away. Thus invisible winds are, in force, the rivals of rivers which are visible. Further, we cannot see smells, heat, cold, sounds. Clothes hung up on a billowy seashore grow moist, and yet they dry when spread in the sun: "The water's then dispersed into small particles that the eyes are quite unable to behold." A ring worn on a finger for years grows thin on the underside; waterdrops from the eaves hollow a stone; the iron ploughshare wears away; and so do stone paved streets under the many feet. "Bronze statues too at the gates show right hands wasted by the touch of many passers greeting them." Yet we do not see what it is that leaves these bodies. The eye fails to see bodies growing or the way that saltspray eats the rocks: "Nature therefore works by unseen bodies."

Later he appeals to the minute bodies glimpsed mingling in rays that slope into the "dark chambers of houses". The particles

> *in unending conflict, skirmish, give battle, fight*
> *in troops with never a halt, all driven about*
> *in frequent partings and meetings. So you may guess*
> *what it is like for the* primordia *of things*
> *to be ceaselessly tossing about in the great void.*
> *As far as it goes, a little thing in turn*
> *may illustrate great things, set you on the path*
> *of knowledge. So it's right that you should note*
> *with fuller care these bodies seen to tumble*
> *in the sun's rays; for those tumblings of theirs*
> *imply that motions of unseen and latent matter*
> *go on for ever beneath. You'll realise*
> *how many things are impelled there by unseen blows*
> *to change their course, and, driven back, return*
> *the way they came, now this way and now that,*
> *in all directions. You must grasp they all*
> *derive this restless state from the* principia,
> *from the* primordia *moving of themselves.*
> *Those bodies forming a small aggregate*
> *are set off by the impact of the invisible blows*
> *and knock in turn on bodies slightly bigger.*
> *So the movement goes on mounting from the atoms*
> *up gradually to the level of our senses*
> *and the bodies go whirling that we see in sunbeams*
> *moved on by blows we cannot clearly distinguish.*

He argues that we need not wonder that the *primordia* are in movement while the sun is seen to rest above. For the nature of first things

> *lies far off from our senses, beneath our ken.*
> *Since they're themselves beyond what you can see,*

they must withdraw their motions too from sight.
And all the more, since things that we can see
often conceal their motions when far away.
Often the flocks of sheep crop the lush pastures,
creep slowly on, drawn this way and then that
by grass that glitters with fresh dew, while lambs,
full-fed, go frisking gaily and butting. Yet,
we, gazing from a distance, see but a blob,
a white patch stationary on the green slopes.

His close observation of the motes in the sunbeam give him the basis on which to describe a phenomenon not actually discovered by the microscope until the first half of the nineteenth century and not reduced to mathematical terms till the early twentieth: Brownian motion:

> When we look at microscopic particles suspended in a liquid or a gas, such as oildrops in an emulsion or dust and smoke particles in the air, we see how they move in a perfectly disorderly fashion, wandering this way and that without rule and without purpose. This indirectly shows us the activity of the atoms in the liquid or the gas which cannot be seen even in a microscope. It is true that in the average taken over a longer period of time the total of all the impacts of the atoms on the microscopic particles is cancelled out. But the statistical deviations from the average occurring at every moment result in the particle's being given impulses this way and that with constant change of direction, and it is random impulse which gives rises to the ceaseless oscillations of the particle. (Sambursky)

In fact the motes are agitated by molecules of the air, so that the intuitive subtlety of the Lucretian passage is startling. We see how the atomic school had brought into scientific reasoning the method of inference. Observation of the motes in light goes back to Demokritos. Aristotle tells us: "Some say the capacity to produce movement is first and foremost the soul's characteristic; but as they hold that nothing can produce movement which doesn't itself move, they've supposed the soul is one of the things that move. Hence Demokritos argues that the soul is fire in some sense and heat. For, forms and atoms being countless, he calls the spherical ones fire and soul, like what are called particles in the air, which can be seen when sunbeams pass through our windows, the whole collection of which he calls the element out of which nature is composed."[21]

There remains to be considered the way in which realisation or intuition of the general movement of their society, or particular aspects of social activity, affected the thinkers. Though by the time of Plato the considerable development of slavery in economic life did much to strength the aristocratic contempt of banausic or manual labour among the thinkers, such a fastidious attitude does not seem to have dominated the Milesian nature-philosophers. Several of the tales about Thales show him busy in commercial and political affairs. Herodotos says that he advised his fellow Ionians to set up a common council and to federate; tradition makes him a trader who travelled in Egypt and perhaps Chaldea, and who made his fortune by selling salt. One year foreseeing an abundant harvest, he rented all the olive trees and made a big profit.

He is said to have been interested in navigation, as he would indeed have been if he were a trader, and to have taken over from the Phoinikians the use of Ursa Minor, instead of Ursa Major as a guide to the north star—hence the calling of Ursa Minor by the Greeks *Phoinikē*. Heredotos further tells us that he accompanied Kroisos, apparently as a military engineer, in his expedition against Pteria. When they reached the Halys they could not get across, so Thales had the river diverted in part into a deep crescent-shaped channel from a spot above the camp and thence round to its rear; the army was then able to pass over the now-shallow waters. Even if some of the stories are inventions, they show the reputation of the man and the sort of milieu in which he grew up.

The fact that the Greek city-state could develop the concept and practise of the rule of law in a way impossible for states under despotic controls meant that the citizens were sure to extend the ideas of law and order in new ways into their whole view of the universe. The social world was governed by man-made law; the natural world by nature-made law. It was some time before these principles matured and grew fully conscious, but they were at work from the outset in Ionian philosophy. We have noted the tradition that Thales was the author of the proposed constitution of the Ionian confederation. We have discussed the

Anaximandrian concept of all things giving justice and reparation to one another, according to the assessment of time; and returning in dissolution to their source, according to necessity. And the medical concept of *isonomia*, applied to the measure of all things, though social in origin. Empedokles said of his elements (roots) that they were all equal. Even when Strife is at its height and each root is "unmixed" (and so, in Hippokratic terms, a "strong substance"), balance is preserved; for each is as strong as any other. Equality prevents "injustice" even when Strife is lord of the kosmos. Aristotle says that he cannot make out whether Empedokles means equality in power or in volume—but in another passage he admits that the equality lies in power. Indeed Empedokles does deal in spatial categories, saying that love is "equal in length and breadth"; but after stating that the roots are equal, he goes on to say that they are equal in age, that each has its own kind of honour, *timē*, and that they rule in turn. His universe thus reveals Alkmaion's formula of health writ large; and even Zeus is no longer supreme; he is simply one of the roots on the same level as an odd and unknown deity, Nestis. Strife is linked in equality with Love. Otherwise there would be no created world, only the nondescript mixture of the Sphairos. We do not hear of Justice, but we hear of mighty Oaths that represent the binding and necessary nature of the alternations; what controls is the decree that is "an oracle of Anankē". We must note that the rule of each root is seen in social terms. Strife has its *timai*, its rights or prerogatives of office, as its share or fate, *aisa*.

This stress on equality has roots far back in the tribal past. In *Iliad* XV it is implied that the heavens, the sea, and the "murky darkness" are equals in rank and portion or share. In Hesiod's *Theogony* earth and heaven are called equal, and an expression of this is the fact that the distance between heaven and earth is the same as that between earth and Tartaros. In the *Odyssey* a well made ship is called "equal", and a wise or balanced mind is also "equal". We see an intuitive sense of symmetry and balance in the universe, not any clear physical theory or model. Later Eukleid uses the term "equally" to express geometric symmetry in his definition of a straight line.

Parmenides lays more stress on Justice. In Being there can be no Injustice, since its limit is an unbreakable chain or fetter that holds it fast.

Justice thus approximates to Necessity, and is seen as an active force. Note how even here Anankē has the servile mark of the fetter. What brings about this necessary Justice in Being is its self-identity, its homogeneity or self-equality: "it is all alike", "it is equal to itself on all sides". But the identification of Being with Necessity in an absolute way leads to the conclusion that in the perfectly just world, thought too is perfectly just (in full harmony with its own nature and the nature of Being), but outside that world it is "forced" to attempt the impossible, to utter the unutterable, to think the unthinkable. Thought becomes "blind, wandering, helpless". This set of contradictions emerges out of the sublime coherence of the kosmos in its necessary totality, which, from the fragmentary or relative angle of actual life, becomes a crushing imposition of Necessity or Slave-Impotence. Here lies the nemesis of abstracting the two opposites of process and putting them together in a metaphysical unity. Each opposite is absolutely self-identical; both of them are equal.

A few words more on Anaximandros. He held that the earth owes its stability to its all-round equality. He made a thorough application of the concepts of Justice to the universe, and of the equality of the opposites. He saw nature as a self-regulative equilibrium, with its order guaranteed by the fixed proportions of its main constituents; and this position of his had great influence on later thinkers. It was clearly social in origin, with the political assumption that justice was an affair between equals. In Herakleitos we find at the core of his politics the supremacy of the common law of the city; the ultimate unity of all human laws is the "common mind". Possibly he himself held to a Solonian position of moderate democracy; he admired Bias of Priene who is said to have remarked that "the strongest democracy is the one in which all fear the law as their master". The laws which men devise to make their life together possible and fruitful is somehow linked with the divine law that "nourishes them"—the law of formative process which Herakleitos keeps trying to define from one angle after another. The divine law is perceptible in all things, and human laws are effective in so far as they coincide with the one law that controls not only a particular society of men but the whole complex of existing things, animate and inanimate. The relationship is not merely one of imitation on the part of human law; divine law plays its part in a concrete manner, as is implied by the term "nourish". Herakleitos says that though the *logos* is common, men live as if they had a private (isolated) understanding. Sextus Empericus tells us, "This is nothing other than an explanation of the way in which the universe is ruled. Therefore in so far as we share an awareness of this, we speak the truth, but in so far as we remain independent of it, we lie."[22]

In the light of what has just been said it is worth while to look again at the Herakleitan passage on the exchange of all things for one another. The word for exchange, *antamoibe*, stresses the aspect of exact reciprocity, and the prefix *ant-* may well have a secondary connotation of repayment or requital, as when Aischylos uses forms of the verb *antameibesthai.* We thus see a close link with the Anaximandrian view of process as a deal between equals, a settlement that involves an equation of compensation to injury. (Here we touch on a concept of tit-for-tat that goes back to tribal life and its system of compensations, before the arrival of law proper.) To gain justice was literally to "get back the equal", as the Odyssean phrase states. To give justice was literally "to pay the equal". The same terms are used for the completion of a trading transaction (sale, barter, loan) as for the full rendering of justice. The pattern of thought was applied to all and any sequences in which one event was followed regularly by its reciprocal and was thus "exchanged" for it. Pindar used it for land that is ploughed and left fallow in turn, and for hooves that hit the ground in regular alternation. Hesiod uses it for the succession of day and night. Plato uses it for the cycle of birth and death, of waking and sleeping. Philon uses it for the cycle of the seasons. The scientific thinkers use it to bring out connections that had not been properly realised: breathing-in and breathing-out (Plato); the stretching of the lyre-string and the vibration when the string is released, or evaporation and precipitation (Aristotle). Anaximandros and Herakleitos, from different angles, extended the pattern to include all process.

We see then that among the pre-Sokratic thinkers there is in general a close and persistent link between their cosmological schemes and the developing systems of democratic government. Without the latter the schemes could not possibly have come into existence. We have only to compare them with the forms of cosmogonic thought thrown up in the societies of the Near East with their autocracies to realise that the intellectual difference is also a social one. "The naturalisation of justice transformed her status," says Vlastos, "and added immeasurably to her stature. But it also transformed nature. These 'ineluctable laws of nature', what were they prior to Milesian physics? Behind the massive stability of heaven and earth had lurked a realm of arbitrariness and terror. The uniform motions of sun and moon could be inexplicably broken by an eclipse; the fertility of earth and womb might mysteriously fail; children could be born 'unlike those who begat them, but monsters'; these and a thousand other things could be thought of as lesions in natural order, special interventions of Zeus and his instruments, vindicating the authority of the supernatural by suspending or reversing the ordinary course of nature. The adventurous reason of Ionian science charted this realm of magic, detached it from the personal control of supernatural beings, and integrated it into the domain of nature. All natural events, ordinary or extraordinary alike, were now united under a common law." We may say then that the concepts of Justice and Equality invaded the cosmological sphere, where thinkers had sought an *archē* (a beginning, also a source of authority). The concept of a single authority or power gave way to that of a struggle of opposites, guided by a principle of justice, inside the rule of law.

This achievement could only have been the work of men involved in the democratic process for the first time in history. The abolition of the distinction between two grades of being, divine and mortal, was also the abolition or weakening of the distinction between lord and commoner, king and subject. There was a basic assumption: justice could not fail to come about in a society of equals. We may cite another branch of theory in which the democratic assumption operated: the *krasis* or mixture of the seasons, developed by medical thinkers. This branch attempted to grasp and define the relation of man to his environment: on the basis of a harmony or equilibrium between environmental forces. Here a certain advance to quantitive analysis could be made by linking the balance or *isomoiria* with the equinox (when day equals night, all the hours of day and night are equal, and the sun rises at a point midway between his most northern and most southern rising-points in the year, the summer and winter solstices). The astronomical equalities here involved were taken as causing one another. The utopian Island of Iamboulos has an equinox throughout the year so as to give it the most temperate of climates. The *isomoiria* was seen as coming about through a rotation in office among the powers, as in the democratic *polis* where (as Euripides puts it) "the *demos* rules by turn". In medical theory the constitution of each season played its part in relieving or worsening diseases; the body's health depended on an orderly sequence of seasonal change, so that even good weather, if unseasonable, could be damaging and the predominances of the humours (phlegm, blood, yellow bile and so-called black bile) could be disturbed.

There is yet another way in which philosophic activity was linked with the democratic process of equalising law. The seventh century, with its rapid advance of many mercantile city-states, saw a remarkable proliferation of constitutions and legal codes all over the Greek world. It has been argued that causal analysis proper is normally preceded by ordering and classification. The classifying tendency would appear in both legal and mathematical matters. We need not accept the exact mathematical or geometric formulations which were later attributed to Thales; but the accounts are true enough in describing the kind of intellectual activity which was generated in the Ionian cities by their trading, monetary, calculating, and legal activities. Anyone who like Thales had learned a little about Babylonian geometry might easily have taken over its method of calculation with demonstration, such as is found in cuneiform texts—for example, the correct formula for the area of an isosceles triangle. Starting off with such statements, he might well have arranged the findings in a more logical order, and thus via classification have advanced towards a grasp of causal relations. In some such way the Greeks made decisive steps in generalisation, interrelating things and attempting to construct models of the world and its workings—an attempt linked at all stages with interest in the crafts and their methods.

A break, which complicated the issues, came with the end of the fifth century, with the breakdown of Athenian democracy under the weight of its inner contradictions, one of which lay in the growth of the slave-economy. Plato was the great exponent of the break in the old unitary concepts. Man is seen as divided between a spiritual element which partakes of the divine, and a bodily element which belongs in a servile way to the realm of necessity. Such a philosophic position was linked with a fierce anti-democratic outlook. Aristotle, though trying in many ways to overcome the new split in thought, succumbed to it at certain points, most obviously in his division of the universe into two sections: one made up of the familiar opposites of process, the other composed of "something beyond the bodies about us on this earth, different and separate from them, the superior honour [*timē*] of its nature being proportionate to its distance from this world of ours". So he saw two kinds of motion: the circular one of the more honourable bodies, the rectilinear one of the lower regions, imperfect and wandering. Justice and Anankē were now separated. There was no way of directly reconciling the existing world with concepts evolved in the old days of the early democratic process—though a new struggle began, carried on by Aristotle and then by the Stoics, and to some extent, in a weakened form, by the Neoplatonists.

The conventional terms in which the idea of *isonomia* was carried on appear in *On the Kosmos*: "In these greater matters nature teaches us that equality is the preserver of concord, and concord is the preserver of the kosmos." But this system now operates under the autocratic will of a deity outside process. The social imagery is kept, but changed to meet the new circumstances.

> He is established in the immoveable and moves and directs all things as and when he wishes, among the varieties of form and nature —just as the law of the city, itself immoveably established within the minds of those who observe it, disposes of the activities of the state. For in obedience to the law the magistrates go to their offices, the judges to their appropriate courts, the councillors and members of the assembly to their appointed meeting-places; and one man goes to the *prytaneion* for his meals, another to the lawcourts to defend himself, a third to prison to die. The law also ordains public feasts and annual festivals, sacrifices to the gods, cults of heroes, and libations to the dead, with other varied activities, all arising from a single ordinance or authority of the law. . . . So it is, we must suppose, with that greater city, the kosmos: God is a law to us. . . .[23]

When we come to lesser aspects of social or craft activity, the observations which are used to clarify natural process are large in number. Thus Galen argues that the kidneys exert traction in drawing in the urine. And he goes on to use the simile of a sieve letting through the wheylike (thinner serous) portion. He cites "the example of milk being made into cheese. For this too, although it's all thrown into the wicker strainers, does not all percolate through; such part as is too fine in proportion to the width of the meshes passes down and is called whey; the rest cannot get down, for the pores of the strainers won't admit it." Arguing in defence of his traction-theory and against the thesis that water is carried towards the rarefied part of the air around us, he declares that peasants, wanting to cheat with their corn-deliveries, which they bring into the town in wagons, "fill earthern jars with water and stand them among the corn, which then draws the moisture into itself through the jar and gains in bulk and weight". Yet, "if you care to set down the same vessel in the very hot sun, you'll find the daily loss to be very little indeed". So the theorists know less "about nature than do the very peasants". Dealing with organs that have to do with the disposal of nutriment, he describes their function as *oikonomia*, house-management or administration.[24]

We saw how Empedokles used the game of Catch-water. Herakleitos said: "Time is a child moving counters in a game; the royal power is a child's." Time, controlling all things, is a child at a game of chance. Here we have an important example of the notion of Time as an active force. Herakleitos uses the word Aiōn, not Chronos. Before him *aiōn* referred to a man's lifetime or to the spinal marrow which was thought at times to be the source of semen; after him it was used of the long or endless life of the gods and of Time or Life as a changer of fortunes. Aiōn was thus originally time in a specifically human sense, an originating force. Clemens identifies him here with Zeus, a typical late misunderstanding. Herakleitos rather is combining the ideas of universal formative process in its unpredictable movements and results, and of time as a seminal force perpetually begetting new and strange forms. The idea of chance or caprice would not be present except as a paradoxical overtone, reminding us how little we understand the deep processes of transformation. (We can make too much of the passage in the Indian *Vishnu Purana*, dated perhaps A.D. 500, where Time-Vishnu is said to "sport like a playful boy, as you shall learn by listening to his frolics".

There is indeed here the idea of Time as a spontaneous force bringing about all sorts of unexpected effects; but the depth of the Herakleitan aphorism is lacking—the contrast of seminal energy and complex structural results.)

Aiōn is playing a game of draughts. The imagery goes back to schemes of Zeus weighing the fates of two combatants, and of two warriors playing draughts before battle; and it leads on to the developed notion of Chance in the Hellenistic period, with the cult of Tyche. Tyche came to be used as the term for the city-guardian, its Fortune. Further, from games of chance came questions of probability, as happened later with Pascal and others—though the ancient world lacked questions coming up from insurance companies to add their pressures! Dice-games of one sort and another were immemorial. Plato in his *Lysis* tells how Sokrates goes into the palaistron on the festival of Hermes and finds young men dicing at the end of the sacrifices. Dice were marked one to six—though the *astragalos*, an ankle-bone of a sheep or goat, was also used, with four irregular surfaces, one convex, its opposite concave, one of the other two slightly shrunken, the numbers being 1, 3, 4, 6. The chances here were multiplied in comparison with the equal-sided dice. Four *astragaloi* were generally thrown together, and each of the possible combinations was given a name, often after some god or hero. In some games the highest value went to a combination of all four numbers (1, 3, 4, 6), though this was more common than a combination of the same numbers. It was however called *Basileus* and was the throw by which the Romans appointed the King of the feast. Or the highest number won (6, 6, 6, 6). No rule made the victory depend on the result of a series of throws, and we see then a lack of interest in the mathematics of chance or probability. (The rise of a theoretical interest in the seventeenth century came from the problems set by games, cards or dice, which were won by the turning-up of a certain number in each sequence of throws.) The ancient players often relied merely on quickness in throwing the wanted number, or just left the whole thing to chance, though much skill was possible, based on a variety of exercises requiring agility and accuracy of eyesight as well as speed. Plato in the *Republic*, treating the professional training of artisans, says, "No one can become a skilled dice-player if he plays only for pleasure and hasn't devoted himself to it." In the last book of his *Laws* the Athenian stresses that all details of the constitution can't be worked out ahead; in many matters a procedure of trial and error must be used: "We must take the risk of throwing 3 times or 6 or 3 times 1." Aristotle remarks, "It is difficult to succeed at many things or many times, for example, to repeat the same throw ten thousand times with the dice would be impossible, while to make it once or twice is comparatively easy". This seems the nearest to an attempt to find a quantitative formula on probability, though we know that, at least later, there were treatises on the subject of dicing, including one by the emperor Claudius, and these must have gone much further than Aristotle does.

An outlook largely based on a desire for clearcut geometrical results distrusted all theories of probability as suggesting a failure in the rule of law. Indeed, one reason why Plato despised all the natural sciences was that they seemed full of uncertainty and conjecture. "I know that arguments based on probability are like cheats, and, if not treated with care, may well mislead us, alike in geometry and in everything else." Aristotle agreed that he was right in calling natural science the doctrine of the probable, and found real proof only from "sure primary principles and sure primary causes. But that doesn't mean we should dismiss those sciences as worthless, only that we should be satisfied with what is to our advantage and within our power." Simplikios adds that Theophrastos held the same views. The latter began to develop the hypothetical syllogism; and Stoic logic in turn was much concerned with hypothetical and disjunctive sentences—if *a*, then *b*; if *a*, then *b* or *c*. These syllogisms had a steadily wider effect in all fields. The Stoics with a clear concept of Fate found trouble with the concept of the possible; and the scientific question merged with moral and psychological ones of predestination and freewill. Refuge was found in the definition of possible events as "those which are not prevented from happening": which shows them on the first steps to the modern idea of probability.[25]

Though the question belongs more to the field of religion than that of science, we may glance at the origins of the idea of a creative or sustaining word in the universe; for here we touch on one of the sources for the concept of universal law. Further, only by understanding something of this matter, can we grasp the development of the word *logos* in Greek. First, then, there is the point that the fullgrown idea of a God who has created the universe can only arrive after (*a*) a fairly high degree of craftsmanship has been reached, involving techniques that shape objects and bring about transformations in the materials used, as in pottery and metallurgy; (*b*) a considerable degree of state centralisation has been attained. In Homer we find no hint of a Greator God. But theogonies of the Near-Eastern type must have been known; and we see their invasion and acclimatisation of the Hesiodic *Theogony*. For a definite elaboration of theology, as distinct from mythological schemes, which can become complex and extended, we need a high degree of intellectual abstraction, involving social division, the growth of a monetary system, and an expansion of mathematics.

One does not mean that all the necessary elements had to be present at the same place or time. After getting rid of the kingship, the Greeks lacked rulers of supreme power who could become the earthly representative or surrogate of a dominant father-god around whom gathered creative functions and who could in due time emerge as the great or sole power in the universe. But, on the one hand, the state was being strongly built-up in the mercantile areas, with law as its unifying factor; and on the other hand ideas were flowing in from regions where the kingship flourished—ideas which fused with those born from a different kind of centralisation.

To turn from the Greeks to the Hebrews. Here we have a people who, except for a fairly brief period under David and Solomon (when no strong imperial power was active in the Near East), did not have a powerful state with a supreme ruler, and who did not own anything at all like Greek mathematics, art, poetry, philosophy, science. Yet ideas and influences moved in from all around and merged with certain strong forces of resistance (often connected with tribal or bedouin ideas about the indivisibility of the land as the heritage of the whole people). The result was the tenacious dream of a come-back, a revival of Davidian power, which powerfully internalised the concept of unity and created Jewish monotheism as it appeared in historical times, from about the sixth–fifth centuries B.C. In the case of the Greeks the complexity of factors prevented any simple monotheism developing and brought about instead the rich unitary concept of natural process, of which man was a part, in the thinkers from Thales to Herakleitos.

We can learn much about the way the concept of a supreme creator-god developed by turning to Egypt. An early stage is represented by the papyrus of Nesi-Amsu, written down about 311 B.C., but in many parts going back to the early years of the Old Kingdom. The tale is recited by Neb-er-Djer, Lord-to-the-Limit, a name of the Sungod of Heliopolis. The all-powerful deity, alone existent, has to create the lesser gods, the universe, mankind, from his own excreta. "I thrust my penis into my closed hand, I made my seed spirt into my hand, I poured it into my mouth, I shat and produced Shu [Air], I pissed and produced Tefnut [Sky]. Thus, I became from One God Three Gods", a Trinity. Neb-er-Djer also declares: "I created multitudes of creation, which came forth from my mouth," and "I laid a foundation in my own heart." These last two statements bring in the word of the mouth and the thought of the heart, and are probably later formulations. The antiquity of the other statements, in which the god produces the universe materially from his own body and its functioning, is proved by a pyramid text: "Atum is he who came into being, who masturbated in On. He took his penis in his grasp so that he might create orgasm by it, and so were born the twins Shu and Tefnut."[26]

Later, as the treatment of the myth became more abstract or spiritualised, the excreta of the god were described as effluences or forces emitted by him. In a hymn to Ptah of Memphis, where the god's titles are those given to him by the priests of the nineteenth and twenties dynasties, we find the physical aspects toned down and stress laid on the word of the mouth:

> You built up your own members and fashioned your body when the heavens and the earth were unmade, and when the waters had not yet come forth. You knitted the earth together, you assembled your members, you embraced your body, and you found yourself in the condition of the One who made his seat and who moulded the Two Lands. You had no father to beget you and no mother to give you birth. You fashioned yourself without the help of any other being and you came forth fully equipped. . . . The words come forth from your nostrils, and the celestial waters from your mouth, and the staff of life [grain] comes forth on your back. . . . You are the moulder of gods and men and everything which is produced.

A slab from Ptah's great temple shows a further stage of abstraction. Ptah begot himself. As the result of a thought he produced Temu (Atem, the Setting Sun), and through his tongue Thoth came to him.

> His heart and tongue gain power over all the other members of the divine company, and he, Ptah, is the heart in every body, the tongue in the mouths of all gods, all men, all cattle, all creeping things; and by thinking with his heart and commanding with his tongue, he makes all living things live according to his will. The Nine Gods of Ptah are before him as teeth and lips. The teeth are the seed and the lips are the hands of Ptah. [We see how the old imagery has been bowdlerised.] The Nine Gods of Temu exist through the seed and fingers of Ptah. They are the teeth and the lips of this mouth which gives names to all things, and from which Shu and Tefnut have gone forth. The Nine Gods have created the sight for the eyes, the hearing for the ears, and the breath for the nose, so that they may make announcements to the heart. The heart it is that arranges for every piece of information to come forth, and it is the tongue which reproduces what the heart has thought out. And so Kau [male] spirits were made, and the Hesmut [female] spirits were ordained, through the decrees which were thought out by the heart, and have come forth by the tongue, and they create all food and all provisions. And thus all handicrafts and all works are done—the working of the arms, the walking of the legs, the movements of the limbs—according to the decree which is decided upon by the heart and brought forth by the tongue, and which makes the significance of all things.

Ptah who created all things by thought and word (supplanting seed and fingers) was also a god of the crafts and their practitioners. He invented all the crafts and craftsmen came under his protection. His highpriest bore the title Lord of the Master-Craftsmen; he himself was identified by the Greeks with Hephaistos. He is represented as a stumpy dwarf, as are the goldsmiths and stone-setters of Memphis. A scrap of dialogue runs: "Hurry up with the necklace, it should be finished by now." "As Ptah loves me, I want to finish it today." In the hymn Ptah was described as "moulding" gods and men: which may refer to forming figures out of clay or to the work of a potter. (Khnum of Elephantine, later transferred to Abydos, was a creator-god who made men on the potters-wheel, with the aid of his wife Heqet.)[27]

We may further note the special relation to Thoth, moongod

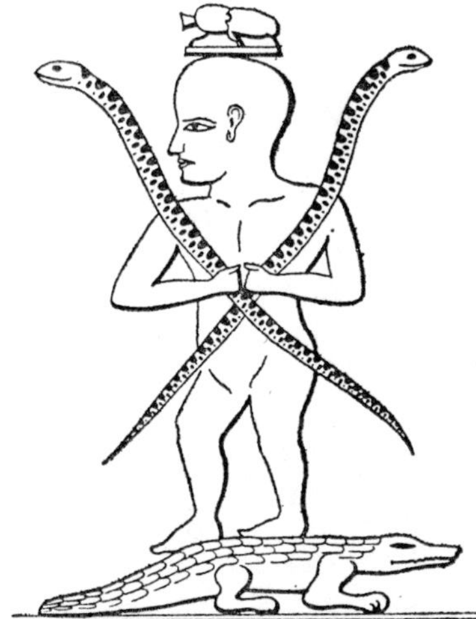

20. Ptah in two forms: as guardian of one of the Arits (regions) of Osiris (Papyrus of Ani), and as Ptah of the Magicians, lord of all primal and creative matter, and master of the great serpent gods of Upper and Lower Egypt (Budge, *From Fetish* 158)

with ibishead, who had charge over all intellectual pursuits, the invention of writing, the separation of languages, the recording of annals and laws. He was the god of the scribes; he made calculations, had command over figures (the reckoning of times) and the divisions of the year, and was depicted, pen and palette in hand, as Clerk of the Court at the weighing of the dead man's heart. He was master of hieroglyphs and divine words, and thus was a magician, the patron of magicians; and as well as being the Tongue of Ptah he was called the Heart of Re. He was thus the Word and the Son of the Creator-god—just as later the Greek *Logos* became the creative word of the supreme god in Judaeo-Greek thought, and finally the Son of God for the Christians, the incarnation of the word that was in the beginning.

An amusing offshoot of the ancient idea of the creator-god masturbating is to be found in grotesque figure, used for apotropais purposes in the Hellenistic and Roman periods. He seems a late form of the god Bes, to whom are added all sorts of apotropaic symbols. He shows a big grimacing head, several arms, four wings and a bird's tail, an aureole of seven animal-heads, a large out-

21. The Allgod or Pantheos of the Magicians, who made in himself the powers and forms of the main cosmic gods; inside the snake (Ouroboros) on which he stands are all the great Typhonic creatures: Leyden Mus. (Hopfner, *Ae id.* 311)

standing penis, eyes all over his body, and masks of lions on his knees. On two amulets a balance hangs at the end of his horizontal penis; on others the lapidary has replaced the penis by the beam of the balance. The explanation lies in a complicated pun. The word used in the Pyramid texts for the creator-god grasping his penis is *iws,' w*—while one of the names for the balance, attested from the Middle Kingdom is *iwsw*. Further, the goddess Iousâas who personifies the hand of the creator-god in the act of grasping his organ to produce the necessary orgasm, in late times would have had her name pronounced very like *iwsw*. Hence the way in which the god's organ, in the moment of its creativeness, is identified with the balance. It is hard to know how much of theory was based on this type of pun, which was felt to be magically potent; but it is possible that the learned folk who worked out the symbolism of the amulets and the spells, may have argued that the act of bringing into existence the material universe was accompanied by a further act which ensured the balance of the elements. Anyhow, in an odd transcendental form we have here the Greek idea of the physical universe, by its very nature, ensuring an ultimate balance in its moving and changing ingredients.

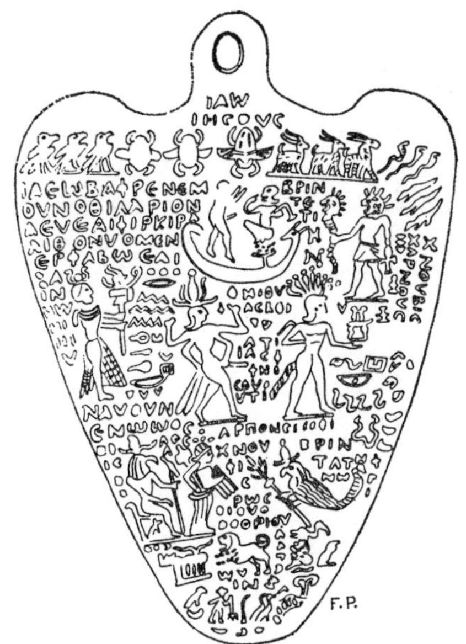

22. The onanistic creative Act of Atum (Petrie, *Amulets* pl. 49)

The abstraction of creative or directive power as the word could only come about after the centralisation of political controls in the person of a supreme ruler who, from the recesses of his awe-inspiring palace, sends out his irresistible commands and dominates the whole life of a people. Because Egypt for a number of reasons, including its geographical position and shape, was able to build the first effective and durable monarchy, we find there the complex development of the figure of the one creator-god. A sophisticated version of the supreme god as the hidden king issuing his words of command appears in *On the Kosmos*. The author bases his account on the Persian Great King of the sixth-fifth centuries and draws much on the Heroditean picture of Dareios' palace at Ekbatana. The king, who symbolises the god, he says, lived in Sousa or Ekbatana, "invisible to all, in a marvellous palace, with a surrounding wall flashing with gold, elektron, ivory. It had a succession of many gate-towers, and the gateways, separated by many stades from one another, were fortified with brazen doors and high walls; outside these the leaders and most eminent men were drawn up in order. . . ." He goes on at lengthy detail to describe how the ruler from his hidden place of power issues his words of command, as does God on "the loftiest crest", and how these words are carried stage by stage into the world where their instructions are put into action. Thus the world is kept in its due order and activity. (The account leads on to the comparison of god with the operator who works a single release-mechanism.)

But though the Word as all-powerful command did not function in the Greek city-state as in the autocratic kingdoms, as part of the split between theory and practice, freedom and slavery, mind and body, the Word as the instrument of persuasion (in poetry, political or legal speech, philosophic discussion) had a very high place. It has been well remarked, "only the tongue was inspired by the gods, never the hand" (Zilsel); and so the Word, the messenger or angel of the mind and tongue, owned a special potence. In Homer *logos* meant simply something spoken, word, talk. But because of the central importance of the spoken word in Greek culture, *logos* came to refer to the powers of thought which it made possible, the system of reasoning by which men organised their thoughts. In Pindar we find it used for rule, principle, law, for proverb and oracle. It took on the sense of relation, correspondence, proportion, ratio; and at least by Herodotos (but doubtless much earlier) it stood for computation, reckoning of moneys handled—as later it meant a banking account and public accounts. By the time of Aristophanes and Plato it was used for plea or case in law, and Plato used it for thesis or hypothesis. Already by the time of Herakleitos it had come to mean the reason or ground of things and processes, and Plato carried on the meaning of an intelligible system as revealed in the world-process. The Stoics deepened afresh the Herakleitan concept of the *logos*.

In all this development *logos* is directly linked with human life and natural process; it expresses various aspects of human reasoning, of the sense of relations and proportions, and also of the intelligible structure of things, events, processes. True, strains develop inside its application, and especially from Plato onwards there is the tendency to equate the "intelligible" with a non-material otherworld. But it is only with the breakdown of the old free city-state, the re-emergence of the kingship after Alexander the Great, the deepening of class-divisions and the vast increase of a sense of helplessness among the commonfolk, the producers, that the *logos* becomes entirely an otherworldly and transcendental force or substance. With the *Septuagint* it turns into the Word of Wisdom of God, personified as his agent in creation and in maintaining world-order. With the *New Testament* it is identified with Christ.[28]

We have seen in this chapter that Greek thinkers made many observations direct from nature, which were of great importance; yet they also drew largely on the methods and products of the crafts in order to understand and explain natural process. They saw the crafts in fact as a reflection or extension of such process; and they explained the latter by models based on craftwork. But at the same time they drew crucially on their social and political world, on their understandings or intuitions of its relations and forces, for the fundamental generalisations through which they ordered their material. And this was not just a matter of society in a general way; it was a matter of a very specific society, its forms and forces—the first democratic society in history, evolved through reconstructions and transformations of tribal bases without any recourse to kingship and organised priesthoods. The social process man saw in the universe was democratic process with its effort to create equality before and in the law as a binding force.

As a result there were certain relative elements in the thought, but we must repeat that the thought is not thereby simply reducible to its social bases. As Parmenides said: "Thinking and Being are the same thing." Thinking expresses the being of the thinker, and that being is at once both in nature and in society: a product of those two spheres, which are dialectically one. "Just thought" in this relation is thought which fuses both nature and society without distorting their connection, their differences and their ultimate unity. The "freedom" and the "equality" which men are experiencing for the first time in the life of settled and developed communities are the keys to an understanding of the simple and yet complex relations active within natural process.

I have not attempted to classify the various ways in which the image or comparison worked to stimulate ancient thought. Clearly some analogies came up as momentarily illuminating a particular problem without any evident relation to an interconnected system. But others struck deep and may be said to underlie the whole movement of thought: to provide its centres of organisation, its essential structures. From nature men took their observations of evaporation and its related processes to explain material changes in quality and composition; and those of fire,

23. Slaves digging for potter's clay (Corinthian plaque of seventh to sixth centuries)

of wind and water, to develop a concept of natural force—with the storm, the typhoon, the tornado, the burst of thunder and lightning as the culminating revelation. They saw in the universe their own democratic struggle for equality within the unifying law; and they saw in their own crafts and creative activities the same formative processes as operated universally in nature. When we realise that it was under these four main headings that they grouped and organised their thoughts about the universe and nature, we can see how the lesser and passing images or analogies have their link with the larger patterns and help to compose a coherent system of thinking. The emphases or interpretations varied strongly, but in the last resort they went on inside certain shared perspectives. Plato, who had hated democracy, was as affected by those perspectives as were the men who had helped to build the early city-states, whatever different twists or interpretations he gave to the common stock of ideas, images, and symbols, or however he developed their inner conflicts as well as their traditional meanings.

The Dangerous Moment

IX

We have been considering how the thinkers used and interpreted craft-activities, but we know little of what the craftsmen themselves thought about their work and its processes. There is however one interesting document, a poem which is certainly a craft-spell; and we shall look at it in some detail for the help it gives us to get right inside the craft-world. In a *Life of Homer*, attributed without authority to Herodotos, there occur several epigrams which the poet is said to have composed, and the spell is one of these. The *Life* itself is often dated to the second or third century A.D., when it was fashionable to imitate the Herodotean style and dialect; but it has been pointed out that the diction here is quite unlike that of the Roman pastiches. Much of it is Hellenistic, and there is an Ionic element which seems derived from the sources used by the compiler: one or more chapbooks on Homer and his life. The compiler put the material together in an attempt to modernise it, and his most likely date lies between 150 and 80 B.C. Some of the epigrams have traditional folk-material: one is a harvest quête-song. However, Homer is depicted as extemporising the dactylic hexameters at various places that he visits in his wanderings. Our craft-spell was attributed to Hesiod for no clear reason by Julius Pollux of Naukratis, Greek grammarian of the later second century A.D., who was given the chair of rhetoric at Athens by the emperor Commodus—for his mellifluous voice, university gossip declared, not for his academic merits.[1]

The *Life* states that while on Samos Homer saw some potters firing a kiln packed with fine vases. They had heard that he was a clever fellow, so they offered to give him some of the vases if he sang for them. So he sang the spell. The author of the *Life* then moves on to the next Samian episode and does not represent the poem as a begging song. The attributions to Homer or Hesiod have no value; the work is certainly a traditional craft-spell. And we cannot trust its location on Samos. There are some non-Ionian elements in the diction; and Samos may have been chosen as the site because of its fame as a ceramic centre. From 200 B.C. to the fourth century A.D. the term Samian Vase occurs in Latin literature: merely, it seems, a cant term for clay vessels as distinct from metal ones. In the seventh century, Isidore of Seville attributes the invention of clay vases to Samos. Athens has been suggested as a better site; but the only supporting arguments are two points of scansion and the fact that there were large numbers of potters in the Kerameikos. Still, Athens remained a centre of fine vase-production for centuries longer than any other ancient Greek site, and so an old craft-spell may well have been preserved there. Here then is the poem:

If, potters, you will pay me for my song,
then come, Athena, hold your hand out over the kiln.
May the pots and all the dishes turn a good black,
be all well-fired and fetching the asked price,
many sold in the market, many sold on the roads,
bringing lots of money, and may my song be pleasing.
But if you potters turn shameless and deceive me,
then I conjure up the ravagers of kilns:
Smasher, Crasher, Unquenchable, Shaker-to-Bits,
and Defeater-of-the-Unbaked, who much trouble the craft.
Stamp on stoking tunnel and chambers, let all the kiln
be thrown in confusion, while loud the potters wail.
As a horse-jaw grinds, so may the kiln be grinding
to powder all the pots stowed there within it.
Come too, Circe of many spells, Sun's daughter,
cast relentless spells, harm them and their craftwork.
And you too, Cheiron, come with hordes of Centaurs,
those who fled from Herakles' hands and those who died.
Trample the pots, kick the collapsing kiln.
And let the potters wail as they watch the villainy,
but I'll rejoice at the sight of their luckless craft.
If one of them stoops to look in the spyhole, let
his face be scorched, so all may learn just dealings.

In line 3 there is a variant reading: "may they turn out well"; but the reference to black glaze would represent the original text. In the second or possibly late third century redware (the so-called Pergamene or Sigillata) was brought in, and in the first two centuries A.D. became generally popular. Hence Pollux has the variant reading. The wares are *kanastra* and *kotyloi*. Hesychios defines the first as "a terracotta vase, a bowl, a basket". An inscription from Lebena, Crete, dated to second century, uses the word for a vase: "This is the *kanasthon* of Artomon." Probably the writer was a bad speller, and should have written: "*Kanastron* of Artemon." Basket was probably the original mean-

24. Greek potter at wheel, attaching a handle (sixth century vase, B.M.)

ing, then the term was applied to vases of the same shape—not to cups, as Pollux mentions *kanastra* with dishes in which food was served. He also calls them "wide-open" or "spread-out", like *phialai*: a description that fits the shallow bowls or one-handlers. The date of this latter type of vase seems to be from about 520 B.C. on till near the end of the fourth century; so a date of between 520 and 325 is possible, with the site Athens; but the archaic period, say 520–480, seems more likely. When one-handlers went out, another name was needed in the chant. No doubt various substitutes for *kanastra* were found; in time what was put in was "very sacred things". The original term, however, seems to have survived in some written text; in the fifth to fourth centuries Athens was the centre of the book-trade (if we may use that term for the circulation of written copies of compositions). Pollux keeps *kanastra*; the *Life* and the *Souda* give us *mal' hira* or *hiera*.[2]

In lines 13–14 we meet the image of the horse-jaws chewing, champing, grinding up the pots. If a vase explodes in a kiln, it is liable to be reduced to powder. The lines remind us of the proverb: "The mills of the gods grind slowly, but they grind extremely small"—that is, to powder. If the spyhole was suddenly opened when the kiln was fired under reducing conditions (with a lack of oxygen inside), there could easily be a delayed burst of blue flame, which could burn a careless potter.

There is no mention in the spell of any invocation to *help* the potters, except that Athena is called on to come if the potters pay the singer. In the Roman world, however, we are told that the potters, when removing pots from the kiln, called on the

25. Athena paying a visit to an Athenian pottery in mid-fifth century B.C.; note female vasepainter

firegod Vulcan three times to save their pots from cracking as they cooled. (A master of ceramics in Etruscan Veii was called Volca, which may be a sort of corporate surname given to a man because of his craft. Volcanus was the more correct spelling of the god's name, with his festival Volcanalia on 23 August. So the name Volca suggests some close relation of craftsman to the god, no doubt through a craft-fraternity.)

The key-part of our charm lies in the names of the five destructive demons, each of which has his own function: Smasher, *Syntrips*, breaks the pots up; Shaker, *Sabaktes*, brings a whole stack down when the lowest one is weakened; Crasher, *Smaragdos*, is the demon who makes the pots burst in the kiln as they're being fired; *Asbestos* is the one who raised the temperature too high; *Omodamos* causes damage while the pots are still unfired. (The interpretation that he strains or harms the shoulder, *ōmos*, of the potter is unlikely.) Unfired pots can crack or sag while drying; but as all the other demons operate inside the kiln as firing goes on, Omodamos must do his work there as well. The explanation of his name is given by Aristotle in *Meteorologika* where he discusses the term *ōmotēs*. He says that substances which are capable of being mastered by heat and of thus gaining consistency, but which have not yet been so affected, are called *ōma*; and he cites potters' clay among his examples. Later he remarks that compounds of earth and water are hardened and made more dense both by fire and cold, and that many substances which have been made hard or dense by cold become moist at first (that is, when they're heated) as does potters' clay. That clay at the start of firing steams and grows softer; as a result it can become distorted in the kilns. Such distortion, then, we may take as the work of Omodamos.

Against this interpretation it has been argued that the general disaster mentioned in lines 11–14 could hardly be the work of this demon. The clay or mud with which Greek kilns were mainly, sometimes wholly, built would have been baked at the first firing and so be safe from Omodamos. But we may reply that the song-charm was meant for the firing of a new kiln, or for the first firing at the end of the rainy season when the kiln was new or repaired. The potter's craft in ancient as in modern Greece would have been seasonal, with winter rains damaging or breaking down many kilns. Also, potters no doubt smeared fresh clay over cracks that showed up during the dry season, and the song would again be considered useful.[3]

Omodamos then is a demon who can wreck individual pots or the whole kiln, which is described as consisting of *pyraithousa* and *domata*. *Domata* refers to the upper and lower chambers, but the first word is not found elsewhere; it is made up of *pyr*, fire, and what seems the participle of the verb *aithein*, to kindle, sometimes to blaze. There is no other example of such a word signifying the place where something is done. We should expect some such term as *pyraitheion*, which is used of Persian fire-temples. *Pyraithousa* is then best taken as meaning fire-porch; for in Homeric diction *aithousa* means porch. In the representations of kilns on votive tablets from Penteskouphia, the stoking tunnel, open in front and closed on top and sides, has the form of a rude porch.

Lines 15–18 are more sophisticated than those dealing with the demons and may well be the work of a later poet, perhaps of the Hellenistic period when learned allusions to local myths were the mode. They do, however, have their interest, Circe (Kirkē) may seem an odd figure to be brought in; but as the haloed daughter of the Sun she may have been thought a controller of heat, and her name means Circle or Ring. *Kirkos* was a kind of hawk or falcon, apparently noticed for its circling flight. *Krikos* was the common prose form, though *kirkos* reappears in the Latin *Circus* with its circular form and round-and-round

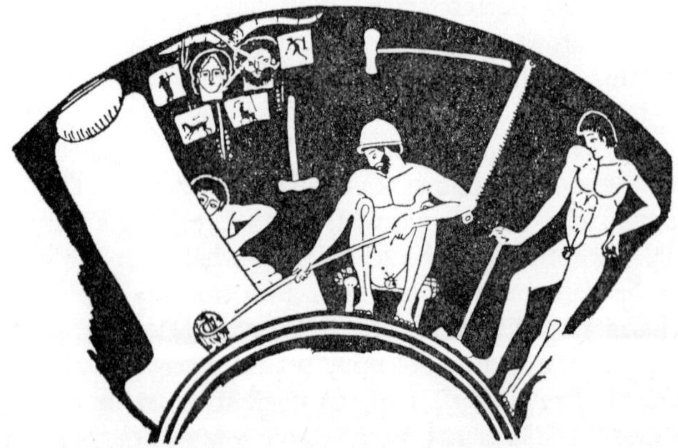

26. Men at a forge with apotropaic masks: redfigured Attic cup

movement of races. *Krikos* had its craft-senses, e.g. as ring of a spanner, a ring bolt, a hoop. The kiln was rounded or oval in shape, so Kirkē may have been taken as presiding deity of its shape and its heat-transformations. She was famous as a witch with transformative powers.[4]

Circe, the circle or circler, may also have some connection with the potters' wheel. Homer, in a simile for the maze-dance, speaks of the potter "sitting by his wheel that fits between his hands, and making trial of it to see if it will run". Legends attributed the invention of the wheel to Talos, son of the sister of Daidalos, to Anarchasis the Skythian, to Hyberbios the Corinthian, and to an unknown inhabitant of Marathon, while an Athenian, Koroibos, was said to have invented earthen pots. The wheel was a heavy strong disk of wood, terracotta, or stone, some two feet in diameter; on the underside a socket fitted over a low fixed pivot. The wheel was balanced to run true, without vibration or wobble. Usually a boy turned it by hand, adjusting the speed at command of the potter; some wheels had notches round the edge for a firm grip. Once the wheel got going, its weight and size gave ample momentum. The potter had both hands free for work, and the wheel provided the energy which he directed. Men did the throwing, as women were not considered the right persons for operating machinery—though at times they painted pots. On a redfigured hydria we see four painters: a man, two lads, a woman. Athena is visiting the studio with a garland, while Victories hold garlands over the heads of the lads.

The other mythological characters brought in are the Centaurs. Generally they were all said to have been killed by Herakles, including the wise Cheiron. Apollodoros, however, says that survivors "fled in different directions. Some came to Mt. Malea, and Eurytion to Pholoe, and Nessos to the river Euenos. The rest were received by Poseidon at Eleusis and hidden in a mountain." Eleusis here seems a Lakonian site, not the mystery-centre in Attika. The Lakonian basis of the myth is supported by the fact that Cheiron at the time of the pursuit is said to have been living in Malea. The only trace of a cult of Cheiron, however, is in an inscription on Thera, an island that the Lakedaimonians claimed to have colonised. Herakles above all represented the young-man-initiate as the triumphant hero of ordeals; but he early took on the character of a culture-hero, liberator and toiler,

27. Herakles attacking drunken Centaurs in the Cave of Pholos: early sixth century skyphos in Louvre (*J.H.S.* pl. 2)

working at such tasks as cleaning the Augean stables and killing off destructive monsters. One line of tradition further made him an Idaian Daktyl. The Daktyls (Fingers) were spirit-attendants, *daimones*, of the Great Mother, who, like the Telchines, were smelters and workers in iron. Herakles thus also had his aspect as craft-guardian; and he was in general opposed to the Centaurs as the civilising hero against the wildmen of the forest. Pindar in dealing with Cheiron still identified *Kentauros* with *Phēr*, Wildman. In the *Iliad* it is the hero Peirithoos who destroys the creatures: "He exacted vengeance on the shaggy Wildmen and drove them from Pelion to the Aithikes." Again we are told: "Mightiest were they [Kaineus and Dryas], and with the mightiest they fought, with the mountain-haunting Wildmen." In the *Odyssey* the Centaurs are opposed to mankind as uncivilised beings, as are the Kyklopes.

The irruption of the Centaurs into the pottery as they escape from Herakles thus represents a barbarous shattering of the craft-processes that have made men human. In the tales the Centaurs were sent mad by drinking wine (which only civilised men, under the controls and releases of the Dionysiac cult, could afford to imbibe); e.g. when Herakles was in the cave of Pholos or when they tried to ravish the bride of Peirithoos during his marriage.

Yet these wild creatures also had their link with craft-processes. The Satyrs came to represent not only the free forces of nature but also the fettered forces of production in a world of slavery and exploitation. In the *Kyklops* of Euripides the satyr carries out agricultural labour; in Aischylos' Promethean satyr-play he is associated with the discovery of metallurgy; in the *Ichneutai* of Sophokles the satyr-chorus are slaves—perhaps of Dionysos; but in effect they belong to the groups to whom Apollo promises reward if they find his cattle: "any shepherd, farmer, charcoal-burner, or nymphborn wildman of the mountain". In the *Amykos* of Sophokles they again are slaves, who in the end are freed. Other plays show them as helots, harvesters, slave-workers. An epigram describes them as chained slaves in the smithgod's forge; and the motif of a satyr-dance to express some new invention or technical development (wine, fire, lyre) brings out their important relation to productive activity.

The craftsman nature of the satyrs intrudes even in a basic fertility scene such as that of the rise of the earth-maiden up out of the earth (the underworld) in the spring. Satyrs are often shown helping the earth to break open, and they do it with heavy hammers, not with some object snatched up from the world of nature. Their rôle here as craftsmen is brought out by the analagous scene of the birth of Athena from the head of Zeus, where the cleaver who breaks open the head to aid the emergence of the goddess is Hephaistos the smithgod, Palamaon, Hermes, or Prometheus. The latter as giver of fire to men was closely linked with the crafts that used fire in transformative process, potters and smiths. Palamaon has been taken as a form of Hephaistos but may merely be one of his *daimones.* (Here the craft-tool merges with the ritual weapon, the double-axe of thunderbolt earth-impregnation.)

The Kyklopes were mythical metallurgists as well as builders of megalithic structures; in the *Odyssey* they are primitive cave-

28. Pandora as Earth-Maiden rising up with Satyrs cleaving the Earth: blackfigured vase (Lenormant de Witte, *Élite des mons. céramographiques* i pl. 52)

dwellers with a pastoral economy. Hesiod tells us that they "equipped Zeus with his thunderbolt; they were the first skilled manual workers, who taught Hephaistos and Athena all the techniques of fine workmanship, such as is wrought under the sky". The Kēres, spirits of doom and death, were regarded as Telchines, who, we noted, were connected with metallurgy: "the first workers to succeed in working iron and copper, since tradition makes the Sickle of Kronos a work of the Telchines" (Strabon).[5]

Cheiron became an emblem of the figure who handed on traditional lores (which would include techniques and craft-spells) to the initiate during his period of withdrawal from normal life—a period in which, in one sense, he went off into the free life of nature, nature being in turn identified with the sphere of the ancestral spirits. Cheiron thus was tutor in his cave to the archetypal hero, Achilles. He had mantic powers; e.g. he told his grandson Peleus how to gain the shape-changing Thetis. He was linked with Prometheus; when struck accidentally by one of Herakles' poisoned arrows he decided to give his immortality to the latter. His link with initiation is brought out by the fact that he was ancestor or legendary president of the family or clan (craft-fraternity) of the Cheironidai, who lived in the region of Magnesia, famed for their lore in medicine and claiming to be his descendants.

There is thus an interesting duality about Cheiron and the other semi-animal figures, as also about the mythical fraternities, the Telchines, Daktyls, Kouretai, who are linked with the cult of the Great Mother. They symbolise the wild and destructive forces of uncontrolled nature, and yet at the same time they are the founders of the main craft-systems, which control and transform nature. So in a way they are seen as doubly fettered. As natural forces they have been taken over and given a new direction by man the producer: and as man the producer they have been reduced to slavery and subjection. The same duality appears in the *daimones* of the Great Mother, who in some aspects are dangerous and malevolent, but in other aspects are her faithful and rejoicing servants, spirits of fertility and of all that enhances life.[6]

In the charm-chant they appear in their destructive guise, since the mechanism of control has broken down. They thus represent the critical moments of change in craft-process—moments which

29. Terracotta plaque from Pheidias' workshop at Olympia: two craftsmen with an apotropaic Herm

can result in a new unity and the factors being transformed, but which, if things go wrong, explode in destruction.

The ambivalence of the *daimōn* as aider and destroyer is well brought out in the apotropaic masks hung in the pottery, on the kilns themselves, on ovens; e.g. a portable one now in the Museum at Athens. Masks were set over the entrance to the pottery so as to keep out all hostile influences; and masks were modelled on the upper sections of ovens, turned to face inwards, over the holes where the fire spurts out. In such an oven we find three masks guarding and controlling the fire-exit. The types of guardian-masks vary. We meet Satyrs with long beards and upstanding ears and hair; the expression seems one of wild fear, to ward off what is feared, but it may be meant merely to look grim and forbidding. Again we meet Kyklopes, with typical worker's caps, tall and conical, and with thunderbolts, their products at the forge, on either side. (Satyrs and Centaurs were closely related; they are found interchanged as types on coins of Makedon in the sixth–fifth centuries. Nonnos a thousand years later recorded this tradition: "The centaurs are of the same race as the shaggy satyrs.") So we find in the masks the *daimones* set on guard who are conjured up in the spell-poem as destroyers. On an Attic vase a pottery is shown; the kiln is being prepared for firing, and over it hangs a satyr-mask. A young man stokes the kiln, while another man approaches with a load of fuel on his shoulders. The owner or foreman, overseeing the work, strolls about with his staff.

The terracotta constructions on which the masks appear may have been braziers as well as ovens. By projecting inwards, the long solid beards could support pots or other utensils. Such objects are found all round the Mediterranean, but cluster on the coast of Asia Minor, at Halikarnassos, on Delos, and at Naukratis. They largely date from the third century B.C. and may have come from a single manufacturing centre, such as Delos. The bearded head is the typical form of the mask-support, with conical cap or ivy wreath; but at times we find depicted on squarish panels goats, oxen, Sirius, thunderbolts, rosettes. The masks or symbols were set on guard over the transformative moments of boiling or baking as well as over those of pot-making.[7]

A scholiast of Aristophanes' *Birds* tells us that figurines of

30. Portable ovens or braziers with apotropaic masks (J.H., *Proleg.* 189)

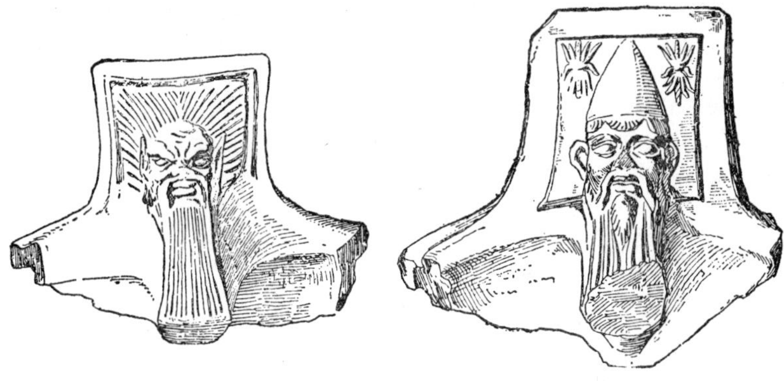

31. More oven-masks

wood or terracotta, representing Hephaistos, were put by a chimney "to watch over the fire". Pollux, commenting on a lost comedy, mentions "the amulet that the smiths put on the chimney", and adds that it was the custom to hang there some obscenely ridiculous object to turn away the evil eye. Another commentator describes a *baskanion* as "a figure in a man's form, summarily recalling its human nature, which artisans hang before their workships to ward from their work the risk of the evil eye". Some notion of these objects is given by necklets made up of amulets; we see threaded there objects in the form of animals, horns, hands making insulting gestures, rather schematic phallic shapes, dwarfs, pygmies, hunchbacks. The fabulist Aisop is said to have been a hunchback, at the sight of whom the other slaves cried out that "their master had acquired a *probaskanion* for them all". A deformity was considered to have the power to drive away the influence of the evil eye. The term "evil eye" here may be taken to mean any malign or destructive force or potence. A terracotta plaque from Pheidias' workshop at Olympia shows two artisans with a herm (a statue with head and block as body) between them, apparently meant to protect their work.[8]

The dwarf-figures remind us of the god Ptah, whom we noticed as a craftsman-creator god of Memphis in Egypt and who was identified by the Greeks with Hephaistos. Herodotos tells how the Persian king Kambyses, on entering the god's temple at Memphis, jeered at his statue. "The statue closely resembles the Pataikoi which the Phoinikians carry about on the prows of their warships—but I'd make it clearer to anyone who's never seen these if I said that it was like a pygmy. He also entered the temple of Kabeiroi, which no one but the priest is allowed to do, made fun of the images there (they resemble those of Hephaistos and are supposed to be his sons), and actually burnt them."

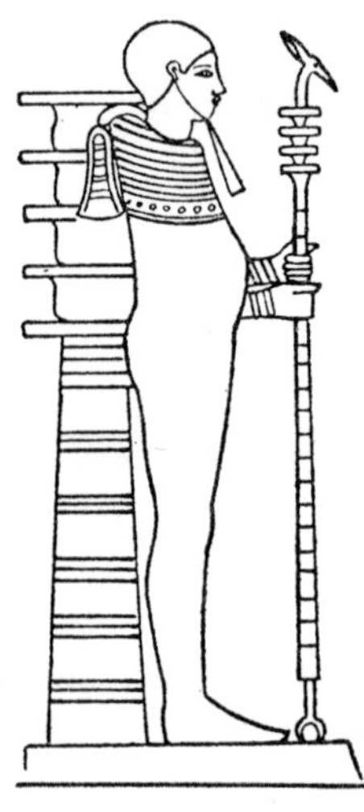

32. Ptah of Memphis in predynastic form standing by the tree of new life and creative energy; he stands on an object representing the measuring reed of a workman (Budge 13)

For the Kyklopes as bogeymen instead of guardians we have an account by Kallimachos in his *Hymn to Artemis*. The goddess visits the volcanic smithy on Lipara, where the Kyklopes are "at the anvils of Hephaistos, standing round a molten mass of iron". They are making a horse-trough for Poseidon. "They lifted their hammers above their shoulders and struck with rhythmic swing the bronze glowing from the furnace, or iron, strongly labouring." The Okeanids are scared.

33. Dwarf goldsmiths (resembling the Kabeiroi, or sons of Ptah) who seem a special feature of the Memphite workshops: Tomb of Merruka

No shame to them. Not even the daughters of the Blessed
look on them without a shudder, though long they've ceased
to be children. But when one of the girls disobeys her mother,
the mother calls the Kyklopes to her child, Arges
or Steropes, and Hermes comes out from the house,
his face rubbed with burnt ashes. And so he plays bogey
and the child runs in to her mother's lap, with her hands over her eyes.[9]

We see then that the masks or figurines used by craftsmen belong to a wide series of grotesques in bronze or terracotta, which were made as *baskania* rather than as genre-pieces or portraits of comic actors. These hunchbacks, these baldheaded and deformed bodies, were felt to represent beings so unfortunate that bad luck turned away from them. Masks were felt to have a specially strong apotropaic force, perhaps because the face or head, with its capacity for strong and terrifying grimaces and with its eyes glaring in a fierce threat, concentrated the thought and aim of a living creature as nothing else could. The mask thus became an emblem of total concentration of spirit-force. And it is interesting to note that Athena, the craft-goddess, had a particularly powerful mask at her disposal, the *gorgoneion*. This mask was in effect inseparable from her person and divine force. Indeed she had a pair of such frightening other-selves: the Gorgon with its tongue stuck out (analagous to the *fascinus* of the Latins) and her Owl with its hypnotically fascinating eyes. The superstitious man, according to Theophrastos, on seeing an owl, cried out as a safeguard: "Athena is stronger!" Thus the goddess protected against her own powers of fascination. After killing the Gorgon, she had appropriated its powers. Aias calls her Gorgopis at the moment when he accuses her of having struck him with distracted wits.

She was Athena Glaukopis—owl-eyed, or bright-eyed; and Athens put her big-eyed owl on its coins. Ausonius mentions an otherwise unknown legend about Iktinos, architect of the Parthenon. He installed in Athena's temple "an owl painted with colours of such magical power as to lure all kinds of fowls and kill them with its stare". Argos had her cult as Oxyderkes (Sharp-eyed); Diomedes was said to have founded the sanctuary to thank his protectress for giving him such sharp and penetrating eyes that he was capable of recognising the gods even in human guise. At

Athens she shared with the other great craft-deity, Hephaistos, a temple, quite small, behind the craftsmen's quarters, the Kerameikos, near a shrine of Aphrodite. At the time of the Peace of Nikias an artist set there on a single base two bronze statues representing the pair of deities. Pausanias gives the one detail that Athena was shown with grey-bright eyes; he must mean that her eyes were made of stones incrusted in the metal. Did the artist want to depict the Glaukopis of Homer or to show that Athena as consort of Hephaistos was Oxyderkes, Ophthalmitis? Her epithet as Hephaistia is not attested before the fourth century, but is certainly earlier.[10]

The Spartan Athena was called Optiletis, which Pausanias translates as Ophthalmitis and which probably has the same value as Oxyderkes. At Teumesos Athena was Telchinia, which shows a connection with the *daimones* of metallurgy, the Telchines, and which was taken to mean *Baskanos*: Witch with the power of the evil-eye. At Elis she was Narkaia, the Petrifier—with the same power as her Gorgonhead. It has been argued that as Baskanos she was a goddess of techniques and that her power was one of vivifying rather than one of magically binding. Perhaps it would be correct to see in her both aspects. A work of art or one of the crafts showed the material bound (petrified) in a new form, and yet at the same time given a new life. Athena's fascinating powers, largely effaced in her myths, thus seem an essential ingredient of her divinity. Iodama, her priestess at Alalkomene, was petrified at seeing her with the *gorgoneion*. At Troy, when her temple burned, Ilos seized the palladion and was blinded; for no man might view this image. At Athens, an Athena Apotropaia is mentioned in an inscription found near the column of Phokas.[11]

We need not here examine the wide range of *gorgoneia* on shields, in tombs, on vases, and elsewhere as amulets. But we may note one that shows the gorgon guarding a statue of which only the two feet remain. On two sides of the triangular base is a gorgonhead, on the third a ramshead (with similar protective significance). The statue was dedicated in the precinct of Apollo at Delos and probably represented the god; the base has an inscription that dates the work to the early sixth century and shows the dedication of a Naxian artist. As for the owl we may look at a Roman mosaic on the Caelian Hill, in the entrance hall to a basilica built by a pearl-dealer, Hilarius, who was head of a college of Dendrophori sacred to the Mother of the Gods. We see fourfooted beasts, birds, and reptiles attacking the Evil Eye, which is also bored through by a lance; as a final touch, a little owl perches on the eyebrow. On a fragment of an early Corinthian pot we see a potter at work before a big domed oven on which a large owl perches, while below, between potter and oven, is the figure of a small grotesque man. The owl here may well be Athena's.[12]

34. Owl of Athena Glaukopis on Athenian coinage; and another brazier mask

We have noted a vase-painting which shows Athena visiting a pottery. In another we see her modelling a horse in clay as the first stage to making a bronze statue. We do not have many craftsmen's dedications to her. The potter Aischines offered "a tenth of his works", probably meaning a fair proportion of his profits. Another potter, Andokides, known from his signatures as a craft-innovator, together with Mnesiades (otherwise unknown), made a joint dedication. We know of only some half dozen, out

35. Evil Eye attacked by birds and beasts, with Owl perching over it: mosaic on Caelian Hill, Rome (cf. *J.H.S.* vi 312)

of a total reckoned as five hundred or more, fine craftsmen in the pottery business of the late sixth and fifth centuries. Pausanias says: "The Athenians are far more zealous in divine matters than other men; they were the first to surname Athena Erganē [Worker]."[13]

The apotropaic mask, guarding organic life or craft-process at a critical moment, may be said to embody both the attacking and the defending forces. As we saw earlier of the satyrs, it expresses both the terrible energies of uncontrolled nature and the human domination of those energies which makes of them the core of the creative process. The concept of the critical moment, which is safely turned and thus made into a fortifying instead of a destructive force, is linked with the whole far-ranging concept of the limit, the correct measure, proportion, balance. The latter concept was embodied in a number of mythological and cult-figures, such as Moira, Nemesis, Dikē (Justice); and so it is no surprise to find the creative-destructive mask connected with such figures. The idea of the due limit or share in things is closely bound up with that of justice and right; and the goddess Praxidike (Justice-exactor) was imaged only as a head, and only heads were sacrificed to her. Pausanias knew her in a multiple (probably triple) form, at Haliartos in Boiotia where, in the open air, was a sanctuary of the Praxidikai, at which oaths of a very binding nature were sworn. At Pheneus was a thing or place called the Petrōma (*petra*, rock) which held the mask of Demeter surnamed Kidaria. The people swore oaths by the Petrōma dealing with the most important matters. We do not know if the mask was of stone, but it seems likely. In any event the link of the Petrōma with penalties for a broken oath suggests the petrifying Gorgon-mask. The priest donned the mask while performing the rites of smiting the Underground People with rods.[14]

The terrible mask in Greek cult and myth has roots going far back into the religion of the Near East. The Medousa-head merges with the mask of Humwawa (Humbaba) whom Gilgamesh meets and conquers. A terracotta shows the hero standing on the cut-off head of the storm-monster, which is depicted as a mask. In the seal of Shaushshatar, king of Mitanni about 1450, we see on the top left hand side what is perhaps the earliest representation of Mitra or Mithras casting or slaying the bull; the figure on the right may then be Varuna, god of waters, with the Nasatya twins (prototypes of the Greek Dioskouroi) in the lower corners wrestling each with a lion. The central figure is a winged woman with lion-limbs in the lower part of her body, holding a pair of lions upside down, probably a form of Ishtar, but certainly the prototype of what became the Greek Lady of Wild Things. At the top of all is the hairy head or mask of Humbaba. In the Sumerian version of the Gilgamesh epic, Humbaba fastened on Gilgamesh his eye, the eye of death; in the Old Babylonian version, he also possesses *milimmu*, a kind of devastating magical gleam. We see here the elements that in Greece appear connected with Medousa (one of the Gorgon triad), Athena, and also Charon, the ferryman

36. Seal of Shaushshatar (Barnett, *Cat. Nimrud Ivories* 83)

of the Styx, whose name seems a poetical form of Charopos, bright-eyed. A direct link is provided by the wide distribution of the Humbaba-type mask in graves; we find the continuous-line type in the sanctuary of Artemis Orthia in Sparta.[15]

With Humbaba we come to a mask directly representing the wildest forces of untamed nature, the stormwind; we may ask if the terrible glare in his eye is not that of lightning. The hero who defies and defeats him has mastered the thunderstorm, the thunderbolt. Hephaistos had his smithy in volcanoes. His forge was in the Lipari islands, and he was closely connected with Mt. Moschylos on Lemnos, a wooded volcano. There he landed when flung from heaven by Hera, and there he learned his craft of metalwork. Aischylos set his forge on the top of Mt. Aitna. It was from Mt. Moschylos that Aischylos, perhaps, and certainly Attius considered Prometheus to have taken fire for men; there seems a connection with the yearly rite of bringing fire to the island. Hephaistos may have been a god of fire rather than of metallurgy, but the distinction has little meaning; for his fire is the transformative fire of craft-process. Prometheus was connected with both Athena and Hephaistos and with both metallurgy and pottery. Plato holds that he took the fire from "the common abode of Athena and Hephaistos".[16]

The significance of volcanic sites in relation to Hephaistos and his smithy does not lie merely in their fiery nature. As we saw with regard to Typhoeus-Typhon, such sites are linked with the conflict of the forces of creation and destruction, of order and disorder. They are the seat of great powers, which can be sheerly destructive but which can only be directed into creative channels. The cavern of chaotic fire becomes the smithy of human creativeness, of craft-process. We find the same sort of trail if we look at the Daktyls of Mt. Ida in Crete, who turn out from one angle to be initiates or shamans living in secret sanctuaries and initiating into thunder-rites. In a fragment of Euripides, Minos, after the birth of the Minotaur, sends for them, apparently to purify the palace and explain the situation. They leave their hidden lairs and come in white robes; they say that they are accomplishing the Thunder (or Thunder-rites) of night-wandering Zagreus and the flesh-devouring banquets, holding the torches of the Mountain Mother; they have each become a Bacchos of the Kouretes. The thunder-rites seem fertility-rites of the sacred marriage when the earth (especially a cave) is impregnated by the thunderbolt, the sacred *labrys* or axe. The Bullroarer, called by the Greeks *rhombos*, was used in such rites and in initiations, to produce the effect of thunder.[17]

What concerns us here is the way in which the fertility-ritual of the sacred marriage is linked with the transformation-moments of craft-process, with thunder as the great powerblast, fertilising and transforming. Again a frightening force of violent destruction, controlled and used by men, becomes creative. The Kyklopes in their rumbling or roaring volcano-workshops represent the thunderpower subdued to human purpose. (The fall of the palladion from the sky and the fall of Hephaistos from Olympos seem to have the same link with the idea of the thunderbolt as something that can and must be controlled by men. The fire from heaven, joining with the underground fire, could produce total chaos; but in the person of the firegod, the *daimōn*-smith, it changes its character and is put to the service of humanity.)

We find the same sort of connection between fire and thunder if we turn to Vulcan. Among the Latins the Tubilustria of 23 May belonged to him. "They purified the Trumpets, his work."

This statement by Ovid has been doubted, but there seems a clear Etruscan link of firegod with metallurgy; e.g. the importance of Sethlans at Populonia where iron ore from Elba was worked, and the tale about the *Tyrhena tuba* being invented by Tyrsenos, son of Herakles, and brought into Italy by Etruscans. Trumpets as a craft-product of metallurgy, which evoked the thunderblast, may well be linked with Vulcan in his Etruscan aspects. He had a strong aspect as the god of ravaging fire and perhaps of earthquakes. He had no temple, but a sacred area, where burnt objects struck by lightning and arms taken from the enemy in war were put to be purified, was devoted to him from early times.[18]

This inquiry into the fears and hopes of potters and of other craftsmen whose work involved the use of fire as a transformative force may seem to have brought up little information that is directly connected with scientific thought. But it has given us much insight into the ways in which craftsmen had built up immemorial ideas around the critical moments of change in their materials. Craft-process is viewed from one angle as a sort of initiation-ritual, during which the worker enters the world of nature, participates in a crisis of change, and either fails lamentably or emerges triumphantly. Hence the way in which the great moments of change in human life—birth, puberty, marriage, death—are seen as expressing or symbolising the crucial moments of change in nature or in the materials of craft-process. The deep unitary and dialectical aspects of Greek thought, philosophic and scientific, can thus be much better understood when we realise how much of the ingrained attitudes they reveal were caused or stimulated by the craft-lore which had been heaped up in the fraternities and which in time became a part of the general heritage. To understand this development we must further return to the analysis of the ways in which among the Greeks, as among no other ancient peoples, tribal forms, by a complex but powerfully fought-out series of conflicts and reorganisations, turned into the forms of urban democracy.

ADDENDUM TO CHAPTER IX

There are yet some further points to be made out of the charm-song. Athena appears at its outset as a protective force, and Circe is a witch from the main stock of myth; but the shattering *daimones* come from craft-lore and with them are connected the Centaurs. We have noted how the *daimones* of metallurgy, which have every sign of antiquity, the Telchines, Daktyls, Kouretes and Korybantes are creatures of the mountainous wilds and the forests, like the Centaurs, as well as being attendants of the Great Mother. There is every reason to believe that the first metallurgists worked in the wilds and that their mystery-rituals were associated with the Mountain Mother. Many craft-rituals thus appear to be closely connected with tribal initiations of an orgiastic character in which shamanist possession by spirits played a central part. Strabon tells us:

> Men probably speak in their myths about the Mountain-Roamings, *Oreibasiai*, of religious devotees and of gods themselves, and of their Possessions, *Enthousiasmoi*, for the same reason that they are prompted to believe that the gods themselves dwell in the skies and have forethought, among their other interests for prognostication by signs. Now the search for metals, and hunting, the search for the things useful for the purpose of life, are manifestly closely related to Mountain-Roaming—whereas juggling and magic are closely related to *enthousiasmoi*, cult-worship, and divination. And such also is devotion to the *technai*, especially to the Dionysiac and Orphic *technai*.

A little before that he has been discussing the Daktyls of Mt. Ida, "who were the first to discover and work iron". The Kyklopes of volcanic craters or caves seem also to represent the early miners and metal-workers, though they have become connected with Hephaistos.

The craftsmen of the cities seem very different characters; but they share one quality with the workers of the wilds. They are considered as in some sense separated from the ordinary body politic. Though in fact they provide the basis on which the civilisation of the city-state is built, together with the trade that accompanies their productions, they are felt as aliens by the men of property. The one great rebel figure in myth who fights the highgods is Prometheus—omitting figures like Typhoeus, who represents simply the forces of chaos. Prometheus who steals fire from heaven for men was closely connected with the crafts using fire for transformative purposes. Before he made men the gift of the crafts, they were like the men whom Parmenides described as "forced" to attempt the impossible by thinking the unthinkable and uttering the unutterable, the full nature of being. They were foredoomed to blindness, wandering, helplessness. "Seeing, they did not see; hearing, they did not hear," says Aischylos. The word for such a helpless condition is *amechanie*, a lack of all *mechanai*: devices, constructions, man-made contrivances. Theognis uses the phrase "attempts lacking *mechanai*" to express man's inscrutable fate, which often makes him do the exact opposite of what he has intended. Thus, the myth declares that without the crafts man is helpless in the snare of nature; but the civilised inheritor of the freedoms and powers created by the crafts looks down on their practitioners as not truly men of the *polis*. Protagoras in the Platonic dialogue sets out an unusual form of the myth connecting Prometheus and the crafts. His brother Epimenides had endowed each species of the animals with its proper *dynameis*—one with strength, another with speed, another with fecundity, and so on—so that a balance was established and they all had a chance of survival; but the human race had been forgotten and were doomed to die out. So Prometheus resolved to steal from the gods the *dynameis* of the crafts and give them to men. He did so and distributed them in the same way as Epimetheus had given qualities to the animals. Each man had his own particular capacity. Some could make clothes, others shoes, others houses, right on through the crafts. Thus men could only subsist by the exchange of the things they made for others that they could not make. By this story, we are told, Protagoras wanted to justify the Democracy of Craftsmen who made up the assembly of smiths, potters, fullers, shoemakers, and so on, at Athens: "That's how it's rightly that the citizens welcome the counsel of smith or shoemaker on public affairs."

Plato is seeking to bring out what he feels is the wrongheadedness of democracy. Yet he has to admit that craftsmen are needed. In the *Republic* he says that society has developed so that no man is self-sufficient and each needs a crowd of others; hence the specialisation and division of labour. But, he asks, does this basis, necessary for a city-state, by its complex interactions create the unity of society? On the contrary, he insists, the division of crafts runs totally counter to the political community of citizens defined as equal or alike, *isoi* or *homoioi*. The essential that binds men is lacking. The craftsmen lack political or soldierly skills; and Prometheus, Hephaistos or Athena cannot provide them. Only Zeus (thus representing the upperclasses, who are assumed to be alone capable in political rule and in war) can give the binding element of *aidos* and *dikē*, respect for one another and justice. (In this system respect implies respect for ruler and soldier on the part of the commoners; and justice is the maintenance of the *status quo*.) So Hermes is sent with these moral virtues down to men, and distributes them in complete equality.

There is thus a contradiction in Plato's system; for respect and justice mean different things to rulers and ruled, yet his view of true community means that they must be equally shared. The craftsman's share does not imply equality with the rulers, but the acceptance of inferiority. This point is brought directly out in the *Republic*, where the Three Virtues are to be allotted to the Three Classes. The rulers duly get Wisdom, the warriors get *andreia* (courage or manhood); but the third virtue, *sophrosyne*, soundness of mind and discretion, sense of balance, is not handed over to the workers, but is declared the common property of all three classes. (*Andreia* too works out as taking over specific aspects of virtue in the name of a unitary conception.) Thus in Plato a strong feeling for a necessary unity in society founders on his insistence that sharp class-barriers are needed. In the *Laws* his position hardens into the rejection of all craftsmen from the ranks of citizens.

Aristotle takes the same philosophic view. The unity of the state implies a complete reciprocity among equals—"as if the shoemakers and the carpenters exchanged their crafts so that the same jobs would not constantly be done by the same hands." And that, he thinks, is the height of absurdity. Every craftsman must be sharply limited to his own speciality or he destroys the inferior order to which he belongs. "Imagine ten thousand men gathered inside the same walls—men who marry among themselves, who exchange their products—some of them carpenters, others labourers, shoe-makers. . . . That wouldn't compose a City." Aristotle declares too that in the ideal state no worker will be a citizen.[19]

There is thus considered to be a complete dividing line between economic or productive activity and social or political existence. As a social being a man has leisure to take part in running his city, to discuss politics and philosophy, to share in the sports and festivities, and so on. The craftsman by the nature of his work is largely barred from these activities, so that his social existence is minimal or ineffectual. In such attitudes we see the aristocratic contempt of banausic labour, which has an element of validity in that it opposes a concept of the whole or all-round man to that of the man crippled by division and fragmentation of labour. But the opposition is made falsely. The master, profiting from the division of labour which he despises, refuses to see the vital part played by productive activity in binding men together in the new community. He sees the whole productive sphere as nothing but an economic mechanism, dehumanised in itself and lacking all social essence. Such a deep division of master and worker could only come about in a slave-society, where the free worker, because of his "dehumanised" function, is hardly distinguishable in idea and emotion from the slave.

Thus the craftsman still continues to be someone outside society in the sense in which society is defined—just as earlier the *demiourgos* had tended to be outside the estate-unit of land, the *oikos*, or was a denizen of the wilds associated with strange and frenetic cults. And as the democratic state developed in the fifth century, he became from the viewpoint of the masters a political danger too. How could there be social unity with division of labour, unless the craftsmen would recognise their subordinate and inferior position? (Behind this question there was the true realisation that class-division destroyed social unity by its very nature; but only some of the early Stoics and Cynics were ready to follow the logic of the situation along these lines.) Hence the desperate efforts of a thinker like Plato to devise utopian systems in which the leisured class, seen as the one section with virtue and intelligence, can impose a system of order, while at the same time for the lower orders there is the rule "one man, one task". Social unity is maintained by imposing its opposite:

> But when a cobbler or any other man whom nature has designed to be a trader, having his heart lifted up by wealth or strength or the number of his followers, or any like advantage, attempts to force his way into the class of warriors, or a warrior into that of legislators and guardians, for which he is unfitted, and either to take the implements or duties of the other; or when one man is trader, legislator, and warrior all in one, then I think you'll agree with me in saying that this interchange and this meddling of one with another is the ruin of the state.[20]

There is yet another point made by the philosophers which links with the question of the critical moment as defined in our charm-song. The charm seeks to bring together the forces needed at any particular moment for the success of the craft-process of transformation. Plato stresses that *technē* does not consist in the simple or rigid application of rules that have been learned. An impulse, both intuitive and analytical, must proceed from the craftsman. He must be able to seize on the right moment, *kairos*, and act in the way that is required by the situation at that moment. If he loses the right moment, he spoils everything. That is why he must never leave his job.[21]

As a result of the complex of attitudes to craftwork which we have been discussing, there is no clear concept of man opposed to nature and transforming it. In Europe the long period of Christian alienation from nature and denunciation of it as something evil was needed before men could set themselves to tame, control, master it through their science and technology. So, far from representing the human distance from nature, the ancient craftsman revealed above all the intrusion of natural forces into the bosom of society. "In his production the craftsman sees his particular activity as 'naturalising' itself. The domain of 'artifice' is another matter; it defines the activities which beget only fictions, as in their trades is done by those illusionists the sophists or the bankers. The work of craftsmen, which is set over against agriculture, felt as more natural, is also integrated in the order of nature and provides a contrast with money-making as does *physis* with *nomos*. But between *physis* and *nomos*, there is no place for the production of a work which, while being completely real, will appear as purely human. Man is not yet sufficiently distinguished from nature for his action to be able to detach itself without thereby at once swinging over to the side of convention" (Vernant). For Aristotle all finance is against nature in that it is not concerned with satisfying a need but seeks money for money's sake. The making of a shoe has a natural end: the wearing or use of the shoe. But the shoe can be turned to an end which is not natural: its sale. All *technē* can be thus distorted from its natural function into money-making. To the extent that it stays enclosed within the limits of natural needs, any exchange is according to nature; but, lacking the nature of a true *technē*, money-making knows no limits. Usury seeks to beget money on money indefinitely—thus chasing an illusion, a mere convention. (Aristotle does not go on to discuss money as an alienating power.)[22]

Before man in a machine-world felt himself finally alienated from nature the typical utopia was one in which nature spontaneously produced plenty for everyone. In a comedy by Krates it is said that in a future world when there will be no slaves, tables will lay themselves, the *kyathos* pour out wine, and so on; in a comedy by Telekleides there is a stream of soup flowing, fishes leap fried on to the tables. When the water-mill was developed in the late Hellenistic period, the poet Antipatros of Thessalonika did not see the machine as transforming and mastering nature, but as a form of activity in which the forces at work were those of the *daimones* of nature:

Cease from grinding, O you toilers. Women, slumber still,
even if the crowing rooster calls the morning star.
For Demeter has appointed Nymphs to turn your mill
and upon the waterwheel alighting here they are.
See how quick they twirl the axle whose revolving rays
spin the heavy roller quarried overseas.
So again we savour the delight of ancient days,
taught to eat the fruits of Mother Earth at ease.

The wheel of mechanism is dissolved in the circling dance where man and nature harmoniously meet—the dance from which the concept of the wheel has been ultimately derived. But we may note that the workers who are relieved of heavy physical toil are slave-girls; a poet might celebrate their release in fantasy, but the masters of their world were not interested in bringing such a fantasy down to earth. Rightly enough, they realised deep in themselves that such a development would completely disrupt their world.[23]

Magnets

X

Magnetic forces must have been observed in very ancient times; but till metallurgy was fairly well developed, there would have been no clarity as to just which minerals could exert them. In Assyria of the seventh century we read in a love-spell that the mineral *sadanu-sabitu*, mixed with oil, should be used to anoint the man's genitals while powder of iron is sprinkled on the woman's. *Sadanu-sabitu* is "the haematite [iron ore] that grasps", i.e. magnetic iron ore, which here is to attract iron filings and bring the woman to the man who wants her. The Greeks with their quest for an active principle at work in the universe could not but be early interested in magnetism; and Diogenes Laertes tells us of Thales: "Aristotle and Hippias both declare that, arguing from the magnet and from amber, he attributed *psyche* [that is, life] even to lifeless things." The term for "lifeless" is *apsycha*, things without *psyche*. We may interpret him as meaning, not that things without life had life, but that things which seemed by our usual criteria to lack life, yet had in them a form of living energy. Hence his saying that all things were full of gods. Aristotle suggests that he thought of the *psyche* as the source of motion, but it is not clear if he considered everything which can move or cause motion to own *psyche*. He may have held that there were varying shares of *psyche* in things, and that the magnet and amber had a particularly large amount. The magnet thus demonstrated what was true in some degree or other of all apparently inanimate things.[1]

To explain magnetism Empedokles used his theory of effluences or emanations, with the assumption of a symmetry between the effluences of one body and the pores of another. Alexandros of Aphrodisias tells us: "Why does a magnet attract iron? Empedokles says that the iron is drawn to the magnet because both give off effluences and the size of the pores in the magnet correspond to the effluences of the iron. The effluences of the magnet thrust away the air near the pores of the iron and set into motion the air closing the pores. When this is driven out, the iron at once follows the stream of its own effluences; for when the effluences of the iron approach the pores of the magnet and fit them in shape, the iron is drawn after the effluences and is attracted."

Demokritos, too, held that life existed to some extent in all bodies. Lucretius tells us: "Democritus says all things own some sort of a soul, even corpses, since it's clear they always share in a certain warmth and power of sensation, though the greater part disperses into air. . . . Democritus thought that dead bodies perceive." Alexandros gives us a long account of his views on magnets and on amber:

> Demokritos himself declares that effluences arise and that like moves towards like, though everything moves towards the void as well. On this basis he holds that the magnet and the iron are composed of similar atoms, the magnet however of finer ones, more widely spaced and enclosing more void than the iron. So, since its atoms are more easily moved, they move faster to the iron (for motion proceeds towards the like), and entering the pores of the iron they set its component bodies in motion by slipping through them on account of their fineness. The bodies thus set in motion leave the iron as an efflux and move towards the magnet, both because of the similarity in particles and because the magnet has more void. Then by reason of the wholesale egress of the bodies and their motion, the iron itself follows them and is also carried to the magnet. But the magnet does not move towards the iron because the iron does not have as many void spaces as the magnet.
>
> But granted that iron and lodestone are composed of like particles, how about amber and chaff? When anyone offers the same explanation for this case too, it must be recalled that amber attracts many things. Now if amber is composed of the same particles as all these, then the latter also are composed of similar particles and should attract each other.[2]

Whatever puzzles they posed, it is clear that the phenomena connected with the magnet and amber had a powerful effect on early Greek thinkers, convincing them of the presence of unseen forces (effluences and the like) and deepening their whole concept of the physical universe.

A passage from Plato's *Ion* more than anything else shows us how these phenomena stirred men's minds imaginatively and made them ponder on the nature of attraction and repulsion. Ion is a rhapsode who recites Homer's epics, but he also is an appreciative critic (about 530). Sokrates argues that if he truly grasps and appreciates Homer's work he must also be capable of doing the same with other poems. Judgment implies standards and criteria; and this generalisation applies to all technical accomplishments, including those of painting, sculpture, musical performances, and the art of the rhapsode. So Ion's grasp of Homer is not "mere skill", but is dependent "on some sublime power which prompts you". He goes on:

> I should compare you with that stone which Euripides calls a Magnet—the Heraklean Stone, to use the common name. As you know, it has power to attract iron rings. More, it invests those rings with a power like its own, so that they can attract other rings, and the result is often a long chain of rings hanging one from another, though in all of them the magnetic power is derived from the original stone.
>
> In precisely the same way human beings are inspired by the Muse, and from those who are inspired a chain of similarly inspired persons is suspended. All the great epic poets uttered their poetry, not in virtue of any skill, but by inspiration and divine possession, and the same is true of the great lyric writers. You may compare them with the devotees of the Korybantes, who dance only when they are out of their senses. In just the same way the lyric poets are out of their senses when they compose their lovely songs. They embark on harmony and rhythm as on a Bacchic Orgy, become possessed, and like the Bacchants, completely out of their senses, draw milk and honey from the rivers.
>
> More, the poets themselves admit a spiritual process of this sort. They tell us that they draw their melodies from the mellifluous springs of the gardens and groves of the Muses, and carry them to us, winged, like honey-bees. Indeed they tell the truth.

He develops this thesis, calling the prophets also inspired, and then returns to the image of magnetism.

> Do you realise that the spectator is the final link in the chain of magnetised rings. You, the rhapsodes and actors, represent the middle link, and the first link is of course the poet. Thus the deity sways men's souls as it will, and attaches them to each other by virtue of its power. As is reflected in the analogy of the Magnet, a rich concourse of dancers, chorus-trainers, and assistant trainers

> attach themselves to that chain which is initially suspended from the Muse.

In his view the deity, the divine force, is transcendent, outside our physical universe; but if we translate his concept back into the unitary systems of the Milesians, we find in his words a powerful development of Thales' position. A current of force runs through nature, strongly manifest in the magnet, and the same current runs through human life, both drawing men together and putting them in an active relation to nature, so that in all "technical accomplishments" the two currents come together and the creative process is seen at work in human activity and expression. The arts have a particularly magnetic quality—they dam up, control, and put into significant form the flow of force; and this force overflows on to all who play any part in them, creative, interpretative, or receptive of their energies. The flow of the current, the tensions and the releases it brings about, all involve harmony and rhythm as a necessary aspect of entry into the deep formative energies and structures of the kosmos.

The account that Plato gives in the *Timaios*, indeed, comes much closer to a Milesian kind of attitude. "As for the flowings of water, fallings of thunderbolts, and the marvels of attraction [*helxis*] in amber and the Herakleion Stone—not one of these ever owns any attractive force [*holkē*]. But as there's no void and these bodies propel themselves round one into another, and, according as they separate or unite, all exchange places and proceed each to its own region, so it's by means of these complex and reciprocal processes that such marvellous things are brought about, as is well clear to anyone properly investigating them." Note the linking of the thunderbolt with the *helxis* of the magnet.

The popular term for the magnet, Herakleian Stone, is said by Hesychios to come from the place name Herakleia in Lydia; but this idea is doubtless a late rationalisation. Far more likely the term means "the stone with a power like that of Herakles". The Herakleian Disease was epilepsy, so-called because in its onset it threw a man about as if Herakles was wrestling with him. It was a form of possession like the inflow of the magnetic current in poetic or prophetic inspiration, in the raptures of the Dionysiac dance, and so on.

Ploutarch claims to have as his authority Manethos, an Egyptian who wrote a history of Egypt from the earliest times up to 323 B.C., under the first two Ptolemies, for the statement that Set-Typhon and Horos symbolised loadstone and iron. Egyptian usages

> often give Isis the name Athena, which has some such meaning as this: I came from myself, which indicates self-impelled movement. Typhon, as we've already said, is called Seth, Bebon, and Smu, names that seek to express some violent and hindering restraint or opposition or turning-back. They still call the magnet the Bone of Horos, and iron the Bone of Typhon as Manethos records. For just as iron is often like a substance which is drawn towards the stone and follows it, so the saving, beneficent, and reasonable [having *logos*] movement of the world turns and attracts, assuaging by persuasion that hardness and Typhonic quality; then, rising up, it [the Typhonic hardness] returns into itself and sinks into its unlimited state.

Set was certainly from ancient times associated with a metal which can hardly be ordinary iron, since the Egyptians did not themselves work iron till the sixth century B.C., but which may be meteoric iron. That kind was the earliest iron known to the Egyptians and was called "iron from heaven". The metal associated with Seth was used, in the form of an adze, in opening the mouth of the dead king, an important part of the mortuary ritual aimed at immortalising him. Since his resurrection was in the form of an ascent into the sky, to the sun, "iron from the sky" would be suitable for the ceremony and would be a sky-clearing force like the thunderbolt. There is, however, no other known reference to Horos and the loadstone. In any event the passage is of importance as linking the action of loadstone-and-iron with the attraction and repulsion of cosmic forces.[3]

Cicero, discussing divination, uses magnetism as an example of forces and causations that exist though we cannot explain them. "If I were to declare that the magnet is a kind of stone that attracts and draws iron to itself, but could give no reason for this happening, would you totally deny the fact?" Lucretius treats the phenomenon at length for the same sort of reason. He has been discussing the union of opposites, fire (heat) and water, as well as action at a distance: heat causing fire without any actual contact from fire itself. Then he turns to the Magnet, so-called by the Greeks from the land of the Magnesians, where magnetic minerals are found. "Men wonder at this stone; it often produces a chain of rings that hang from it below; sometimes you see suspended five or more, one after the other, tossing in light airs, one strung from another, attached to its lower side, each in turn feeling the stone's binding power: with such a continuous current the force pervades." He gives many examples of unseen forces; argues that every object sends out streaming *corpora* that strike on our eyes and create our vision; says that smells, cold, heat and sound also stream: a continual effluence and interaction of what we might now call an electro-magnetic field. Some effluences are not suited to the things on which they impact; the sun parches earth, thaws ice, melts wax. Fire melts metals, but shrivels and draws together hides and flesh. Then comes the theme of pores, which differ from one another: each sense "takes into itself in its own peculiar way its own special object". Again, "one thing is seen to stream through stones, another to pass through wood", and so on. The poet decides that from the magnet must stream "many seeds, or a current if you will, which drives off with blows all the air lying between the stone and iron". The *primordia* of the iron "fall headlong into the void in one body, so that the ring itself follows". Moreover, the air behind the iron pushes it. This air "makes its way with much subtlety through the frequent pores of the iron to its minute parts, and then thrusts and pushes it on, as the wind a ship and its sails". All things have some air inside, "as they are of a rare body and air surrounds and is in contact with all things. So the air in the innermost recesses of the iron is ever stirred into restless motion and therefore beats the ring without a doubt and agitates it within, you know. The ring is carried in the direction in which it has once plunged forwards—into the void part to which it has made its start." But sometimes the iron is repelled. "I've seen Samothracian rings of iron jump up, and iron filings go mad in bronze basins together when this magnet stone was set under. Such strong desire the iron feels to flee away from the stone." The reason is that the current, *aestus*, of the bronze has filled the pores of the iron, "and there is no room for the magnet's current, which then dashes against the iron texture". (This is incorrect; the interposition of bronze does not change the attractive power.) Some persons wonder that the magnet cannot attract other things such as gold, which "stand steady by the power of their weight"—while other things have too rare a body and the current flies through it: e.g. wool.

Lucretius goes on with examples of things not so alien to one another that they fail to stick together, such as cement and stone, and wood and bull's glue, wine and water (though oil and pitch won't mix); purple dye and wool; bronze soldered to bronze with tin. Here the textures have a mutual correspondence, so that the cavities of each fit the solids of the other. The union of magnet and iron suggests a fastening with hooks and eyes. In all this exposition he is no doubt following in general the line of Demokritos and Epikouros.[4]

Plinius gives us much information about the magnet. He speaks of "the hatred and the friendship felt by deaf and insensible things", the relation which the Greeks call sympathy. He instances magnets and iron and the *adamas* "breakable by the blood of a goat", and argues that medicine and magic alike have originated from the relationship of love and hate, concord and discord, that exists between natural simples. The magnet is called Heraklean because of its strength, but probably also from the Lydian town of Herakleia not far from Magnesia. Iron "is clasped and held in its embrace"; he endows it with hands, feet, and *mores* (properties, ways of its own). It was named by its discoverer, a shepherd on Mt. Ida, according to Nikandros of Kolophon, who found the nails in his sandals and his staff-tip caught by it. Sotakos of the early third century B.C. described five kinds—from Ethiopia, Magnesia on the borders of Makedon, Hyettos in Boiotia, near Alexandreia on the Troad, and Magnesia in Asia Minor. A stone was also found in the land of the Cantabrians, in Spain, which, though it attracted iron, was not considered a true magnet. Most important was the distinction between male and female magnets: the female stones were not permanently magnetic. Next came colour: the Macedonian magnet-stones were red and black, the Boiotian more red than black, the Troad black and female, the Asianis white and lacking in power to attract iron (this last was apparently talc, called *magnetitis lithos* by Theophrastos). The bluer stones were the better. "The palm goes to the Ethiopian variety, which in the market is worth its weight in silver; it is found in the sandy district of Ethiopia called Zmiris. There too is found the haematite magnet which is blood-red in colour and when ground produces not only blood-red but also saffron-yellow powder." Probably red and brown haemetite were found together—or possibly goethite, a species of brown haemetite. But haemetite has not the same power of attracting iron as the magnet. The test of the Ethiopian magnet was its ability to draw another to itself (as would happen if unlike poles were presented to one another).

All magnets were valuable as eyesalves if used in the correct quantities, says Plinius. They stopped acute watering. Also, when ground and calcined, they cured burns. Near the Indus was a magnetic mountain from which one could not detach one's feet; and there was also another mountain nearby with a force that repelled iron. There is folklore about an anti-magnet, called the *adamas* (a name used for the diamond and other stones). Placed close to a magnet, the *adamas* "prevents the iron from being attracted away from itself; or if the magnet is moved towards the iron and grips it, the *adamas* snatches the iron and takes it away". All this has no basis in fact; it was apparently devised out of the need felt to have some opposite to the magnet. Augustine repeated the tales of Plinius about the magnet and about the breaking of the *adamas* by the application of goat's blood. He cited such matters to show that the pagans were inconsistent in rejecting the miracles of the Bible.[5]

Philostratos in his *Life of Apollonios of Tyana* tells of a fabulous stone with magnetic properties in his account of the wonders of India. The sage produces a stone that attracts and holds other stones; he points to his own thumb and says that the largest specimen is exactly the size of its nail.

> And it's conceived in a hollow in the earth at a depth of four fathoms, but is so strongly invested with *pneuma* that the earth swells up and breaks open in many places when the stone is conceived in it. But no one can get hold of the stone as it runs away unless scientifically [according to *logos*] attracted. We can secure this *pantarbē* [all-fearer]—that's the name given to it—partly by the performance of certain rites, partly by certain forms of words. In the night it glows like day, just as a fire might; for it is red and emits rays. And if you look at it in the daytime it smites your eyes with a thousand glints and gleams. And the light in it is a *pneuma* of mysterious [*arrhetos*, unspeakable] power; for it absorbs everything nearby. But why do I say nearby? You can sink anywhere in river or sea as many stones as you like—not even near one another, but here, there, and everywhere—and then if you let this stone down among them by a string, it gathers them by the diffusion of its *pneuma*, and the yielding stones cling all round it in a bunch like a swarm of bees.

Then the sage demonstrates the powers of the stone. The stone behind the fantasy may be a ruby mentioned by Ktesibios. Charikleа in the romance of Heliodoros has a ring: "its bezel is set with a stone called *pantarbē*, and it bears an inscription in certain sacred characters which, we may believe, is instinct with a celestial sanctity and thus, I imagine, confers on the stone a certain power of repelling fire and of keeping its wearers unscathed in conflagration."

From Euboulos we see that anything attracting desire could be called magnetic. "It's hard, if Cyprian loaves are spied, past them to ride; for magnet-like they draw the hungry to their side." Inevitably the analogy with love-attraction was stressed. The romancer Achilleus Tatios tells how a lover wants to talk about love in the hearing of his Leukippe; so he chats with a servant of the house about the peacock making a display to attract his hen. Not only birds are stirred by love: "That would be nothing unusual, for you know that Love himself has wings. Creeping snakes and plants too, and I believe even stones. At least the magnet loves iron; and if it only sees and touches it, it attracts it as though it owned something amorous in its depths. Can't we call this the love-embrace of the loving stone and the beloved metal." He goes on to say that the palm among trees is especially susceptible; there are male and female, and the enamoured male withers if set too far from the female. When that happens, the gardener goes to some high point and notes the direction in which the tree droops; he thus locates the beloved, takes a shoot from her, "and grafts it into the very heart of the male". The tree that seems on the point of death recovers and gains new vigour from his joy at the embrace of his loved one. "It's a kind of plant-marriage."

Claudian, a poet of considerable intellectual curiosity, describes the loadstone and a model of Venus and Mars, in which she was carved from a Magnet and he from Iron. There can be no doubt that the model really existed, and it may have been used for cult-purposes, or at least in some display on occasions, at a temple of Aphrodite, probably at Alexandreia—of which town the poet seems to have been a native.

Bring me the man who sweats to scrutinise
the world, the seeds from which all lives arise,
the cause why suns are dusked and moons expire,
why comets show their threat of crimson fire,

where winds are laired, what forces shake and cry
from bowelled earth or jag the splitting sky,
why thunder glares or rainbows flower with light—
then, if our minds can grasp such things aright,
I'll ask a question.

There's a common stone,
dark-hued and drab: the Magnet. It's unknown
on glistening throats of girls or braided hair
of kings or jewelled belts that soldiers wear.
But note its marvellous properties, you'll claim,
though dull, it beats a gem of lustrous flame
or pearls from seaweed on the Red Sea shores.
It sucks at iron through its stony pores;
iron with eager kiss it hugs and needs
if it's to wake; its hidden power it feeds
with iron's rasping contact. Left alone,
it languishes, a feeble famished stone,
and all its fluid strength is drained away.

Mars with his spear of blood creates dismay,
and Venus gives us comfort in despair.
A common shrine of gold these lovers share.
Each has an image. Mars in iron stands;
Venus a magnet carved by skilful hands.
Duly the priest enacts the marriage-day.
A torch leads on the choir: the doors are gay
with myrtle; spilth of roses hides the bed;
and scarlet marriage-cloths are fitly spread.
Then lo, a miracle! Her beauties draw
the lover up—the scene that heaven saw
when under him with wanton breasts she gasped.
Her arms enfold his helm; she keeps him clasped
from head to foot and stirs with close embrace.
He feels afar her breath of summoning grace,
the secret net his jewel-bride has cast.
Then Nature signs, and, wedged, the iron's fast.
The pair are mated suddenly at last.

What is the pulse of warmth that thus controls?
What harmony compels these stubborn souls?
The stone desires the touch, beholds its mate;
the iron gently feels the urge of Fate.

Thus Venus in her beauty can assuage
the fiery god who longs for wars to wage,
and draws his flashing sword to whet his rage.
Alone she dares to face the snorting horses,
to calm his stormy heart with softer forces.
Then peace returns. Forgetting battle-dooms,
he bends to kiss her, helmed with ruddy plumes.

Terrible child, has then your might no end?
Snatching the bolt of power, from heaven you send
the Thunderer to bellow in the deep.
Now crags and shapes wherein no senses sleep
you master: now your arrows wound the stones.
Rocks show obscure desires, and iron owns
your magics, which through veins of marble creep.

We have some slight evidence that magnetic experiments were made with statues, which must have been quite small. The architect Timochares is said to have planned to put an iron statue of Arsinoe, sister and wife of Ptolemy II, in the temple to be dedicated to the two rulers. The statue was to hang in air, with magnets above and below, or on all sides, attracting it with equal force. But both architect and king died before the temple was built. Ausonius in his *Moselle* has a garbled version, mistaking the architect for Dinochares who had devised the lay-out of Alexandreia. "Here too the man who designed Ptolemy's palace, Dinochares, builder of the pyramid towering above to a fine point, devouring its own shadow—he who, bidden to commemorate the incestuous love of Arsinoe, poised her image in mid-air, under the roof of her Pharian temple: from the vaulted roof a loadstone breathes its influence and draws the girl up to itself by her iron-wrought hair." The *Souda* states that in fact the same kind of device was operated in the temple of Sarapis at Alexandreia; and Rufinus tells us that a figure of the Sun, magnetically poised, hung in that temple till it was destroyed by the Christians in A.D. 391. A similar figure of Mercurius is said to have been one of the wonders of Trèves, Augusta Treverorum, which stood on the Moselle—though it has been suggested that it was actually suspended by a very fine wire: as perhaps was also the case with the Sun in the Serapeion.

Though Claudian says that the magnet had no decorative

value, haematite was common enough in magic gems, and Theophrastos tells us:

> Certain stones have powers [*dyameis*] of the kind already mentioned, in that they do not react to extraneous forces: for example, they cannot be carved by iron tools, but only by other stones. Generally speaking, even the larger stones differ greatly in the methods of working that they admit. As we said before, some can be sawn, and others carved or turned on the lathe, like this *magnētis*, which indeed has an unusual appearance and is admired by some for its likeness to silver, though in no way akin to it.

But what he is talking about is in fact talc.[6]

Naturally, with its mysterious powers, the magnet was much used in magic. The *Lithika*, an Orphic poem said to be based on the prose treatise of Damigeron (second century B.C.), declares that it was used by the witches Circe and Medeia; and an unchaste wife could not stay in the bed where one had been put. Agathias cites against gout and epilepsy the herb nightshade and the stones magnet and aetites (eaglestone), swallow's blood and boy's urine, and so on. Hippolytos, in his attempt to unmask magicians and their tricks, states that they use trapdoors and mirrors to show demons in cauldrons; they make the moon appear indoors and imitate the starry sky by fixing fishscales to the ceiling; they get the effect of an earthquake by burning weasel-dung with magnetstone on an open fire; they make a false skull from the caul of an ox, wax, and gum, and make it speak by means of a hidden tube, then cause it to collapse and vanish or burn up. Here such power is attributed to the magnet—and Hippolytos himself is taken in by this belief—that if subjected to fire it is thought to release forces capable of splitting the earth. We recall how Plato linked thunderbolt and magnet.[7]

The magnet is used in the spell called the *Sword of Dardanos* in the great magical papyrus now at Paris; the spell is called a *praxis* "in which nothing is equal". *Praxis* means doing, business, transaction, but in late times it gained a special sense of "spell"; Dardanos was a mythical ancient whose works, buried with him, were said to have been disinterred by Demokritos. The performer of the *praxis* must take a magnet which breathes, which has *pneuma*, and engrave on it a design of Aphrodite seated on a soul (? shown as a butterfly) as though on a horse, binding her hair up with her left hand and having above her the inscription *achmagerarpepsei.* Under her stands Eros on a globe, burning Psyche—a common art-type shows him applying a torch to Psyche (depicted as girl or butterfly). Under him in turn is a name that includes Adonai, Jacob, and Iao. A *teletē* or consecration is needed to make the charm active. It is not set out at once but seems given later: an offering of fragrant spices and the like, drenched in sweet-smelling wine. *Teletai* were similarly applied to herbs. Here the rite is said to give life to Eros. The Egyptians believed that an offering of incense animated divine images; a magical papyrus describes how to put life into a wax Eros.

After consecrating the stone, the performer puts it under his tongue and turns it round with the aim of gaining his desire, uttering the incantation which begins: "I call on the Archiegetes [chief leader, founder, author] of all *genesis*. . . ." This being is described as "life-giving, breathing-in, power-of-*logos*, uniting all things with his *dynamis*, firstbegotten, founder of all, gold-winged, whose light is darkness". There follows a series of antithetical phrases: a doxological passage celebrating the Archiegetes as the uniter of all opposites. The tone is Orphic. The strange term *melamphaes*, merging light and dark, is repeated, as is *logismos* which infers an innate character of *logos* in the Archiegetes, who is the infuser (of *pneuma*), dark, and *oistron*, which means gadfly but also mad passion; he is "lord of all pneumatic sense or knowledge [*aisthēsis*] of all hidden things".

Eros is thus all possible creative forces. The *Sword* is to be inscribed on goldleaf. The user must write down: "One [is] Thouriel Michael Gabriel Ouriel Misael Irrhael Istrael"—a formula modelled on the common "One is Sarapis". The leaf is to be swallowed by a partridge. The user then kills the bird and recovers the leaf; he inserts *paiderōs* (a herb, perhaps here chervil) and wears it round his neck. Next comes the prescription for the *epithyma*: "that which is to be magically burnt", the sacrificial victim.

And there are instructions for gaining an assistant spirit. Make a small mulberry wood image of Eros wearing a chlamys, with his right foot set forwards, his back hollowed. In the hollow put a small bit of gold foil on which the girl's name is written with a Cyprian stylus—a stylus that has been hammered when hot, then hardened by being dipped in cold water. Go to the girl's home, strike her door with the image, and utter a spell to make her dream. Eros is to take the shape of the god or spirit she most reveres, and tell her of the spell-user's desire. Going home, the latter puts flowers on a table covered with clean linen, sets the image there, and offers it incense, all the while repeating the incantation. Eros will certainly do as he wishes. But it's best to send a dream in this way on the night of the day when the magnet has been used.[8]

Another spell may be cited in full to bring out the full cosmic imagery of the rite in which the magnet as a repository of force plays the final part.

> You are the Unquenchable Fire set beside the Great God Osor-[on]ophris Osor. . . . You ministered to him when he fell in love with his own sister Senephthys [Isis and Nephthys] and ran 6 times 60 leagues and encompassed 6 times 60 mountains. Even so minister to me NN in regard to NN or else I'll utter the 8 Letters of the Moon that have been fixed on the Heart of the Sun; and if I'm about to speak and you've then gone off, I'll go inside the 7 Gates round Dardaniel and shake the Foundations of the Earth and the 4 Elements of the World will be merged together so that their product will become nought.
>
> May you be dissolved in your own Nature and mix with the Air, go to NN daughter of NN and bring her to me with your Thundrous Fire. I adjure the Great God, set in the pure Earth, by whom the Fire is set unquenchable for ever *athouin athouin athouin iathouin silbelthiouth iatet atatet adonai.*
>
> (A safeguard: wrap 3 peonies round your left arm and wear them.)
>
> Come to me, God of Gods, Manifestation from Fire and Pneuma, who alone wear Truth on your head, who cleave the Darkness, Lord of Spirits *loth mouloth pnouteu esioth* Hail Lord *lampsoure iaso iassin.*
>
> (Say this three times and if as you proceed the Phantom. . . .)
>
> Open Heaven, open Olympos, open Hades, open Abyss, let the Darkness be divided at the bidding of the Highest God and let the Sacred Light come forth from the Infinite into the Abyss.
>
> (If he again delays, speak thus aloud . . . your boy:)
>
> *Abra a o na babrouthi hie barache* Approach O Lord God and give me an answer about the things I beg of you.
>
> (On the margin: Hail Sacred Light, Hail Eye of the World, Hail Ray of Dawn upon the World. And ask what you wish.)

(Release) I thank you that you have come at God's command and beg you to keep me whole, unscared, unspectre-struck, *Athathe athatachthe adonai*. Take yourselves to your hallowed Seats.

(. . . on a cup, into which you have put a *kotyle* of good oil, and place it on a brick, and inscribe these characters on a Live Magnet. These characters are made. [Inscribed at the foot of the column.] Set the Stone outside on the left of the cup, and, grasping them with both hands, proceed as was explained to you, and put into the cup at its bottom the membrane of a bitch called white or [?] of a dog that's become white . . . and write with myrrh on the boy's breast *karbaoth*.)

The magnet is used in alchemical recipes, but not as often as we might expect from its fame as a source of unknown power. Thus, we find lead, through one of its derivatives called magnesia, begetting three other metals: copper, tin, and iron. The mystics used the magnet to express spiritual powers. The *Krater* declares: "For contemplation owns a power all its own. Those who have already once contemplated, it takes possession of, and it draws them to itself as men say the magnetic stone draws iron." Here we meet a weak form of what Plato set out passionately in *Ion*. Hermogenes, a Christian heretic of the Marcionite sect, held the view that matter, in a chaotic ferment, was as eternal as God, but God exercised over it a creative attraction analogous to the influence of the magnet or of Beauty. (Aristotle had said of the supreme good that it affects or moves as the beloved does the lover.)[9]

We may now return to the efforts made in scientific thought to use the concept of the magnet. The astronomer Ptolemaios in his *Tetrabiblos*, dealing with the question of reversible and irreversible effects, uses the folk-fantasy of garlic binding up the forces in a magnet. Some things, he says, have such numerous and powerful causes that they are inevitable; others with weak and simple causes may be averted. Physicians can tell which ailments are going to be fatal, and which admit of help. "We must believe the physician when he says that a sore will spread and cause putrefaction, and the miner [*metallikos*] for instance when he says that the Magnēs Stone attracts iron. Each of these left to itself through ignorance of the opposing forces, will inevitably work out as its original nature compels; but the sore won't cause spreading or putrefaction if it gets preventive treatment; nor will the magnet attract the iron if it is rubbed with garlic. And these very deterrent measures also have their resisting powers both by fate and by nature." He is grappling with the Stoic problem of the relation of fate and natural law, which are identified; as noted, some Stoics tried to find ways of justifying freewill. Ptolemaios is working towards the idea that freedom is the knowledge of necessity.

Galen had pondered much on the magnet. He inherited the dynamic views of the Stoics. He drew on Aristotle and Theophrastos, and recognised their valuable contribution; but he felt a deeper debt to the Hippokratic school of medical writers who were "the first to recognise what Nature does". He saw the elements, not as mere ingredients variously mixed, but as "acting upon and acted upon by one another". Questions of attraction played a considerable part in his theories. For instance, he writes:

37. Smith magnetising iron by hammering it to the north; an experiment with the basic idea of rock magnetism: Gilbert's *De Magnete* 1600

"It is not only kathartic drugs that naturally attract their special qualities, but also those that remove thorns and arrowheads such as are at times deeply imbedded in flesh. Those drugs also that draw out animal poisons or poisons applied to arrows, all have the same *dynamis* as has the Herakleian Stone." His weakness is that like practically all ancient thinkers who did not turn to a total determinism he sees the formative principle in matter as a vital activity with its end already implicit in its first stages. There is a great and important truth in such a concept; but the principle was abstracted and no attempt was made to seek out systematically the concrete ways in which it extended itself, moving from simple levels of organisation to more complex ones through a continual interplay, both dynamic and dialectical, with its environment. That is, each organism was treated separately, even when thinkers such as the Stoics saw that it existed dynamically as part of its surroundings. And so nothing like an evolutionary theory could develop, despite some general intuitions that all life had begun at a much lower lever.

As a result the idea of the relation of ends and means, and of adaptation to environment, remained on a metaphysical level, though some thinkers, and Galen above all, developed a fine sense of the organism as a vital whole. Galen saw growth as occurring through a unity of conflicting and interpenetrating opposites, and he posited specific aspects of attraction and repulsion for every material existence, organic or inorganic—again not in mechanical interactions but by means of a continual transformation in which the full relation of an object and its environment had always to be taken into account. As a physician, he was naturally concerned with the states of individual organisms, their healthy or diseased movement, and he concentrated on the processes of nutrition, assimilation, and rejection.

> If there were not an inborn *dynamis* given by nature to each of the organs at the very beginning, then animals would not go on living for a few days, far less for the number of years they actually do live. Let us suppose there was nothing to guard their condition and that they lacked *technē* and *pronoia*. Let us suppose they were steered only by material forces and not by any special *dynamis* —attracting what is proper to it, rejecting what is foreign, and causing alteration and adhesion to the matter intended to nourish it—if we suppose all this, I am sure it would be ridiculous to discuss

> natural *energeiai* and still more physical ones—or indeed life as a whole.

Note that he uses the term *technē* for formative forces at work in an organism. *Pronoia*, forethought, must be understood, as we saw earlier with regard to the Stoics, as the inner guiding principle, not as some outer or imposed goal. For material forces he uses *ropai*, which orginally meant turn of the scale, fall of the scale, pan, weight; balancing, suspense, decision or outcome; decisive influence or moment, crisis. (A late use was for discount deducted from payment.) *Repein* means to turn the scale, sink, incline one way or another. So by *ropai* Galen means forces taken in their purely mechanical aspect, measurable, weighable. He rejects *ropai* as giving us no insight into the living formative process. "Nature," he says elsewhere, "is *technikē* and the substance of things is always tending towards unity and also towards alteration [change, transformation] because its own parts act upon and are acted upon by one another. . . . This *technikē* nature has powers which attract, appropriate, and expel alien matter."

He attacks Asklepiades, who had denied attractive forces altogether—and so magnetism. Epikouros, however, despite atomism, "allows that iron is attracted by the Herakleian Stone and chaff by amber", but his explanations are untenable; he said that "atoms flowing from the stone are related in shape to those flowing from the iron, so that they become easily interlocked. So, after colliding with each of the two compact masses, the stone and the iron, they rebound into the middle and thus become entangled and draw the iron after them." Galen applauds Epikouros also for seeing a similar process at work in the magnet and in animal bodies in "the dispersal of nutriment and the discharge of waste matter, as also in the action of kathartic drugs". We saw, above, Galen's views on such drugs. He goes on to discuss the atomic theory: "that some of the particles flowing from the loadstone collide with the iron and rebound, and that it is by these that the iron becomes suspended—that others penetrate into it and rapidly pass through by way of the empty pores or channels", and "that these then collide with the second piece of iron, but are unable to penetrate it, though they penetrated the first piece, and that they then course back to the first piece and produce entanglements like the former one". Galen says that such a theory is refuted by its own absurdity; he has seen five styles of iron attached in a line, though only the first was in contact with the loadstone and the *dynamis* it transmits.

He uses the term *dynamis diaplastikē*, formative force, which he states to be also *technikē*. The best and highest *technē* "does everything for some purpose, so that there is nothing ineffective or superfluous or capable of being better disposed". Turning to the magnet he says that if filled out with effluences it would disintegrate. Epikouros claims the effluences are very small—then how can they hold up the iron? Galen discusses the notion of hooks, but himself feels that magnetic force is merely a strong manifestation of the power of like to attract like. In all his arguments we find a confusion between the idea of a vitalist force acting in varying degrees in all things and that of a unitary process with a hierarchy of levels, in which each level has its own specific structures and qualities. Such a confusion is inevitable where there is no concept of evolution.

Dealing with bodily growth we find Galen once more struggling with the concept of the *technē* of nature and the function of (magnetic) attraction.

> Praxiteles and Pheidias and all the other statuaries used to decorate their material only on the outside in so far as they were able to touch it; but the inner parts they left unembellished, unwrought, unaffected by *technē* [*atechnos*] or forethought, since they couldn't penetrate there and handle all the portions of the material. It's not so, however, with Nature. Every part of a bone she makes bone, every part of the flesh she makes flesh, and so with fat and all the rest. For there's no part she hasn't touched, elaborated, embellished. Pheidias on the other hand couldn't turn wax into ivory and gold, nor yet gold into wax; for each of these remains as at the beginning, and becomes a perfect statue simply by being clad externally in a form and *technikos* shape.

But Nature works everywhere in an organism, shaping, changing, developing. Galen goes on:

> Just as Pheidias owned the *dynameis* of his *technē* even before touching his material, and then activated [*enērgei*] them in connection with his material—for every *dynamis* remains inoperative in the absence of its proper material—and so it is with semen. Its *dynameis* it has owned from the start, while its *energeiai* it didn't get from its material but reveals them in connection with it.

The semen is the craftsman or *technitēs* "analogous with Pheidias, while the blood corresponds to the statuary's wax. It wasn't the task of the wax to discover for itself how much of it is needed; that's the business of Pheidias. So the *technitēs* will draw to itself as much blood as it needs." Now the magnet is brought in: "If we retain the two principles—that of proportional attraction and that of non-participation of *logismos*—we'll ascribe to the semen a *dynamis* for attracting blood similar to that possessed by a loadstone for iron." He has stated that we must not credit the semen with *nous* or treat it as if it were "an actual living animal". Hence the *logos*-power is not present, even though the semen acts according to *logos*. Similarly the magnet lacks *nous*. Here then we meet a quantitative formula. The semen draws in just as much blood as it can deal with; the quantity attracted is exactly proportional to the attractive power. It follows that a similar quantitative formula applies to the magnet.[10]

In the work *Questions and Solutions*, attributed to Alexandros of Aphrodisias (though it may be by a later writer of the third century A.D.), we find a critical survey of the positions of Empedokles, Demokritos, and Diogenes of Apollonia. The author then sets out his own position. Of what Empedokles said, he remarks: "Here, assuming that one accepts the theory of effluences, the question can be raised as to why the magnet doesn't follow its own effluences and move towards the iron. For on the basis of this theory there's no reason why the magnet shouldn't be attracted by the iron rather than the iron by the magnet." If there is complete symmetry in the system, there is not sufficient reason to make one force control the other. The author is arguing that while, according to Empedokles, mutual attraction exists, there is also simultaneous and equal action and reaction.

These points were not brought out into the open in antiquity, at least in part because the magnets tended to be relatively large and heavy pieces of magnetite, while the bits of iron were small and light. Another factor that obscured the reciprocity of action was the friction involved. Plato in the *Timaios*, however, had insisted that what happened was "complex and reciprocal processes", but not in the relation raised by our author. Further, the point made by the latter was in harmony with the general doctrine of the atomists, who saw in certain conditions of symmetry and similarity a necessary prerequisite for mutual action. As for the question of repulsion (raised by Lucretius in an incorrect form, and also by Ploutarch), it was only later that inquirers noted that any one magnet had two locally distinct spots revealing the polar faculties of attraction and repulsion. Philoponos commented: "By what faculty of the elementary substance does the magnet attract the iron, or is the stone supposed to have the opposite faculty of blowing away and of repelling?"

The phenomenon which the ancients described was that of ferromagnetism. They used the mineral loadstone, magnetite, an oxide of iron. Nickel and cobalt, also ferromagnetic, were discovered only in the eighteenth century; and though the magnetic quality of nickel was soon recognised, not till 1845 was the similar quality of cobalt proved by Faraday. Magnetite or magnetic iron ore is a black opaque mineral with metallic lustre. It is found widely, especially as a constituent of igneous rocks, and is also present in detrital deposits, not being prone to decomposition.[11]

Magnetism played its part in developing the idea of impetus as opposed to Aristotle's false notion of motion as maintained only as long as a force acted directly on an object. The impetus theory was the transitional stage between ancient ideas of motion and those coming to a head under Galileo.

The idea of impetus, of transmission and storage of motive power, had indeed been suggested by Aristotle himself, though in a fantastic form. He assumed that parts of the medium in contact with a missile (i.e. the air) both pushed it and maintained its motion. But if the mover and the thing he moved acted together and then ceased acting simultaneously, the notion of the pushing masses of air behind the missile was untenable. So Aristotle had to suggest that the thrower imparted to air "the power of being a mover". The air indeed "ceases to be moved when its mover stops imparting motion to it, but it goes on being a mover and thus moves whatever is adjacent to it". That is, when the intermediate agent ceases to be moved (to be directly acted on by a force), it can still impart motion to its neighbour, so that the series goes on till it gradually weakens and ends. Hipparchos, dealing with the question of falling bodies and weight, developed the idea of a throwing force which (for instance) carries a body up into the air "as long as it is stronger than the power of the thrown body; the stronger the throwing force, the swifter the object moves upward. Then, as the force lessens, the upward action goes on with a reduced velocity till the body starts to move down under the influence of its own natural pull, although the projecting force persists in a certain way; as this fades out, the body moves downward more swiftly, achieving its greatest velocity when that force has totally disappeared."

But it took a long time for this outlook to get a grip on men's minds. Alexandros, about A.D. 200, while trying to hold fast to Aristotle's ideas, spoke of air moving without being moved and so self-moved, reluctantly bringing in a ghost of impetus. Themistios next brought out more clearly the idea of storage of power. Here the magnet and the ponderings on it played their part. Themistios contrasted with the idea of storage the relation between magnet and iron when the iron loses its temporary power of attraction after being separated from the magnet:

> Perhaps the neighbouring air is not only moved but also gains for itself the power of moving, in direct analogy, I believe, to the case of a material heated by fire. It not only becomes hot, but also gets a power of its own to heat and passes it on continuously for some time. After a while comes a time when the power borrowed from the fire fades out in the process of transference. Similarly air and water . . . become, so to speak, selfmoved and thus for some time are simultaneously both moved and moving. However, they are not moved by the thrower, but rather by their own power, which they received as a signal from the projector, exactly as water heated by fire not only stays warm after the fire has been removed, but conserves for a long time the power of heating.

Simplikios carried the idea further, suggesting that "the moved object receives a kinetic power from the moving one". He even suggested the dropping of the "motion of the air" out of the problem. But he failed to work his idea fully out, and it was not till Philoponos, nearly seven hundreds years after Hipparchos, that the full consequences of the idea of a "throwing force" were worked out. From Philoponos the notion of impetus was passed on to the Arabs in the twelfth century, and then on to Ockham, Buridan, and Oresme in the west in the fourteenth century.[12]

Jet and amber also received a certain amount of attention for their attractive powers which, however, were not so dramatic as those of the magnet. *Elektron* had a double sense: yellow amber and an alloy of gold and silver. The word is connected with *ēlektor*, the beaming sun, which is used by Empedokles for fire as an element. Thales mentioned amber together with the magnet, as did Plato. Plinius says of the alloy: "All gold contains silver in varying proportions. When silver enters as a fifth, the metal takes the name of *electrum*. *Electrum* is also made by adding silver to gold." In fact the proportions of gold and silver in it varied a lot; and with the purification of metals *elektron* as an alloy fell into disuse, though we still find the name in alchemical lists. The link of amber and the alloy no doubt came through the colour, which was associated with solar light and fire. Kallimachos compares the sparkle of the alloy to jetting water. We are reminded of the identification made in Plato's *Timaios* between chemic water and metals; and a scholiast to Aristophanes assimilates *elektron* to glass. The *Souda* defined it as a form of gold mingled with glass and precious stones. Later the sense of the word changed, and it was applied to various yellow and brilliant alloys; according to Du Cange, medieval authors used it for a mixture of copper and tin; and we find it as a synonym for brass.

The solar relation is brought out in the myth that drops of amber are the tears of the Heliades, daughters of Helios, who stand as poplars weeping drops that are hardened by the sun in the sand. They grieve for their brother Phaethon. The site was the river Eridanos, the Po. Apollonios Rhodios adds that the Celts called amber the Tears of Apollo—tears wept when he left heaven at the chiding of Zeus and went to the sacred race of the Hyperboreans, "angry about his son whom divine Koronis bore in bright Lakereia at the mouth of Amyros". The pseudo-Aristotle in *On Marvellous Things Heard* says that the amber-dripping poplars are on the Elektrides Island on the Adriatic, silted up by the Eridanos. There Phaethon, mismanaging the sun-chariot, was struck by the thunderbolt and fell into the lake of hot stinking water at which no animal drinks; any bird that tries to fly over drops in, dead. The poplars grow in this lake or marsh. To these islands came Daidalos in his flight from Crete, and here he set up two statues, one copper and the other tin, to himself and his son Ikaros. As Ikaros had failed in his wing-flight, the island and its amber were connected with two falls from the sky, one of which was the result of a thunderbolt.

Amber, a fossil resin, has the property of acquiring electrical charge by friction; and it must have been this power, which seemed magical, that brought about the extensive trade in very ancient times in pieces fetched from the Baltic (where it is mainly found in the promontory of Samland in East Prussia). The legendary link of the Hyperboreans with Apollo on Delos and at Delphoi (originally no doubt with Leto his mother) seems to be based on the amber-routes to the north. Amber was thought to hold apotropaic powers, so that even raw bits of it are often found in ancient tombs; at Vasto in Italy we find female amber masks of the seventh century B.C.; the Picena culture of this period is the richest in amber finds in all Italy. At Belmonte, for instance, up to a hundred fibulae with pieces of raw amber attached can be found in a single tomb. Amber amulets include phallic pendants.

The strong link with the idea of a fall from the sky, from the sun, is shown by the statement of Chares that Phaethon died in Aithiopia, where there is a temple of his and an oracle, and where amber is produced. As far back as the *Odyssey* amber is described as shining "like the Sun". Nikias says that it is a liquid produced by the setting rays of the sun: the rays, at the exact moment of sunset, strike with greatest force on the surface of the soil and leave on it an unctuous sweat, which, carried off by the tides of Ocean, are cast upon the shores of Germany. Theomenes says that near the Greater Syrtis are the Gardens of the Hesperides and Lake Elektron; on the banks are poplars from the tops of which amber falls into the waters below, where the Hesperidean nymphs gather it. Plinius, discussing the remedial powers attributed to amber, says that "amber to be of high quality should present a brightness like that of fire, and not flakes resembling those of flame". The most esteemed was called Falernian after the wine: "it is perfectly transparent and has a softened transparent brightness." We see the persistent relation to the sun and its light; the statement that it falls from the tops of poplars, tall spiring trees, again stresses the fall from the sky. There seems then a link with such phenomena as lightning, thunderbolt, tornado, but apart from the mythical connection with the bolt-stricken Phaethon there is no statement by ancient writers which brings the point out. Rather, it was linked with the magnet. Plinius says, "When a vivifying heat has been imparted to it by rubbing it between the fingers, amber will attract chaff, dry leaves, and thin bark, just in the same way as magnet attracts iron. Pieces of amber, steeped in oil, burn with a more brilliant and lasting flame than pitch or flax."[13]

Through connecting amber with magnets the ancients made no atempt to isolate its particular qualities of attraction. The first person to study those qualities was William Gilbert (later sixteenth century), who found that they were shared by other substances; he called them *vis electrica*. The first person to use the term electricity was Walter Charleton in his *Ternary of Paradoxes*, 1650. Bodies owning the power of attracting light objects were said to be electrified or charged with electricity. In 1729 Stephen Gray found that the power could be transmitted by contact from one body to another and that it was transmitted from one part of some bodies to all other parts. The bodies through which the power was freely transmitted were called conductors by Desaguiliers in 1736. About 1733 du Fay, superintendent of the Gardens of the French king, found that there were two "kinds" of electricity, with unlike kinds attracting and like kinds repelling each other.

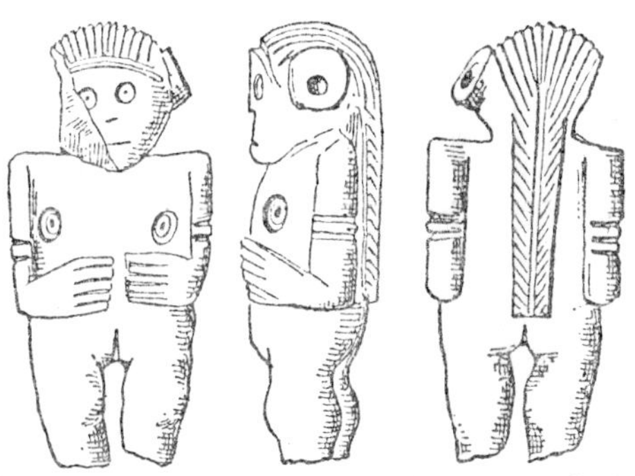

38. Female figurines of amber from tombs at Vetulonia (today Colonna), Italy (L.A. Milani, *L'arte e la religione*)

Because of its link with the sun and with sky-bolts, amber was thought to have great fire-power; and as experiments to devise powerful or explosive fire-materials began, amber was used. The evidence comes from the medieval period, but would certainly have much earlier roots. In *De Alkimia*, attributed to Michael Scot, the Cambridge MS. has a section dealing with the preparation of colours, Greek Fire, sulphur, oil of turpentine. There may well be some material from Scot here. Ingredients of Greek Fire include sandarac, sulphur, amber, and naval pitch; distillation is used and the result is applied to incendiary arrows tipped with cotton and fustian. Amber powder was used in a kind of improved Greek Fire of 1340, employed at St. Omer. Amber appears in the manufacture of saltpetre in the fifteenth century; and the *Mittelalterliche Hausbuch*, compiled about 1480 in south Germany, gives recipes with or without amber and camphor. A manuscript dated about the fifteenth century has a recipe for inextinguishable fire that includes sulphur, colophony, turpentine, amber.[14]

Jet was a lesser substance with attractive powers. The name, *gagates*, came from a town and river in Lydia; but in Roman days the main source was from the Whitby lias in Yorkshire, with craftsmen carving it at York. With its magical reputation it was much in vogue for decorations (as in Victorian England); it was used for hairpins and distaffs, bangles and necklaces, and medallions depicting family-groups, as well as in gorgon-headed amulets for warding off the evil eye. Plinius notes that water ignites it and oil quenches it, that it leaves a sulphurous smell, and that the fumes dispel hysterical affections, detect epileptic tendencies, and test virginity.[15]

ADDENDUM TO CHAPTER X

The most interesting account of electricity is to be found in Claudian's poem on the Electrical Ray, Crampfish, or Torpedo. This fish forms an isolated family in the rays, possessing large paired electrical organs formed of vertical hexagonal columns and set between the pectoral fins and the head. With these organs it can give powerful shocks, which are used in self-defence or in the killing of prey. The head and trunk of the fish form a circular disc, with a short stout tail. (When, in 1805, the American Robert Fulton experimented with the use of gunpowder-charges below water to blow in the side of a ship, he called his device a torpedo; and though it took some time for a moving underwater mechanism with an explosive to be developed, his name was kept for it.) Claudian writes:

Who has not heard of the craft that nothing tames
in the dread torpedo, the powers its name proclaims?
Softbodied, slow, it scarcely marks the sand

on which it sluggishly crawls; but Nature's hand
has armed its flanks with a numbing venom-store:
a chill to freeze live things lies at its core.
Its own strange winter in its heart it hides;
with guile aids Nature; in its power confides,
its crafty skill; in seaweed stretcht, obeys
its sense of touch; attacks; unmoving stays.

If, cheated, it takes the bait which out of sight
holds the bronze jagging hook, it still won't fight
or vainly bite the line. Shrewdly it goes
closer. Though caught, its venomed might it knows:
wide effluence from its veins leaps scattering;
out of the sea, along the line, to sting
the far-off fisher. The dread force expands,
climbs paralysing; on the slack line it steals;
slips down the jointed rod. The blood congeals
suddenly in the cocksure fisher's hands—
he drops the dangerous burden. The rebel prey
he leaves and rodless takes his homeward way.

The terms used for the discharge are *venemum* (poison), *vis* (force), and *ars* (which has the same meaning as *technē*); the Latin name *torpedo* refers to the numbness, *torpor*, caused by the shock. That the torpedo could shock a fisherman is true, but its current would act only in water. Walsh in a paper of 1773 tells of a fisherman who "always knew when he had a torpedo in his net, by the shocks he received while the fish was at several feet distance; in particular, he said, that in drawing in his nets with one of the largest in them, he received a shock when the fish was at twelve feet distance, and two or three more before he got it into his boat. His boat was afloat in the water, and he drews in the net with both hands. It is likely that the fisherman

39. Line-fisherman: Pompeian painting (Reinach, *Peintures* 276)

might magnify the distance; but, I think, he may be so far believed, as that he felt the shock before the torpedo was drawn out of the water. . . . Some electricity would pass through the net to the man's hands, and from thence through his body and to the bottom of the boat, which in all probability was thoroughly soaked with water, and perhaps leaky to the water under the boat." Claudian's account hardly fits in with all these details; but he had doubtless heard true stories of fishers receiving shocks.[16]

Mechanics

XI

Many craft-techniques were already well-developed in early times. Homeric carpenters were skilled in making swing-doors and their fastenings. In the period of Thales an engineer, Eupalinos, constructed on Samos a tunnel (more than 900 feet long) passing under the hill of Kastro; the miners started out at opposite sides of the hill at the same time and met almost exactly in the same line as modern excavation has shown. The Pythagorean Archytas is said to have made many mechanical inventions and to have discovered the pulley in south Italy: the tradition at least shows that the early Pythagoreans were interested in such matters. In physics the ancients recognised as forces fire, air, gravitation, and magnetism. Of air they knew that it tends to rise or descend with heating or cooling; and then when compressed it escapes with violence. They knew that if the air is sucked up from a half-immersed tube, the water rises in the tube. They explained the fact by the theory of bodies being superimposed in order of density—solids and liquids at the bottom, then air, then fire—and their always tending to follow one another in this order without leaving any space between. Also, the force of attraction was not the same between all these elements: it was little exerted between a liquid and a solid but much more between a liquid and the air, so that the air sucked out of the tube attracted the water strongly and counterbalanced its weight. There was an equilibrium when the weight of the column of water drawn up was equal to the force of attraction of the air.

The Greeks also knew that sound is propagated in the air in spherical waves and that it can be thrown back by an obstacle to produce an echo. They knew too that light is propagated in a straight line, and is reflected on a polished surface at an angle with the surface equal to the angle of incidence. Plato seems to have known this law, which was clearly set out by Eukleid, who showed its main consequences. Refraction was studied, chiefly by Ptolemaios. Further, the Greeks knew and used the property that concave mirrors have of giving an enlarged image; they knew of magnifying lenses, but did not combine them into telescopes. In Aristophanes' *Clouds* Strepsiades undertakes to use a lens for wiping out the writing on a tablet of wax; Seneca says that small letters appear magnified when looked at through a glass-ball full of water. The Greeks knew that movement can be transmitted by means of toothed wheels and endless screws, and that great effects can be got with little force by the use of a system of pulleys. They knew that water cannot be compressed.[1]

Though there were many specialisations in the crafts, a wide number of skills must have been generally shared. The Roman army did not depend on a corps of trained engineers; from Caesar we learn how the legionaries were capable of all sorts of construction-work in wood and stone; they could build ships or pile-bridges across rivers in short spaces of time. Trajan's Column shows us soldiers at varied tasks. Later the army built up its groups of technicians, especially after the arrow-shooting ballista came in early in the second century and the stone-throwing onager perhaps a little later. Special legions of *ballistarii* of men who understood machinery and could operate and maintain the artillery were raised in the fourth century; one unit perhaps had about fifty pieces of ordnance. As the third century went on, the supply of men suitable for technical training had lessened, and it was doubtless difficult to keep the artillery sections up to strength. But at least in earlier years specialisation was not at all

40. Soldiers building a fortified camp: Trajan's Column

rigid. Men like Vitruvius or Sostratos (who built the Lighthouse at Alexandreia) were as much engineers as architects. Vitruvius shows the all-round nature of professional skills: "An architect should be equipped with knowledge of many branches of study and varied kinds of learning, as it's by his judgment that all work done by the other crafts is put to the test. This knowledge is the child of practice and theory." Scholarship must be added to manual skill. The architect must "be educated, skilful with the pencil, instructed in geometry, knowing much history and having followed the philosophers with attention, understanding music, owning some knowledge of medicine, acquainted with the opinions of jurists and with astronomy and the theory of the heavens". He explains the reasons for these lores. For instance, arithmetic is useful in computing costs and measurement, "but difficult questions involving symmetry are solved by means of geometrical theories and methods. A wide knowledge of history is needed, since among the ornamental parts of his design for a work there are many, the underlying idea of which he should be able to explain. As for philosophy, it makes an architect highminded and not self-assuming, but rather tends to make him courteous, just, and honest without avarice." Also he needs to know physics. No man should claim the profession of architect "without climbing from boyhood the steps of these studies, without having reached the heights of that holy ground of architecture nursed by the knowledge of many arts and sciences".

The sculptors Kleoitas and Aristeides modified the machinery for the starting-gate in the stadion at Olympia. Carpenters working on the Delphic sanctuary thought nothing of turning their hand to the construction of lifting-devices that could transport stone from quayside to cart, or from ground-level to the required place on high in the edifice. Many difficult problems must have been tackled as challenges without any direct experience of the necessary procedures, as with the Samian tunnel or the boat-bridge built by Mandrokles. Diades, an engineer, seems to have invented drawbridges for ships so that Alexander, at the protracted siege of Tyre, might land troops near a breach in the walls made by ship-artillery; at the same siege the citizens devised huge wheels that whirled round and stopped or broke the bolts from the catapults. We have examples of craftsmen expanding their range. The painter Protogenes was for long a ship's painter;

the greater inventor Ktesibios began in his father's barber-shop. Such facts as these need to be recalled and weighed against the aristocratic contempt of work, of practical activity, which dominated so much of the intellectual tradition.

A poor man, even a slave, if he had intelligence, pertinacity and a certain amount of luck, might become a philosopher. Bion, who began as a member of the Platonic Academy and ended as a Cynic, had been a slave.

> My father was a freedman who wiped his nose on his sleeve [meaning that he was a dealer in saltfish], a native of Borysthenes, with no face to show, but only the writing on his face, a token of his master's severity. My mother was the sort a man like my father would marry, out of a brothel. Afterwards he cheated the revenue in some way and was sold with all his family. And I, then a not ungraceful youngster, was bought by a rhetorician, who on his death left me all he had. And I burned his books, scraped everything together, came to Athens, and turned philosopher. *This is the stock and this the blood from which I boast I've sprung.* [*Il.* vi, 211]. Such is my story. It's high time then that Persaios and Philonides left off prattling about it. Judge me by myself.

The Stoic Kleanthes of Assos was a pugilist, according to Antisthenes in his *Successions of the Philosophers*. "He arrived in Athens, as some say, with four *drachmai* only, and meeting with Zenon he studied philosophy most nobly and adhered throughout to the same doctrines. He was renowned for his industry, driven by extreme poverty to work for a living. By night he drew waters in gardens; by day he exercised himself in arguments. Hence his nickname Phreantles or Well-lifter. He is said to have been brought into court to answer the inquiry how so sturdy a fellow as he made his living, and was acquitted on producing as witnesses the gardener in whose garden he drew water, and the woman who sold the meal he used to crush." The court voted him a donation of ten *mnai*, but Zenon told him not to take it. Once at a public show the wind blew his cloak aside and showed that he lacked a shirt, so the people applauded him. Zenon bade him hand over an obol from his wages, then later produced a handful of small coins and said that Kleanthes could even maintain a second Kleanthes if he wished, "while those who possess the means to keep themselves yet seek to live at the expense of others, and that too though they have lots of time to spare from their studies". So Kleanthes was called a Second Herakles. Here we see great admiration of the union of intellectual and manual labours.

We must add too that many thinkers made instruments and machines, e.g. Archytas, Eudoxos, Menaichmos; Aristotle admired mechanical toys and Aristoxenos had a liking for technical detail. Archimedes made machines and wrote about the mathematical aspects of his mechanics. Geminos, among others, held mechanics to be a branch of that section of mathematics "concerned with and applied to things perceived by the senses"; Karpos was one of many scientists who considered that geometry was not injured by association with the *technai*; Pappos declared that the science of mechanics is "justly esteemed by philosophers and diligently pursued by all who are interested in mathematics". We find inscriptions recording the names of inventors. Even after 200 B.C., when the interest in research declined, free men at times studied and mastered techniques, and it was not held unworthy for such to use their hands in scientific work.

The main extant authors who give us information about mechanics and their applications are Aristotle, Ktesibios, Archimedes, Biton, Vitruvius, Athenaios, Heron, Pappos, and Oreibasios:

For Aristotle's ideas in detail we need to go to a treatise which has come down under his name but which was probably written not long after his death by a member of his school, perhaps while Straton was its head. Thirty-five problems are considered. In this chapter we shall treat this work as if it was by Aristotle himself, since it cannot be far from his ideas.

Ktesibios, who probably flourished about 300–270, worked under the Ptolemies. He invented the cylinder and plunger, the force-pump, the water-organ, a catapult worked by compressed air, another kind of catapult and a scaling ladder, a waterclock, and many mechanical and pneumatic devices such as singing birds to call the hours.

Archimedes, who died in 212 at the age of about 75, has only come down to us in some theoretical work, but we know that he wrote a book on practical mechanics (how to build a spherical planetarium) as well as explaining the mathematical basis of his mechanical procedures. He is said to have invented the water-snail, the endless screw, the compound pulley, and cranes and other machines of far greater power than any known previously, for the defence of Syracuse. The attributions in general may be accepted.

Biton has left six chapters dealing with four catapults (non-torsion artillery), a scaling ladder, and a siege-tower. He states that his devices are taken from four previous inventors: Poseidonios, who made his siege-tower for Alexander the Great, Zopyros the Tarantine, who seems a Pythagorean, Damis of Kolophon, who made the ladder, and Isidoros of Abydos, who was *nauarch* or admiral under Antiochos in 191. (Damis may be the Damios who was nauarch of Eumenes II about 168.) Biton's book is exceedingly obscure.

Vitruvius, who composed his discourse on Architecture about 25 B.C, tells us in his last book much about transport and various technical matters useful for a builder.

Athenaios the Mechanician wrote on the capture of fortified towns about the same time.

Heron of Alexandreia wrote on Pneumatics, Automatic Theatres, a Dioptra (combined theodolite and waterlevel), and Catapults; he also compiled a textbook on Geometry. All these works have come down in Greek; but we have in addition an Arabic translation of his textbook on Mechanics.

Under Diocletian, Pappos made a compilation which in Book VIII deals with mechanics and gives many fragments from earlier writers.

Oreibasios, physician to the emperor Julian, wrote on medicine and described machines for resetting dislocated limbs. The sliding parts of these machines are called tortoises as they move slowly; they were constructed so that the stretchings worked gently and did not cause lesions of the patient's members. They were usually moved by screws, but we also find an axle turned by a handspike. We may add that an anonymous writer of the later fourth century addressed a memorandum to the government in which he advised several technical improvements.[2]

Aristotle held that only two sorts of simple movement exist: the circular (movement of rotation) and the rectilinear (movement of translation). The circular movement is that of the heavenly bodies; the rectilinear is that of bodies in the sublunar region, which are subject to genesis and passing-away. (In mechanics, to translate means to cause a body to move so that all its parts follow the same direction.) The simple movements of translation are of two kinds: the rectilinear centripetal or downward movement towards the centre of the universe, which naturally affects the heavy bodies whose position of equilibrium is the centre—and the rectilinear centrifugal or upward movement, which belongs to light bodies situated in the concavity of the lunar orbit. So heaviness and lightness impart rectilinear movement to the bodies with those qualities; but the movements stop as soon as the bodies have reached their position of natural equilibrium. So this position possesses a certain power, and that is why the fall of heavy bodies is accelerated. The force of the weight increases in proportion as the body nears its position of equilibrium. The natural movements here described are in opposition to violent movements, which result from external constraint or force, and which are not directed towards the position of natural equilibrium. But whatever kind the movement may be, it must be circular, rectilinear, or a composition of the two.[3]

Aristotle may be said to have here forestalled an important theorem in modern kinematics: in its most general form an infinitely small movement of a solid body is made up of an infinitely small rotation round a certain axis and an infinitely small translation parallel to this axis. But, not being able to take into account the infinitesimal, Aristotelean dynamics could not but fall into hopeless errors. Aristoteleans, considering the fall of a stone cast up by a sling, could only describe the trajectory as made up of two straight lines joined by a circular arc, not as a parabola.

Aristotle saw two influences on a moving body: a force and a resistance. Without the force the body could not move; without the resistance the movement would be instantaneous to the point to which the force impelled it. The velocity of a moving body then depended both on the magnitude of the force and the magnitude of the resistance. On this basis he worked out the following law. The force F moving a body is equal to the resistance R which acts on the body, multiplied by the velocity V imparted by the force: $F = RV$. (In fact the equation does work within its bounds for empty space, since in a vacuum an infinitely small applied force will produce eventually an infinitely large velocity, and indeed there are plans for using the principle to power interstellar spaceships—using the force of solar light on large sails to build up, over weeks or months, a colossal velocity. But in essence the equation would only be valid at infinity.) Again, according to Aristotle's system R and F manifest themselves differently in natural and violent movement. In the first, the body seeks its position of natural equilibrium, and the only resistance is that of the traversed medium. Also, observation shows that the natural movement, in so far as it is rectilinear, is accelerated. Thus, a stream of water falling from a height seems continuous near its start, but soon acceleration detaches drops of water from one another and they reach ground separately. A stone falling from a height strikes an object more violently near the end of its fall than at the start or the middle: which is a sign of its increased velocity. All this is right according to theory. A moving body passes from a zero velocity to a given velocity through acceleration, which continues for the same reason as it began, and ends only when the body has reached its goal, its position of equilibrium.

In violent movement—traction of a cart or towing of a ship—resistance is represented by the weight of the object, and force by the motive power continuously acting on that object. In the movement of a projectile, as we saw, the air supplies the motive power.

What most interests us here is the law of proportions established between V, F, and R. The same force will move a heavier body more slowly than a lighter one: the velocities of the movements imparted to those bodies will be inversely proportional to their weights. "The velocity of the lighter body will be to the velocity of the heavier body as the weight of the heavier body is to the weight of the lighter body." But when this law is applied to the free fall of bodies in space it fails. A light body like a feather falls more slowly than a heavy body like a bit of lead; but if we take two falling bodies of the same shape and size weighing respectively 1 lb. and 2 lb., we ought to get: 1 lb. = RV, and 2lb. = R2V. That is, the body of 2 lb. should fall twice as fast as that of 1 lb., since the air resistance is the same. But experience shows this formulation to be wrong. However, Aristotle's assumptions carried on till Galileo, when the atomists and Lucretius were proved to be on the right lines. The latter wrote: "So the atoms in spite of their unequal masses, must move in empty space with equal velocity."[4]

Then take the case of a body steadily subject to an unchanging force, while the resistance grows till it equals the force. We know from experience that at a given moment the velocity becomes nil; but according to Aristotle's law we have the constant $V = \frac{F}{R}$, so that what we know to happen, cannot happen. Aristotle tried to get out of the difficulty by saying that a small force cannot move a large body. "Because a whole force moves a body along a certain distance, it doesn't follow that half this force moves that body along any distance during any time. If that were so, one man could move the ship that all the haulers pull, if, the force of the haulers being divided by a certain number, the traversed distance was also divided by that number." By his theory Aristotle could not explain why it was easier to use a given force to move a cart with large wheels than one with small wheels.

The treatise on mechanics is almost all about the lever, which it derives from the circle. Some things, it says, occur according to nature, others are done contrary to nature, by *technē*. As the poet Amphion said: "By *technē* we gain mastery over things in which we are conquered by nature." When a smaller weight lifts a greater one, as is done by the lever, it's against nature. "The original cause of all such phenomena is the circle," which is remarkable for the way in which it combines a series of opposites. Thus the centre is at rest while the circumference moves; the periphery is at the same time both concave and convex; when a wheel turns, one part goes forward, the other part backwards at the same time; the moving radius comes back to the point from which it started; and different points along the same radius move at different speeds; if two wheels touch one another, one turns one way, the other turns the other way. These two wheels are "like the wheels of bronze and steel that are dedicated in temples". The same principle can be applied to series of wheels or circles, only one of which is moved. So, making use of the property inherent in the circle, craftsmen make an instrument concealing the original circle, so that "the marvel of the machine is alone apparent, while its cause is unseen." (Heron describes this device, called *hagnistērion*. "A wheel of bronze placed at the entry to the temple: this is what those who enter the temple use to turn." The touch of the metal was thought to purify. A part of the mechanism was hidden, so that several wheels were seen to turn in varying directions of their own accord.) No cogs or teeth are mentioned, and there is no need to assume them, as the resistance to be overcome would be slight. In the treatise the lever is further derived from the balance, and the balance, turning about an axle or a string, is derived from the circle, the wheel.

From the formula F = RV Aristotle concluded that the properties of the lever and the balance were related to velocities with which circular arcs are described. Two forces are equivalent if by moving unequal weight with unequal velocities they give the same value to the product of the weight by the velocity.

> If we take a rectilinear lever divided by a fulcrum into two unequal arms, to the ends of which two unequal masses hang, when the lever turns round its fulcrum, the two weights will move with differing velocities—the one furtherest from the fulcrum will describe in a given time a greater arc than the one nearest to it. The velocities with which the two weights move have the same ratio to each other as the lengths of the arms of the lever.
>
> When therefore we wish to compare the forces of the two weights, we must find, for each of them, the product of the weight by the length of the arm of the lever. That one which corresponds to the greater product will outweigh the other; and if the two products are equal, the two weights will remain in equilibrium. (Duhem.)[5]

Thus it is that Aristotle managed to extend his theory of the lever, to show that the various operations of the mechanisms can be understood simply by considering the velocities with which certain circular arcs are described. He in this way, it has been noted, foreshadowed the principle of virtual velocities. The treatise was able to claim: "The properties of the balance are reduced to those of the circle; the properties of the lever to those of the balance; and the greater part of the peculiarities of mechanical movements are reduced to the properties of the lever."

But his application of the principle was all too rigid and oversimplified; and the results were sadly inadequate when he tried to deal with complex problems. At the outset he ran up against a strong contradiction. The line described in a movement of the lever through the point of application of the force of resistance is a circumference of a circle; it does not coincide with the vertical line along which that force or resistance acts. Aristotle made the feeble excuse that a balance was more accurate the longer its arms were, for then the circular arc described approximated more nearly to a vertical line. He argued that a small rudder could turn a big boat because "the point at which it is attached to the ship is the fulcrum, the whole rudder is the bar, the sea is the weight, and the helmsman is the motive force".

The treatise tries to apply the basic Aristotelean principle in dealing with balances and weights, pulleys and rollers, nutcrackers, swingbeams in wells, windlasses and grummets on a lyre-yoke, wedges, the way men stand up, the way one man puts timber on a shoulder, the way two men carry a weight between them on planks. It asks why the rowers in the middle of a ship contribute most to the movement, why the higher the yardarm the faster the ship travels with the same sails and the same wind, why round and circular bodies are easiest to move, why burdens are carried more easily on rollers than on wheels, why a missile travels further from the sling than from the hand, why it is that the greater the radius the faster the movement, why seashore pebbles are round when they were originally long stones or shells, why pieces of timber are weaker and more bendable the longer they are, what makes the power of a small wedge, why dentists remove teeth more easily by applying the weight of the forceps (i.e. to loosen the tooth) than by using the bare hand, why it's easier to move what is stationary. Then there is a brief and weak attempt to answer the questions: Why do thrown objects ever stop travelling? Why does a body travel at all by its own motion when the discharging force doesn't follow and go on pushing it?

There is much confusion about problems of movement and there are often wrong assumptions behind the questions; e.g. about round pebbles. The author goes wrong as to the way that pulleys work, though he knows both the simple and compound forms. What is of interest is the way his mind keeps playing around problems of rowing or sailing a ship, of using pulleys and wedges on construction work or wheels and rollers in transport. On all such matters he seeks with much ingenuity to impose his theory of the circle-derived lever. That lever is shown at work in rudder, forceps, nutcracker, wedge—the latter tool being seen rather ineffectively as two levers opposite to one another.

The treatment of the thrown object, the force driving it on and the resistance slowing it down, might be said to hover insecurely round Newton's first and second laws of motion: that every body continues in its state of rest, or of uniform motion in a straight line, unless compelled by the application of a force to change that state, and that to every action there is equal and opposite reaction. But for several reasons, one of which is his incorrect theory of the pushing air, the author cannot fully formulate these points or see the need to do so. (Although in writing of the heavens, Aristotle has assumed that circular motion is simple, the author of the *Problems* seeks to analyse it into two rectilinear motions. He himself had briefly suggested that whirling is compounded of pulling and pushing; but no attempt was made to apply such an idea systematically with regard to the heavens till Kepler and Newton.) The treatise ends with the analysis of an object caught in an eddy. In view of the importance of the idea and image of the eddy in the cosmogonic theories and the fascination of the *prēstēr*, we may take this passage in full.

> Why do objects travelling in eddying water all finish their movement in the middle? Is it because the travelling object has definite magnitude so that it is moving in two circles, one less and one greater, each of its ends being in one of them? The greater circle, then, since it travels more quickly, turns the object round and drives it sideways into the smaller circle. But since the travelling object has breadth, this second circle produces the same effect, and again drives the object into the next inner circle, until at last it reaches the middle. There it stays, for, being in the middle, it is in the same relation to all circles. In each circle the centre is the same distance from the circumference.
>
> Or can it be because objects which the travel of the whirling water cannot control on account of their weight (that is, the weight of the object overcomes the speed of the revolving circle) must get left behind and travel more slowly? But the smaller circle travels more slowly; for the large circle revolves to the same extent in the same time as the smaller circle, when the two are concentric. So the object must be left in each lesser circle in turn till it reaches the centre. In cases in which the travel prevails at the beginning, it will do the same until it stops. For the original circle and then the next must prevail by its speed over the weight of the object, so that it will pass in turn to each smaller circle all the time. An object that doesn't prevail must be moved either inside or outside. For that which isn't overcome cannot continue travelling in the circle in which it is originally. Still less can it remain in the outer circle; for the travel of the outer circle is more rapid. The only thing left is for the object which isn't controlled by the water to

> shift to the inside. Now each object always inclines not to be controlled. But since its arrival at the middle puts an end to the movement, the centre is the only part at rest, and everything therefore must collect there.

We may pause here to note a mechanical theorem which, though not explicitly stated, is in general assumed by many Greek thinkers, especially the later ones: that cause equals effect. This assumption normally underlies conservation-theories; and behind it is a notion of permanence, which on analysis turns out to be metaphysical and to reduce time to an abstraction. In such a system the causal continuity of an isolable process is to be found in a ceaseless sequence of equal causes and effects, and this sequence constitutes an aspect of unchanging permanence behind the changing appearances. The fundamental nature of permanence, conservation, and equality of cause and effect is assumed in such statements as that of Plato: "How can that be real which is never in the same state?"—or that of Aristotle: "In pursuing the truth one must start from things that are always in the same state and never change." Even Demokritean atomism, which posited an endless scurrying of elements or atoms, had only shifted the angle from which permanence was viewed; now it appeared in the unchanging constituent units.

With such an outlook, the question of change could only be approached from a mechanist angle in which the notion of the absolute seemed to have abdicated but in fact had merely changed its idiom. True, the Greeks never followed out the logic of the position to its full mechanist conclusions; but this aspect of their thought prepared the way for Galileo and Newton in due time, when the quantitative analysis became possible. That analysis had the same assumptions as are shown in those quotations from Plato and Aristotle. Process was to be defined by abstracting from it an invariant which was in essence timeless. The cause-effect relation was formally declared to be symmetrical; and so the relation between the earlier and later states of any process was symmetrical in respect of the causal factors determining its course. The particles and the total mass and energy were the same in earlier and later states.

> So remarkable has been the success of this assumption that few have noticed that it is an assumption, and fewer still have seen

> grounds to question its adequacy. Some have expressed the view that scientific method can only cover the permanent and quantitative aspects of phenomena. Others have even suggested that the human intellect is biologically so conditioned that the intrinsic character of process must for ever escape rational comprehension. We shall see that these views are wrong. The causal continuity which relates earlier and later states in any process may itself be a form of process, a universal pattern of one-way change which recurs everywhere. The invariant factor in process need not itself be timeless, but may consist in a universal tendency towards a defined end-condition. The clue to the order of nature may not be a principle of permanence, but a universal pattern of process displaying an invariant one-way tendency. For it is not change, but only arbitrary change, which eludes the rational intellect (Whyte).

We might say that Aristotle's triadic system of potentiality, *energeia*, and full actualisation, with its abstract teleology removed, provides us with a genuine approach to the real world of one-way change (in which cyclic systems may be also involved).[6]

Ktesibios seems to have been the most important inventor of antiquity, but we have to rely mainly on accounts of his work by others. The best description of his clock comes from Vitruvius. Incidentally it brings out that not all Greek intellectuals belonged to the propertied classes and that those who had direct contact with the craft-world were capable of experimenting. Vitruvius begins by saying that "Berosos the Chaldaean is said to have invented the semicircular dial hollowed out of a square block and cut according to the latitude; Aristarchos of Samos the Bowl or Hemisphere, as it is said, also the Disk on a level surface", and he goes on about the inventors of several other types of dials—with names such as the Spider, the Ceiling, the Dial for Consultation, the Dial for All Latitudes, the Dovetail, the Cone, the Quiver. These men also devised the Conical Spider, the Conical Ceiling and the Antiboreum (Turned-to-the-North); "many have left instructions for making the Hanging Dial for Travellers". There was clearly no lack of dial-systems. The same writers have also worked at ways of constructing waterclocks, "and first, Ktesibios of Alexandria, who also discovered the nature of wind-pressure and the principles of pneumatics". Vitruvius adds that it is worth a student's while to learn how the discoveries were made, so it is clear that he approves of experiments.

Ktesibios was the son of a barber. "He was marked out by his talent and great industry and had the name of being especially fond of mechanical contrivances. On one occasion he wanted to hang the mirror in his father's shop in such a way that when it was pulled down and pulled up again, a hidden cord drew down the weight; and he used the following expedient. . . ." He fixed a wooden channel under a ceiling-beam and inserted pulleys; along the channel he took the cord into a corner where he fixed upright tubes, in which he had a lead weight let down by the cord. So, when the weight ran down into the narrow tubes and compressed the air, the air was forced down through the mouth of the tube into the open; and meeting an obstacle, "it was produced as a clear sound". Ktesibios then went on to apply these principles to the making of hydraulic machines. "He also described the use of water-power in making automata and many other sorts of curiosities [*deliciae*]: among them the construction of waterclocks." Wanting materials that wouldn't be worn by the water or dirtied and clogged, he made a hollow tube of gold or pierced a gem. "The water flows smoothly through the passage and raises an inverted bowl which craftsmen call the cork or drum. The bowl is connected with a bar on which a drum revolves. The drums are made with equal teeth, and the teeth, fitting into one another, cause measured revolution and movements. Further, other bars, and other drums toothed in the same way, driven together, cause in their revolving various kinds of movements in which figures are moved, pillars are turned, stones and eggs are let fall, trumpets sound, and other such sideshows." Vitruvius explains some of the details of the waterclock:

> The hours are marked on a column or pilaster; and these are indicated by a figure rising from the lowest part and using a pointer throughout the day. The shortening and lengthening of the pointers was brought about through the addition or removal of wedges for each day and each month. [The wedges were used for adjusting the pointers.] To regulate the supply of water, stopcocks are thus formed. Two cones are made, one solid, one hollow, and so finished by the lathe that one can enter and fit the other; the same rod, by loosening or tightening them, produces a strong or gentle

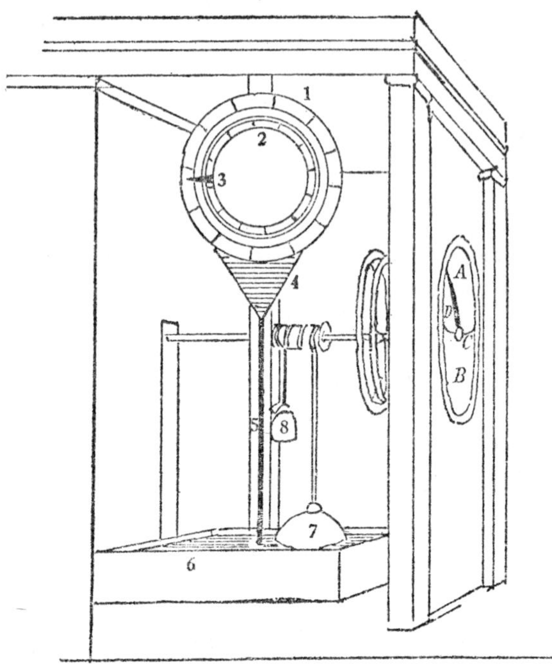

41. Ktesibean Water-Clock (Loeb Vitruvius, ix 8, 8): 1, outer circle of signs; 2, inner moveable circle of months; 3, point moving with inner circle; 4, cistern for water from rotary valves of 2; 5, pipe delivering into 6; 6, main cistern; 7, drum or cork; 8, sand; A, hours of day; B, of night; C, dividing line; D, clock-finger

current of water flowing into the vessels. Hence by this methodical contrivance, waterclocks are set up for winter-use.

But if by adding or withdrawing wedges the shortening or lengthening of days is found to be incorrectly marked by the use of wedges (very often the wedges are faulty), the following solution must be adopted. The hours are to be indicated crosswise on a small column, in accordance with the *analemma* [sun-dial showing the latitude and longitude of a place]. The lines of the months are also to be marked on the column. And this to be made to revolve without interruption, so that it turns to the figure and the rod—with which rod the figure as it moves on shows the hours—and so causes the shortening and lengthening of the hours in their respective months.

There are also winterclocks called Anaphorica. (Dials were little use in the winter.) An *analemma* is described, the hours being marked by bronze rods, starting from the centre of the clockface; on the *analemma* circles are described, which limit the spaces of the months. Behind the rods is a drum on which the firmament and zodiac are drawn, with the twelve signs. Starting from the centre, the spaces are greater and less. On the back part, in the

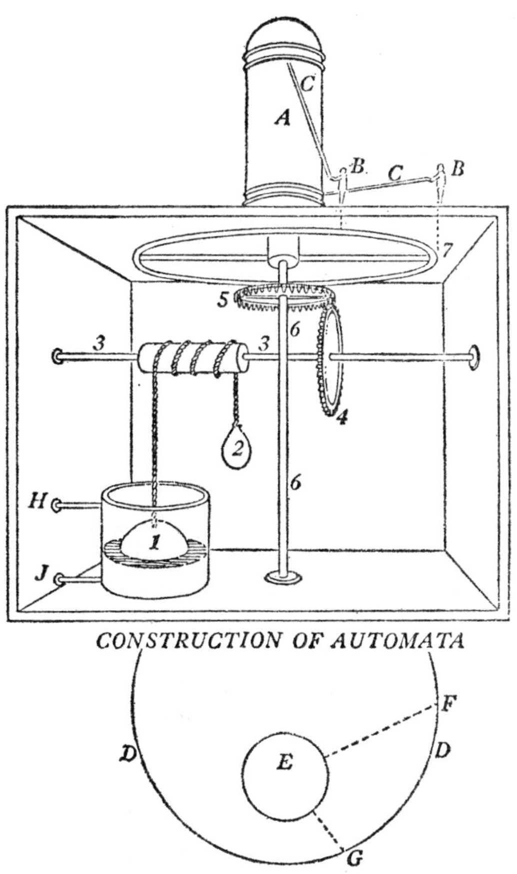

42. Ktesibean Automatic Machine (Loeb Vitruvius, ix, 8, 5): 1, drum or cork; 2, sand; 3, axle turned by 1; 4, toothed wheel turned by 3; 5, ditto turned by 4; 6, axle turned by 5; 7, wheel revolving on 6; A, pillar; B, figure in two positions; C, jointed rod attached to B; D, plan of large wheel; E, position of pillar; F, position of B; G, position of B; H, inlet to cistern; J, outlet

middle of the drum, is fixed a revolving axle, on which is coiled a pliable brass chain. At one end hangs the cork or drum raised by the water; on the other a counterpoise of sand equal in weight to the cork. So, as far as the cork is raised by the water, the counterpoise drags down and turns the axle, and the axle turns the drum.

> The turning round of the drum at times makes a greater part of the zodiacal circle to indicate the proper length of the hour; at times a lesser part for this purpose. For in the various signs holes are made to the number of the days of the various months; and the pin, which in dials seems to represent the sun, marks the spaces of the hours; and moving from one hole to another, it completes the course of the passing month. So, as the sun, traversing the spaces of the constellations, lengthens or shortens the days and hours, so the index, moving along the dial-holes in the opposite direction to the revolving drum, passes daily at times over longer, at times over shorter spaces. Thus it effects over the monthly periods the representation of hours and days.

For the water-supply a cistern is set aside, behind the dial, with a hole in its bottom; a pipe lets the water in. Against the hole is fixed a bronze drum with an opening for the water to flow in. In this drum is a smaller one, joined to it by tenon and socket. "The lesser drum, turning round inside the bigger, like a stop-cock, fits closely and smoothly in its revolution." On the edge of the big drum 365 points are marked off at regular intervals. The small drum on its outer circumference has a tongue with its tip directed towards the points. It also has proportionate perforation, since the water flows in and guides its workings. The zodiacal signs are on the edge of the big drum, which does not move.

So, when the sun is in Capricorn, the tongue touches daily the various points in Capricorn on the part of the big drum. The greatest weight of the running water is vertical and so is quickly delivered through the big drum's perforation into the vessel. The vessel is soon filled and arrests and contracts the spaces of the days and hours. But when by the continuous revolution of the small drum the tongue enters all points in Aquarius, the perforations leave the perpendicular, and after the downpour the water is forced to send out its current more slowly. Thus, the slower the flow by which the vessel receives the water, the more it stretches out the length of the hours. The Greeks and Romans did not divide

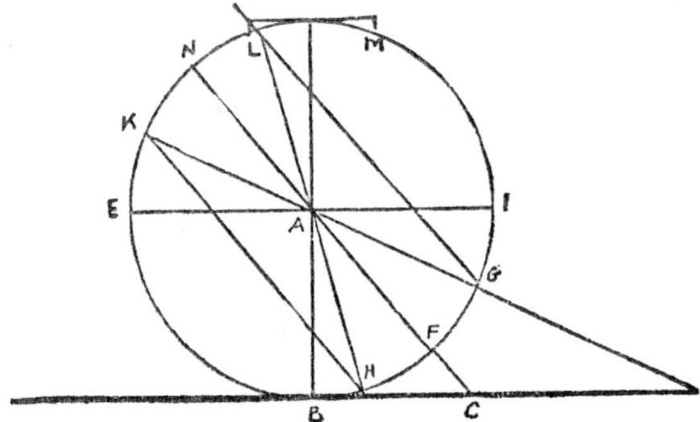

43. Analemma: Latitude of Rome. AB, Gnomon; BC, shadow; EL, Horizon; CFAN, Equinoctial ray; GAK, Winter Solstice; HAL, Summer Solstice (Vitruvius ix 7, 1)

day and night into 24 equal hours; the daylight was divided into 12 equal hours, and the night (darkness) into another set of 12 equal hours; so that, except at solstices, the lengths of the hours of a day and that of the hours of its night were never the same. Hence the need of complicated mechanisms which varied the lengths of the days and their hours, using an adjustable scale and later an adjustable water-flow.

Ktesibios used rack-and-cogwheel systems and was probably the first man to do so. He did not use a pointer moving across a scale, as was later done; but he gave much thought to make his clock impressive and even theatrical. Puppets emerged; cones, half black, half white, were turned to show the hour; pebbles or balls were dropped rattling into a bronze basin; horns were blown, no doubt at noon. For the reasons mentioned above, the system had to be daily restarted; the container was emptied and the float let down to the bottom. As the movement could not be continuous there was no circular dial. All later clocks, except the anaphoric type, stuck to the pointer moving along a straight line, up and down, or across. The anaphoric clock, probably devised by Hipparchos, introduced a sky-map with constellations and adjustable sun; but here too movement could not be continuous. The disk was brought each morning back to its first position.

Ktesibios also invented the water-organ. Heron gives us a clear account of it. Wind was supplied by pumps; a row of pipes sat on a channel into which air was driven. For each pipe there was a valve made of a square chamber closed by a square wooden slide; if the slide was pushed in, a hole in it connected the pipe with the channel below. Vitruvius, however, mentions several channels or registers, each closed by its own valve, and no individual chambers for the pipes are described. The slides, quite long, seem to have slid along each other—each one serving a pipe in every channel.

Another of Ktesibios' inventions was an engine of bronze for raising water to a height. Vitruvius described it with some difficulty, as terminology for this sort of engine was lacking through a false notion being attached to it: that air had something to do with the force-pump even when it was pumping water.

> At its roots [lower part] are twin cylinders, set not far apart, with outlet pipes converging like fork-prongs and meeting in a vessel placed in the middle. In this vessel valves are to be accurately fitted and attached by a well-wedged pin; the valves, by closing the pipe-mouths, retain what has been forced by air into the vessel. Above the vessel a cover like an inverted funnel is fitted and attached by a well-wedged pin, so that the force of the incoming water won't cause the cover to rise. On the cover a pipe, called a trumpet, is jointed to it and made vertical. The cylinders, below the pipe-mouths, have valves inserted above the openings in their bases. Pistons are now inserted from above, rounded on the lathe, and well-oiled. Thus enclosed in the cylinders, they are worked with piston rods and levers.
>
> Since the valves close the lower openings, the pistons drive on the air and water in the cylinders. By such inflation and the resulting pressure they force the water through the orifices of the pipes into the vessel. The funnel receives the water and forces it out by pneumatic pressure through a pipe. A reservoir is provided, and thus water is sent up from below for spouting [i.e. for fountains].

If we omit the remarks about air, we see that there are two cylinders with plungers or pistons which are worked by horizontal levers and vertical connecting-rods. As the cylinders are close to one another, there is most probably more than one lever. The word for valves is *asses*, pennies. Heron, some seventy-five years later, uses two kinds of valves: square vertical flap-valves, and round flat horizontal lids. The first kind seems the earlier.

The earliest reference to Ktesibios, by the poet Hedylos, mentions one of his minor devices, the sort of thing we find in Heron's *Pneumatika*. Athenaios says that drinking-horns, *rhyta*, were carried by the statues of Arsinoe, sister-wife of Ptolemaios II. The one devised by Ktesibios made musical sounds and was in the form of the grotesque god-dancer Bes, a squat dwarf: "Come drinkers of strong wine, regard the Horn in the shrine of gracious Arsinoe, the Westwind's lover. It's in the shape of the Egyptian Bes, who gives a shrill note when the spout opens to pour. Not a battle-signal, but a call for carousal and feast, comes from the golden mouth. Like the ancestral tune that the Lord Nile evokes from the divine waters, dear to the initiates who bring him offerings. So, if you honour Ktesibios' clever device [*sophon heurema*: wise finding or discovery], come here, young fellows, to Arsinoe's temple." Philon of Byzantion tells us that Ktesibios invented two catapults; and Athenaios the Mechanic that he devised an apparatus for storming walls.

Vitruvius goes on to say that many other devices by Ktesibios were still current; e.g. many "driven by water-pressure. The pneumatic pressure [*spiritus*] will be shown to bring about effects borrowed from nature, both notes of blackbirds by the motion of water, and walking automata, little figures that drink and move, and other little things that flatter the pleasure of the eyes and the use of the ears." The blackbird-device is recorded by Heron. That Ktesibios wrote books is shown by a comment of Vitruvius: "The man who reads the Works of Ktesibios and Archimedes, and of others who have composed manuals of the same kind, will not be able to make out their meaning unless he has been instructed in these matters [the nature of things] by philosophers."[7]

Archimedes, we saw, in theory concentrated on problems of statics. Here we see the typical prejudice or limitation of the Greek thinkers who considered the circle the supreme form and equilibrium or the mean the perfect condition. The phenomena of equilibrium, unlike those of kinematics, were capable of treatment along simple lines, with a method similar to that used by Eukleid in his *Elements*. Archimedes only needed the acceptance of two propositions: that two equal weights applied at equal distances from the fulcrum are in equilibrium, and that two unequal weights applied at unequal distances from the fulcrum are not in equilibrium, and the more distant weight descends. Next, the law of equilibrium is thus easily established in the case of a lever: $pL = Pl$—the relation in which the greater force P is exerted at the shorter arm l of the lever. To demonstrate the relation all we need to do is to replace the weight 4 lbs by an arrangement of two weights of 2 lbs each. Then there will be symmetry round the fulcrum and therefore equilibrium.

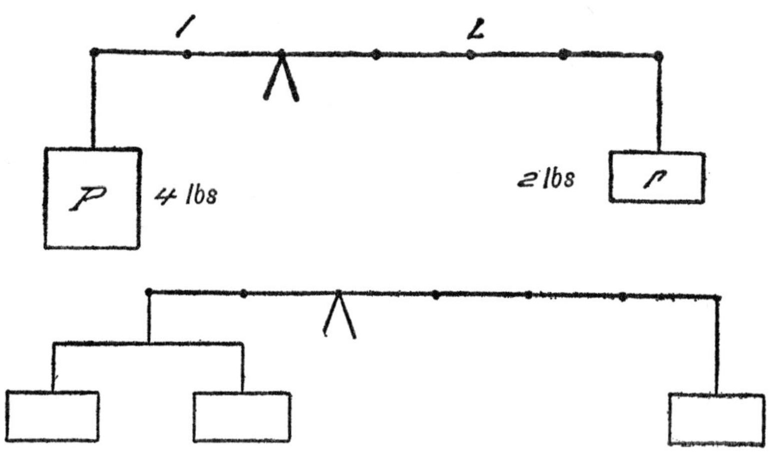

44. Fulcrum with different arrangements of weights

Archimedes used this law of the lever to inquire into the centre of gravity of various surfaces such as triangles, trepeziums, and segments of a parabola. He used a similar method, plus a new hypothesis, to demonstrate a series of propositions in hydrostatics, proving among other things that a body put into a fluid of equal density to its own is wholly immersed, but remains suspended in the fluid, while a solid floating in equilibrium on the surface of a liquid displaces a weight of this liquid equal to its own weight. The laws about two heavy bodies hanging from the arms of a lever were based on hypotheses solely applicable to that problem; they could not be used to deal with cases of equilibrium in quite different conditions; and no analysis of them can suggest the lines leading to new hypotheses. The law of the lever indeed was little more than the disguised verification of a fact. So the problem of the equilibrium of floating bodies had to be tackled by unrelated principles.

We can see the weakness of his law if we replace one of two equal weights, A and B, hanging from two equal arms of a lever by two smaller weights (*a* and *b*), which are in equilibrium and which in sum are equal to A. We cannot know from the law what will now happen. Take for instance a compound pendulum made of a rigid rod (of very little weight) to which are hung a weight of 2 lbs at a distance of 4 inches, and another of 2 lbs at a distance of 8 inches. The moment of force acting on the pendulum when held in a horizontal position is $2\times4+2\times8 = 24$. Using Archimedes' system we could replace the two weights by a single weight of 4 lbs, fixed at a distance of 6 inches. The moment of force would still be 24: i.e. 6×4. But if we let the pendulums oscillate, we *should* find the duration of the oscillations to be the same—in fact we find nothing of the sort. The conditions of symmetry for a system in motion is not at all what it is for a system in equilibrium. The changes in the pendulums did not affect the static moment of their systems, but it changed the moment of inertia.

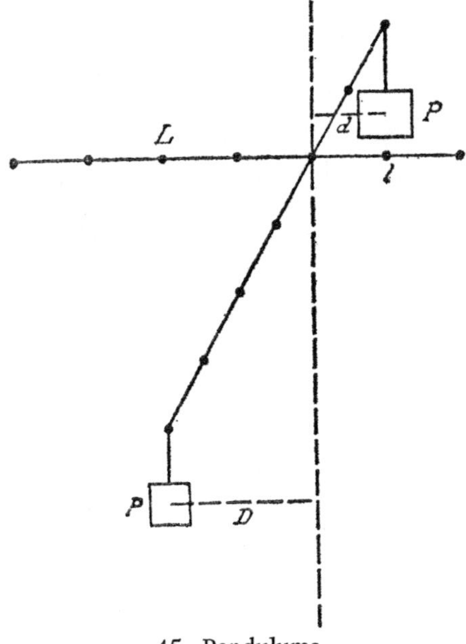

45. Pendulums

For a lever to keep equilibrium, it doesn't matter if we hang the arrangement of two weights higher or lower than the weight it replaces, or if we put the arrangement parallel or perpendicular to the direction of the lever. That was the ideal situation which Archimedes had in his mind; and he was basing his argument on a relation, itself based on the moment of forces, that was not clearly set out till the end of the medieval period. He was intuiting that the effective power of a force at a given moment is equal to that force multiplied by its distance from the vertical axis which passes through the fulcrum: $Pd = pD$—which was equivalent, in a horizontal position, to the relation $Pl = pL$

The limitations then inherent in the approach of Archimedes explain why he made no attempt to work out the theory of the various ballistical engines he devised. (A tradition among the Arabs, we may note, attributed to Eukleid some treatises on the lever and heavy and light bodies. Whether or not his work, they seem to have been written about the same time. While looking to Aristotelian dynamics, they use the same sort of axiomatic method as does the *Elements*, though on simpler lines than in the work of Archimedes. The author follows Aristotle in connecting the law of the lever with the size of the circles described by its extremities; he also attempts a theory of the balance, taking account of the lever itself and assuming that a part of it may be supposed to be detached and replaced by an equal weight hung from the middle point of that part.)

The one model that Archimedes described, according to Karpos, was his planetarium. Claudian in a poem tells of it: "An enclosed force in the sphere directs the stars' courses and drives the living work with definite motions. A fabricated Zodiac runs through a year of its own, and month by month a toy moon waxes and wanes. Now bold invention rejoices to make its own heaven revolve and sets the stars in motion by human wit. Why wonder at harmless Salmoneus with his fake thunder? Here man's small hand has proved to be Nature's rival." He was doubtless celebrating the work merely in terms of its traditional fame, though he may have seen some later efforts to imitate it.

Archimedes made important inventions: the screw, the steelyard, a winch (*tripastos*); in him there was indeed the union of mathematical insight and inventive capacity that could have transformed the whole ancient situation, if there had not been so many adverse pressures. Moschion ascribed to him the snail-screw, the *kochlias*, which was used for raising water; and added that by means of a screw-windlass he shifted the ship of Hieron. Plinius gives us some information about developments in the use of the screw:

> Our fathers drew them [press-beams] down by means of ropes and leather thongs and handspikes. Within the last hundred years there have come into use presses invented in Greece, some people putting handles on the spar, others making the spar lift up chests of stones: which is very much praised. Within the last twenty-two years it has been discovered how to press with shorter presses and smaller-presshouses, with a shorter spar straight in the middle, bearing down with full weight from above on the lid laid on the grapes. . . .

The three stages which Plinius cites are the windlass-and-lever press, the screw-and-lever press, and the direct-screw press. He says that the first use of the screw in Italian presses was about 25 B.C.; and the invention in Greece cannot have been much earlier. The direct screw-press was first used at Pompeii about A.D. 50. This sort of press necessitated a proper female screw. For a lever press the screw was not an essential or very evident part of the machine. The direct-screw seems to have been used in the ancient world only for oil, wine, and fuller's presses. The first attempt to make a standing part through which the screw could turn may well have been the work of the physician Andreas, a contemporary of Archimedes, who devised a bone-setting clamp worked by a direct-screw. Here only a small force was needed; the make-shift female screw wouldn't have been capable of working a heavy press.

A strong case has been made out for Archimedes having noted water-drums at work in Egypt and realising how his studies of screw-lines and spirals could be used to modify the drum. That is, he adapted an existing instrument instead of inventing a new one at a clean sweep. Vitruvius describes a water-snail in which there were eight wooden spirals, though snails found in Spanish mines have a single spiral of copper. The explanation seems to lie in the fact that Archimedes used this system in taking over and adapting the water-drum.[8]

That he had great inventive powers we cannot doubt. Polybios,

Livius, Ploutarch tell how he invented cranes with far greater power than previously known; cranes that could send stones weighing some 260 kg. down on to the enemy ships or raise those ships out of the water and dash them on the rocks. Ploutarch tells how he had the defence-works handed over to him. He had told King Hieron of Syracuse that "if he had another earth, he'd move this after he'd taken his place on the other one", and to prove his point, he offered to move a three-masted cargo-ship which many men had laboriously hauled ashore, with crew and cargo aboard. He "drew it along, smoothly and evenly as if it were floating on water, not with great toil, but seated some way off, gently swinging with his hand the end of a compound tackle". The story was elaborated by turning the ship into the great cargo-ship presented to Hieron by Ptolemaios of Egypt, and making Archimedes himself superintend the building of it. No one knew how to launch the huge hull, so Archimedes did it with a screw of his own invention. Tzetzes gives the ship a cargo of 50,000 *medimnai* (one *medimna* being a corn measure of about 54 litres), and makes Archimedes draw it with his left hand, using a triple pulley; Proklos says that he let Hieron launch it himself.

Simplikios says that "when Archimedes made the weighing instrument called *charistion* [a steelyard] by the proportion of that which is moving, that which is moved, and the way travelled, as the proportion went on as far as it could go, he made the famous boast: Somewhere to stand and I'll move the earth." He doesn't say that Archimedes used the steelyard to draw the ship, which would have been absurd. He says that he invented it according to the golden rule of mechanics, and by following out the principle arrived at his boast. But the principle also worked in the pulley, rope, drum, gearwheel, and endless screw. Pappos adds that Archimedes found the law by which a given weight can be moved by a given power—and thus was stirred to his claim.

What he must have used in drawing the ship was a compound pulley worked by a windlass containing a screw. He certainly didn't launch the ship. His famous remark must have been made in showing Hieron how the endless screw worked and how it embodied so astonishingly the golden rule. If he wound a rope round a drum (circumference one metre), and the drum was turned by means of an endless screw engaging a toothed wheel

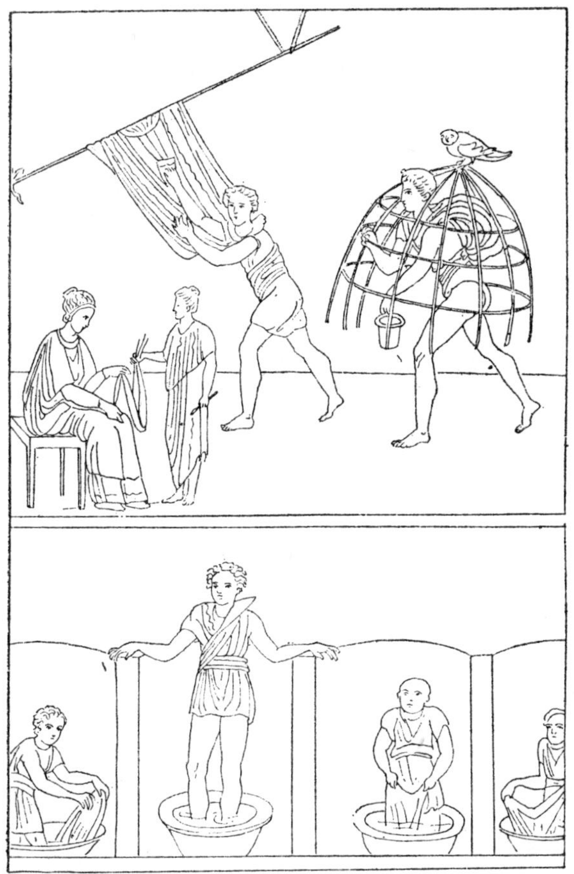

46. Fulling Press: Pompeii, House of the Fullers. Note the Owl on the drying frame

of fifty teeth, and the screw-handle travelled one metre at each turn, the power was in the proportion 1:50. If a pulley of 5 sheaves were added, the man would pull for 250; and if the screw were turned by means of another endless screw giving the same proportion, the pull would be 1:2500. Add another screw and we get 1:125,000. No doubt Hieron, astounded, said that there must surely be some limit to such leaps in the power obtained; and Archimedes replied, "No limit. Give me another earth to stand on, and I'll move the whole of this one."

It becomes clear indeed when we examine the evidence that Ploutarch's account of him as considering ignoble and vulgar "the craft of the engineer and every craft that ministers to the needs of life", is baseless. We can find the explanation of this misunderstanding, which came easy to a man who himself carried on the Platonic contempt of banausic activities, in the words of Archimedes in *On the Method*. There he wrote that while a mechanical perception or *theōria* does not provide a proof, it often helps a man to find the proof if he has a clear notion of what is to be proved. Eudoxos was the first to prove that the cone had a third of the volume of a cylinder, the pyramid a third of the volume of a prism, in each case of the same base and height, yet Demokritos deserved honour for being the first to announce the fact, though he could not prove it.

As there has been so much misunderstanding on this point, we had better cite his own words, addressed to Eratosthenes:

> Since I know you, as I have already said, to be a learned and excellent master of philosophy, and, if need be, you can appreciate mathematical researches, I have thought it well to explain to you the particulars of a method through which you will find it possible to gain a certain facility in treating mathematical matters by mechanical means. Besides, I am convinced that this method will be no less useful for the demonstration of the theorems themselves as well. In fact I myself saw some things for the first time through mechanical means, and then I demonstrated them geometrically; for the research done in this way is not a real demonstration. But it is certainly easier, having in that way gained a certain knowledge of the question, to find the demonstration, instead of seeking it without any preliminary knowledge.
>
> This is why with the theorems of the cone and the pyramid, which Eudoxos first demonstrated—that is, that the cone is the third part of the cylinder, and the pyramid the third part of the prism, having the same base and the same height—a fair share of the credit should go to Demokritos, who first declared, without demonstrating it, that the figures had these properties. In my case too, the theorem which I am now publishing was discovered in a way similar to that of the theorem I have mentioned. And on this occasion I have decided to set down the method in writing, both because I had said I would do so and because I am persuaded that it will be of some use to mathematics. I think, in fact, that now and in the future, other theorems which I have not yet thought of may be

> discovered through this method. In the first place I am going to put down one which first came to me by mechanical means, that is that every section of a rectangular cone is equal to the four thirds of the triangle having the same base and the same height, and after that some of the other results gained by this method. At the end of the book I explain the geometrical demonstration of the theorems which I have already told you about.

Probably Demokritos used a mechanical experiment, turning a cylinder and a cone out of wood or clay, and then comparing their weights. Archimedes probably did the same. He made a parabolic section and a triangle out of thin plate, and then compared their weights—to his surprise finding that they were commensurable. But in his writings he did not tell us of this procedure because in all he wrote he wanted to state things in terms of mathematics. So, after going through the physical and mechanical experiment, he translated the whole thing into mathematical terms. And because Ploutarch found mathematical descriptions in his writings, he assumed that he was not interested in the mechanical aspect. We can make out a series of four books by him: On the centre of gravity in solid bodies, On the centre of gravity in plane figures. On the equilibrium of plane figures, On the squaring of the parabola—the four composing a single work, though the first three books seem to represent what he called his *Mechanics*. In the *Book on Uprights*, he showed how to use the idea of a centre of gravity in straight lines for the purpose of finding the distribution of the weight of a beam, or of a wall supported by two or more pillars placed anyhow, or of a balk carried by any number of men. He proceeded to hang weights on the beam, then to deal with plane figures, showing the distribution of weights in their angles, and next setting weights on them as well. All matters of much practical importance. Indeed, the picture that emerges is one of an engineer concerned deeply with the mathematics of the mechanical problems he tackled—the kind of scientist that we do not meet again for well over a thousand years, in the later medieval era.

The anaphoric clock, which we described in connection with Ktesibios, was probably the invention of Hipparchos in about 150. It has clear similarities with the astrolabe. Often the astrolabe is regarded as the original, but it seems clear that the clock preceded it. The plane astrolabe (first described by Philoponos) consisted of a brass disk, which could be held vertically by a triangular lug with a ring; on the back were two lines engraved at right angles—one vertical, one horizontal, when it was suspended. One of the upper quadrants was divided into 90°, and a small diopter (*alhidade*) was set on a stud in mid-disk. Here was the actual Star-Catcher or *Astrolabos*, which was used to find the height of a star, the sun or the moon above the horizon. On the front was a narrow raised rim divided into 360°, starting straight below the suspension-ring. Inside the rim were several flat disks, one for each climate, engraved with lines that defined in planispheric projection the tropic of Cancer and the equator as concentric circles, while the disk-edge stood for the tropic of Capricorn. A vertical line stood for the meridian; an arc for the horizon of the respective climate. Hour lines were given by the meridian and five short curves each side of it below the horizon; above the latter were curves representing parallels to the horizon (*almucantaras*)—90 of them in the big astrolabes. On top of the disk was put the Spider, *Aranea*, which contained the planispheric projection of the sky reduced to a skeletal form so that as much as possible of the plate beneath it could be seen; in the middle it is solid, to fit a stud in the middle of the instrument.

In operation, first the *alhidade* on the back was used to find the height of sun or a clear star; then the Spider was moved till the star touched the height curve (*almucantar*) in question. Then one had the position of the sky at the moment of observation.

The reason for taking the astrolabe as later than the clock is the fact that the Spider certainly represents a late phase in its development. The primitive form would doubtless use, say, a vertical wire for the meridian, with a horizontal line for the horizon of the sky seen from somewhere on the equator. Then would come the planispheric projection; then the zodiac—with the tropic of Cancer, the equator and the parallel lines for the zodiacal months. Clock and astrolabe were at this point differentiated. In the clock the map was turned by water and the sun's place defined by one or other of 365 holes, while the astrolabe indicated the sun's place by a graduated circle (divided into signs, each of which was subdivided by 300). As more and more *almucantaras* were added to determine the height of sun or star, the thickness of the wires became a nuisance for the user of the astrolabe. So the places of the map and the lines were changed; on the plate lines could be engraved finely, and the zodiac and a few special stars would be shown by slight pointers. Thus appeared the second astrolabe, that of Ptolemaios. (The hypothesis here set out is the work of Drachmann, and gains support from the fact that, if it is correct, we see how the term Spider arose—from the network of lines on the Hipparchan astrolabe, which suggested a spider-web. After the change, which put the lines behind, the name was retained for the sliding part. In the description of an Hipparchan astrolabe by Synesios the star-map seems to be in the background.)

Vitruvius has shown how a serious architect of his day attempted not only to master the artistic tradition of his discipline and to know as much as possible about the practical problems of building, but also to see his art as incomplete unless it embodied a thorough knowledge of mathematics, geometry, science, and philosophy. There are limitations in his own grasp of such a wide field, but his aim is none the less admirable. Art or craft is seen as a dead thing unless it can grasp in its own terms something of the general formative processes of the universe. At the same time Vitruvius is writing for the foreman and the works-manager. He is concerned with experimentation. He tells of the use of a lighted lamp as a test for foul air in a well, and of how the vibration of bronze in response to the impact of iron tools in a neighbouring tunnel led to the taking of military precautions. He deals with the effects of white lead on those who work it, and the danger of lead pipes for water-supply. He is interested in the application of water-power to clocks and organs—an application controlled by a balancing weight in sand. He seeks to understand the principle of equilibrium involved, which furnishes the difficult problem of virtual velocity; and also the principle of the balance and of the lever. We may note that we find slave-labour brought in to work the capstans of pulleys, the water-wheels, the treadmills; but the status of the plasterers and paviours is not so clear. Building workers often worked in gangs of ten under a foreman, and were organised in *collegia*, craft-guilds or benefit societies.

He defines a machine as a continuous (coherent) material system or structure (*coniunctio*) with great powers for moving burdens or weights. "It is moved by the art [*ars, technē*] of the turning

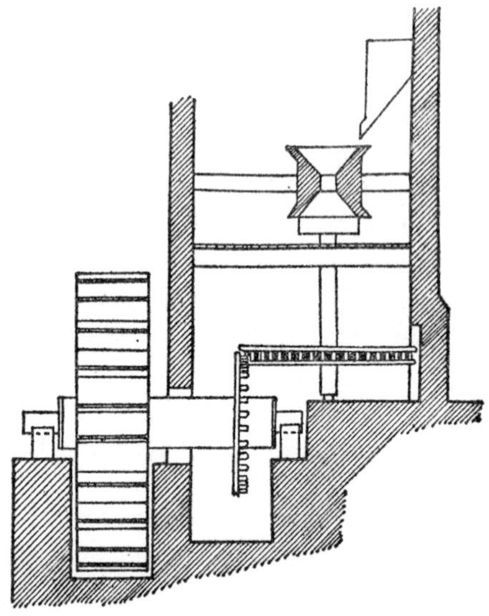

47. Watermill for grinding corn, according to Vitruvius

of circles, which by the Greeks is called *kyklike kinēsis*. The first kind of machines is of ladders; the second is moved by the wind [*spirabile*, in Greek *pneumatikon*]; the third is by traction." In Book IX he describes the circular courses of the stars, which provide the pattern for all engines. In Book X he repeats: "All machinery is generated by Nature, and the revolution of the universe guides and controls." He divides machines into mechanisms and organs. The first term seems to mean engines made up of different kinds of powers, like catapults, where the compound pulley is used to draw back the arm that hurls the missile, or the winepress where the winch pulls on the beam working as a lever. An organ then would be a simple engine, a term that fits the differential gear, though hardly the hand-ballista or small catapult which he also cites as an example.

He tells of cranes, including one with differential gear. For very heavy weights a double rope and double tackle-blocks were used. We meet three parallel sets of pulleys on a crane, worked by three slave-gangs. A heavy crane is set up by means of its own winch. Instead of capstan a treadwheel with men inside it can be used. He adds that the engines he has been describing can be used also "for loading and unloading ships, some being upright, some horizontal, placed in fittings that turn. Likewise, also without the setting-up of beams, the haulings of ships are carried out on level ground in the same way and by an arrangement of blocks and ropes." He tells stories of how particularly hard jobs were done. Chersiphron, faced with the problem of transporting the shafts of column from the quarry to the temple of Artemis at Ephesos, put pivots in their ends and rolled them along the soft ground. The frame consisted of two beams behind, two in front, and two cross-beams that held the bearings. But the epistyles set a yet harder problem. Chersiphron's son solved it by rearranging the system; he made wheels about 3·5 m. across, with the ends of the epistyles put in the middle of the wheels, and created a structure like that by which "rollers smooth the walks of the sports grounds". More recently one Paconius had to transport a base for the "enormous Apollo" in the temple to replace one worn out by age; he used a similar frame but with a single rope that failed to give the big bobbin the right direction; perhaps two ropes and two teams of oxen would have brought it off.

48. Treadmill (human power) for erecting column: relief found in ruins of Capuan amphitheatre

Vitruvius deals further with the theory of the effects of wheels, pulleys, and levers; the raising of water by means of a drum "tarred like a ship and turned by treading men"; a sort of paddle-wheel for taking water from a flowing river; gears and water-snail; a hodometer for measuring distances, in which the wheel is so huge and unwieldy that he does not seem to be discussing something he has himself seen. He ends with military devices, catapults, ballistae, battering-rams, moveable towers, borers, a climbing machine, a grappling hook, also called the crane, for demolition of walls, tortises for filling ditches, and defence-machinery.[9]

We had best keep Heron for treatment in a separate chapter and continue here with war-engines. In this field alone was there a consistent effort made to develop; but the engines and devices that were worked out were almost wholly connected with sieges, with static systems of warfare. All the artillery was based on the bow. From the long bow was developed the crossbow or stomach-bow, the *gastraphētēs*. For a while there was exploration of the

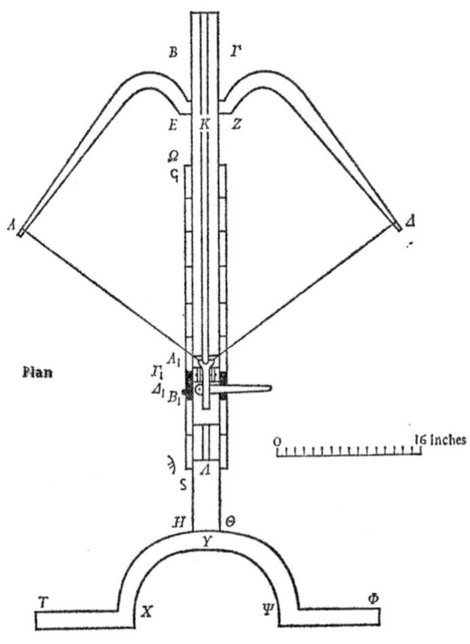

49. Stomach bow (Marsden)

possibilities of a composite bow made up of three main layers: a central strip of wood with a band of animal sinew on its outer side, and pieces of horn glued on the inner side. The handles or tips of the arms had little resilience, but the two outward curves close to the central binding had a great deal of it and were the springs, *tonoi*. Heron tells us how stomach-bow was adopted:

> Originally the construction of these engines developed out of hand-bows. As men were compelled to project by their means a some-

> what larger missile and at greater range, they increased the size of the bows themselves and of their springs—I mean the curved portions running inwards from the ends; i.e. the resilient parts running inwards from the horns. As a result they could hardly be persuaded to bend and needed greater force than the pull exerted by the hand.

So a form of bow was devised which the shooter stretched by resting his stomach on a concavity at the rear-end of the stock and then pressing forwards with all his strength: the bow was fixed to the stock; a board that slid in a dovetail groove stuck out beyond the bow; and the archer, as he leaned on the curved stock, drove this slider into the stock. A hook on the slider caught the bow-string; and two pawls, moving over racks, held the slider when the bow was spanned. An arrow was set before the string; the archer took his sights and pulled the trigger. Then the slider was slid forwards to catch the string again and the bow could be re-spanned.

The catapults, which made up the standard artillery of Greek and Roman times, were substantially based on this system, though they were much enlarged and set stably on the ground. A smaller type, *euthytonon*, had the stock mounted on a tripod on two axles (one horizontal, one vertical), so that it could be sighted by hand; it shot arrows. The larger type, *palintonon*, was fixed to a stand, so that the whole contraption had to be turned for sighting; but it was mainly used for hurling stones, bolts, and the like against walls. The two spanner frames were not square but rhomboid. In a bow the wood was elastic and could bend; but the two arms of the catapult were of hard wood, since it needed great strength. The elasticity was provided by a long rope of plaited sinews, wound many times round two bolts that were set across holes in a strong frame, e.g. two boards with four cross-pieces. A bundler was thus formed into which the end of the arm was thrust. Like the stomach-bow, the catapult had a slider projecting out, with a hook on its inner end that caught the bowstring; it was drawn back by a winch at the inner end of the stock; in the bigger catapults pulleys increased the winch's power. Otherwise the system was the same. The stock in which the slider moved was called the pipe; in a *euthytonon* it was a solid board with an undercut groove for the slider. In the *palintonon* we find the sinews held in two separate frames which are linked by a frame above and below; the stock (ladder) consists of two parallel planks with cross-pieces at intervals.

Later came the *onager* (wild-ass), an engine with one arm which moved in a vertical plane and flung a stone from a sling; the motive power was still a rope of sinews. The Romans called the arrow-firers *catapultae*, the stone-throwers *ballistai*; but in the fourth century *ballistae* and their compounds were used as arrow-firers, and the stone-thrower was the one-armed *onager*. It has been argued that Heron's *Cheiroballistra* gives instructions for making a machine of the same type as the artillery on Trajan's Column: an arrow-firer, a type that could easily be built in the palintone form that had previously been used for stone-throwers. So, though the new machine was an arrow-firer, it had the form that the engineers were used to call a *ballista*. For a while then, it seems, round the reign of Trajan, the army had two sorts of *ballistae*: the old two-armed stone-throwers with wooden metal-plated frames to hold the springs, and the new engines with iron frames. Anyhow, by the fourth century the old kind of stone-throwers were replaced by the *onagri*. No doubt it had been found that stone-throwers on all-metal frames could be efficiently constructed. Certainly from about A.D. 100 the Romans had developed the most powerful arrow-shooting engines ever made in the ancient world, and the most suitable for fieldwork.

The weak point of the catapults was the sinew-rope, which had to be loosened when the machine was not being used, then tightened again. It changed tension according to humidity; and if the two bundles didn't have exactly the same tension, the missile wouldn't go straight. Philon described how to alter the tension by using wedges instead of bolts. He tried to replace sinews by springs made from hammered bronze-plates—a system ascribed by him to Ktesibios, but probably devised by himself; in his discussion, however, it is to swords (made in fact of steel) that he refers for examples of the resilient properties of metals. He suggested using compressed air—the inner ends of the arm pressing on two pistons to compress the air in two cylinders. This last proposal seems to have been worked out only in theory, but it was none the less interesting as an example of the readiness of the engineers to consider new forms of power. It is possible indeed that Ktesibios did consider the possibility of getting more power by using metal springs instead of sinew or hair after the *gastraphētēs* and its derivatives had been superseded by torsion systems which in turn had been carried more or less as far as was feasible. But he would have used alloys of iron, it seems probable; and because of the failure to get a really strong and efficient metal spring, he seems to have tried multiplying the number of springs. Certainly we may say that if the *gastraphētēs* had had a steel bow, there would have been little pressure to develop torsion artillery; and even if the latter were used, they would not have found it easy to drive out the *gastraphētēs* type.

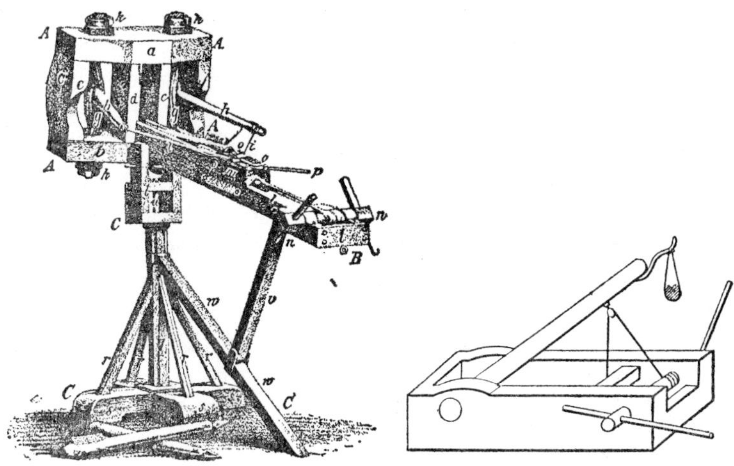

50. Catapult (Baumeister); an Onager type of missile-thrower

Philon mentions also an invention by Dionysios of Alexandreia, a sort of arrow machine-gun. The handler had only to turn the winch forwards and backwards to launch a succession of arrows. The latter came out as fast as the handles could be worked. But sighting had to be done once and for all at the outset; the catapult was fixed in its position. Philon saw it in action at Rhodes, but did not know all the details; he merely saw that the man in charge had to press down hard on a handle. The lock probably held some kind of wedge. The slider was moved to and fro by a pin carried by an endless chain running over two pentagonal wheels, one at each end of the pipe. The claw gripped the string by itself and was then automatically locked until the slider had been brought back and an arrow had been dropped before the

51. Machine-gun nest made of trimmed saplings: Trajan's Column

string. The string was automatically released, the arrow was shot, and the slider was brought forward once more. The arrows were put in a container above the pipe; a cylinder with a groove to take one arrow at a time formed the bottom; the cylinder was turned by an arm on a chain engaging a curved furrow on its outside. Philon tells us: "It shot at longest range slightly more than 200 yards," one stade. Not a great range. And the thing had disadvantages. As the sighting couldn't be changed, its effect in battle was generally negligible, except on closely massed troops close at hand. "Perhaps the argument that it is useful for firing into a group," Philon comments, "might persuade many; but this too would be found not to work. The missiles won't have any spread, since the window [aperture] has been laid on a single target and produces a trajectory more or less along one segment of a circle. Nor will the missiles have a very elongated dropping zone." The arrows weren't notched, as they fell before the string as best they could—and, indeed, Philon admits it was a hard and time-consuming job to notch arrows. The machine "has not found a noteworthy use. We must direct most of our research, as I've strongly insisted, to achieving long range and to tracking down whatever parts of the engine impair efficiency. By the means I've just described I see no advance in these respects."[10]

Not even the strongest catapults could smash strong walls down. Attackers had to come directly up under a solid roof—a tortoise—which was wheeled up. Then they could use a ram, which at times was turned by means of rope laid round it. The ram could thus drill holes in the defences. It was an enlargement of the hand-drill turned by string held in a bow: a very old device. We hear of such a wall-drill moved up on rollers. Scaling ladders were at times set up by winches. Apollodoros, about A.D. 120, has a bucket-chain which was used for pouring boiling water or pitch over defenders on a wall.

Steady thought then could be given to the mechanisms useful for the army because the latter was a large and stable organisation necessary for the state; but the development went on within the severe limitations set by ancient presuppositions. In the last resort military mechanisms could not forge ahead if the engines and devices of normal industry failed to develop and expand. That there were inventive persons about is suggested by the memorandum *On Matters of War*, written perhaps 266–75, by an unknown man, who seems a knowledgeable citizen not at all of the upper levels of society: he remarks pointedly that the high nobility are not interested in technical innovation. He is concerned at the failing manpower of the empire, impressed by the technical achievements of the barbarians, and sets out several projects, of which the most striking are scythed chariots, a warship in which yoked oxen turn paddle-wheels, and a bridge made out of inflated skin-bladders with hooks and eyes to hold them together. Other inventions include a *ballista* worked by a single soldier, which, he claims, can shoot the width of the Danube. One of his scythed chariots has "automatic lashes to urge the horses on and is defended with shields surrounded by iron spikes as on a battlement"; it needs only one driver for the two horses. The government does not seem to have been in the least interested by his proposals, though Valentinian, says Ammianus, was an "inventor of new weapons".[11]

The only other field where there was anything like consistent development, however patchy, was that of agriculture. In the two Roman centuries covered by Cato, Varro, Columella, there were invented the Gallic reaper, the screw-press, and the watermill. Yet none of these three writers mention those devices. Only Columella raises the question of slaves and productivity, in a passage dealing with corn-growing. To corn-land "a tenant-farmer can do no great harm, as he can to plantations of vines and trees, while slaves do it tremendous damage. They let out oxen for hire and keep them and other animals poorly fed: they don't plough the ground with care and they charge up the sowing of more seed than they've actually sown; what they've committed to the earth they don't foster so that it will make the proper growth; and when they've brought it to the threshing-floor, every day during the threshing they lessen the amount by trickery or by negligence. For they steal it themselves and don't guard against the thefts of others; and even when it's stored away they don't enter it honestly in their accounts. The result is that both manager and hands are offenders, and the land generally gets a bad name." However, he advises the use of skilled slaves for jobs like vine-dressing, where they are well under control. The rough-and-ready ox-powered reaper was devised in northern Gaul (probably by local Celtic farmers), but it was not noted and used elsewhere; nor did it inspire attempts at similar sorts of labour-saving devices for other aspects of fieldwork. Yet estate-management was the one activity of the masters, outside the army, which was held in ancient esteem, with books on it written by Greek, Carthaginian, and Roman landlords.

Mining was the one industrial activity which needed a large number of men, a diversity of skills and implements, and an overall management; it involved tunnelling, ventilating, underground lighting, processes in washing, crushing, and smelting, with use of by-products. Already in the fifth and fourth centuries B.C., at Laureion in Attika, it had reached its full development. In that district the geological basis saved the exploiters from having to tackle difficult problems of drainage; but when such problems came up, as in the west and north of the Roman Empire, the challenge was evaded, despite some use of the screw. Drainage systems were too inefficient to enable men to mine much below the ground-water level. Water was mainly got out by slaves who hand-baled, as ore was carried up on their backs in leather-bags. Even the ancient writers were shocked by conditions in mines when they happened to come up against them.[12]

Heron of Alexandreia

XII

Heron was not a thinker in any way comparable to such men as Ktesibios and Archimedes; but he has been luckier in that several of his works have come down to us and we thus know more of his ideas in detail. His *Mechanics* consists of three books: an introduction, an exposition of the theory of the Five Powers—windlass, lever, pulley or tackle-block, wedge, and screw—and some examples of their use. It mingles theory and practice, and was meant for use by architects and builders. Though it is generally well-arranged, some chapters have got out of place. Thus it opens abruptly with an account of the *barylkos*, a machine for lifting heavy burdens: "Let us make the burden we want to lift 1,000 talants and the moving power 5 talants." Pappos succinctly describes the system. "He moves the given weight by a given power through a combination of toothed wheels, where the diameter of the wheel has a ratio to that of the axle as 5 to 1." Pappos himself sets out a similar engine using the ratio 2: 1 for the wheels and pinions; and ends by fitting a screw, as is done in the version of the engine that Heron gives in his *Dioptra*.

Later Heron tells us that if we don't want to use gearwheels we can use ropes instead. In fact we find gearwheels actually used only in watermills and in the instrument brought up from the Antikyra wreck; in the first case very great power was needed, in the second case hardly any at all. Not one gearwheel is mentioned in Heron's *Automatic Theatre*, or in the machines of Oreibasios. We can assume that it was only in theory they were used for lifting burdens.

The rest of Book I carries on consistently as an introduction to the science of mechanics as one of haulage and lifting. So we are first instructed about wheels. Heron clears up a problem that the Aristotelean treatise failed to comprehend. Two wheels of different sizes are fixed to the same axle; if they turn round once, rolling along the circumference of the bigger wheel, the smaller one travels the same distance (which is larger than its own circumference); if the smaller one does the rolling, the bigger wheel travels a distance shorter than its own circumference in the one turn. Heron comments without being bothered: One wheel rolls, the other both slips and rolls. We see how much more a practical sense has grown up since Aristotle's days. Heron deals with the parallelogram of forces (which appears as the Aristotelean Problem 23); and explains how to construct similar figures on a larger or smaller scale, describing a sort of pantograph for the work. How to transfer a given plane figure from one place to another, and so on; how to copy the back of the figure and make inverted copies.

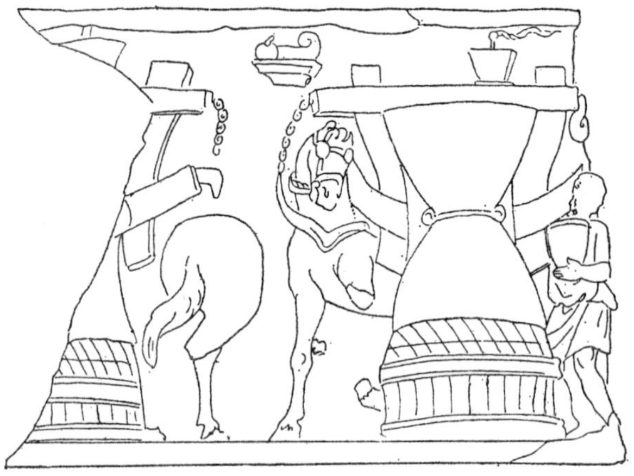

52. Horses turning mills (Jahn, *Dorstellung* pl. XII, 2)

Then comes the theory of mechanics in general: problems of moving burdens by a small power; e.g. down inclined surfaces, over smooth and greased planks, and so on. We meet three passages from lost works of Archimedes: on the centre of gravity, on the balance, on the distribution of the weight of a wall set on columns or of a piece of timber carried by a gang of workers. Haulage and lifting are treated. We see that transport and building are the bases on which mechanics have developed in the ancient world. In this respect there is no change between the Aristotelean line of approach and that of Heron. "Next we shall treat of the Five Powers by which burdens are moved, and explain their principles and their natural function, and treat other matters that are of use in the handling and lifting of burdens. Here ends Book I of the Treatise of Heron on the Lifting of Heavy Things." His reader, we find, was a practical builder, concerned not only with the distribution of weights on a row of pillars, but also with the way that a gang of workers could most efficiently carry timber. Yet this reader must also know a lot of mathematics and be interested in such problems as the nature of gravity and its centre. He must be able to design buildings, make complex drawings on paper, and have a thorough knowledge of the workings of his machines. Such a man was the *architekton.* Vitruvius we saw was a good example of the profession.

Book II describes the five powers and their use, the theory of each machine's function, the general theory of their function, and examples of their combination. Heron glances at several of the Aristotelean Problems and gives their solutions. (Aristotle or his school is not named; we may assume that in other chapters Heron is similarly disposing of problems set by various unnamed thinkers.) The rest of the book is taken up with problems in statics, finding the centre of gravity in figures such as a triangle or a polygon, or working out how the weight is distributed in such figures when they are supported by their angles and bear a weight at some arbitrary point. We may take one passage to show his method:

> As for the wedge, the blow must move it during a given time, for there can be no movement without time, and this blow works by a mere touch, which does not remain with the wedge, not even for the shortest time. And it's evident to us from this that the wedge moves on after the blow has ceased. And we learn this also in another way: during a certain time after the blow there come from the wedge noises and splinters from the splitting by its edge. And that the blow, though it does not stay on the wedge, not even for the shortest time, has its effect on it, as is evident to us from the stones and the arrows [probably a rendering of *belos,* missile], whether flung by hand alone or by some other engine, because after the stone leaves the hand we see it reach a far-off place with power, though the hand does not [any longer] propel it. And from this it is evident to us that the blow does not stay on the wedge for even the shortest time, but that the wedge after the blow begins to move.

The analogy of the wedge and the hand-thrown missile is correct enough, though the law of inertia is only slightly grasped. However, by making the transmission of force through the wedge instaneous—the blow "does not stay in the wedge for even the shortest time"—Heron is avoiding the problem of how the stone is propelled after it leaves the hand. On the other hand it might be argued that as the wedge "begins to move" after the instantaneous blow it is no longer pushed by a force in contact with it, as the air is supposed to go on pushing the missle with which it is in contact. In this case we are on the edge of the impetus-theory.[1]

We find the Aristotelean stress on circle and balance. "That the five powers that move the weight are like the circles round a single centre is clear from the figures drawn in the preceding chapters. But I think their shape is nearer to that of the balance than to the shape of the circle, since in the beginning the first explanation of the circles came from the balance. For here it was shown that the ratio of the weight hung from the smaller arm to that hung from the greater arm is like the ratio of the larger part of the balance to that of the smaller." And: "We contend that the circle is of all shapes the one with the greatest movement and ease, whether it is a circle moving round a single centre or moving along a surface at right angles to it. And so the shapes that are near it. I mean the balls and the cylinders, their movement is a turning, as explained in the previous Book."

Book III deals with the accessories needed for the practical use of the five powers, and "which also help in the moving of the heavy bodies. We also explain the engines used for pressing, since these also need a great power when used." He deals with the tortoise: "a solid body made of a square piece [or pieces] of wood, the ends of which are turned up." He describes cranes with one to four masts, with grabs for lifting stones, called crabs. Another lifting device uses pegs and axle, and Heron comments: "In this method we must guard against using too hard iron, lest it break, and we must guard against what is soft, lest it bend and twist because of the weight of the stone; but we must use iron that is in between, neither too hard nor too soft; and it's also necessary to guard against a bend in the end, a fold in it, or a crack that it got when it was made. The fault in it is serious, not only because the stone may fall, but because it may hit the workers if it falls." What he wants is steel that isn't glass-hard. He deals further with ways of hanging heavy stones or the like without cranes. Thus stone blocks are let down from "the top of high mountains" by means of pulleys. A column is shifted on its base by means of a lift built across a wall or a house, with a counter-weight on the other side. The presses for crushing grapes use male and female screws, beams, and heavy stones; there is also a twin-screw press. From the way that the text is written, it seems that

53. Relief from temple-tomb of the Haterii, Rome, showing crane at work in its construction

the screw-cutter was rather new; and it has been suggested that Heron invented it himself.

A citation from Herakleitos by Hippolytos has an obvious interpolation about the screw: "Straight too he says and twisted are the same. Of letters he says the way is straight and crooked; the turning of the instrument called the screw in the fuller's shop is straight and crooked, for it moves upwards and in a circle together. It is one, he says, and the same." The straight-and-crooked seems to refer to a line of script. The screw-interpolation is of interest in showing how Herakleitan concepts continued to be reinterpreted in the light of technical changes.[2]

Now for the five powers: winch or capstan, toothed wheels, lever, pulley, wedge, screw. Lever and wedge had been used immemorially The lever is the oldest tool for increasing the power of man, Heron says. As always, it was used for all sorts of odd jobs, moving small weights, getting objects into position, overturning them, and so on. An example of its use in simple form was the well-sweep: "Why are well-sweeps made the way they are? They put the lead as extra-weight on the beam, while the bucket is the weight itself, whether empty or full. They do so because the work is divided into two stages—for the bucket has to be dipped, then drawn up—and it happens that it's easy to lower the empty bucket, but difficult to draw it up full. So it pays to have it go down a little more slowly and then have the weight much lighter when it is to be drawn up." The wedge had long been used to split wood or stone. Pappos in the fourth century A.D. calls it a power "of great service, in large presses for perfumery and the very great joints in carpentry, but most of all when it comes to detaching the stones from the quarry face. None of the other powers can do this. . . . But the wedge does it alone by any sort of blow."

An Assyrian relief about 850 B.C. shows a single pulley used for letting a bucket down a well. Pulleys were early used on ships. About 200 the compound pulley was devised; Vitruvius speaks of the triple pulley and the pulley with five sheaves. The winch was widely used; for example, on presses. In cranes and the like it was combined with the pulley, gaining extra power, but the winch itself might be geared. Heron uses the latter device in his *Theatre*. He also uses it in his system for shifting a weight of 1,000 talants by a power of 5 talants, though he adds that you can try ropes instead—then bids you put the axles and wheels into solid posts and set them up on a firm piece of ground. It doesn't seem that the system with toothed wheels worked. (Endless chains and ropes were not used, except for bucket-chains in Vitruvius.) The winch appears in catapults, with pulleys to help it in the bigger structures.

Cogwheels created a difficulty in that an effective shape for the teeth was not easily found; the friction was very high, or else the gear would not work. Until A.D. 1675 the teeth had to be worked out by trial and error. Neither Vitruvius nor Oreibasios used cogwheels engaging one another for machines that hoisted or pulled; they did not use parallel gearwheels at all.

> It would seem, then, that the use of the cog-wheel began with the rack-and-pinion arrangement of Ktesibios, and the endless screw of Archimedes, while the direct transmission is first known from the Antikyra instrument, which is from the second century B.C. The first mention of gear-wheels is from Vitruvius, about 25 B.C., in the water-mills, with the wheel at right angles. Next comes Heron, about A.D. 60, with the *barylkos*, which I refuse to take as a working engine. The gear-wheels then were developed by trial and error, big wooden ones in the water-mills and, later, windmills; small metal ones in clockwork. (Drachmann)

The Antikyra instrument, devised to show the movement of the heavens, consisted of a large number of brass gearwheels, in which the teeth were all shaped like equilateral triangles—they could not have stood up to any heavy work.

The screw-line, "the snail on the cylinder", was first constructed, says Pappos, by Apollonios of Perge, who, living about 265–170, was a younger contemporary of Archimedes, and took over the idea for his water-snail and his endless screw. Heron says that the screw can be used for lifting burdens or pulling a rope; but the endless screw could not be used in larger machines except by surgeons. The female screw was devised for presses.

The five powers then dominated practical work and the theory of mechanics. They were connected with transport and building, with the work done mainly by beasts of burden like oxen or by slaves. There was no link of the theory with questions such as velocity and acceleration; nothing like the problems of ballistics drawn from firearm and cannon that thickened in the medieval world from the fourteenth century on. Where questions of movement were discussed, as in the Aristotelean *Problems*, they were mistakenly regarded as matters of leverage.[3]

We may note, however, that a more kinetic outlook is arriving if we compare some of the arguments in Heron's *Mechanics* with those in the Aristotelean *Problems*. Thus, from Aristotle's time it had been recognised that two simultaneous motions of a body, taking place in different directions, added vectorially to a resultant along the diagonal defined by the two directions. In his *Physics* he expresses in general terms the fact that two such motions do not cancel each other out, but produce a motion in another direction. The *Problems* give a purely geometrical account of two displacements along two sides (AB, AC) of a rectangle ABCD. But Heron takes a more kinetic approach to the question of the parallelogram of forces. "Let the point A move with constant velocity along AB and the line AB move with constant velocity along the lines AC and BD . . . and let the time in which A reaches B equal the time in which AB reaches CD," and so on. When we come later to Philoponos we find a dynamical concept in his commentary on the passage from Aristotle: "Let a rectangle be given and two bodies in motion, one starting downwards along one side, the other starting laterally along the other side. If they meet near the earth they won't stop each other but will collide and move with an oblique motion in the direction of the diagonal of the rectangle." But Philoponos still feels too respectful to Aristotle to cut quite adrift from his positions. He adds, "Obviously these are not contrary motions, since they don't stop each other, but are, so to say, sub-contrary, since they hinder each other in their original direction but not in their motion as such." He introduces the term sub-contrary (borrowed from logic) to express a case of oblique collision. It had taken near a thousand years for this advance from a static geometrical outlook to a dynamical one to come about.[4]

As an example of the lack of any urgent relation between theory and practice, we may take the instruments used. In Philon's *Pneumatika* we meet an experiment to show how a siphon works. One container, in which we are to watch the water rising, is made out of horn scraped till it is diaphanously thin; but in all experiments to show how the air keeps out the water when a jar is dipped, bronze or clay vessels are used. At the time glass was made only with coloured or opaque consistency, or in lumps for ornaments. (Where clear glass is here mentioned, we must suspect a later intrusion.) But in Heron clear glass is cited several times, though, when his dipping experiments come from Philon or Ktesibios, there is no mention of glass despite the fact it would have served better.

As an example of the ingenuity of many of the mechanics described by Heron we may take from his *Dioptra* the surveyor's instrument, which combined theodolite and water-level, and which could be fitted on to the same foot. The foot however is not explained, though we may take it to have been a wooden table or tripod. The device itself was mostly of bronze. A holder stood up bearing a round plate, horizontal, which was set round the lower end of a vertical pivot. Round the latter turned a toothed wheel, which was engaged with a screw (mounted on brackets on the plate). This screw had its furrow cut away by a longitudinal groove as broad as the wheel was thick. When the wheel was opposite, the wheel turned freely; but a slight turn of the screw could lock it at any time. Both theodolite and water-level were built on a hollow column that fitted the pivot and had on its underside three pins fitting holes in the toothed wheel; so they both could be mounted on the holder. The column of the theodolite ended in a Doric Capital, which carried a toothed bronze half-circle turning between two flat rulers and engaged by a screw also between those rulers. On top of the vertical half-circle was fixed a full circle that bore the sighting apparatus, an *alhidade* with a pointer at each end. On the horizontal disk were scribed two lines at right angles, one coinciding with the half-circle below. The water-level also was made of a hollow column with three pins; it carried a long horizontal rod hollowed-out to take a bronze tube, which was turned up at each end to take a small tube of glass. Water was poured in; and the water-levels in the two glass tubes determined an horizontal line. Round each tube was fixed a frame along which a bronze plate, touching the glass, could slide up and down. There were sighting-slits in each plate; and a horizontal line could be determined by adjusting these slits opposite the water-level in the glass tubes. Screws going through the rod steered the plates; they passed through a smooth hole where a pin from the side engaged the screw-thread. The screws were too thin for female screws to be made for them. For staff there was a post

54. Heron's Stationary Theatre of Apotheosis

with a big shield, half white, half black, which slid up and down a dovetail groove and was kept in position by a cord. Heron most likely invented the instrument himself.

The *Dioptra* also has an account of an hodometer. A small pin is fixed to the hub of the carriage-wheel and at each turn it moves a horizontal wheel with spaced teeth. A complicated system of toothed wheels and endless screws transmits the movements and turns the hands of the meters that mark units of different magnitudes. Some details about pointers, however, raise practical difficulties and suggest a purely theoretical device. But it is possible that Heron added these details later in an effort to elaborate a working instrument. He makes suggestions about testing the screws, which would hardly be in place in a mere paper-construction; but he may have imported these suggestions from experience with another machine that actually did work.

In his *Katoptrika* (extant only in a Latin version) Heron gives proof of the proposition that, of all rays impinging on a mirror and reflected at the same point, those reflected according to the law of equal angles of incidence travel the shortest distance. He remarks that this fact is "in accordance with reason". Much later Olympiodoros deals with the same subject, though he is not directly copying Heron. He sees in the law an example of the truth "that nature produces nothing in vain nor labours in vain". Here we have the first direct statement of the principle of least action (set out by Maupertuis in mid-eighteenth century and reformulated by Hamilton as a basic instrument of physics).[5]

The Automatic Theatre is again highly ingenious. No cog-wheels appear; the whole thing is done by drums and strings. There are two constructions: a small stage that moves into view, presents a puppet-show, and retires, and a stationary stage presenting a play in many acts. The motive force is a heavy weight that fits into a container packed with millet or mustard-seeds. When the seeds dribble out through a small hole, the weight descends at a determined rate and turns an axle from which it is hung by a cord. Strings from this axle control and bring about all the movements in the theatre. Thus a puppet is turned by a string going round a drum; to make him turn back, the string is passed over the drum and wound round the other way; to make him move, stop, move again, there's a length of slack string between two windings, and this slack is fixed on to the drum with wax to prevent it hanging

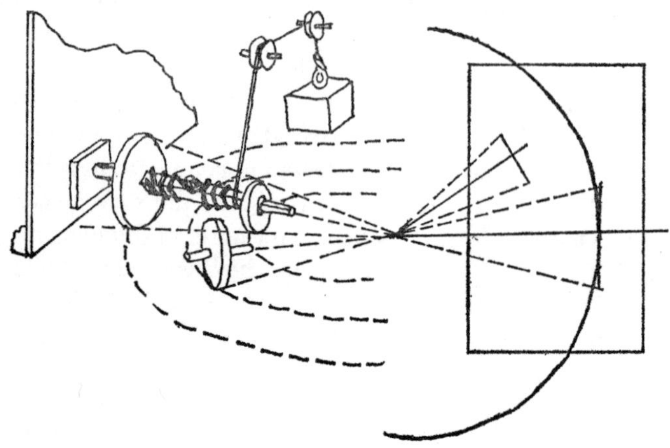

55. Device for movement in the theatre

down and becoming entangled in the rest of the machinery. If something has to be done only once—for instance, the dropping of a backcloth—it may be worked by a separate weight that's released by a string pulling out a pin. There are three wheels to bring the stage in or out; another set of wheels, lowered or lifted by a screw-furrow engaged with a peg, enable it to move backwards and forwards. Pins on a wheel, acting on the short end of a lever, control the arm of a puppet and produce the required gestures; —e.g. of hammering. In one scene a ring is made to turn round a temple by means of strings, and bacchantes in wild dance-postures go round and round.

This last effect is part of the repertory of the stationary theatre; not that the theatre itself stays in one place. "The automatic apparatus is installed in a certain place from which one immediately withdraws. Very soon after, the Theatre starts off moving to another determined spot, where it halts. Then the altar set in front of Dionysos lights up, and at the same time milk or water spirits from his *thyrsos*, while his cup spiils wine of the panther. The four faces of the basement surround themselves with wreaths, and to the sound of drums and cymbals the Bacchantes dance in a circle round the little shrine. Soon, when the noise stops, Dionysos and Victory (who stands on the top of the structure) together make a turn round. The altar, which has been behind the god, is then seen in front and it in turn lights up. Again the *thyrsos* and cup overflow; again the Bacchantes dance round to the sound of cymbals and drums. When the dance is over, the theatre returns to its first station. Thus ends the Apotheosis."

Water has been put in a vase held in the support, while another is filled with milk. The conduits leading from these reservoirs are hidden in a column. They can be opened or shut by a double cock which at the same time puts them in communication with *thyrsos* and cup. The liquid runs into a central cylinder from which it can be voided. The cock turns under the impulsion of a counter-weight that also puts into action the platform where the god stands as well as the pulley supporting Victory. A big reservoir of water is hidden at the top of the theatre. It keeps on filling a recipient (called in physics the Vase of Tantalos), which is emptied rapidly by a siphon at the very moment it is about to overflow. Its weight thus keeps on varying. It is now heavier, now lighter, according to

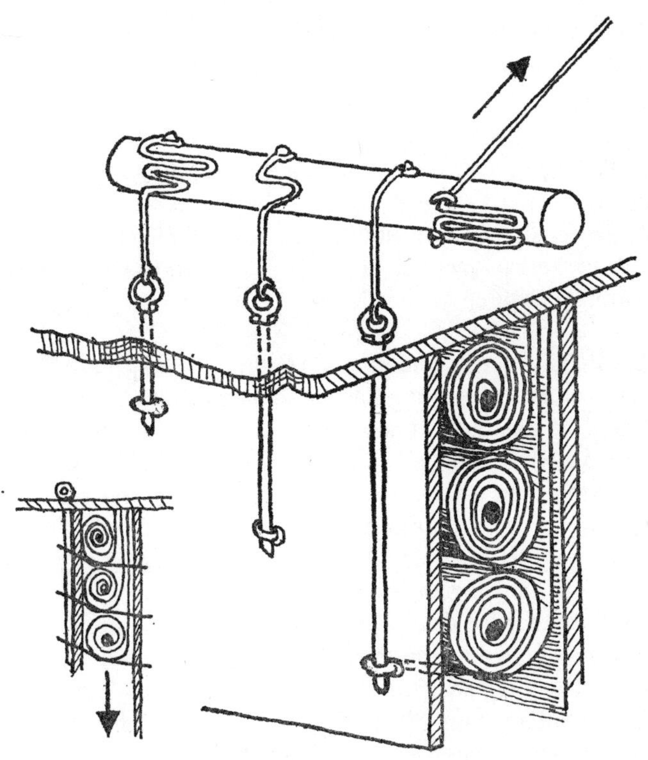

56. Device for controlling scenery, etc.

the weight to which it is bound, and it thus forces that weight to go up or come down. (The system was reused in 1452 when Count Borso d'Este entered Reggio, but Dionysos was supplanted by St. Prosper, patron of the town, and the Bacchantes by Angels.)

The theatre of moving figures staged plays such as that of Nauplios, which depicted episodes of the Greeks returning from Troy and the storm that met them off Euboia.

> 1, The Greeks repair their ships; a dozen workers are at work. 2, The ships are set afloat. 3, The ships go off one by one. We see dolphins sporting about them and the sea growing rough. 4, Nauplios is seen with torch in hand. Athena appears at his side. The man and the goddess join in the same act of vengeance: Nauplios makes the Greeks pay for the death of his son Palamedes by drawing them with a trumpet signal on to the Kaparean Rocks, and Athena punishes the impious excesses committed by the conquerors after the city's fall. 5, The ships are wrecked; Aias, swimming in the waves, is struck by lightning and disappears.

Backgrounds were painted on canvases which were unrolled in turn at the changes of scene; the noise of thunder was got by letting wooden balls escape from a trap and fall on a series of inclined planes inside a column. These systems were carried on by the Arabs and Persians, and then by the West in the Renaissance; especially, a large number of constructions which decorated the various seigneurial gardens of Italy, France, and Germany were directly inspired by the Heronian tradition.

A mere listing of the contents of Heron's *Pneumatika* will show the large number of experiments and applications of physical force, and at the same time an extraordinarily restricted idea of what to do with them all. The work opens with an account of siphons: the bent siphon; the enclosed siphon; the siphon discharging liquid with uniformity; a vessel for withdrawing air from a siphon; a vessel for holding or discharging a liquid at pleasure; another for discharging liquids at different temperatures at pleasure; another for discharging liquids in varying proportions; a waterjet produced by compressed air; a pump-valve; a model in which libations on an altar are produced by fire; a vessel from which the contents flow when filled to a certain height; two vessels from which the contents flow when liquid is poured into one of them; a model of a bird made to whistle by flowing water; another of birds made to sing and be silent in turn; trumpets that are sounded by flowing water; sounds produced by the opening of a temple door; a drinking horn from which either wine or water will flow; a vessel that holds an unvarying level of water though a stream flows out of it; another that stays full when water is drawn from it; a sacrificial vessel that flows only when money is introduced; a vessel from which a variety of liquids flow through one pipe; a pipe from which wine and water flow in varying proportions; a vessel from which wine flows in proportion as water is taken off; a vessel from which wine flows in proportion as water is poured

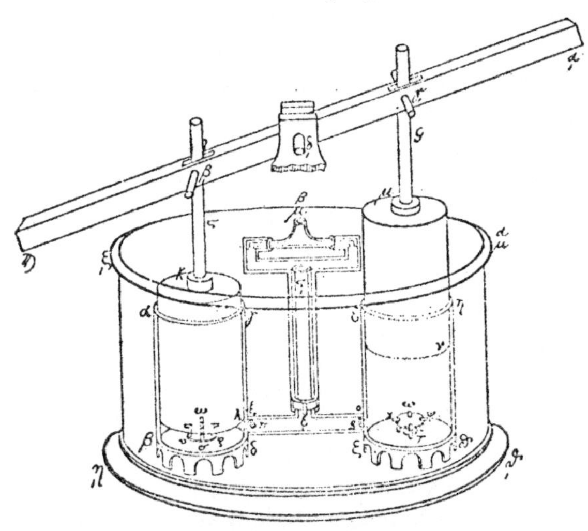

57. Engine for extinguishing fires

into another; a fire-engine; a model that drinks at certain times only, on a liquid being presented to it; another which may be made to drink at any time; a third that will drink any amount that is presented to it; a temple-wheel which on being turned liberates purifying water; a vessel holding different wines, any one of which may be liberated by putting a certain weight in a cup; a self-trimming lamp; a vessel from which liquid will flow when any portion of water is poured into it; another that will hold a certain quantity of liquid when the supply is continuous, but will only take a portion of it if the supply is intermittent; a model of a satyr pouring water from a wineskin into a full basin without making the contents overflow; temple-doors opened by fire on an altar; a vessel from which wine flows but stops at the introduction of water, but flows again when the water-supply ceases; a model of Herakles who, at the lifting of an apple, shoots a dragon which then hisses.

So it goes on and on. We are told how to make a vessel from which only uniform quantities of liquid can be poured; a water-jet actuated by compressed air which is blown into it; a bird-model that produces notes at intervals through an intermittent stream of water; several birds that emit notes in turn; a steamjet supporting a sphere; a model representing the earth in the cosmic centre; a fountain made to trickle by the sun's rays; a *thyrsos* made to whistle by being submerged in water; a figure holding a trumpet which is made to sound by compressed air; the steam-engine; a vessel from which flowing water can be stopped at pleasure; a drinking-horn with an oddly-shaped siphon; a vessel in which water and air ascend and descend alternately; a model of a satyr holding a wineskin from which water is driven by compressed air; a vessel with trick-flowings (water flows out as it is poured in, then stops if the supply is withheld and won't flow again till the vessel is half-filled; then on the supply being again stopped, there is no flow till the vessel is quite filled); a cupping-glass with an air-exhausted compartment; a syringe; a vessel from which a flow of wine ceases when a small measure of water is poured in; another from which wine or water may be made to flow together or separately; a model in which libations are poured on an altar and a serpent is made to hiss by the action of fire; a trick-siphon; a vessel that emits a sound when liquor is poured in; a water-clock which controls the quantities of liquid flowing from a vessel; a drinking-horn from which pure water or a mixture of wine and water can be made to flow alternately or together, another from which wine or water may be made to flow separately or mixed; a cup into which wine is discharged in any quantity; a goblet into which as much wine flows as is taken out; a shrine over which a bird may be made to revolve and sing by devotees turning a wheel; a siphon in a vessel from which the discharge ceases at will; figures made to dance on an altar by fire; a lamp in which the oil can be raised by water contained in its stand; another in which the oil is raised by blowing air into it; a third in which the oil is raised by water as required; a steamboiler from which a blast of hot air or of hot air mixed with steam is blown into the fire and from which hot water flows on the introduction of cold; a steamboiler from which a hot blast may be driven into the fire; a blackbird made to sing, or a triton to blow a horn; an organ blown by manual labour; an organ blown by means of a windmill; and, finally, a model of an animal which has its head apparently cut off by a knife but which keeps the head attached, and then at once drinks.

One point of interest is that we find in Heron the term *energeia*

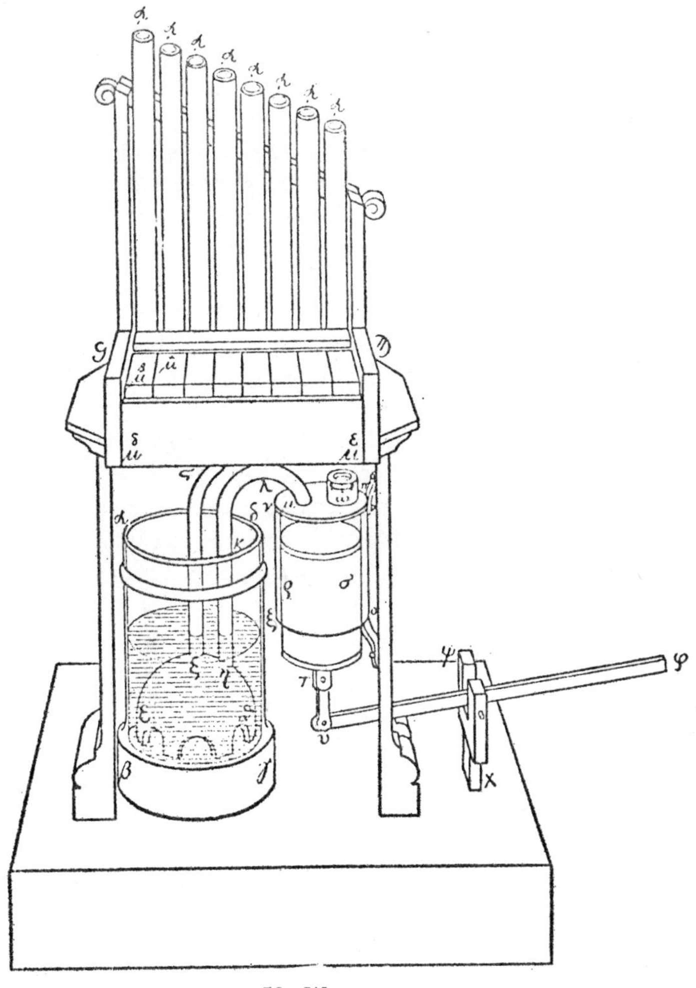

58. Water-organ

narrowing down from its Aristotelean significance and getting a more directly mechanical connotation. In Galen it takes on the sense of function; e.g. the natural blending of the four elements in their correct proportion is said to bring about the normal functioning or *energeiai* of each organ of the human body. Heron in his *Pneumatics* uses *energeia* to mean function when he is speaking of the working of the siphon. The term refers to the mechanism of an automaton, as when he says that the *energeia* of a static automaton is safer than that of a mobile one. Later, Philoponos interprets Aristotle's *energeia* as a kinetic phenomenon proceeding from object to eye, and he applies the laws of geometrical optics to the phenomenon. "The *energeia* move in a straight line towards our eyes. . . ."

Some of the devices may have been worked out only on paper; but there is much likelihood that the ones connected with temples were put into practice. The wheel which on being turned releases holy water would clearly be of much use to a priesthood, as well as the sacrificial vessel that flowed only when money was put in. The lift- and force-pump for use in putting out fires is made up of two cylinders with pistons, valves and tubes. The tube through which the water is ejected can be turned round and the jet directed as wished by the inclination of the mouthpiece. Two toothed wheels at right angles turn the bird on top of a casket; and the self-snuffing lamp works by a rack-and-cogwheel system. In the various models the mechanism is mostly hidden under the altars or other structures and communicating with them. Currents of hot and cold air, or streams of hot and cold water, or at times compressed air, are used to make the systems work. A fire is lighted on an altar; it heats the air and the water that works the hidden mechanism, which acts on the statues, doves, and so on, which the people watch at their mysterious movements. In one model hot air coming out through four bent pipes from the hollow altar makes puppets dance.

In the case of the animal that appears to be beheaded, the head is held on by a wheel with dovetailed cross-section, which consists only of three sectors of about a sixth each of the whole circumference. One sector holds the head; the other two are inside the body. The knife, sliding through, turns the wheel, which holds on all the while. The pipe for the water is opened for the knife to pass, then closed again by means of the sectors of wheels operating

59. Altar-fire opens Temple-door

two racks. There is also a model in which puppets are moved by floats by means of levers. The automaton serving guests with water for washing their hands has a spout with a hand holding a ball of pumice stone above. When the guests take the pumice, the hand disappears and water flows. After a while the water stops and the hand comes out with another bit of pumice for the next guest. The explanation is somewhat obscure but it is clear that the hand, released from the weight of the stone, gets by its own movement another piece of pumice, which it takes back. (Much later the same idea was used in a complex waterclock.)

The vessel from which water flows when a coin of five drachmai is introduced is thus described:

> Let ABCD be a sacrificial vessel or treasure chest, with an opening A in its mouth; and in the chest let there be a vessel FGHK, containing water, and a small box, L, from which a pipe LM, leads out of the chest. Near the vessel place a vertical rod NX, about which turns a lever OP, widening at O into the plate R parallel to the

> bottom of the vessel, while at the end P is hung a lid, S, that fits into the box L, so that no water can flow through the tube LM. This lid however must be heavier than the plate R, but lighter than the plate and coin together. When the coin is thrown through the mouth A, it will fall upon the plate R and, by its greater weight, will turn the beam OP and raise the lid of the box so that the water will flow. But if the coin falls off, the lid will come down and close the box, so that the discharge stops.

The more complicated of the devices for opening a temple-door by a fire on the altar runs thus:

> The construction of a small temple such that, on a fire being lighted, the doors will open of their own accord and shut again when the fire goes out. Let the temple stand on a pedestal, on which lies a small altar. Through the altar insert a tube with its mouth inside the altar and the mouth contained in a globe below, reaching nearly to its centre. The tube must be soldered into the globe, in which a bent siphon is placed. Let the door-hinges be extended downwards and turn freely on pivots; and from the hinges let two chains, running into one, be attached by means of a pulley to a hollow vessel, which is suspended—while other chains, wound on the hinges in an opposite direction to the former, and running into one, are attached by means of a pulley to a leaden weight, on the descent of which the door will be shut.
>
> Let the outer leg of the siphon lead into the suspended vessel; and through a hole (which must be carefully closed afterwards) pour enough water into the globe to fill a half of it. It will be found that when the fire's grown hot, the air in the altar becomes heated and expands into the larger space. Passing through the tube into the globe, it will drive out the liquid contained there through the siphon into the suspended vessel, which, descending with its weight, will tighten the chains and open the doors.
>
> Again, when the fire is extinguished, the rarefied air will escape through the pores in the side of the globe, and the bent siphon (the end of which will be immersed in the water in the suspended vessel) will draw up the liquid in the vessel so as to fill up the void left by the particles removed. When the vessel is lightened, the weight suspended will grow the heavier and shut the doors.
>
> Some instead of water use quicksilver, as it is heavier than water and easily disunited by fire.

Then there is the system for making a trumpet blow when a temple-door is opened:

Behind the door let there be a vessel holding water. In this invert a narrow-necked vessel, shaped like an extinguisher, with which at the lower end let a trumpet communicate, provided with bell and mouthpiece. Parallel with the tube of the trumpet and attached to it, let a rod run, fastened at the lower end to the narrow-necked vessel and having at the other end a loop. Through this loop let a beam pass, thus supporting the vessel at a sufficient height above the water. The beam must turn on the pivot, and a chain or

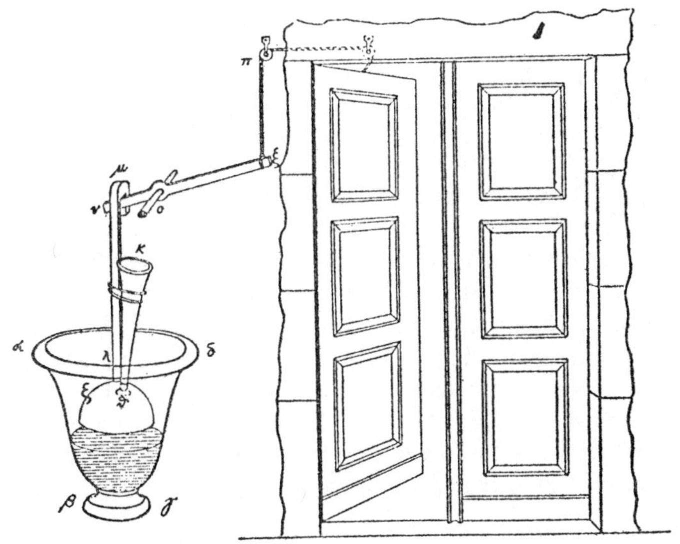

60. Trumpet blown by opening Temple-door

cord, attached to the further extremity, be fastened by means of the pulley to the hinder part of the door. When the door is opened, the cord will be stretched and draw up the end of the beam, so that the beam no longer supports the loop. And when the loop changes its position as a result, the vessel will descend into the water and produce the sound of a trumpet by the expulsion of the air contained in it through the mouthpiece and bell.

The temple-wheel is thus described:

In the porticoes of Egyptian temples revolving wheels of bronze are placed for those who enter to turn round—from a belief that bronze purifies. There are also vessels of lustral water, from which the worshippers may sprinkle themselves. The task then is to construct a wheel so that on its being turned round water will flow from it to sprinkle the worshippers as described. Behind the entrance-pillar let a vessel of water be hidden with a hole A perforated at its base. Under the base fasten a small tube with a hole bored opposite A. And in this tube set another tube, soldered to the first (larger) tube at the end away from the wheel, with a hole again opposite the hole A. Between these two tubes let a third tube be closely fitted, with a hole opposite the hole A. Now if the holes are all in a single line, when water is poured into the vessel, it will flow through them all and out through the innermost tube. But if the middle pipe is made to revolve so as to change the position of its hole, the discharge will stop. Attach the wheel to the outer end of the middle tube, and if it is repeatedly made to revolve, water will gush out.

Two of the devices are particularly interesting, since they sharply bring up the question of why the inventive capacity was not applied to the productive world. For his water-organ Heron uses a small windmill to work the pump. A rod is attached to a piston; it can move up and down as it is fixed to a vertical rod by a pin about halfway along its horizontal length. The windmill stands nearby on its support and turns a disk with projecting pegs; these pegs strike on a small plate at the end of the horizontal rod away from the piston and drive it down, so that the piston is lifted up. As they leave the plate the pressure is ended and the piston goes down. Heron remarks that the frame holding the axle-rod of

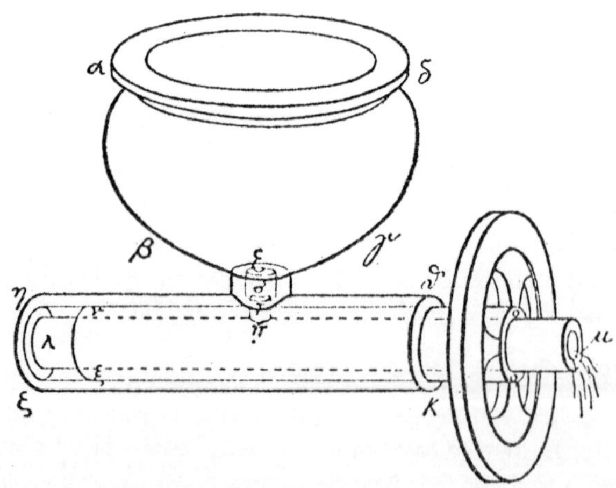

61. Mechanism for turning the Temple-wheel

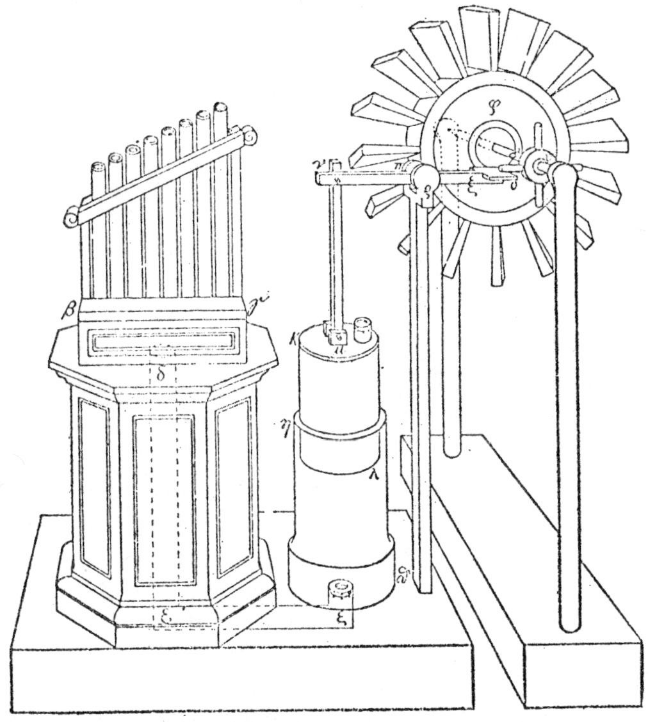

62. Windmill operating Organ

the windmill should be turned always to the prevailing wind, "so that the revolution may be more uniform and rapid". Since the windmill did not appear in western Europe for about a millennium later, this scheme has been taken to be a late interpolation to the manuscripts. But the suggestion is untenable, as the same text and figure is found in a pseudo-Heron, whose date cannot be later than about 500 A.D. Much more likely Heron devised his little windmill for this one specific task and did not realise the wider potentialities, as was also the case with his readers. The *Pneumatics* exists in a rather incomplete state, and it is possible that Heron did not live to finish it. (It has been suggested that the eight-sailed turret-mill found in the Aegean Islands derived from Heron, since it is not at all like the four-sailed postmill, which later appeared in the west.)

Then there is the steam-engine. "Place a cauldron over a fire: a

63. Heron's steam-engine: front and side view

ball is to revolve on a pivot. A fire is lighted under a cauldron containing water and covered at the mouth by a lid. With the cauldron a bent tube communicates, the end of the tube being fitted into a hollow ball. Opposite the point where the tube enters set a similarly-shaped pivot with its lower end resting on the lid and its pivoting end keeping the ball in place and able to turn. Into the ball are set two pipes at the opposite ends of a diameter and bent in opposite directions—the ends being at right angles. As the cauldron heats it will be found that the steam, entering the ball through the tube in the lid, passes out through the bent tubes towards the lid and causes the ball to revolve, as in the case of the dancing figures." With this engine are linked two other models. In one a jet of steam supports a globe. "Under a cauldron containing water and closed at the top, a fire is lighted. From the covering a tube runs upwards, at the end of which and communicating with it is a hollow hemisphere. If we put a light ball into the hemisphere, it will be found that the steam from the cauldron, rising through the tube, lifts the ball so that it is suspended." In the other model figures dance (or rather they are carried round in a ring in dancing postures). "When a fire is kindled on an altar, figures are seen to dance. The altar must be transparent, of glass or horn. Through the altar-hearth a tube is let down, turning on a pivot towards the base of the altar, and, above, on a small pipe attached to the hearth.

Communicating with this tube, and attached to it, are smaller tubes lying at right angles to each other, and bent at the extremities in opposite directions. A wheel or platform on which the dancing figures stand, is also fastened to the tube. When the sacrifice is kindled, the air grows hot and passes through the pipe into the tube and then is forced from it into the smaller tubes. There, meeting with resistence from the sides of the altar, it causes the tube and the dancing figures to revolve."

We see that the ancients had clearly grasped the motive power of steam, but felt no impulse to use the power except in such toys. That is, in Heron's works are set out the principles on which wind-power, water-power and steam-power were to be developed and to bring about the industrial revolution more than a millennium and a half later; further, the knowledge is not at all merely abstract since it is applied in simple but effective models. Once again we

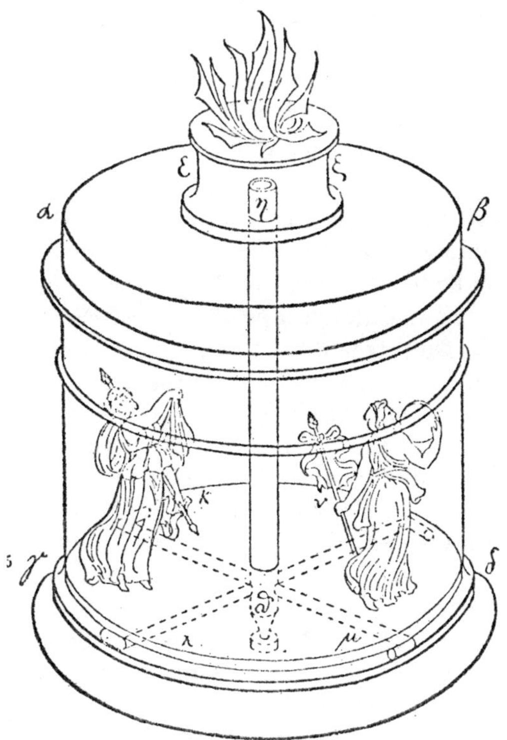

64. Fire-device to make dancing figures revolve

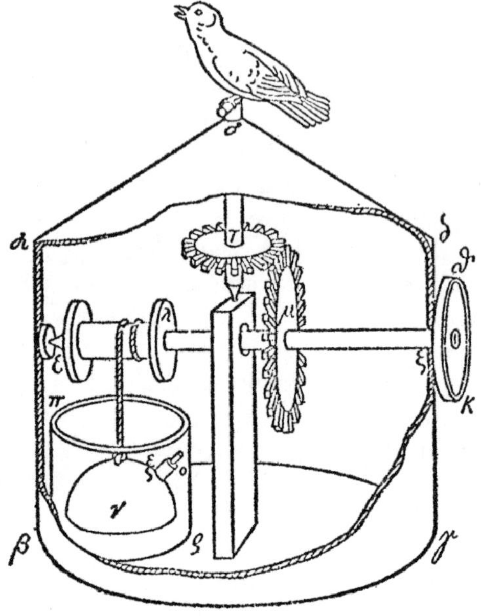

65. Device for artificial singing-bird

are up against the problem as to why the ancients averted their minds and did not make the extended applications. Certainly part of the answer lies in the statement that steam-engines of an industrial kind had to wait till it was possible to make iron pipes and put them together with screws. But that is not the whole answer. The ancients did not develop metallurgy for the same reason as they did not make any serious attempt to develop industrial power (apart from the watermill in the later centuries). One does not mean that by a slight adjustment of their minds they could have leaped into the industrial revolution. What one is pointing out is that no attempt was made to combine the inventive faculty, so evident in a range of thinkers from Ktesibios to Heron, with such possibilities as were present in the existing technological level, especially in metallurgy. Then the inventions and the technology would have begun to interact and fortify one another as happened only fitfully and sporadically in the ancient world.

The introductory remarks in the *Pneumatics* show that Heron was not unaware that his devices could have a valuable practical use. He says first that he has undertaken the work to make an orderly arrangement of the schemes handed down from the past, together with his own discoveries; he also wants the treatment to correspond with the method he has used in his treatise in four books on Waterclocks. "For, by the union of air, earth, fire, and water, and the concurrence of three, or four, elementary principles, various combinations are effected, some which supply the most pressing wants of human life, while others produce wonder and alarm." But he goes on to discuss the question of a void and the way that transformations of the elements occur. "That something is consumed by the action of fire is manifest from coal-cinders, which, preserving the same bulk as they had before combustion, or nearly so, differ very much in weight. The consumed parts pass away with the smoke into a substance of fire, air, or earth. . . ." And so on. There is little new in his remarks, though he discusses compression of air and the creation of artificial vacuums. He concludes that "every body is composed of minute particles, between which are empty spaces less than the particles of the body". But the question of the combinations that "supply the most pressing wants of human life" is not raised, nor does any ghost of it appear elsewhere in the work.[6]

Yet we cannot say that ancient scientists were unaware of the value of experiments, and they must have known that at least many of their models could be developed on a much larger scale and used in various ways. Experiments were made in mechanics, optics, acoustics, physiology. Especially from the work done in acoustics we see that the thinkers were aware of the concept of "two sets of experiments". Philon Mechanikos was conscious of the value of repeated experiments and also of the effect of social conditions on mental attitudes. "The ancients did not succeed in determining this magnitude by test, since their trials were not carried out on the basis of many different types of performance. But the engineers who came later noted the errors of their predecessors and the results of subsequent experiments, and so they reduced the principle of construction to a single basic element. . . . Success in this work was recently achieved by the Alexandrian engineers, who are heavily subsidised by kings eager for fame and interested in the *technai*." (But his branch of work, concerned with warfare, was the one branch, as we have seen, in which there was anything like a steady pressure for advance.) Philoponos investigated the laws of falling bodies in the same way as Galileo; work here was known to Renaissance scientists and played an important part in the controversy over their theories.

We find also, as in Philon's words, a sense of change in attitudes and of progress in methods. Heron hoped that from his collection of earlier inventions, to which he had added his own, there would result "much advantage to those who will hereafter devote themselves to the study of mathematics". Archimedes had said, "I consider it necessary to expound my method . . . for I'm convinced that it will be of no little service to mathematics. I apprehend that some of my contemporaries or of my successors, will, by means of the method when once established, be able to discover other theorems in addition, which have not yet occurred to me." Seneca could even exclaim, "The day will come when our children will wonder at our ignorance."

We thus find strange and glaring contrasts. On the one hand the Greeks founded, in forms that are still recognisable today, the

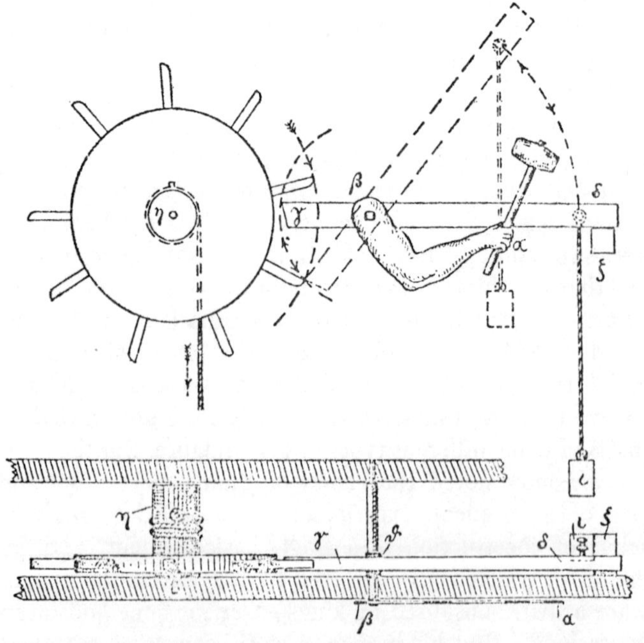

66. Mechanism for moving arm in the automatic theatre

sciences of mathematics, astronomy and mathematical geography, physics, chemistry and chemical terminology, geology, and meteorology, botany, biology, medicine, physiological psychology—whatever shortcomings or confusions may be found in the treatment. And especially in mathematics or medicine the thinkers had a strong sense of belonging to a coherent tradition with a steadily expanding horizon. Yet the fully effective encounter of life and science never came about. In such applications of mathematical and physical knowledge as we see in the models, there was indeed a sense of penetrating into the secrets of natural process, but the sense was liable to dissipate itself in what we can only call an emotion of childish wonder. "The craft of those who contrive marvellous devices", or "the art of the sphere-makers", who construct "a model of the heaven with the help of the uniform circular motion of water", says Pappos, were subdivisions of mechanics. *Katoptrika* was "clearly a science worthy of study and at the same time produces spectacles which excite wonder in the observer. For with the aid of this science mirrors are constructed which show the right side as the right side, and similarly the left side as the left side, whereas ordinary mirrors by their nature have the contrary property and show the opposite sides."

Certainly a major reason for the failure of science to become an activity linked with society and its problems—except in the cases of medicine and artillery—lay in the small number of persons who carried on the tradition. This small number had to make their researches unaided and on their own initiative. There were many festivals, contests, and prizes for literary men, but nothing whatever of the same sort for scientists. After the Sophists came into fashion in the fifth century, a thinker of any kind could draw some attention and interest by giving his ideas a rhetorical dress and by lecturing. But it was only at a few capitals, after Alexander, that any public facilities were provided. The groups thus fostered at Alexandreia or Pergamon were small, and only a small section of them could claim to be scientists proper. Even with medicine, for which there were schools such as that of Kos, there was no system of licensing or proving status: the physician had to develop a technique for convincing laymen of his professional claims rather than to set out a prognostic on purely scientific grounds. In such a situation men working in one field would hear only by chance of what others were doing in it; forms of collaboration or ex-

67. Device for throwing up a ball and balancing it on steam

changes of ideas were hardly possible; results achieved at one time and place were liable to be lost through never becoming generally available. In the last resort the forms of alienation created by slavery and the attitudes of the ruling class were responsible for this situation.

Thinkers were aware to some extent of the limitations under which they worked. Plato remarked that since no city held solid geometry in honour, "these studies are languidly pursued", and he suggested that if the state superintended and honoured such work, "continuous and strenuous investigation would bring out the truth". Diodoros of Sicily says that in Babylon knowledge is handed on from father to son; pupils are "bred in these teachings from childhood up"; afterwards they are "relieved of all other services to the state"—while in Greece the student "who takes up a large number of subjects without preparation turns to the higher studies only quite late, and then, after labouring at them to some extent, he gives them up, distracted by the need to earn a living;

and only a few here and there really strive for the higher studies and continue in pursuit of them as a profitmaking business, and these are always trying to make innovations in connection with the most important doctrines instead of following the paths of their predecessors". He is speaking of philosophy, which would, however, include the sciences. Perhaps by his last remark he means that through the lack of any systematic teaching, newcomers are unaware of what has already been done and are liable to blunder all over the place. The Hippokratic treatise *On the Technē* attacks the attackers of science; and the author knows that all the other *technai* and sciences are threatened—he expects their representatives to defend them. He is writing in the midst of the new sophistic, and we see how the craftsman who wanted to be a scientist had a difficult job in vindicating his position. His task was made more difficult by the tradition that the free citizen's judgment should prevail in all matters—a tradition which had its good aspect in being based on an ideal of all-round knowledge, but which did not work when the citizen had no basis at all for his views. Plato shows the worst possible attitude: that the judgment which mattered was that of "the user of the *technē*". Thus the

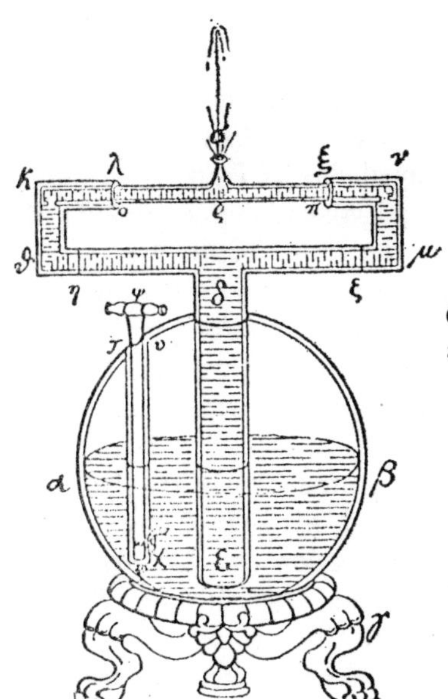

68. Waterjet worked by compressed air

consumer (especially the rich or noble one) was elevated over the producer, craftsman or scientist. Aristotle expresses the same idea; only the consumer fully appreciates the end or purpose of the object; the craftsman's activity deals with the means.

One aspect of the situation we have noticed is that each school tended to fight hard exclusively for its own position and to be uninterested in finding common ground with other schools. A change appeared in the Hellenistic period. There was now much more exchange of ideas, and organisation emerged to a limited extent. The individualistic formula was less the rule and there were a certain amount of convergences, though the old sharpness of rival formulations persisted to a considerable extent. After about 200 B.C. the work of research slowed down. By the second century A.D. we meet much activity in collecting and systematising, with a certain amount of criticism of past thought in the effort to reach a synthesis. Galen declares that he does not wish to defend any sectarian dogma and add to the "wide dissention" in medicine, but to show how one can work out "the best sect". But all that does not mean that now we have only epigones collating past writings. We have noticed how Galen makes important advances in the concept of the formative process; and men like Proklos and Philoponos were far from being mere backward-looking scholars. True, the old adventurousness has largely gone; but the results are not merely negative. From one angle the thinkers now expressed the politically unifying trends of the Roman Empire; Galen was proud at having unified medicine as Trajan had unified Italy by his system of roads. General education was making big strides, with facilities provided by the state; public schools and universities appeared; examinations for scholars were introduced and professorships were endowed; there was a strong tendency to standardisation of instruction. But the crushing political controls prevented these developments from having a widely fructifying effect.

The author of *De Rebus Bellicis* stated clearly the isolation of the man with any originality of mind, his lack of any relation to the world of power: "In this connection one has always to examine what a man means rather than what he says. For it's universally agreed that in the technical arts, among which we include the invention of weapons, progress is due not to those of highest birth or immense wealth or public office or eloquence

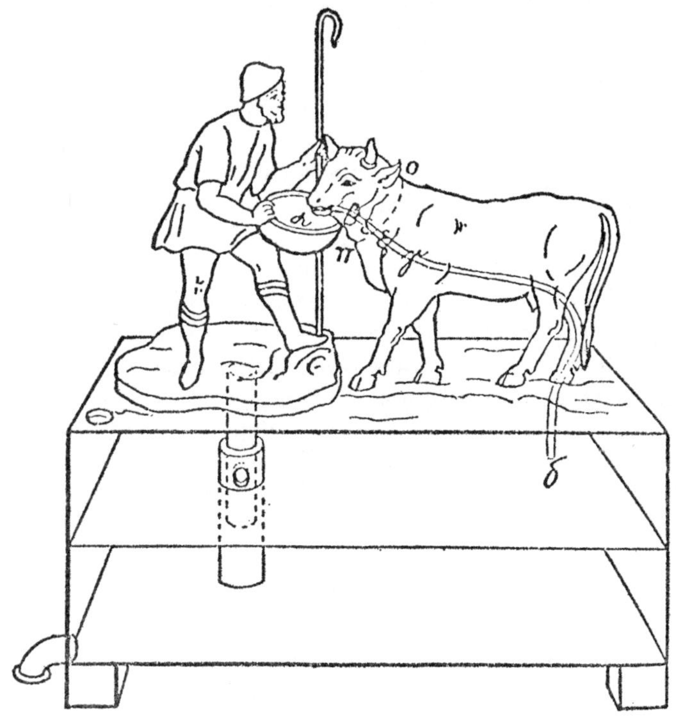

69. Mechanism for cutting through a bull's neck

derived from literary studies, but solely to men of intellectual power, which is the mother of every excellence, depending as it does on a happy accident of nature. And indeed this is a quality which we see granted without respect of persons. For though the barbarian peoples derive no power from eloquence and no illustrious rank from office, yet they are by no means considered strangers to mechanical inventiveness, where nature comes to their assistance."[7]

We have noted that at times it seems as if there was a deliberate refusal to consider ways and means of increasing production, at least on the part of the ruling class. Thus, Seneca, dealing with inventions, says that one cannot admire together Diogenes and Daïdalos—the ascetic philosopher who tried to reduce his needs to a minimum, and the craftsman obsessed with devices. Contemporary inventions, such as the making of transparent glass, the development of heating systems, stenography, are all the work of the basest slaves, with penetrating wits in their own way, but lowly creatures turned to the earth. The inventions are works of reason, it is true, but not of the right reason. The luxury of superfluous devices merely submits the body to the soul, and the slave becomes the master. We may then correctly say of the Greeks: "Their ethic takes on the character of an asceticism, by means of which, in place of working to conquer things so as to extract enjoyment from them by force, one sets oneself to know and to be able to do without such things" (Laberthonnière). But many of the exponents of this ethic were rich men like Seneca, who owned an abundance of slaves to carry out or satisfy any whim.

The ancients also were not unaware that devices, constructed for a worthy purpose, could also be used for evil ends. The medical writer of the treatise on Articulations, remarks about the apparatus built to deal with dislocations that "they are so powerful that, if one wished to use them to cause harm, one would have an irresistible force at one's disposal through them". And in fact the instruments of torture used in the Renaissance were direct imitations of the Hippokratic apparatus. Finally, we note that the one attempt to prove that the work of the inventive engineer is close

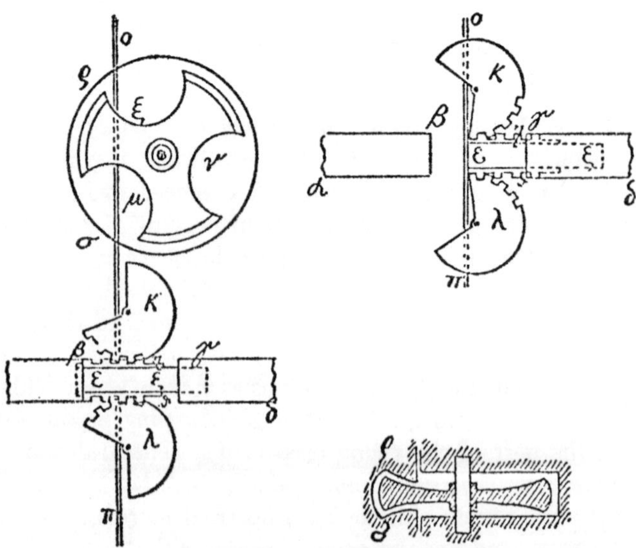

70. Inner devices of the mechanism

to that of the philosopher—by Heron—does not appeal to the sphere of production. His war-machines, he claims, can procure for men the peace of the spirit, *ataraxia*, by guaranteeing them a protection from invasions or seditious uprisings. They thus preserve the *status quo* and do not attempt to change it.[8]

Blast Power

XIII

If we take a long view, we see that two matters played a key-part in human development and finally came together effectively: the mechanism of propulsion and the dream of using solar or thunder power, blast-power. Throughout, a dominating rôle was played by destructive and violent hopes and fantasies. A crucial moment had arrived, far back in the palaeolithic, when men discovered a more powerful way of projecting a missile than by throwing it from the hand. The throwing-stick and the bow were the weapon-tools which gave men this great advantage. Among Australian natives, the spear-thrower, like the bull-roarer, has a great magical potence; for unknown reasons it gave added power to the spear. "I have myself seen an Australian spear, with the help of the spear-thrower, fly a hundred and fifty yards, and strike true and deep at the end of its flight" (Marett). The bow was the first composite mechanism that men devised; the total energy gradually expended by the archer's muscles was stored up in the bent wood or horn so that it could be concentrated at one point and released all together at the same moment. The Aterians and Capsians in Africa, and doubtless their Asian and European contemporaries. used the bow; the Magdaleneans and probably other palaeolithic societies used the thrower. The small communities settled west of the Nile in the fifth millennium B.C. on the shores of the lake then filling the Fayum depression left an immense amount of flint arrowheads, bone-harpoons, and bone dart-heads. Right up to the end of antiquity the bow, with the various forms developed from its principle, such as the catapult, remained the one long-distance weapon that was mechanically propelled. As warfare had been extended, incendiary material had been attached to the heads of arrows; later they were catapulted into enemy camps or towns. But the true fusion of propulsive power and explosive or inflammatory force could not arrive till the discovery of gunpowder.

The dream of achieving that fusion however went back as far as we can see. Australian witchdoctors or shamans thought they could capture solar power in a box and direct it against someone at an indefinite distance away. The commonest form of destruction-magic was by pointing bones or sticks. An instrument from Queensland is typical. The *munguni* consists of a short pointed bone attached to a string which passes into and through a small hollow receptacle of bone or wood; it comes out at the opposite end, which is then closed. To have its effect, the *munguni* is held in one hand with the bone pointed towards the victim, who may be many miles away. A double action is thought to take place. Some of the victim's blood is drawn into the receptacle and sealed up there; and at the same time a deadly force passes out of the *munguni* into the victim. To kill him, the *munguni* with its contents must be burned; to keep him wasting, it may be warmed now and then. He will not recover till it has been thoroughly rinsed out. Another form of the power-killer is the *tchintu*, a small lump of resin with two teeth in it and a long string attached. By being sung (spelled), the heat of the sun can be drawn in. Then the *tchintu* is set in someone's tracks; the heat follows the victim, catches him up, enters his body, and kills him. We may note that it is resin to which the killing solar power is akin; the solar teardrops of amber were connected with the thunder-stricken fall of Phaethon and later used in explosives.[1]

Concepts of this kind are generally linked with shamanist cultures. Among the Warao of Venezuela, where tobacco is used ritually as an hallucinogen, the initiate swallows a stick, which travels past the spirit in his chest and is "born" white through a mystical hole in the palm of his hand; a second stick similarly comes out through the palm of the other hand. The sticks are reswallowed, pass through the chest and arms, and this time are born as white crystal beads. The shamans can emit magic arrows to kill or cause sickness; they see these projectiles flying through the air like fireballs and know that some other shaman has malevolently sent a bit of glass, a twig, a human hair, a rock, or some other object into the body of his victim. The way that the projectile is sent is as follows. The shaman (*bahanarotu*) ingests the chosen missile, lets it pass through his chest and arms to the wrist, where it waits, moving slowly to the exit-hole in the hand. The *bahanarotu* takes a deep pull at his cigar, lifts the hand with the missile to his mouth, belches out a ball of smoke and sends the missile off. Such a practitioner is called the Master of the Arrows; and he does his shooting at night so that he can watch the glowing puff of tobacco smoke in which the missile travels. The image is of a tube in the arm which shoots out the arrow through the hand-hole. An anthropolgist records of the Barama River Caribs of Guyana:

> It is believed that a tube somewhat like the barrel of a gun extends from the *piaiyen*'s [shaman's] neck to the elbowjoint, and from the latter point to a small opening between the bases of the first and second fingers. . . . With the "shots" held above the elbowjoint, the *piaiyen*, when ready for action, takes a long inhalation of tobacco smoke and extends the right forearm in the intended direction. The force of the smoke is believed to be the physical agency necessary for the ejection of the shot. (Gillin)

The way of the smoke-blast along which the missile travels is also the way on which the shaman goes in his voyage to the spirit-world.

When a full scheme of an afterworld is developed by a class-divided society like that of the ancient Egyptians, the accumulated emotions of fear, hate, envy, resentment find expression in fantasies of torments inflicted on the damned. *The Book of the Gates* tells of the passage through the twelve sections of the Tuat or Underworld, each Gate represented by a serpent standing on its

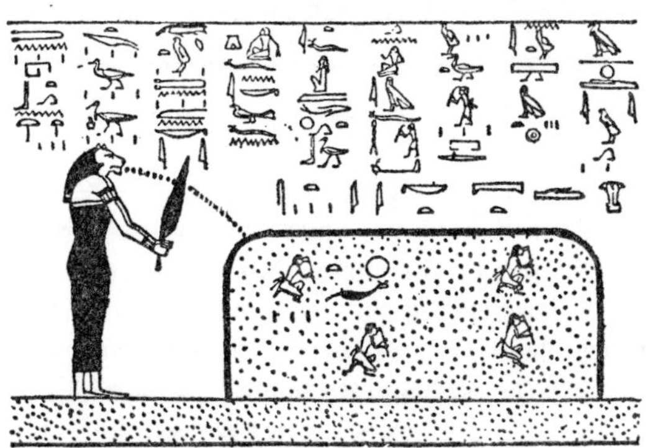

71. Fire pellets blown at the Damned immersed in Pits of Fire (Book *Ami Tuat*)

tail—perhaps the spirit of the pivoted doorleaf. The dead man, going through the western antechamber, is accompanied by Khepri, the Beetle in a Disk, which is surrounded by the convolutions of a serpent with its tail in its mouth; the Beetle is in its own boat, with Saa (god of knowledge) in the bows and Hekaa (god of magic) in the stern. (Thus the sun of tomorrow enters in embryo the Tuat, with Afu-Ra, the Body of Ra.) After the Sixth Gate comes the Judgment Hall of Osiris. The Boat of Afu is received into the Seventh Gate, but then the opposing forces, seeking to prevent the sun's rebirth, thicken. After the Eighth come the Waters of Nun, the primeval Ocean, then the Fiery Lake of Serser, then the Fire burning the enemies of Osiris. A drawing shows Flesh-of-Osiris, wearing Amun's plumes and seated under a canopy which is formed by the body of the serpent Mehen. Mehen blasts off the heads of kneeling and fettered captives. The blast is pictured as globules of fire.

72. The Dead being blasted in Pits of Fire (Book *Ami Tuat*)

The Book of Ami Tuat again shows us the night-journey of the sun. In the eleventh hour we meet the Firepits where the souls, shadows, and bodies of the enemies of Ra and Osiris are burned. In one pit the damned are shown immersed up to their necks in consuming fire. Goddesses maintain the fire by spewing it out of their mouths into the pits; and we see the fire-globules curving from a mouth down on to the heads below. We also hear Afu-Ra's boat in its progress, guarded by Mehen and lighted by twelve *uraei* who pour out fire from their mouths. The fire-shot is solar power; we

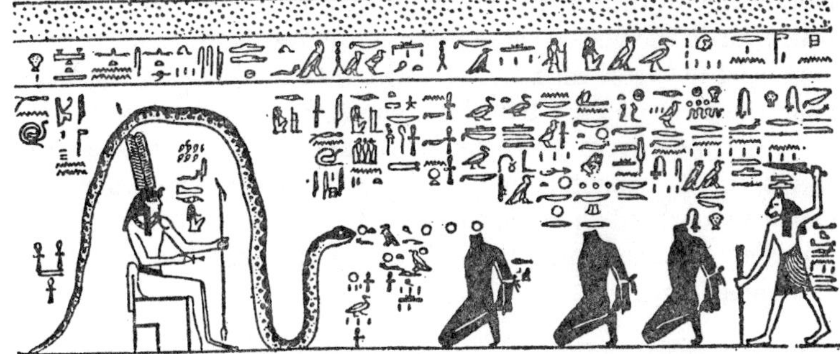

73. The Serpent Mehen (under whom sits the Flesh of Osiris with the plumes of Amun) blasts off the heads of captives (*The Book of Gates*)

see a sophisticated version of the Australian *munguni* or the Warao smoke-missile. The imagery of the fiery pits was taken over by the Christians for their vision of hell.[2]

The idea of trapping solar heat, concentrating it into a sort of laser-beam, and using it to strike down the enemy at a distance is only one aspect of the fantasies of blast-power that evolved. Another idea of blast-power draws its strength from a different sphere, which is nevertheless still of the sky—the sphere of storms, thunder and lightning, thunderbolts. Here nature (the world of the ancestral spirits) has set the example; and the aim of man is to imitate her. But with religion proper the shaman as weather-controller gives way to a highgod like Zeus, who wields the thunder and who strikes down Salmoneus when he tries to carry on the shamanist function (see figure 74).

Thunder is the one recurrent phenomenon of vast violence and fury, apparently cosmic in its dimensions to the mind of primitive or ancient man; it creates a corresponding fear. "It was fear that first made gods in the world, when lightning fell from high heaven, the world's ramparts were rent in flame, and stricken Athos blazed," declared Petronius.

The seeds of this idea go back at least as far as Demokritos, who is cited as saying: "When the men of old beheld the disasters in the heavens, such as thunderings and lightnings and thunderbolts and collisions between stars and eclipses of suns and moons, they were terrified, imagining the gods to be the causes of these things."

Kritias, one of the Thirty Tyrants of Athens in 404, gave the twist which made the gods a mere invention linked with thunder. Early men lived in bestial anarchy, so a wise man made up a story about gods whom he set in "the place where they could most frighten men, the place from which he knew came both terrors and easements to all men of labouring life—that is the vault above, in which there dwell the lightnings, he beheld, and terrible claps of thunder, and the starry face of heaven spangled by that skilful craftsman Time."

74. Salmoneus with his own Thunderbolt defying Zeus: fifth century krater (*A.J.A.* iii 331)

Where later a highgod was seen flinging bolts from on high, the primitive saw a powerful shaman inside the phenomena. The shamans of the Australian Dieri are called Kutchi; when a tribesman sees a circling duststorm near the camp, he is terrified. What he sees is Kutchi in person at his dangerous work. He hurls his boomerang and kills Kutchi, then flees in dismay: "Kutchi growl along a me, by and by me tumble down." To obtain a maximum of blast-power and be able to stand up against thunderstorm and tornado meant an ability to rival the thunderbolt. The bullroarer, a piece of flat wood whirled round at the end of a string, was used at initiation-ceremonies to summon up the dreaded and coveted force in a controllable form. Among the Wiradthuri, before initiation no boy might see a bull-roarer; he was told that its noise was the roar of Dhoromoolan. He and the women could hear the unearthly sound only from a distance. During initiation the novices were covered closely with blankets and the terrible roaring came up on to them in complete darkness. Afterwards the boys were allowed to see, and handle, the bull-roarer, and to learn how to twirl it. That was the great moment of revelation. Among the Aranda, at one point in the initiation the bull-roarers were heard nearing; the women fled while the novice, on his back, had poles piled on him and banged up and down by the old men, who sang: "Night, twilight, a great clear light, a cluster of trees skylike rising red as the sun." As the boy was being circumcised in the darkness by a fire, the bull-roarers sounded all the time, so loudly that the women and children in the camp could hear them. These latter believed it was the voice of the great spirit Twanyirika come to take the boy away. The spirit was thought to enter the novice's body after the operation and bear him off into the wilderness till he had recovered: then he left the boy, who could return to the camp. We must try to understand the very powerful emotion generated by the bull-roarer as thunder-power on the novice undergoing such rites.

The thunder-roar as a destructive force appears in many of the tales told about the bull-roarer's origin. The Wiradthuri said that the highgod Baiame destroyed his disobedient deputy Dhurraloolan and put his voice into the trees of the forest (soughing and roaring in tempest). The Kaitish said that the Tumana, the spirits of the bull-roarer, were killed by wild dogs. Murtu-murtu, the bull-roarer spirit of the Warramunga, was a man torn to pieces by wild dogs, and the trees from which bull-roarers were made grew where his flesh touched the earth. But at the same time the bull-roarer as a thunder-surrogate was a part of the life of nature, which was one with the spirits of the ancestors. It was called Grandfather by the Kai and by the Kurnai. Balum means a spirit, an ancestor, and the bull-roarer. Among Central Australians the bull-roarer was rubbed on a man's stomach so that it might communicate virtue and make him good, happy and strong.[3]

We find it distributed practically all over the world: England, Ireland, Scotland, Wales had it. In many areas it survived as a toy with names such as boomer, buzzer, whizzer, swish, and so on. In

Scotland till recently it was used by herdsmen to call the cattle home; as soon as the cattle heard it, they rushed for the byre. It was also considered there a "thunner-spell", a charm against thunder. It can be traced along Central Europe through Switzerland, Germany, Poland, past the Carpathians. In America it has been found among the Eskimos, and scattered over the northern half of the continent down to the Mexican border. It turns up again in central Brazil. From the Malay Peninsula and Sumatra it stretches over a great arc, from Africa west and south, to New Guinea, Melanesia, and Australia, together with New Zealand and Polynesia. Analagous instruments like the buzz fill other regions such as the eastern coastlands of Asia. On New Guinea and in north America a human face was carved on it. In West Africa it was held to contain the voice of a very god, while in Australia it was connected with the highgod. In a few places—Galicia in Europe, the Malay Peninsula, and among African Bushmen—it was used to drive and scare animals, wild or tame; but its main use was in connection with initiation and fertility ritual; e.g. rainmaking.

The Greeks knew it and called it *rhombos*, cognate with *rhembein*, to turn round and round. They used it in the Mysteries. The term *rhombos* is also used for a toy and the magic wheel described by Theokritos in the lovespell of the second Idyll; also for the tambourine or drum used in the worship of the Great Mother and of Dionysos. As a magical instrument whirling and producing a thunder-noise the word was naturally used of heavenly motion and of the course of the sun. A scholiast to Clemens describes it as "a bit of wood to which a string is tied, and it is whirled round and round at initiation rites to make a whirring sound". Strabon, dealing with the Kouretes, says that Aischylos in his (lost) *Edonoi* tells how the instruments of Kotys were used by the Thrakians in their Dionysiac orgies. Kotys is the Thrako-Phrygian form of the Mountain Mother to whom the Cretan *mystes* held aloft his torch; she was called also Bendis, Thea, Kybele. Aischylos describes the noise made by the "mountain gear" of Kotyto, the maddening hum of the *bombykes*, the clash of the bronze cymbals, the twanging of strings—"and the bullvoices roar from somewhere out of the unseen, fearful semblances, and from a drum an image as it were of thunder underground is borne on the air heavy with dread". We see that in the Greek Mysteries as much as in the Australian initiation-rites it was felt necessary to use the bull-roarer to create thunder-noises, which were felt to express the most powerful and shattering forces in the universe. In the early religions of the Near East the stormgod as a heavenly bull played an important part.

On the lines of the Egyptian cosmogonies which saw the universe as the creation of a single god out of the products of his body, thunder was a sort of vast flatus from the divine anus, just as rain was imaged as the highgod pissing. Common among the Australians and other peoples at what we may call the shamanist level is the belief that a shaman is full of stones-of-power, crystals. In the Mara tribe all the shaman's internal organs are thought to be taken out and replaced by those of a spirit. The *boglia* in western Australia has a quartz crystal in his stomach, which embodies and concentrates his power. The crystal itself is called *boglia* and at the shaman's death it passes into his son's stomach. We are also told that the human body, and especially the anus, is the sole source of *boglia*. In southern Australia the *mundie*, a crystal, is considered to be the excrement of the deity, and is used in initiation and held sacred.

The glittering crystal is a stone of light, of the sun; linked with stomach and anus, it is seen as a sky-excrement. It belongs to a series of life-giving magical substances that include gold; and it has a very wide distribution as an object helping in divination.[4]

Thunder had certainly once been in Greece a divine force without any special connection with a highgod. We saw how the thunder-noises were used in the mysteries of the Great Mother. Pausanias noted in Arkadia, famed for its archaic cults, sacrifices on the Alpheios to Lightnings, Storms, and Thunders. In art thunder-bolts are set on the Chair of the highgod without Zeus, and they are connected with the divine child of the Great Mother. On a terracotta relief (see figure 75) we see the three dancing Kouretes or Korybantes who clash shields (another thunder-simulation) over the baby Zeus; by him on the ground as a sort of double or other-self lies a thunderbolt. When Kronos is going to swallow the baby, Rheia gives him a stone in swaddling-clothes, which he swallows and later vomits out. (The tale is primitive enough, but it has a yet more primitive form in which the god takes the thunderstone into his stomach, like the shamans, and later excretes it. In initia-

75. Relief of the Kouretes dancing round the Divine Babe (Zeus) and Thunderbolt (J.H., *Themis* 23)

tion-myths the presiding god is often said to swallow the initiate, then vomit him out.) Hesiod tells us that not till the stone was got rid of by the god's body were thunders, thunderbolts and lightnings let loose. "Before that, huge earth had hidden them." It was by such a Thunderstone that Pythagoras was purified; on such a stone he gazed in the Diktaian Cave of Zeus.

Thunder-magics long continued. The timely thunderstorm that saved the Roman army in the campaign against the Quadi, under Marcus Aurelius, was attributed to the magic of the younger Julianus, whose father was the first man we know to have been called a theurge. In the version of Psellos, Julianus makes a human mask of clay which discharges "intolerable thunderbolts" at the enemy; and Sozomen tells of his splitting a stone by magic. Claudian describes the battle as one in which heaven flung bolts in defence of the Romans. "A scorched horse bore trembling its rider on its smoking back; another sank beneath his fire-wasted helmet; spears glowed molten by lightning and swords vanished in sudden smoke."[5]

An odd tale is told by Prokopios of the architect Anthemios from Tralles, who belonged to a family with high intellectual attainments; one brother was a lawyer at Rome, two were doctors, one a grammarian. Anthemios, who was also a mathematician, was asked by Justinian to Byzantion, where he designed the cathedral of St. Sophia. Once he had a quarrel with his neighbour in a contiguous house over the walls and windows; he lost his case through the eloquence of the other, who was named Zenon. In revenge he arranged in a lower room several cauldrons of water, each covered by the wide bottom of a leather tube. The tubes went on up till they were stuck somehow among the joists and rafters of the next house. A fire was put under the cauldrons, and the steam, collecting in pockets of Zenon's house, exploded and shook the whole place. Its inhabitants wondered in terror why they had a private earthquake. Perhaps Anthemios did manage to make some use of suddenly-expanding steam. He is also said to have tormented Zenon's guests at dinner with lights flashed into their eyes from mirrors; and he scared them with noises produced by the collision of certain minute and sonorous particles. Zenon announced to the Senate that a mere mortal must yield to the power of someone who shook the earth with Poseidon's trident and imitated the thunder and lightning of Zeus.

There were theatrical machines for producing effects of thunder and lightning. Lines from the opening of Claudian's *Rape of Proserpine* have been taken to refer to the use of such machines at Eleusis: "I see the shrine reel, its foundations totter, while the threshold glows with radiant light announcing the god's advent. And now I hear loud roaring from the earth's depths, the temple of Kekrops re-echoes and Eleusis waves its holy torches." But though the poet had a special interest in strange devices and unexplained natural forces, he is here surely expressing the state of wild inspiration he feels. Another poem of his has been taken to refer to fireworks. He is describing games: clown, mime, musician with flute and lyre, comedian, tragedian, player of the water-organ who elicits low music "from those pipes of bronze that sound a thousand diverse notes beneath his wandering fingers", and who "with a lever stirs to song the labouring waters". Acrobats hurl themselves through the air like birds and form a pyramid on the apex of which a boy dances. "Let the counterweights be removed and the mobile crane descend, and let the lofty scene rotate, flames scattering various in chorus-fashion. Let Vulcan force fireballs to roll harmlessly across the boards, let the flames seem to play about the sham beams of the scenery and a tame conflagration, given no rest, wander about among the untouched flowers." The description is obscure and perhaps refers to light-effects gained by mirrors; in any event fireworks cannot be involved.[6]

The thunderbolt was taken as the emblem of the most terrifying blow of fate. "Though the bolts strike one man alone," says Ovid, "not only one is terror-stricken." The bolt was especially thought to strike down the lofty. "It is always the great buildings and the tall trees that are struck by lightning," says Herodotos. "It's God's way of bringing the lofty low." Seneca stresses the fear of the thunderstorm. "Are you demented and oblivious of life's fragility that you fear death only when it thunders? does your life depend on escaping the *fulmen*?" He goes on about other forms of death. "But you tremble at the crash of the heavens. You tremble at the emptiness of the clouds and whenever anything lightens you expire. What then? Is it nobler in your opinion to perish by despair than by the *fulmen*? Rather, arm yourself with courage against the menaces of heaven; and when the world takes fire in every part, recall that not a single atom of this vast mass will be lost for you. If you think that it's for you the heavens are confounded and there is a stormy discord, and that it's on your account the clouds, pouring forth and clashing, crash together, if you think so great a force of fires is agitated for your end, console yourself with the thought that your death merits such a disaster. But even that thought will be impossible: the bolt strikes too quickly." He stresses also the stinking nature of thunder. It congeals wine, and the man who drinks such wine will die or go mad. For the *fulmen* owns a *vis pestifera*, a pestilential power. It makes oil and all perfumes stink; even its mere exhalation can kill. "Wherever thunder falls, a stench of sulphur is sure to be; and the smell is so strong that to inhale it too copiously is to lose one's mind." Lucretius says that the nature of the bolts is shown "by the strokes, by the traces of their heat burnt deep into things, the marks exhaling the noxious vapours of sulphur". A smell is indeed left by ball lightning. There suddenly appears a dazzling ball of fire, usually hazy in contours, which floats spinning, pulsating with an odd hissing sound, and scintillating with red sparks. It moves off on an irregular path, then explodes with a blinding flash and deafening concussion, leaving a sharp smell as of burning sulphur. The phenomenon occurs mostly near the end of a storm. The smell has often been attributed to nitrogen oxides, but is almost certainly ozone. The stress on the smell by ancient writers, which also appears strongly in European folklore, is, however, at least in part due to the feeling that there is an analogy between blast-power and bodily flatus. In folktales we find the stink associated with a blackening of bodies. Even earthquakes were recorded as stinking:

> At Bologne in Italy, *anno* 1504, there was such a fearful earthquake at about eleven a clock in the night (as Beroaldus in his book *de terrae motu*, hath commended to posterity) that all the city trembled, the people thought the world was at an end, *actum de mortalibus*; such a fearful noise it made, such a detestable smell, the inhabitants were infinitely affrighted, and some ran mad. . . . At Meacum, whole streets and goodly palaces were overturned at the same time; and there was such a hideous noise withal, like thunder, and filthy smell. . . . (Richard Burton, *Anatomy of Melancholy*)[7]

In the theory of thunder and lightning there was much stress on a rotatory movement. Lucretius links this idea with the image of a furnace. The winds shut in the clouds growl like wild beasts in a cave. They "seek an exit, whirl, and roll together out of the clouds the seeds of fire; they gather a host of them into a single mass and make them rotate in the hollow furnace within till they've burst the cloud and glitter out in forked flashes". He also shows the idea of compressed air sending out a missile. The idea in a general form is implicit in many ancient theories of thunder; but interestingly he links it with the idea of a leaden ball as a projectile. "At times the force of the wind, aroused from outside, falls on a cloud hot with a full-fledged bolt; and when it has burst, at once the *vortex* falls down, fierily eddying—which in our tongue is called *fulmen*. The same takes place on every side to which the force in question has borne down. At times, also, the power of the wind, though discharged without fire, yet chafes afire in the course of its long travel; and while it is passing on, on its way it loses some large bodies that can't get through the air as the others do, and out of the air itself it gathers and carries along other bodies, minute, which mix with it, producing fire by their flight. Very much as a leaden ball gets hot in its course as it loses many bodies of cold and takes up fire in the air." Bodies, *corpora*, here are corpuscles or atoms. Aristotle had taught that leaden shots in their flight through the air grew hot as they melted; but Lucretius is the first we know who links such shots with thunder-power or fire.

Plinius mentions the thunderbolt-stone, *keraunion*, in which magicians were much interested. He cites Sotakos as saying that it was used to destroy towns and fleets. It was probably pyrites, the nodular masses of which are still called thunderbolts. *Keraunion* appears in the recipe for automatic fire given in a work attributed to Julius Africanus (born A.D. 160–180); but the passage comes from a section of the book that is later than 550 (as Belisarios is mentioned), and probably earlier than mid-tenth century. Such mixtures had, however, long been known. The fire consists of equal parts of native sulphur (*vivum* or *theion*: which has not been melted), rock salt, *konia* (dust used for quicklime and for incense distilled from resinous trees—we may take the latter meaning here as it is equivalent to *manna* in older manuscripts), *keraunion* or pyrites—all ground in a black mortar in the noon sun, and mixed with equal parts of the resin of the black sycamore and liquid asphalt of Zakynthos to a greasy paste. "The mass must be stirred at noon with care and the body protected, for the composition easily bursts into flame. It must be kept in bronze boxes with tight covers, sheltered from the rays of the sun till it's wanted. If the engines of the enemy are to be burnt, they are smeared with it in the evening, and when the sun rises, all will be burnt." We see here strong links with the sun, the heat of which sets it off; the mixture is to be ground at noon; an ingredient is resin (recall what was said of amber). In fact the sun would not affect the mixture, but exposure to heavy morning dews or light rain might set it off.[8]

In the imagery of the ancient world concerning cosmic disasters we inevitably find that much is drawn from great storms, earthquakes, volcanic eruptions, tornadoes, floods. Water and fire are the two great forces to which a total breakdown or change is attributed. Zeus strikes down enemies or wrongdoers with his bolt. In the cosmic conflict with Typhōeus (Typhon) we see storm, earthquake, and eruption mingled. Both the fighters, says the Hesiodic account, thunder. We have cited some of the phrases above in Chapter VI; but may add here that "the whole earth seethed, and sky and sea. And the long waves raged along the beaches, about and about, at the rush of the deathless gods; and there arose an endless shaking." Zeus triumphed with "his arms, thunder and lightning, and lurid thunderbolt". When Typhon is struck, "a great part of huge earth was scorched by the terrible vapour and melted as tin melts when heated by man's *technē* in channelled crucibles; or as iron, hardest of things, is softened by glowing fire in mountain glens, and melts in the divine earth through the strength of Hepaistos", the firegod. Iron was smelted on Mt. Ida, perhaps one of the reasons why the *daimones* of metallurgy were attached to the Great Mother, the Mountain Mother. "Even so, the earth melted in the glow of the blazing fire."

Nowadays such passages read like prophetic accounts of the destruction wrought by napalm, atomic bombs, and the like; and indeed the fantasists, who have revived the notion of superior civilisations blotted out in the remote past and lost to history, have claimed that in accounts like that of the *Theogony* we have mythologised versions of actual calamities, caused by men in forgotten phases of history or by invaders from outer space on flying-saucers or rockets. In fact there is a real link between the ancient stories of cosmic disaster and the modern weapons of devastation; but the link lies in the tradition of destruction-fantasies that go back to the magical devices of the palaeolithic shaman and that have been actualised by the modern scientist.

Let us look at some of the past pictures to see how remarkably ancient fantasy forecast the horrors to come as the science of a world of alienation reached its maturity. In the *Arthasatra*, attributed to Kautilya (about 300 B.C.) but with interpolations reaching at least to the fifth century A.D., nitre and "a salt extracted from fertile soil" appear, as well as explosives (*agniyoga*, inflammable powder). Machines are installed in forts; "fiery spies" carry out all sorts of feats; firepots, "explosive fire", poisonous or explosive substances are daubed on chamberwalls; "seafoam", mixed with burning oil, is put underwater for an outburst of fire; showers of firebrands with thunder-noises come from the sky; there are poisonous smokes. Smoke is sent out through blowpipes. The tricks include a body burning with magical fire in the dark, a body smeared with burning oil, the image of a god covered with a layer of mica on which burning oil is smeared. The powder of firefly, mixed with oil of mustard seed, emits light at night. Many of the methods (blowing fire through tubes or reeds, sending out columns of smoke from the mouth) suggest the rituals of the shamans in

America who used tobacco as an hallucinogen. Recipes are given. The poisonous smokes, some of which are scented, are made of arsenic sulphides or green vitriol, and powders from plants (some poisonous), insects, animals, reptiles. Other materials employed include vegetable oils and juices, perhaps petroleum, dungs, wax, the powder of "all the metals" as red as fire, lead tin (or zinc?), turpentine, charcoal.[9]

The destruction of Sodom and Gomorra has been claimed by modern fantasists as the work of a prehistoric atomic bomb; and all sorts of actual and workable inventions have been claimed to lie behind such accounts as that in the Indian *Samarangana Sutradhara* of how to build a *vimana* or flying-chariot:

> Strong and durable must the body be made, like a great flying bird, of light material. Inside it one must place the mercury-engine with its iron heating apparatus beneath. By means of the power latent in the mercury which sets the driving whirlwind in motion, a man seated inside may travel a great distance in the sky in a most marvellous manner.
>
> Similarly, by using the prescribed processes one can build a *vimana* as large as the temple of the God-in-motion. Four strong mercury containers must be built into the interior structure. When these have been controlled by fire from the iron containers, the *vimana* develops thunder-power through the mercury. And at once it becomes like a pearl in the sky. More, if this iron engine with properly welded joints be filled with mercury, and the fire be conducted to the upper part, it develops power with the roar of a lion.

The imagery of the driving whirlwind, thunder-power, and power-with-the-roar-of-a-lion, show clearly enough the basis of the *vimana* in the traditions of *pneuma* and *prēstēr*-force we have been unravelling. The Indian epic *Mahabharata* is full of such fantasies. There is the mysterious weapon *brahmastra*, when "the fury of two fiery darts acting against each other, overspread the heavens and earth and grew strong like the burning rays of the sun". We hear of:

> a single projectile charged with all the power of the universe. An incandescent column of smoke and flame, as bright as ten thousand suns, rose in all its splendour. . . . It was an unknown weapon, an iron thunderbolt, a gigantic messenger of death which reduced to ashes the entire race of the Vrishnis and the Andhakas. . . . The corpses were so burned as to be unrecognisable. Their hair and nails

> fell out; pottery broke for no apparent cause, and the birds turned white. After a few hours all foodstuffs were infected.

Here are further Indian fantasies:

> Then Vayu (the presiding deity of that mighty weapon) bore away crowds of Samsaptakas with steeds and elephants and cars and weapons, as if these were dry leaves of trees. . . . Borne away by the wind, O king, they looked highly beautiful like flying birds . . . flying away from trees . . . (*Drona Parva: Samsaptaka-Badha Parva*)

> Meteors flashed down from the firmament. . . . A thick gloom suddenly shrouded the host. All points of the compass were enveloped in that darkness. . . . Inauspicious winds began to blow. . . . The sun seemed to turn round; the universe, scorched with heat, seemed to be in a fever. The elephants and other creatures of the land, scorched by the energy of that weapon, ran in flight. . . . The very waters being heated, the creatures rising in that element began to burn . . . hostile warriors fell down like trees burnt down in a raging fire—huge elephants burnt by that weapon, fell down on the earth . . . and the chariots also, burnt by the energy of that weapon looked . . . like the tops of trees burnt in a forest fire. (*Naryanastra Mokshana Parva: Drona Parva*)

> Meteors, showering blazing coals, fell on the earth from the sky. . . . The Sun's disk seemed to be always covered with dust. . . . Fierce circles of light were seen every day around both the sun and the moon. . . . A little while after the Kuru king, Yuhishshira heard of the wholesale carnage of the Vrishnis in consequence of the iron bolt . . . a fierce iron bolt that looked like a gigantic messenger of death. . . . In great distress of mind the king caused that iron bolt to be reduced to fine powder. Men were employed, O king, to cast that powder into the sea. (*Mausala Parva*)

We have here visions of cosmic disaster in which the thunderbolt plays a central part. "In considering the marvellous works of the thunderbolt," said Seneca, "no one can doubt that there is in it a divine and finely accurate [*subtilis*] power." He ends Book III of his *Natural Questions* with a vision of world-end through water. What makes the Indian passages so striking is the fact that nowadays men have learned to harness the thunderbolt and the tornado —indeed, have learned how to manufacture far greater disasters; and the significance of the Indian visions is not at all lessened if it could be shown that news of cannon and firearm had reached medieval India and helped to stimulate the image of the *brahmastra*.

Sometimes the account of a violent shamanist experience may be merged with what can be legitimately interpreted as the account of a tornado or thunderstorm. Thus *Ezekiel* (i–x) has been translated into modern meteorological terms; and the "likeness of four living creatures", which are also described as four wheels and four cherubim, has been taken to be in fact a quartet of tornadoes raging with a lot of electrical activity. "And I looked, and behold, a whirlwind formed to northwards, a great cloud, and fire infolding itself, and a brightness was about it, and out of the midst of it as the colour of amber, out of the midst of the fire." And again, in a passage which has been said to be an excellent description of magneto-plasma-dynamic phenomena: "Their appearance was like burning coals of fire, and like the appearance of lamps; it went up and down among the living creatures; and the fire was bright, and out of the fire went forth lightning. And the living creatures ran and returned as the appearance of a flash of lightning." The experience is said to have occurred on the banks of the Chebar near Babylon "in the thirteenth year, in the fourth month, in the fifth day of the month" (probably 590 B.C.) as the prophet was "among the captives". In such a situation a shamanist trance-vision might well have been merged with the fury of light and noise in the tornadoes. "And their whole body, and their backs, and their hands, and their wings, and the wheels were full of eyes round about, even the wheels that they four had. As for the wheels, it was cried to them in my hearing, O wheel. . . . And when the cherubim went, the wheels went by them; and when the cherubim lifted up their wings to mount up from the earth, the same wheels also turned not from beside them."

The image of the thunderbolt has inevitably dogged the development of explosive power. Petrarch in a dialogue, usually dated 1344, mentions bronze shells of a small size fired from wooden guns. "I am surprised that you have not also those bronze acorns which are cast with a jet of flame and a horrible noise of thunder. It is enough to have the anger of an immortal God thundering in the vault of heaven, but O, cruel mixture of pride, man, sorry creature, must also have his thunder. Those thunders which Virgil thought to be inimitable, man, in his rage for destruction, has come to imitate. He hurls them from an infernal machine of wood as they are hurled from the clouds. Some attribute this invention to Archimedes. . . . This scourge was so rare that it was considered a prodigy, but now that minds are apt to invent the worst things, it is as common as any other kind of arms."

Milton, with a true poet's insight, gives the invention and use of gunpowder the setting of cosmic conflict, but outdoes the Indian epics by an explicit description of the devilish device. Hard-put, Satan teaches his followers how to mine 'deep underground, materials dark and crude, of spirituous and fiery spume", which, brought into the light of day, show themselves "pregnant with infernal flame, which into hollow engines long and round, thick-rammed, at th'other bore with touch of fire dilated and infuriate, shall send forth from far with thundring noise among our foes such implements of mischief as shall dash to pieces, and o'erwhelm whatever stands adverse, that they may fear we have disarm'd the Thunderer of his own dreaded bolt". He was perhaps elaborating with deep mythological force Spenser's attribution of fire-arms to the Devil. He describes the seraphs standing with fiery reeds ready to set off their cannon against heaven. The "roar embowell'd with outrageous noise the air, and all her entrails tore, disgorging foul their devilish glut, chain'd thunderbolt and hail of iron globes".[10]

Interestingly, the first realisation that the new forces of destruction might bring about a real world-end was evoked by the Gunpowder Plot aimed at blowing up James I and his Parliament. The king saw it as a Doomsday by Fire, paralleling the earlier Doomsday by Water of God; and Vicars called it: "Sulphurious, furious hels dooms-day." Dekker spoke of it, in *If This be not a Good Play*, as aiming to hew down "a whole land at one blow, and at once drowne in a flood of flames". Ben Jonson, whose *Catilina* was in many ways a symbolic account of the Plot, tells there of Conspiracy outdoing the "transcendent furies", "the fall of torrents, and the noyse of tempests, the boyling of Charybdis, the seas wildnesse, the eating force of flames, and wings of winds". Catilina says of one of his followers that he would "go on upon the Gods; kiss lightning, wrest the engine from the Cyclops, and give fire at face of a full cloud". Carrying on the theme in *The Staple of News*, Jonson tells how a former General of the Jesuits is said to have become the Order's Cook so as to invent an Egg-Bomb: "All the yoke is wildfire, as he shall need to beleaguer no more towns, but throw his egg in"; "It shall consume palace and place; demolish and bear down all strengths before it"; "Never be extinguished, till all becomes one ruin." His fantasy foresees both napalm and atomic bomb, the power to take over the thunderbolt, wrest the engine from the Cyclops. King, Lords and Parliament being seen as the earthly hierarchy that mirrors God and His Powers, their destruction by gunpowder at one fell swoop was imaged as a cosmic disaster.

The attempt to unite fire and projectile went back far, but for long could only express itself by tying some fiery material to a missile. All savage races known in modern times, who use the bow, also at times seem to have tried incendiary arrows. On Assyrian reliefs we see incendiaries used in the siege of towns in the ninth century B.C.; torches, lighted tow, burning pitch and firepots are thrown down on the attackers. The *zikkim* of the Old Testament seem to be some sort of incendiary arrows: "A madman who casts fire-brands, arrows and death" (*Proverbs*). "Sharp arrows of the night with coals of juniper" (*Psalms*). *Isaiah* is more obscure: "All you that kindle a fire, that compass yourselves about with sparks, walk in the light of your fire and in the sparks you have kindled." The Persians used arrows tipped with burning tow in the capture of Athens, 480 B.C. We don't hear of the Greeks themselves using them till 429, when the wooden walls of Plataia had to be protected with skins. Resinous torches and fireships were used at the sieges of Syracuse, 413, and Rhodes, 304. At the siege of Delion in 424 the Boiotians, to destroy fortifications, used a long tube made of hollow sailyard and iron moved on wheels, bearing a vessel with burning charcoal, sulphur, and pitch, and large bellows behind the vessel. This is the first attempt that we know of to use a tube in some sort of engine for projecting fire or fiery materials. A similar apparatus using powdered coal (? charcoal) was described by Apollodoros, architect or engineer of Hadrian. After the flame has been played on stone walls, they crack when vinegar or other acids are poured on them. This seems the first mention of the use of powdered coal, which comes up again in accounts by Heron of Byzantium in the tenth century.

But clearly from the fourth century B.C. experiments with

dangerous fires were going on. Aineias tells how burning materials like pitch, tow, and sulphur are to be used to destroy engines being brought up against a besieged town. "Let sticks be prepared, shaped like pestles but much larger"—the pestles here meant were big utensils used for stirring meal and dough in kneading-troughs: three cubits long according to Hesiod's advice—"and into the ends of each stick drive sharp irons, larger and smaller, and around the other parts of the stick, above and below, separately place powerful combustibles. In appearance the pestle-ends should be like bolts of lightning drawn by artists. Let this be dropped upon the engine as it is being pushed up." These fire-contraptions, thrown from above to stick in the wood of the engine and burn furiously away, are thus made to look like what thunderbolts were imagined to be. Fire-fighters "must have a protection for the face, so they'll be less disturbed when flame darts up at them". The fire itself is to be "powerful and quite inextinguishable, made of pitch, sulphur, tow, granulated frankincense, and pine sawdust in sacks". The date of Aineias is about 360 B.C.[11]

Fire-arrows seem to have become common among the Greeks in the fourth century, especially after the death of Alexander the Great in 323. Arrian describes Phoinikian fireships at the siege of Tyre; and we hear of fire-arrows and firepots at the siege of Rhodes. Virgil writes of fire-arrows. No javelin could have hurt Bitias, but a "fiery dart" with a great hissing noise pierced his shield and corselet; it came like a *fulmen*. His fall was like the crash of a huge rocky structure into the sea, "drawing ruin with it". The seas were "all embroiled and the black sand heaved up"; the underground confines of volcanic Typhon shook at "the roaring noise". The idea of the fire-missile summons up the thunderbolt and the setting of cosmic strife. Tacitus tells of fire-lances thrown by machines; Ammianus of fire-arrows, *malleoli*, which water made more fiery, but which sand put out. He adds that they must be shot slowly or they went out. Vegetius in the late fourth century says the mixture was of sulphur, resin, bitumen, and tow soaked in petroleum; it was enclosed between an envelope, *tubus*, and the shaft of the missile, a large iron-headed spear, called *falarica*. The head was up to three feet long. Fire-arrows were used by Visigoths at the siege of Nîmes in 673. Indeed it was long before they died out. The English army used them till at least 1599, shooting them from both long bows and crossbows. Lances tipped with incendiaries were used at the siege of Bristol in 1643. The Chinese were still shooting fire-arrows at the French in 1860.[12]

Fire-ingredients were becoming complicated. Petroleum had long been known, from Samosata, Ekbatana, and other places, and in legend was linked with Medeia. The discovery and use of naphtha, bitumen, petroleum stimulated strongly the hope of powerful fiery missiles; and the knowledge of such materials increased and spread much after Alexander the Great. Pseudo-Aristotle tells us:

> In Media and the district of Psittakos in Persia there are fires burning, a small one in Media, but a big one in Psittakos, with a clear flame. So the Persian king built his kitchen nearby. Both are on level ground, not in high places. They can be seen night and day, but those in Pamphylia only by night. . . . [? natural gas]
>
> At Apollonia, near the country of Atlantinoi, they say that bitumen and pitch is buried and springs up out of the earth just as water does. . . . It smells of sulphur and vitriol. . . . There is also continuous burning in Lykia and near Megalopolis in the Peloponnese. . . .

Ktesias of Knidos (about 398), a Greek physician at the Persian court, tells of oil from a huge Indian worm that set everything on fire. Captured, the worm was hung in the sun a month and the dripping oil was collected in earthenware pots, then sent to the king in sealed jars. The jars were cast into besieged towns and set everything afire when they broke. Nothing could resist the combustion except mud or sweepings, which put it out. Later, Ailian cites Ktesias as saying that no battering ram or military engine could withstand the oil. Philostratos says the white worm was found in the river Hyphasis in the Punjab; the oil got by melting it down could only be kept in glass vessels, and once on fire no ordinary means could extinguish it. The king used it to burn walls and capture cities. The sage Apollonios asked the Indians why Alexander had not attacked the Oxydrakai, a Punjab people living between Hyphasis and Ganges; he was told that these holy folk repulsed even Herakles of Egypt and Dionysos, using "prodigies and thunderbolts"—*skēptoi*, which is also used for hurricanes and dust-storms. As soon as the enemy approached, "they were driven off by *prēstēres* and thunderbolts, *brontai*, hurled obliquely from above and falling on their armour". The mysterious oil was no doubt naphtha, mythologised with the worm or dragon-crocodile

(? fire-breathing). Note the name of the people, Oxydrakes, which means "with sharp flashing eyes". They thus have dragon-qualities and may be linked in this respect with Medousa, Charon, Athena Glaukopis.

Strabon says that Alexander found at Ekbatana in Media a naphtha lake; a street, sprinkled with it, flashed into flame from one end to the other at a light. A body soaked in naphtha of Sousiana could only be put out by mud, vinegar, alum, glue. A little water made it burn more, but a lot extinguished it. Strabon also cites from Poseidonios the Babylonian white and black naphtha, or liquid sulphur—the black naphtha being asphalt, which was burnt in lamps. *Naphtha* is a Persian word (*naft*, petroleum), but the derivation of *asphaltos* is uncertain. White naphtha (white bitumen, filtered asphalt) has been taken as distilled petroleum, though distillation is usually considered a later invention. It is however mentioned by Dioskourides in a rough form. The preparation of white naphtha may have been by some purifying process or filtration (e.g. by fullers' earth); distillation appears in an Arabic text of 1225. Hippolytos mentions Indian naphtha that kindled at the mere sight of distant fire; Plinius, a bituminous liquid skimmed from salt brine in Babylonia and used in lamps, also a liquid bitumen from Zakynthos, Babylon (white), Apollonia, and Agrigentum (used in lamps). He mentions naphtha separately but says that some put it among the bitumens, though "its burning properties and its susceptibility of ignition render it quite unfit for use". Fire darts on it instantly. He adds that in Samosata on the Euphrates is a pool discharging inflammable mud, *maltha*, which adheres fast to any solid; the people defended their walls with it against Lucullus and burned soldiers in their armour.

Prokopios says that the Greeks called naphtha Oil of Medeia, who lived in Kolchis, between the Black and the Caspian Sea, a petroleum region. In the legend she killed off her rival Glaukē with a garment which burst into flames. But there may also be a reference to Media, the land between the Caspian Sea and Mesopotamia, the petroleum of which was well known, especially after Alexander captured Babylon in 324. Kinnamos speaks of Median Fire.

Vitruvius was the first we know to describe petroleum, in the river Liparis in Kilikia, where it covers bathers, in lakes of Ethiopia and India, and in a well at Carthage, where the oil smells of lemon and is used for anointing cows. Dioskorides refers to the liquid bitumen swimming on waters at Agrigentum. Other areas cited by Plinius include Aitna, Baktria, the fields of Aricia near Rome, perhaps at times he refers to an escape of natural gas; Ailian tells of the spring near Apollonia that constantly emitted flames. Ancient extinguishers included water, sand, dry or moist earth, manure, urine, and especially vinegar. Vinegar, however, would have been little more effective than water, though salty sauces may have been included in the term, and the salt left on the burning wood might have helped to put out the fire. Plinius mentions that Gauls and Germans used salt water on burning wood. Alum was also used on wood, and was indeed effective. Roman siege-engines were fire-proofed with alum in the war with the Persians in A.D. 296. Mixtures which had sulphurs in them, with or without tar or thick petroleum or resins, would stick fast to objects, would resist water, and would yield only with much trouble to sand.[13]

At the siege of Aquileia, says Herodianos (A.D. 240) the folk threw on the soldiers and their engines pots with a mixture of sulphur, *asphaltos*, and pitch, and shot arrows with metal heads and shafts smeared with burning pitch. The Vandals in 468 used braziers with incendiaries against the Roman fleet. Proklos the Philosopher is said by Malalas to have advised the emperor Anastasios in 515 to use sulphur against the ships of Vitalianus; but Zonaras says Proklos the Dream-Interpreter used mirrors to fire them. Persians, besieged in Petra in Kolchis in 551, used mixtures of sulphur, bitumen, naphtha. We see then that the use of incendiaries had become widespread.

The kind we have been considering may be called simple; napalm and thermit are their descendants today. We enter a more complex chemical field with the kind which combined quicklime with petroleum or sulphur. On account of the heat generated by the hydration of the quicklime, the mixture was liable to burst into flames when wetted with water. Plinius thought it a marvel that water should cause fire. Augustine explained the effect by saying that limestone on burning takes up part of the nature of fire, which is retained in a latent form on cooling; water, the enemy of fire, disengages the heat, though oil, the food of fire, fails to do so. II *Maccabees* tells of a "thick water", *nephthai,* from Persia, which, poured over wood on the altar or on big stones, inflamed when the sun shone on it. (The events were of 169 B.C., though written about in 135–106.) The trick was used to impress devotees at the yearly kindling of the lamps in the Sepulchre at Jerusalem, which began in the eighth to ninth century. Pausanias, about A.D. 150, tells of ashes, *tephra*, of a special kind (perhaps incense mixed with quicklime) on an altar in a Lydian temple; a magician put dry wood on them, assumed a tiara, and spoke spells in an alien tongue—at which the wood burst into fire.[14]

The phrase spontaneous or automatic fire, *pyr automaton*, first occurs in Athenaios, who tells how a wonderworker or conjurer, Xenophon, astonished the world with his tricks and made *pyr automaton* issue from himself. Hippolytos tells of a conjurer who put burning tow into his mouth and then blew out sparks.

We have already noted the recipe attributed to Julius Africanus. Quintus Curtius (first century A.D.) tells of red-hot sand that penetrated armour-chinks, and powdered quicklime. The latter ingredient continued to be used in pots slung at the enemy well into medieval times. More important was Greek Fire, which appears from the seventh century at a time when a siege of Byzantion was carried on for seven years. At Kyzikos the Arab fleet and sailors were destroyed, partly by storm, partly by the fire invented by the architect Kallinikos of Syrian Heliopolis, who had fled to the Romans (Byzantines). After that the Romans were victorious through the invention of Sea Fire. Kallinikos seems to have developed his device at Byzantion, but he may well have gained his lore in Syria. His fire was able to benefit from the use of more effective siphons, which had been fitted to ships shortly before. Later, the emperor Constantine Porpyrogenitus declared that the fire-recipe had been revealed by an angel to Constantine the Great; Kallinikos merely devised the art of projecting liquid fire through siphons. A treatise attributed to the emperor Leon tells of the emission of "thunder and burning smoke through siphons", which set ships on fire. It also mentions hand-siphons discharged behind iron shields "recently manufactured in our dominions". A small handpump projecting Greek Fire is shown in an eleventh-century MS.; and a Spanish Moslem physician in a book on surgery depicts a cylindrical syringe with piston, and states that liquid can be sent out from it "as with that tube by means of which naphtha is thrown in sea-battles". (*Siphon* has various meanings: a double-action force-pump or fire-engine which was invented by Ktesibios and improved by Heron; a water-pump for putting incendiaries out; a bent tube for transferring liquids, as in many of Heron's devices; and a pipe through which water was forced like a fountain.) At Thessalonika in 904 liquid fire was said to be blown from siphons by means of compressed air; and a late fifteenth-century MS. shows a defender of Byzantion holding a pipe about five feet long with flames coming from the funnel-shaped mouth. Probably on ships the pump was connected by a flexible tube of leather with the metal tube from which liquid fire was sent. Leo tells us: "The front part of the ship had a bronze tube so arranged that the prepared fire could be projected forward to left or right and also made to fall from above. This tube was mounted on a false floor above the deck on which the specialist troops were accommodated, and thus raised above the attacking forces mustered in the prow. The fire was thrown on the enemy's ships or into the faces of the attacking troops." Greek Fire was used in 941 against Igor the Russian who was attacking Byzantion. Liutprand of Cremona, whose nephew was then ambassador in Byzantion, says that a mere fifteen boats throwing the fire on all sides, from prow, stern, and sides, defeated a fleet of several thousand ships. Anna Komnena describes a sea-battle of 1103. Each Byzantine galley had in the prow a tube ending in a brass or iron head of a lion or some such beast of prey, gilded, frightening; through the open mouth fire was ejected by means of some flexible apparatus, which seems to have been able to swivel. An enemy ship was rammed in the stern and the fire pumped over it.

> This fire they made by the following arts. From the pine and certain such evergreen trees inflammable resin is collected. This is rubbed with sulphur and put into tubes of reed, and is blown by men using it with violent and continual breath. Then in this manner it meets the fire on the tip and catches light and falls like a fiery whirlwind on the faces of the enemy.

These blowpipes with an igniting device on the tip (perhaps a small torch of resinous wood) were an advance version of Leon's micro-siphon, which was a small handpump. Their effect would be to send out a cloud of fire. Greek Fire was considered a Byzantine state-secret. Old methods, of pots of liquid pitch and naphtha, were also carried on. Leon mentions the throwing of pots of powdered quicklime that formed a dustcloud and suffocated or blinded the enemy; there were also baskets full of live scorpions and serpents. The Crusades saw a large expansion of fire-missiles.

With the great attention paid to incendiaries and fire-mixtures of all sorts by the Byzantines and Arabs, and later by the westerners, it could only be a question of time before gunpowder was invented. Alchemy does not seem to have played a direct part in the discovery; but its interest in chemical combinations must have contributed to the general trend. A character like

76. Incendiary developments as shown in a fifteenth-century work made for a Mamluk Sultan of Egypt. Top from left: incendiary arrow, bomb (?), pedestal of incendiary cartridges, ball (centre) for throwing from a short *midfa*, a *midfa* with ball on carrying stick, bomb, gunpowder container or naphtha jar. Below from left: footsoldier with sprinkling club, fireproof clothes with firework cartridges attached, rider fireproofed with spear (cartridges attached), the horse also fireproofed with cartridges, soldier with naphtha flask and short *midfa* with ball

Kallinikos may well have had links with Syrian alchemists. And for our purposes it is not important to discuss the rival claims of Europe and China as to the first making of gunpowder. What is clear is that in the Graeco-Roman and Byzantine worlds there was a steady convergence of social, political, military, intellectual, and technical factors towards the advent of gunpowder. If the Chinese Taoists truly record the mixture of carbon, sulphur, and saltpetre in 919, and if this recipe spread from China to the West, things would certainly have been speeded up a little. Since the Chinese used their techniques and recipes in this field for fire-works, we see that they lacked the war-pressures, the continual experimentation with fire-missiles, which were driving the Byzantines and westerners on and which had gunpowder as their logical conclusion. Whatever the exact details, round about 1300 came the crucial developments leading into firearms, cannons, and the use of explosives in an increasingly destructive way. In the west, unlike China, the close integration of physical theory, mechanics, ballistics, and war-pressures led to the new science of the sixteenth and seventeenth centuries.[15]

Probably the basis of the earliest Greek Fire was liquid rectified petroleum or volatile petrol projected in hand-grenades, or ordinary petroleum in tubs shot from *ballistae*.

> In Leo's time this liquid was projected from jets to which it was pumped through flexible leather tubes by a force-pump, the jets being either fixed in brass figureheads on ships, or manipulated to turn in various directions. The burning liquid could also float and burn around the ships. Since the petroleum was imported, its nature could be kept a semi-secret among the Byzantine officers, but its use as an incendiary in warfare must soon have been learned from experience of it by the Arabs (if they did not know it already), who then began to use it themselves. (Partington.)

To thicken petroleum and prevent it dissipating or failing to reach far enough, resinous substance and sulphur would have been added. The precise proportions in the mixture and the mechanical systems of projection were what made up the secret of Greek Fire.

What concerns us here is the way in which there was a steady progression from, say, the Assyrians with their fire-arrows to the Crusaders with their incendiaries. The revolutionary turning-point in this development came with gunpowder; but that discovery was not something intruding from outside. It emerged in a close context with Greek Fire and the related experiments with combustibles. In the *Bellifortis* of Conrad Kyeser of Eystadt (died about 1405) a recipe for gunpowder is called Greek Fire because it contains also the old ingredient, petroleum. The quest for ever more effective fire-missiles was linked in turn with development of the impetus-theory, fire-arm ballistics, and ultimately with Galilean mechanics.

Another aspect of ancient thought which at every point underlies the developments of Greek Fire and gunpowder was the concern with heat and its transformations, the effort to devise models of blastpower in Hellenistic and Roman times. And behind the physics and the models, as we have seen, lies the immemorial fascination with solar and storm power, the desire to be able to rob Zeus of his thunderpower. The high skygod, we saw, took to himself the shamanist fantasy-powers which had been expressed in primitive magic and ritual. Now the scientist, the shaman reborn with far greater technical resources, was taking back the solar and thunderbolt powers. What had been fantasy becomes all-too-real fact. The Arabic *bunduq* originally meant hazelnut, then a clay pellet, then a lead bullet shot from some kind of bow, finally a firearm.[16]

It may be worthwhile to pause here and turn back to the final book, VI, of Lucretius' great epic, which sums up a great deal of ancient thought on the themes we have been following, and which provides the last word of judgment on man's tendency to take the wrong turning in scientific enquiry and technological application. It would be unfair to the ancient world to record its ideas and practices without outlining this tremendous vision.

The poet has been making a long consideration of the thunderbolt as the most powerful and violent force in nature. He discusses the part played by the winds in this phenomenon, then the winds in their underground caverns, earthquakes, eruptions (which he correlates with fevers and burning diseases in our bodies), lakes with pestilential vapours, noxious smells and fumes; e.g. charcoal, which, when it has been burning "with more than usual force", can fill all the rooms of a house so that "the fumes of the virulent substance act like a murderous blow". Inside the earth "sulphur is generated and asphalt forms incrustations of a noisome stench".

When men go digging deep for gold or sliver, "what mischief do goldmines exhale". The toils appear in the faces and skins of the workers, who often go blind or die. Next the seeds of fire and water are discussed; the magnitude and the minuteness of corpuscles or atoms; the way that certain things combine or fuse. Finally, the nature of disease, when the noxious seeds gather together and come down in clouds and mists, or rise up from the earth tainted with "unseasonable rains and suns". After thus linking the disintegrations or evil combinations in the physical world with the forces that can rot and kill the human body, he turns to the Plague in Athens (during the Peloponnesian War), which he generalises from the account in Thoukydides into a symbol of human disaster.

It has often been thought that his epic ends with the account of the plague because he died and did not complete the work—whether his death was a suicide or not. Certainly the poem ends almost in mid-sentence. But that fact does not disprove his choice of the episode as culminating point of his exposition. He may indeed have meant in his general plan to revert to Epikourean optimism, but have been so overcome with pessimism that he broke off and soon after killed himself. But as we shall see, the episode in many ways makes a fitting conclusion to his vision of life and of man's place on earth.

If we compare his version with that of Thoukydides we can learn much. He omits matters that limit or localise the theme: the details of how the plague broke out, the charge that the Pelopoponnesians had poised the wells, the toll taken of the doctors, the futility of appeals to priests and the fears, the immunity of sufferers to a second attack, the resistances put up by the body, the freedom of the year otherwise from diseases. He thus leaves out all details that make the plague a specific misfortune which occurred by mishap, and so on.

He alters details with the same aim of universalising the situation. The disease attacks the seat of life (*cor*). We do not hear of sufferers being tended or gaining relief from cold water. Men fling their naked bodies in streams or wells. The symptoms and stages of the plague are in general worsened. Thoukydides says that survivors were afflicted with the loss of their extremities; Lucretius says they were castrated through fear of death. He concentrates the Thoukydidean account of widespread depression and of contagion to a single point: that of utter despair. The idea of nemesis appears in phrases like *morti damnatus*. He stresses the staring at death, the universal terror. Where Thoukydides shows things worsened by the countryfolk crowding into the city, Lucretius makes the disease spread out through the countryside. Rustics, already infected, come in to swell the number of the stricken. We get a steadily darkening picure of hopeless calamity, with inner as well as outer aspects underlined. He increases the list of symptoms by drawing on Hippokratic writings. Dogs, faithful beasts, catch the contagion—whereas in Thoukydides they are afflicted through devouring corpses. Lucretius wants to show the infection of man pervading nature and to make the disease not a chance biological misfortune but the inescapable result of man's inner unbalance. What has happened to Athens is something that threatens mankind all the time.

The internalisation of the experience is built up by such words as *metus, timor, maeror, maestus, angor*. Each stage of breakdown is defined in terms of a mental state. "He begins with the outward signs, and advances to the inner meaning, just as he revealed *res caecae* from *res apertae* in the first books. Eventually the physical side is little more than a symbol of the internal; the real struggle, the real decay and death is in the spirit" (Bright). We may say that "the line between biological disease and social disease becomes thinner and thinner until it vanishes". Men's response to the situation is irrational; the victims and those who should attend to them are controlled by the sort of fallacious reasoning condemned in Book III; they cling to a life they cannot prolong or enjoy. "The failure of reason is subtly emphasised as well by the early and persistent attack on the senses and faculties: sight, speech, hearing, touch, smell (the tainted blood from the nose). This I take to be part of the reason for the interpolation from the Hippocratean writings: the assault on the senses without which man cannot obtain a sound view of reality." Society breaks down under the pressures of fear and greed generated or brought to a head by plague.

We may claim then that here is a picture of the pollution of the earth by man's inability to find a living and harmonious relation with nature. The destructive forces are fear (fear of the unknown, fear of death, fear of the truth), together with the greed and powerlust thus created. The society that destroys itself and pollutes nature is one crazed with unresolved conflicts that issue in war and greed. The meaning here in Book VI is brought out by a comparison with Book I. The end of the poem stands in complete contrast with the opening.

Book I opened with the glorification of Venus, the positive life-spirit, whose advent clears away the winds and clouds of heaven, bringing into action all the healthy and creative forces. The goddess is heralded by the birds; in the last book birds are killed off by noxious fumes and effluences, then by the lethal contagion that man has spread in nature. Now they flee before man as the winds and clouds fled from Venus. The animals are inspired by Venus and she inspires in all creatures the desire to propagate. In the last book the men do not vie in bringing more life into the world, they compete in burying the dead. Epikouros in Book I follows Venus as representing the consciousness of all that she implies, of the right relation to nature; the counter-movement is represented by the war-mad king Agamemnon who slaughters his own daughter out of powerlust and greed, as in Book VI men castrate themselves in a final suicidal hope. Many more such correspondences or antitheses could be drawn to show the link with the last Book, which defines disintegration and self-destruction as the first sets out the way of happiness and integration.

This analysis is of the utmost importance in bringing out how a great poet judged his world and its tendencies, and how he saw a false consciousness (which would involve a distorted science and a misapplied technology) supplanting the true consciousness of man's place in the kosmos. But there is for us a more specific point. The plague-sequence comes directly out of the passages dealing with the thunderbolt and its noxious blast, together with a discussion of the other cataclysmic or poisonous aspects of nature. The *fulmen* represents in nature what the plague (pollution, irrationality, fear, greed) represents in society. We must recall that earlier in the Book he correlated the shattering effects of thunderbolt and eruption with symptoms of fever in the individual body, as if in preparation for the extended use of the plague-symbol. One is not claiming, of course, that Lucretius in any simple way foresaw the advent of gunpowder, atomic bombs, Galilean mechanics, and all the rest. But with deep poetic intuition he is grasping the inner meaning of the deepest formative forces at work in his world, and he realises the essence of the choice that men are confronting. It is natural enough then, and right, that two thousand years later his cautionary vision of a polluted earth, of men giving themselves up to the guidance of fear and greed, has even more truth than it had in his own day. He moves from the thunderbolt to the plague, not because he foresees the future explosive powers, but because the thunderbolt was the emblem of supreme power, of the highgod in whom men had projected their own fear of life, their deepest self-alienation—and because, as the expression of supreme power or force, it stirred the most intense terrors of mankind. But because of the totality of ideas and impulses which we have traced in connection with tornado and thunderbolt, and which were moving slowly but surely towards the day of gunpowder and then of the atomic bomb, he was also condemning with every fibre of his being those elements in human culture which were already implicating the destructive and polluting forces that we in our world lament and seek to dethrone.[17]

Ballistics and Mechanics

XIV

Ballistical problems did not come up strongly in the ancient world on account of the relatively short distance to be covered by the missiles. The object to be hit was well within sight, unless the problem was one of lobbing fire-tubs and the like over a wall. The range of a piece of artillery could be altered by pulling back the arms to varying distances or tightening the springs in varying degrees, while keeping the same angle of projection. Or that angle could be changed, while the machine kept the same amount of pull-back and the same tension in the springs. Gunners seem mainly to have used the latter method. Heron tells us how the engine was laid, for line and for elevation. "They pull back the slider, raise the case [the stock] from the rest, traverse [or line] by means of the universal joint, depress and elevate through the pin, look along at the target, load the missile, and pull the trigger." He also says: "Aim well at the target by looking down the length of the case." (Formal sights were not brought into artillery before 1801; till then the sighting was done by looking along "the line of the metal", the outside edge of the barrel.) By looking-down or looking-along Heron meant looking through the aperature between the centre-stanchions. The firer peeped round the shield of his machine to see where his shot fell.

Ancient artillery seems to have been quite accurate within its limits; but it depended on the practical experience of the firers. And such experience also decided the most suitable dimensions for the components of a given catapult, especially the sinew-springs. Considering the springs as cylinders, the engineers asked if they'd get the best results from a squat thick cylinder or a tall thin one, and what size of cylinder went best with a certain length or weight of missile. Philon tells us: "Later engineers drew conclusions from former mistakes, looked exclusively for a standard factor with subsequent experiments as a guide, and introduced the basic principle of construction: the diameter of the circle that holds the spring." He meant the diameter of the spring-cylinder. But several solutions to distinct problems were attempted. The engineers worked out the best relation between the diameters and the heights of the springs, and the optimum rise for springs of a machine shooting an arrow of given length or a shot of given weight; and they showed that all measurements of a given machine could be conveniently described as depending on the spring-diameter—that is, of the hole in the frame through which the spring passed. As a result they arrived at two calibrating formulas, one for euthytone arrow-firers, one for palintone stone-throwers, with corresponding lists of dimensions. The engineers knew that a catapult's strength depended on the size of the hole at the end of the frame, with its bolt; they worked out the diameter of the hole from the length of the arrow or the weight of the stone, and used this calibre as the module for all the catapult's dimensions. Arrow-length provided the technical term for the size of engine.[1]

Circular trajectory is mentioned in Philon's account of the arrow-machinegun; but though trajectories must have been taken into account by experienced gunners, we do not meet any working-out of their theory. It has been suggested that a range of 150 yards was the limit of accuracy and that only large targets beyond that distance were shot at. But even if the performance was not bad up to 400 yards, the range was still quite short in comparison with that of firearm and cannon. We see why so little attention was paid to ballistics proper.

The word *tonos* is at root connected with the pull and strain of tendon and sinew, then with straining, pulling in general; but the Stoic use of it to express tension in a wide range of phenomena, and in particular with the dynamic continuum, may well have been stimulated by its use in connection with the composite bow and the stomach-bow leading on to largescale artillery. It was the *tonos*, the sinew-tension of the bow, that launched the missile and thus created a fast and purposeful form of motion. Though tension could be tested by callipers as the strands were stretched, the best method seems to have been the plucking of a strand and the comparison of its note with that emitted by the first or second one. This method was all the more efficient in that different parts of the spring-cord (sinew or hair) might vary significantly in thickness. Vitruvius stresses the need for the artillery-man to be musical. "A man must know music so as to have acquired the acoustic and mathematical relations, and be able to carry out correctly the adjustments of *ballistae, catapultae*, and *scorpiones*. For in the crossbeams on right and left are holes of halftones, through which ropes twisted out of thongs are stretched by windlasses and levers. And these ropes are not shut off nor tied up, unless they make clear and equal sounds in the ear of the craftsman. For the arms that are shut up under these tensions, when stretched out, ought to furnish an impetus evenly, and alike on either side. But if they don't give an equal note, they'll hinder the straight direction of the missiles."

Thus the *tonoi* of the artillery was merged with the *tonoi* of music, with the pitch, key, and measure of things, the living rhythm. "Impact [impetus] of fire is *tonos*," says Kleanthes, "and if there is enough of it in the *psyche* to complete its aims, it is called strength and force." The word here used for impact or impetus is *plēgē*, which Hesiod used for lightning-stroke. Vitruvius in the above passage uses the cognate term *plaga* for the impetus of the projectile. Kleanthes seems to say that *tonos* launches the soul on its activity; a fiery impact imparts impetus. The suggestion then of a link between the Stoic concept of a universal dynamic tension and the tension giving impetus to the missile gains some direct support.

Though artillery-problems thus may well have had repercussions in philosophical thought, there seems to have been little stimulus for the growth of a new theory of impetus. Men used to handling the war-engines would no doubt have had little respect for Aristotle's theory of the air pushing the missile along, if they ever heard of it; but what interested them were the practical issues connected with the force and direction imparted to the missile by the machine. Still, it is likely that the increasing attention in Byzantion paid to defensive artillery did much to break down the prestige of the Aristotelean ideas. Byzantion (Constantinople) was like Alexandreia an important cultural centre; and here from the fourth century on was the seat of government. Besides, it was repeatedly attacked, especially by sea, unlike Alexandreia. There was thus much more pressure on thinkers and technicians to find ways of linking their ideas with the needs of the state. We saw how Kallinikos, described as architect, found ways on his arrival in the capital to serve those needs by inventing Greek Fire. The development of models or toys on the system of Heron's *Pneumatics* continued at Byzantion; and the only official document dealing with labour-saving devices, which we noticed earlier, was composed in an eastern province where Latin was spoken, perhaps Illyricum. The author shows a practical approach to social and economic problems (in so far as they affect the army), which is remarkable; but though he is much interested in missiles, he shows no sign of any theory as to their flight through the air.[2]

The decisive turn came with John Philoponos in the first half of the sixth century. He realised that what happened to a missile was a "kinetic power" transferred at the moment of throwing from the thrower to the thing thrown, and it was this power that kept the thing moving in its "forced motion". The medium of air did not help; on the contrary the missile would move more easily in a vacuum. Philoponos called the impetus incorporeal. The Stoic would have objected that every quantity capable of physical action was corporeal. But Philoponos seems to have wanted to distinguish as strongly as possible between air as a material agent and his kinetic power. We may compare the modern vectorial term momentum or the scalar term kinetic energy. He made use of two comparisons. First, the concept of his kinetic power, he says, is no more difficult to accept than the fact that "we can see form from the colours which stain solid bodies exposed to them, and that certain forces of an incorporeal form are emitted when the sun's rays pass through a transparent coloured object". He thus viewed the emission of light as involving another sort of impetus, radiated from the luminous source and transferred to the illuminated object. Secondly, he attacked the ideas of Theodoros, bishop of Mopsuestia in Kilikia, that angels move the sun, moon, and planets, angels "who either pull them like beasts in draught, or push them, or both together, like people rolling loads in a circle, or else bear them on their shoulders, which would be even more ridiculous". Instead, he applied the impetus theory to the heavenly bodies. He went on: "There is no reason why the angels should force them into motion, for all things that do not move naturally have a forced motion that's contrary to nature, and bound to come to an end. How then could the motion of so many great bodies last if they were pulled by force?"

Perhaps we can trace the beginnings of a breakdown (far as yet from completion) of a slave-economy in such an outlook. Force or labour-power is no longer to be exerted by human beings who are compelled to carry on heavy tasks by masters who live a quite different life of leisure. The impetus theory forecasts instead a mechanical force that is to do the work. This attitude is further reflected in the use made of the terms *dynamis* and *energeia*. We have noted how the distinction, so sharp in Aristotelean theory, was beginning to blur. For Aristotle, *dynamis* set the action going, but the action (the work) was not at all the same as the force that precipitated it. *Dynamis* is the master who holds the power; energy is the slave who carries out the work that power has initiated. This distinction breaks down with Philoponos, who calls his impetus either *dynamis*, kinetic power, or *energeia*, kinetic force. This sort of position had been given a metaphysical prelude by Plotinos. Matter now is seen as something dead, which can never become anything and which remains unaffected—a concept close to that held by Plato of Space (comparable to a mirror or a screen). Plotinos takes over Aristotle's idea of the relation of energy and potency, but, by removing it from the actual world of change and becoming, he gives it a twist that robs it of its Aristotelean significance; the concept of *energeia* is used to describe the nature of the One. The trinity of *ousia*, *dynamis*, *energeia* (being, emitted potency, actualisation or fulfilment) is first met in Porphyrios, and is further used by Proklos; from these Neo-Platonists it was taken over by the pseudo-Dionysios and was adopted by the Christians. The three exponents just mentioned regarded the ideas involved to be so obvious and familiar as to require no explanation. John of Skythopolis was the Christian who first felt that this was necessary, and St. Maximos the first to expound the triad fully, in Christian terms.

When the triadic aspect of change in the real world has been thus abstracted and made God's property, we have the metaphysical basis on which a purely mechanical theory of motion can be erected. The complex qualitative as well as quantitive unity of the object, organic or inorganic, is disintegrated; since matter is seen as no longer an aspect of the experienced physical universe, it can be abstracted as something subjected to a force outside itself and energy can be visualised simply as a body's power of doing work by virtue of its motion—the motion being imparted by an external force. Thus the ground was cleared for Galileo and Newton, for modern science, and Philoponos made the first definite steps in the new direction.

The overcoming of certain erroneous conceptions in ancient thought was made at the expense of all that was most vital in that thought. True, only the first steps had been taken on a long journey. The use of gunpowder, the development of ballistical

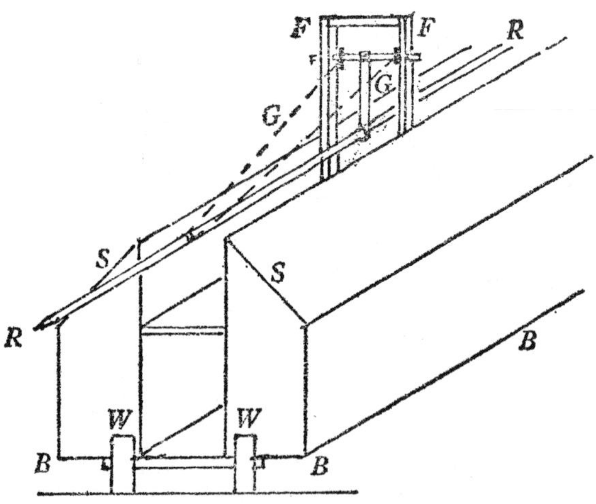

77. Tortoise or Siege-Engine (front elevation and isometric projection): F, Frame; B, Base; G, Guiding ropes; W, Wheels; R, Ram; S, Sloping roof (Vitruvius X, 15)

theory, the revival of Platonism in the Renaissance, the first stages of the capitalist cash-nexus, and so on, had to come about before the full possibilities for mechanistic science could be exploited. But the crucial turn had been taken, the abandonment of ancient concepts of wholeness, the alienation of man's creativeness into a supernal being outside time and space. What complicated the full historical dialectics of the situation was the fact that a direct movement into capitalism was impossible; the movement had to be devious and zigzagging, involving the passage through feudal society. That passage was regressive in some aspects, but it was the only way in which a new society, fully eliminating ancient slavery and preparing the primary forms of capitalist organisation, could come about.[3]

Let us now turn to the medieval world into which gunpowder irrupted. What more than anything else upset the systems of medieval ideas were the new projectiles. They burst into a world of "natural rest", the feudal system of interlocking balances. Aristotelean tradition, which ruled the scholastic world, held that the interfering forces resided in the medium (air, water) where the motion took place; the medium did not move but was charged with the capability of moving; it resisted movement but was defeated by the application of constant force, though it continued to limit the attainable velocity. Such theoretical positions involved contradictions; they reduced a body to rest, yet protracted movement after the effect of the forces had ended. Grossetete at Oxford and William of Ockham made a new approach to dynamical problems possible. Ockham laid down that the sole aim of a scientific theory was to describe observed facts as correctly and economically as possible. The simplest assumption was that a body in motion would keep on moving unless it met resistance; the scientific problem was to give a true mathematical account of the changes in the body's spatial relations with neighbouring bodies.

The road was thus cleared for the impetus theory; and the ideas of Philoponos reached the west just at the time they were needed. Jean Buridan, rector at Paris University in 1327, used the term impetus for the imparted velocity that would carry on indefinitely, he claimed, as long as no opposing force slowed or halted the moving body. What applied force did was to produce acceleration, not maintain velocity. The impetus of a moving body could alter the state of rest or motion of other bodies along its path; falling bodies accelerated because every instant gravity added increments of impetus which begot increments of velocity; the measure of a body's impetus was its quantity of matter (determined by relative density) multiplied by its velocity. This definition corresponded to Newton's of momentum; Galileo used *impeto* and *momento* as synonyms. But Buridan held that the impetus of the heavenly bodies worked to maintain a circular motion, while Newton's inertial motion kept a straight line.

By the mid-fourteenth century there was a pressing need to grapple with the ballistical problems raised by the new explosive force. But cannon needed to be made of metal; and so war-needs played their part in many areas of technology. In mining there were the questions of raising ore from the depths, ventilating mines, pumping water, developing the crude damp-blast method (dominant till the fifteenth century) into blast-furnace production; and these matters involved problems of the arrangement of windlasses and blocks: that is, a variety of simple mechanical devices. Ventilation demanded the study of aerostatics, a section of statics; piston-pumps demanded a study of hydrostatics as well; water-wheels raised questions of hydrostatics and dynamics; airbellows stimulated the study of the movement and compression of air; the mill made men think about the nature of friction and the mathematical arrangement of cogged transmission-wheels; the construction of presses, hammers, using the force of falling water, involved mechanics. But the key-pressures leading to Galileo and Newton came from the sphere of war, from ballistics. The broad effect of the new war-problems is shown by a work like the 1335 MS. of Guido de Vigevano, a court-physician, who worked at human anatomy and developed the application of mechanical skills to the art of war in a way foreshadowing Leonardo da Vinci and the applied science of the Italian Renaissance.

> Ultimately it was the effects of gunpowder on science rather than on warfare that were to have the greatest influence in bringing about the Machine Age. Gunpowder and the cannon not only blew up the medieval world economically and politically; they were major forces in destroying its system of ideas. As Mayow puts it: "Nitre has made as much noise in philosophy as it has in war." In the first place they were something new in the world; the Greeks did not have a name for them. In the second place, the making of gunpowder, its explosion, the expulsion of the ball from the cannon, and its subsequent flight furnished problems, the practical solution of which led to a search for causes of a new kind and the creation of a new science (Bernal).

John Mayow (1641–79) of Cornwall was interested in nitre, and his work shows well how its "noise" stimulated thought in all sorts of fields; he wrote on respiration, combustion, fermentation. Chemically, the phenomena of solution and crystallisation had sharp attention drawn to them. The explosion disrupted medieval physics and chemistry, for, though an action of fire, it did not need air. Men speculated whether the air was provided by the nitre or air held nitre—or at least a nitrous spirit. The explosion became the model for all later attempts to explain combustion and with it breathing, the animal need of air. In the end it led to the discovery of oxygen and the whole of modern chemistry. The explosive force and the projection of the ball stimulated the notion of using natural forces, especially fire, and hence inspired the development leading to the steam-engine. (It thus provided the stimulus that was lacking in the world of Ktesibios and Heron.) The machinery devised to bore cannon was used to make the accurate cylinders without which the early steam-engines could not have proved their efficiency. And the notion of the projectile led to the new concepts embodied in Galilean dynamics. The ancient scientists had studied bodies at rest or bodies acting on one another with relatively steady forces; now came the urgent problem of bodies in violent motion—in a world which itself was in violent motion, moving into a kind of society, that of industrialism, which had no sort of previous parallel.

The impetus-theorists had used the (incorrect) analogy of heat. Bodies are generally of the same temperature as their environment; but if they are heated above that level, the unstable state is only gradually ended. A moving body acquires impetus, said the theorists, as a body acquires heat. Neither heat nor impetus vanish at once; the acquired impetus was the cause of the residual motion, and only when it was used up did the body come to rest. Still, this attribution of an intrinsic power of movement to inert matter was a necessary first step to getting rid of old conceptions and advancing to mechanistic views. Buridan saw that there was no need to install a guiding intelligence in each heavenly body; those bodies, perfectly smooth and frictionless, moved upon each other without effort or resistance. But before the insufficiencies of the impetus-theory could be overcome, it was necessary to find mathematical techniques for describing rates of change. Scholars at Oxford devised a way of treating such rates by regarding motion as a discontinuous quantity, the increase or decrease of which could be expressed numerically as well as graphically. They proved arithmetically, and Oresme proved geometrically, that in a given time a body moving with uniform acceleration covered a distance equal to that covered by a body moving uniformly with the velocity reached at the midpoint of time. Oresme's proof implied that the area under the curve represented the distances covered.[4]

The ancient world had been concerned with motion as the orbits of the heavenly bodies (thought to be circular about the earth*) and the flight of the arrow. Now the motion to be considered was that of the cannon-ball with its varying speeds, ranges, trajectories; and the new ideas thus developed, about velocity and free fall, could not but impinge on the ideas about the heavenly motions. The cannon-ball knocked the heavenly bodies out of their (circular) orbits. Oresme in *De Caelo* denied that the fixedness of the earth followed naturally from the movement of the heavens; he anticipated Galileo, setting out the arguments for a daily movement of the earth by axial rotation and pointing out that all the phenomena of motion seem the same in a moving ship as in a ship at rest. Similar issues came up in the fifteenth century with Nicolas of Cusa, and in the sixteenth century before Copernicus. The ground was steadily prepared for Galileo.

One reason why the impetus-theory failed to make much headway was the fact that it remained largely theoretical. Only with the considerable economic and social advances, plus the extension in the use of gunpowder, was the necessary fusion of theory and practice brought about, and the impetus theory descended to the earth of precise mechanics. What were the main questions raised by the existence of cannons with their ballistical problems?

Intrinsic ballistics involved the study of the processes occurring in a firearm when fired, the need to find out how to combine its stability with the least weight and to adapt it for a suitable and effective aim. Extrinsic ballistics involved the study of the trajectory of a ball through a vacuum and through the air, of the dependence of air-resistance on the ball's flight, and of the ball's deviation from its trajectory. The first aspect required a study of the compression and extension of gases, a study which at its basis was a work for mechanics; of the phenomenon

* With the exception of the Pythagoreans, who saw earth, planets, stars, sun, and moon, as all together orbiting the central fire of the Universe. Recent observations of the Andromeda galaxy have failed to resolve its nucleus, thus giving birth to the hypothesis that the nucleus of our own galaxy, as that of the Andromeda galaxy, is in fact in the nature of a "super sun"; i.e. one vast star rather than a concentration of more normal ones. This corresponds closely with the Pythagorean "central fire".

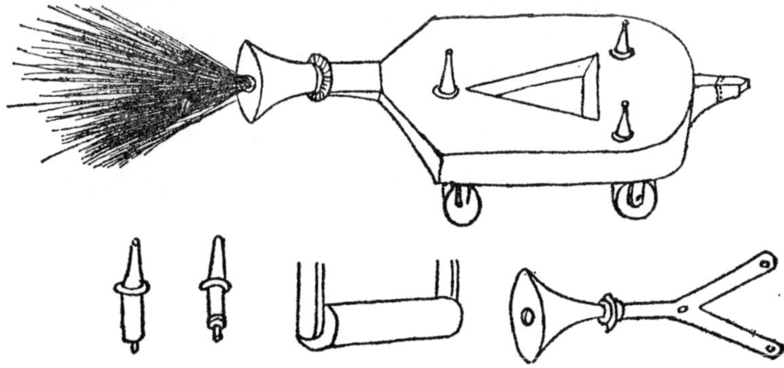

78. A jet-propelled car from a manuscript of Fontana of the earlier fifteenth century (at Munich)

of recoil; of the law of action and reaction; of the resistance and durability of materials, a problem of importance at this stage in the art of construction in general, and one which was also resolved by means of mechanics—Galileo gave it much attention in his *Mathematical Demonstrations*. The problem of a ball's trajectory through a vacuum consisted of resolving the problem of a body's fall under the influence of gravity, and the conjuncture of its progressive movement with its free fall. Hence Galileo was much preoccupied with the free fall of bodies; and the close relation of his theoretical work here to ballistics and artillery may be read in the *Address to the Florentines* with which he opens his *Demonstrations*. He praises the activity of their Arsenal, pointing out what a rich material it provides for scientific study.

Further, the ball's flight through air is an aspect of the general problem of the movement of bodies through a resistant medium and of the resistance's dependence on the speed of the movement. The deviation from an estimated trajectory can occur only as the result of a change in the ball's initial speed, a change in atmospheric density, or the influence of the earth's rotation. All the questions thus raised are purely of mechanics. Accurate tables governing aim can be drawn up when the problems of extrinsic ballistics are solved and a general theory of a ball's trajectory through a resistant medium is attained.

So we see that apart from the manufacture of cannon and ball —a problem for metallurgists, though involving constructional questions that lead back to mechanics and ballistics—all the key-problems of artillery in this epoch lay in the mechanical field; and all the important steps taken by mechanics were in turn dictated by the problems of ballistics. Galileo made his advance because he moved from the largely untested generalisations of the impetus theory to a clear grasp of what the practical issues were, and then sought to recombine theory with practice on a new level of unified comprehension.

A forerunner was Tartaglia, a selftaught engineer, surveyor and bookkeeper, who tried to apply the impetus theory on practical lines. In 1537 he attempted to establish the trajectory of a shot and found that the angle of 45° allowed the greatest horizontal distance of flight; he was the first who tried to compare cannon-

79. Drawing at the start of the *Feuerwerkbuch*, appendix to Vegetius, *Vier Büchern von der Ritterschaft*, Augsburg, 1529

ranges by means of tables derived from mechanical theory. He was Galileo's precursor too in that he showed a dynamical theory must be quantitative and able to make precise mathematical predictions. He laid down that impetus-force and gravity-force acted together on a projectile throughout the course of its flight. Further work on these lines was done by Benedetti at Padua and by Steven of Bruges (1548–1620) who was book-keeper and military engineer. In 1586 Stevin, before Galileo, disproved the Aristotelean view that heavy bodies fall quicker than light ones, and he had some grasp of the parallelogram of forces (explicitly formulated by Newton and Varignon, 1687). Note the link of the new mechanical outlook with the new systems of monetary calculation in men like Tartaglia and Steven. Biringuccio studied casting processes and in his *Pirotechnia*, 1540, he introduced improvements in weapon-manufacture; both he and Agricola (*De Re Metallica*, 1556) dealt with the extraction of saltpetre and the making of gunpowder.

The impetus theory, like the Ptolemaic cosmic scene, had now been driven to its limits. The existing structures of thought had to be broken, and new ones put in their place. Galileo himself, in his *On Motion* of 1592, began from the impetus theory, but found that he had to make fundamental reconstructions. The old theory, limited to rectilinear motion, had halted at the effort to give reasons for the continuance of motion after the projecting agent ceased to be in contact with the moving body; it could not work out precise definitions of force, velocity, acceleration. A so-called accidental levity was said to cause the decelerating ascent of the projectile; an accidental gravity, the accelerating descent. As proof was adduced the fact that the projectile on impact had effects equal to those caused by a body at rest of much greater weight. The old distinctions of natural and violent or forced motion were still unchallenged, and it was held that the two types could not be compounded. As a result there was much difficulty in describing a projectile's track; the ascent and the descent were qualitatively different, and needed different approaches. We find the ascent pictured as a straight line, the descent as a curve, though Tartaglia and Leonardo instinctively drew a continuous curve, which they could not have theoretically defended.

Impetus theorists could not develop a concept of inertia, as they did not believe that a body, gaining an impetus, would go on moving at a uniform velocity; and they could not invoke the vacuum, since, like Aristotle, they denied its existence. Galileo, however, concluded that the accelerations of different bodies down an inclined plane were the same under ideal conditions. In experiments described in his *Discourses* he rolled a bronze ball down one of two equiangular inclined planes making a shallow V, and found that it climbed up the other plane to a point equal to that from which it had started. He then deduced a fundamental proposition diametrically opposed to that of the impetus theory. What the Parisian philosophers had taken to be a slowly dying impetus was now seen to be in essence inexhaustible, except when restrictive forces came into action. In the ideal situation he had invented, rest and uniform motion in a straight line with any velocity were equally "natural" conditions for a body. "The principle of inertia took shape in this statement" (Feathers). With regard to local motion near the earth's surface, however, he went wrong and failed to universalise his conclusion; Descartes did the universalising on general grounds and Newton made his position a part of an effective system of dynamics.

Galileo was thus able to deal with acceleration and at last to grapple with the basic problems of ballistics. And he was able to show, as thinkers like Oresme and Albert of Saxony had failed to do, what he called the supreme affinity between time and motion. Indeed meditations over time and motion seem to have given him his clue, and by 1609 he had reached his solution. He inserted in his *Discourses* a passage stating that the "natural" idea of velocity is a rate of change in time, with acceleration thus a rate of change of velocity in time. Gilbert's idea of gravity as a sort of magnetic attraction had perhaps affected him and led him to separate out natural acceleration (from the causal angle) from spatial considerations.

The law of acceleration and the basic theorem deduced from it were the foundation of dynamics, which dominated the growth of scientific method in the seventeenth century. Soto had anticipated the idea, but in an impetus context. What made all the difference was the context of dynamical theory (with the impetus concept swallowed up in the law of inertia) together with the extreme degree of abstraction that Galileo achieved. We have considered above the social forces making such intellectual abstractions possible: increased division and fragmentation of labour, class division and exploitation of labour, and above all the levelling effect of the cash-nexus with its abstract criterion of value. What had been operative in bringing about Greek philosophy, science and mathematics was again operative in the sixteenth century in a vastly extended form. Where in one case the product had been a slave-economy, in the other there was the movement into capitalist industrialism.

There then lay the two essential aspects of Galileo's thought with its shattering impact. On the one hand was the direct linking of dynamical theory with practice, with ballistics; and on the other, the method of abstraction, of explanation by means of functional relationships reduced to their most abstract aspects. Galileo eliminated as irrelevant the many aspects of motion which are always present in any concrete situation: resistance, friction,

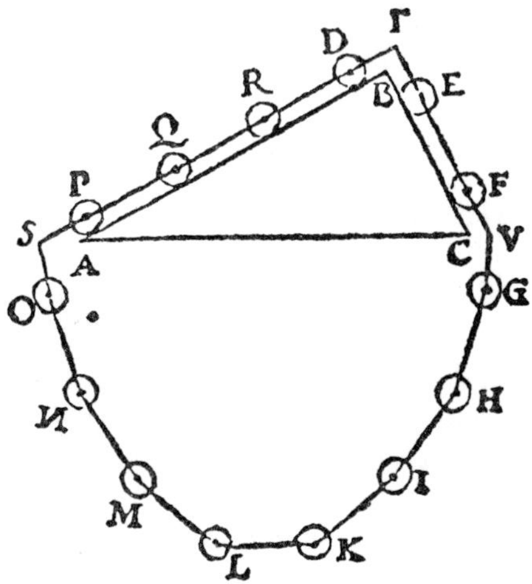

80. Stevin's proof (1586) of conditions of equilibrium on inclined planes. Round the vertical angle of an upright triangle (of which the opposite side is horizontal) hang a ringchain. It will be in equilibrium —or there would be perpetual motion. Remove the suspended loop; there is still equilibrium. So weights on planes inclined to each other are in equilibrium if they are proportional to the lengths of the planes as cut by the horizontal

causation. Such a statement of functions made quantitative analysis and calculation possible; it made them indeed the whole thing. Nothing in Greek thought revealed a reduction or abstraction so bleakly drastic.

In his *Two New Sciences*, 1638, Galileo stated that he had no intention of investigating "the *cause* of the acceleration of natural motion, concerning which various opinions have been expressed by various philosophers". His contempt breaks out: "It is not really worthwhile." His aim was merely "to investigate and demonstrate some of the properties of accelerated motion, whatever the cause of this acceleration may be". He therefore had devised an ideal world in which there was no resistance, no friction from the air: where pendulums swung to and fro on cords without weight. Here was the only world in which his perfectly spherical ball could run down one perfectly inclined plane and up the other to the same height, and in which, if the planes were horizontal, the ball would run on for ever.[5] The new science, based rigidly on quantitative measurements, from the outset, then, by its very nature of abstraction, needed to establish an ideal and unobservable world behind the world it observed. That was why, as we noted, such a science could only come into existence when the ancient concept of wholeness had been driven from the centre of thinking and feeling, and when a metaphysical outlook had flattened out the real world. Paradoxically, the Christian God, taking over from the Platonic, had to abstract the Aristotelean triad of being-becoming and put the cause of motion (of life, of all concrete reality) outside the kosmos, before a thinker like Galileo could turn with contempt on the question of "the *causes* of the acceleration of natural motion" and proceed to reduce everything to quantitative relations. That is, the universe of thought-and-feeling had to be split into two irreconcilable halves, one vital but transcendental, the other actual but lacking all concreteness, before the science of Galilean mechanics could be founded.

The ideal world of mechanics, being quite dead, was one of perfect symmetries and exactly reversible processes—something totally unlike the real world with its turmoil of symmetry and asymmetry, its processes going on in poignantly irreversible time. Time in effect has been eliminated, reduced to a coordinate of the same character as space considered in abstraction from time. In fact, what we get here is a double set of abstractions, one inside the other, for real space is inseparable from time. Modern quantitative science has as its basis and material a world that never existed and never could have existed, a world which with its abstract entities belongs rather to the region of religion (the transcendal sphere of *ousia*) than to that of science at all. (In saying that, however, we are assuming the existence of a concrete unitary science capable of dealing with wholes in all their qualitative and quantitative complexity; and no such science has yet been created. It would then be more correct perhaps to say that science has developed in a state painfully crippled by religion, by metaphysics; and that what we appeal to is the element of concreteness that keeps reasserting itself despite the deforming method, the metaphysical murder of reality that goes on all the while.) We may recall how Carnot founded thermodynamics by imagining a perfect power-machine which in fact could not exist.

How then, it may be asked, has this method been so fruitful in producing the technology that has brought us to the present situation of atomic bombs, rockets, and universal pollution? The answer is that the idealist or metaphysical method is suitable for dealing with stable states and closed cyclic systems, in which symmetry can be assumed or imposed. As L. L. Whyte has remarked:

> In Classical Dynamics the main invariants were conserved dynamical quantities, i.e. quantitative parameters expressing conserved functions of the measurable aspects of motions in closed cycles. The principles of the conservation of mass, momentum, and energy are mathematical definitions of the invariants used in this theory, and as Planck pointed out, the principle of the conservation of energy only possesses an unequivocal empirical content in relation to closed cycles. The fact that these definitions were so effective showed that many processes could be treated as lacking any one-way character. For a brief period towards the end of the nineteenth century it was thought that these dynamical invariants offered the final key to the understanding of nature.
>
> But the concepts of mass and energy are limited in their theoretical and empirical scope, for they cannot alone cover such properties as scale, structure, orientation, and one-way succession. In classical dynamics conservation was the main criterion of the isolability of any system, and there was no reason for any stable system to be

> of one size rather than another, or for any kind of ordered relationship to develop between one entity and another. Bodies were treated largely as points; their relations were supposed to depend only on their distance, structure and orientation being neglected; and the principles of dynamical conservation, in denying the existence of any one-way tendency in conservative systems, emphasised the possibility of cyclic and reversible states of motion.

The "success" of this method proved indeed that nature owns a widespread dynamical aspect; that closed (or relatively closed) dynamical cycles do exist; and that for many purposes scale, pattern, and one-way succession may be ignored. But if we omit scale, pattern and one-way succession, we omit life—even if life also involves cyclic systems.

The mechanics of Galileo and Newton then returned to the ancient notion of cyclic systems, but with very different results due to the sharp limitation of the relationships considered and their reduction to quantitative abstractions. The first serious sign of a breakdown occurred through the development of Field Theory which used a new kind of invariant, an unchanging mathematical relationship (differential field-equation) between changing quantities associated with every point of an extended region. But Field Theory shared with classical dynamics the assumption of the universal availability of a unique coordinate-frame of space and time. A fuller crisis emerged in the twentieth century, represented by Planck, Einstein, Relativity Theory and Quantum Mechanics. This crisis showed that the Galilean assumptions had reached the limit of their valuable application and extension. But, while bringing out many of the insufficiencies of classical dynamics, it has not at all resolved the problems that it raises. We are still as far as ever from the new unifying concepts that will overcome the crisis and put the whole issue on a new level. We are in the position of the astronomers of the late middle ages before Copernicus, devising more and more epicycles to hold the movements of the universe together, and warding off the new generalisations that will simplify the whole situation. The world of the particles skurries under the surface of our concepts, creating more and more strain on the hypotheses that attempt to make sense of it and relate the movements and changes, the deaths and births, the obstinate tangle of transformations.

All that, however, is a matter into which we cannot venture

here; what concerns us is the nature of Galilean dynamics and the fact that an unresolved crisis has broken out in its assumptions.

We can, however, clarify further some of the points we have been making by a glance back at the seventeenth century. We need to couple any analysis of Galileo with another of Kepler, a man of an infinitely richer mind, who reveals all the strains of his situation—a deep conflict between the new abstractions and a persistent sense of wholeness. (Interestingly he had a mother who was accused of witchcraft and a father who was a gunner. He felt sympathy for his mother as a person and was antagonistic to his father. "1578: a hard jar of gunpowder burst and lacerated my father's face.") He took in what we may call the new ballistical dynamics, but a strong element of medieval concreteness in his mind resisted many of its implications. He belonged to the line of thinkers haunted by a sense of the fullness of life, which runs from Bruno, Spinoza, Goethe, on to Hegel and Marx—a line that never succumbs to the new abstractions and fights hard to vindicate a method of thought more vitally and dialectically comprehensive.

From the fertile welter of Kepler's ideas there emerged the three laws that laid the basis for Newton: The planets have elliptical orbits; a planet's motion is not at uniform speed but goes on in such a way that a line drawn from planet to sun sweeps over equal areas in equal times; and the squares of the revolution of any two planets are as the cube of their mean distance from the sun. He reached out towards the enunciation of Newtonian gravitation, but sheered off in repugnance. He continued struggling to find out what was meant by forces, and to apply the notion of two antagonistic forces at work on the heavenly bodies—though he completed his scheme gravitationally only for earth and moon. At times his idea of what constituted a force came closer to the concept of an electromagnetic field than to the Newtonian idea. Essentially he had arrived at an understanding of gravity which included the Newtonian positions, but which refused to abstract those positions as laws, because of his quest for some more comprehensive and concrete system.

In the Copernican system the Aristotelean idea of each kind of matter being attracted to its own place in the universe broke down; but the order of the universe could still be explained by transferring the attraction from the place to matter itself. The Greek principle of like attracting like could be directly applied. Gilbert the magnetist made this application and saw a universal system of gravity, but with gravity differing in different bodies. He showed that the magnetic force which a loadstone exerted on a piece of iron increased with its size and that the action was reciprocal. Kepler took up where he left off. He insisted on the material as opposed to the mathematical: "A mathematical point, whether it be the centre of the universe or not, cannot move heavy bodies either effectively or objectively, so that they approach it." It

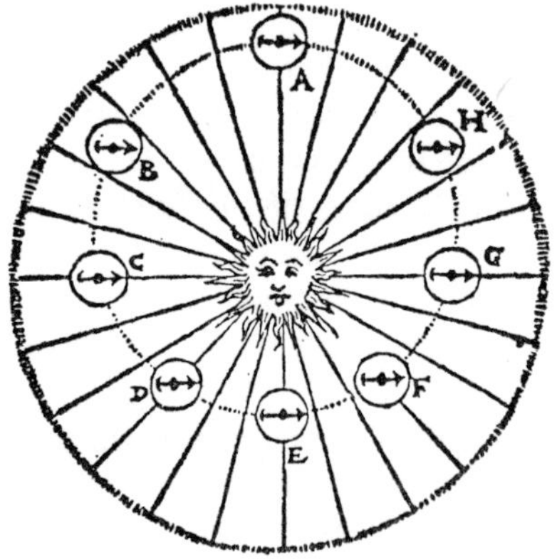

81. Kepler's idea of the way that the Sun acts on the planets

is impossible "that the form of a stone, moving its mass [*corpus*], should seek a mathematical point or the centre of the world, except with respect to the body in which that point resides". And he argued, for the first time, that all attractions, as gravity, were mutual. Hegel, declaring that Newton's law of gravity took no account of the sun's and the planet's quality-endowed matter, *qualifizierte Materie*, contrasted his abstracting method with the method of Kepler, who saw sun and planets in a concrete unity, as movements which did not exclude quality. For Kepler the ellipse was not an abstract curve with two foci, but a dialectical magnitude formed by two real points of the revolving body's reversal of direction.

We may note too that his restless attemps to link the mathematical analyses with the formative process of nature made him feel that harmonic proportions must play a key-part in the unitary cosmic order. He was seeking for integrative systems that went clean past the dynamics of gravitation. In 1619 he published *Harmonices Mundi.* He resurrected Pythagorean and Platonic ideas in the new situation; he experimented with the only five possible regular solid figures (with equal sides and equal angles), and in 1596 he tried to relate them to the five intervals between the six planets which he knew. However, he soon found that he had wrongly estimated the distances of the planets from their centre, and he had to drop his attempt. (Since then we have had the efforts of Titus and Bode to show that the distances of the planets from the sun are related in a simple way to the successive powers of two; and the periodic table of the elements. In about 1927, Pauli noted that if we assumed that no two electrons circling about a nucleus could have the same four quantum numbers, we could arrive at an explanation of the periodic system of the elements; Fermi extended his idea. The concept of harmonic proportions and their rôle, of rhythmic interrelations in the kosmos, in large and small matters, is as yet however in its infancy. We may hope some day to learn a great deal from this field, but not until a new science of unitary dialectical process has been created.)[6]

We need not here discuss Newton's ideas in any detail. Many more lines of thought and discovery were drawn together in his work than in that of Galileo; but we may say that in essence he added to Galilean dynamics the Keplerian concept of opposing forces—gravity pulling the planets to the sun and centrifugal forces counteracting the pull. However, what was dialectical in Kepler has been brought down to the level of mechanics so as to merge effectively with the Galilean system. All observable motion in the universe is reduced to four basic laws: those of inertia, acceleration under impressed force, reciprocal action and reaction, and gravity. Newton's first law generalises Galileo's theory of uniform motion; his second law is involved in Galileo's theory of projectiles; his third is implied in many of Galileo's positions and in his definition of momentum—it is suggested in an early work of his, published after his death, as well as being worked out in his latest ideas on percussion.

The relation of Newton's conception to Galileo's work on projectiles is omnipresent. Newton identified the Keplerian orbit of the moon with the Galilean orbit of a projectile that was falling to the earth, but unable to reach it through its fast forward motion. In his *System of the World* he thus sets out his line of reasoning. If a projectile is fired horizontally from the top of a mountain, it will be deflected from its straight path by the earth's attraction. According to the initial velocity imparted it will follow the curves ABCD; but if the initial velocity exceeds a certain critical value, the projectile will describe a circle or ellipse and "return to the mountain from which it was projected". Further, by Kepler's second law, "its velocity when it returns to the mountain will be no less than it was at first; and retaining the same velocity, it will describe the same curve over and over by the same law . . . and go on revolving through the heavens just as the planets do in their orbits". Newton's gravitational theory is thus in essence a ballistical one; and his account of the projectile sets out in simple form the theory realised in our day by the sputnik. He adds, in Galilean idiom, that in the *System* all was done "in a mathematical way, to avoid all questions about the nature or quality of this force, which we would not be understood to determine by any hypothesis".

We can now estimate the central rôle played by artillery and ballistics in producing the Galilean abstraction and dynamics, and all the scientific consequences for the next three or four centuries. The question of acceleration had become the key-issue; and the series of abstractions, gathering round this question, finally issued in the Newtonian laws, determining their particular limitations. Bodies obey those laws reasonably well under conditions of constant or zero acceleration; but when other kinds of conditions arise, the strain on the laws grows worse and shows them up as ever more inadequate. Strictly they apply only to mathematically abstract and infinitesimal particles, or to perfectly rigid bodies—neither of which actually exist. What the Newtonians took to be exact laws, we now know to be statistical laws that hold as long as they are applied to averages. The first law is unverifiable. Even the development of the infinitesimal calculus had behind it the pressure of ballistics, both in a general and a particular way. The ideas of men like Harriot and Descartes were quickly applied to mechanics. In ballistics by the late seventeenth century men were able to discard the cumbrous method of working out a tangent by supplying the needed constants in geometric constructions—as

Galileo had done. They could now use the function appropriate to the parabolic trajectory.[7]

One key-point is that in the now-abstract universe of science man is banished; all sensuous or qualitative aspects are irrelevant; all value-judgments are nonsense. The system tells us how the system works; and workability becomes the only test—as profits become the only test of capitalist activity. What can be done must be done. The system impels man; and paradoxically, the greater the powers that the system operates, the less becomes the rôle of man in the working-out. Man's powers are alienated into the machine, as once they had been alienated into God. The science and technology based on the reductive abstraction turns out to be one with the mysteriously controlling cash-nexus, which has its own abstract criteria. Time loses its concrete quality and becomes a mere coordinate with an equally abstract space. There is no distinction between past and future in a universe where all processes, becoming mere mathematical equations, are reversible. The thermodynamical laws of entropy-increase, which seemed for a while to contradict pessimistically the picture of action-and-reaction-equal-and-opposite, turn out to represent only the probability of a certain distribution.

We might go much further in showing how the impact of gunpowder and cannons affected other branches of science. But it is enough to point to the link of the development in chemistry, in the theory of combustion, and so on, with the emerging industrial system and its technology, its concept of work-power, which leads on to the steam-engine, to the internal combustion-engine, to systems based on electrical power, and finally to the generation of power by means of atomic fission. Here, in varying ways, the fantasies of canalising and directing blast-power, of mastering the thunderbolt, are at last actualised. The ideas which tantalised the ancient thinkers and remained for them on the level of wild dreams or general theory have been recklessly brought down to earth. The choices which the ancient world both could not take and refused to take are accepted by the bourgeois world as the first condition of its existence. As a result the bourgeoisie have realised as fact what began as a shamanist fantasy, linked with the spirit-world journey and murderous spells, and which became a vision of hell before becoming a part of everyday life. The argument of this book is that the development of shamanist fantasy into atomic bombs and worldwide pollution is not an accident; it has proceeded out of certain deep pressures of fear and hate embodied in human societies, affecting the individual and in turn affected by him. From this angle the growth of scientific theory and practice appears as almost an unadulterated evil. That appearance, of course, is only half the truth. At every point, closely involved with the fear and the hate, have been brotherly elements seeking for security and harmony. Impulses that treat nature as an enemy realm to be ruthlessly trampled and looted have been mixed with the desire to live happily on the earth, in concord with one's fellows and with nature. But if there is any truth in the analysis we have made it is clear that at certain crucial points, where decisions affecting the whole human future have had to be made, the ruthless forces that express and deepen alienation have had the last word. The problem then is not anything so simple as that we need to scrap science and technology as they have developed to date; it is that we must somehow achieve a new vital synthesis of man and nature (which in turn is linked with creating a society without exploitation, division, and alienation). This synthesis alone can provide the critical perspective enabling us to sort out what is valuable in past thought and its applications from what is linked with power-fantasies of the wrong kind. We cannot have a truly human society without the right and harmonious relation with nature—and vice versa. In the last resort the destructive orientations of science, the abstracting and dehumanising trends, are linked with all that makes for alienation in the society that begets them. The problem is too acute and far-reaching to be solved by patchwork and makeshift tinkerings, by saying that we will make only positive and peaceful application of the techniques and ideas that have brought us to our impasse. As temporary palliations in a transitional period such procedures may have their virtue; they are obviously far better than a continuance with the directly and hopelessly destructive activities that range from pesticides to nuclear fission. But only a radically new approach can truly arrest the descent to hell and provide a basis for science and technology free from the old obsessions with blast-power.[8]

Some Further Points and Conclusions

XV

Returning to the Greeks, we may consider again the reasons for the remarkable contribution to philosophy and science that they made, and the reasons for their inability to move beyond a certain point. At the outset they needed to take in the accumulated lores of the Near East. Not that the process of assimilation went on in a single burst. For millennia there had been contacts in the Aegean world; with Anatolia, with Syria and with north Africa. In the long period between the Early Minoans and the Ionian settlements along the Anatolian coast there had been phases of advance and breakdown. Many cultural gains had been lost in the dark ages out of which the Homeric epics emerge. The decisive moment creating the historical Greeks came when the Ionian settlements developed into city-states which rejected both the kingship and the priestly corporation, and which set busily about expanding trade, using the alphabet, making calculations, and establishing money in a definite and mature form. The rejection of the kingship and the turning of the city-aristocracy to trade brought about the need for systems of law, which in turn involved methods of codification. The new kind of society thus built up did not consist of cities existing in countrysides under some central despotism with organised priesthoods. The system that the citizens steadily brought about was one based on slave-production, with prolonged conflicts between the peasants and the clan lords. The slave-basis of such industrialisation as could occur in this situation was what gave new expansive possibilities and laid down the limits to the expansion.

But in thus finding the essence of the Greek situation in slave-production, we must be careful not to make a crude and mechanistic interpretation of the way that things worked out. The economic facts were inextricably entangled with mental and emotional attitudes which were bred from the system and perpetuated it. We are only looking at one side of the process when we generalise:

> Once slavery has spread from the home to the mine and the workshop, it appears to rule out the development of an advanced industrial technique. For the kind of slaves employed in the big productive processes, such as agriculture or mining, are not capable of operating complicated machinery or advanced methods of natural exploitation, still less of improving them. Hence slavery militates against the development of mechanical power; and at the same time it brings few advantages in the concentration of industry, and therefore offers little opposition to the tendency of production to fly outwards to the periphery of the economic area. Furthermore, when slaves are there as an alternative, the producer has no incentive to economise labour; and the bargaining power of the poor free worker is automatically reduced where the two classes are in competition, as they frequently were in the Hellenistic Age. (Walbank)

Some of these points can be challenged. In such enterprises as the mines where there was continuous employment, slaves wholly ousted hired free labour; but in much casual employment slaves and free men seemed to have been hired indifferently. The master who hired out his slave wanted as much as he could get. The reason why unskilled slave-labour was so profitable, it has been argued, lay in the extremely cheap price of slaves—as long as wars and piracies went on. But, however the details are threshed out, it is clear that on the whole slave-production heavily hindered the development of machinery. The more that city-democracy expanded—that is, the more that society progressed—the more slave-production grew. And psychologically this meant that men felt crushed by Necessity.

The very existence of this tendency made Greek society quite different in quality from any previous society. The master-class was distanced from the world of production in a way that had not previously appeared—even though, by the increase of market-systems and of money-dealings, it was from another angle much more directly implicated in economic activities. Hence the way in which the abstracting faculty operated in a highly powerful yet limited way. The abstract criterion at work inside society had its deep and wide effects, as we have seen, but could not advance to anything like the point reached by Galileo in his proto-capitalist

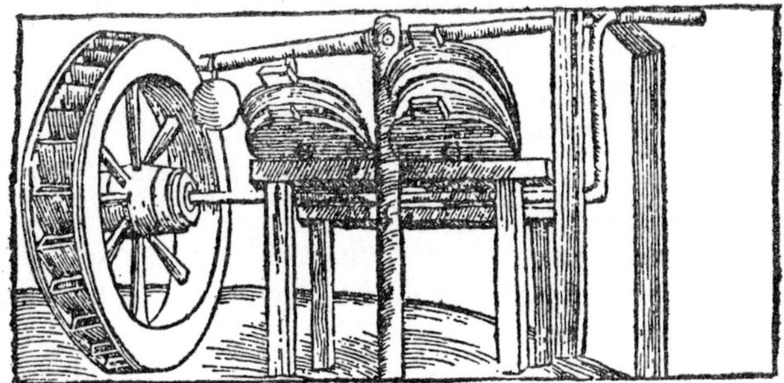

82. Forge-bellows driven by water: V. Biringuccio (1480–1539), *Pirotechnia*

world (if we may be allowed to use that term for the final phase of medievalism when the old system was in a state of extreme tension with the values of the new system that was emergent but not yet triumphant). As Marx says of the Greek situation:

> There was an important fact which prevented Aristotle from seeing that to attribute value to commodities is merely a mode of expressing all labour as equal human labour, and consequently as labour of equal quality. Greek society was founded on slavery and had therefore for its natural basis the inequality of men and of their labour powers. The secret of the expression of labour, namely, that all kinds of labour were equal and equivalent because and so far as they are human, labour in general cannot be deciphered until the notion of human equality has already acquired the fixity of a popular prejudice. This, however, is possible only in a society in which the great mass of the production of labour takes the form of commodities, in which, consequently, the dominant relation between man and man is that of owners of commodities. The brilliancy of Aristotle's genius is shown by this alone, that he discovered in the expression of the value of commodities a relation of equality.

The implication of the masters in production gave rise to such a realisation as that of Aristotle; the distancing from the producers led to the attitude that all manual labour, which included even the work of the sculptor or the scientist using models for practical purposes, was disgraceful and degenerative. The craftsman by his nature was denied all possibility of moral or political virtue. As Xenophon said, "banausic activities are held in complete disdain in the Greek cities". With the unconscious egoism of the master-class he identifies his own class with the city, and does not consider the views of craftsman, free or servile, as worth considering. Banausic activities "spoil the bodies of the workers and the overseers, because the nature of their work forces them to sit indoors, and in some cases to spend the day before the fire. Softening of the body leads to softening of the mind." Aristotle declared, "No man can practise virtue who is living the life of a mechanic," and adds that "in the oligarchies no labourer can ever be a citizen". The same attitude is set out by Plato, Cicero, Seneca. Loukian, who was apprenticed to a sculptor, wrote that if you were a stone-cutter you were a mere worker, doing hard physical labour. "You'll be obscure, earning a small wage, a man of low esteem, classed as worthless by public opinion, not courted by friends, feared by enemies, or envied by your fellow-citizens, but just a common worker, a craftsman, a face in a crowd, one who makes his living with his hands." Ploutarch is mildly surprised that one of his class can find pleasure in works of art, yet despise their producer as a mere craftsman. States with a strong aristocratic tradition refused to grant citizenship to craftsmen, as we know of Sparta, Thebes, Thespiai. Even when a man like Archimedes wrote mathematically of his work in mechanics, the aristocratic tradition, as exemplified by Ploutarch, refused to recognise the fact and attributed to him a "lofty spirit" and "profound soul" which despised such matters.[1]

The connection of work with the servile state was what mattered; what the upper levels despised was not manual work in itself, but the stigma attached to it. Xenophon in a tale about one Euhemeros makes clear that what this man objected to was the position of dependence, the control of a master or employer. Manual work was thus equated with loss of freedom, and in turn freedom was equated with a way of life in which no manual work was done. The intellectual ideal was then one of contemplation of phenomena, social or natural, from outside. We get many signs that in cities where the earlier Ionian attitudes were most strongly carried on, the aristocratic prejudice was not so evident. Herodotos, saying that the Greeks have accepted the low ranking of craftsmen by Egyptians and "almost all foreigners", adds that "the feeling against handicraft is least strong in Corinth". And in the fourth century we find the Ephesians granting citizenship to two Athenian potters. But the conviction that any connection with

83. Wheel-driven machinery for hoisting in mines (Agricola, *De Re Metallica*, 1561)

manual labour was somehow a mark of slavery was powerful in the dominant thinkers and thus largely underlay the intellectual tradition after the early days.

It was then the form of alienation active in a slave-society that was the main factor inhibiting any consistent connection of science with technology, or any movement towards the full exploitation of the economic possibilities, in both organisation of the labour-process and in working out even the practical possibilities present.

There is yet a more particular instance in which we may see how the banausic (servile) concept of productive labour operated to curb ancient developments. We have noted already how important for the Greeks was the notion of limits, which from one angle was bound up with the glorification of the mean. We saw also how the craftsman was looked on as in a sense an alien in the body politic. One aspect of this attitude expressed itself in elevating the consumer as judge of the end or purpose of craft-processes over the actual producer. When a flute is to be made, says Aristotle, it's the musician who commands and the craftsman who obeys. Hence the idea that the craftsman is not truly constructing or inventing, but is trying to imitate a form or *eidos*, which either lies in nature or in somebody's mind, already pre-established. (Plato's theory of Ideas or *Eidē* carries this attitude to its final metaphysical conclusion.) Plato declares that for everything there exist three kinds of *technai*: its use, its manufacture, its imitation. These *technai* belong respectively to the consumer, the craftsman, the painter. The painter knows a thing only by its external appearance, which he reproduces by artifice; the craftsman makes it, but, in so far as he is craftsman, he does not truly know its *eidos* (its function, its purpose, its full nature); the consumer alone has full competence. *Technē*, then, consists in knowing how and when to use rightly a *dynamis* which acts as a sort of natural force. The *eidē* of the manufactured objects appear as their natures—something that exists outside and above the producers, who act only as a sort of intermediary. Making or *poiēsis* appears as an operation of an instrumental type. By the term *poiētika organa* Aristotle means what is capable of producing something—the tools of a trade and also the craftsman who works with them and who has not much of a superior existence. The worker is here submerged in nature, as later he became alienated in the machine. (Descartes was in time to state that the worker knew his trade because he knew the mechanism of his machine.) We see that the vitalism of the ancient view, turned inside out, reveals a mechanistic position.

The inability then to conceive of the use of technology for social advance is linked with a preconceived idea of limits. Each worker is limited to his particular trade; and that trade has its own inner limits determined by the *eidē* it serves. And this idea of limits, which has far-ranging effects in the whole realm of thought, comes back to the concept of the craftsman as little more than a thing, than his own tools, and the full extension of the concept into the slave as worker, the slave who is juridically a thing.

Indeed, Aristotle directly treats the worker as a thing, a tool. At the start of his *Politics* he declares: "The *technē* of the householder like any definite craft cannot dispense with its proper instruments, if its work is to be adequately performed. But instruments can be animate or inanimate. In the case of, say, a pilot, the tiller is an inanimate instrument, the lookout an animate one; indeed in every *technē* an assistant is virtually an instrument. Thus we conclude that any given property as a whole is a mass of instruments, a slave is an animate property, and every assistant may be described as a single instrument doing the work of several. For suppose that every instrument could obey a person's orders or anticipate his wishes and so fulfil its proper functions like the legendary figures of Daidalos or the tripods of Hephaistos, which, if we may credit the poet, 'Entered selfmoved the meeting of the gods'; suppose, I say, that in like manner combs were in the habit of combing and quills of playing the cithern of themselves, master-craftsmen would have no need of assistants or masters of slaves."

Here the assistant, whether slave or free, is assimilated to the status of the slave and becomes a mere tool or means to an end; all labour is seen as essentially servile. And again the fantasy of automatic tools and instruments, or robots, intrudes as apparently providing the only alternative to the use of slaves. (Behind the fantasy is the correct statement that only a universal use of automation can release men from the division of labour which is linked with division into groups or classes of varying privilege and power.)

The idea of a progressive expansion of production can hardly be said to have emerged at all. Cato in his *De Agricultura* gives as his main counsels: don't waste labour-time, or equipment; own just as much of both as you need, not a tittle more; and keep thinking up

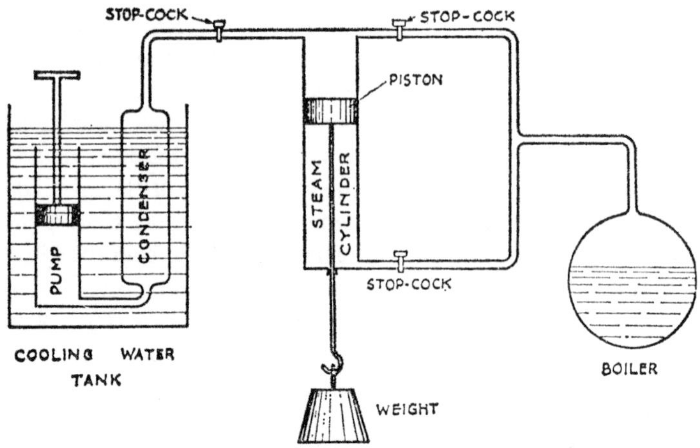

84. Diagram of Watt's model, illustrating the condensing principle for a steam-engine, 1765. In older engines the cylinder was cooled at each stroke after the steam's entry; Watt attached condenser and "air-pump" to empty the cylinder, thus enabling it to be kept at steam-heat while the vacuum produced by condensation did its share of work and increased the engine's efficiency

ways of seeing that men and tools are employed all the while: next, sell and don't buy; produce or make on your estate as much as you can to meet its needs of consumption. He thus found in practice that he could not determine which operation was or was not economically profitable. Xenophon's discussion of labour-division arises from the context of the superiority of meals in the Persian palace on account of the staff of kitchen specialists. He is concerned, not with expanding the quantity of production, but with raising its quality. Apart from the Anon's worry over failing man-power in the army, we find only Plinius raising the question of labour-saving devices (in relation to the Gallic reaper): "The diversity of methods employed depends on the quantity of the crops and the scarcity of labour." But the "diversity of methods" hardly came about. Even the watermill spread slowly, and does not seem to have come into anything like general use till the very late fourth century.

So it is clear that the pressure from the failing man-power, which included the lack of slave-labour, could not by itself transform the system. Though from one angle it was theoretically possible for considerable advances to be made by applications of even the rudimentary forms of water-power, wind-power, steam-power known to Heron and others, from another and decisive angle, the application simply could not be made. The medieval interlude had to come, during which a vast new series of social and economic forces were developed, and new attitudes of mind slowly built up, before the attempts at application could be made. Among the necessary new attitudes of mind, we have noted, were those brought about by the long domination of a theology which set the source of power outside the world of the senses and thus, to its own ultimate downfall, made possible the Galilean abstractions.

But how, it may be asked, was Greek thought so vital and creative if it reflected a society of slave-owners with a deep split between masters and producers? The answer lies in the bases laid down in the first great burst of Greek philosophy in the mercantile city-states on the eastern side of the Aegean. Here, while the transition from tribal ways to city-life was going on, slavery was still largely undeveloped in the productive sphere and there is no sign among the thinkers of the later contempt for banausic activities. The social atmosphere was in general incomparably freer than in previous cities—apart from the Phoinikian mercantile cities which did so much to create the alphabet and which may be taken as halfway-stages between the older types of cities and the Greek city-state. The tension of surviving tribal outlooks and the new busy mercantile systems, in such a situation, had an incomparably stimulating effect, and the result was the unitary concept of natural process from which mythology had been essentially eliminated. The bases thus laid down were never quite lost in the ancient world, despite the powerful effects of Platonic idealism. We have seen how Greek thought always tended to look to the crafts for its illustrative material, its explanatory systems. After the considerable increase in slave-production during the fifth century, with a corresponding crisis in the whole nature and functioning of the city-states, there came the much extended dialectical systems of Plato, Aristotle, and the Stoics, which grappled with the problems of structure and inner conflict in a way far beyond the range of the Ionian thinkers with their simpler universe. Herakleitos represented the cryptic halfway stage between the Ionians with their unitary systems and the thinkers who sought to define a much more complex pattern of movement, conflict and unity. The Stoics, who expressed the deepened sense of human unity which resulted from the collapse of the city-states and the attempt of Alexander to create a universal monarchy, lacked a social basis for their doctrines after it became clear that such efforts as those made by Agis, Kleomenes, and Nabis in Sparta could not avail against the new kingships. They clung to what they felt to be the potentiality in the situation, and thus made their remarkable contribution to scientific theory, their concepts of fields of force and of a tensional dynamic continuum, but were unable to move from theory to practical applications.

85. Bronze-workers, statues, vase-painter at work, bronze statue of Athena seated, another bronze-worker (probably the master) with tools and Hephaistean cap on wall: Athenian redfigured vase-painting, early fifth century B.C., from the Akropolis

In a sense, then, it was the general inability of Greek thought to grapple with the unity of theory and practice in the scientific field that preserved the concrete purity of the concepts inherited from the Ionians. We see at various points a development which promises to narrow down to a basis from which mechanics in the Galilean sense might emerge. But it never happens. The contact with the world of work is never fully established. The primacy of the human being and of human experience in its qualitative fullness reasserts itself. Where the isolation of the individual thinker from the productive life of his world is to be seen is in the inability to advance from ideas about growth, change, movement in an

86. The Birth of Athena from the Head of Zeus: present are Hephaistos and Eileithyia (birth-goddess), Artemis, Poseidon, and others; Hephaistos holds the cleaving axe: redfigured Athenian vase, B.M.

individual body, to any general concept of evolutionary development. The object remains concrete, but at the cost of being essentially isolated in its own pattern of potentiality, actualisation, fulfilment. The individual lives in ceaseless *energeia*, but energy as a dynamical aspect of work eludes him.

In the army was the only stable body of organised workers and directors or engineers, with an accumulated body of experience connected with machines (artillery). Here then alone do we meet a slow but steady readjustment of theory to deal with the dynamics of motion. The climax of this development appears in John Philoponos, whose work provides the basis on which the first thinkers of the west try to grapple with the new world of gunpowder and to reach a general dynamical theory through the problems of ballistics. The explosive power of gunpowder matures together with the expansion of the bourgeois cash-nexus to bring about the dynamics of Galileo and the gravitational theory of Newton. Thus a dehumanised scientific basis is created on which the expansion and application of blast-power can be carried out.

The Galilean and Newtonian concepts need as their social correlative a system in which each individual is conceived as living an atomic existence, apart from all others, impacting and being impacted on, but revealing in the last resort an egoist entity. Hence the Protestant ethic of the individual soul concerned only with its direct relation to God, the principle of transcendent power. The ideal conditions with which classical mechanics was concerned were the conditions of the free atomistic bourgeois soul. Thus Newtonian mechanics asserted that a point-mass left to itself moved with uniform velocity in a straight line. But such a conception omits all reference to a definite (that is, real) coordinate system. Nature in fact gives us no coordinate system with reference to which a uniform rectilinear motion would be possible. As soon as we connect a material coordinate system with any body large or small, the first condition of the law of inertia ceases to be fulfilled: the condition of freedom from external influences. For at once there occurs a mutual gravitational effect of the bodies.

Pure inertial motion is thus a pure abstraction, a mental construction. We see why it came up at the time it did, and why it played such an important rôle. The object with a pure inertial motion was the bourgeois individual, or rather his deepest fantasy of himself, which was also a pure abstraction, a mental construction. So we see also why the science based on the Newtonian abstraction carried on without serious question or alteration while the bourgeois system itself was on the whole operating freely—that is, advancing and expanding in terms of its own inner momentum. The crisis in the Newtonian system arrived only in the epoch of imperialism, with deep inner conflict in the capitalist system and with the effective rise of a rival system that challenges the bourgeoisie. So we reach the Einsteinian position which recognises that it is not meaningful to talk of the motion of "a body" in space as long as only one body is present, and to grant such a body attributes like inertial mass, which arise only from our observation of several bodies moving relatively to one another.

I give this as a simple example of the correlation of scientific ideas with the patterns of history. Why did it take two hundred years for this fact about inertia to force its way into the scientific consciousness and to make scientists admit that no absolute significance whatever can be attached to the concept "inertial mass of a body"? Was it merely that the possibilities of the Newtonian concept took just that time to work themselves formally out? or was it that those possibilities were at all points linked with an actual historical situation, a situation of people, with complex pressures stirring the minds of scientists to one set of relationships and closing them up tightly against others? We must repeat that to link thought-processes with social processes is not to make them simply relative to the latter or to make their actual content subjective; for social process is itself the expression of a large set of objective relationships, man with man, man with

87. Workshop of Sculptor and Stone-cutters, at work on late Roman sarcophagus (Jahn, *Darstellungen*, pl. vii, 1)

nature. In any scientific theory playing an active part in the life of a period there will be found an element of objective truth, and certain limiting factors, of which people are unconscious and which express the limitations of that society in its movement towards the realisation of a free and full humanity, a securely harmonious relationship to nature.

When we have realised the unity of the thought-processes and the social life of a period, we have then not discredited the findings of the first; we have seen them in terms of a larger dynamic whole, which includes the totality of men's relations to nature. We are at last able to separate the wheat from the chaff, and to distinguish what is true from what is merely the expression of various unconscious assumptions, and more, to make out what kind of truth is involved.[2]

There are a few more comments to be made about the thunderstorm as the supreme form of power which human endeavours have sought to master and imitate.

First we may note that the Protestant divines of the Renaissance welcomed and praised artillery. They pointed out that according to

Exodus, 'The Lord is a man of war," and he showed his soldiers how to use their weapons. "Blessed be the Lord my strength which teacheth my hands to war, and my fingers to fight" was the text on the titlepage of an artillery manual. Several clerics wrote books designed to show that the Bible was as good a source of military information as the much-consulted classical textbooks of Vegetius, Frontinus and Caesar. "The whole Bible is a book of the battles of the Lord," one clergyman said, while another was annoyed that most men accepted the value of these secular military works, "but do lightly prize the Scriptures' history of wars, the right art military indeed, which was commanded to be penned by that great man of war, the only chief and highest commander, whose name is the Lord of Hosts". These writers admitted that the calling up of a plague of frogs was beyond the competence of a modern general, but claimed that in all normal military matters the Bible was the best textbook. True, gunpowder was not mentioned there, but there was no doubt that God had meant it to be legitimately used. A Tudor preacher declares, "As Saint Paul gives a Christian in his welfare the whole armour of God, so in this kind of modern war we must improve all things whatever the bowels or face of the earth can afford for our defence." So the Christian was right in using iron for guns and saltpetre for gunpowder. Another cleric said that God had given beaks to birds and claws to beasts, so man, lacking such natural weapons, must use whatever his God-given brain might invent; and in his use of these inventions he must follow his instincts, as in the use of subterfuge and terrorism —as long as the war was just—a proviso that hardly mattered since no nation or group has ever admitted to fighting an unjust war. The clerics said that a man should forgive his personal enemies, but he could use any means against God's, against those who refused to see the light. They let themselves go especially when preaching a sermon for the Artillery Company of London. An odd example was chosen to show men taking the model for their weapon from the sky. Had not God shown a special favour to the English, it was asked, by encouraging the invention of the longbow, that materialisation of the Rainbow?

In the eighteenth century increasing attention began to be paid to electricity. The main way of producing it was imitated from amber. Electrical machines were devised that reproduced the events caused by rubbing a glass rod with silk, or an ebonite rod with fur. In either case light particles of matter were attracted to the charged rod. What for long baffled inquirers was the phenomenon now differentiated as positive and negative electric charge. Two glass or ebonite rods, charged, would repel one another; brought close together, they attracted one another. The tendency was to argue that there were two opposing kinds of electricity. Franklin, however, insisted that there was a single electric fluid. He went on with an attempt to explain the similarity between static electricity (as developed by the crude machines of the period) and lightning. In a letter of 16 October 1752 he told how he sent up into a thunderstorm a kite with a wire attached, and with a key at the end of the twine holding the kite: "To the end of the twine, next the hand, is to be tied a silk ribbon, and where the silk and twine join, a key may be fastened." The silk must not get wet. "As soon as any of the thunder clouds come over the kite, the pointed wire will draw the electric fire from them, and the kite with all the twine, will be electrified, and the loose filaments of the twine will stand out every way, and be attracted by an approaching finger. And when the rain has wet the kite and twine, so that it can conduct the electric fire freely, you will find it stream out plentifully from the key on the approach of your knuckle. At this key the phial may be charged; and from electric fire thus obtained, spirits may be kindled, and all the other electric experiments be performed, which are usually done by the help of a rubbed glass globe or tube, and thereby the sameness of the electric matter with that of lightning is completely demonstrated."

Others had conjectured that there was a connection between thunderbolt and electric shock; Franklin was the first to provide a formal and definite proof. He went on to show that the charge in the thundercloud may sometimes be positive, sometimes negative. We may add that with the growing interest in electricity, the torpedo fish was investigated by Cavendish among others, and it was doubtless because of this attention paid to the fish that the underwater explosive or projectile was later called a torpedo. Papers on the fish were published in the 1770s; and in 1775 Cavendish read *An Account of some Attempts to imitate the Effects of the Torpedo by Electricity*.

Napoleon, who, we must remember, was trained as an artillery-officer, remarked, "When you can use the lightning, it's better than cannon." His comment was far from being a mere fantasy-aside.

Many theories have been set out as to the cause and composition of ball-lightning: that it results from confined plasma, electromagnetic radiation, cosmic rays, free electrons at low temperatures closed in a small volume by exchange forces, a d.c. nonlinear phenomenon (a corona discharge in midair). The last named suggestion seems to meet most of the problems connected with the event. If a dielectric (insulating, non-conductive) inhomogeneity is introduced into a uniform d.c. electric field, such as exists over sizeable regions between thundercloud and ground, there develops a tendency for lines of force to concentrate within the inhomogeneity. A conducting inhomogeneity would also tend to concentrate lines of force towards it, but would itself have little field within its volume.

> If the field were high enough and the focusing effect great enough, it would be possible to have a local breakdown giving rise to a localised discharge of plasma. Such a plasma would itself be an inhomogeneity of high conductance. This in turn would further concentrate lines of force which in turn would increase the volume of the plasma. The feedback cycle would continue until a stable size was reached, where there would be a maximum concentration of energy of the field surrounding the plasma. In a word, the theory says that ball lightning is a corona discharge in mid-air. Mathematically, the current depends on the electric field as follows: $i = \sigma E$, but σ depends on whether or not there is a breakdown, that is $\sigma = \sigma(i)$. (Cade)

Lasers provide sources of electromagnetic radiation ten thousand to a hundred thousand times more intense than those previously available through microwave generators. Already the U.S. army has a laser-rifle capable of blinding a man or setting his clothes on fire at a range of about a mile; the maximum firing rate is once every ten seconds. And this is only the crude beginning of what can be further developed. Another type of weapon uses plasma jets, and is based on the particle-accelerators of the kind used in ion-meters or plasma jet-engines for spacecraft-propulsion. These weapons could only be effective in outer space; and when fired they might disturb the orbit of the artificial satellite on which they were lodged. One idea is to set them in balanced pairs so that, firing in exactly opposite directions the mechanical reactions would cancel out. An attempt has also been made to produce a synthetic thunderbolt out of magnetically controlled plasma. Kapitza in

1955 suggested a model for ball lightning; he took the shape to be a spherical plasmoid, with a resonant frequency corresponding to that of some external radio-frequency field. He proposed that an intense source of microwaves should be focused into a confined space, considering that the resulting spherical plasmoid would have a diameter approximately equal to one quarter of the wave-length of the radio-frequency field. His theory stirred much controversy, and later work went on along different lines, though accepting the idea of a nonlinear phenomenon due to an external field. In California a plasma gun has been built, which generates a plasma of deuterium. The plasmoids are expelled with a velocity of about 120 miles a second.

> It has been proved possible to generate small plasmoids resembling lightning balls, and it has been shown that other forms of plasmoids can be projected magnetically with great velocities. If it eventually becomes possible (and some American military authorities are confident of this) to project large synthetic thunderbolts, containing the same destructive force as is shown by the natural variety, then a defence weapon of immense potentiality will have been produced (Cade).

We may ignore the term "defence weapon" as a euphemism, like the "just war" of the Protestant clerics. The destructive potentiality of such a weapon is obvious. With it we come full circle from the dreams of the shamanist about blast-power.

We must now face up to the protest: "Even admitting that there is truth on the point about the shamanist dream being slowly but steadily brought true over the millennia, the scientists were not working in a fantasy-world since their discoveries and the technological applications have worked. What alternative was there?"

We have continually, in discussing Greek thought, come up against the fact that it resisted the quantitative approach because it held fast to living wholes with their integrated bundle of qualities and quantities. That attitude suggested a different kind of science than the post-Galilean; but we still have no proof that that kind of science is practically possible. We can indeed point to integrative ideas and methods in science over its long history, but the dominant forces have been reductive and quantitative. The enormous development of technology in the world of industrialism has been in effect wholly the work of these forces. What can we say to prove that a contrary movement is possible and that it would be rewarding?

Inevitably we cannot prove how far such a contrary movement would go in providing man with a secure and happy life on earth, for the facts of the case are that the reductive movement has triumphed and has led us into a terrible situation. We can only say that the logic of things suggests that the unitary and integrative outlook would have had diametrically opposite effects, but we cannot outline these effects in any detail. The very fact that we can make a detailed analysis of the shortcomings and delusions of the principles underlying the quantitative method, however, suggests that there is a possible alternative which would work. In support of this position I should like briefly to outline two recent formulations, one general, the other more particular. Both formulations, quite unrelated, are based on the inequality of cause and effect and seek to arrive at conclusions which get rid of the metaphysical assumptions lying behind conservation-theories with their symmetrical systems.

First there is the unitary principle of L. L. Whyte which has been worked out and applied in some detail to physics and biology. Let us take here some of the opening remarks, which look back to the statement by Pierre Curie in 1894 that an asymmetry in causes may disappear in their effects, so that the symmetry of the effects may be greater than that of their causes.

> Inequality is a more general relationship than equality, in the sense that it covers a wider field and approaches equality when the inequality becomes vanishingly small. This is an example of the fact that the field of an asymmetrical relation, such as greater than, often includes the corresponding symmetrical relation, here equal to, as a special limiting case. Thus the field of inequality includes equality, non-simultaneity includes simultaneity, and spatial asymmetry includes spatial symmetry, each as a logically degenerate limiting case of a wider field of relations. The asymmetrical relations of quantity, time, and space (greater than, earlier than, etc.) are more general than, and can be used to define, the corresponding symmetrical relations (equal to, simultaneous with, etc.) which form the basis of quantitative physics. The science of inequality, succession, and asymmetry—which has still to be created—is more comprehensive than the science of equality, reversibility, and symmetry, and can

> include the latter as a special branch. The science of quantity and equations is a part of the more general science of order.
>
> We have therefore to discover the most general possible relation of inequality between cause and effect which can provide a basis for science. This is equivalent to discovering the necessity and sufficient characteristics of scientific causality.

On this basis Whyte works out his general principles, taking the tendency of asymmetry to disappear as a unitary formative process which is present at inorganic and organic levels alike. The principle of conservation is relegated to its correct sphere, that of closed cycles. The full application of Whyte's ideas, which is perfectly feasible, would soon lead to revolutionary effects in science in all its branches and would break through the metaphysical impasse of purely quantitative science. Hints of the new approach can be found in some aspects of quantum mechanics and in the new physics of particles; but they can only remain hints until a systematic application of new principles is made—principles for which Whyte provides a generous blueprint. No doubt as the work of building up the new science goes on, many insufficiencies, over-simplifications and gaps will be found in his system, and the formative principle will take on a fullness and richness which no preliminary sketch can hope to achieve. But as a stimulating set of guides for the first steps on the new road his formulations are invaluable.

My second example is the work in physics of the Soviet astronomer N. A. Kozyrev. He has done important work in his own professional field. By observing fluorescent areas on the moon's surface, he was able to argue that that surface had no magnetic field: as was later proved by Lunik II. In his physics he insists that science must take notice of the world of concrete experience, of real time, with its asymmetries; and he has set out his conclusions in what he calls Causal Mechanics. He declares, in mathematical terms, that cause and effect cannot be simultaneous in time and must be separate in space; and he goes on with an attempt to work out a positive system that will surpass Newtonian principles, including the quantum modifications. He argues that, whatever the time and distance between cause and effect are in fact, the ratio between these two factors provides a constant. This ratio, a measure of speed, is a universal constant as important as the speed of light. It may be called the speed of the transformation of cause into effect. Naming it the Progress of Time, he denotes it by the symbol o_2. He then looks round for other constants which, when multiplied together or divided into one another, provide a quantity also measurable as a speed; and he selects the electric charge carried by an electron, *e*, and Planck's constant *h*. Squaring the electric charge carried by an electron and dividing it by *h*, we get a constant measurable as a speed; its value is 350 km./sec. Taking *K* as a numerical factor, which Kozyrev claims to have found experimentally to be about 2, we obtain the equation: $o_2 = K.e^2$. 350 km./sec.

In Newtonian mechanics the physicist takes for granted that there is simultaneity of cause and effect, of action and reaction; for he has in fact reduced the two bodies concerned to abstract or ghostly points. He assumes o_2 to be infinitely large. This assumption, as can be seen from the above formula, is the same as assuming that Planck's constant, *h*, is zero: which is the approximation made in converting quantum mechanics into classical or Newtonian mechanics. (In Planck's formula, quantum of energy = *h* times frequency.)

Mathematically, in Newton's terms, we cannot decide, in the case of a car's collision with a wall, which is car and which is wall. Is the car knocking the wall or the wall the car? (It is interesting to note that the ancient sceptics on such matters reached a position analagous to that of Newtonian mechanics. Sextus Empiricus argues: "The hoop moves and the hoop-trundler also moves. Why then should the trundler move because of the hoop rather than conversely the hoop because of the trundler?" And he goes on to argue along these lines that the agent and the object of the action are equally the cause of movement.) If, however, there is a time-gap in accordance with the principle of Kozyrev's time-progress, we can distinguish in theory as well as in practice which hits which, or which moves which. The same principle enables us to make a distinction of right and left hand. In Newtonian mechanics, any geometrical design or construction, any conceivable form, is the same as its mirror-image, so that we cannot tell left from right. Chiral problems have kept on coming up as we get deeper among the particles, and they occur at other levels as well. Thus, all naturally occurring amino-acids own a left-handed configuration and the process of basic protein synthesis is chiral, converting point-centred and planar inorganic atoms or molecules into organic molecules of a chiral character. Kozyrev embodies the power to express left- or right-handedness in our formulations by determining the sign of time-progress in our system of measurement. He goes on to argue that the time-progress for spinning bodies differs from the usual value by an amount equal to the speed of rotation, which must be added or subtracted according to the direction of rotation. The change in the time-progress by virtue of rotation gives rise to unbalanced forces, and so can be used as a source of energy. That is, the passage of time releases energy. Kozyrev believes that it is possible for us to grasp the moments of real change, in which asymmetry appears in a system, and to harness those moments, to draw out of them the energy which internally would have gone to the reassertion of the system in some extended pattern.

It is of much interest then that fundamental aspects of his thought have close affinities with those of Whyte's, though the two thinkers have been quite unaffected by each other. We may note what Whyte says of living protein. The stability in protein systems expresses the capacity to form linearly symmetrical chains which can be folded into a variety of other symmetrical structures. But on the other hand the tendency to undergo characteristic changes after a slight stimulus arises from the asymmetrical (polar or polarisable) side- and end-groups that can be strung on these chains—the interaction of these polar groups with their changing environment determining the manifold transformation of the protein molecules. So the protein chain serves as a relatively stable carrier of specific polar (or polarisable) groups, the processes of which determine the changes which the chain itself undergoes.

> But living protein displays a further all-important property. The polar or polarisable side-groups are arranged regularly, and establish a continuous resultant field through each functional region (and throughout much of the animal organism) so that one normalising process dominates the region, and alternating pulses of depolarisation and polarisation are propagated without interruption along channels of identical or co-operative molecules. We shall see later that this property provides the clue to the co-ordination of local processes as components of one extended normalising process. It is the continuity of induction of polarisation throughout the functional regions of the organism, so that one normalising process composed of a pattern of local normalising processes controls the whole system, which underlies the developmental and functional stability of the organism.

One consequence of Kozyrev's theory is that the Second Law of Thermodynamics is seen to be incorrect. Against that law it has already been argued that the sun's energy-reserves are used to replace the losses, acting as a sort of accumulator: the energy being liberated by a fusion-process involving hydrogen. Kozyrev adds the suggestion that the time-progress is what supplies the energy and brings about the re-charges. He suggests further that the processes converting time are possibly electrodynamic; they may also come about through the creation of matter which is later burned away. Another consequence of his concept is that forces should act along the axis of a rotating body such as a planet.

> In the case of the Earth, the forces operate towards the South pole in the central cylinder surrounding the axis of rotation and towards the North pole at greater distances from the axis, as shown in the figure. The result should be that the planet is deformed into a "heart-shape". In fact, geodesists have calculated from observations on one of the American satellites (Vanguard I) that the Earth is deformed in this sort of way, but they conclude that the South pole is squashed and the North elongated—the exact opposite of Kozyrev's conclusion. However, he explains the difference as being due to the method of calculation employed.
>
> In other ways observations on earth seem not incompatible with Kozyrev's prediction. The gravitational constant is larger in the Antarctic, as he suggests. And experiments on falling bodies carried out as long ago as the seventeenth century support his prediction that they will fall to the south of the vertical line. Kozyrev has himself measured the asymmetric forces in the Crimea, in Pulkovo, and in the Arctic circle, and claims to have shown that the direction of the forces reverses from north to south at 75° 05′ N., as the theory demands.
>
> His observations on Jupiter, which has a rotating velocity at the Equator of 11,000 m./sec. (as compared with 450 m./sec. at the Equator on Earth), show that it, too, is heart-shaped, and his measurements are said to bear out the theoretical calculations. And he claims the same, too, for his measurements on Saturn. (Margerison)

His ideas about rotating bodies may turn out to provide key-links between physics and biology. His equations dealing with time-progress and the direction of rotation link with the laws governing the basic synthesis of natural proteins, the molecules that guide process possessing a unique primary axis and a characteristic univocal spiral process about that axis. "The pulsation of each molecule involves a chiral, non-propagated polarisation cycle and cyclic changes of shape, which prevent stable association into extended structures, but provide the necessary condition for basic synthesis," to cite Whyte again. Kozyrev's equation links further with the wider range of asymmetries that Whyte considers. In both Kozyrev and Whyte we find the same sort of non-reductive interrelation between the laws of physics and those of biology, as we would expect of truly unitary science.

And as we might further expect of such a science, Time, which in the Newtonian (and even the Einsteinian) world is totally robbed of its real nature and made an abstract coordinate, turns out to be the most concrete factor of all, the true source of energy. Since Time is precisely what distinguishes real process from abstracted patterns and metaphysical entities, it must indeed be in Time that the clue to the real universe lies. Concrete Time cannot but be the central and comprehensive reality which unifies all other processes and events, and gives them their ultimate meaning.

Unfortunately Kozyrev, despite his prestige as an astronomer, seems to have been unable to continue his work in physics in the U.S.S.R. The atomic physicists, including Kapitsa, have taken advantage of their privileged position to attack his theory of time-progress as "one false hypothesis after another", and as "a flippant chase after sensations". They have thus had him deprived of facilities to carry on his work in physics. We can only hope that their attitudes will soon be condemned and serious attention paid to Kozyrev's ideas. As a pioneer attempt, those ideas may contain errors or weaknesses; but if there is any truth in the attitudes set out in this book, they have enormous importance as pointers to the new kind of science we need if we are to survive.

I have introduced this necessarily brief and rough account of the ideas of Whyte and Kozyrev to answer the objection that the post-Galilean scientists had taken the only possible line. The only possible line, indeed, in terms of their world and its pressures, its assumptions, but not the only possible line for science when once those assumptions are radically challenged. Greek science, in part because it never got down to the job of linking theory with practice, shows a strange mixture of reductive and metaphysical elements with intuitions of the fully concrete universe of process. The modern world, with its basis in the sixteenth and seventeenth centuries, took the reductive line and, because this line is essentially dehumanised and alienated in its outlook, the result was a science leading into ever more devastating weapons, into nuclear fission, and into universal pollution and destruction of the environment. Now, in a reaction against this line and its consequences, and as part of the work of building a world-society in which the harmony of man with man is only another aspect of his harmony with nature, we need to return to the unitary and concrete aspects of ancient thought. Without discarding what valuable lessons can be learned from the epoch of quantitative science, we must set ourselves the task of evolving methods of thought that can deal with wholes without reducing them to the mechanical level. Methods of thought which can grasp Time in its fully concrete nature.

Notes

Abbreviations used in Notes and Bibliography

A: *Antiquity.*
AA: *American Anthropologist.*
AAA: *Annals of Arch. and Anthrop.*, Liverpool.
ActA: *Acta Archaeologica.*
ACIHS: *Actes du Congrès International d'Histoire des Sciences.*
AGP: *Archiv f. Gesch.d. Philosophie.*
AIHS: *Archives Internat. d'Hist. des Sciences.*
AJP: *Amer. Journal of Philology.*
AM: *Mitteilungen des deutschen archaolog. Instituts, Athenische Abteilung.*
APA: *Amer. Association, Proceedings.*
ARW: *Archiv f. Religionwiss.*
AS: *Abhandlungen d. Säch. Akad. d Wissen., philol.-hist. Klasse*, Leipzig.
AZ: *Archäol. Zeitung.*
BCH: *Bull. de correspondence hellénique.*
BIFAO: *Bull. de l'Inst. franç. d'Archéol. orient.*
BSA: *Annual of British School at Athens.*
BSGW: *Berichte d.k. sächs. Gesch. d. Wiss.*, Wien.
BSR: *Papers of British School at Rome.*
C: *Centaurus.*
CAG: *Commentaria in Aristotelen Graeca.*
CE: *Chronique d'Égypte.*
CP: *Classical Philology.*
CQ: *Class. Quarterly.*
CR: *Class. Review.*
CRAI: *Comptes rendus des séances de l'Inst. des Inscriptions.*
CS: *Colloques de Strasbourg.*
CZ: Cook, *Zeus.*
DK: Diels-Kranz, *Die Fragmente d. Vorsokratiker.*

Dox.: Diels, *Doxographi Graeci* (3rd ed. 1958).
EHR: *Economic History Review.*
EJ: *Eranos Jahrbuch.*
EP: *Études de Papyrologie.*
H: *Hermes.*
HSCP: *Harvard Studies in Class. Philology.*
HT: *A History of Technology* i 1954.
HTR: *Harvard Theolog. Rev.*
IC: *Inscriptiones Creticae*, M. Guarducci.
JDAI: *Jahrb. d. deut. archäol. Instituts.*
JEA: *Journal of Egyptian Arch.*
JHI: *Journal of the Hist. of Ideas.*
JHS: *Journal of Hellenic Studies.*
JHSC: *Journal d'Hist. des Sciences.*
JP: *Journal de Psychologie.*
JRS: *Journal of Roman Studies.*
MEFR: *Mélanges de l'École franç. de Rome.*
MH: *Museum Helvetian.*
MKNA: *Mededeelingen d. k. Nederl. Akad.*
NC: *Numismatic. Chron.*
NHJ: *Neue Heidelberger Jahrb.*
NJKA: *Neue Jahrb. f.d. klass. Alt.*
P: *Phronesis.*
PAPS: *Procs. Amer. Philosophical Soc.*
PBA: *Procs. Brit. Acad.*
Ph: *Philologus.*
PR: *Phil. Rev.*
RA: *Revue archéol.*
REG: *Revue de Études grecques.*
RhM: *Rhein. Museum f. Philol.*
RHS: *Revue d'hist. des sciences.*
RM: *Mitteil. d. deut. archäol. Inst., röm. Abteilung.*
RMet: *Revue de Métaphysique.*
RRI: *Rivista del Reale Istituto d'Arch. e Storia dell'Arte.*
SB: *Sitzungsber. de preuss. Akad. d. Wiss., ph.-hist. Kl.*
SKGG: *Schriften d. k. Gelehrter Gesselschaft.*
YCS: *Yale Class. Studies.*

Aetius: Aet.
Aristotle: Ar.
Cicero: Cic.
Demokritos: Dem.
Diogenes Laertius: DL.
Empedokles: Emp.
Herodotos: Hdt.
Herakleitos: Her.
Parmenides: Parm.
Ploutarch: Plout.

Sextus Empiricus: SE.
Simplikios: Simp.
Theophrastos: Th.

Drachmann: Dr.

George Thomson: GT.
Jane Harrison: JH.
Jack Lindsay: JL.
Partington: Pa.
Sambursky: Sa.

I. Energy Ancient and Modern

1. Hdt. viii 26; Ar. *Met.* viii 3. Megareans: DL ii 106–112 and ii 30; Cic. *Acad.* ii 4; Plout. *de frat. am.* xviii.

2. Ar. *NE* 1098b; *Rh.* 1411b28; *Met.* 1042b10; 1043a20, etc.

3. Peek, p. li; for pathogenic *dynamis*, W. H. S. Jones i (Hippok. *arch. iatr.* xxii 3f, and xiv and iii). Cf. Pl. *Tim.* 33a, "hot things and cold and all things that have strong powers", Vlastos (4) 157. Also *Tim.* 54b and 32a. Power over a thing: Ar. 1045b35 to 1046a11; 1048a 25 to b4.

4. Causes: Lloyd (1) 105–7; Ross 71–5; effects of these ideas, Sa. (2) 50f. Octave: *Phys.* 194b27; *Met.* 1031a28. For *dynamis*: Souilhé; W. H. S. Jones (2), medicine. There is a difficulty in fully unifying the concept of dynamis at organic and inorganic levels: Lloyd (4) 265.

5. *Morphe* is rather used for shape; for Ar. form is more or less identified with both efficient and final cause.

6. Local matter in heavenly spheres exists without the three latter changes; intelligible matter (spatial extension) never exists without sensible matter: a point made only in *Met.* Opposition: GC 329b7ff.

7. A fifth element is needed as one that moves naturally in a circle and so explains what he took to be the eternal circular movement of heavens: Lloyd (1) 107ff. Scheme: Ross 106; *GC* 331ff: against Emp. who held the four elements incapable of transformation.

8. Cic. *Nat. Deor.* ii 22.

9. Vernant (1) 18–20. Also Ar. *Pol.* vii 1325b15; *NE* 1140a; *Met.* 1048b 18ff and 1050. Pl. *Charm.* 163bd; *Prodikos*. Also see

Demiourgos: Aymard 139. Also Vernant 23–5. Xen. *Oik.* i 16, cf. Ar. *Pol.* vii 1325 a 32. Xen. i 21; iv 2, v 13, v 4ff; iv 24 (Kyros); vi 7—cf. Ar. *Oik.* i 1343a25. Xen. also xv 10, xviii 10, xv 4, vi 9. Gods: v 19f and 12, xx 14, cf. Menandr. (Stob. lxvii 5); Ar. *Oik.* i 1343a30.

10. Lazare Carnot: Cardwell. Also Ubbelohde (1) 128f, 143; water-level and heat-temperature, 130f.

11. Kant: conservation of quantum of substance implied by any appearance: N. K. Smith, *Critique of Pure Reason* 1933 224. Young: *Lectures* 44: "The quantity mass (velocity) has been conveyed by the term living or ascending force. . . . The same idea is somewhat more concisely expressed by the term *energy*, which indicates the tendency of a body to ascend or to penetrate to a certain distance in opposition to a retarding force." See also Clerk Maxwell, *Theory of Heat* 1899 94. G. Jones for Joule's early experiments.

12. Whiteman 23, 332ff.

13. Ubbelohde (1) 209f and (2).

14. *Ib.* 45, 53. Watt: Cardwell. Other scientists and engineers: Otto von Guericke 1678, R. Hooke 1678, Huyghens 1680, Papin 1690. T. Newcomen's steam piston-engine patented in combination with Savory; he was an ironmonger and blacksmith of Dartmouth, living 15 miles from Savory's house.

15. M. le Comte Laplace (2) 3f. For caloric theory: R. Fox. It shows how hard the idea of fire or heat as substance died; caloric was a weightless subtle highly elastic fluid of heat, with many distinctions (free, combined, latent, radiant); caloric was thought responsible for the supposed repulsion between gas particles. The theory was active in first two decades of 19th century; its decline was perhaps linked with decline of Laplacian physics.

16. 1380: Pa. (1) 59f, 174. Fontana: Hart 52ff, Vienna codex 3064 on, Hart 59f.

II. More on Aristotelean Energeia

1. *Phys.* 200b12–5; 32f.
2. *Met.* 1065b, cf. *Phys.* 201 a 27–31.

3. Note many passages in Ar. where *energeia* retains force of verb *energein*. In general, Leclerc 108ff.

4. *Od.* x 303; with ref. to Dem. D 176 and 276 (animals); Her. D 112 and 123. In opposition to *noos*, Pind. *N.* vi. 6; Emp. 8, 1 and 110, 5 D. Pl. *Laws* 889b, *Rep.* 381b. *Nomos-physis*: opposition taken over by Sophists; Pl. *Gorg.* 482e. Archelaos: DL ii 16. Pupil of Anaxagoras, he held that there were two causes of *genesis*, heat and cold; things were produced from slime, *ilys*; what is just and true depends not on nature but on convention. See also Philolaos D9. DL viii 85, Pythag. treatise begins: "*Physis* in the kosmos was composed, *harmochthē*, of limitless and limiting elements, and so the whole kosmos and all in it." Note Latin *natura* (*nasceri*, to be born). Ar. *Met.* 1014b17f.

5. Leclerc 336. In general, Whiteman, L. L. Whyte, Burtt, etc.

6. *Met.* 1071b7–10.

7. Leclerc 341–5; Ar. 1071b18–23, to 1072a25. The concept of the physical as the actualisation of the mathematical is not same as that of Descartes (identifying physical and mathematical), or that of Newton (in which math. features like measurability are derived from the physical through its existing in a place as a "container"), or that of Leibniz and Kant (in which the physical is math. only ideally, by virtue of thought).

8. Leclerc 347f.

9. *Tim.* 32bc; *On Kosmos* 396f, cf. Plout. *Prim. frig.* 946d; Maguire 137–9. *Isobares* in Chrysippos: Achilleus *Isag.* 32, 9; Plout. *Stoic. rep.* 44; Maguire 137 n53; Philon *Aet. mundi*; Tim. Lok., FPG ii 52a, cf. 39a; DL viii 26. Ocellus Lucanus: Maguire 138 n55. *On Kosmos* 397. More conservation-views; Lucret. i 294–307; Epik. *Ep. ad Hōt.* i 39; Parm. fr. B8, 7.

10. Plato: A. W. Porter 4; Ubbelohde 127. Ar.: Ross 205. Galen: *nat. fac.* i 11, 25; ii 4, 89. Anaxim.: Hippol. *Ref.* i 6, 6; Diod. i 7, 3. Thales: Ar. *Met.* 983b 23f. Parm.: Th. *Sens.* iii–iv; Stratton 64, 157–9, cf. Th. on Dem. on *symmetria* in soul's composition. Philol.: *Iatrika* of Menon (Anon. Lond. xviii 8, p. 31). *On Reg.* i 32f; *Fleshes* 9.

11. *Anc. Med.* 13 and 16 (47, 12ff). Soul: Ar. *An.* 405b24ff; Philolaos and phlegm (Anon. Lond. xviii 41ff) as hot (against usual belief) through supposed link of *phlegma* and *phlegein*.

12. Galen, *Epid.* vi 48, xvii A 1002K (fr. 67); Ar. *GA* 723a24f; Censorinus 6, 6 (DK 31A81) has probably got it wrong: see *GA* 765a3ff. Lloyd (3) 61n19 and (4) 102. Ar. *GA* 765b8ff and 28ff; Platt's note *ad loc.* (Oxf. transl.) Deformed male: *GA* 737a27ff; Lesky 151f. Blood: *PA* 648a5ff. The positions are linked with upper-lower, left-right opposites: *PA* 648a11ff, cf. 653a277. *On Reg.* i ch. 34.

13. *Pneuma,* e.g. Alex. Aphr. *de anima* 26, 16; *de mixt.* 224, 15. Active: Galen *nat. fac.* i 3, 8; Nemesian. *de nat. hom.* v. Activity of air as cold: much confusion, I. Duering (3) 81; Plout. *prim. frig.* 951f (cold air: Posedonios).

14. Cic. *nat. deor.* iii 22. Sa. (1) 133 thinks the movement is from organic processes to others including craft. DL vii 156 for *technikos.*

15. Lloyd (1) 111; as connected with earlier and later pneumatic theories, Jaeger (1).

16. Cornford (5) 93f.

17. Wheelwright (1) 122 n8, and 41.

18. Ar. *Phys.* ii 1f; *de caelo* 299a15; *Met.* 1061 ab and 1020a7–14; *Cat.* 4620. Continuum: *De an.* 409a4; Newton, Intro. *De Quadratura*, par. 27.

19. *An. post.* 75b14–7, 76a9–25, 78bff, 87. *Phys.* 193b25–30, 184a 7–12; *Met.* 997b20 to 998ab, 1073b5 to 1077ab, 1078a14–7; Ross 46 and 70.

20. *On the kos.* 398b. Host of workers: *polycheira.* Date: Furley, Maguire. Pohlenz thinks it addressed to Tib. Alex. governor of Egypt soon after A.D. 63; Duering, written about time of publication of Ar.'s works by Andronikos, c. 40–20 B.C.

21. Philon, *op. mund.* 117, cf. Pl. *Tim.* 75d. Maguire 150f and 151 n77 (not from Poseidonios). Shows: *thaumata.*

III. Opposites

1. JL (6) and (7) ch. 3; also in general (1), (2) and (3); GT (2); Lloyd (4) chs. i–ii for many more examples. For "different modes" of opposition: Lloyd ch. ii.

2. Kroef; Lloyd (3) 57.

3. Evans-Pritchard 234ff; Lloyd *l.c.*; Hertz 100. Perry for his material, not his thesis. Maoris and Australians, on the other hemisphere, also take right as the good side; GT (1) 66, 262.

4. Fourfold: *Il.* xv 189ff; Hes. *Theog.* 106f, 736f and Stokes 25ff; Wet, dry: *Od.* vi 201, xxiii 187; xiii 398, 430. Cf. Soph. *El.* 819. Hes.: *Works* 460. Athena: *Od.* xiii 392–8, cf. 430. Cold, hot: Lloyd (4) 100f. Hes. *Works* 504ff, 582ff. Ar. *Met.* i 3, 6. Pandora: *Works* 60ff (c. *Il.* vii 99), made of earth and water. Emp.: Kahn 134ff. Moisture and sex: Onians 200ff. Life and wetness: Aisch. fr. 229; Orph. fr. 32(ab): note libations for the thirsty dead. Lloyd (4) 44–6.

5. Lloyd (4) 99f, esp. n29; Hippol. *Ref.* i 6, 6; Aet. v 19, 4.

6. GT (1) 260f; Ar. *Met.* 986a15 and 22ff; GT (3) on Orphic relations. DL viii 83, Kirk (4) 236–9.

7. Pl. *Laws* 717ab, even and left (chthonian), odd and right (Olympian). Refs. in Lloyd (3) 60f. Tables of opposites in Parmenides and Empedokles: Lloyd (4) 63.

8. *De Caelo* 284b24f and 35ff; *IA* iv 705b29ff; *PA* 671; Lloyd (1) 61.

9. Lloyd (1) 62 n26 and 63 n30; difference of temperature on three heart-chambers, 63; failure to note other creatures have hearts on left, 64. Upper parts: *PA* 656a 10ff; *HA* 494a26ff; *IA* 706a 19f. Sex and left-right in Parmenides, fr. 17; Lloyd (5). Galen held: sex of animals determined (1) by side of body from which male seed comes (2) by side of womb where embryo lies, right being hot and male, left cold and female: *On Use of Parts* xiv 7, ii 302ff, esp. 309f (Helmreich); and *On Seed* ii 5, iv 626ff Kühn, cf. *Epidemics* iv. ch. 48 seems to take the Hippok. view to be similar.

10. *Laws* 794d–795d; Ar. *NE* 1134b33f; *MM* 1194b31ff.

11. Fr. 4 and 12; Lloyd (4) 95f. Anaxag. on interdependence of hot and cold, fr. 8. Qualities as substances: Lloyd (4) 82n1.

12. Lloyd (4) 94f. Critical: Heidel, Cherniss (1), McDiarmid, Hölscher 266. Upholding Ar.: Kahn 119ff, Guthrie (2) and (3), Cornford (4) 34.

13. Hölscher 266; Lloyd (4) 96f for refs. The basic opposites may be bright and dark.

14. Simp. *Phys.* 24, 13 (D12A9); Sa. (1) 8. Cf. Her.'s union of fire and justice: see later. Fire will overtake (D28 and 66, By. 118 and 26; W71–2), *katalambanein* in future middle, suggesting both take by surprise and legally condemn.

15. Solon iii 11ff (D. fr. 24); Kirk (4) 117–21; Simp. *Phys.* xxiv 17, certainly citing Th.—Vlastos (4), following Cherniss on return to Unbounded. I cannot accept Albright (1) 234f emendation of *helikia* for *adikia* (based on *aetas* of Aug. *CD* viii 2), but he rightly notes link of *kosmos* and Latin *mundus* (probably via Etruscans).

16. *On kos.* 396b. Kirk (3) fr. 10, pp. 67–79. Relation to *de victu*, *ib.* 169, and see index "opposites". *Eth. Eud.* 1235a25 (DK 22A22).

17. Painters: Plin. xxxv 50; Rumpf *JHS* 1947 lxvii 16. Polygnotos not one of them?: Pollitt 228 14 (though Cic. thought so). Emp.: Santillana (1) 125; DK no 23. Pollitt, 169, 221, 228. For harmony, perhaps *harmonia* did not get this sense till 5th c., Kirk; Wheelwright 107. See index, JL *Helen of Troy*.

18. Cic. *Brut.* 70; Lloyd (1) 48; Th. *Sens.* 73ff.

19. *Colour* 791a; Plin. xxxv 29 *Tonos*: *teinein*, stretch. Hdt. vii 30 as tightening, strain, tension (of hopla). Sinews of tendons, twisted skein of guts in torsion; engines; power of contracting muscle; mental or physical exertion, force, intensity.

20. *On Reg.* i ch. 33, four ages.

21. *De Cael.* 286a25f; *GC* 318b16f; privation, Ross 63–6. Wet and female: Lloyd (4) 105; *PA* 548a33ff, cf. 24a. Ar. notes the disagreements and problems.

22. *Phys.* v 1.

23. Ross 82f. In *Phys.* iii 1, Ar. uses movement as synonymous with change, and so includes generation and destruction, 200b32 on. Here he restricts movement so as to exclude "change in respect to substance", i.e. generation and destruction.

24. Ross 101; *GA* i 4 and *Phys.* 245b3ff; *Cat.* 8b25 on; *GA* 319b12–4.

25. Ross 101. Mean: *NE* 1107a6–8 on to 1109b26.

26. Heidel (1) 337; Ar. *Phys.* 190b; Sa. (2) 11–3; *GC* i 10. Kant: Joachim 124.

27. Reinhart (2) 223; Gigon (2) 99; Vlastos (4) 165; Snell; Kirk (3) 149ff; Wheelwright 34, 106f: frs. D126, By 39, W 22; D76, By 25, W34; D67, By 36, W 121. Base: Fraenkel (2), Diels, Burnet (fire); air, Zeller; olive oil, Snell; wine, Schuster. Opposites in Her., Kirk (4) 191–6. "Cold warms, etc." suggests strong reciprocity in change, with measure, metron, involved. The balance of nouns and verbs in the first two clauses suggests transformation; in the last the variation seems more a stylistic play. Also the phrasing gives a sense of direct personal impact of the changes. Contradictions: Ar. *Top.* 159b30ff, *Met.* 1005b23ff, 1012a24ff, 1062a31. Lloyd's attempt (4) 99–102 to "defend" Herakleitos is therefore not to the point.

IV. Cycles of Time

1. Fr. 1 Meineke; Cornford (2) 104. Circular ideas: Thornton 112–4; Webster (1) 32. Year Comes Round: *Od.* xi 295, cf. Hes. *Works* 383, 617; Emp. Diels B17, 28; B26, 1. Hdt. iv 155, ii 121; Eur. *Or.* 1645, *Phoin.* 477, 544, *Hel.* 112; *Orph. fr.* 2246 Kern on cycles; Hor. *Sat.* ii 6, 26. Idea of cycle obstructive: Goldbeck, Haas; no, Reymond 222f, Cornford (6) 87.

2. Spencer-Gillen NT 387f; Roheim 133f, 95 (ancestral time); JL (7) 36f.

3. Berndt 22f.

4. Babylon: Brandon esp. 113f and 146f, Sumerians 68ff; Frankfort 325f, 331f; Pallis 184–97, 99; Thureau-Dangin 134.

5. Fraenkel (1); Thornton 82f.

6. *Il.* xxii 212; *Od.* ix 16ff; *Il.* xvi 831.

7. Her. fr. D106, By. 120, W94; Plout. *Camillus* 138a; Sen. *Ep.* xii 7; Hes. *Works*, esp. 822ff; Onians 412. Also Her. fr. D57, cf. Hes. *Theog.* 124, 748. Galen: *Dox.* 626; Wheelwright 47f.

8. DL ix 16; Stob. *Ecl. phys.* i 9, 43 (p. 264); Athen. xi 461f; Plout. *Op. Mor.* 402, 705.

9. Behind: *Il.* v 352; Thornton 95, also for further discussion.

10. Thornton 106f. Ovid *Fasti* i 27f, iii 99f; Frazer (1929 ed.), ii comm. on i 28 and pp. 15f, citing O. E. Hartmann. Circular time: Otterlo 16ff; van Groningen ch. 3; Bassett 150ff; Fraenkel; Onians; Kleon *de motu circulari*. ed. Ziegler. For Pherekydes: DL i 119; Damask. *de princip.* 124; Kirk (4) 54–72 and 39. Willamowitz thought cosmogonic Time impossible in 6th c. *Zvran* was a refinement of Mazdaism, not early. Orphics: Kern fr. 68. For Time in Pherek. and in Iran, India, Sidon: West (2) ch. 2; Ogenos and Zeus 50–2. Kronos: Plout. *de Is.* 32. The names of the Greek months were local (or shared by a small group) and named after some god or festival: Wehrli. For Typhoeus: Stokes and West (2). Emp.: fr. B30, 3, cf. Pl. *Soph.* 242d; *Polit.* 272d.

11. JL (7) 20. Circling rites in Attic birth-rote of *amphedromia*, Roman marriage, *confarreatio*, etc.

12. Neolithic town: *The Times* 20 Sept. 1972. Myrtos: Warren 213f; Minoan type household shrine 215f, communal tombs 266, bull rhyton 220. Samarra: JL (7) 130 and D. Davison, *Story of Prehist. Civilisation* 1951 figs. 11–2. Potter's wheel seems invented late 4th millennium; in use in Sumer by 3250; Egypt, c. 2750; in Troy (IIb) c. 2500: Noble 6.

13. Music: JL (7) 104. *Tim.* 40c, *Epin.* 982e. *On kos.* 391b and 399a. Aet. ii 7, 7 (DK 44A16) "Around the [Pythag.] centre the divine bodies dance", Kirk (4) 260, cf. Eur. *Ion.* 1079, Soph. *Ant.* 1146f, etc. Ptol., *Hypoth. planet.* ii 8 (120, 33); Sa. (4) 144f. Wheel-magic as in Theokritos ii. Note twirled inside hole (dynamic circle). See also Pl. *Phaidr.* 247a; Stob. i 49, 3ff W.

14. Maze-dance, see JL, *Helen* and (7) 121f; totemic centre (7) 40. Homer: Kirk (4) 10–2; Egypt: Pritchard 3 and 60f; Kirk (4) 13; E. A. E. Reymond esp. 276f; JL (7) for multiple series of world-mountains, sky-pillars, etc. Pl. *Laws* ii 665: "Order in movement is called Rhythm and order in vocal sounds (the combination of high and low notes) Harmony, and the union of these two is called a Performance by a Choros," cf. 653f. Maths.: Michel 542.

Bab. Map: *BM Guide Bab. and Assyr. Ant.* 1922 120f; J. Lewy *Hebrew Union Coll. Annual* 1942–3 xvii 10ff; West (2) 50. Okeanos: West; Gisinger *RE* xvii 2309; Favorin. fr. 82 Barigazzi (Krates); Kirk (4) 103f; Sarton i 82, 84. The *apeiron* of Anaximandros may have been circular or spherical: Cornford *CAH* iv 542, cf. Aisch. *Ag.* 1382; Kirk (4) 110 denies. Cylinder: Ps. Plout. *Strom.* 2; Hippol. *Ref.* i 6, 3. Note the Greek *omphaloi* (navels) as world-centres, ritually based.

15. *Laws* 680; *Soph.* 242de. Platonic Great Years Adams, *Rep. Plato* ii 304. Wheelwright 51–6. Scholars seeing an *Ekpyrosis*: elder Gomperz, Zeller, Gigon, Stock (transl. of Aristotle), Mondolfo. Against: Burnet, Fraenkel, Kirk, Cherniss. Also see West (2) 134, 152, 155, 163; Sa. (1) 198ff; Guthrie (1) ch. iv; Plout. *Stoic. rep.* 1052c on cosmic metabolism, in *ekpyrosis* the kosmos is wholly soul-like, cooling begets the tension of the *pneuma*, etc.: Simp. on *de caelo* 279b15–7, with Stocks *ad loc.*; *CAG* vii 294; Stob. *Dox.* 283f; *On kos*, 401a8ff. These later commentators may well have been influenced by Stoics.

16. J. Soustelle, *Daily Life of Aztecs* 1964 ch. 3; G. C. Vaillant *The Aztecs of Mexico* 1950 194–6; Eliade (2) esp. ch. 2. Sacredness (5040), Pl. *Laws* 771ab in relation to division of tribe (also 4s and 3s); *CQ* 1952 4–12. Cycle 216 years for Pythag. transmigration (DK 14, 8). Mind rotating: Anaxag., Simp. *Phys.* 164, 24; 156, 13; 300, 31, 35, 14; Ar. *Phys.* 187a23. Parmenides' rings of rare and dense: Aet. ii 7, 1. Dem., whirl and rotation, DL ix 31; Aet. ii 7, 2.
    Disasters in general, Lovejoy. Flood, Guthrie (1) 115 n17; Diod. i 6, 3 (cf. Censorin. *de die nat.* 4); Polyb. vi 5 (cf. Lucret. v 338ff); Ar. *Pol.* 1269a4. Apollodoros (late 2nd c. B.C.) "And the whole of time is passing, just as we say the year passes, on a larger circuit." Sa. (1) 106. See also Pl. *Tim.* 39d and 22; *Krit.* 109de; *Laws* 676a and 781e; Cornford (2) 116f; R. G. Bury; Koster 55ff; Heath (2) index Great Year; van den Waerden (1); Mugler (1) 68f; *CR* 1955 46–8; Ar. *Meteor.* 339b27 and 1329b25; Philoponos *Nik. Isag.* i 1.

17. Ar. 223a29 on; Ross 91. Genesis: *An. post.* 95b. Time: *Phys.* 223b. Clocks: Sa. (1) 239f; Ar. *Phys.* 788, 36 on.

18. Ross 89f; *Met.* 1048b9–17; *Phys.* 219ff.

19. *Phys.* 225b20; SE *Pyrrh. Hyp.* iii 19 (136f); Simp. *Phys.* 788, 36 on; Sa. (2) 98–107. Simplikios says the term interval used by

Archytas, but he is probably citing ps-Archytas. Ar. *Phys.* 218b14, 221b7. Stones: Stob. *Ecl.* i 104, 7 and 106, 5.

SE *l.c.*; *Tim.* xx 37d on and 47a. School of Ainesidemos called Time corporeal "differing in nothing from being and the prime body"; others (Stoics), incorporeal. SE *l.c.* who argues for time's unreality. Also SE *Phys.* ii 216. Sea-changes and cyclical theory of Xenoph., Kirk (4) 178.

20. Sa. (2) 102; S. Pines 111f (Galen). Also Sa. (2) 104; Proklos *in Tim.* 271d; and Pl. *Tim.* 38b.

21. Zenon: Ar. *Phys.* vi 9; Sa (2) 89ff. Antiphon: Simp. *Phys.* 55, 7 and 55, 22; Plout. *Plat. quaest.* 1004b; *Vorsok.* ii. 594; Themist. *Phys.* 19, 6–17. Zenon: Gigon (1) and (2).

22. Eudoxos: Reymond (1) 133–6; Tannery (1) 96; Zeuthen 142; Heath (4) 4, 191, 193f.

23. *De caelo* 168; Heath (4) 198f. The tract on Indivisible Lines is not by Ar., attributed to Th.

24. Xenok.: Ar. *Phys.* 187a3; Simp. *Phys.* 138, 3–8; *de caelo* 665, 5f; Philopon. *Phys.* 83, 19f and 84, 15f. Sa. (2) 91f compares with the differential in maths. and theoretical physics occasionally used by Leibniz. See also SE *Maths.* ix 418–25; Heath (3) 11. Dem.: Sa. (2) 92f; Heath (4) 119f. Archimedes: Sa. (2) 91; for layers cf. Archim. *Method.* And Dem. on pyramid and prism, also with idea of infinite layers, Heath *l.c.*

25. Sa. (2) 95f: I summarise his argument, see his book for full account. Ar. *Phys.* 212a2–30; Plout, *de comm. not.* 1080e.

26. Itard 213. Berkeley: Struick 190 and 195f. Marx and Hadamard's position: V. Glivenko, *Post Znamenem Marksisma* 1930 (no 5) and *Unter dem Banner des M.* 1935 (no 9) 102–110. For Marx's position, cf. F. du Bois Reymond, *Die allgemeine Funktionentheorie* i 1882 141.

27. SE *Pyrrh. Hyp.* iii 19, 137 (Demetrios on Epikoureans). Proklos iii 29; Cornford (2) 104. Sen. *Ep.* xii 6–8.

West (2) 154–64, 190–2, tries to reconstruct the Herakleitan Great Year with cycles—*Dawn* (sea into earth, prester) sun = *Birth*: semen converted into body, soul. *Day*: sun steadily progressing: soul steadily growing. *Sunset*: sun turns back to sea =

15th year, *Puberty*, soul converted into semen. *Night*: advent of many small fires constantly turning back to sea: intermittent conversion of soul to semen *Dawn*, new sun = 30th year, *Marriage*: new soul thrown off. The Great Year has 10,800 years Censorinus)—360×30. Underlying this scheme is the pattern of tribal initiations.

V. Numbers and Atoms

1. Sa. (1) 27f; Milhaud (1) 88; Heron (4) 44, 13; Reymond (1) 122f; SE *Maths.* iv opening. Moral: Brunschvig 34.

2. Boutroux (1) i 5.

3. JL (2) 72f. Gnomon on sundial: Kirk (4) 99, 102f. Babylonian knowledge of Pythag. theorem: Price 12f; Neugebauer (3) 36; Sarton (1) i 73; Archibald *Isis* 1936 xxvi 79.

4. Ar. *Anal. pr.* 41a; *Pl. Theait.* 147d; Tannery (1) 52; Heath (6). Egyptians: Heath 111, Tannery ii 37–42; sch. Pl. *Charm.* 165e; *Laws* vii 819ac. Plato too had his doctrine of the golden mean or due measure, *to metron*, e.g. *Philebos.*

5. *De Is.* lvi; Griffiths 207f, 50–11. Pl. *Tim.* 50cd, *Rep.* i 546b (Adams *ad loc.*). *Teleios*: Heath (5) i 241; Guthrie (2) i 225. Eukleid's definition of a perfect number (7, *Def.* 22) was one "equal to (sum of) its own parts", i.e. all its factors including 1; but before him the term was used to indicate other properties. In general; Wedberg and R. M. Jones 95. *Panta* and *pente* have no etymol. connection. Griffiths for Egyptian alphabet.

6. Experiments: Sa. (1) 35f. Noise: Ar. *de caelo* 290b; *on kos.* 399a.

7. Philol. fr. D44B4 and B6, cf. B11.

8. *Met.* 1092b8 and 1090b5; Th. *Met.* 11, 6a19 (DK45, 2). Usener; Alexandros *in Met.* 827, 9; Kirk (4) 313–6; Raven (1) 101–11, 150–8. And Ar. *Met.* 1028b15, 1036b8. Mosaic: P. Fisher.

9. Pollitt 89; Ar. *Met.* 968a8; Philol. fr. 11 (Stob. Ecl. i 1, 3). Galen *de plac. Hipp.* v (Kuhn v 448), cf. *de Temp.* i 9. Lysippos also wrote a Kanon. Burkert CQ 1963 177: Orestes' footprint (Wil-

lamowitz Aisch. *Oresteia* ii *Das Opfer* 1986 174ff) sees medical theory in *Cho.* 183f; sees in print the theory of perfect proportions underlying the recognition.

10. Philon M., *Syntaxis* iv 1 (49, 20: Schoene 1893): Vorsok. 40B2. Pollitt 92 n111. *Para mikron* is also taken as "from a small unit", i.e. a module; "gradually", "little by little". Schulz; Stuart Jones 129; R. Carpenter 124. Pliny uses *quadratus*, citing Varro (Greek would be *tetragonos*), xxxiv 55, for the way P. threw weight on one leg; square-built, Carpenter 107. Ferri sees a ref. to balancing of 4 cola in a sentence through a paratactic or chiastic scheme. But it could be square as the perfect structure.

11. Vitr. iii 1, opening; he goes on to deal with units of measurement taken from human body: finger(inch), palm, foot, cubit, which are "grouped into the perfect number called *Teleon* by the Greeks".

12. Sa. (1) 41f; citing his examples.

13. Epikouros *On Nature of Things* ii 217–60; Farrington (2) ch. 11; GT (1) 312f; Kirk (4) 376.

14. Cic. *de fin.* i 6, 20. Mins on Marx's doctoral thesis. Marx says Epik. sees atomism, "with all its contradictions, as the natural science of the self-consciousness, which is an absolute principle under the form of absolute particularity," while for Demok., "the atom remains a pure and abstract category, an hypothesis which is the result of experience, not its animating principle, and which thus remains without realisation, just as it no longer determines real natural inquiry."

15. Sa. (1) 127; Ar. *Met.* 985b; GC 315ab. Lucret. ii 1007–22, cf. 760ff.

16. Aristox. 81; Philol. *in Pl. Phaid.* 85e–86; GT xx (1) 259 n22. Aisch. *Eum.*, 696–700 (693–7) Cic. *TD* ii 23; Ar. *NE* 1106b, "Virtue is a sort of middle attitude in that it aims at the mean." For Plato: Michel pt. ii, golden section, last ch. there.

    Pythags. in general: Minar sees P. as antidemocratic and links him with landed nobles, 111. Vlastos (2) 423, as originally opposed to nobles. Popular revolt: Polyb. ii 39. Archytas of Taras may have accommodated himself to democracy. See in general von Fritz 97ff; GT (3) 210ff; Delatte. Alkmaion: Hippok. *Anc. Med.* 16; Kirk (4) 232–8, 238; Aet. v 30, 1; Ar. *Met.* 985b23ff (on opposites); Iambl. *VP* 257; Vlastos (1) 364 n84.

Isonomia: Vlastos (1). Solon, fr. 3D; Demosthenes vi (2 *Phil.*) 25; xxiv (*ag. Timokr.*) 75f; Aischines i (*ag. Timarch.*) 4. Hdt. iii 80ff, debate. See esp. Vlastos, with Larsen, Debrunner, Ehrenberg (1), (2) 89, and (3).

Alkmaion as Pythag.: Ehrenberg (1) 535; Larsen 9; Zeller i 562; indefinite, K. Freeman 135. Not Pythag.: Vlastos; Heidel (3); Ar. *Met.* 986a26ff, Ross *ad loc.*

17. Leukip. Diels 67B2; Ar. *Phys.* 194b27; Medicals, Sa. (2) 51f.

18. Her. fr. 8; Parm. i 14, viii 14 and 37, x 6; Pl. *Rep.* 616c. See my *Helen* for discussion of Share-concept in fate-terms; also GT (1) 158, 170.

19. Wheel: JH (1) 588f; Cook *Zeus* i 255f; Clem. Alex. *Strom.* v. 242. Grammarian Dionysios the Thrakian wrote book, *The Interpretation of Symbolism that has to do with Wheels.* Prokl. *in Tim.* v 330. The Orphic imagery of soul in body seems to reflect aspects of the miner's dark buried life. Emp. 115, 124. 146f. Prometheus: GT (4) and (3) 319f for P. in penance in Hades; Emp. an exile from the abode of the blessed "because I put my trust in insensate strife."

20. Soph. *El.* 339f; GT (1) 356; Aisch. *Cho.* 77. Chance: GT 370f. *Anankē*, connected with fetters, *desmoi*, already appears in Hesiod and Semonides: *Theog.* 615; Sem. 7, 115 Diehl, if. Parm. B8, 14 and 31.

21. Gillespie cited by Medawar, *Listener* 3 August 1972.

VI. Air and Fire as Force

1. Anax., Guthrie (1) 59; Aisch. *Eum.* 568; Ar. *Prob.* 948b25. Tylor i 432f for refs. and more examples.

2. Homer: Otto 17; *Il.* xxii 161; Tyrtaios fr. 7 Diehl. Breathe out: Bichel 258, 232; Boehme 113, Obscure: Jaeger (2) 222n19. Out of mouth: *Il.* ix 409, xvi 856. Note *psychein*, blow. Anaximenes: Aet. i 3, 4, Anax. B2; Kirk (4) 158 breath-soul. Bickel (1) thinks Anax. revived the original sense of psyche as his own; Hdt. and Anaxagoras continue to use psyche for "life". Changes: Onians 23ff; Snell (2) ch. i.

3. Xenoph., Ar. *Phys.* iv 6 (215b22); *Pythag.Schule* B30. SE *maths.* ix 247; Sa (2) 2; Galen (Arnim) ii 787, cf. ii 446, Diels 24B4, cf. Alkmaion. Orphics: Ar. *de an.* i 5 (410b22): *Orph.* B11.

4. Plout. *prim. frig.* 951f, 949b, 951e. Ar. *Meteor.* 382b5; Duering (3) 81.

5. Clem. *Protr.* 68: i 52, 16 (St.); *Strom* v 103 (ii 394, 21 St.). Dem., B30. Diog., fr. B8, cf. Hippok. *Sacred Dis.* 19; Sa. (2) 10; Diels 64B2 and A5. Archytas: D47B1, explaining high or low pitch in notes in terms of speed.

6. Huxley (1) 93f; JL (3) 102.

7. Ar. *Probl.* xvi 8; xxv 1.

8. Farrington (1) i 33; Reymond (1) 26; Tannery (2) 88; J. J. Hall; Aet. ii 20–1 (DK12A21) and ii 25 (DK12A22); Kirk (4) 135f; Hippol. *Ref.* i 6, 4; Ps. Plout. *Strom.* 2 (DK12A10); from Th. Kirk (4) 131f for difficulties. Probably movement of sun on ecliptic was through winds, also declination of moon and wanderings of planets; east to west movements due to rotation of wheels in the planes of their circumference. In the fire-holes of Diogenes of Apollonia (Aet. ii 13, 5ff, Kirk (4) 438f) heavenly bodies are like pumice stone, "the breathing-holes, diapnoai, of kosmos." Other invisible stones, circling, sometimes fall.

9. Nozzle: Diels *Dox.* 25ff; Lloyd (4) 313ff doubts; AR iv 775–7; Il. xviii 372, 412, *automata* 468ff. West(2) 88 (cf. his note to Hes. *Theog.* 863) takes as bellows. *Physa*: *Il.* xviii 372, 409; Ar. *Pr.* 962a35, and Hippok. *Peri Phys.*; Strab. xiii 4, 11. Connected with verb meaning to puff, blow, distend, blow up or out: ? link with *physis.*

10. Aet. iii 3, 1f(DK12A33, 13A17); Tannery (2) 92 for lightning analogy; Kirk (4) 138f. Her. fr. D30. By20, W29; Clem. *Strom.* ii 396; Ar. *Met.* i 3 (984a7). Except in a broad way, and in astronomy, the regularity was not explored. Fr. D65, By24, W30 (*pyr* as *phronimon*). Aspects of fire: Heidel (1) 351, and rel. to Emp.

11. Fr. D31, By21, W32, cf. Aet. iii 3, 9(DK22a14).

12. *Meteor.* 371a15ff, 370b22; Hall 37. W. N. Shaw, *Manual of Meteorology* ii 356; Kahn 12.

13. Hes. *Theog.* 843ff, also 307, 869; *Il.* ii 782. JL (3) index Typhon. *Typhein*: to smoke or consume in smoke, burn slowly. See also Pherekydes here.

14. Arrian fr 3 (Stob. i236, 8ff W). Suck up: Aristoph. *Lys.* 973ff; Ar. *Meteor.* 371a14ff. Hall asks if Th. provides the metaphor; most unlikely. It certainly goes back to Milesian thinking. Witnesses: Plass, citing Clyde Orr 58f. *Tropai*: Kirk (3) 325–44. Xenoph., DK21A33; 12A27. Plout. *de Is.* 40, cf. Hdt. ii 11f, Plin. xxxi 7, 81, Wiedermann 74ff and Wellmann 253 n1; Griffiths 454. Earth-sea: Philon *Aet. mund.* 23–6 (derived via Stoics from Th.); Ar. *Meteor.* i 4 Primordial isle: Guthrie (1) 38.

15. Epik., C. Bailey (2) 71, cf. 308; Ep. ii 104f; on clouds, DL x 99; Lucret. vi 451–96. Zenon: DL vii 154. *On Kos.* 394a–395a. Streaks in the sky are called Torches, Planks, Jars, Bits.

16. Lucret. vi 423ff; Bailey (3) *ad loc.* Plin. ii 131–4; Sen. *NQ* v 13, 3; *Dox.* 275B2.

17. *Il.* i 481, xvi 350, *Od.* ii 427. Hdt. ii 42 (linking with *brontai*); Th. *Ign.* 1 (with *keraunos*). Taken to infer fire present: Burnet (2) 148f; Kirk (3) 325–31.

18. Sen. *NQ* ii 58; Kirk (3) 349ff; fr. D76, By25, W35; also D64. Cf. Plout. *On E at Delphoi* 292c and Her.'s idea of sun alternately kindled and quenched, *Dox.* 626.

19. Fr. D31, By23, W33. Diels takes it as continuation of the *prēstēr* aphorism, but the citations are widely separated: Clem. *Strom.* ii 396. *Dox.* 276. Anaxim., fr. 3, DK thought it not the original word. Sun condenses air: Dem., according to Th. *Sens.* 54. Ar. *Phys.* 203b7 says that all physicists who postulate an infinite primary stuff, but no separate cause of motion, hold it "enfolds all and steers all," Kirk (4) 114f.

20. Fr. D41, By19, W120; D32, By65, W119. Scholars: Kirk, Gigon; Cic. *ND* ii 15, 41; Pohlenz (3) citing Dion Prous. *Or.* xxxvi 56. Cherniss (2) 331 says Her. Fire is not a mere symbol of universal process, nor substrate persisting identical through qualitative changes; it is a token for exchange, yet involved itself in change. It seems the one existing phenomenon that is nothing but change.

21. Weapon: Gigon (2) 145f; Kirk (3) 355f. Orphics: Rheinhardt (2) 198f, *Hymn* 19. Cults: IG v 2, 288 (p. 58); Usener *Kl. Schr.* iv 471ff (*RhM* 1905 lx 1ff); RA (3rd s.) xl 388, Homs. Cf. Appian

Syr. 98; Galen *Plac. Hipp.* iii 8. Kirk (3) 355. Darting: *Il.* xv 80, Emp. B134, Pl. *Krat.* 412e–413c; West (2) 142–4. Her, fr. D16 (against *Il.* iii 277 etc.) and D28 (W 73 and 71). Zeus as Air: Philemon, fr. Kock (DK64C4). Dikē and Sun: West 158.

22. *Logos* in Her.: Kirk (4) 198f; GT (1) 275; fr. D50 and D72; Marc. Aur. iv 46; Asklep., *CAG* vi 25; Alexandros *CAG* i 45 and 670; Simp. *CAG* vii 621; Wheelwright (1) 121.

23. Moist: fr. D12, By41f, W44; Wheelwright 61–5. Also fr. D115, D118, D77; smoke, D7 and 98. West (2) 149–51.

24. *Kykeon*: fr. D125, By84, W50; Th. *de vertig.* 9; Walzer 154—visual images and motion of head. Posset, and tale of Her. drinking it: Kirk (3) 255–7; *Il.* xi 638, *Od.* x 234 (with honey). More dynamic than Pythag. idea of soul as attunement of opposites, held together in due proportion like strings of lyre: though that idea involves tensions. Pl. *Phaid.* 85e–86d, 61e and 98d. Burnet (3) 152; GT (1) 259f.

25. SE i 129 Log.; Wheelwright 69f. Intelligent: *noetos*. Exact opposite idea that soul is active when body sleeps. Pind. fr. 131; Aisch. *Ag.* 189–91 (179–81); Ach. Tat. i 6; Hippok. *on reg.* iv 86. Source probably Pythag. GT (1) 260. Fr. D73, "One should not speak or act as if asleep." D89, "The waking have one world in common; sleepers have each a private world." D21, "Whatever we see awake is death; asleep, is dreams" (lit. "is sleep"). Awake one is part of the dialectics of life and death, of shared reality. See Pl. *Laws* vii 800a.

26. Ar. *de an.* i 5 (411a7f); also 403a19. Simp. *CAG* xi 73; *on Kos.* 399b. Her. fr. D62, By67, W66. Note D5, By126, W66: "They pray to images as if they should talk to houses; for they do not know the nature of gods and heroes."

27. Fr. D103, By70, W109; Wheelwright 148 on W81, D114. Wheelwright 100f. Also fr. W80–3. *Peras*: Ar. *Met.* iv 17.

28. Suppl. *CAG* vii 621, 7ff; Ar. *de caelo* iii 5 (304a10ff).

29. Fr. D48, By66, W115. Wheelwright 100, 153.

30. Fr. D90, By22, W28; Plout. *On the E.* 988e; Kirk (3) 345; Diels *ad loc. Theog.* 371. Bury *Isthmian, ad loc.*; Willamowitz *Berlin Akad.* 1909 826f. Pythermos: Huxley (1) 112.

31. Solon i 16, 71; Theog. 189ff. Marx *Capital* 1946 i 129. Ar. *Pol.* i 9, 13 (1257b); GT (1) 233, on *Metron* and relation to *Moira.*

32. Alk. fr. 101D; Soph. fr. 85 and *Ant.* 295; GT (3) 352. Isok. viii 7; Hipp.*Aph.* i 3; Pl. *Rep.*563e, cf. Bacchyl. *Epin.* xiv 59; Aisch. *Ag.* 990. Also JL, *Helen.*

33. Fr. D125a, W96; D94, W122. Plout. *on exile* 604a, cf. *de Is.* 370d. Fr. D51, W117, By45; Wheelwright 153f. Fr. D8, W98. Her. attacks Pythags. in D40, By16, W128, see also D81, W136. Relation to Pythag. Hippasos: Ar. *Met.* i 984a7; *de Caelo* iii 303b12; DL viii 6; Wheelwright 114; Gomperz (1) i 146, 371; Zeller 195; R. D. Hicks, *ad loc.* DL; Prokl. *Comm. Eukleid.* Friedländer 426; Kirk (4) 231; *Souda* DK 143; Burnet (2) 94 n2; Iambl. *VP.*

34. Fr. D80, By62, W25–7; Simp. *CAG* viii 412; Ar. *EE* vii 1235a26; Philod. *Dox*, 548. "Seekers after gold dig up much earth and find little," D22, W4. "To extinguish *hybris* is more needful than to extinguish a fire," D43, W88, DL ix 2. *Philosophos* (D35, W3): term is thought to be Pythag. Clem. Alex. *Strom.* ii 421 (St.), iii 119 (Dind.). Dialectical concepts: Pl. *Soph.* 153c; Taylor 387; GT (1) 320.

    In general, there is certainly a link of Her. concepts of fire and those in Near East, esp. Zoroastrian: West (2) 165ff with refs. It is of importance to investigate these, but here what concerns us is the difference in the Greek ideas. West 173–85 (including Dikē and Sun); strife, 189f; Great Year 190–2; the idea of Prophet 192–6; Her.'s death 196–201.

VII. Pneuma as Force

1. Her. obscure: *On kos.* 396b20, *ho skoteinos*; DL riddling, *ainiktes*; Tertullian, *ille tenebrosus*; Clem., "He loved to conceal his metaphysics in the language of the Mysteries." Ar. *Rhet.* 1407b 13–5, punctuation; Wheelwright 12–6. "The hidden harmony is better than the obvious," D54; "nature loves to hide," D123. West (2) 111–3; GT (1) ch. 13; Kirk (3) 7–11. Her. saw unity of all knowledge. Relation to Parm., West 113; Vlastos (1) 341 n11; GT 297. Dedications: Wheelwright 115f.

2. Sa. (2) 1; Galen *de multit.* iii (Arnim ii 439f). The reader should read the whole of Sambursky's illuminating account of the Stoics.

3. Stratton 159–63. For Pythags. vision goes out, for Dem. effluence comes in (no doubt Emp. too). Ar. 437b23ff; *Dox.* 403; Vors. i 253; Aet. iv 13, 4. Anaxag, and opposites: Th. *Sens.* xxvii–xxxvii; Kleidemos on transparency, xxxviii; Diogenes and air, xxxix–xlviii; Dem. xlix–lviii. Stoics. DL vii 157; Aul. Gell. v 16, 2; Galen *Hipp. et Plat. plac.* vii (Arnim ii 865, Müller 641); Reinhardt 18ff; Cic. *ND* ii 85. Alex. Aphr. *de an.* 130, 15, and 131, 32. Sa. (2) 27f.

4. Plout. *Stoic. rep.* 1034d; Galen *de loc. affect.* v 1 (Arn. ii 876). Pneumatist medical school: held *pneuma* brought by inbreathing into left side of heart, where it was converted into natural vital and psychic *pneuma*, and distributed through the nervous system: Galen *nat. fac.* ii 6.

5. Stob. *Ecl.* i 166, 4 (Arn. i 99); Sa. (2) 7f; Plout. *Stoic. rep.* 1053f citing Chrysippos on physical states. Galen: Arn. ii 716; Philon; Arn. ii 458 (*Leg. alleg.* i 20; *quod deus* 35).

6. Sa. (2) 13; extereme dilution 13f; arguments of Alex. Aphr. and Plotinus, 15. DL vii 138–40, 85, 107f. Galen: *nat. fac.* ii 6 (97f) and iii 15 (211 and 213); central cavity or separate caverns 212, cf. cavernous tissue.

7. Sa (2) 19. Ar. on relative: *Met.* iv 15 (3 modes); quality, *ib.* 14 (4 modes); quantity 13.

8. Aet. iv 19, 4 (Arn. ii 425); Sa. (2) 23f. Arguments over terms: mechanism of presentation, *phantasia*; impression as seal or modification of psyche: SE *Pyrrh. hyp.* ii 70. Idea of circular waves also applied to sound.

9. Sa. (2) 29; Philon *de sac. Abel* 68 (Arn. ii 433). Simultaneous: Alex. Aphr. *de mixt.* 224, 24; Galen. *Hipp. et Pl. plac.* vii. *Hexis*: Sa. (2) 31; Galen and tensional motion, 32f; field of force, 35–40, with comparison with modern concepts, Descartes, Newton. Plout. 924d; Sa. (2) 42f. Pythags. (esp. Philolaos) seem first to assign "earthlike" qualities to the moon: Aet. ii 30, 1. Stob. *Ecl.* i 155, 24 (Arn. ii 471) uses terms *symphyia* and *syntaxis* to describe Chrysippos' *dynamis* of the *pneuma*.

10. Sa. (2) 55. Fate as *dynamis pneumatikē* 58; antecedent and operative causes 60f; human impulse to act as innate cause of motion in man 63; divination and induction 65–71; many-dimensional 77; failure to arrive at probability: Sa (3) and (1) 82; Clem. *Strom.*

viii 9. Stoic dialectic as a form of modern calculus of propositions: Lukasiewicz 77; Enriques (1) 30–46; Bochenski.

11. Simp. *Categ.* 257, 29ff and 264, 34f; Clem. *Strom.* viii 9; Sa. (2) esp. 85f.

12. Simp. *Categ.* 264, 54ff; Sa. (2) 85–8, the comparative propositional as a logical tool of inductive science; 93–8 calculus.

13. SE *Pyrrh. hyp.* iii 245–9, 199f, 207. The Cynics carried on this sort of total rejection of convention. Political relations: Cerfaux 167, 274, 306f, 320, 380, 405, 472; *ib.* 129 on idea of king as god above laws; Kaerst ii (2nd ed.) 306n3; Goodenough (1) 58; DL vii 122; *Stoic. vet. fr.* 617–9, 521, 690f; M. H. Fish; Tarn, *Alexander* 417–31; L. Delatte 141; A. Delatte 121; Köstermann, Cic. *Leg.* iii 1f; Chalkid. *in Tim.* 175; Stob. iv 7, 61.

VIII. The Sources and Bases of Greek Scientific Thinking

I wrote the earlier part of this book, including this chapter, before reading G. E. R. Lloyd's *Polarity and Analogy*. I have left the text of the chapter as it was so that it might serve as an independent approach to the questions of "imagery in Cosmological Factors" which he raises in his ch. iv. Similarly my chapter on Opposites should be read with his valuable analysis of "different modes of opposition" in ch. ii, and "theories based on opposites", ch. i. In my book these issues are considered only as the preliminary to grappling with Greek science, its virtues and its limitations. I have used Lloyd (4) in the notes.

1. See for example Heidel (1) 340f, 342, 346–8; West (2) 122f; Ar. *Meteor* 983b. Aet. i 3, 1 (Ar. *Met.* 983b18). *Dinē*: Heidel (4). Anaxim.: Simp. *Dox.* 476f. Her.: Ar. *de an.* 405a25; DL ix 9; *Vors.* 88, 10.

   Od. xxiii 188ff; Burford 199; Aymard (2) 31ff. Also *Od.* vi 58, iii 464–7. i 108, xx 160f, xiii 222f, xxiv 226, 242ff, xviii 366ff; *Il.* xiv 166 etc. Divine: *Il.* v 59–61, vii 220ff, xv 411ff, xxiii 85; *Od.* iii 425, vi 232–4, viii 373, xvii, 382–6, xix 56f. Demiourgos also called *Poiētes*, Maker, Poet, and he works with Pythag. proportions and numbers: *Tim.* 31c. Jesus: L. G. Rylands, *Evolution of Christianity* 1927 163f (*Mark* vi 3). Ar. *GC* 33ob. Plato and crafts: Schuhl (2) on *Gorgias* 303d, 506d (craftsman keeps the whole in mind), *Philebos* 55d (math. sciences superior), *Soph.* 120e, *Pol.* 279d. In general: Mondolfo and Espinas. Hellanikos *FHG* 112, 11: "Lemnian armourers were the first *demiourgoi* in Greece." Prometheus: Vernant (2) 427. No distinction of artist as Wise Man and as Technician before Plato: E. A. Havelock, *Preface to Plato*; A. E. Taylor 38–40; E. Schaper, *Prelude to Aesthetics* 1968 ch. 2; *Ion* 533e.

2. Ar. *Prostrept.* (Jaeger *Aristotle* 74f); *Meteor.* 381b7; PA 639b15ff etc. Hippok, *de victu*: Kirk (3) 21, 26 (Heraklean reminisces?). *Plants* ii 1 (822a): we have a poor translation of a medieval copy, itself a poor version from Arabic. Union: *henōsis*. Philon: *Alleg. Gen.* i 28–30: *energēsai*.

3. *Hylē*: *Phys.* 191a8–12, cf. *Met.* 1036a 9–12; Leclerc 114–21; *Met.* 984a 22–5. Growth: 337b, 334a on (wax making sphere or pyramid as emblem of way that any part of flesh could make fire or air). Building metaphors: Ar. *Phys.* ii 3 (195ab), i 7 (190b, 191a), ii 1 (193a) etc. Dubarle 218f. (Modelling in Pl. *Tim.* 50afl, 50c2; stamping, 50c5 and 4; fermentation 74cd. For the academic argument: Taylor on *Tim.*; Cornford (2); Skemp (1); Herter; Hackforth; Vlastos (6); Cherniss, *Ar.'s Criticism of Plato* 1944; 423ff. For technological imagery in Aristotle, Le Blond (1).

4. *On kos.* 399b. Statue: ps. Ar. *de mir. ausc.* 846a19; Plout. *Perikles* 31; Cic. *TD* i 13, 54; Val. Max. viii 14, 6 (Plout. and Cic. mention the picture). Keystone, *on kos.* 399b29: probably Stoic source, Lorimer (2) 99; Sen. *Ep.* 90, 32; God the Cutter, *Tomeus* in Philon, *Quis heres* 215ff, 188; but Goodenough (3) 132, 146f shows neo-Pythag. source.

5. Gudea: JL(2)7f; Albright (1) 225 and (2); A. Heidel JNES 1948 vii 98–105 etc. Anaxim.: Burnet (2) 77 n4; Guthrie (2) i 135ff. Nails: Aet. ii 14, 3 (DK13A14); O'Brien (3) 117n25. Rivets, fr. 33 (fig juice: *Il.* v 902f); O'Brien (1) 155f. Ar. *de gen. anim.* 747a on, 729a9–14, 737a12. 739b20, 771b18, 772a22. Four metals: Galen xv 32 Kühn, DK 31A34. Baker: Bignone (2) 27f; O'Brien (1) 156 n69. Copper and tin, fr. 92; *choanoi* for melting metal, fr. 96 vf. 84; welding fr. 34, cf. 96; hammered-out, fr. 30. O'Brien 155f; Lloyd (4) 30. If *petala* are metal plates, West's fine image (2) 106f and 100, of the leaves of the world-tree is spoilt.

Aristotle: *GA* 731a24; *PA* 652a31; *PA* 683a22 contrasts Nature and the smith who makes a various-purposed article. More building images: pile of stones on foundation-lines (blood as material of body): *PA* 668a16; vessels as framework, *PA* 668b24 and *GA*

764b30 (in this case, frame used by modellers). Stomach as manger (Pl. *Tim.* 70e; Ar. *PA* 650a19), diaphragm as partition-wall (*Tim.* 69e6, and Ar. *PA* 672b19). Use by Ar. of sculpture, architecture, medicine for the four causes: Lloyd (4) 287ff.

6. *Colour* 792b, 793b on, 795b, 797a, 827a. Touchstone, 793ab; Theognis 447–50; Pind, *P.* x 67. Simonides uses it of Time: Stob. *Ecl.* i 8, 15. *Col.* 827b, 795–6, 797b; 826b, green smoke; 816b, breath. For earth breathing: Heidel (1) 355; O'Brien (1) 166f in general; Pl. *Tim.* 77c8, 78e3, 70cd and 80d; cf. Ar. *Parv. Nat.* 312, breathing cools and irrigates the body.

7. Mixture: Jaeger (2) 157f, (4) iii 5ff. Galen, *nat. fac.* iii 7 (166–8), discussing traction, *holkē*, of stomach 168ff, and circular fibres; kidneys and traction 57f. Tin: Ar. *GC* 328b; size, 320a. Plout. *Cess. Oracles* xli. Natron the natural carbonate of soda got from Egyptian lake; kermes, JL (1). Alex. Aphr. *de mixt* 216a14ff; Stob. *Ecl.* i 54; Sa. (2) 121–3. Ar. *GC* 322a, also 321b.

8. *Thyreos:* Heath (4) 265, 348; Eukleid, *Phainom.* Other shapes: Heath 428, 444, 222, 72, 67, 223, 300f. *Od.* ix 240, 313; Prokl. *in Eukl.* i Deff. 3, 8; Disc: IG xi (2) 287, 3rd c. B.C. Eukleid and definition of line: Caruccio (1) 81f; Amaldi 42–4.

9. Reymond (1) 116–9. Samos: DL viii 1. Building: Sorel 198ff. Boutroux (2) 38–40. Descartes *Geometry* Bk. 2 (ed. Adam and P. Tannery vi 388). Plato: Mayerson 101. Sorel sees "parallel lines" as interpolation, as Greek geometers tried to avoid direct use of infinity; Eukleid should have defined the parallelism of the two lines as the function their equidistance. Rainbow interpreted by image in mirror: *On kos.* 395a.

10. Ear: Stratton 166f, 72, 84; Soph. *Aias* 17. Alkmaion: Stratton 88, 175 n6f; noise in shell? Eye: Stratton 70, 98; Ar. *de sensu* 437b; O'Brien (1) esp. 140–6, 161–7.

    Hippok. comparisons: Lloyd (4) 345–60: fever-yawn and steam from boiling cauldron; fever-sweat and condensation; membrane round seed in womb and crust on bread; humours of heated body stirred and separated as in milk-churning butter comes to top etc.; cold on body and figjuice curdling milk; sediment in cup and in the bladder; stone in bladder and iron-smelting; nutrition in plants and animals; drugs in the body likewise; rupture of foetus and bursting of corn-ear; tree deformed by lack of room, same with foetus; growing of embryo and tree; milk from breasts at pressure of unborn babe as oil squeezed from a soaked hide; mixture of fat and wax to illustrate theory of strong and weak seeds; relative evaporation of oil and water, comp. with bilious and watery humours in fever; flow of water between communicating vessels used to illustrate how humours travel in body; experiment with bladder and pipe to show how parts of the body are formed, etc. For more on Plato and Ar., Lloyd 360–80: curdling imagery 369.

11. SE *Maths.* vii 228, 372; *Pyrrh. hyp.* ii 10; Diels 64B2. Sa. (2) 25–7 and 10. Term goes back at least to Diogenes of Apollonia: "All existing things are modifications of the same thing." Acoustics: Cohen-D. 573.

12. JL (10) 389ff. *Typos*, hollow mould or matrix: Ar. *PA* 676b9. *Charaktēr*: Körte, Ussher 26ff.

13. Anax.: Aet. ii 20, 1 and 24, 2; ii 13, 7 (D12A21 and 18). Image is not of compressed air from bellows and fire from forge, as Sa. (1) 15 takes it. Parm.: Lloyd (3) 981 Aet. ii 7, 1 (DK28A37); Heath (2) 66ff. Ixion: Sch. *Od.* xxi 303; Hyg. *fab.* 33, 62; Serv. *ad Aen.* vi 601, *Georg.* iii 38, iv 484; Sch. Venet. *Il* i 266. Anaxim.: West (2) 99–102. Bark: Clem. *Strom.* 2 (D12A10). For efforts to explain bark-image, West (2) 89f, 95. Lid: Ar. *de caelo* 294b13; Kirk (4) 153; Pl. *Phaid.* 99b.

14. Ar. *de caelo* 295a13; Kirk (4) 334. Anaxag.: Hippol. *Ref.* i 8 (D59A42). Cic. *de fato* 42; A. Gell. vii 2, 11. Chain of physical events: Sa. (2) 61f. *On Kos.* 398b on throwing out from height a sphere, cone, cylinder; water-beast, land-animal, winged creature —all follow "natural" motion. Used, if not thought-up, by Stoics to illustrate idea of fate. Chrysippos (Cic., A. Gell.) seems only have cited a cylinder, which obeys its *formae volubilitas*, though thrower gave it *initium praecipitantiae*. Alex. Aphr. *de fato* 13 seems use same source as *On kos*. Latter applies it to single revolution that started off whole heavens.

15. *On kos.* 391b. Aristoph. *Th.* 54; Plout. *Aem.* 37. Diminutive in Delian inscr., 3rd c B.C., IG xi (2) 161a105. Lathe: Aisch. fr. 57, 3. Polos: Hdt. ii 109; Pl. *Tim.* 40c; Ar. *de cael.* 285b9 and b21; *Meteor.* 361a33. Sphere, Aisch. *PV* 429. Pole-star: Eratosth. *Kat.* 2; orbit, Pl. *Epin.* 986c. Crown of head: Hesych.; the head itself, Pollux. See JL(1)189–93 on spine and head. *Pelein*: for sense cf. German *werden*, cognate with Latin *vertere*. *Vertex*, pole: Cic.

ND ii 41, 105; Virgil *Georg.* i 242; whirlwind; Lucret. i 293, vi 444. vi 298; Liv. xxi 58, 3. *Aen.* xii 673; also crown of head or head.

16. Ar. *de caelo* 295a; Aet. ii 22, 1 (*petala*); Sa. (1) 188f. D13A7,4; D13A14; 13B2a; cap, 13A7,6. Kirk (4) 154, 156f. Cf. Dioskouric cap as hemisphere.

17. Ar. *GC* 334a; Diels fr. 54. Anaxag.: D59B4 and B12. Theory of similarity of composition: Ar. *GC* 314ab. *Pansperma*: Ar. *de caelo* 303a16; Pl. *Tim.* 73c.

18. Emp. DK82 (scaly crocodiles?); Ar. *Plants* 822b, 824b; Sen. *NH* iii 24; O'Brien (1) 156n68, though the comparison may be Seneca's. Imagery: O'Brien 156f, 176. Note Plato's fish-trap: *Tim.* 78b; Lloyd (4) 360.

19. Archimedes: Vitruv. *praef.* ix 9–12; Prokl. *Comm in lib.* i *Euk.* ii 3; Ar. *Plants* 823a. Thales. Ar. *de caelo* 294a; Sen. *NQ* ii 74. Ar. *Met.* 983b6; Kirk (4) 87–9, Bab. and Egyptian rels. 91f; Hölscher 385–91; Plout. *de Is.* 34. *Skaphē*: Heath (4) 270. In Homer, *Od.* ix 223, small milkpails, skiff in Aristoph. *Knights* 1315; sundial, Vitruv. ix 8, 1 etc. Bowl on fire-altar: West (2) 175f citing Duchesme-Guillemin, *RE* Suppl. ix 1585. Image of earth-ship or sun-ship led to idea of *logos* or *nous* as pilot, cf. *On kos.* 400b; so to idea of ship of state, Alkaios etc. See Lloyd (4) 276. Her.: Kirk (3) 263, 269ff, 276ff, 281, 285, 287, 290, 316, 334; commentators, esp. sch. Pl. *Rep.* 498a. Sun's circle: *koilos* (Reiske). Alex. *in Meteor.* 72 (Hayd); Olympiod. *in Meteor.* 136 (Stüve); DL ix 9–11, probably citing Th. Mimnermos: fr 10 Diehl, cf. Stesich. fr 6 Diehl. Kirk (4) 14f. JH (4) 370f. Anaxim. and lightning like oar-flash in water: Lloyd (4) 315–7.

20. Emp. DK100 (transl. J. Burnet); Ar. *Prob.* 914b9; Kirk (4) 341f. See O'Brien (1) for lengthy analysis, also Wilkens and Last CQ 1924 xviii; Lloyd (4) 324ff; Furley (2). Poros in *Il.* is riverford or ferry, in Hes. narrow part of sea; paths of sea, *Od.*; bridge. Hdt.; pathways in general, Aisch.; pore or body duct in Hippokratics, various physiological meanings. Water: Pl. *Symp.* 175d. More comparisons in Emp., Lloyd (4) 333–6: swung cup, sea as earth's sweat. See same for sterile mules; pun on milk and pus; fruit and eggs. The link of hair, leaves etc. may be meant to point to a functional likeness.

21. Spider: Her. fr. 67aD; Chrys. Arnim ii 879 (Chalkid. *ad Tim.* 220); Sa. (2) 24. Ar. *GC* 526a and 316b; *Phys.* 231a. Lucret. i 255ff, ii 112ff, 308ff; Sa (1) 115–7. Ar. *de an.* 403b–404a, cf. 405, goes on to Leukippos and Pythags. Melissos of Samos (Simp. *de caelo* 558, 2), follower of Zenon of Elea, refers to finger wearing away iron, but to deny validity of senses—against Anaxagoras?—but in his reduction-to-absurdity of plurality he opens way to atomists: Kirk (4) 304–6.

22. Thales; Hdt. i 170 and 75; DL i 26; Huxley (1) 94f; Dicks; JL (2) 66; Lloyd (4) 232f, 306–8; Guthrie (2) i 45–71; Kirk (4) 74–98. Albright (1) 229f thinks *naus* omitted after *phoinikē*, also Neugebauer (3) 143, 147ff. Emp.: Ar. *GC* 333a. Her.: Kirk (3) 48ff, verb *trephontai*, basic sense of thicken or clot. Rotation, Kirk 54. See fr. 2 in Kirk 57–64 and 33ff; SE *maths.* vii 113. Ionia: archaeology show advanced mercantile developments: Albright (3) 144–64 (4) 269f; Hanfmann (1) and (2). JH (4) 532–4 for Themis and Physis, but she sees only the moral aspects.

Equal: *Od.* viii 43ff, xi 337, xiv 178 etc., Hes. *Theog.* 126, 719–25; Stokes; Cornford (4) 15f; Vlastos (4) 168. Probably there was a sense of equivalence between the visual horizon and the base of the sky's hemisphere. Emp.: Vlastos (4) 158–61; Ar. *GC* 333a19–34, *Meteor.* 340a14. Emp. fr. B17, 20 (Love; length); Tannery (2) 314 overstresses spatial aspect, cf. Parm. fr. B8, 19, 8, 44 (spatial and dynamic eqilibrium) Cornford 64, cf. *Il.* xv (the 3 gods). Nestis: Willamowitz (2) i 20. Time: Ep. fr. B17, 27 (oath, cf. Pind. O. vi 65; Soph. *Aias* 660ff). Ar. *Met.* 1975b6–7.

Parm.: Vlastos (4) 161–4. Anaximandros: Ar. *de caelo* 295b11; Vlastos (4) n 52 and 57 and pp. 168, 173, for rels. to *apeiron* and *kosmos*. Note Pl. *Symp.* 188e, assumption that injustice or encroachment equals destruction. Her.: Vlastos (4) 167, 175. Bias: DL i 88; Plout. *Mor.* 154d, Vlastos (4) n112–4 and n51. For the Oath in Emp. as a social contract, Lloyd (4) 218.

Exchange: Vlastos n158; Pind. *N.* vi 9, *P.* iv 226; Hes. *Theog.* 749; Pl. *Phaid.* 71–72; Philon. *incorr. mund.* 109; Pl. *Tim.* 79e; Ps. Ar. *Mech. prob.* 803a13; *Meteor.* 355a28. Demokritos loses interest in equality: Vlastos 178. Medical: Vlastos 158f, cf. Pl. *Symp.* 188a, *Laws* x 906c; DL viii 26. Eur. *Suppl.* 406. Analogies of city-state and individual: Pl. *Rep.*—Lloyd (4) 396f; Ar. *Pol.* 1295a40f, *MA* 703a29ff, cf. *GA* 771a11ff. So we get the full set of micro-macro-cosmic systems: Lloyd (4) 267.

23. *On kos.* 400b; Albright (1) 230; Babylonians, van Waerden (2). Classification, Weyl 286. Brother of Alkaios captured by army

of Nebuchadnezzar, Dec. 604, later went home to Lesbos: J. D. Quinn. *Bull. Amer. Schools Orient. Research* lxiv 1961 19f.

Her.: Wheelwright 140; Kirk (1); Teichmüller 2ff and others stress only physical aspect as if Her. merely carried on idea of primary stuff. *Archē*: Lloyd (4) 230–2; Zeus as reflecting the Homeric King, 196–9.

24. Galen *nat. fac.* 58, 55f, cf. 67, evaporation; nutriment 20; slaves that thieve, bold or abashed, 66f.

25. Aiōn: West (2) 158f, 192; Taylor on Pl. *Tim.* 91a2–4; Onians 200ff; Eisler *Weltenmantel* 507; *Vishnu Purana* i 2; Great Year: West 191. Vulgarisation of theme, man as plaything of gods: Pl. *Laws* 644de, 803c on, etc. Alkman *Melici* 58, Anakreon *ib.* 398.

Her. fr. W24; JL (10) 51–5; Ar. *HA* ch. 21 Plout. Q. *Symp.* 680a; Cic. *de fin.* iii 16 (54). Sa. (1) 176–81, (2) 80. Pl. *Phaid.* 92d. cf. *Theait.* Simp. *Phys.* 325, 24. Names: Pollux ix 99, 117; Eustath. *Il.* xxiii 88; Suet. *Aug.* 71; Mart. xiii 16. Throws: Plaut. *Curc.* ii 3, 78; Cic. *de Div.* ii 59(121). Mart. xiv 14; Euboulos fr. 57 M. Invoke god or mistress: Plaut. *Capt.* i 1, 5; *Curc.* ii, 3, 77–9. Divination, Suet. *Tib.* 14. Treatises: Ov. *Trist.* ii 471ff; Suet. *Claud.* 33.

26. Budge 139–44: BM Pap. 10188; Pritchard 5; Faulkner *Pyr. Texts*, Utterance 527, cf. 1248; *Book of the Gates*. Cf. Chronos and his spilt seed in Pherekydes: Kirk (4) 57, 59.

27. Hymn: Budge 259–61; Lepsius *Denkmäler* vi 118; Slab: BM 797; Read and Bryant, *Procs. Soc. Bibl Arch.* xxiii 160–87, xxiv 206–16. 300; Erman, *Sitz.d.k. preuss. Akad.* Berlin 1911 916–50, etc. P. Montet (2) 150–2. Dwarfs: Montet 102f; Hdt. iii 37 (Kabeiroi as Ptah's sons and dwarfs). Budge, 149–62 and Pap. of Ani 343. 114, 120 etc. Temple of Imhotep, Imouthes, identified with Asklepios, near Memphis.

28. Bes-Pantheus: Derchain (1) Puech *RHR* cxx 116f; Ste Fare Garnot, *Religions of Antiquity* 17. Identified as Homerty (von Bissing); Aion (Festugière); Horos and Sopdou (in naos of Saft el-Henneh); Min-Horos or Amun. Lore of intaglio cutters: Derchain (2) and (3) intro. 17; Derchain (1) 34 for further pun on whip (crack, ejaculate).

On kos. 397b–398ab, cf. 399b, image of trumpet call in war sounded in camp and setting off multiple actions: so the cosmic unseen force. *Logos* and world-process, Pl. *Rep.* 500c; Plot. ii 3, 13; iii 8, 2. Stoics: Zenon, Arnim i 24; Chrysippos, *ib.* ii 264, cf. 169, iii 4. M. Ant. vii 53. See LSJ Dict. for large amount of sub-meanings developed. There is perhaps not much to be said for connection of logos with Bab. word for water, which meant originally voice, loud cry; Thales would then have got from East his water principle: S. Langdon *J. R. Asiatic Soc.* 1918 433–49; *Isis* 1921–2 iv 423.

Tongue: Zilsel (4) 22.

IX. The Dangerous Moment

1. Willamowitz (1) 413–39; Noble 102; JH (1) 190; Rose 220; Pollux; Philostr. *Vitae Soph.* ii 12. Texts: Willamowitz (3); Allen v; Noble 106f; R. M. Cook (1) and (2); *Souda* sv Homeros. Nature of poem: begging songs, Noble 106; Burford (3) 122. Scansion: short first syllables in *kalos* and *technēi*, lines 4, 10.

2. Discussion of the wares: Noble 108–110; Schwyzer (2) no 7483; Edgar no 111 pl. v; dates Cook (2); "kanasthon" on sherd from Naukratis, lettering dated second half 5th c. Artemon: Meisterhans 81f, 4b and n 703; Schwyzer (1) 532, 2 and 533, 36. Description: Pollux x 85f; Cook (2), Noble 110.

3. Grind: Leutsch i 444. no 48; ii 199 no 85; Noble 111f. Vulcan: Burford (3) 167f; Delcourt (1) 212, 211n3. Craft-fraternities: see *Telchines* in Roscher. Ar. *Meteor.* iv 380b6ff, 383a14ff. Porch: Noble fig. 232. Medieval copyists seem to have thought P. the name of a female fire-demon.

4. Circe: *Od.* xiii 87; *Il.* xxii 139; Aisch. *PV* 857; Ar. *HA* 206a18; Oppian *Kyn.* i 64. Plural *kirka* as spells: P. Mag. Lond. 121, 299; as buds or sprouts of black poplar, Hesych.; rowing as motion back and forwards, *kōpolatēs*, Hesych., Phot. *Kirkos* as kind of wolf: Opp. iii 304 (? circling prey). Lykos Wolf was one of the Telchines, and Apollo assumed wolf-form to destroy the T. Circe's island Aia seems a version of the primal rounded isle in Ocean.

5. *Il.* xviii 599–601. Maze-dance, JL, *Helen.* Invention: Richter 89f. Wheel: Noble figs 73, 78, and p. 54f; Beazley (1) 97–9 and (2) 571 no 75. R. Green suggests wrongly they work on metal. Apollod. *Lib.* ii 5, 4; Eleusis, Willamowitz (2) 396 n1 and 396f, Malea. Thera: IG xii fasc. 3 no 360. Daktyls: Delcourt (1) 166; fire 167; evil eye 170. JH (4) 370, 403. Centaurs: *Il.* ii 741 and i 269 (*phēr*), *Od.* xxi 303. Satyrs: JL (3) 356. Kyklopes: Hes. fr. 178; Burford (3) 195; JL (3) sv index. *Kēres*: JL (3) 195; JH (1) 172; Stesich. makes two kinds.

6. Apollod. *Lib.* ii 5, 4; 5, 11. Cheiron linked with Thetis in prophecy about her son-to-be. Apollod. iii 13, 5 (prophecy also attributed to Themis and Proteus. Both Cheiron and daughter of Proteus give information about shape-changing. Aisch. *PV* 908ff; sch. *Il.* i 519; Q. Smyrn. v. 338ff; Hyg. *fab.* 54 and *PA* ii 15. Clan: Pl. *Symp.* iii 1; Müller, *Orchom.* 249. Birth of Athena: brought out by Hephaistos (Pind. *O.* vii 35) Prometheus (Eur. *Ion* 455), Palamaon (sch. Pind. *O.* vii 35) another name of Hephaistos—with hammer or double axe. Prometheus in general: JL (3), Vernant (2). Tale of birth: Hom. *hymn* 28; Pind. *l.c.* with sch. (Hermes also appears): L. Malten RE viii 313, 43; Apollod. i 20; Rose *HB* 108f. Satyrs and Korē: JH (1) 69; Epimetheus, 281 fig. 71.

7. Oven: Conze (2); Furtwängler Taf. i and ii, p. 110. Masks: JH (1) 188f; JL (4). Conze sees simple apotropaic forms; Furtwängler sees Kyklopes; F. Mayence BCH 1905 373. Satyr-centaur: Nonnos xiii 43; JH (1) fig. 30. Attic vase: Noble 73 fig. 230; JH (3) 9 fig. 1. Types: Walters p. xix. Braziers and cooking utensils: B. A. Sparkes *JHS* 1962 121–37. Names on inscribed examples: Hekataios, Nikolaos, Philostratos. Italian potters of 16th c. lighted kilns "always in the blessed name of God" or with "prayers offered to God with all the heart", or "in the name of Jesus Christ: Pa. 158 n 91, citing Piccolopasso.

8. Sch. *Birds* 346; Pollux vii 108 (*geloion ti*, Latin *turpiculum*); Delcourt (1) 113; Aristoph. fr. 51; sch. *Clouds* 436; Phryn. *Anecd. Bekk.* 30, 5; *Life of Aisop* iii 12; Aristoph. *Wasps* 566, 1401; *Birds* 651. Lobeck 970ff; O. Jahn (1) 67; Baumeister, *Denkmaler* i 76 fig. 76; Seligmann i 273–337 and ii 118–88 (apotropaia). Graffito drawing: Burford (3) pl. 32.

9. Hdt. iii 37; Delcourt (1) 112; Furtwängler (2). *Hymn* 67: JH (2) 26. Rhythmic swing, *amboladis*: sch. says "in succession or alternately", but sch. Pind. N. x 62 says "not continuously", *amblēdēn, amboladēn*. Note *Il.* xxi 364; Hdt. iv 181 suggests splintering, with *zeionta*.

10. Welsford 61 and ch. 3; Wace; Yeames; Allardyce Nicoll 47–9; Suet. *Aug.* 83 etc. Gorgopis: Delcourt (1) 142f—see the whole of this book for rel, of magic and craft. Th. *Char.* xvi; Soph. *Aias* 450; Delcourt 195 (statue with eyes of precious stone); Eur. *Ion* 987; *Hel.* 1315; Aus. *Mos.* 308–10, *magico perlitis fuco*. Temple: Frazer (1) ii 124 (against thesis of temple of H. in ps.-

Theseion); Picard (1) 382; (2) 138; (3) ii 74 and 572; IG i (2nd ed.) 1, 371; Delcourt 191f. Incrusted eyes: Picard (3) i 184, 206. Note Falcon of Horos in black granite with white inlaid eyes: BM 1226, about 1250 B.C.

11. In general Roscher (despite meteorolog. thesis); Paus. ii 22, 4; iii 18, 2; *Il.* v 128; Plout. *Lyk.* xi. Elis: Farnell (1) i 264, 315 (thinking that as N. she absorbed hero Narkaios in local legend son of Dionysos and Physkoa); Paus. ix 19, 1; v. 5, 17; Stob. *Flor.* 38, 56. Tales: Paus. ix 34, 2; ps. Plout. *Little parall.* xvii 309 and *Q. Gr.* iii; Inscription: CIG 5939.

12. Statue: JH (1) 192f; Homolle; Burford (3) 11 and pl. 1. Caelian: JH (1) 196f, cf. relief on back of a Corinthian marble, *JHS* vi 1885 31; modern, Tuchmann, *Mélusine* 1885. Eros and mask of Seilienos: Deonna (6). Masks in general: Kerenyi (1) and (2); Guntert 114ff etc. At Sousse a threshold is protected by a phallic fish and two snakes menacing evil-eye: Picard (4) 93; Deonna (2) 131. Defecation and evil-eye: Deonna (1) 93. Corinthian pot: Pernice 75; JH (1) 191f.

13. Potters: Burford (3) 170; Raubitschek no 48. High status of some, Burford 150; dedication of potter Kittos, early 4th c., IG ii (2nd ed.) 4921a. Patroness Athena: Soph. fr. 760, 844; Paus. i 24, 3. With Hephaistos: Pl. *Laws* 920e, *Symp.* 71.

14. Moira etc. see JL, *Helen.* JH (1) 188; *Od.* xi 633. Rhodian plate with gorgonheaded *potnia theōn*: JHS 1885 pl. lix. Triad of Gorgons and Graiai. Island gems (Boardman) 50f, 131, 135, 157 gorgons; centaurs 54f, 131–6 etc.; Medousa 135.

15. TC: Louvre AO 12475 said to be from Ashnunnah: Larousse, *Myth. gén., myth. assyro-bab.* 61; in general S. Smith *AAA* 1924 107ff; R. D. Barnett 147. Seal: Barnett. For Sparta, JL *Helen.* Homer knows one gorgon, cf. Eur. *Ion* 989; but Hes. *Theog.* 278 has three living in western ocean (i.e. other-world), later put in Libya. Serpents: *Shield Herak.* 233; Aisch. *PV* 794, Cho. 1050, wings and bronze claws, huge teeth, cf. Paus. v. 18, 1. Tradition in Athens of head of Medousa buried under mound in agora: Paus. ii 21, 6; v 12, 2. Lock of her hair: Paus. viii 47, 4; Apollod. ii 7, 3. For Perseus: JL (8).

16. Lipari: Theok. iii 8. Lemnos: Delcourt (1) 41; JL (3) esp. 87, 94f, 175, 177f, 184, 188f, 191; Aitna, ib. 43–6 as cosmic centre.

Temple of H. at Athens was small till mid-5th c. when he got large Doric building, almost certainly the biggest he had anywhere. The site was previously inhabited by potters and bronzesmiths. Was he celebrated as god of fire or god of craft? In any event the fire was seen as transformative force in craft. Dissmoor 129; Homer Thompson *Hesperia* 1936 126. Prometheus: JL (3) 175–80; Vernant (2). Servius *ad ecl.* vi 42 speaks of P., "after creating man", with Minerva's help "ascending to heaven and there lighting a torch at the Wheel of the Sun".

17. Daktyls: Delcourt (1) 165–70; JL (3) 190f; JH (4) 50–2. *Labrys*: see JL *Helen*; JH (4) 177, 58f, 61f, 115, 130. Bullroarer: JH (4) 61ff; Frazer GB (2nd ed.) iii; A. Lang 39–41, 31–5; Marrett; Gennep (1) pp. lxviii ff; Paus. viii 29, 1; Appian *Syr.* 58.

18. Tubilustrium: Ov. *Fasti* v 725; doubted, Wissowa, Warde Fowler. Altheim (1) 187–90; (2) i 39; Delcourt (1) 211. Tale of magical recipe against thunder, made of onions, hair, little fishes; Faunus and Picus taught it to king Numa: see further Delcourt 210f. Relation to Prometheus in the duping of the high god. Ravaging fire: Delcourt 210 n1. Volcanus with hammer and anvil on Roman-Gallic relief: Burford (3) pl. 34.

19. Aisch. stresses that Prometheus represents *all* crafts, though special emphasis is put on fire: Vernant (2). Strabon x 473–4, xii 564; Jeanmaire (1) 182; Hdt. iv 76. Division of labour: Pl. *Protag.* 320e ff; *Rep.* ii 369 and iv 428; *Laws* viii 846; *Alkib.* 127ab (Eris). Aisch. *PV* 45–50. Ar. *Pol.* ii 1261a35, vii 1329a35, iii 1280b20ff; Schuhl (1) 10–4. Xen. *Oik.* vii 22 craftsmen are like women (work inside and often sit), cf. Ar. 1343b28; 1252a30ff. Parm. fr. B6, 5–6, B8, 54; Aisch. *PV* 447f, cf. Theog. 140, 1078; Vlastos (4) 163.

20. Vernant (1) 27ff; Gouldner 216ff; *Rep.* 436; Finch in general. Each man has predestined job, *Rep.* 374b, cf. 370bc; contrast Ar. *Pol.* 1260b; but he speaks like Plato, 1252b. Note *Od.* xiv 228. Division of labour in Nubian mines: Diod. Sic. iii 12, 14. Xen. *Kyrop.* viii 2 notes lack of specialisation in small town. In mock epic Margites was a Jack of all trades good at none; contrast *Exodus* xxxi 1, 11; xxxv 30ff; G. Dumezil *Tarpeia* 208–46.

21. Pl. *Pol.* 299d–300a; *Rep.* ii 370b; Ar. *NE* ii 1104a9, *kairos*, Vernant (1) 34. Note Latin *neg-otium*: business as the negation of leisure (culture).

22. Vernant (1) 35f; Ar. *Pol.* 1257a6ff.

23. JL (7) 242f; *AP* ix 418; Finley (1) 36; Moritz 131; Schuhl (1) 19f, 87.

X. Magnets

1. Campbell Thompson 9. DL i 25; Kirk (4) 96; Ar. *de an.* 405a19; Huxley (1) 98; Burnet (2) 50 is not right.

2. Emp.: Alex. Aphr. *quaest. et sol.* ii 23. Dem.: G. H. Clark in Nahm; Santillana (1) 163–5. Samothracian rings: Plin. xxxiii 23; Isid. *Orig.* xix 32–5 golden *sed capitulo ferreo*; JL (3) for ring and Samothracian mysteries, Prometheus, 178. Pores, *viae apertae.*

3. Pl. *Ion* 533dff; Warry 69–72; *Tim.* 80c; Epik. fr. 293. Heraklean *pathos* was elephantiasis; herakleia, huge drinking cup. Griffiths 78–82, 217, 522f; JL (8) ch. 12; Wainwright 6, 32; thunder, 10, 22, 77. Plin. xxiii 64 and Thorndyke (1) i 213 on attraction-repulsion.

4. Cic. *de div.* i 39; Lucret. vi 906ff, sea welling up through fresh water (Strab. 754, Plin. ii 227).

5. Plin. xx 1, xxviii 41, xxxvii 15; xxiv 51; xxxix 17; sympathy, xxviii 84 and 187; xxxvii 59. Heraklean, xxxvi 126; discovery ii 211—Burford (3) 191ff, first discoveries. Magnesia: some 25 miles ENE of Smyrna. Mountains, Plin. ii 211, xx 2. Folklore, xxxvii 59, 55, 60f, repulsions attributed to other metals, medical value of adamas against distraction; theamedes xxxvi 130. Ethiopian: Sil. Ital. iii 265. Also, Th. *Lap.* 41; Athen. ii 112f; *Souda* sv; Alex. Aphr. *Prob.* 2; Porphyr. *de abs.* iv 20. Also, Diosk. iv 147; Ach. Tat. i 17; Plin xxxvi 127; Strab. iv 703; Pl. *Tim.* 80c; Louk. *Imag.* i; a throw of the dice, Hesych. Fused with glass, probably for dark tint, Plin. xxxiv 147, xxxvi 192. False haematite, Diosk. v 147; Galen xii 204 K. Augustine *CD* xxi 4–6 (*PL.* xli 712–6).

6. VAT iii 46f; Ktesib. fr. 57, 2 (C. Müller); Heliod. viii 11; Athenaios iii 112f (Koch ii 192); Ach. Tat. i 17f—goes on about marriage of streams crossing salt sea; love of land-viper and sea-snake. Claudian: JL (9) 150–2. Aus. *Mos.* 311ff; Plin. vii 125; xxxiv 148; H. G. Evelyn-White, Loeb Auson. i 249, term used is agate,

achates. *Souda*, sv *magnites*. Th. *Lap*. 41; Eichholz 115. Gems: A. Jacob in *DS Dict*. iii 937. List in Derchain (3) 345–50.

7. *Lithika* 317ff; Thorndyke i 581, *De Imp. et Rebus Gestis Justiniani* 1869 149. Later: Thorndyke 750, *Liber Lapidum* of Marbod bishop of Rennes; against melancholy, 756, Constantius Africanus; draws out iron nails from passing ships 756; magnet and vacuum, recipe for gold, *Mappae Clavicula* 766; Aldhelm's Riddle 636; also 646, 657. Hippol. *Ref*. iv 39.

8. Paris Pap. 1716ff; Nock (1); JL (3) 149, 187f; Dieterich 6f. Pneuma, cf. Paris Pap. 2631; Parthey ii 18; Kroll, *Ph*. liv 365; J. Röhr, *Ph*. Suppl. xvii (1), 94. Aphr. on seal: Nock 154n3. Wax Eros: P. Leid. v 1, 14 (794f). Nock for more details. Partridge sacred to Aphr., Cook *Zeus* i 727; *paideros*, Paus. ii 10, 6, Frazer *ad loc*., Diosk: says it's another name for akanthos; Plin. thought it Greek for chervil, but adds it is a kind of smooth-leaved akanthos. Demetrios Phaleros dyed his hair with it; phallos-bearers in theatre wore a sort of bonnet made of it and creeping thyme with myrtle wreath, etc.

9. Warren Mag. Pap., see A. S. Hunt for details. Peonies: *selonogona*. Phantom: *phasma*. Alchemy: Leyd. pap. no 65, pp. 86, 232; M. Berthelot, *Coll. des anc. alch. gr*. 1887–8. Krater: *Corpus Hermet*. iv 11. Hermogenes: C. T. Crutwell, *Lit. Hist. of Early Christianity* 1893 i 241.

10. *Tetrabib*. i 3 (15): Plout. on garlic, Thorndyke (1) i 213. Galen *nat. fac*. (Loeb. A. J. Brook): drugs i 12 and 14 (47, 55); ropai, ii 3 (80); artist i 14 (46); Asklepiades i 14 (44–56); *technē* i 46, 81, 98, 29f, Praxiteles ii 3 (83–5); *holkē* used for attractive force (in fact, tractive), quality attracted 55, 42, 30.
11. Alex. of Aphr. 72, 17; Sa. (4) 119f; Philoponos *Phys*. 403, 22. Magnetite belongs to a group of minerals with formula corresponding to 72·4% iron, hence value as iron-ore product.

12. Simp. *de caelo* 264, 25 (73f); *phys*. 1347, 3 (71). Themist. 234, 27; 235, 8 (71f). Simp. *phys*. 1348, 36 (72), 1349, 26 (72). Sa. (4) 71ff, and 102, idea of action at distance growing up in neoplat. circles.

13. Amber. *Il*. v 513, xix 39. Emp. 22, 2. As alloy, *Od*. iv 73, amber *Od*. xv 480, cf. xviii 296; Virg. *Georg*. iii 522. AR iv 603ff, cf.

Diod. v. 2, 3; Hdt. iii 115; *Od.* iv 72–5, xviii 294f, xv 459ff; Th. *Lap.* 16; ps. Ar. 81 and 102 *de mir. ausc.*; Hyg. *fab.* 40, 44. Spekke, pl. vi, also for ancient texts, charms 34f, urine of lynx (piercing-eyed) 35. Soph. tears of birds, meleagrides, named after Meleagros, in India. Statue of Augustus, Paus. v 12, 7. Amber axe in Vistula, first half of 2nd millennium B.C.: E. Sturms, *Die Neolith. Plastik*; Spekke 7. Statuette of Baltic amber in Assyria (9th c.), Spekke 27; amber-beads in foundations of temple towers, Assyria, Asher, Babylonia; mentioned in Assyrian jewellers' lists dating back to first millennium B.C. Roman ladies used amber balls to cool hands.

14. Partingdon, 87p9, 103 n113, 314, 158 n93–4.

15. I. Richmond in J. S. Wacher, *Civitas Capitals of R.B.* 1966 83f; RCHM *Eburacum, R. York* 1962 pl. 68. Exported to Cologne, not worked there. Plin. xxxvi 34–6 (c. Alb. Magnus *de mineral.* ii); magic, Plin. xxv 5, on redhot hatchet; if it doesn't burn, things will happen as wished. Solin. *Coll. rer. mir.* xxii 11.

16. Claudian: Shorter Poems xlix (xlvi). Cic. *ND* ii 50; Varro *LL* v 77 (M); Plin. ix 42, 67 (143), xxxii 1, 2 (7). See my edition of Priestley's *Memoirs* 23 for experiments; Berry ch. 6; *Philosophical Trans.* 1776 lxvi (read 18 Jan. 1775) pt. i 196–225; Walsh *ib.* 1773 461–77; J. Hunter 1777.

    More on Magnets: Gilbert in his book of 1600 cites in Bk ii, ch. 3, several ancient authors: Aristotle, *de Anima*; Anaxagoras; Epikouros; Plato (*Timaios*); Galen; Lucretius; Ploutarch (*Quaestiones Platonicae*); also the latter on amber in ii ch. 2; in i ch. 6, Plato's rings. Mottelay, edition of Gilbert, 75, speaks of the ancient lynkourion as the tourmaile or topaz, citing Davy, *Mem. Sir Hum. Davy* 1836 i 309, and takes it as "gold magnet" of Heliodoros and the stone of Philostratos (also the stone in the ring of Gyges). For *lynkourion* (urine of lynx) see Disok. ii 81; SE *Pyrrh.* i 119; Hesych. sv *elektron*; Str. iv 6, 2; Th. *Lap.* 28; IG xi (2) 161B49 (Delos, 3rd c. B.C.), and 2 (2nd ed.) 1534, 100; Str. iv 5, 3; Aet. ii 35.

XI. Mechanics

1. Od. xxi 42. Eupalinos of Megara under tyranny of Polykrates: Farringdon (1) 39f; Hdt. iii 60, cf. vii 22; Paus. i 40, 1; Plin. vii

195; for eastern precedents, J. Goodfield. Archytas: Aul. Gell. x 12 (I do not discuss here his "bird"); sound, Vitruv. v; *Clouds*, act 2, sc. 1; Sen. *QN* i 6, 5. In general: Milhaud (2) 257; Diels (1) 34; R. Berthelot; Reymond (1) 178–83 etc. My main debts are to Drachmann.

2. Olympia: Paus. vi 20, 14; Sostratos, Burford (3), E. J. Wisemann, *R. Spain* pl. x, 102; Plin. xxxvi 83; CIL ii 761; Boat-bridge, Hdt. iv 87f; Burford (3) 172. Tyre, Diod. xvii 43, 1; Diades, Arr. *Anab.* ii 23, 1f; Diels (1) 30; Tarn 107; Marsden (2); Athen. Mech. W10, 10ff. Protogenes: Plin. xxxv 101 "till his 50th year"; Pollitt 176–9.

   Ketsib.: Dr. (5) only one of the name; Susemihl 734ff. Archimedes: Dr. (8) and (12). Also Edelstein (1) 579f; Rhem; Plout. *Q. Conv.* viii 2, 1 (718c); Ar. *Pol.* 1340b26. Aristox.: Geffken (2) 92; Cohen-D. 2, 5, 195, 183. Use hands: Blüh. Contrary view, Farrington (1) i 45, 114, Zilsel (2) 329. Inventions: Rostovtseff (1) 124, Lovejoy-Boas 200, 382ff. Heron (Cohen-D. 184) says mechanicians had to learn at least one craft. Oreibasios: Dr. (1) 171–85.

   High esteem of *technai* in general in Hippok. treatises (late 5th, earthy 4th cs.), e.g. *VM* i; *CMG* i 36, 7 and i 9, 2; *de arte* i Heinimann (2); Festugière (4) pp. xv ff.

3. Duhem (2) i 108; Reymond (1) 183–92; Ross 62–95; Mansion; Carteron. Natural position: Jouget i 3; Ar. *Phys.* 208b10, 261b25.

4. Theorem: Duhem (1) i 171; Reymond 186f; Sageret 214. Empty space: *Phys.* 216b; Duhem i 192–7. Acceleration: Simp. *in Ar.* v 6, 916 Diels. Stone: Duhem i 388; Sageret 214; *Phys.* 230b25. Law: *de caelo* 301b; Lucret. ii 235.

5. *Phys.* 250a10; Duhem (1) i 194; Reymond 191 citing Duhem i 7.

6. Ar. 848a11. Contradiction: Duhem (2) i 9; Jouguet i 35; Whyte (1) 14–16; Pl. *Tim.* xxvii. Circle and rect. motion: *de Cael.* i 2; *mech.* 848b35 and 852a7; whirl, *Phys.* 244a2ff; Cohen-D. 201; Lloyd (4) 269.

7. Ktesibios: Vitruv. ix 8 (mentioning also Eudoxos, Apollonios, Skopinas of Syracuse (see Vitr. I, i 17 and 6), Parmenio, Theodosios of Tripolis in Lydia, who wrote on spherical trigonometry (1st c. B.C.), Andreas, Patrokles, Dionysodoros of Melos (Str.

xii 548). See also Heron, Schmidt, i 491–4, drawing on same sources; Heiberg (2) 73.

Sideshows: *parerga* (extra ornaments). Clocks: Dr. (13), 20–31, and (7). Counterpoise: Vitruv. x 1, 1. Cistern: *castellum*, cf. Plin. xxxvi 121. Works: Vitruv. i 1, 7. Organ: Vitruv. x 8, 3; Schmidt i ch. 42; Dr. (1) 194f (*choragium*, error for *korakion*), and (13) 9, (1) 196. Rhyton: Dr. (5) 1f; Athen. xi 497b. Water-machine: Vitruv. x 7; Granger ii 311–3; Schmidt (1) i 494; Heron *pneum.* i 10f and 28. Dr. (1) 155. Valves: *asses* (coins); term *spiritus* used; pipe-mouths, *nares*, nostrils; pistons, male plungers, *emboli masculi*. Suction-pump not yet known. *Catinus*: air-chamber (Dr.) but here can have no air. Blackbird: Schmidt i 91.

8. Archmides: Mach (2) 18; Duhem (2) i 11f; Reymond 193f; Dr. (14). Karpos: Pappos iii (tom. 1) 1026 (F. Hultsch 1878). Eukleid: Duhem (2) i 67; Heath (4) 269. *Katoptrikon* of (?) Eukleid: Heath (4) 268. Claudian: Shorter poems li (lxviii): Salmoneus, JL (3) index. Practical: summarising Dr. (14), against Klemm 20 and Farrington (3) 216, 309.

   Kochlea: Dr. (11); Athen. v 208f; Str. xvii 807 and 819; Diod. i 34; v 37; Tannery (2) 207; Heron *Mech.* iii 15, 19, 21; Plin. xviii 37; Dr. (6) on oil mills and presses; Kirk (3) 98 n1, as simple roller. Snail: Dr. (1) 153f and (12); Vitr. x 6. Archimedes: Rufini; Enriques (3) 360f; Geymonat; Caruccio (1) ch. 6, and the sand-reckoner, 115f.

9. Move earth: Dr. (8); Rehm 1466 n28; Plout. *Marcell.* 14–7; Polyb. viii 3–7; Liv. xxiv 34; Athen. v 206d–207b; Tzet. *Chil.* ii hist. 35, 107 and 128; iii 66, 80. Prokl. *Proleg.* 2, 237 (*in Eukl.* 63 Fr.); Simp. 1110 (*Phys.* Diels); Papp. *Coll.* viii 10 (1060 Hultsch).

   Astrolabe: Dr. (7) and (13); Neugebauer (4); Philoponos, *RhM Philol.* 1839 vi 127–71; Synesios, *PG* lxvi 1577–88. Dr. supposes that the Hipp. and Ptol. types coexisted for some time.

   Vitruvius: experiments ii 191, 367, and 189; slaves ii 285, 303, and 309; free (?) ii 95 and 83. Owner as own manager: ii 9. Machines: x 1 (ladder, *akrobatikon*); nature x 1, 4; ships x 2, 10; water-drum, Dr. (1) 150–4; hodometer, Dr. (1) 157–9—another more workable, Heron, *Dioptra*: Dr. 159–70.

10. Heron *Bel.* W75–81; Marsden (1) 7f; Dr. (1) 186–91. Names: Dr. (1) 188; Marsden 10. Description: Philon, Vitruv., Heron. *Onagri*: Marsden (1) 189. Philon: Marsden 7; Schramm (1) 62—air-spanner as invention of Ktesibios. Repeater: Philon *Bel.* 73–6.

Schramm found the 5-screw wheels would not pull the chain in his model, but with a bicycle chain it went well. No evidence that Caesar's *onager* at Avaricum was a repeater, Marsden 94; Schramm 62 n1, no; Lammeet, yes; Dr. (9) no.

11. Dr. (1) n110. Ladders: Biton and contemporaries: Rehm (2); Schneider; Schramm. Anon: Thompson. Amm. Marc. xx 9, 4. Also S. Reinach; Seeck; Berthelot (2); Naher; Köchley i 410–19.

12. Colum. i 7, 6f; Finley (1) 43, 30. Reaper: Thompson 80f; Renard, Kolendo. Ptolemaic Egypt an except. in its agricultural advances; it was a special case with its semi-serf peasants and its strong organisation, its closed-in geography, its irrigation: Rostovtseff (1) i 363; JL (11) and (8). Mining: Finley (1) 30, 43; Davies; Ardaillon; S. Laufer 1125–46. Mills: Dr. (16); Mortiz; Forbes (1) ii 86–95. Finley (1) 31 for spread of pottery-moulding and of the pottery industry.

XII. Heron of Alexandreia

1. His date: *Isis* 1939 xxx 140, 1947–9 xxxiii 263–6, 1938 xxix 243; Sarton (1) i 73. Pappos: Dr. (1) 22–32, 82ff. Gearwheels, *Mech.* ii 21, Dr. (1) 83. Vitruv. x 2, 5–7; two wheels, Dr. 32. Book ii: Dr. (1) 50ff. Citing ii 14 (Dr. 72).

2. Dr. (1) 81f. Lenticular screw used for the screw and cog-wheel, Oreibasios, ib. 81. Book iii: Dr. (1) 94ff; Steel, 106; shift column, 107f. Herakleitos: Hippol. *Ref.* ix 10, 4; Kirk (3) 97ff. Fuller's press: Mau 388 fig. 229.

3. Dr. (1) 199ff. Lever: Dr. (6). Well-sump: Dr. (1) 18. Babylonians of late 3rd millennium B.C. knew among other such matters how to measure the volume of the frustrum of a square pyramid. Their formula was not as simple as the Egyptian, but the two were equivalent. Heron, two millennia later, tackled the same problem, his solution was the Babylonian one: *Works* 1914 v. 30–5; Sarton (2) 40 and 73.

4. Assyria: Laessoe 6. Pulleys: Dr. (1) 204. Wedge: Pappos *Math.* 1122, Dr. (1) 55; Mau 352 fig. 185, Taf. ix fig. 1. Winch: Schmidt i 398–40 (ch. 18). Theatre; *Mech.* ii 21 (Dr. (1) 91). Catapults: Marsden 13–5, 31f, 56. Cogwheels: Feldhaus (1). Dr. (1) 202.

Antikyra: Price (1). The Pompeian painting of press has two screws; an actual specimen, from Herculaneum, has only one: Feldhaus (2) 121. Screw for holding down: Dr. (1) 205.

Baryllion (for finding weight of liquids): Heron. *Spir.* i 39. Parallelogram of forces: Sa. (4) 88f. Ar. *Phys.* 262a12; ps. Ar. 848b15.

Heron *Mech.* i 8; Philopon. *Phys.* 842, 22.

5. Surveying instrument: Dr. (1) 198 and (10). Hodometer: Dr. (1) 27, 159ff, 202; Price (4) 84; ship's instrument probably by another author, Dr. (1) 165–8.

Theatre: Dr. (1) 197; Schmidt i 335–453; Prou; Diels (4); Chapuis (1) i 44f and (2) 36–8. (In actual theatre, *mechanē* or crane for swinging actors in air; *stropheion* for apotheoses; *bronteion* for thunder: Poll. iv 127, 130, 132.)

Katoptika: Sa. (4) 118f; Olympiod. *Meteor.* 272, 5. Maupertuis, *Essai de Cosmologie* 1751 221f, Fermat 1657 *Oeuvres* (1891) ii 354: principle of least time and nature acting by shortest course.

6. Windmill: Dr. (1) 206; Forbes thinks an intrusion. Temple-wheel: JH (1) 590f, see earlier about Orphic Wheel.

Heron and *energeia*: Sa. (4) 110, 114; Philipon. *De an.* 331, 1. Galen *nat. fac.* ii 126; Heron *Pneum.* i 40. *Energeia* and *dynamis* tend to become interchangeable.

7. Experiments: Cohen-D. 211, 249–52, 268, 294f, 479; Philon 318; Heron 249; Archimedes 71. See also Sen. *NQ* vii 255; Wohlwill; Olschi 160. Progress: Zilsel 328 thinks Ptolem. (*Almagest* i 1: Heiberg 4) and Sen. (*NQ* vii 25, 31), exceptional. Edelstein (1) 583f. Cohen-D. 184, 262, cf. 351, 249, 342, 574–6. Experiments: Aristotle and Hippol., author of *On Nature of Child*, xxix, detailed investigation of growth of embryo chick by examining eggs at different stages of development: Lloyd 379; HA 561; GA 752.

Individual basis of science: Burckhardt 140ff; Neugebauer (3) 25.

Pl. *Rep.* 528b; Diod. ii 29; Hippok., Edelstein (2). Galen, *On Scientific Demonstration*: Edelstein (1) 602f; J. v. Müller, Intro. Teaching of science was rudimentary: Marrou 160ff, 225ff, 243ff. Public libraries rare in cities: Christ-Schmidt ii 1 (1920) 19. For the Mouseion: RE xvi (1) 1933 807ff. Support by Alex. Great to science much exaggerated: Regenbogen 1459ff. Roman Empire: Edelstein (1) 604. Scholasticism in ancient thought: Praechter, Tenkin (medicine). In general: Regenbogen (2), Blüh, Diller. Galen only investigated what served his purpose: Kühn ii 286.

8. Sen. *Ep.* 88 and 90; Laberthonnière ii 348, cf. Cresson 44, 51ff. Torture: Espinas (1) 132 n2. "What use now is courage?" asked Archidamas on seeing catapults from Sicily. Aristotle replies that a brave man can still use such things in defence against heavy odds: Schuhl (7) 7. Note rejection of machinery (building) by Vespasian: Suet. *Vesp.* 18—in a passage praising him for being "a great encourager of learning and the liberal arts". Defence: Heron *Bel.* ch. 1. Plato in *Gorgias*, after stressing the great value of the engineer in preserving cities from attack, adds: "Still, you despise him and his craft, you call him *mēchanopoios* only by way of insult, and you wouldn't want to give your daughter to his son nor yourself to marry his."

XIII. Blast Power

1. Thrower; Marrett (2) 231f. Bow: Childe (1) 38 and 52. Australia: W. Ramsay Smith, *Aust. Enc.* 1927 i 27.

2. J. Wilbert in Furst, 55–83, esp. 71f. Caribs: J. Gillen. *The Barama River Caribs* 1936 (Peabody Mus. xiv, 2). Budge (1) 368ff and (2). Ani: Budge (2) and (1) 357ff, 366; (3) 147. Dead man plays draughts against Mehen: (1) 42; M. in the Boat 96. See also the inscriptions at Philai (J. F. Borghouts *JEA* xlix 114–49, on Evil Eye of Apopis), e.g. "Sakhmet, the great one, mistress of the fire of Bigeh, the flaming one, mistress of the House of Flame, who burns him whose-character-is-evil with her flaming eye, the great flaming goddess, who scorches the rebels when the fire breaks out against them in a quick leap." Again, "sending out heat against the rebels of her father," 136; cf. Tefnut 137; shooting by Hathor, probably burning glance.

3. Salmoneus: J.L. (3) ch. 9. Petronius: *PLM* 76; Dem. and Kritias: SE *phys.* i 24 and 54; D. *Vors.* 571. Kutchi: Howitt 446; JH (4) 67. Aranda: Spencer (1) 244–6. Baiame: R. H. Matthews *JRAI* xxv 295. Wild dogs: Roheim 394f, 435. Kai: C. Keysser *Aus dem Leben der Kaileute*: Neuhauss, *Deutsch New Guinei* iii 38. Kurnai: Howitt. Balum: Neuhauss iii 410–4. Rub stomach: Marrett (2) 207.

4. J. Matthew 171f; Spencer-Gillen (2) 480, 488. West Australia, D. R. Salvado, *Memorie storiche dell' Aust.* 1851 299; Oldfield 235. Mudie: Angas ii 224. Life-giving: Perry (1) 162 etc.

Bull-roarer. Distribution: Marrett (1) and (2) 125–9, 207; Haddon; Lang. *Rhombos*: Eur. *Hel.* 1362; Theok. ii 30; Archyt. 1; Arist. *Frogs* 303; Diog. Ath. i 3; *AP* vi 165; *IG* ii (2nd ed.) 1456, 49, cf. 1517, 207. Penis: P. Lond. 1821, 164. Wheel: Pind. *O.* xiii 94, *I* iv (iii) 47 (65) eagle swoop. Tympana: Oxy. Pap. 1604. Sky: Kritias 19, 2D. Sun in *Orphic h.* 8, 7; Alastor with Nemesis, *IG* xiv 1389 ii 34. Lozenge and a figure composed of two cones on opposite sides of same base. Description: Sch. Clem. Alex. *Cohort.* 5; JH (4) 61f; Van Gennep (1) pp. lxviii ff; Strab. x 470.

5. Late example, Appian, *Syr.* 58. Baby Zeus on ivory relief, JH (4) 59; dance, *ib.* fig 3. Hes. *Theog.* 459ff; JH (4) 60; G. Murray (1) 86. Gaelic Cailleach, Old Wife of Thunder; Mackenzie 165. Dunbar rescribes thunder and lightning coming from her body, "flew from her hippis". Julianus: Dodds 283–5; *Souda* sv Ioulianos; Claud. *de VI cons. H.* 348f; CZ iii 324ff. Confusion (?) with J. who commanded against Dacians under Domitian; Dion K. lxvii 10; JL (8) 215, Harnuphis. Sozomen *HE* i 18.

6. Prokop. *de aedif.* i 1, 2–3. He tells how A. and Justinian both saw in a vision the same plan for stopping a flood; a stone quarry at Jerusalem revealed to J.; an angel tricked into perpetual custody of St Sophia; also Anon *de Antiq. C.P.* i 4, 70; Preger 88.
   Theatre: Pollux iv 127, 130. Claudian *Rape of Pros.* 9–11. De Pauw, *Philosoph. Dissertation on the Egyptians and Chinese* 1795 i 306–8. Claudian *de Manlii Theod. Cons.* 326; Pa. 10. *Thaumata* —Th. *Char.* vi, xxvii (Ussher 230 n10, 74 n7). Xen. *Symp.* ii 1; Isok. *Antidos.* 213; Pl. *Rep.* 514b, *Laws* 658c; Ar. fr. 83 (Rose). Organ: Cic. *TD* iii 18, 43; sculpture in Arles Mus.

7. Ovid *ex ponto* iii; *remedia amoris* 369; Hdt. vii 10; Aisch. *Ag.* 468. Sen. *QN* ii 59 and 53. *Fulmen*, bolt, opposed to *fulgar*, lightning. Lucret. vi 219ff. Burton: i 2, 4, 3. Sir T. Brown, *Enquiry into Vulgar and Common Errors* ii 97f (1658 ed.) links Thunder and Gunpowder: "This is the reason not onely of this fulminating report of Guns, but may resolve the cause of those terrestrial cracks, and affrighting noyses of Heaven; that is, the nitrous and sulphurous exhalations, set on fire in the Clouds."

8. Lucret. vi 219ff, 271ff, 295ff. Ar. *de caelo* ii 7 (289a); Ideler i 359; Pa. (1) 33 n30–1. Problems of friction and heat. Plin. xxxvii 9 (5); Pa. 7–9. The theory that sulphur and charcoal were present (making up gunpowder) cannot be accepted. Rocksalt gives a strong yellow flame and looks hot.

9. Hes. *Theog.* 819ff: note the winds, some godsent, some sent by Typhon. Epigrams of Homer ix 2–4. End by fire in *Elder Edda*, etc. *Arthasatra*: Pa. (1) 209–11, 230 n110; legends of early gunpowder in India 211. For Gunpowder Plot: B. B. de Lina, *Jonson's Romish Plot*, 1967.

10. C. Berlitz, *Mysteries of Forgotten Worlds* 1972; L. Pauwels and J. Bergier, *The Eternal Man*, 1972, as examples of fantasy reconstructions. Berlitz 31f, 214–6. Fuller details in W. R. Drake, *Gods and Spacemen in the Anc. East* 1968, where every fantasy of flight is taken literally. *Mahabharata*: Eliot vi 473; Pa. (1) 212, 221. Sen. *QN* ii 31. Petrarch: Pa. (1) 103, refs. 135n119. Note *nochus*, hazelnut, used in Germany for projectiles from machines: Pa. (1) 142 n331. Milton, *PL* v 478ff; Spenser *FQ* i 7, 13, cf. Ariosto *OF* ix 28. Ezekiel: Bathurst; Cade 24; possible relation to Bab. imagery, West (2) 88f.

11. Savage races: Feldhaus (1) 320. Assyrians: Layard. *2nd s. of the Mons. of Nineveh* 1853 pl. 21 and 39; Pa. (2) 225; Berthelot, *Rev. des deux mondes* 1891 cvi 786 (no petroleum or resins). *Proverbs* xxvi 18; *Psalms* cxx 4; *Isaiah* l 11; Hime 139. Hdt. viii 52; Thouk. vii 53; Diod. xx 86 and iv 100–4; Romocki i 8. Apollodoros: R. Schneider (1) 18–2; Pa. (1) 2. Heron of Byz., Wescher 219, 224. Aineias. xxxiii–v (also describes use of vinegar and birdlime, cf. xxxviii–xlvi) and Philon *Mech.* v 90, 17, Schöne; Th. *Ign.* 61; Plin. xxxiii 94. Hypera: Hes. *Works* 423. Incense: *manna libanōton.* Hdt. for hemp round Persian arrows at Athens; hollow heads for fire later: JSA—A iii 1960, 22–4.

12. Arrian, *Exped. Alex.* ii 19. Bauer 326; Diod. xx 48, 88, 96f. Aen. ix 707; Liv. xxi 8; Tac. iv 23; Amm. Marc. xxiii 4, 14f; Veg. *Res Mil. Inst.* iv 1–8, 18; Oman 47; Hime 139f.

13. Medeia: Pa. (1) 3. Naphtha: Strab. xvi 743 etc. See Pa. (1) 3–5 for details and refs. Petroleum: Vitruv. viii 3; Diosk. *MM* i 99; Plin. ii 110; ps. Ar. *de mir. ausc.* 35f, 113–5, 127; Ail. *NH* xiii 16. Ktesias in Photios: Oppert 55; McCrindle; Lassen; Plin. ix 17; Ail. v 3; Philostr. *VAT* iii 1; ii 33; von Bohlen ii 63–6; Maclagen. *Skēptoi*: *On kos.* 395a28; Eur. *Androm.* 1046; Athen. v. 219e. Extinguishers: Pa. (1) 5; Hdt. ii 180; A. Gell. xv 1; Amm. *Hist.* xx 6, 13; Lenz 11.

14. P(1) 4f; Herodian viii 4; Lebeau vii 16, *Hist. du Bas-Empire* 1827. Malal. *Chronog.* xvi (PG xcvii 597, 583); Dinsdorf 1831, 403f, 675,

394, 474); Zonoras, *Ann.* xv (PG xxxiv 1217); Agathias *Hist.* iii 5; Gibbon ch. xlii; J. B. Bury *Hist. LRE* 1889 i 447.

Plin. xxxvi 25(53); Aug. *CD* xxi 4, ii *Macc.* i 20–36, cf. i *Kings* xviii 3–8; Pa. (3), mixture of sulphur and quicklime also inflames when water-sprinkled. Trick: Eisler *Orph.-Dionys. Mysteriengel.* 1925 ii 135–8; Liv. xxxix 13; Paus. i 27.

15. Athen. i 35; Hippol. *Ref.* iv 28–41. Greekfire: Theophanes, *Chronog.* ed. de Boor 1883–5 i 353f; Romocki i 5; Hime 27; Pa. (1) 12, cf. Anastasios: Pa. 36n125. Kallinikos is a Greek name, but that proves nothing. Const. Porph. *de admin. imp.* xiii, xlviii (Bekker); Prokop. *BG* xxcxiii 183, 367, 369; Kallinikos from Egypt (?), Pa. (1) 14. Leo: Pa. 15 ref. 140, and 15f, refs. China: Pa. (1) 246, 254f, 260, 262ff, 277. Needham refs. Pa. (1) 161 n95. For air-gun Hoff.

16. Refs. Pa. (1) 31f and 15f; also 205 n97.

17. Lucretius: I owe the basis of this discussion to Bright. Serene gods: Bignone ii 318–22 on *isonomia*. Despair: Borle. Disease: Bright 609, 617, 619, 620. Three levels: physical disease, mental, social (fear and greed), Luc. vi 647ff. The poem ends with detail showing distortion of event that should unite men in love and piety (funeral of kin) into social violence. "And the sudden pressure and poverty impelled to many terrible acts. With a vast tumult they would set their own kin on the funeral pyres of others and put torches to them, often brawling with blood profusely shed rather than leave the bodies." Note that Ar. related human spasms to earthquakes. See Lloyd, *Polarity*, as to Aristotle linking earthquakes and flatus spasm.

XIV. Ballistics and Mechanics

1. Aim: Marsden 91f, accuracy 93f, no precise sighting system 88. Heron. *Bel.* W89 and 86, 7. Philon *Bel.* 49–51 cf. 58. Calibration: Marsden 25–9 for various developments. Theorem of two mean proportionals 39–41; Vitruvius 41–3. Bow-range: W. MacLeod *JHS* 1970 197f; N. G. L. Hammons *ib.* 1968 17; *Hesperia* ii 1933 344; iv 1935 114–7.

2. Philon: Schramm (1) 25f; Marsden 93–5. *Tonos*: Heron *Bel.* W83; Marsden 17; Vitr. i l, 8; A. Gell xvi 18, 5. (In Vitr. *hemitonia* may

be error for *homotonia*, equal tones: Philander.) Kleanthes: Arnim i 128; Plout. *Stoic. rep.* 1034d; Sa. (2) translated "limit".

3. Sa. (4) 75f; Philop. *Phys.* 641, 13 and 29; 642, 9. Angels: *opif. mund.* i 12 (28, 30). Plot. *Enn.* ii 5 (25), iii 6 (26). Light, Philoponos and Plot., Sa. (4) 112f, 113–5. Porph. (Iambl. *de myst.* p. xxxii Parthey); Sheldon-Williams 431, 455, 459n4, 460, 492f. Prokl.: Dodds (2) 167, 169; *de dec. dub.* 22, 13–9, Boese. Plotinos, Alex. Aphr. and Aristotle: P. Henry.

4. Buridan: Crombie (2) 10. Medieval scholars weak at statics: Hall (1) 21; Menut v 213f; in general Hessen. 1335: Hall 7. Bernal 238f; Mayow, *Isis* xli 1950 32. Men of Oxford etc.: Crombie (1) 26; Hall 19; Menut. Marsile of Ingham (in Paris 1379) made the heat analogy; he saw movement as distinct from impetus.

5. Oresme: Hall 56ff; Menut v 271ff. Mechanism: Hessen 14f, Galileo and impetus: Koyré. Feathers 125. D. Soto, a Spanish theologian in 1555 saw the issues clearly, defining accelerated motion (uniform difform motion), not velocity, as proportional to time; and declared this kind of motion proper to projectiles and free-falling bodies: Clagett, Galileo: "Using the same proof as Oresme, he showed that the velocity (v) of a falling body was a function of time (t) such that $v = \frac{1}{2}gt^2$, g being a constant determined by gravity. This function gave a sufficient scientific explanation of the dependence of v on t", Crombie (1) 26f. Newton's "essential qualities", McGuire. Descartes, conservation and determination: Knudsen.

6. Whyte 40f. Koestler on Kepler. Hegel: Bloch; Burtt 53; Kepler's causality as Aristotle's final cause reinterpreted in terms of exact maths. Kepler and proportion: Hall 259–61; *Astron. Nova* (C.W. iii 14–7); Singer (2) 238f; Wittkower 142; Cassirer i 383ff.

7. Newton's projectile: Koestler 504. His laws, Davis 99, Bondi 908. Man banished: Lindeman 145; Burtt; Whyte 50 etc. Caudwell and Hessen for social relations: atomised selfsufficient bourgeois individual in the Newtonian system.

8. Unfortunately, on account of a number of pressures etc. (including the war-danger) Marxism in the S.U. and elsewhere has not yet begun to develop an all-round critique of bourgeois science, but has been concerned only with its pragmatic extension. An

example of backwardness: Kedrov in 1962 on Galileo's law of free fall: "It states a generalisation of all the cases that have taken place and all the cases that under given conditions can or will happen." But there have been some serious attempts to grapple with symmetry-asymmetry, e.g. at Kiev in 1960 papers by Gott and Depenchuk, with Savchenko's criticism.

XV. Some Further Points and Conclusions

1. Wallbank (1) 16; GT (1) 332f. Demurring: A. H. M. Jones; Finley (2). See further: Edelstein (1) 580–4; Zilsel (3) Farrington (1) ii 166; Cornford (6) 93; W. L. Westermann *RE* Suppl. vi 1935 894–1068; Laistner 289f, 535 (failing slave-supply); Rostovtzeff (2) 303, 178 and (1) 1258, 1205ff; Childe (1) 1942 235ff, 250ff, 272; Rehm 158ff; Westermann *Slave Systems* 1955. Marx, *Capital* 1946 i 28; GT (1) 330. Xen. *Oik.* iv 2f; Ar. *Pol.* 1278a, example Thebes etc.; Herakleides Pontikos, *Pol.* 43. Thespiai, Kyrene, *SEG* ix 1; Burford (3) 12, 25, 34; Louk. *Dream* i 8; Plout. *Perik.* ii 1 and *Agesil.* xxvi 4f. Archimedes: Edelstein (1) 589f; Cohen-D. 315, 317; Rehm 145 n27.

   Ar. *Pol.* 1258b33ff on practical maths., "there are books by several writers", but to dwell on such matters would be "in poor taste". Inventions in Plin. vii include laws, customs, morals as well as arts and crafts.

   Note in Hes. *Works* 60ff, Zeus directs Hephaistos in making Pandora; he is above menial work?—cf. Pl. *Tim.* 41aff the Demiurge directs other gods in certain tasks, but here the intention is to explain imperfections in the cosmos. Note Ar. *Pol.* 1337b17ff, a thinker can do manual work for his own sake or that of friends; it is the servile or dependent status that matters.

   Limits: Vernant (1) 36f; Ar. *Pol.* vii 1328ff and iii 1277b; Pl. *Rep.* x 601c on; Edelstein (5). The school of scepticism and the notion of periodic destructions may have helped to sap interest in relating science to technology. Democracy as basis of culture: Plout. *max. cura princip. phil. esse*; Loukian *Quomodo historia conscrib.*; Strab. iii 4, 13 (political falsification).

2. Burford (3) 34; Hdt. ii 167; Ephesos, E. Preuner. Inertia etc.: Caudwell 48; GT (1) 313; Freundlich 37–44; H. Planck *Ann. d. Phys.* 4 Folge 138, 26; M. Abraham *Electromagnet. Energie d. Strahlung*, 4 Aufl. 1906 etc. Einstein found mass and energy con-

vertible into one another, according to his equation (Energy = mass multiplied by velocity of light squared); we know that the conservation of energy holds only for systems with no change of mass.

Limitations: Finley (1) 35f, 43f, who also discusses lack of true craft gilds, longterm business corporations etc., also Finley (3). Mills: perhaps a marble—slicing mill in Ausonius *Mosella* 362–4. Many mills were powered from aqueducts, e.g. Suet. *Calig.* 39. Plin. xviii 300. Vitruv. xx v 10, 1 has a single labour-saving suggestion: the same heat-source for hot-water rooms in baths for men and women, but only one short par., x 5, 2, for corn-grinding watermill. Roman engineers contributed hydraulic concrete; they realised that by adding materials such as pozzolana or Santorini stone they enabled conventional mortar to set very hard and quick in absence of atmospheric carbon.

3. Clerics: Hale. Franklin: Hurd ii 191–3. Napoleon: Cade 28. (Note that Nap. was an artillery officer. When he passed out of military school, his examiner was Laplace, whom Nap. took later on his Egyptian expedition, with Berthelot, who noted the salt-lakes as "a vast laboratory where nature prepares a vast amount of soda," by means of chemical reactions contrary to current ideas of chemical affinity." This led him to revolutionise those ideas by a 1799 paper. Financial aid from Nap. enabled him and Laplace to carry out researches at the country house, Arceuil, in Paris suburbs, gathering a brilliant group. Rapid growth of French science led to a complex growth of scientific institutions, and developed in France, earlier than elsewhere, the professional in science. Nap. kept a close eye on what went on.)

Thunderbolt, Cade 96ff, 103: Finkelstein and Rubinstein 1964. Applications, Cade 142–7, Whyte 16f and 165.

Motion was fourfold for Aristotle; with 17th c. it referred only to change of place, e.g. Sebastian Basso, *Philosophia Naturalis* 1621; Galileo added the need to see motion in a quantitative math. aspect. Kepler tried to integrate mech. motion, purposive development, and archetypal controls—inevitably with many idealistic aspects in his ideas, but showing the intuition of a true science of structure and development.

Kozyrev: Margerison. He published another paper on Causal Mechanics in 1963. Protein: Whyte 87. SE *Phys.* i 228; he is arguing there is no such thing as a cause.

Note on Eudoxos and Archimedes

Eudoxos shows the Greeks could not meet head-on the challenge of the paradoxes of Zenon of Elea and had to have recourse to stratagems. He began by setting out a theory of proportions which, while taking into consideration geometrical continuity, could be applied to all ratios of magnitude, whether commensurable or not. If (A, B) and C, D) are two pairs of magnitudes, the proportions A/B and C/D will be equal if, whatever may be the whole numbers m and p, we always have:

$$\frac{mA}{pB} = \frac{mC}{pD}$$

Thus the ratios of magnitudes were geometrised and were no longer arithmetical, as they had been with the Pythagoreans.

On this basis Eudoxos built up his method of exhaustion, grappling with the problem of how to pass gradually from a regular figure to the figure circumscribing it. The method had two principles: (1) if two magnitudes a and b are unequal and if we repeat the lesser enough times (n), it will finally equal or exceed the greater one; i.e. if $a < b$, $na > b$; (2) if we take from a magnitude more than its half, and then again from the remainder more than its half, and so on, in the end we get a remainder less than any given magnitude.

By this method Eudoxos showed, for example, that circles have areas proportional to their inscribed squares. And this proposition is true for regular figures of 4, 8, 16, 32 . . . sides, which are successively inscribed in the circles. At each operation the difference between the areas of the circles and those of the inscribed polygons is diminished by more than half. It tends to become zero. So the properties established for polygons hold true for circles.

Archimedes powerfully extended the method of exhaustion. Eudoxos had shown how a certain figure could be considered as the limit of another figure progressively increasing. But he could not evaluate the successive terms of the progression. Archimedes tackled this problem and found ways of making the calculation; e.g. he determined the circumference of a circle by defining it as the boundary of two polygonal perimeters, inscribed and circumscribed, of which the number of sides is indefinitely increased. On these lines he also calculated the curvilinear areas or arcs bounded by curves—showing that any segment bounded by a straight line and a parabola is equal to four-thirds of the triangle with the same base and same height as the segment. To escape using the passage to the limit here, he proved that it was absurd to suppose the area of the parabolic segment to be greater or less than four-thirds of the triangle with the same base and height.

He applied his method in various ways, as to find the volume of a sphere and a segment of it. He made the circumscribed and inscribed polygons revolve about the axis, found the volumes of the circumscribed and inscribed solids of revolution respectively, and then, by increasing the number of sides in the polygons respectively, he compressed the solids into coalescing with one another and with the included sphere or segment, finally confirming the results by the usual method of exhaustion. The contents of the inscribed and circumscribed figures were got by adding the content of "solid rhomboi" and differences between such. Along these lines he proved that the volume of the sphere is equal to that of a cone having for height the radius of the sphere and for base a circle equal in area to the surface of the sphere—so that it is $\frac{1}{3}r.4\pi r^2$ or $\frac{4}{3}\pi r^3$. It followed that the volume of a cylinder circumscribing the sphere is $\frac{3}{2}$ that of the sphere. And so on.

The method of exhaustion proves its logical exactitude by a *reductio ad absurdum*; and this way of looking at things, this reliance on methods of logic, closed the minds of geometers and mathematicians against looking in another direction to find the solution of the problems of areas and curvilinear volumes. It meant that Archimedes based his method of integration on the comparative study of the static moments of two figures; and this approach necessitated the use of an infinite number of lines or parallel planes. Then by the comparison of suitably selected sections he obtained the *equation of equilibrium* between the known surface or volume of one of the figures and the unknown surface or volume of the other. In the problem of the sphere mentioned above he had to have four cones with the great circle as their base and the radius of the sphere as their height; the sphere than had a volume four times greater than that of the cone constructed with its radius.

> "On the one hand, the condition imposed on the difference (line or surface) of always diminishing by more than its half ensures that this difference can become less than any given quantity, after a finite number of operations. On the other hand, the method of construction employed in each problem ensures that the law of diminution is really obeyed by the decreasing magnitudes; hence the terms which form the numerical representation of these constitute a series the convergence of which is evident and has no need of proof. In every way the direct use of infinity, which results from dichotomy, and which Zenon has criticised, is avoided" (Reymond).

But the method the Greeks had evolved was one difficult to manipulate and expand. To make the application more general, they would have had to examine the nature of the progressions that represent the decomposition of the geometrical figure—as did Cavalieri, Fermat, Pascal. Then they would have had to establish the conditions which the progressions must meet if they were to be used for solving any problem of quadrature. (Heath (4) 300f, 314–7, 320–2 and 120, 191–4, 157f; Reymond (1) 132–6.)

We must repeat, however, that they were not merely obstinate or blind, however much they were hypnotised by the concept of the mean and of equilibrium. They also felt that to tackle the problem along the lines mentioned above—the lines actually taken from the 17th century on—was to limit the problem so severely as to lose its essence, to destroy the concrete nature of physicalised geometry and the dynamic pneumatic continuum. Here is the problem that we brought up in connection with Marx's critique of the infinitesimal calculus. That critique was based ultimately on the view that somehow a method could and must be found to bring the "ghosts of departed qualities" back into the mathematical method instead of seeking to banish them ever more completely.

Bibliography

Aeneas Tacticus (Aineias): Loeb ed. 1923.

Albright, W. F. (1) *PAPS* cxvi (3) 1972 225–42 (2) *J. Biblical Lit.* 1922 xxix 143–51 (3) in *The Aegean and the Near East* 1956 (4) *History, Archaeology and Christian Humanism.*

Alexander Aphrodisiensis, *Scripta Minora* ed. I. Brun (2 vols.) 1887–92.

Allen, T. W., *Homer* 1912.

Altheim, F. (1) *Gr. Goetter* (2) *Röm. Religionsgeschichte* 1931.

Amaldi, U., in Enriques (3) i pt. 1.

Angas, F., *Savage Life and Scenes in Aust. and N.Z.* 1847.

Ardaillon, E., *Les mines du Laurion dans l'antiquité* 1897.

Arnhim, J. v., *Stoicorum veterum frag.* (4 vols.) 1921.

Arrigo, A. d', *Natura e tecnica nel mezzogiorno* 1956.

Aymard, A. (1) *Rev. d'hist. de la phil. et d'hist. gén. de la civilisation* 1943 124–46 (2) *JP* 1948 29–50.

Baeumker, C., *Das Problem d. Materie in d. griech. Philosophie* 1890.

Bailey, C. (1) *The Gr. Atomists and Epicurus* 1928 (2) *Epicurus: The Extant Remains* 1926 (3) ed. of Lucretius 1947.

Bailey, K. C., *The Elder Pliny's Chapters on Chemical Subjects* 1929.

Baldry, H. C. CQ 1932 xxvi 27–34 (Embryolog. analogies).

Balme, H. C. (1) *CQ* 1939 xxxiii 129–38 (2) in *Aristote et les problèmes de méthode* (Symp. Aristot. 1960: Louvain-Paris 1961) 195–212 (3) CQ n.s. 1962 xii 81–98.

Bambrough, J. R. in Laslett, 98–115.

Barie, G. T., *L'esigenza unitaria da Talete a Platone* 1931.

Barigazzi, A., ed. *Favorino di Arelate* 1966.

Barnett, R. D., in *CS* 22–4 Mai 1958 (*Éléments orient. dans la relig. gr. anc.*).

Barrow, R. H., *Plutarch and his Times* 1967.

Bassett, S. E., *The Poetry of Homer* 1938 (Sather Class. Lecture xv).

Bathurst, G. B., *Weather* (R. Meteor. Soc.) xix no 7.

Bauer, in I. Müller iv 1.

Beare, J. L., *Gr. Theories of Elementary Cognition from Alcmaeon to Aristotle* 1906.

Beardslee, J. W., *The Use of Physis in 5th c. Gr. Lit.* 1918

Beazley, J. D. (1) *PBA* xxx 1946 (potters, painters at Athens) (2) *Attic Red Figure Vase Painters* (2nd ed.) 1963.

Benoît and J. Schwartz, *EP* vii 1948.

Bernal, J. D., *Science in History* 1954.

Berndt, R. M., *Djanggawul* 1952.

Berry, A. J., *Henry Cavendish* 1960.

Berthelot, M. (1) *Annales de Chimie et de physique*, s. 7, xix 1900 289–420 (2) *J. des Savants* 1900 171–7.

Berthelot, R., *L'idée de physique math. et l'idée de physique evolutionniste chez les philosophes gr. entre Pythag. et Platon.*

Bevan, E., *Holy Images.*

Bickel, E., *Schriften d. Königsberger Gelehrten Gessellschaft Jahr.* Heft 7 1925 (Homer. Seelenglaube).

Bignone, E. (1) *Storia della lett. latina* 1945–6 (2) *Empedocle* 1916.

Bloch, *Subjekt-Objekt Erläuterungen zu Hegel.*

Blüh, O., *Amer. J. of Physics* 1948 xvii 384ff.

Blum, C., *EJ* 1946 xliv 315ff.

Blümner, H., *Technol. u. Terminologie d. Gewerbe u. Künste bei Griechen u. Römern* 1875–87.

Boardman, J., *Island Gems* 1963.

Bochenski, I. M., *Ancient Formal Logic* 1951.

Boehme, J., *Die Seele u. das Ich im homer. Epos* 1929.

Bohlen, P. von, *Das alte Indien* 1930.

Bondi, H., *Listener* 29 Nov. 1962 (gravity).

Booth, N. B., *JHS* 1960 lxxx 10–5.

Borle, J. P., *MH* 1962 xix 162–76 (Lucretius).

Bourgey, L., *Observation et Expérience chez les médicins de la coll. hippocratique* 1953.

Boutroux, P. (1) *Les principes de l'analyse math.* (2 vols.) 1914 (2) *L'idée scient. des mathematiciens* 1920 (3) *RMet* 1921 657.

Bouché-Leclercq, A., *Hist. de la divination.*

Boyer, C. B., *The Concept of the Calculus* 1939.

Brandon, S. G. F. (1) *Creation Legends of the Anc. Near East* 1963. (2) *Time and Mankind* 1951.

Bréhier, É. (1) *Chrysippe et l'anc. Stoicisme* 1951 (2) *RHS* 1950 iii 201–9 (3) *Les idées philos. et relig. de Philo d'Alex.* 1925.

Bright, D. F., *Latomus* 1971 xxx (3) 607–32.

Brommer, F., *Vasenlisten zur griech. Heldensage* 1956.

Broughton, T. S., *An Econ. Survey of Anc. Rome* iv 1938.

Browning, R., *JRS* 1952 xlii 13–20.

Brunschvicg, L., *Les étapes de la philosophie math.* 1922.
Buber, M., *Rev. of met.* xi 1958 359–79 (what is common).
Budge, E. A. W. (1) *From Fetish to God in Anc. Egypt* 1934 (2) *The Egyptian Heaven and Hell* 1925 (3) *The Book of the Dead: Pap. of Ani* 1960.
Burckhardt, J., *Ueber des wiss. Verdienst d. Griechen* (ed. E. Dürr 1914).
Burford, A. M. (1) *EHR* s.2 1960 xiii 1–18 (heavy transport) (2) *Procs. Camb. Phil. Soc.* n.s. 1965 xi 21–34 (temple-building) (3) *Craftsmen in Gr. and R. Society* 1972.
Burnet, J. (1) *PBA* 1915–6 235ff (soul) (2) *Early Gr. Philosophy* 1892. 4th ed. 1928 (3) *Gr. Philosophy, Thales to Plato* 1914.
Burtt, E. A., *Metaphysical Foundations of Mod. Physical Science* 1924.
Bury, R. G., *CQ* 1951 xlv 86–93 (Plato and history).
Buslepp, in Roscher sv *Talos.*
Butterfield, H., *The Origins of Mod. Science* 1949.
Byers, H. R., ed. *Thunderstorm Electricity* 1953.

Cade, C. M., and D. Davis, *The Taming of the Thunderbolt* 1969.
Cajori, F. (1) *Amer. Math. Monthly* 1915 xxii 143–9 (Zenon's paradoxes) (2) *A Hist. of the Conception of Limits and Fluxions in G.B. from Newton to Woodhouse* 1919.
Campbell Thompson, R. C., *Ambix* ii 3–16 (Assyr. Chemistry, 7th c.).
Capelle, W., *NJKA* 1905 xv 529–68.
Cardwell, D. S. L., *From Watt to Clausius.*
Carpenter, Rhys, *The Esthetic Basis of Gr. Art* 1959.
Carteron, H., *La notion de force dans le système d'Aristote* 1924.
Cary, M., *A Hist. of the Gr. World from 323 to 146* B.C., 1932.
Caspar, M., *J. Kepler* 1948.
Cassirer, E., *Das Erkentnisproblem* 1911.
Casson, S., *Progress and Catastrophe.*
Caudwell, C., *The Crisis in Physics* 1938.
Cerfaux, L., and J. Tondriau, *Le Culte des Souverains* 1956.
Chaignet, *Hist. de la Psychologie des Grecs.*
Chalmers, J. A., *Atmospheric Electricity* 1957.
Chapuis, A. (1) with E. Gélis, *Le monde des automates* (2 vols.) 1928 (2) with E. Droz, *Les Automates* 1949.
Cherniss, H. (1) *Aristotle's Criticism of Presocratic Philosophy* 1935 (2) *JHI* 1951 xii 319–45.
Childe, V. G. (1) *What Happened in History* 1954 (2) *Man Makes Himself* (3) *Progress and Archaeology* 1944.
Christ-Schmid: W. Christ and W. Schmid, *Gesch. d. griech. Lit.*
Cichorius, C., *Die Reliefs d. Traianssäule* i 1896.

Clagett, M., *The Science of Mechanics in the M.A.* 1959.
Clerc, C., *Les théories relatives aux cultes des images chez les auteurs grecs du 2e s. après J.-C.* n.d.
Cohen, J. (1) *Human Robots in Myth and Science* 1966 (2) *Books and Bookmen* Jan. 1971.
Cohen, M. R., with J. E. Drabkin, *A Source Book of Gr. Science.*
Collitz, etc. *Sammlung d. griech. Dialektinschriften.*
Commager, H. S., *HSCP* 1957 105ff.
Conze, *JDI* 1890 (Gr. Kohlenbecken).
Cooper, L., *Aristotle, Galileo and the Leaning Tower of Pisa* 1935.
Cook, R. M. (1) *CR* 1948 lxii 55–7 (2) n.s. 1951 i 9.
Cornford, F. M. (1) *Essays in hon. G. Murray* 1936 (space) (2) *Plato's Cosmology* 1937 (3) *From Religion to Philosophy* 1912 (4) *Principium Sapientae* 1952 (5) *Before and After Socrates* 1960 (6) *The Unwritten Philosophy* 1950 (7) with P. H. Wicksteed, Loeb. Ar. *Physics* 1929 (8) *CAH* iv 1926 522–78 (9) *The Laws of Motion in Anc. Thought* 1931.
Costabel, P., *JHSC* 1950 iii 315–56 (hist. of moment of inertia).
Cresson, A., *Le problème moral et la philosophie* 1933.
Crombie, A. C. (1) *Augustine to Galileo* 1952 (2) *Discovery* Jan. 1953 (3) *Med. and Early Mod. Science* 1959 (4) *R. Grosseteste and the Origins of Experimental Science* 1953.
Crosland, M., *The Society of Arceuil.*
Cuillandre, J., *Le droit et la gauche dans les poèms homeriques* 1943.

Davies, O., *R. Mines in Europe* 1935.
Davis, W. O. (1) *Analog* Aug. 1962 (2) *Amer. Phys. Soc.* 23 April 1962 (with others).
Dauvillier, A., *Atmospheric Electricity* 3 March 1959.
Debrunner, in *Festschrift f. E. Tièche* (Bern) 1947 11ff.
Deichgräber, K., *Hippokrates ueber Enstehung u. Aufbau des menschlichen Körpers* 1935.
De Lacey, P. H., *CP* 1939 xxxiv 97–115 (causation in Plato).
Delatte, A. (1) *Essai sur la politique pythag.* 1922 (2) *Les conceptions de l'enthousiasme chez philosophes présoc*, 1934.
Delatte, L., *Les traités de la royauté d'Ecphante* etc. 1942.
Delcourt, M., *Héphaistos* 1957.
Denk, P., *Sitz. Phys. Med. Soc. Erlanger* 1940 lxxi 353–68.
Deonna, W. (1) *De Telesphore au moins bourru* 1955 (2) with M. Renard, *Croyances et Superstitions de table* 1961.
Derchain, P. (1) CS 16–8 Mai 1967 (Relig. en Eg. hellénistique) 1969 31–4 (2) *CE* 1964 xxxix 183–5 (3) with Delatte, *Les intailles magiques* 1964.

Derry, T. K., with T. S. Williams, *A Short Hist. of Technology* 1961.

Dicks, D. R., *CQ* n.s. ix 1959 294–309.

Diels, H. (1) *Antike Technik* (3rd ed.) 1924 (2) *Die Frag. d. Vorsokratiker* (5th ed.) 1934–7 (3) *Doxographi Graeci* 1929 (4) *Abh. d. Akad. d. Wiss.* Berlin 1917 (Heron's theatre).

Dieterich, *Kleine Schriften.*

Diller, H., *H.* 1932 lxxvii 14ff.

Dilthey, W., *Pädagogik, Gesch. Schriften* 1934 ix 72ff.

Dingle, H. (1) *Science and Human Experience* 1931 (2) *Through Science to Philosophy* 1937 (3) *Nature* 1939 clxiv 808 (4) *ib.* 1940 clxv 427 (5) *The Scientific Adventure* 1952 (6) *The Special Theory of Relativity* 1946.

Dinsmoor, W. B., *Hesperia* Suppl. v. 1941 125ff.

Diogenes Laertius, *Vitae Philosophorum* (Loeb) ed. A. D. Hicks 1950.

Dodds, E. R. (1) *The Greeks and the Irrational* 1959 (2) Proclus: *Elements of Theology* 1933.

Dossin, G., *La divination en Mésopotamie anc.* 1966.

Drachmann, A. G. (1) *The Mechanical Technology of Gr. and R. Antiquity* 1962 (2) *ACIHS* 1953 (catapults) (3) *C.* 1961 vii 145–51 (windmill) (4) *JHS* 1936 lvi (screwcutter) (5) *C.* 1951 ii 1–10 (Ktesibios) (5) *Kgl. Danske Videnskabernes Selskab. Archaeol. Kunsthist. Meddelelser.* Bind 1, Nr. 1, 1932 (7) *C.* 1954 iii 183–9 (astrolabe) (8) *C.* 1958 v 278–82 (Archimedes) (9) *ACIHS* (1959) 1960 203–5 (Caesar's scorpio) (10) in Singer (1) iii 1937 609–12 (dioptra) (11) *ACIHS* (1956) 1958 iii 940–3 (13) *Acta hist. scientiarum natur. math.* iv 1948: *Ktesibios, Philon and Heron* (14) *C.* 1967 xii 1–11 (15) *C.* 1968 xiii 220–4 (16) *Ancient Oil Mills and Presses* 1932.

Drake, St., *Discourses and Opinions of Galileo* 1957.

Drioton, E. (1) *L'Ethnographie* n.s. xxiii (15 April 1931) 57–66 (2) *CE* xii July 1931 259–70.

Dubarle, D., *Rev. des Sciences philos. et. théol.* 1952 xxv 205–30.

Dugas, C., *BCH* xxxix 1915.

Dugas, R., *Hist. de la Mécanique.*

Duhem, P. (1) *Le système du monde* i, ii 1913 (2) *Origines de la statique* 1905–6 (3) *Études sur Leonardo da Vinci* 1906–10.

Düring, I. (1) *Notes on the Hist. and Transmission of Aristotle's Writings* 1950 (2) *Aristotle in Anc. Biog. Tradition* 1957 (3) *Aristotle's chemical treatise Meterologica Book IV* 1944.

Edelstein, L. (1) *JHI* xiii 573–604 (2) *Problemata* 1931 iv 105ff (3) *Quellen u. Studien z. Gesch. d. Naturwiss. u.d. Medizin* iii 253ff (4) *RE* Suppl. vi sv Methodiker 367ff (5) *Bull. Inst. Hist. of Medicine* 1937 224ff.

Edgar, C. C., *BSA* 1898–9 v. 56.

Ehrenberg, V. (1) *Historia* 1950 i 515ff (2) *Aspects of the Anc. World* 1946 (3) *RE* Suppl. vii 293ff.

Eichholz, D. E., *Theophrastus de Lapidibus* 1965.

Elder, J. P., *TAPA* 1954 lxxv (Lucretius' suicide).

Elkin, A. P., *Aboriginal Men of High Degree* 1946.

Eliade, M. (1) *The Two and the One* 1962 (2) *The Myth of the Eternal Return* 1954.

Elliot, H. M., with J. Dowson, *The Hist. of India as told by its own Historians* 1875.

Enriques, F. (1) *Per la Storia della logica* 1922 (2) with Santillana, *Storia del Pensiero Scientifico* i 1932 (3) *Questioni riguardanti le mat. elementari* 1924–7.

Erman, A., *Die aegypt. Religion.*

Espinas, A. (1) *Les origines de la technologie* 1897 (2) *RMet.* 1903 703.

Evans-Pritchard, E. E., *Nuer Religion* 1956.

Evelyn-White, H. G., *Hesiod, the Hom. Hymns*, Loeb 1929.

Evrard, E., *Bull. ac. r. de Belge, Cl. d. Lettres* vi 1955 299f (Philoponos)

Farnell, L. R., *Cults of the Gr. States* 1896–1909.

Farrington, B. (1) *Gr. Science* i 1944, ii 1949 (2) *The Faith of Epicurus* 1967 (3) *Gr. Science: Its Meaning for us* 1961 (4) *Head and Hand in Anc. Greece* 1947 (5) *Science and Politics in the Anc. World* 1965.

Faulkner, R. O., *The Anc. Egyptian Pyramid Texts* 1969.

Feathers, N., *The Physics of Mass, Length, and Time* 1961.

Feldhaus, F. M. (1) *Die Technik d. Vorzeit, des geschicht. Zeit u. d. Naturvölker* 1914 (2) *Die Maschine im Leben d. Völker* 1964 (3) *Die Technik d. Antike u. des Mittelalters* 1931.

Ferguson, J., *Bibliotheca Chemica* 1906.

Ferri, S., *RRI* 1940 vii 117–52 (Canon).

Festugière, A. J. (1) *Personal Religion among the Greeks* 1960 (2) *La révélation d'Hermès Trismégistos* 1944–54 (3) *REG* 1945 lviii 1–65 (4) *Hippocrate* 1948.

Finch, H. L., *The Gr. Idea of Limitation* 1951 (Doct. Diss. dept. Philos. Columbia).

Finley, M. I. (1) *EHR* n.s. 1965 xviii 29–45 (2) ed. *Slavery in Cl. Antiquity* 1960 (3) *Pol. Sc. Q.* 1953 lxviii 249–68.

Fisch, M. H., *AJP* 1937 lviii 59ff, 129.

Fischer, P., *Mosaic* 1971.

Fontaine, J. *Mél. A. Piganiol* 1965 iii 1711–29.

Forbes, R. J. (1) *Studies in Anc. Technology* 1964 on (2) *Metallurgy in Antiquity* 1950 (3) in *Hist. Technol.* (Oxford) ii 1957 (3) *Hist. of Science and Technology* (with E. J. Dijksterhuis) 1963.

Fox, R., *The Caloric Theory of Gases.*

Fraenkel, H. (1) *Wege u. Formen frühgriech. Denkens* 1955 (2) APA 1938 lxix 230ff (3) *Dichtung u. Philosophie d. frühen Griechentums* 1951.

Frankfort, H., *Kingship and the Gods* 1948.

Frazer, J. G. (1) Paus. comm. (2) *Golden Bough* (3rd ed.) 1911–5 (3) Ovid's *Fasti.*

Freeman, K., *Ancilla to the Presoc. Philosophers* 1948.

Freundlich, F., *Foundations of Einstein's Theory of Gravitation* 1924.

Fritz, K. von (1) *Pythag. Politics in S. Italy* 1940 (2) *CP* 1945 xl 223–42, 1946 xli 12–34.

Furley, D. J. (1) *Aristotle On the Kosmos* etc. 1955 Loeb (2) *JHS* 1957 lxxviii 31–4.

Furst, P. T., *Flesh of the Gods* 1972.

Furtwängler (1) *JDAI* 1891 110 (2) *ARW* 1907 x 320–32.

Gadd, C. J., *Divine Rule.*

Gagé, J., *Basiléia* 1968.

Galileo, G. (1) *Dialogue of the World Systems,* transl. Salisbury, ed. Santillana 1953 (2) *On Motion and Mechanics*, transl. Drabkin and Drake.

Ganschinietz, *Texte u. Untersuch.: Hippolytos' Capitel gegen d. Magier* 1913.

Geffcken, J. (1) *ARW* 1919 xix 286ff (2) *H.* 1929 lxiv.

Gellius, Aulus, *Noctes Atticae* (Loeb) ed. J. C. Rolfe 1948.

Geymonat, L., *Storia e philosofia dell' analisi infinitesimolo* 1947.

Ghilioungui, P., *Magic and Med. Science in Anc. Egypt* 1963.

Gianelli, *Culti e miti della Magna Grecia* 1928.

Gigon, O. (1) *Der Ursprung d. griech. Philosophie* 1945 (2) *Untersuch. zu Heraklit* 1935.

Gillispie, C. C., *Lazare Carnot, Savant.*

Glotz, G., *Le travail dans la Grèce anc.* 1920.

Gnudi, M., *The Pirotechnia of V. Biringuccio* 1943.

Goldbeck, E., *Die Antike* 1925 i 72ff.

Goldschmidt, V., *Le système stoicien et l'idée de Temps* 1953.

Gomperz, T., *Greek Thinkers* i 1901.

Goodenough, E. R. (1) *YCS* i (2) *By Light, Light* 1935 (3) *YCS* iii (4) *Political Philosophy.*

Goodfield, J., *Scient. American* 1964 (6) ccx 104–12.

Göttling, K. W., *Opuscula Academica* 1869 182–8.

Gouldner, A. W., *Enter Plato* 1965.

Granger, F., Vitruvius (Loeb) 1933.

Green, R., *JHS* 1961 lxxxi 73–5.

Greene, W. C., *Moira* 1963.
Griffiths, J. W., *Plutarch De Iside* 1970.
Groningen, B. A., van, *La composition litt. archaique grecque* 1958.
Guérin, P., *L'idée de la justice dans la conception de l'univers chez les premiers philosophes grecs* 1934.
Guignet, M., *St Grégoire de Nazianze* 1911.
Guiraud, P., *La main d'œuvre industrielle dans l'anc. Grèce* 1900.
Güntert, H., *Kalypso* 1919.
Guthrie, W. K. C. (1) *In the Beginning* 1957 (2) *Hist. of Gr. Philosophy* i 1962 (3) *JHS* 1957 lxxvii 35ff.

Haas, A. E., *AGP* 1909 xxii 80ff.
Hack, R. K., *God in Gr. Philosophy to the Time of Socrates* 1931.
Hackforth, R., *CQ.* n.s. 1959 ix 17–22.
Haddon, A. C., *The Study of Man.*
Hale, J., *Listener* 17 Aug. 1961.
Hall, A. R. (1) *The Scient. Revolution* 1954 (2) *From Galileo to Newton* 1963 (3) *Ballistics in the 17th c.* 1952.
Hall, J. J., *JHS* 1969 57–9.
Hamelin, O., *Le système d'Aristote* 1920.
Hanfmann, G. M. A. (1) *AJA* 1948 lii 135–55 (2) *HSCP* 1953 lxi 1–37.
Hanson, N. R., *Patterns of Discovery* 1958.
Harris, H. A., *Greek Athletics* 1964.
Harrison, J. (1) *Prolegomena* 1922 (2) *Myths of the Odyssey* (3) *Gr. Vase Paintings* (4) *Themis* 1963 reprint.
Hart, C. (1) *The Dream of Flight* 2972 (2) *Kites* 1967.
Hassenstein, W., *Das Feuerwerkbuch von 1420* 1941.
Heath, T. L. (1) *Maths. in Aristotle* 1949 (2) *Aristarchos of Samos* 1913 (3) *The Works of Archimedes* 1897 (4) *Manual of Gr. Maths.* 1963 (5) *Hist. of Gr. Maths.* 1921 (6) *Diaphantus of Alexandria* 1964.
Heiberg, J. C. (1) *Mathematisches zu Aristoteles* 1904 (2) *Gesch. d. Math. u. Naturwiss. im Altertum* 1925.
Heidel, W. A. (1) *AGP* 1906 xix 333–79 (2) *Procs. Amer. Acad. Arts and Sc.* 1910 77–133 (3) *AJP* 1949 lxi 1ff (4) *AJP* 1940 li 1–33 (5) *AGP* xiv 390ff (6) *CP* i 906 i 279–82 (7) as (2) 1913 xlvii 681–734 (7) *HSCP* xxv 1914.
Heinimann, F. (1) *Nomos u. Physis* 1945 (2) *MH* 1961 xviii 105–30.
Henry, P., *Entretiens Hardy* v 429–49.
Heron of Alex. (1) *Pneumatica u. automata*, W. Schmidt 1899 (2) *Mechanica u. Catoptrica*, L. Nix and W. Schmidt 1900 (3) *Rationes dimet. et comm. dioptrica*, H. Schöne 1903 (4) *Definitiones*, J. L. Heiberg 1912 (5) *Stereometrica*, Heiberg 1914.

Herter, H., *RhM* 1957 c. 327–47.
Hertz, R., in *Death and the Right Hand* (transl. R. and C. Needham) 1960 89ff (2) *Rev. Philos.* 1909 lxviii 353ff.
Hessen, B., in *Science at the Crossroads* 1931.
Hett, W. S., *Arist. Minor Works*, Loeb 1963.
Hime, H. W. L., *Origin of Artillery* 1915.
Hirzel, R., *Themis* 1907.
Hoff, Arne, *Airguns and Other Pneumatic Arms*, 1973.
Hoffmann, B., *The Strange Story of the Quantum* 1963.
Hölscher, V., *H.* 1953 lxxxi 257ff, 385ff, 415–8.
Homolle, T., *BCH* 1888 xii 464.
Hopfner (1) *RE* sv Mageia 347ff (2) OZ (*Gr. aeg. Offenbarungzaube*).
Hopper, R. J., *BSA* 1953 xlviii 200–54 (silver mines).
Howitt, A. W., *Native Tribes of S.E. Australia* 1904.
Hunt, A. S., *Studies pres. to F. Ll. Griffith* 1932 233–40.
Hurd, D. L., with J. J. Kipling, *The Origins and Growth of Physical Science* 1964.
Huxley, G. L., *The Early Ionians* 1966.

Ideler, ed., *Aristotle's Meteorologica.*
Itard, J., *RHS* iii 1950 210–3.

Jaeger, W. W. (1) xlviii 29–74 (2) *Theology of the Early Gr. Philosophers* 1947 (3) *Aristoteles* 1923 (3a) engl. transl. (2nd ed.) 1948 (4) *Paideia* i 1945, ii 1943 NY, 1944 Eng., iii 1944 NY 1944 Eng.
Jahn, O., *BSGW* 1885.
Jähns, M., *Gesch. d. Wiss. in Deutschland* 1889–91 xxi pts. i–iii.
James, M. R., *The Apocryphal N.T.* 1945.
Jeanmarie, H., *Dionysos* 1951.
Joachim, H. H. (1) ed. *Arist. Gen. et Corr.* 1922 (2) *J. of Philol.* 1904 xxix 72–86 (Ar. and Chem. Combination).
Jones, A. H. M., *EHR* 2nd s. ix 1956 185–99.
Jones, H. Stuart, *Anc. Writers on Gr. Sculpture.*
Jones, R. M., *The Platonism of Plutarch.*
Jones, W. H. S. (1) Loeb Hippocrates (2) *Philosophy and Medicine in Anc. Greece* 1946.
Jouguet, E., *Lectures de mécanique* (2 vols.) 1908–9.

Kaerst, J., *Gesch. des Hellenismus* i 1927, ii (2nd ed.).
Kafka, G., *Die Vorsokratiker* 1948.
Kahn, C. H., *Anaximander and the Origins of Gr. Cosmology* 1960.
Kapp, E., *Greek Foundations of Traditional Logic* 1942.

Kelsen, H., *Society and Nature* (2nd ed.) 1946.

Kember, D., *JHS* 1971 xci 70–9.

Kemmer, E., *Die polare Ausdruckweise in d. griech. Lit.* 1903.

Kepler, J. (1) *Gesamm. Werke*, ed. W. V. Dyck and M. Caspar (2) *Seinen Briefen*.

Kerenyi, C. (1) *EJ* xvi 1948 183 (2) *Dionisio* 1949 17.

Kerkford, G. B., *P.* 1955; 3–25.

Kirk, G. S. (1) *Mind* 1951 lx 35–42 (2) *AJP* 1949 lxx 384–93 (3) *Heraclitus, the Cosmic Fragments* 1954 (4) with Raven, *The Presoc. Philosophers* 1957 (5) *CQ* n.s. v 1955 21–38 (6) *AJP* 1951 lxxii 225–52 (7) *AJP* 1949 lxx 384–93 (8) *Camb. Phil. Soc.* 1956–7 n.s. 4 clxxxiv 10–12 (9) *MH* 1957 xiv 155–63.

Kleingünther, A., *Protos heuretes, Ph. Suppl.* xxvi Heft i 1933.

Klemm, F., *Hist. of Western Technology* 1959.

Kline, M. (1) *Maths. in Western Culture* 1954 (2) *Maths. and the Physical World*.

Knight, W. F. J., *Cumaean Gates* 1936.

Knudsen, O., and K. M. Pedersen, *C.* 1968 xiii 183–6.

Köchly, H., and W. Rüstow, *Griech. Kriegsschrift.* i 1853.

Koestler, A., *The Sleepwalkers* 1959.

Kolendo, J., *Annales* 1960 xv 1088–1114.

Körte, *H.* 1929 lxiv 69ff.

Koster, W., *Mythe de Platon, de Zarathustra et des Chaldéens* 1951.

Kostermann, E., *PH* 1932 lxxxvii 358ff.

Koyré, A. (1) *Études galiléennes* 1959 (2) *From the Closed World to the Infinite Universe* 1957.

Kraeling, C. H., *Anthropos and Son of Man* 1966.

Kranz, *H.* xlvii 132ff.

Kranz, W., *Kosmos u. Mensch im d. Vorstellung d. früh. Griechentums* 1938.

Kroef, J. M. van der, *AA* 1954 lvi 847ff.

Kroll, J., *Lehren des Hermes Trismegistos*.

Kromayer, J., with G. Veith, *Heerwesen u. Kriegführung d. Gr. u. Römer* 1928.

Kühn, J. H., *System.-u. Methodenprobleme Corpus Hippoc, Hermes Einzelschriften* xi 1956.

Kuhn, T. S., *The Copernican Revolution* 1957.

Laberthonnière, *Études sur Descartes* 1935.

Laessoe, J., *J. Cuneiform St.* vii 1953.

Laistner, M. L. W., *Survey of Anc. Hist.* 1929.

Lammeet, F., *RE* sv *Skorpion* 1927 585–6.

Lang, A., *Custom and Myth* 1884.
Laplace, M. le Comte (1) *Essai philos. sur les probabilités* 1795 (2) 3rd ed. 1816.
Laslett, P., ed. *Philosophy, Politics and Society* 1956.
Larsen, J. A. O., in *Essays in Pol. Theory pres. to G. H. Sabine* 1ff.
Lassen, C., *Indische Altertumskunde* 184.
Last, H., *CQ* 1924 xviii 169–73.
Lauffer, S., *Die Bergwerkssklaven von Laureion* i 1955 .
Le Blond, J. M. (1) *Logique et méthode chez Aristote* 1939 (2) *Aristote, philosophe de la vie* 1945.
Leclerc, I., *The Nature of Physical Existence* 1972.
Lefebure, *Rites égypt., Construction et protection des édifices* 1890.
Lenz, *Mineralogie d. alt. Griechen u. Römer* 1861.
Lesky, E., *Die Zeugungs-u. Vererbungslehren d. Antike u. ihr Nachwirken* 1951.
Leutsch and Schneidewin, *Corpus paroemiograph. Gr.*
Levy, H. (1) *Mod. Q.* i (1) 1938 (2) *Philosophy for a Mod. Man* 1938.
Lindemann, F. A., *The Physical Significance of the Quantum Theory* 1932.
Lindsay, J. (1) *Origins of Alchemy* 1970 (2) *Origins of Astrology* 1971 (3) *Clashing Rocks* 1965 (4) *Pottery Q.* no 8 1955 130–8 (5) *Life and Letters* Oct. 1945 (6) Totemism Reconsidered, *Hommages à Marie Delcourt* 1970 (7) *Short Hist. of Culture* 1961 (8) *Men and Gods on the Roman Nile* 1968 (9) *Song of a Falling World* 1948 (10) *Leisure and Pleasure in Roman Egypt* 1965 (11) *Daily Life in R.E.* 1963.
Linforth, I. M., *The Arts of Orpheus* 1947.
Lloyd, G. E. R. (1) *Early Gr. Science* 1970 (2) *JHS* 1962 lxxxii 56ff (3) *ib.* 1964 lxxxiv 92–106 (4) *Polarity and Analogy* 1966 (5) *JHS* 1972 178f.
Loane, H. J., *Industry and Commerce in the City of Rome* 1938.
Lommatzch, *Die Weisheit des Empedokles.*
Lorimer, W. L. (1) *The Text Trad. of Ps-Aristotle De Mundo* 1924 (2) *Some Notes on the Text of ps.-Ar. De Mundo* 1925 (3) *Aristoteles De Mundo* 1933.
Lovejoy, A. O. (1) *PR* 1909 xviii 369–83 (2) with G. Boas, *Primitivism and Related Ideas in Antiquity* 1935.
Luce, G. G., *Body Time* 1972.
Luck, W., *Die Quellenfrage im 5 u. 6 Buch des Lukrez* 1932.
Ludwich, A., *RhM* lxxi 1916.
Lukasiewicz, J., *Comptes-rendus Soc. Sciences Varsovie* xxiii 1930, fasc. 1–3.
Lynch, J. P., *Aristotle's School* 1972.

Mach (1) *Science of Mechanics*, transl. McCormack 1920 (2) *La Mécanique* 1904.
McCrindle, J. W., *Anc. India as described by Ktesias the Knidian* 1882.
McDiarmid, J. B., *HSCP* 1953 lxi 85–156.
Maclagan, R., *J. Asiatic Soc. Bengal* 1976 xlv 30–71.
McGuire, I. E., *C.* 1967 xii 231–60.
Mackenzie, D. A. *Scottish Folklore and Folk Life* 1935.
Maguire, J. P., *YCS* 1939 vi 109–67.
Maier, F. G., *Griech. Mauerbauinschriften* 1961.
Mansion, A., *Intro. à la physique aristot.* 1913.
Marett, R. R. (1) *Hibbert J.* Jan. 1910 (2) *Anthropology* n.d.
Margerison, T., *New Scientist* 26 Nov. 1959.
Mariolongo, R., *Atti d. R. Acc. dei Lincei* xiii 1960 (phys. ser.).
Marrou, H. J., *Hist. de l'éducation dans l'antiquité* 1948.
Marsden, E. W. (1) *Gr. and R. Artillery* 1969 (2) *Gr. and R. Artillery Technical Treatises.*
Mates, B., *Stoic Logic* 1953.
Matthew, J., *Two Representative Tribes of Q'land* 1910.
Matson, W. I., *RMet.* 1952–3 vi 387–95 (Anaximandros).
Mau, A., *Pompeji in Leben u. Kunst* 1908.
Mayerson, M. E., *Bull. Soc. fr. de philosophie* Feb.-March 1914.
Meisterhans and Schwyser. *Grammatik d. attischen Insch.* i 1939.
Michel, P. H., *De Pythagore à Euclide* 1950.
Mieli, A., *Archeion* xxi 1938 (Galileo).
Milhaud, G. (1) *Les philosophes géomètres de la Grèce* 1900 (2) *Étude sur la pensée scient. chez les grecs et chez les modernes* 1906 (3) *Nouvelles études sur l'hist. de la pensée scientifique* 1911.
Milne, M. J., in Noble 106–13.
Minadeo, R., *Arion* 1965 iv 444–61.
Minar, E. L., *Early Pythag. Politics* 1942.
Mins, H. F., *Sc. and Soc.* 1948 (1) xii 157–69.
Mondolfo, R. (1) *En los origines de la Filosofie* 1942 (2) *L'infinito nel pensiero dei greci* 1934.
Montet, P. (1) *RA* 1952 xl (2) *Eternal Egypt* 1965.
Moret, A., *Ann. Musée Guimet* xiv 1902.
Moritz, L. A., *Grain-Mills and Flour in Class. Antiquity* 1958.
Mossé, C., *The Anc. World at Work* 1969.
Mottelay, P. F., *De Magnete*, W. Gilbert 1958.
Mugler, C., *Devenir cyclique et pluralité des mondes* 1953.
Müller, I., *HB d. klass Altertumwiss.* 1887.
Müller, J. V., *Abh. Akad. München* 1894 xx 405ff (Galen).

Nahm, M. C., *Selections from Early Gr. Philosophy.*
Needham, J., *Science and Civilisation in China.*

Neher, R., *Der Anon. de Rebus Bellicis* 1911.

Nestle, W., *Vom Mythos zum Logos* 1942.

Neugebauer, O. (1) *Ueber eine Methode zur Distanzbestimmung Alexandria-Röm bei Heron* 1938 (2) *PAPS* cxvi 1972 243–51 (3) *The Exact Sciences in Antiquity* 1962 (4) *Isis* 1949 xl 240–56.

Nicoll, A., *Masks, Mimes and Miracles* 1931.

Nidditch, P. H., *The Development of Math. Logic.*

Nilsson, M. P. (1) *Gr. Piety* 1948 (2) *Gesch. d. griech. Religion* (3) *HTR* 1945 xxxviii.

Noble, J. V., *The Technique of Painted Attic Pottery* 1966.

Nock, A. D. (1) *JEA* Oct. 1925 154–8 (2) *HTR* 1934 xxvii 53ff (3) *ARW* xxiv 1926.

O'Brien, D. (1) *JHS* 1970 xv 140–79 (2) *ib.* 1968 lxxxviii 93–113 (3) *ib.* 114–27.

Oldfield, A., *Trans. Ethnol. Soc.* iii 1865.

Olschi, L., *Gesch. d. neusprach. wiss. Literatur* iii 1927.

Oman, C. W. C., *Art of War in M.A.* 1905.

Onians, R. B., *The Origins of European Thought* 1951.

Oppert, G., *On the Weapons, Army Organisation . . . of the Hindus* 1880.

Orr, Clyde, *Between Earth and Space* 1959.

Otterlo, W. A. A. von, *MKNA* vi–vii 1943–4.

Otto, W. F., *Die Manen oder von den Urformen des Totenglaubens* 1923.

Pallis, S. A., *The Bab. Akitu Festival* 1926.

Pappos, ed. Hultsch 1876–8.

Partington, J. R. (1) *Hist. of Gr. Fire and Gunpowder* 1960 (2) *Origins and Development of Applied Chemistry* 1935 (3) *Nature* 1927 cxx 165 (4) *ib.* 1947 xx clix 784.

Payne-Galloway, *The Crossbow* (2nd ed.) 1958.

Peck, A. L. (1) Loeb, *Aristotle, Generation of Animals* 1943 (2) *CQ* 1931 xxv 27–37, 112–20 (3) *CQ.* 1952 n.s. ii 32–56.

Perdrizet, P., *BCH* 1900 292.

Pernice, *Festschrift f. Benndorf.*

Perry, W. (1) *Children of the Sun* 1923 (2) *Megalithic Culture of Indonesia* 1918 (3) *JRAI* 1914 xliv (orientation of dead, Indonesia) (4) *Origin of Magic and Religion* 1923 (5) *Growth of Civilisation* 1924.

Philoponos, Ioannes, *In Arist. Physicorum livros comm.* ed. H. Vitelli 1887.

Picard, C. (1) *CRAI* 1929 (2) *REG* ii 1939 (3) *Manuel archéol. gr.* ii (4) *MEFR* lviii 1941–6.

Pines, S., *Procs. Amer. Acad. Jewish Research* xxiv 1955.

Plas, P., *JHS* 1972 179f.

Plische, H., *Nachshricten von d. Gesell. d. Wiss. zu Göttingen, ph.-hist. Kl.*, N.F., Fachgr. 2, vol. 2, no 1, 1936.

Pohlenz, M. (1) *Die Stoa* 1948 (2) ed. Plout. *Moralia* 1952 (3) *H.* 1940 lxxv 119.

Pohlmann, M., *Untersuch. zur alteren Gesch. d. ant. Belagerungs-geschützes* 1912.

Pollitt, J. O., *The Art of Greece* 1965.

Poppelreuter, *Zur Physchologie des Aristot., Theoph., Strato.*

Porter, A. W., *Thermodynamics* (3rd ed.) 1946.

Poulsen, F., *ActA* xvi 1945 178–95.

Praechter, K., *Byz. Zeits.* 1909 xviii 510ff.

Prantl, C., *Aristoteles ueber die Farben* 1849.

Preuner, E., *JDAI* 1920 69–72.

Prévost, P. (1) *Sur l'équilibre du feu* 1792 (2) *Du calorique rayonnant* 1809.

Price, D. J. de Solla (1) *Science since Babylon* 1962 (2) *Scient. American* June 1959 cc 60–7 (3) *Year Book of Am. Philos. Soc.* 1959 518f (4) *U.S. Nat. Mus. Bull.* 218 (Washington 1959) (5) in *Heavenly Clockwork* (Monograph no 1, Antiq. Horolog. Soc.) 1960.

Pritchard, J. B., *Anc. Near Eastern Texts* (2nd ed.) 1955.

Prou, V. (1) *Les théâtres d'automates en Grèce* 1881 (2) *Notices et Extracts des MSS de la Bibl. Nat.* etc. xxvi (2) 1877 1–319 (chiro-baliste d'Héron).

Pyke, M., *The Boundaries of Science* 1963.

Raubitschuk, A. E., *Dedications from the Athenian Acropolis* 1948.

Raven, J. E. (1) *Pythagoreans and Eleatics* (2) *CQ* 1951 xlv 147–52.

Regenbogen, O. (1) *RE* Suppl. vii 1950, Theophrastos (2) *Quellen u. St. zur Gesch. d. Math., Studien* i 1930 131ff.

Rehm, A. (1) *Archiv f. Kulturgesch.* xxviii 1938 135–62 (2) *Bitons Bau von Belagerungsmaschinen*, with E. Schramm 1929.

Reinach, S., RA 1922 xvi 205–65.

Reinhardt, K. (1) *Kosmos u. Sympathie* 1926 (2) *Parmenides u.d. Gesch. d. griech. Philosophie* 1916 (3) *H.* 1942 lxxvii 1–27.

Renard, M., *Techniques et Agric. en pays trévois et rémois* 1959.

Rey, A., *La Science dans l'Antiquité* 1930–48.

Reymond, A. (1) *Hist. of the Sciences in G.R. Antiquity* 1927 (2) *RMet.* July 1911 (infinite) (3) *Logique et Mathématique* 1900.

Reymond, E. A. E., *Mythical Origin of the Egyptian Temple* 1969.

Richter, G. M. A., *The Craft of Athenian Pottery* 1923.
Ridgeway, W., *The Early Age of Greece.*
Rivaud, A., *La principe du devenir et la notion de la matière dans la philosophie grecque* 1906.
Rodier, G., *La physique de Straeton de Lampsaque* 1890.
Rohde, E., *Psyche* 1921.
Roheim, G., *Australian Totemism* 1925.
Romocki, S. J. von, *Gesch. d. Explosivstoffe* 1895.
Roque, B. de la, *Fouilles de l'inst. fr. d'arch. orient. du Caire* 1921 *Rapp. prélim.* iv. 1 *Mehamud.*
Rose, H. J., *Primitive Culture in Greece* 1925.
Ross, D. *Aristotle* (5th ed.) 1949.
Rostovtzeff, M. (1) *Social and Econ. Hist. of Hellenistic World* ii 1941 (2) *ib. Roman Empire* 1926.
Rufini, E., *Il Metodo di Archimedes* 1926 and 1961.

Sackur, *Vutruv u. Poliorketiker* 1925.
Sageret, J., *Le système du monde* 1913.
Sambursky, S. (1) *Physical World of the Greeks* 1956 (2) *Physics of the Stoics* 1959 (3) *Osiris* 1956 xii 35ff (4) *Physical World of Late Antiquity* (5) *Osiris* 1958 xiii 114f.
Santillana (1) *The Origin of Scient. Thought* 1961 (2) with F. Enriques, *Storia del Pensiero scient., Il Mondo antico* 1932.
Sarton, G. (1) *Intro. to the History of Science* 1927–48 (2) *Hist. of Science* i 1953.
Schink, D., *F. Vegetius Renatus: Die Quellen d. Epitome Rei Militaris, Klio Beheft* 22 1930.
Schmidt, W., *Heronis Alex. Opera* 1899–1914.
Schneider, R. (1) ed. *Anon. de Rebus Bellicis* 1908 (2) *NJKA* 1910 xiii 327–42 (3) *Griech. Poliorketiker* (4) *Die antike Geschütze d. Saalburg* 1931 (5) *RE* 1910 sv *Geschütze* 1321.
Schöne, H., see Heron (3).
Schonland, B. F. J., *The Flight of the Thunderbolts* 1950.
Schott, G., *Magia Universalis Naturae et Artis* (4 vols.) 1657–9.
Schramm, E. (1) see Schneider (4) (2) *SB* Berlin 1917 718ff (Vitruvius). (3) in Kromayer 209ff (4) *RhM* 1906 xxi 142ff (Heron's ballista).
Schrödinger, E., *Nature and the Greeks* 1954.
Schuhl, P. M. (1) *Machinisme et philosophie* 1938 (2) *REG* 1953 465–72.
Schulz, D., *H.* 1955 lxxxiii 215ff (Canon).
Schweitzer, B. (1) *AM* 1930 lv 107–18 (2) *SKGG* 1932 1–52 (3) *NHJ* n.f. 1925 esp. 107ff (3) *Ph.* 1934 lxxxix 286–300.

Schwyzer (1) *Griech. Grammatik* i 1939 (2) *Dialectorum Gr. Exempla Epigraphica Potiora.*

Scott, W., *Hermetica.*

Scranton, R. L., *Greek Walls* 1941.

Seeck, O., *RE* i 1894 2325 sv Anon (3).

Seligmann, S., *Der böse Blick u. Verwandtes* 1910.

Seltmann, C. T. (1) *Gr. Coins* 1933 (2) *Book of Gr. Coins* 1952 (3) *NC* ix, 1.

Sextus Empiricus: Loeb (4 vols.) ed. R. G. Bury.

Sheldon-Williams, I. P., in *Camb. Hist. Later Gr. and Med. Philosophy* 1967.

Silberg, P. A., *J. of Applied Physics* 1961 (1) xxxii 30–5.

Simplikios (1) *In Ar. Categ. comm.* ed. C. Kalbfleisch 1907 (2) *In Ar. Phys. lib. comm.*, H. Diels 1882 (3) *ib.* 1895.

Singer, C. (1) *Hist. of Technology* 1956 (2) *Short Hist. of Scient. Ideas* 1959 (3) *Studies in the Hist. and Method of Science* 1921 (4) *Greek Biology and Greek Medicine* 1922.

Skemp, J. B. (1) *Theory of Motion in Plato's Later Dialogues* 1942 (2) *Plato's Statesman* 1905.

Snell, B. (1) *H.* 1926 lxi 356ff (2) *The Discovery of the Mind* 1953 (3) *H.* 1926 lxi 353–81.

Solmsen, F. (1) *Studi di Filol. Classica* xxiv 235ff (2) *HSCP* lxiii 1958 265ff (3) *Philos. Rev.* 1941 l 410–21.

Sontheimer, *Vitruvius u. seine Zeit* 1908.

Sorel, G., *De l'utilité du pragmatisme* 1921.

Souda (Suidas), ed. A. Adler.

Souilhé, J., *Étude sur le terme dynamis dans les dialogues de Platon* 1919.

Spekke, A., *The Anc. Amber Routes* 1957.

Spencer, B. (1) with F. J. Gillen, *The Native Tribes of Central Austr.* 1899 (2) *Northern Tribes* etc. 1904.

Spengler, O., in *Reden u. Aufsätze* (Herakl.) 1951.

Stahl, W. H., *Roman Science.*

Stewart, J. A., *Myths of Plato* 1905.

Stokes, M. C., *P.* 1962 vii 1ff.

Stratton, G. M., *Theophrastus and the Gr. Physiological Psychology* 1917.

Strohm, H., *MH* 1952 ix 137–75 (Platonic elements in *On kos*).

Struick, D. J., *Sc. and Soc.* 1948 (1) xii 181–96.

Susemihl, F., *Gesch. d. griech. Lit. d. Alexandrinerzeit*, Bd. 1, 1891.

Tannery, P. (1) *La géometrie grecque* 1887 (2) *Pour l'hist. de la Science Hellène* (2nd ed.) 1930 (3) ed. of Diophantos.

Tarn, W. W., *Hellenistic Naval and Military Developments* 1930.
Taylor, A. E., *Plato the Man and his Work* (2nd ed.) 1927.
Teichmüller, G., *Neue Studien zur Gesch. d. Begriffe*, Heft 1, 1876–9.
Tenkin, O., *Bull. Inst. Hist. of Medicine* 1935 iii 405ff.
Thompson, E. A., *A Roman Reformer and Inventor* 1952.
Thomson, G. (1) *The First Philosophers* 1955 (2) *The Primitive Aegean* 1952 (3) *Aeschylus and Athens* 1941 (4) *Aeschylus, Prom. Bound* 1932.
Thorndyke, L. (1) *Hist. of Magic and Experimental Science* 1932 on (2) *AIHS* 1955 viii 21ff.
Thornton, H. and A., *Time and Style* 1962.
Thureau-Dangin, F., *Rituels accadiens* 1921.
Thurston, R. H., *Hist. of the Growth of the Steam Engine* 1895.
Tomlinson, C., *The Thunderstorm* 1959.
Trouillard, *La procession plotinienne* 1955.

Ubbelohde, A. R. (1) *Man and Energy* 1963 (2) *Time and Thermodynamics* 1950.
Usher, A. P., *Hist. of Mechanical Inventions* (2nd ed.) 1954.
Ussher, R. G., *The Characters of Theophrastus* 1960.

Vassails, G., *JHSC* 1950 iii 222–41 (weight of fire).
Vaux, C. de (1) *Notices et Extraits des Mss Bibl. Nat. etc* 1903 xxxviii 23–235 (2) *J. Asiatique* (9th s.) i 386–472 (3) *ib.* 1893 ii 152–269, 470–514.
Vernant, J. P. (1) *JP* 1955 19–38 (2) *ib.* 1952 419–29.
Vitruvius (1) ed. F. Granger 1962 (2) ed. F. Krohn 1912.
Vlastos, G. (1) *AJP* 1955 lxxvi 337–68 (2) *CP* xli 1946 (Solon) (3) *Philos. Rev.* li 1942 (4) *CP* xlii 156–78 (4) *Gnomon* 1955 xxvii 65ff (5) as (3), slavery in Plato's thought, 1941 280–304 (6) *CP* 1939 xxxiii 71–83 (Disorderly motion in *Tim.*).
Vogel, W., *Leonardo da Vinci als Ingenieur* 1954.

Waagé, F. O., *A.* 1937 xi 46–55.
Wace, A. J. B., *BSA* x 1903–4.
Waerden, B. L. van der (1) *H.* 1952 129ff (2) *Bull. soc. math de Belgique* 1957 (1) ix 10–3.
Wagner, H., *Aristoteles, Physikvorlesung* 1967.
Wailes, R., in Singer ii 623–8 (windmills).
Wainwright, G. A. (1) *The Sky Religion of Egypt* 1938 (2) *JEA* xviii 1932 (iron in Egypt).
Walbank, F. W., *JHS* lxiv 10.
Walters, H. B., *Cat. of TCs in BM.*

Walzer, R., *Eraclito* 1939.

Warren, P., *Myrtos* 1972.

Warry, J. G., *Gr. Aesthetic Theory* 1962.

Weber, L., *Le rhythme du progrès* 1913.

Webster, T. B. L., *Sophocles* 1936.

Wedberg, A., *Plato's Philosophy of Maths.* 1955.

Wehrli, *Dikaiarchos* 1944.

Wellmann, *H.* xxxi 1896.

West, M. L. (1) *CQ* 1963 xiii 157–75 (2) *Early Gr. Philosophy and the Orient* 1971.

Weyl, H., *Philosophy of Maths. and Nat. Science* 1949.

Wheelwright, P. (1) *Heraclitus* 1959 (2) *The Burning Fountain* 1954.

White, K. D., *Agric. Implements of the R. World* 1968.

Whiteman, M., *Philosophy of Space and Time* 1967.

Wiedemann, *Hdt. II.*

Wilkins, K., *H.* 1967 xcv 129–40.

Willamowitz-Moellendorf, U. von, (1) *Das Ilias u. Homer* 1916 (2) *Der Glaube d. Hellenen* i 1931 (3) *Vitae Homeri et Hesiodi* 1916.

Wimmer, F., *Works of Theophrastos* 1866.

Winnefeld, *Philosophie des Empedokles.*

Wittkower, R., *Architectural Proportions in the Age of Humanism* 1962.

Wohlwill, E., *Physikal. Zeits.* 1906 vii 23ff.

Wolf, E. *Symposium* 1948 i 35–7 (Anaximin. and Herakl.).

Woodbridge, F. J. E., *PR* 1901 x 359–74.

Wundt, M., *AGP* 1907 xx (Herakl. and Ionia).

Zeller, E. (1) *Hist. of Gr. Philosophy from the Earliest Period to the Time of Soc.* 1881 (esp. ii 1–116, Herakl.) (2) *Aristotle and the Earlier Peripatetics* 1897.

Zeuthen, H. G., *Hist. des maths. dans l'antiquité et le m.a.* 1902 (transl. J. Mascart).

Zilsel, E. (1) *PR* 1942 li 245–79 (physical law) (2) *JHI* 1945 vi 328ff (3) *Amer. J. of Sociology* 1941–2 xlvii (3) *Die Entstehung des Geniebegriffes* 1926.

Zonneveld, J. J., *Angore Metuque* 1959.

Index

PERSONS

PLACES

SUBJECTS